No Longer Property of
EWU Libraries

European Perspectives on
Consumer Behaviour

No Longer Property of
EWU Libraries

European Perspectives on Consumer Behaviour

edited by
Mary Lambkin
Gordon Foxall
Fred van Raaij
Benoît Heilbrunn

PRENTICE HALL
London New York Toronto Sydney Tokyo Singapore
Madrid Mexico City Munich Paris

SCL
HF5415.33
.E85E95
1998

First published 1998 by
Prentice Hall Europe
Campus 400, Maylands Avenue
Hemel Hempstead
Hertfordshire, HP2 7EZ
A division of
Simon & Schuster International Group

© Prentice Hall Europe 1998

All rights reserved. No part of this publication may be reproduced,
stored in a retrieval system, or transmitted, in any form, or by any
means, electronic, mechanical, photocopying, recording or otherwise,
without prior permission, in writing, from the publisher.

Typeset in 10/12pt Ehrhardt
by Dorwyn Ltd, Rowlands Castle, Hants

Printed and bound in Great Britain by
T.J. International Ltd

Library of Congress Cataloging-in-Publication Data

European perspectives on consumer behaviour / edited by Mary Lambkin
 . . . [et al.].
      p.   cm.
   Includes bibliographical references and index.
   ISBN 0-13-552382-6 (pbk.)
   1. Consumer behavior—Europe.   2. Consumer behavior—Research–
–Europe.   I. Lambkin, Mary.
HF5415.33.E85E95   1997
658.8'342—dc21   97–12767
                                                                  CIP

British Library Cataloguing in Publication Data

A catalogue record for this book is available from
the British Library

ISBN: 0-13-552382-6 (pbk)

---

1 2 3 4 5   02 01 00 99 98

EASTERN WASHINGTON
UNIVERSITY LIBRARIES
CHENEY, WA 99004

Contents

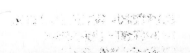

General introduction

●●●

This collection of readings aims at drawing a representative overview of twenty years' research on consumer behaviour in Europe. The project bears some similarities to *Perspectives in Consumer Behavior*, edited by Harold Kassarjian and Thomas Robertson, which has earned a unique place in the literature on consumer behaviour. It was first published in 1968[1] at the dawn of the development of consumer behaviour as a separate subject and has made a continuing contribution to the development of that subject by providing a showcase for articles that have had a formative influence in that field, and by identifying leading-edge papers that point towards the future direction of the subject. A perusal of the content of the fourth edition[2] points up one significant omission, however: the absence of contributions from European authors. Out of thirty-one articles in that volume, only one is of European origin.[3] This obvious imbalance provided the impetus for this book whose title, *European Perspectives on Consumer Behaviour*, clearly identifies the nature of its content. The main objective which guided the present volume was to provide students, lecturers and the general public with a selection of articles which take account of both the richness and the variety of studies on consumer behaviour on the European continent.

Criteria for selection

In our attempt to gather articles that can be considered as representative of the European mainstream, an effort was made to include as many different European countries as possible, to account for the variety of European research on consumption. The editors of this volume are all marketing scholars with a strong interest in consumer behaviour and represent four different countries and cultural traditions in Europe – Ireland, the United Kingdom, the Netherlands and France – which gives a wide breadth of perspective and ensures familiarity with the current work in universities and research institutes around Europe. This breadth of coverage is considered very important because the fragmentation of writing and research in Europe, often accentuated by language differences, makes it difficult to achieve an extensive knowledge of the work that exists. As editors, we have tried to make sure that we have identified contributions from each of the European countries and were both surprised and delighted at the wealth of material that emerged from this search. This very exercise has enhanced our repertoire of knowledge and will no doubt filter through in the courses we teach and in other writings.

Given our objective to bring together articles which represent an important added-value either by introducing new research horizons or by providing an interesting synthesis of the literature on a given topic, specific criteria were imposed, namely:

1. **Theoretical importance** – articles were considered that made a significant contribution to knowledge already existing, or are very likely to influence the course of development in the future. We also felt it important to stress the specificities of European approaches through the influence of such disciplines as psychology, anthropology and economic psychology.
2. **Review characteristic** – preference was shown for articles that are broadly based, summarizing and developing a particular topic area rather than very narrow studies.
3. **Empirical studies** were accepted where the scale and import of the data are of real significance. The choice of articles also reflects a good balance between studies based on a quantitative approach and works that are influenced by a qualitative approach.
4. **Readability** – while this book is primarily directed towards an academic audience, normal requirements for clarity and readability were employed in the selection process.

Structure of the book

The initial plan was to follow the structure of Kassarjian and Robertson's book quite closely, with similar chapter headings. As the literature was compiled, however, it became obvious that in some of the topic areas European authors had not contributed much or not significantly, while other areas emerged which European authors had made uniquely their own. The volume is organized according to a very simple structure which views consumption behaviour as a process that is largely determined by various types of influence. This process is analyzed through the study of such stages as motivation, perception, cognition, attitude formation, decision-making, etc.

To help the reader progress through the different stages, the book has been divided into four parts. Part I introduces the main concepts and theories involved in the study of consumption. Part II considers the consumer as an individual and examines the major aspects involved in any purchase decisions. Part III considers the social interactions which might affect the consumer in his or her choices. This scheme, which is relevant to most approaches on consumer behaviour, would not be complete without acknowledging alternative views on consumption. Part IV hence takes into account such approaches as economic psychology, semiotics, postmodernism, etc.

The final design thus offers some chapters that parallel the American volume quite closely, with the addition of several that are unique. As might be expected perhaps, the parallel chapters deal with long-established topics, such as personality and motivation, information processing, decision-making and socio-cultural processes. The chapters which stand alone in this book deal with the nature of the European market and strands within it, some distinct theoretical models, economic psychology and semiotics. Broadly speaking, three types of article will be found in this volume:

1. Articles that represent a major breakthrough in a given research field such as the double jeopardy effect (Ehrenberg *et al.*, chapter 2), the facets of involvement (Laurent and Kapferer, chapter 4) and the behavioural perspective model of purchase and consumption (Foxall, chapter 2).

2. Articles that propose new and original research paradigms such as the study of the non-buyer consumer (Bon and Pras, chapter 3), the application of the implicit personality theory to product perception (Pinson, chapter 4) or the application of structural semiotics to the study of supermarket shoppers (Floch, chapter 8).
3. Articles that constitute a very good synthesis of a topic of interest such as the role of personality in consumer research (Foxall and Goldsmith, chapter 3), the article on consumer culture (Featherstone, chapter 6), and the article on macro and micro perspectives on economic psychology (van Raaij, chapter 7).

This volume will thus interest various types of reader. First, readers who are looking for a good overview of the major topics involved in the study of consumers. Second, readers who wish to strengthen their knowledge in a particular field of consumer research. This book is also intended to serve both as a textbook for courses in consumer behaviour, and as a source of reference. Most of the articles are easily accessible for MA students and require little experience in data analysis. Moreover, each chapter is preceded by an introduction which lays the ground for the articles that follow and guides the reader through the various research paradigms and concepts discussed in the chapter.

Formative influences on European research on consumer behaviour

The editors acknowledge that the study of marketing in general, and consumer behaviour in particular, started later in Europe than in North America, and that both the number and quality of articles written were less, certainly up to the 1980s. As Lars Gunnar Mattson and Philippe Naert explain, 'an important historical fact is that during the formative years for research in marketing in Europe, i.e., during the 50's and 60's, the research contributions have typically been virtually unknown outside the individual country (or, in some cases, region, e.g. the Nordic countries) where the research took place' (1985: 5). Since then, however, there has been a burgeoning of activity in both fields, and there is now an abundant and rich literature available, much of which is of noteworthy quality and interest. Thus, while it might be forgivable for compendiums of readings in marketing and consumer behaviour to have a North American bias in the 1960s and 1970s, that is no longer the case.

The variety and richness of European research on consumption also reflects the fact that many European scholars had a very strong influence on both the inception and development of consumer behaviour research in North America, being at the origin of those concepts that gradually gained a wide popularity among American scholars. This scenario, acknowledged by many researchers, has been briefly developed by Kassarjian in a recent article.[4] Consumer research originally consisted of 'economic theorizing, perhaps analyses of secondary data, and at times, naïve attempts at experimentation and surveys' (Kassarjian, 1994, p. 265). This naive view of consumption rapidly changed after the Second World War, mainly because of the rising influence of alternative approaches being proposed by European scholars. A good example is the influence of *economic psychology*, which derived originally from George Katona's psychological approach to economic behaviour. Psychological variables, he contended, may contribute to a better understanding of the behaviour of economic agents. The perception and evaluations of economic reality, as well as consumers' expectations and attitudes, play a leading role in their economic behaviour. This approach was crucial in the sense that it motivated marketers to look at consumers' motivations, expectations, etc. It also contributed to the view that consumption is an extremely complex and unpredictable phenomenon which could not be reduced to the theoretical and objective observations of *homo economicus*. A new approach to the consumer, which started in the 1960s, showed that consumer behaviour could not be predicted and explained by looking at economic laws without considering any behavioural 'disturbances' or psychological processes of evaluation, decision and choice.[5] A new consideration for the behaviour of consumers (as opposed to very general economic rules) hence allowed other disciplines to infuse marketing thought and shed new light on the behaviour of consumers.

Granted that the consumer was not a *homo economicus* rationally engaged in a process of utility maximization, psychological research soon provided a conceptual framework to analyze such irrational and affective determinants of consumption choices. Largely based on Freud's seminal work in psychoanalysis, which laid the ground for the study of unconscious motives underlying the way human beings perceive reality and act, the psychological approach soon became a major paradigm in consumer research and largely influenced the fields of investigation and the methodology. A good example is the development of motivation studies in the 1950s. The Austrian Ernst Dichter (1964) was also very influential in showing that consumers make most of their product and brand choices on the basis of emotional and deep-seated reasons they might not always be aware of (Sheth *et al.*, 1988). He was the first to use clinical psychology experiments which relied heavily on focus group interviews and personal interviews to interpret consumers' motivations to buy. The impact of psychology on consumer behaviour can be discerned throughout chapter 3, as well as in articles dealing with the predominance of affective factors in consumers' choices.

Some specificities of the European approach to consumption

The individual chapters represent a distinct European view of the world and expose the biases in education and research tradition that have influenced our approach. It thus seems important to stress the various specificities of European research as opposed to the American tradition.

First, it has been argued that the approach taken by European researchers reflects the relationships between business schools and the universities. Locke (1983), for example, has stressed the importance of the very early links of the German business schools to the universities, an explanation for the strong scientific approach to business education and a propensity to favour mathematical model-building as a basis for research. Such an emphasis is clearly visible in the large literature on stochastic models of consumer behaviour which, in fact, is probably the branch of European research that is best known to our American colleagues (Mattson and Naert, 1985). This tradition is based in the centre of Western Europe – mainly Belgium, Germany and the Netherlands. A related point is that many of the business schools in mainland Europe grew out of the economic departments within their parent universities, and economics, particularly microeconomics, continues to play a large part in their business education (Mattson and Naert, 1985). In many European business schools, business administration is referred to as 'economics of business'. It is hardly surprising, therefore, to find that much marketing and consumer behaviour research draws on economic models for its structure. A particular example is the large and impressive body of work which has developed in the area of brand management, notably the Dirichlet model which has long been considered a very important contribution to the modelling of consumer behaviour (see chapter 2). Another significant and influential example in the same chapter is the model developed by Foxall to analyze the situational determinants of consumer behaviour.

Secondly, and quite paradoxically, an important aspect which characterizes the European approach to the study of consumer behaviour is the strong influence of social and human sciences on the research approach. Whereas the American approach was initially largely influenced by economic theory, European research always showed strong affiliations to such disciplines as psychology, sociology, psychoanalysis, anthropology, etc. The epistemological influence of the human and social sciences can easily be perceived through the citation of such names as Katona, Dichter, Lévi-Strauss, Barthes and Baudrillard in European consumer behaviour literature.

A cognate discipline which is highly visible in European consumer behaviour literature is sociology, which readily provided tools to analyze such phenomena as socialization processes, the influence of reference groups, the spreading of rumours, etc. Baudrillard's early work on the political economy of the sign, for instance, offers crucial insights into the power of consumption and how it plays an important role in organizing contemporary societies around objects, needs and commodities. In our society, advertising, packaging and window displays linked to the proliferation of commodities, increased the quantity of signs produced and resulted in the proliferation of what Baudrillard calls 'sign-value'. Hence, commodities cannot be characterized solely by use-value and exchange-value (as has long been the case in marketing), but rather by sign-value (that is, an expression of their prestige, style, power, etc.), which becomes an essential, constituent part of the commodity. Chapter 8 accounts for studies largely influenced by these sociological paradigms.

The importance of 'sign-value' underlies semiotics, which Europeans have embraced with great vigour and creativity and have more or less made their own. Semiotics, which attempts to interpret how goods are encoded within systems of signs and meanings, can be regarded as one of the most important contributions of European research to the study of consumption. This is one of the most exciting new topics which is listed in Part IV, 'Alternative Perspectives', and the selection includes well-known articles from established authors as well as contributions from talented, young scholars.

The rising influence of human sciences can also be perceived in the emergence of alternative views on consumer behaviour. In this European tradition, the consumer has gradually been perceived as an individual, whose consumption decisions do not solely derive from the principle of utility. Consumption has hence been viewed as a set of practices by which the individual creates meanings, seeks for experiences, lives emotions, etc. This new approach to consumption comes through clearly in chapter 8, which is an attempt to introduce emerging streams of research in the field of consumption.

Thirdly, a key epistemological difference needs to be stressed between the American and European approaches to consumption. The American approach to behaviour traditionally relies on nomothetic methods, which are factual, orderly, clear-cut and satisfyingly systemic.[6] On the other hand, Europeans have been characterized by an eminent American researcher, Sidney Levy, as being 'traditionally more willing to explore depth, to enjoy analysis of symbols, to cope with ambiguity'.[7] Nevertheless, the richness of the European approach stems from its ability to integrate various research perspectives. From an epistemological point of view, the articles selected represent two opposite research traditions.[8] Many articles, especially in Part II of the book, represent a positivist approach based on experiments and surveys largely driven by quantitative data. The focus is on buying decisions through the analysis of the various stages which end with the purchase decision. Other articles, especially in Parts III and IV, represent a non-positivist approach in which the focus is on consuming rather than simply on buying. This research tradition is essentially concerned with the analysis of emotions, affects and meanings.

The richness of the European tradition in consumer research lies in its diversity and its ability to integrate very many different research approaches and paradigms. A good illustration of the possible coexistence of opposite paradigms is the coexistence of two successful research methods in Europe over the last twenty years: the phenomenological approach and the structuralist approach. The phenomenological method, committed to a new form of 'concrete thinking' which privileges the intentional relation of consciousness to the meanings of the world by returning to the origin of ideas in our lived experience of things themselves, is a good example of a philosophical approach which infused consumer research and contributed to new ways of embracing knowledge. The influence of phenomenology can be seen in such research areas as the experiential approach, the analysis of such phenomena as gift giving, possession, self-extension through objects, consumption addition, etc. Phenomenology represents a field of research categorized under the concept of the 'etic' approach, that is, a mode of investigation attempting to study consumption practices in their surface structure.

Opposed to this, the 'emic' approach considers elements of sign structures with respect to their function within the code. Structuralism, which represents an emic approach, jointly became a dominant intellectual paradigm in Europe in the 1960s and infused consumer research in its anthropological and semiotic dimension. The successful coexistence of such diverse approaches accounts for the originality and richness of the European approach to consumer behaviour, which undoubtedly constitutes a valuable source of references for anyone interested in the study of consumption.

Notes

1. Kassarjian Harold and Robertson Thomas, 1968, *Perspectives in Consumer Behavior*, Glenview, IL: Scott, Foresman and Co.
2. Kassarjian Harold and Robertson Thomas, 1991, *Perspectives in Consumer Behavior*, 5th edition, Englewood Cliffs, NJ: Prentice-Hall.
3. In the previous edition of the book only one European author is referenced, that is, Fred van Raaij, 'Economic psychology', originally published in the *Journal of Economic Psychology*, 1(1981), 1–24.
4. Harold H. Kassarjian, 1994, 'Scholarly traditions and European roots of American consumer research', in Gilles Laurent, Gary L. Lillien and Bernard Pras, *Research Traditions in Marketing*, International Series in Quantitative Marketing, EIASM, Kluwer Academic Publishers, 265–79.

5. For more details on this topic, see chapter 7 on Economic psychology and Fred van Raaij, 'Economic psychology', originally published in the *Journal of Economic Psychology*, 1(1981), 1–24.
6. These are the characteristics applied by Gordon Allport to American psychology, quoted in Levy (1994).
7. Commentary by Sidney Levy to Kassarjian's presentation: 'Scholarly traditions and European roots of American consumer research', in Gilles Laurent, Gary L. Lillien and Bernard Pras, 1994, *Research Traditions in Marketing*, International Series in Quantitative Marketing, EIASM, Kluwer Academic Publishers, 283–7.
8. This opposition is largely developed by Russel Belk, in 'Studies in the new consumer behaviour', in D. Miller (ed.), 1995, *Acknowledging Consumption. A Review of New Studies*, London: Routledge, 58–95.

References

Baudrillard, J., 1981, *Pour une critique de l'économie politique du signe*, Paris: Gallimard, 1972; translated as *For a Critique of the Political Economy of the Sign*, St Louis: Telos Press.

Belk, R., 1995, 'Studies in the new consumer behaviour', in D. Miller (ed.), *Acknowledging Consumption. A Review of New Studies*, London: Routledge, 58–95.

Dichter, E.,1964, *The Handbook of Consumer Motivations*, New York: McGraw-Hill.

Kassarjian, H. H., 1994, 'Scholarly traditions and European roots of American consumer research', in Gilles Laurent, Gary L. Lillien and Bernard Pras, *Research Traditions in Marketing*, International Series in Quantitative Marketing, EIASM, Kluwer Academic Publishers, 265–79.

Kassarjian, H. H. and Robertson, T., 1968, *Perspectives in Consumer Behavior*, Glenview, IL: Scott, Foresman and Co.

Kassarjian, H. H. and Robertson, T., 1991, *Perspectives in Consumer Behavior*, 5th edition, Englewood Cliffs, NJ: Prentice-Hall.

Levy, S., 1994, 'Commentary to Kassarjian's presentation': 'Scholarly traditions and European roots of American consumer research', in Gilles Laurent, Gary L. Lillien and Bernard Pras, *Research Traditions in Marketing*, International Series in Quantitative Marketing, EIASM, Kluwer Academic Publishers, 283–7.

Locke, R. R., 1983, 'The influence of past systems of management education on current systems – The German case', Working Paper, 83–14, European Institute for Advanced Studies in Management, Brussels.

Mattson, L.G. and Naert, P. A., 1985, 'Research in marketing in Europe. Some reflections on its settings, accomplishments and challenges', *International Journal of Research in Marketing*, 2(1), 3–25.

Sheth, J. N., Gardner, D. M. and Garrett, D. E., 1988, *Marketing Theory. Evolution and Evaluation*, New York: Wiley.

van Raaij, W. F., 1981, 'Economic psychology', *Journal of Economic Psychology*, 1, 1–24.

Acknowledgements

● ●

A collection of readings such as this is a collaborative effort which requires the goodwill and co-operation of many people and organizations. We have been most gratified by the interest and assistance extended to us by all those approached and we would like to acknowledge this assistance.

Firstly, we must thank all of the authors for allowing us to publish their work. We have derived much benefit and enjoyment from our search of the literature and we are most grateful for this opportunity. We have come away from this exercise with a sense that the study of consumer behaviour is alive and active around Europe and that there is a considerable volume of good research in existence which deserves to reach a wider public. We were impressed by the originality as well as rigour of the material uncovered and we feel that translation difficulties may have denied some of this material the attention it truly deserves. We feel pleased if this volume helps in a small way to achieve recognition for the valuable work of our colleagues around Europe.

We must also thank the publishers of the journals who kindly allowed us to reproduce their material. In particular, we would note the *International Journal of Research in Marketing*, the *European Marketing Academy*, the *Journal of Economic Psychology*, *Recherche et Applications en Marketing*, the *Journal of the Market Research Society*, the *Journal of Marketing*, the *Journal of Marketing Research*, the *Journal of the Academy of Marketing Science*, *Sociology*, and the *Journal of Personality and Social Psychology*. We wish to express our thanks to Julia Helmsley, Alison Stanford and their colleagues at Prentice Hall. Their patience and support throughout the rather extended timeframe of this project was exemplary and their efficiency and professionalism in the execution of the publishing process was an important contribution.

As in all of our working lives, we owe a great debt to our families for allowing us the space and time to devote to this project. Additionally, our motivation and achievements benefit in no small way from the valuable and enjoyable interactions with the friends and colleagues with whom we work. We hope that they, in turn, will find some interest and value in the contents of this book.

Finally, we must acknowledge that the choice and arrangement of material in this book is our own and we accept full responsibility for any errors or omissions. We hope that the end result is a worthy addition to the consumer behaviour literature and we look forward to updating and revising it in response to the feedback we receive as time progresses.

Mary Lambkin   Fred van Raaij
Gordon Foxall   Benoît Heilbrunn

The publisher gratefully acknowledges the following sources for permission to reproduce material in this book previously published elsewhere. Every effort has been made to trace copyright holders, but if any have been inadvertently overlooked the publisher will be pleased to make the necessary arrangement at the first opportunity.

Chapter 1. Pinson and Jolibert: © Economica, 1997.
Chapter 2. Ehrenberg: © reprinted by permission of The Market Research Society and A.S.C. Ehrenberg, 1991. Ehrenberg, Goodhardt and Barwise: © reprinted with permission from *Journal of Marketing*, published by the American Marketing Association, 1990. Foxall: © G.R. Foxall; reprinted with permission of *Journal of the Academy of Marketing Science*, 1992.
Chapter 3. Bon and Pras: © reprinted with kind permission from Elsevier Science – NL, Sara Burgerhartstraat 25, 1055 KV Amsterdam, The Netherlands, 1984. Foxall and Goldsmith: © reprinted by permission of The Market Research Society and G.R. Foxall and R.E. Goldsmith, 1988. Derbaix and Pham: © C. Derbaix and M.T. Pham; reprinted with permission of *Recherches et Applications en Marketing*, French Marketing Association, 1989.
Chapter 4. Laurent and Kapferer: © reprinted with permission from *Journal of Marketing Research*, published by the American Marketing Association, 1985. Pinson: © reprinted with kind permission from Elsevier Science – NL, Sara Burgerhartstraat 25, 1055 KV Amsterdam, The Netherlands, 1986. Derbaix and Vanden Abeele: © reprinted with kind permission from Elsevier Science – NL, Sara Burgerhartstraat 25, 1055 KV Amsterdam, The Netherlands, 1985.
Chapter 5. Webley and Lea: © reprinted with kind permission from Elsevier Science – NL, Sara Burgerhartstraat 25, 1055 KV Amsterdam, The Netherlands, 1993. Böcker: © F. Böcker; reprinted with permission of *Recherches et Applications en Marketing*, French Marketing Association, 1992.
Chapter 6. Featherstone: © M. Featherstone, 1990; reprinted with permission of M. Featherstone, The British Sociological Association and Cambridge University Press. Van Raaij: © reprinted with kind permission from Elsevier Science – NL, Sara Burgerhartstraat 25, 1055 KV Amsterdam, The Netherlands, 1993. Schwartz and Bilsky: © 1990 by the American Psychological Association; reprinted with permission.
Chapter 7. Antonides: © reprinted with kind permission from Elsevier Science – NL, Sara Burgerhartstraat 25, 1055 KV Amsterdam, The Netherlands, 1989. Van Raaij © reprinted with kind permission from Elsevier Science – NL, Sara Burgerhartstraat 25, 1055 KV Amsterdam, The Netherlands, 1984.
Chapter 8. Nöth: © reprinted with kind permission from Elsevier Science – NL, Sara Burgerhartstraat 25, 1055 KV Amsterdam, The Netherlands, 1988. Heilbrunn: © B. Heilbrunn, European Marketing Academy Conference, Paris, May 1995. Floch: © reprinted with kind permission from Elsevier Science – NL, Sara Burgerhartstraat 25, 1055 KV Amsterdam, The Netherlands, 1988.

Part I

foundations

Introduction: The development of consumer research in Europe

1

Pinson, C. and Jolibert, A., 1997, 'Consumer behaviour: An overview of current approaches and issues', in Y. Simon and P. Joffre (eds), *Encyclopédie de Gestion*, 2nd edition, Paris: Economica

Introduction

The purpose of this first chapter is to provide an overview of the consumer behaviour literature emanating from the European continent. This is a formidable task for several reasons. First, the range of potential topics that might be considered to belong within the subject of consumer behaviour is so large that it is difficult to keep the introduction within reasonable bounds and to decide which material to include or exclude. Secondly, a focus on the European literature does not mean that ideas coming from other sources, particularly North America, can be ignored. In fact, the opposite is the case; a good review of European writing must place it in the context of the total literature on the subject. Thirdly, the authors must attend to two dimensions of the literature simultaneously: namely, actual differences in the real world, i.e. behaviour of European consumers compared with other regions of the world, and differences in the concepts and research methods that European scholars bring to bear on their subject matter.

Fortunately, Christian Pinson and Alain Jolibert, the authors of the overview of the development of consumer behaviour contained in chapter 1, are well placed to meet these challenges. They are both distinguished scholars with an acknowledged interest and reputation in the area of consumer behaviour and they have an encyclopaedic knowledge of their subject from extensive teaching and research in the area. Their overview ranges across most of the main headings covered in consumer behaviour texts, presenting core ideas and identifying particular contributions by European authors. They cover traditional topics such as personality and self-concept, lifestyles and values, social class and reference group influences and decision making within the family, but with a refreshing originality coming from the inclusion of citations from hitherto unfamiliar authors. They also address the newer topics concerned with individual behaviour and decision making, notably product involvement and brand attachment, sensory detection and attentive processes, information processing and decision making, choice criteria and choices made.

This chapter also provides a useful organizing framework for the more narrowly focused papers in succeeding chapters. Having read this introductory chapter, subsequent papers can be easily placed within context and can perhaps be interpreted more accurately by interested readers. A further benefit comes from the fact that this chapter identifies sources of data on European consumer markets and provides an exhaustive reference list which is likely to be helpful to both marketing practitioners and academics.

Consumer behaviour: An overview of current approaches and issues

●●

Christian Pinson
Professor of Marketing, INSEAD and University of Paris-Dauphine

Alain Jolibert
Professor of Marketing, University Pierre Mendès-France of Grenoble

Summary

Current approaches to consumer behaviour (Robertson and Kassarjian, 1991; Kroeber-Riel, 1992; Dubois, 1994; Filser, 1994; Foxall and Goldsmith, 1994; Engel, Blackwell and Miniard, 1995) are generally based upon three fundamental postulates:

- consumers do not strictly obey the principles of economic rationality as commonly defined;
- consumers do not, however, behave in a random manner and their behaviour cannot be adequately described by stochastic models;
- consumer behaviour stems from innate and acquired needs and involves a complex combination of conscious and unconscious processes as well as rational and emotional factors.

Consumer behaviour may take the form of an impulsive purchase or may be preceded by a lengthy decision-making process. In all cases, it is the expression of a conscious or unconscious search for the satisfaction of physiological, economic or socio–psychological needs. This article offers an overall presentation of the major individual and situational variables which help explain consumer behaviour.[1]

1. The importance of economic and socio-demographic factors

Consumption is of course dependent on inescapable economic, demographic and social realities. Indeed, the economic situation, together with the evolution of mentalities and lifestyles,[2] has a decisive influence on consumer general spending and on the demand for certain goods and services. Table 1 illustrates how the structure of household consumption

---

This is an abridged and slightly modified version of the article 'Le comportement du consommateur', in Y. Simon and P. Joffre (eds), *Encyclopédie de Gestion*, Paris: Economica, 1997, chapter 22.

Table 1   Consumer expenditure by object in Europe (1993)

Units: % of Total Household Budget	Food, Drinks, Tobacco	Clothing and Footwear	Housing and Household Fuels	Household Goods and Services	Health	Transport and Communications	Leisure	Others
Austria	20.4	9.3	18.8	8.3	6.0	18.2	8.2	10.8
Belgium	21.9	7.7	16.5	11.3	12.6	13.0	4.8	12.3
Denmark	20.2	5.3	27.8	6.1	2.2	14.9	10.4	13.0
Finland	22.2	4.6	21.2	5.9	4.9	13.7	9.1	18.4
France	18.6	6.0	21.1	7.5	10.3	15.9	7.5	13.0
Germany, East (1992)	25.0	4.5	15.8	11.7	5.9	20.1	7.8	9.2
Germany, West	16.8	7.8	22.5	9.2	5.2	17.0	10.4	10.9
Greece	37.4	8.2	13.0	8.0	4.1	15.7	5.9	7.8
Ireland	35.6	7.1	12.3	7.2	4.2	12.9	12.5	8.2
Italy	19.6	9.8	15.8	9.6	7.0	12.5	9.0	16.7
Luxemburg	18.6	5.9	20.0	11.3	7.7	20.1	4.5	11.9
Netherlands	14.7	6.8	18.0	6.9	13.2	13.2	10.1	17.1
Norway	25.3	6.2	19.3	6.4	5.6	13.0	8.7	15.6
Portugal (1986)	32.7	9.2	7.8	5.4	2.6	12.3	5.3	24.7
Spain	21.0	8.9	13.0	6.9	4.6	16.4	7.0	22.2
Sweden	18.6	6.2	29.6	6.6	2.0	15.5	9.5	11.9
Switzerland	25.0	4.0	19.3	4.5	12.7	11.2	9.9	13.4
United Kingdom	21.1	5.5	16.2	6.1	1.5	9.8	10.2	29.7

Source: Based on 1995 European Marketing Data and Statistics, Euromonitor, London.

budgets varies across European countries. The predictive power of these macro-variables is, however, more problematic when they are no longer used to describe or explain macro-consumer behaviour, but rather to predict the choice of specific products or brands.

Some general trends in European society are worth mentioning. These changes have created market opportunities for some industries and stable or declining demand for others. For example, the increase in the number of working women has clearly accelerated the development of mail order sales and more generally speaking of any new selling formulas or products (frozen food, for example) which make it possible to save time. The decrease in [the] size of the family due to cohabitation, divorce, diminishing birth rate, has led to changes in food consumption, packaging, the demand for housing, furnishings, etc. The increase in unemployment has caused a decrease in expenditure connected with the individual dwelling and clothing, and has led to an increase in do-it-yourself, barter and the appearance of a type of consumption characterized as 'tribal' by some observers (Maffesoli, 1988; Badot and Cova, 1995; Cova, 1995). Serious concerns regarding the economic situation could lead to more fragmented forms of consumption in which production and consumption interpenetrate each other. Rochefort (1995), in a recent book, describes the development of this new generation of consumers that he calls the 'entrepreneurial consumers'.

The ageing of the population (120 million Europeans are over 50 years of age) has also become a major problem in Europe. A French statistical study (Darmon *et al.*, 1991) suggests that this ageing has indeed had a significant effect on areas such as health, food, leisure and transportation. The market for those over 50 years of age has thus become a prime target today (see Treguer, 1994; Burt and Gabbott, 1995; Guérin, 1995, as well as the July–August 1994 issue of *Admap*). According to Rybarski (*Marketing Week*, 2 July 1993), 80 per cent of individual assets in Britain belong to people over 50 years of age. Banks, insurance companies, press and travel agencies have been among the first businesses to attempt to develop new products and services for older consumers. In France, a study run by CREDOC (a state agency) found that while their life expectancy has been lengthened, their purchasing power has increased fivefold, between 1960 and 1990; that of those under 50 years of age has increased threefold.

Elderly consumers typically purchase in small quantities, often in stores close to their residence, favour traditional food preparations, earlier meal-times, have specific service needs in terms of home delivery, product installation and repairing; they are overconsumers of the daily press and of TV and radio broadcasts. Their behaviour is, none the less, quite varied and it would be wrong to consider this segment as homogeneous. This point is well illustrated in a study carried out by CREDOC on the eating habits of seniors (Greiveldinger *et al.*, 1990) as well as in a special report presented in the 16 October 1995 issue of *CB News*. Only after 65–70 years of age should age be considered to be a discriminating factor in consumption. The age felt, or what has been called 'cognitive age', seems to be the influential factor rather than actual age. Cognitive age is influenced by various factors, such as retirement, the departure of children, the death of a spouse, one's state of health, purchasing power, involvement in non-professional activities and a certain number of personality traits (Schiffman and Sherman, 1991; Wilkes, 1992; van Auken and Barry, 1995; Guiot, 1996).

The concept of [the] family lifecycle is commonly used, not only in marketing, but also in the economics, psychology and sociology literature to describe changes in the size and structure of the family. The underlying idea is that individuals follow a natural progression characterized by modifications in marital status, in the size of the household, in the age of the head of the family, in the presence of young or old children, etc., which all lead to important modifications in the organization of daily life, interaction processes and in the allocation of household resources (Wilkes, 1995). The epistemological validity of the family lifecycle concept and of the household typologies obtained when using it has been questioned (Lemel and Verger, 1986). To be really useful, the concept needs to be enlarged to take into account some of the recent social trends, such as the increase in the number of unmarried couples, working women, the divorced and changing roles in the family (Courson and de Saboulin, 1985; Hoffmann-Nowotny, 1987; De Gaulejac and Aubert, 1990). The model presented by Gilly and Enis (1982) takes into careful consideration late marriages and births, the absence of children, remarriages, cohabitation,[3] single-parent families and different cases in which the individual finds himself or herself alone. A recent study (Schaninger and Danko, 1993) has demonstrated the empirical interest of this model.

The notion of social class raises similar problems. Regardless of the method used to divide the total population into classes – using such criteria as possessions, occupation, source of family income, education, social interactions and affiliations (Marshall *et al.*, 1988; Rossides, 1990; Bottomore, 1991) – the central hypothesis is that these classes can be arranged in terms of some measure of social status or standing, to form a hierarchical division of society. Whereas American commercial consumer researchers do not hesitate to use subjective criteria such as the prestige of a given profession or the place of residence in addition to more objective criteria, in France, social classes are essentially identified by using the four socio-professional categories defined by the state agency INSEE (Bénéton, 1991; Lemel, 1991). These four classes, generally called A, B, C, D, are described below:

A. the upper or [dominant] class which include people having either hierarchical (e.g. senior managers) or intellectual (e.g. university professors or upper professionals) or economic power (e.g. company owners);
B. the middle class or lower 'bourgeoisie' which includes middle managers and civil servants, and also middle businessmen and employees;
C. the lower class, which is composed of blue-collar workers, the vast majority of farmers;
D. the class of the economically weak composed of active elements (low-paid manual labourers and farm workers, minimum wage-earners), or inactive (unemployed living on welfare, poverty-stricken retirees).

At the European level, the ESOMAR Association has recommended the harmonization of the different national systems to come up with a common European system where seven social classes are distinguished (for a more precise description of this fairly complex system, see Marbeau, 1992; Quatrezooz and Vancraeynest, 1992).

Assuming, as is often the case, that members of a given social class share the same central values, purchasing behaviour should be relatively similar within one social class, while it should differ across classes. Bourdieu (1979, p. 141), among others, has shown that social class and lifestyle can be used to explain the possession of certain goods. Moingeon (1993) offers a presentation of the potential contribution of Bourdieu's idea to marketing. An INSEE study (see Herpin, 1986) demonstrates that within the same [. . .] revenue brackets, clothing and fashion behaviour are strongly influenced by social class; a phenomenon also very visible in the domain of cultural and leisure activities, household equipment, media consumption and stores patronized, just to cite some classic examples. More than forty years after the introduction of the concept of social classes in marketing, we have to admit, however, that reality is much more complex than it may seem. In comparing the predictive power of income and social class, it appears, in fact, that the concept of social class is only an indicator of consumption when the 'sign-value' of the goods bought and the retail outlets used is taken into consideration (Grønhaug and Trapp, 1989; Kanwar and Pagiavlas, 1992; Labich, 1994). This seems to be due to two related factors:

● membership in a social class – as commonly measured – and income level are very imperfectly correlated;
● social status stems more from an individual's professional activity and his/her social position than from his/her income.

Thus the impact of social class on consumer behaviour mainly concerns those products and services which correspond to functional needs specific to a socio-professional category (deep freezers for farmers or personal computers for company executives, for example) or which benefit from a large social visibility: these products play a symbolic function in the sense that they signal the social class to which the consumer feels they belong or with which they aspire to be identified.

2. Reference groups and the process of social influence

The concept of 'reference group' is often used to explain the influence of some groups of individuals on purchasing and consumption behaviour. These groups can be real (family, friends, professional acquaintances . . .) or imaginary. Their influence can be positive or negative.

As de Montmollin (1977) noted, the process of social influence involves two distinct phases: one centres on how receptive the individual is to the normative information transmitted by diverse social groups (see Bearden and Rose, 1990), the other, on the form taken by the individual's response to this information. Uncertainty plays a fundamental role in both these steps. Indeed, social influence can occur only if the individual is uncertain as to the behaviour to be adopted in particular purchasing or consuming situations. This uncertainty may refer to the norms of the reference group to which the individual wishes to be associated, but also to the importance accorded, by this same group, to these norms and their desire and ability to make them respected. In other words, along with the question 'What must I do?' is a second type of [question]: 'Did I do the right thing?' and 'What is the sanction or the reward which awaits me?'.

A variety of factors will have a bearing on how dependent the consumer will be on one or several reference groups. Some of these factors are product- or brand-specific; others concern the individuals themselves. The more the possession and use of the product are visible to others (de Chernatony *et al.*, 1995), the more likely the individual will be subject to social pressure. Consumers, just like any other individuals, have to arbitrate between, on the one hand, a concern to affirm their membership to this or that social group, and, on the other, a need, which can be equally strong, to manifest their difference. Some products have so much the status of social symbols (McCracken, 1986; Belk, 1988; Manrai and Manrai, 1995) that they constitute a real semiotic system for the consumer (Nöth, 1988; Semprini, 1995; Douglas and Isherwood, 1996). The conspicuous consumption of these symbols serves a two-fold objective: first, they give a certain idea of [the] self to others ('social self'); they can also be used, according to social identity theory (Dittmar, 1992; Kleine *et al.*, 1993), as reference points in the construction of social reality and to anticipate the reactions of others and to define social roles.

'Symbolic interactionism' and 'self-concept' theories are useful to understand how the image that the individual builds for himself or herself (Sirgy, 1986; Oppenheimer, 1990; Burkitt, 1991; Hatie, 1992; Wiley, 1995) is based on subjective impressions. Reflexive appraisal theory explains that what people really think of you is actually less important than what you believe they think of you (Ichiyama, 1993). The self has been conceptualized as a knowledge structure which plays, in the memory, the role of a prototype, of a 'schema', of an associative network that the consumer may use in processing data (Olson and Zanna, 1990; Nystedt *et al.*, 1991; Piolat *et al.*, 1992; Debevec and Romeo, 1992). There is no single self-concept but many evolving self-concepts (real self, private self, social self, self as perceived by others . . .) which are more or less conscious (Rimé and Le Bon, 1984). The consumer engages in more or less 'self-monitoring', depending on a variety of contextual and individual factors (Brewer, 1991; Larkin, 1991; Kuhl, 1992; Monteil, 1993; Banaji, 1994; Bakhurst and Sypnowich, 1995). The self-concept clarity scale developed by Campbell *et al.* (1996) makes it possible to determine to what degree the dimensions underlying the self-concept are clearly defined by the subject, as well as their level of coherence and stability.

As suggested by Aron *et al.* (1991, 1992), individuals can include in their 'self-concept' individuals other than themselves as soon as those are sufficiently close. The self-concept can therefore take on a 'plural' or 'collective' dimension (Trafimov *et al.*, 1991). It is this dimension which we find, for example, in the 'us-concept' which has been proposed (Castellan, 1993; Zouaghi-Bensedrine, 1996) to explain the influence the family plays as a reference group. The 'us-concept' is a mental representation which individuals hold of the identity, personality and lifestyle values of their family. Depending on whether this representation is positive or negative, they will try to reproduce or, alternatively, avoid the types of consumer behaviour which, they believe, characterize their family.

As noted by Rochefort (1995), the importance of the symbolic factor of consumption has drastically increased in France during the 1980s at the expense of the functional value of goods. For Rochefort, this 'immaterial component', as it is termed, stems more from a need for reassurance and increased concerns for such traditional values as health, ecology, permanence of time and security, than from a need to produce a public self-image, as was the case in the so-called 'showing-off years'. For example, the success of the *Espace* and *Twingo* cars from Renault is interpreted by Rochefort as a need to extend the family universe in the face of the aggression of road traffic and of social issues.

3. The impact of personality

Although these two dimensions are indissociable, personality research emphasizes either the overt, directly observable aspects of human conduct (the *persona*),[4] or the inner aspects of human conduct (the *anima*). Personality, as conceived by Sigmund Freud, is the product of the interaction of three elements: the id, the ego and the superego. The id corresponds to primary needs, to often instinctive drives, buried in the unconscious. The superego reflects the rules, values and norms imposed by society; in a certain sense, it acts as an individual's moral and social conscience. The ego represents the interests of the individual. It ensures the necessary arbitration between the demands of the id and the constraints of the superego. Freud further distinguishes the three following psychosexual types:

- The *erotic type* within whom the dominating function is that of the id.
- The *obsessional type* whose dominating function is the superego.
- The *narcissistic type*, who is characterized by a constant worry to affirm his or her ego.

Also according to Freud, the sexual evolution of the child involves three stages of libidinal development: the oral stage, the anal stage and the phallic stage. A fixation at one of these stages results in the adult individual in certain expectations and dominant types of behaviour. For example, in her excellent psychoanalytic study of smoking behaviour, Lesourne (1984) explains that beyond the 'initiatory' function of the first cigarette which allows adolescents to state publicly that they have attained adulthood, cigarettes allow smokers to 'regress' towards infantile experiences marked by 'oral avidity, anal mastery, phallic ambition'. Smoking, especially when it is done in excess, is also to enact something dangerous, which makes it possible to play with death and to imagine that one exercises a magical power over it.

Jung (1921) is the author of the well-known categorization of people as 'introverts' and 'extroverts' and of a classification into eight 'psychological types' based on four psychic functions: thought, emotion, sensation and intuition. This typology is often operationalized by using the Myers-Briggs test (Murray, 1990) and has been the object of several consumer research applications (e.g. Gould, 1991; Hyman and Tansey, 1991).

Ernest Dichter (1960) and a myriad of so-called motivation research studies have contributed to popularizing the vision of a consumer researching the satisfaction of id-derived, primitive needs (very often of a sexual nature); these needs are very often suppressed (in the Freudian sense of the term) and were described as being essentially unconscious, socially disreputable and incompatible with the idea of a 'rational' consumer. After having been very popular for more than two decades, and although still being used by many European market researchers specializing in so-called 'qualitative' studies, motivation research has become virtually non-existent in academic circles where it has literally lost its respectability and credibility. This disappearance can be explained by the two-fold criticism aimed against it. A first and enduring attack on motivation research (Packard, 1957; Guyon, 1984; Haineault and Roy, 1984) is that it gives unscrupulous marketers the possibility of manipulating consumers through the exploitation of deep motivations of which consumers are scarcely or not at all conscious. The validity and reliability of the methods used by motivation researchers have also been the object of strong attacks coming for the most part from supporters of the positivist and empiricist approach. It is only recently that certain academic circles (e.g. Holbrook, 1988; Albanese, 1990) have called for a renaissance of psychoanalytic theory in consumer research.

Psychoanalytical personality theories were extended through the development of approaches which place more emphasis on the social and cultural determinants of personality. Here we find those authors that Clapier-Valladon (1991) refers to as 'cultural psychoanalysts'. For Alfred Adler (1938), individuals' behaviour is directed by a will to overcome an 'inferiority complex' and a feeling of insecurity. This can be achieved through very subjective and indirect psychological means, for example, through the selection of occupations, social positions, activities and products carrying a strong social image. Karen Horney's (1950) approach is also based on the concept of basic anxiety resulting from the more than imperfect relationships which parents maintain with their children. Throughout life, the individual will seek to allay this anxiety, by being compliant, aggressive or detached. The CAD (Tyagi, 1983) is a test of interpersonal orientation which makes it possible to classify individuals into these three categories (compliant, aggressive, detached).

While 'social learning' theorists consider that human behaviour can be explained by a wealth of social motivations acquired through conditioning, others such as Carl R. Rogers (1961) or Abraham H. Maslow (1964) attribute a real force of self-fulfilment to man. For the 'interactionists' (e.g. Endler and Parker, 1992) the instability of behaviour from one situation to the next is the rule and it is necessary to take into account the interaction between the individual and his or her surroundings as well as the similarity of situations if one is to find some coherence or stability (Mischel, 1990).

Finally, certain authors – the factor structuralists – view personality as the sum of personality traits which can be statistically inferred from observable quantifiable differences in behaviour. Their objective is not to discover the unconscious reasons behind individual behaviour, but more to identify individual differences which are sufficiently stable to be called personality traits. These differences are drawn from personality inventories or from the lexical analysis of the terms most commonly used in natural languages to describe the personality of individuals. This research has long been dominated by the results obtained by Cattell (1983) and Eysenck (1967). While Cattell arrived at a factor structure of twelve, then sixteen, factors, Eysenck proposed the following three super-factors: (a) 'neuroticism', which corresponds to the level of emotional stability of the individual, (b) 'extroversion–introversion', and (c) 'psychotism', i.e. the extent to which the individual is (or is not) aggressive, antisocial, cold, self-centred. These two structural models of the personality are currently replaced by the so-called 'Big-Five Factor Model of Personality'. These five super factors are generally described as follows:

Factor E   *Extroversion*
Factor A   *Agreeableness*
Factor C   *Conscientiousness*
Factor N   *Neuroticism or Emotional Stability*
Factor O   *Openness to Experience*

These factors have been uncovered not only in questionnaires identical or similar to those used by Cattell but also in lexical analyses carried out in extremely diverse linguistic and cultural contexts.[5] Costa and McCrea (1992) have now developed a 240-item questionnaire *The Neo-Personality Inventory* (Neo-PI-R), which makes it possible to measure these five factors directly.

Although the consensus on the interest presented by the 'Big-Five Factor Model' is very strong, it is far, nevertheless, from being complete. The theoretical and methodological debate focuses on the contexts and research methods used, the number, nature, importance and interpretation of the factors revealed by factor analysis (Ben-Porath and Waller, 1992; Briggs, 1994; Costa and McCrea, 1995; Eysenck, 1992; McAdams, 1992; Wiggins, 1992; Zuckerman *et al.*, 1993; Block, 1995; Westen, 1996). In the light of this debate, we can conclude with John and Robins (1993) that the 'Big-Five Factor Model' is less a conceptualization of personality as it may exist and develop within an individual than a statistical representation describing the principal monothetic dimensions which underlie major trait differences as observed among individuals after testing or through spontaneous evaluations.

Apart from the theoretical debate on the true structure of personality, marketing researchers have long made efforts to find a link between this or that personality profile and this or that purchasing behaviour. As an illustration, the results of a psychoanalytically-oriented survey concerning the attitudes of French women to cosmetic products are presented in Table 2.

Several empirical studies in psychology (Larsen and Ketelaar, 1991; Watson and Clark, 1992) have demonstrated that extroversion correlates positively with positive affective reactions, while neuroticism is closely associated with negative affective reactions. This double relation has also been evidenced by Mooradian (1996) in the field of affective

Table 2 A psychoanalytic view of perfumery: French women's attitudes towards cosmetic products

Segment 1: *The sensual* Hedonists, they take care of their body and their appearance first of all for themselves.	25%
Segment 2: *The perfectionists* Only place importance on their body because it reflects their moral strength. Buy cosmetics only because they have to.	23%
Segment 3: *The detached* Their ideal would be to have a body which would go unseen. They place the least amount of importance on it and look after it only out of necessity.	11%
Segment 4: *The seductresses* Hedonists who exist through what they perceive others' judgements to be.	29%
Segment 5: *The social* Ready to make all efforts to make the most of their assets. A tool for social reference, their body must express the image they want to give of themselves.	12%

Source: Summary of a SOFCO study, Fédération de la parfumerie, 1982. Cited in *LSA* **883** (1 April 1983), 86–92.

responses to advertisements. In another study, Allsopp (1986a, 1986b) using the conceptual framework and the test developed by Eysenck and Eysenck (1975), has demonstrated that a positive correlation exists between extroversion, psychoticism (i.e. aggressive, antisocial nature . . .) and the consumption of beer and cider by young drinkers (18–21 years of age). Another interesting application of personality research is the study carried out on the choice of perfumes by Mensing and Beck (1988) at the Institute of Applied Aesthetics of Freiburg (Germany). These researchers, in collaboration with the Haarmann and Reimer Company, have found that a relationship exists between, on the one hand, individual colour preferences and certain personality traits (identified by the Eysenck test) such as extroversion–introversion, neuroticism (i.e. emotional stability) and, on the other hand, perfume preferences. This research project has led to the development of a test (The Haarmann and Reimer Colour Test) which makes it possible to orient women perfume-buyers towards fragrance 'notes' corresponding best to their needs. These needs are revealed by the coloured 'rosette' which the consumer chooses among those shown to her. Again, the underlying hypothesis of the test is that there is a relation: (a) between the choice of certain perfumes and personality, (b) between the choice of certain colours and personality, and then (c) between the choice of certain colours and certain perfumes. The reader will find in Table 3 a summary presentation of the seven segments in the women's perfume market (there is also a masculine version of the test), as identified by Mensing and Beck.

As the majority of marketing researchers and experts harbour no doubt that consumers first and foremost seek products conforming to their personality, it may seem strange that this relationship is so difficult to establish empirically. A meta-analysis (Lastovicka and Joachimsthaler, 1988) on 44 studies using personality variables demonstrates that, on the average, their effect is limited (r = 0.15). To quote Albanese (1990, p. 3), 'the paradox, quite simply stated, is that we all have a personality, but we do not know how it is systematically linked to our consumer behavior'. The reasons most often given for this state of affairs refer to the lack of [a] strong conceptual foundation, [and] the poor quality of the *ad hoc* research tools most often used. It is also probably illusory to hope to identify a simple, strong link between general personality traits and such or such an isolated act. It is rather in understanding behaviour in its globality and longitudinally that we may hope to find the role played by personality.[6] A personality type or trait may only trigger a particular type of behaviour if the context or situation justifies and permits it. For example, dogmatic consumers will express all the more differentiated behaviour when confronted with purchasing contexts to which they are accustomed (see Foxall, 1988). In the same way, the emotionally unstable (factor N in the 'Big-Five Factor Model') or aggressive (factor A) consumers can be distinguished from emotionally stable or cooperative consumers only in situations where these personality differences find a reason or an opportunity to express themselves. As emphasized by the interactionists (see the study of van Heck *et al.*, 1994), one should have a representative sample of subjects *and* situations in order to obtain a better idea of the personality–consumer relationship and to measure the essentially 'moderating' role of personality variables.

The new personality theory proposed by Mischel and Shoda (1995) seems to offer some highly interesting perspectives on how to integrate past research: according to these authors, there exist relatively stable individual differences which would explain the particular

Table 3   The psychology of women's perfume selection: the seven main segments identified by the H & R Color Test

Segments	Dominant Personality Traits	Major Individual Characteristics	Preferred Fragrance Notes	Examples of Corresponding Perfume Brands
1	Extroversion	Maximum search for stimulation, great sociability, willing to take risks	Fresh-floral	Ô de Lancôme
2	Introversion	Minimum search for stimulation, minimally sociable, rather self-centred	Oriental	Shalimar, Opium
3	Emotional ambivalence	Romantic, sentimental, interested in fashion trends, likes to dream	Floral-aldehydic-powdery	Rive Gauche, Nahéma
4	Emotional ambivalence with tendency towards extroversion	Flexible, modern, satisfied with their life, spontaneous, idealistic	Floral-fruity	Anaïs Anaïs
5	Emotional ambivalence with a tendency towards introversion	Strong need for security and protection, searching for an ordered lifestyle, protected from conflicts	Floriental	Must de Cartier
6	Emotional stability with a tendency towards extroversion	At peace with themselves, socially very active	Chypre	Miss Dior
7	Strong stability with a tendency towards introversion	Strong self-control, traditional values, reject everything which is excessive	Aldehydic-floral	Chanel No. 5

Source: Compiled from J. Mensing and C. Beck (1988) and Haarmann and Reimer, *Book of Perfume*, Gröss Verlag, Hamburg, Germany.

manner with which an individual perceives a given situation, activates certain cognitive and affective processes (in terms of coding, creation of beliefs, expectations, emotions, goals, values, projects . . .). In turn, these processes unleash, through mechanisms unique to each individual, other reactions which finally result in a type of behaviour.

4. Consumer lifestyle and values

Consumption behaviour may become so characteristic and stable as to achieve the status of consumer lifestyles. These styles result from the conditions of life to which consumers are subjected and from the major socio-cultural trends which they wish to follow. Through their consumption, people express not only their needs, but also their support (conscious or unconscious) of certain social values.

In the United States, 'psychographic' studies correspond to an attempt to gather data on consumers' activities, interests and opinions in order to understand their attitudes and behaviour regarding one, two or several products and to allow a segmentation of the market. This approach is characterized by a relative absence of theory in that it focuses on the simple statistical description of market segments at one point in time. The *Yankelovich Monitor* and the VALS approaches seem to be more concerned with the identification of the fundamental values and motivations underlying consumer behaviour. The VALS system has, however, been the subject of some criticism in academic circles and its validity (both convergent and discriminant) has not yet been clearly demonstrated (Beatty *et al.*, 1988; Lastovicka *et al.*, 1990).

The creation of [the Single] European Market on 1 January 1993, allowing the free movement of goods, capital and persons, has prompted many practitioners and academic researchers to look for large groups of 'Euro-consumers', who would consume more or less the same Euro-products and services, which would, in turn, help develop 'pan-European' marketing strategies. In spite of the fact that European needs and lifestyles tend to converge, there still exist in Europe such economic, demographic, social and cultural disparities that one cannot yet speak of a common European identity.[7] This has led some authors (e.g. Valette-Florence, 1991) to wonder if the very idea of a Euro-consumer is perhaps more of a myth than a reality. At the same time, one cannot deny the universal nature of certain socio-demographic (education, revenue, profession . . .), psychological (personality . . .) and spiritual (ethical, religion . . .) factors, nor underestimate the long-term impact of the standardization of institutions and regulations throughout Europe.

The CCA (Centre de Communication Avancé, HAVAS Group) and Europanel, a group composed of ten European market research firms, have identified sixteen 'euro-sociostyles' corresponding to six major families called 'mentalities': the 'socio-contestors', the 'socio-ambitious', the 'socio-dreamers', the 'socio-notables', the 'socio-withdrawn', and the 'socio-militants'. Each mentality is then divided into two or three 'socio-styles' (see Cathelat, 1990; Voller and Winckler, 1991). These sixteen socio-styles are represented on a three-dimensional map (see Figure 1). The first axis ('movement'–'settlement') concerns the extent to which people are open to new ideas. It contrasts the spirit of adventure, mobility, flexibility, modernism, with the desire for security, tradition, conservative values. The second axis ('valuables'–'values') opposes materialism to a more intellectual, spiritual life

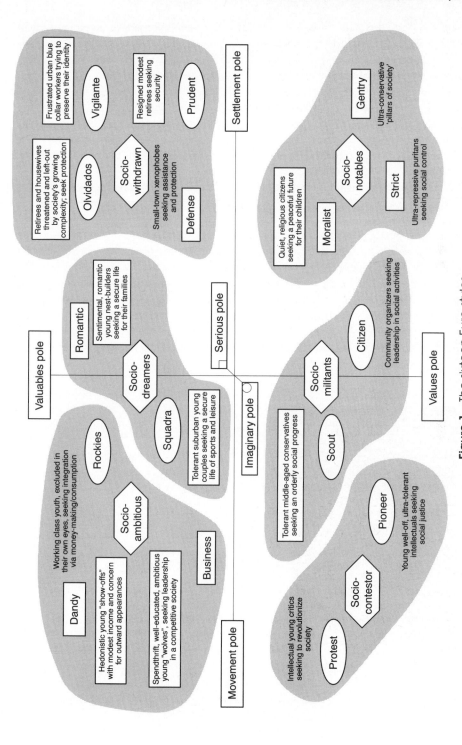

Figure 1 The sixteen Euro-styles.
Source: Based on Cathelat (1990) and Voller and Winkler (1991).

orientation. The third axis ('imagery'–'serious') plots one's impulsive emotions against more rational, planned or reflective behaviour.

The framework and data proposed by RISC (Research Institute on Social Change) offers another medium for observing sociocultural changes in Europe. Recent RISC studies (Hasson and Ladet, 1994; Ladet, 1994), suggest the emergence of two strong dimensions: a tendency towards openness as opposed to resistance to change and the spread of hedonism – as opposed to moral codes. These two main dimensions or axes are in fact the combination of about 39 trends (e.g. ethnocentrism, involvement in society, etc.). They are then used to identify ten cells, each rather arbitrarily containing approximately 10 per cent of the total population, as shown in Figure 2.

The analysis of the consumption densities of a given product or brand in each of the ten cells allows [us] to measure the extent to which there exist consumer similarities across segments (cells) as well as possible brand strengths or weaknesses in this or that segment. To illustrate, Figure 3 presents an application for the car manufacturer BMW. It shows the proportion of people stating that BMW is their first choice to replace their current car (2.9 per cent in France, 8.3 per cent in Germany, 4.8 per cent in Italy, 3.2 per cent in Spain, 6 per cent in the UK). In each of the ten cells, an index indicates the extent to which consumers belonging to that cell intend to buy the product. The index value 100 corresponds to the average intention to buy. If the index value is greater than 100, then this suggests that consumers belonging to this segment (cell) are more favourable towards the brand than the average consumer. Figure 3 shows that the segments which are the most

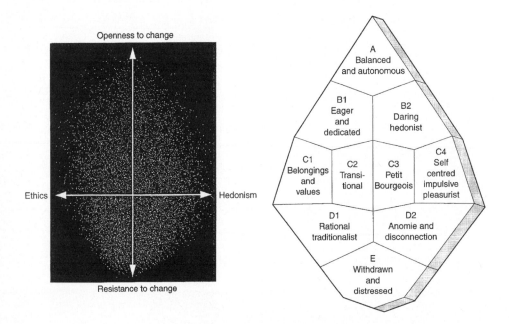

Figure 2   European socio-cultural territories identified by RISC (1995).
Source: RISC (December 1995).

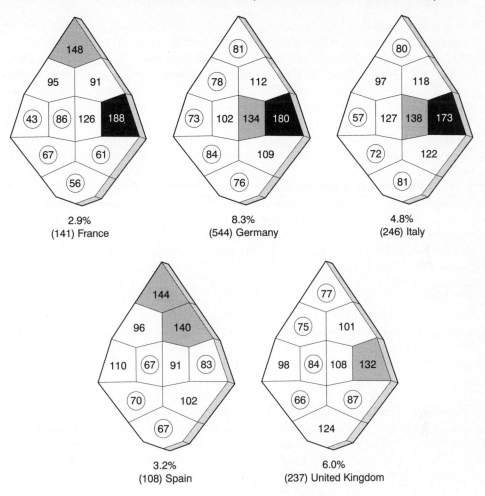

Figure 3   An RISC study of the socio-cultural territories of BMW in Europe.
Source: Hasson (1995, p. 79).

open to hedonism in France, Italy and Western Germany are primarily choosing BMW. On the contrary, in Great Britain, the BMW brand is mostly chosen by the most conservative segment and in Spain by the segment which is the most sensitive to change (Hasson, 1995).

   The methods and inventories used by the CCA and other similar institutions have often been criticized. They do not appear to lead to convergent results, amalgamate causes and effects of changes in society, and are, moreover, protected through confidentiality rights which do not facilitate the evaluation of their scientific validity (Valette-Florence, 1986, 1994a). A number of empirical studies have also cast a doubt on their predictive power, compared to inventories which simply include socio–demographic variables (Kapferer and Laurent, 1981; Valette-Florence and Jolibert, 1985).

This has encouraged some researchers to focus their studies on the values held by consumers (Kahle *et al.*, 1986; Valette-Florence, 1989b; Valette-Florence and Jolibert, 1990; Kamakura and Novak, 1992; Aurifeille and Valette-Florence, 1992; Schwartz and Sagiv, 1995), but this approach too is not without its own conceptual and measurement problems (Jolibert and Baumgartner, 1995; Odin *et al.*, 1996). Another option has been chosen by the EVS (European Value Survey) inventory which uses a very broad set of psychological and sociological values (Tchernia, 1995). Another development concerning consumer values has to do with the identification of the 'means–end chains'. Introduced by the work of Reynolds and Guttman (1988), these methods identify through the use of in-depth interviews, the 'latent benefits chains' sought by consumers in a product, the psychological and functional consequences of buying the product and the possible links with personal values. Three critical reviews of these methods and of the applications are available (Valette-Florence, 1994b; Gengler and Reynolds, 1995; Grunert and Grunert, 1995). The interested reader should also consult the special issue of the *International Journal of Research in Marketing* (1995, vol. 12, pp. 189–278) devoted to the topic.

5. Consumer product involvement and brand attachment

The concept of involvement refers to the intensity, the direction and the nature of the interest held by the consumer regarding a product, a product category or any relevant marketing activity. This interest is a function of certain individual variables, the products and the purchase situations concerned, and can be either permanent (enduring) or temporary.

Depending on the authors, involvement has been conceptualized and studied as a pre-disposition, a state, a process, a response; was defined in relation to a product class, a specific product, a brand, but also a purchasing situation or task (e.g. the reception of an advertisement). The consequences of consumer involvement may either be cognitive, affective, behavioural; enduring, temporary, contextual; conscious, unconscious; immediate, delayed; controlled, automatic. The result of this extreme heterogeneity is a concept which is perceived by some as vague and ambiguous, and a literature which is difficult to synthetize (see Valette-Florence, 1989a; Laaksonen, 1994). It is, therefore, hardly surprising to note the diversity of the measures proposed (Day *et al.*, 1995). The scales most used to measure enduring implication are those of Zaichkowsky and of Laurent and Kapferer.

Zaichkowsky's (1985) 'Personal Involvement Inventory' (PII) is unidimensional and aims to measure enduring involvement regarding a specific product or product class. This scale has been the subject of many analyses and revisions (McQuarrie and Munson, 1992; Goldsmith and Emmert, 1991; Zaichkowsky, 1994). For McQuarrie and Munson (1992), the importance attached to the product and the interest generated by it represent two related, but distinct aspects of involvement. For them, the concept of involvement, as measured by the PII scale contains at least two dimensions, which amounts to saying that the scale is probably not unidimensional, a point of view shared by other researchers (Mittal, 1995; Jain and Srinivisan, 1990; Cristau and Strazzieri, 1996).

Laurent and Kapferer (1985, 1986), Kapferer and Laurent (1986, 1993) have adopted a totally different approach. Instead of attempting to identify the components of involvement to compose a unidimensional scale, they have taken up the task of identifying and measuring the antecedents of involvement. The four antecedents retained are:

(a) the *interest* or importance which the individual personally attaches to the product;
(b) the *perceived* risk associated with the product purchase, which has two aspects: (i) the perceived importance of the negative consequences of a bad choice, (ii) the subjective probability of making a bad choice;
(c) the *hedonic* value of the product, i.e. its emotional appeal, its ability to provide pleasure;
(d) the *perceived sign value* of the product, the degree to which it expresses the person's self.

For these authors, these four variables correspond to distinct yet related 'facets' of involvement; combined, they allow [. . .] involvement profiles. This approach has been criticized by Mittal (1995), who regrets that Kapferer and Laurent have confused the concept of interest or importance, very closely related in their opinion to that of involvement, with three other variables (perceived risk, hedonic value and sign value) which are, for them, clearly antecedents of involvement. Various researchers (Rodgers and Schneider, 1993; Valette-Florence, 1989a) as well as the authors themselves (Kapferer and Laurent, 1993) have studied the structure of the scale and noticed that in certain product purchasing contexts, the interest and pleasure factors often, but not always, appear as one single factor, as if consumers often tend to like what interests them, and vice versa (Valette-Florence, 1988).

An additional problem concerns one of the two facets of the risk factor (the probability of making a bad choice). Kapferer and Laurent (1993) indicate that in numerous empirical studies they have found that this factor was only weakly linked to the four others. While their recommendation is, nevertheless, to retain it, Strazzieri (1994) and his co-workers have chosen to exclude every risk element associated with the purchase of the product, in order to better focus the measurement of involvement on its enduring dimension. Such a conception of involvement may be explained by the complex role played by the risk factor which is at the same time an antecedent of situational involvement and a consequence of enduring involvement (Volle, 1995). The PIA (Pertinence, Interest, Attraction) scale proposed by Strazzieri (1994) is thus based on the principle that measurement of enduring involvement must not include perceived risk (and, notably, its uncertainty element). For this author, perceived risk determines the stakes of a purchase decision but not the importance which the product has taken on for the consumer. The PIA scale is short (six items), is apparently unidimensional, has good internal consistency and is already the subject of a number of interesting applications (Strazzieri and Hajdukowicz-Brisson, 1995; Cristau and Strazzieri, 1996).

If it is generally acknowledged that high involvement leads to greater attention and greater efforts to process and elaborate the information gathered (Eagly and Chaiken, 1993; Smith and Buchholtz, 1991) as well as increased importance for opinion leadership and diffusion of information (Venkatraman, 1990; Cristau and Strazzieri, 1996), one should not forget to take into account the emotional, symbolic or utilitarian character of the product. In fact, involvement combines cognitive and affective elements. The cognitive component may be viewed as the reflection of essentially utilitarian needs, which are 'rational' and centred on the functional characteristics of the product, while the affective component corresponds to the existence of emotional needs that the product is called to satisfy. Here we touch once more on the symbolic and expressive function of consumption (Baudrillard, 1968; Moles, 1972; Csikszentmihalyi and Rotchberg-Halton, 1981) in which the object consumed or used in a conspicuous manner serves as an indicator of social integration and differentiation.

The importance taken by the product in the life of the individual may be such that it becomes difficult to describe it by means of the simple concept of high involvement. A number of researchers have studied situations in which objects or tasks serve primarily to define and reinforce the individual's self-identity (Babin *et al.*, 1994; Richins, 1994). In this case, it would seem more judicious to substitute the concept of involvement with the concept of 'attachment' (Ball and Takasi, 1992; Belk, 1992; Kleine *et al.*, 1995) to explain that some consumers may develop true affective and emotional bonds to products and brands. These bonds may be so strong that they lead to a real personalization of the product (Fournier, 1994; Heilbrunn, 1995, 1996).

6. Decision-making within the family

The privilege of making a particular decision often belongs to more than just one person. Numerous purchases require or encourage the participation of several family members. According to the circumstances and the course of the buying process, family members can play one, two or many of the roles presented in Table 4.

The identification of the exact role played by each family member at each step in the decision-making process is a delicate task (Madrigal and Miller, 1996). It is [. . .] difficult to find a method to measure influence which is scientifically reliable, relatively easy to use and as 'neutral' as possible. The researcher is, in fact, confronted with the extreme subjectivity

Table 4 The diverse consumer decision-making roles

1. The *inspirator* is at the origin of the idea to buy the product.

2. The *informant* takes charge of, or is charged with, the collection of information and its diffusion within the family.

3. The *persuader* attempts to influence family members (is either for or against the idea of purchasing the product).

4. The *consultant* is available to provide advice, an opinion or information.

5. The *decider* makes the decision to buy or not to buy.

6. The *buyer* proceeds to the formal act of buying.

7. The *preparer* prepares, assembles or instals the product for use by family members.

8. The *initiator* initiates family members in the use or the consumption of the product.

9. The *user* uses or consumes the product.

10. The *manager* is responsible for the maintenance and upkeep of the product and signals when it requires replacement or renewal.

of the perceptions by the different family members of the chronological course of the purchasing process and of the actual contribution made by each member in the final decision. This accounts for the often contradictory nature of the information provided by households (Peterson *et al.*, 1988; Foxman *et al.*, 1989). This is particularly true when the research methods used are limited to opinion surveys and do not involve cross-checks or direct observation.

The study of household decisions is inseparable from the cultural and social norms to which the family is bound (Ford *et al.*, 1995). These norms define the place of the family in society, its preferred modes of functioning, as well as the socially acceptable role of each family member.

Based on concepts already introduced by, among others, LePlay (1871) and Laslett and Wall (1972) to describe familial organization, Todd (1990) distinguishes four major traditional family systems in Europe. These are obtained by considering, on the one hand, parent–child relationships (these may be of the liberal or of the authoritarian type) and, on the other hand, the relationships between siblings (these may be egalitarian or non-egalitarian). The combination of these two variables makes it possible to determine the four[8] major types of family presented in Figure 4:

1. 'Absolute nuclear family': the relationships between parents and children are of the liberal type, the relationships between siblings are not egalitarian (for example, there is no egalitarian division of inheritance between siblings). The term nuclear indicates that the family does not develop beyond the 'parent–child' core, which is to say that the children leave the parental residence when they marry.
2. 'Egalitarian nuclear family': the relationships between parents and children are of the liberal type while the relationships between siblings are of the egalitarian type; at the time of marriage, the children leave the parental residence and at the time of parental death, the inheritance is divided equally.
3. 'Community family': the relationships between parents and children are of the authoritarian type, and the relationships between siblings are of the egalitarian type. There is equality among sons and when they marry, the 'nuclear' family may evolve towards a greater structure, in which married brothers co-reside. These community forms are relatively rare in Europe.
4. 'Founder family': the relationships between parents and children are of the authoritarian type and the relationships between siblings are of the non-egalitarian type; the essential part of the inheritance goes to only one of the sons, who remains at the parental residence; the others continue to reside there only if they are single.

The most traditional types, i.e. those corresponding to enlarged, authoritarian and non-egalitarian families, are especially typical of ancient rural societies; modernity has caused them to evolve towards types which are more nuclear, liberal and egalitarian. However, the theory defended by Todd is that even if modern European societies have, for the most part, eradicated their peasant foundations, the disappearance of the ancient succession rules, egalitarian or not, has not led to changes in fundamental attitudes. For that, the ancient family model, to which this or that 'modern' family is attached, still explains a good part of how people behave in the ideological, religious and economic domains. For example, a

1. The Founder Family
(authoritarian and non-egalitarian)

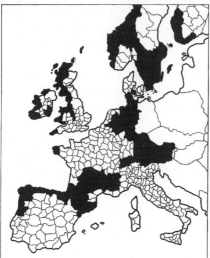

2. The Community Family
(authoritarian and egalitarian)

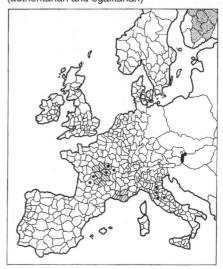

3. The Egalitarian Nuclear Family
(liberal and egalitarian)

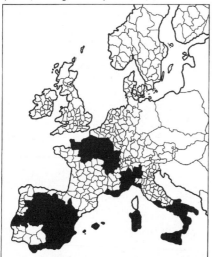

4. The Absolute Nuclear Family
(liberal and non-egalitarian)

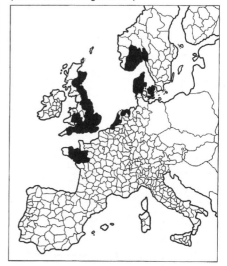

Figure 4   The four major traditional family systems in Europe, as distinguished by Todd.
Source: E. Todd, 'Le poids des structures familiales', *Sciences Humaines*, **58** (February 1996, p. 37).

family of the 'founder' type will be marked by a patriarchal organization of consumption, while greater autonomy regarding purchasing and consumption will reign in an 'egalitarian nuclear' family.

Todd's classification is not the only one proposed by historians or sociologists (see Kellerhals and Roussel, 1987; Segalen, 1993). For example, Kellerhals (1987), in an attempt to classify the various types of interaction within the family, proposes to distinguish four fundamental processes corresponding to: (a) the search for internal cohesion of the family, (b) its social integration, (c) the definition of priorities, and (d) the modes of regulations adopted. Roussel (1991) suggests the existence of three family types: the 'alliance family' (characterized by a sort of social pact guaranteeing family and social integration), the 'fusion family' (in which individual fulfilment and collective success overlap) and the 'association family' (marked by the equality in status, the lack of task differentiation and the self-sufficiency of members). Olson and McCubbin (1983) propose a 'circumplex' model made up of two main aspects: the level of family cohesion graded in four levels ('disengaged', 'separated', 'connected' and 'enmeshed') and the adaptation capacity of the family, graded also in four levels (rigid–structured–flexible–chaotic). The classification suggested by Donati (1985) considers the extent to which the family identifies with society. While the 'amoral' family favours internal solidarity, the 'organic' family values a sense of responsibility and is set up as a mirror of society; the 'acquiring' family places prime importance on the social attainment of its members and favours the acquisition of social skills and advantages. The 'expressive' family emphasizes the satisfaction of individualistic needs, with the other possible functions of the family (acquisition, protection, socialization . . .) being considered to be more the responsibility of society than of the family. Finally, Kellerhals and Troutot (1986) propose [. . .] three major family types: (a) 'stronghold' families, which are characterized by a fusional type cohesion, a normative type regulation based on fairly general, invariable rules and a pronounced withdrawal into themselves; (b) 'guild' families which are also characterized by strong cohesion, but which are run by discussing situations one by one, and which practise open-mindedness towards the outside; and (c) 'negotiation' families: extremely open to the outside, their cohesion is founded on the autonomy and specificity of each of its members, which explains that family decisions occur only after each particular case has been discussed.

Individual autonomy and open-mindedness on the part of the family seem to be more common, at least in France, in middle- or upper-class families than in lower- or working-class ones. The explanation proposed by family sociologists (de Singly, 1991, 1993b; Kaufmann, 1988; Kellerhals et al., 1982) is that the more resources are available to the families, the less they feel the need to withdraw into themselves, and the less the married couple plays a significant role in the development of one's self-identity and in giving sense and stature to each of its members. De Singly (1993a) cites the example of spouses who, not being able to have the same summer vacation dates, wonder what they are going to do: the solution to take part of their vacation separately is only [taken] by two out of ten persons in the lower classes, four out of ten in the middle classes and five out of ten in the upper classes.

Any given domestic organization reflects how power is distributed according to the interests, values and resources of each family member. These resources can be cultural, social, intellectual, psychological or economic (Kranichfeld, 1987; Roussel, 1989). The family is often described as having essentially three functions: to ensure the economic well-being of its members, to provide them with psychological support, and finally, to contribute to their social integration (Becker, 1991; Castellan, 1993; Popenoe, 1993; de Singly, 1993b). The influence of each individual is therefore often assumed to be directly proportional to his or her contribution to one or more of these functions (Pahl, 1990; Burgoyne, 1990). This power is none the less modulated by the individual's time-budget: the individual who possesses some power must have the time necessary to exercise it. The means and strategies used by family members to resolve possible family conflicts and to make their particular point of view prevail, have been the subject of a number of theoretical and empirical studies (Bergadaà and Roux, 1988; Divard, 1992). They show the extent to which decision-making can take a very political form.

In their study of domestic organization in France (see Figure 5), Glaude and de Singly (1986) make a distinction between the domains which are equally shared by spouses and those which are exclusively reserved for one or the other spouse. Their results confirm various international studies (Böcker, 1987; Maurin, 1989; Lemel, 1991, 1993; Lavin, 1993) which indicate gradual advancement towards more egalitarianism within the couple, even if certain tasks continue to be allocated to women (e.g. cooking, cleaning, upkeep). If the social class of the couple is taken into account, it appears that working-class families are closer to the 'women administrator' type, while upper categories mainly opt for the 'house-wife' model. The middle class live more in an 'egalitarian woman' style than the other classes. Egalitarianism is more common in couples in which both spouses work outside the home, with the active woman attempting to disassociate herself from traditional household tasks. Working women must take care of their professional life plus the majority of domestic tasks, household finances, the family's social relationships, the children's education, her married life, etc., in addition to personal projects. This entanglement of activities and social roles leads to a variety of tensions, conflicts and compromises (Ott, 1992; Dubar, 1991). The demand for personal territory will bring into play a whole range of confrontations, negotiations and legitimizations (Schwartz, 1990; Commaille, 1992; Kaufmann, 1992).

Egalitarianism decreases as the number of children increases (Glaude and de Singly, 1986), while the likelihood of domestic specialization rises with the age of the household, as if the family was able to come to an agreement on how to divide tasks and allocate domestic power based on the preferences and abilities of each family member. Retirement, which brings with it an increase in free time, may increase the probability of having joint decisions (Heslop, 1990) or may lead to a total redistribution of tasks, carried out up to then by one of the spouses. This may result in a different period of renegotiation and readjustment (Keating, 1980).

Children and adolescents play an extremely active role in a significant number of family decisions bearing not only on products which essentially concern them (toys, clothing, leisure, food), but also on domains involving the family as a whole, for example, the choice of a restaurant, a car, a television, a computer or a leisure activity (Doulhitt and Fedyk, 1988; Foxman et al., 1989; Fosse-Gomez, 1991; Brée, 1993). To illustrate, we present in Figure 6 a study carried out by Dubois and Marchetti (1992), on 600 Brazilian families, to measure the influence of the father, mother and children on the purchase of twelve household electronic products.

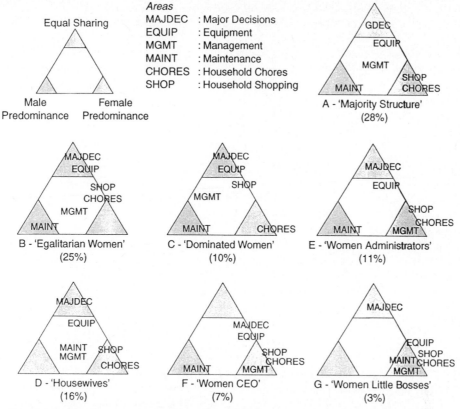

Note: The seven types of family organization shown here were obtained by using automatic classification methods. For each type, the average position of each of the six decision domains were projected onto a triangular graph with respect to three zones: 'equal sharing', 'male predominance', 'female predominance'. For example, for households corresponding to the 'majority structure' (type A), 'major decisions' are equally shared. A decision domain is considered to fall into the 'equal sharing' zone if on average 60% of the responses are: 'my husband and me equally'.

Figure 5   Seven types of domestic organization in France.
Source: From Glaude and de Singly (1986, p.14).

The process by which children and adolescents acquire consumer values, skills, attitudes and behaviour has been studied under the terms of 'consumer socialization' (Moschis, 1987; Peracchio, 1992; Easterling *et al.*, 1995; for a synthesis see Ribadeau-Dumas, 1995). One classification often used to describe this process is that of Becker (1964). Becker uses three basic dimensions to describe the parent–child relationships, i.e. strict character vs. permissiveness; hostility vs. human warmth; detachment vs. anxiety, to arrive at eight parental types: authoritarian, rigid, directive, democratic, permissive, neglecting, overprotective and neurotic. Two studies by Carlson *et al.* (1992) and Hamou-Poline (1997) suggest that the influence of children in the decision-making process depends on parental types. Children

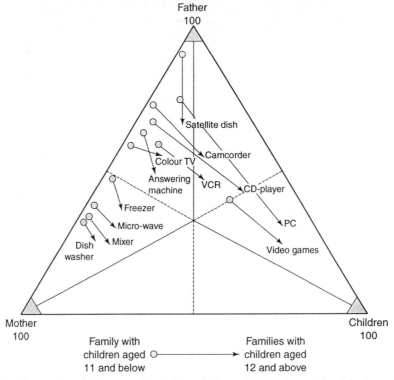

Changes in the average influence observed within families with children aged 11 and below and those with children aged 12 and above

Father
100

Satellite dish

Camcorder

Colour TV

Answering machine | VCR | CD-player

Freezer

Micro-wave | PC

Dish washer | Mixer

Video games

Mother
100

Children
100

Family with children aged ○──────► children aged
11 and below | Families with children aged 12 and above

Method: The question asked for each of the twelve products was: 'To what degree did each family member play a role in the decision-making process (concerning the product under consideration)?' The respondents had to distribute 100 points (constant sum method) to indicate the degree of influence of each member. The arrows indicate how the influence process is modified by the age of the children.

Figure 6 The influence process in the family: a study of buying decisions concerning twelve household electronic products.
Source: Dubois and Marchetti (1992/93).

have more influence in families belonging to the 'neglecting' or 'permissive' type and, naturally, less influence in a family of the 'authoritarian' type. As noted by Mangleburg (1989), other factors explain variations in the influence of the child. These have to do with the decision stage (children have a greater influence on problem recognition than on the choice itself), the individual characteristics of the parents, the importance attached to the education of the child (the more the parents are concerned with their children's education, the less they have a tendency to give in to their demands), the age of the child (the younger the child is, the less the parents are influenced), and finally, the characteristics of the family.

A number of studies (for example, Carlson *et al.*, 1992; Hong, 1994) have demonstrated that it is also necessary to take into account the type of parent–child communications which characterize the family. In the families characterized by a 'social orientation', communication is based on deference to parental values and, thus, on the respect of certain norms regarding consumption (Allsop, 1988); others have a more 'conceptual' orientation, the objective of which is to develop the autonomy and skills of the children as consumers. The contrast between these two types of social orientation is particularly clear when one compares Oriental and Occidental families. In an Oriental culture (for example, Chinese, Korean, Japanese . . .), the family is viewed as a micro-representation of society in which family members are linked to a set of codified norms, rules and obligations (Pan and Vanhonacker, 1993; Chu and Ju, 1993; Hong, 1994). In the most traditional of these families, a strict adherence to Confucian principles will translate into an absolute respect of the father, strict obedience by the wife to the husband, parents-in-law and (in the case of death of the husband) to the eldest son, and the duty imposed on adult children to take care of their aged parents. Social relationships within the family are supposed to follow the 'way of the golden mean' characterized by the respect of the values of tolerance, deference, harmony, discretion and submission to authority. By contrast, in an Occidental society of the North American type, the family is not seen as an extension of society, but rather as an extension of one's self-concept (Laslett, 1984). The American family encourages personal success and independence of its members. To quote Pan and Vanhonacker (1993), for Chinese, 'the family is a part of society, while for Americans, it is a part of themselves'.

7. The identification of choice criteria and decision-making rules

One important objective of consumer behaviour research is to identify the product characteristics which play a key role in consumer product judgements. As the specialized literature suggests (Payne *et al.*, 1992; Maule, 1994; Westenberg and Koele, 1994; Harte and Koele, 1995), one can regroup available approaches into three major categories: 'direct citation', 'process tracing' (e.g. information display boards and verbal protocols) and finally 'structural modelling' methods.

Compensatory models rely on the hypothesis that consumers evaluate diverse brands or products through an evaluation of the totality of the attributes of the brand or brands under consideration. The best-known compensatory model is the 'expectancy-value' model (for a review, see Eagly and Chaiken, 1993). Its popularity is such that researchers who use it often forget its underlying hypotheses and limitations, although these factors are well identified by specialists (see Brehmer, 1990; Saris, 1993; Grunert, 1989, 1990; Eagly and Chaiken, 1993). Contrary to compensatory models, non-compensatory models argue that the consumer is capable of limiting himself or herself to certain key attributes. The number of attributes examined may even be reduced to one or two key attributes, such as the 'construction-by-aspects model' presented by McGuire [1986].

A number of empirical studies indicate that consumers rarely use one single decision-making model, but rather a combination depending on the context and their level of familiarity. The greater the complexity of the judgement to be made, the greater the tendency to proceed by stages (Gertzen, 1992). A non-compensatory type model is first used to eliminate non-acceptable brands. The set of alternatives (products or brands) *a priori* judged acceptable by the consumer makes up the 'evoked set' or the 'consideration set'. Only those alternatives stand a chance to be later selected, after an evaluation process which often is described as involving a compensatory model. In a series of studies Chandon and Strazzieri (1986) and Strazzieri and Chandon (1994) have shown how the 'evoked set' concept may be used to measure the 'intensity of competition' and 'competitive fields' which operate between brands in the consumer's mind.

Although reduced, the total number of brands under consideration is positively influenced by a certain number of factors, among which we find the number of brands known (Brown and Wildt, 1992), the use situations considered (Aurier and Jean, 1996), the level of education (Lapersonne *et al.*, 1995; Aurier and Jean, 1996), the type of habitation (Aurier and Jean, 1996), the level of brand loyalty (Grønhaug and Troye, 1983; Lapersonne *et al.*, 1995), age (Aurier and Jean, 1996) and finally tolerance of ambiguity (Malhotra *et al.*, 1980). The relation between the level of involvement and the number of brands under consideration is more complex in so far as the factors involved are exercising opposing influences (see Divine, 1995); a highly involved consumer is more expert, more demanding, and therefore more likely to have a narrower 'evoked set'; but at the same time we may imagine that a higher level of involvement will translate into a more 'exploratory' behaviour which then should result in more brands being considered.

The formation of a favourable attitude or intention does not automatically trigger a purchasing action. This simple observation has nourished a long tradition of research in psychology (see Eagly and Chaiken, 1993; Krebs and Schmidt, 1993; Olson and Zanna, 1993) and in marketing (Fazio *et al.*, 1989; Bagozzi *et al.*, 1989). Numerous explanations have been offered to account for the presence or absence of a link between attitude, intention and behaviour, such as the impact of personal, economic factors, the time interval between observations, social influences, various situational variables, the volitional capacities of the individual, the perceived 'cost' of the transition from intention to act, the fact that at a given moment, attitude is more or less 'accessible' (Berger, 1990; Fazio, 1990) or that it is accompanied or not by emotions, by a direct experience of the product, etc. This literature is much too voluminous to be presented here (see Petty *et al.*, 1991; Eagly and Chaiken, 1993). Among the most often advanced theoretical explanations are those which are articulated around the 'theory of planned behaviour' (see Ajzen, 1991) which have been the subject of numerous studies in marketing (e.g. Bagozzi and Warshaw, 1990; Bagozzi *et al.*, 1990; Netemeyer and Bearden, 1992; Ajzen and Driver, 1992). Briefly stated, this theory explains that behaviour is released by the combined effect of: (a) the attitude towards the behaviour concerned, (b) social norms towards that behaviour, and (c) the control that the individual perceives to have over behaviour. Resuming the work of Kuhl (see Kuhl and Beckman, 1994) on the distinction between individuals who are 'action-oriented' versus those who are 'state-oriented', a number of researchers have shown unsurprisingly that 'action-oriented' consumers allow themselves to be guided more by their own attitudes, while others ('state-oriented') are more influenced by social norms. The interest of this line of research is less in the results obtained than in the impetus given to a deeper investigation of the nature of volition and of its underlying processes. An initial step in this direction is represented by the conceptual model developed by Bagozzi (1993).

8. Consumer information-processing

The study of the processes used by consumers in acquiring and analyzing information to arrive at a decision (to purchase or not to purchase) has traditionally favoured the so-called cognitive approach. For many years, the dominant paradigm corresponded to a 'cognitive–affective–conative' sequence and emphasized the limitations of the consumer as a 'perfect information processor'. While retaining the cognitive psychology achievements, more recent approaches have rehabilitated and reintroduced the affective, emotional and occasionally irrational and unconscious, dimensions of the decision-making process (Derbaix and Vanden Abeele, 1985; Cohen and Areni, 1991). Most researchers, who have attempted to integrate this body of knowledge, have focused on stimuli of the persuasive type. An examination of the major 'models' presented (Petty and Cacioppo, 1985a; MacInnis and Jaworski, 1989; MacInnis et al., 1991; Mick, 1992; Mick and Buhl, 1992) show the importance granted to three key factors: the opportunity, motivation and ability of the subjects to process the information they are exposed to. Information processing has been discussed in terms of 'levels' or 'depth' (see Lockhart and Craik, 1990) to emphasize that subjects may consciously or unconsciously mobilize all or various parts of their aptitudes to respond to incoming stimuli.

Beyond differences in the terminology used, the major stages[9] of information processing, which one can traditionally distinguish, concern: (a) sensory detection and registration, (b) the focusing of attention, leading to the perception and categorization of stimuli, (c) the search for meaning, and finally (d) a large variety of elaborations and inferences through which consumers 'go beyond' the information received to arrive finally at personal conclusions and to appropriate it. In the following section, some of these aspects of consumer information processing will be selectively addressed.

8.1 Sensory detection and registration

The individual is first solicited by sensory registers through the intermediary of (primarily innate and automatic) sensory processes (Bonnet et al., 1989a; Sekuler and Blake, 1994). There is 'sensory arousal' if the stimuli with which the consumer comes into contact surpass 'absolute thresholds'. Studies on sensory discrimination have also demonstrated the existence of 'difference thresholds': they correspond to the minimal variation which must intervene in the intensity of the stimulus for the individual to feel a variation and distinguish one stimulus from another. This notion of 'just noticeable difference' is often illustrated in the following manner: it is easier to perceive a variation of light when a second candle is lit, than when an eleventh candle is lit while ten candles are already burning. By multiplying this type of experiment, Ernst Weber[10] was able, in 1834, to establish his famous formula: $\Delta I = KI$, where ΔI is the difference threshold, I is the intensity of the stimulus and K a constant (the so-called Weber fraction) which varies according to the solicited sensory receptors.[11] Although Weber fractions have been verified in a good number of psychophysiological experiments and in various sensory contexts, they seem to describe more aptly what occurs when the intensity of the stimuli used is average than when it is low or high.

It was Fechner who in 1860 first described the relationship between variations in stimulus intensity (I) and the intensity of the sensations (S) felt by the subject: $S = W \log I$, where W is a constant which depends on the Weber fraction. Further, Stevens and Stevens (1975) have proposed the following relationship: $R = KI^n$, when R is the intensity of the sensation or psychological reaction, I the stimulus intensity, K a constant and N is an exponent which differs according to the sensory modalities studied: 0.6 for sound, 0.33 for brilliance, 0.55 for the odour of coffee, 1.3 for sweet or salty flavours, etc. (Weil-Barais, 1993). Stevens' approach has been extended to the case where the stimuli are not physically present – in this case, judgements are based on sensory memories (Wiest and Bell, 1985) – and to situations in which individuals are no longer asked for their sensations but for their preferences. If Stevens' fraction is generally accepted by researchers in psychophysics as a reasonable approximation of the stimulus intensity–sensation felt relationship (Krueger, 1991), this relationship in the commercial world of product choice is considerably complicated each time that physical sensation is masked or altered by other information, such as that, for example, of the image which consumers have of products.

Signal Detection Theory[12] (see McMillan and Creelman, 1991) focuses not only on the detection abilities of individuals, but also on their decision – is the signal present or absent? – when the stimulus is ambiguous and its detection difficult. Thus, in a given situation it is necessary not only to consider the objective characteristics of stimuli and the individual's detection thresholds, but also a certain number of personal and situational factors which will have an impact on the decision to accept as probable or improbable the signal's presence. It is in that sense that researchers can speak of 'response strategies and 'decision-making style' characterizing an individual faced with a certain discrimination task.

Information collected by the senses is initially, and very briefly, stored in registers, codes or sensory memories. Visual information is, for example, placed in the 'iconic memory' where it is preserved intact for a short period of time – around a few fractions of a second (Loftus *et al.*, 1992). Recent research (e.g. Irwin *et al.*, 1990) suggests that iconic memory cannot be reduced to simple retinal persistence. It is an analogous visual representation of the impinging stimulus which does not exceed 300 ms and also an 'informational' persistence which is available at the disappearance of the stimulus and which later enables its categorization. For a synthesis of accumulated, fundamental knowledge on other sensory modalities, such as sound, smell, touch and taste, the reader should consult Hirsch and Wetson (1996), Engen (1991), Schab (1991), Béguin and Costermans (1994), Heller and Schiff (1991) and Bartoshuk (1988). Surprisingly little consumer research on this topic has been published.

There is subliminal stimulation or 'subception' when an individual is subjected to stimuli which, because they are below the individual's perceptual thresholds, cannot be detected, but whose intensity is, none the less, strong enough to provoke sensory registration; for example, superimposed images flying by at the speed of 1/2000 of a second, thus in principle undetectable by the eye which functions at the speed of 1/15 of a second. The possibility of using subliminal stimuli in a persuasion context has led to a lively controversy. Indeed, some empirical studies suggest that, under certain conditions, subliminal messages can effectively produce certain positive effects (e.g. Weinberger and Hardaway, 1990; Borstein and Pitman, 1992); this has often been explained by a phenomenon of 'unconscious familiarity' (Borstein, 1992a, 1992b; Murphy and Zajonc, 1993).

The dominant position of advertisers and communication specialists is, however, that: (a) such subliminal manipulation, generally illegal, is not practised, and that (b) it is much less effective than when using normal, i.e. supraliminal, stimuli (Pratkanis and Greenwald, 1988; Rogers, 1992–93; Rogers and Smith, 1993; Smith and Rogers, 1994; Haberstroh, 1994; Trappey, 1996). An examination of the specialized psychological literature yields the same conclusion, i.e. the efficiency of supraliminal stimuli is superior to that of subliminal stimuli (Merikle, 1992; Greenwald, 1992; Jacoby *et al.*, 1992). The only interest represented by subliminal persuasion would be the possibility to circumvent perceptual defence mechanisms (Borstein, 1989, 1992a; Weinberger and Hardaway, 1990). But, even in this case, these effects appear to be extremely limited: perhaps sufficient when dealing with simple physical stimuli or injunctions, subliminal stimulation appears totally ill-adapted when more complex stimuli or messages are present.

The fact that consumers may be unconsciously influenced by supraliminal stimuli to which they do not remember having been exposed and which they will perhaps not even be capable of recognizing later is well established (Lewicki *et al.*, 1992; Greenwald and Banaji, 1995). This research, which focuses on the so-called 'mere exposure effect' and 'implicit memory' phenomena, is to be distinguished from that just discussed because it involves, in the great majority of cases, supraliminal stimuli, to which subjects were accidentally exposed or which were situated 'outside attention' or in situations of divided attention.

The 'mere exposure' concept has been introduced by Zajonc (1968) to explain the fact that mere exposure to stimuli may later, when they are again presented, cause a slightly more positive response than that generated by new stimuli, even if these stimuli have not been identified at the time of initial exposure. An entire line of psychological research (see Bornstein, 1989b) and in marketing (see Janiszewski, 1990a, 1990b, 1993) demonstrates the existence of this phenomenon. Zajonc's explanation that the favourable affective response is mechanically linked to a simple repetitive effect producing object familiarity, without any cognitive mediation, has been contested (see Cohen and Areni, 1991) and other hypotheses have been proposed (Anand and Sternthal, 1991; Vanheule, 1994). These hypotheses all presuppose some minimum level of information processing.

The concept of 'implicit memory' (Schacter, 1992; Sanyal, 1992; Schacter *et al.*, 1993; Nicolas, 1994) has been introduced to explain that the accomplishment of certain tasks may be facilitated by former experiences which the subject does not remember. Schacter *et al.* (1989) have proposed the 'retrieval intentionality' criterion to distinguish implicit memory tests from those which measure explicit memory (see Jacoby, 1991; Basden *et al.*, 1993). The two forms of memory (implicit vs. explicit) seem to function in an independent manner. A series of marketing applications demonstrate the interest that the concept of implicit memory may represent for a better understanding of consumer behaviour (Perfect and Askew, 1994; Friestad *et al.*, 1993; Perfect and Heathley, 1996). The debate, none the less, is far from being closed with regard to the type and level of processing exactly required to produce an implicit memory effect of interesting magnitude, without nevertheless falling into the domain of explicit effects (Krishnan and Shapiro, 1996).

8.2 Attentive process

Any refined analysis of the information registered in sensory memories presupposes a focus of attention. This focus will occur very rapidly, if the consumer is in a state of vigilance. It may, on the contrary, appear quite late or not at all, if the consumer shows strong indifference.

Regardless of the definitions used for defining the concept of attention (LaBerge, 1990; Kinchla, 1992), the central idea in attention research is that it requires some mental effort and that it is more or less selective and focused depending on the motivations of the individual and the demands of the task (Usai *et al.*, 1995). While sensory registration of stimuli is often passive, initially unconscious[13] and relatively unlimited as far as abilities are concerned, the attention process is more active, controlled, conscious and limited in terms of aptitudes than the individual is capable or ready to mobilize.

Focused attention will bring about the intervention of information decoding processes, certain of which are sequential, hierarchical, controlled, while others remain parallel and still automatic.[14] As explained by Theeuwes (1994), there exist different types of visual selection processes: one is 'endogenous', that is to say controlled by the individual, the other 'exogenous', that is to say, triggered by some unexpected stimulation. A series of empirical studies by Eriksen *et al.* (1990) demonstrated that when an individual focuses his or her attention on a stimulus which has already been the subject of automatic processing, the information already extracted and very superficially processed seems to be totally ignored, as if the stimulus were being presented for the first time. This reinforces the idea that the two types of processing (automatic vs. focused) differ vastly and are largely independent. Naturally, not all the tasks require focused attention to be well carried out; in fact, quite often relatively automatic processes prove to be sufficient, for example, when the task is very familiar, very simple. If it were otherwise, it would be difficult to imagine how individuals, in general, and consumers, in particular, could deal with the enormous quantity of information available in their environment.

The extraction and conscious use of information may be studied by using traditional survey methods, or other approaches involving, for example, verbal protocols or information display boards. When this extraction corresponds to automatic and partially unconscious processes, it is necessary to rely on more complex research apparatus (Bagozzi, 1991) such as the eye movement camera, commonly used in psychology and increasingly in marketing (see Kroeber-Riel, 1979, 1992; von Keitz, 1988; Russo and Leclerc, 1994). The eye movement camera allows the recording of eye movements (saccades) and fixations and therefore the determination of what has been seen (and for what length of time). It does not, however, provide any information on the conclusions recorded by the individual nor on the reasons for a particular eye movement pattern. Its use seems valuable also for finding out what has not been seen. How much information contained in advertising material, on a label, or packaging, is invisible to the consumer to whom it was destined?

8.3 The emergence of meaning

As Weil-Barais recalls (1993), a sensation becomes a perception only if the individual grants significance to the source responsible for the sensation. Unlike a sensation, a perception is always built. The level and types of processes which come into play are a function of the task, the needs, the motivations, the habits, the concepts most easily accessible, the personality, the cognitive and non-cognitive aptitudes of the individual, as well as a number of defence mechanisms (Krohne, 1993; von Hippel *et al.*, 1994; Roskos-Ewoldson and Fazio, 1992; Lecas, 1992).

Consumers use the information received to form an opinion or to arrive at a product judgement (Bettman *et al.*, 1991). They process information to give it a general, then a personal, sense (Debevec and Romeo, 1992). To this, they engage in a series of constructive elaborative and inferential processes which are strongly charged with (more or less conscious and controlled) emotions, mental images, evocations and associations. If the information available seems insufficient to them and if perceived risk is high (Verhage *et al.*, 1990; Volle, 1995), consumers will engage in external search for information (Gemunden, 1985). The information gathered is compared and eventually integrated with information already contained in the memory.

The individual disposes of multiple memory systems, specialized and distinct, although often complementary, to resolve the extreme variety of tasks facing him or her (Cantor *et al.*, 1991). Other types of memory have been added to the classic distinction between long-term and short-term memory or working memory. Declarative memory (Squire, 1992) corresponds to the conscious, explicit memorization of facts and events of either a semantic (semantic memory) or episodic (episodic memory) nature. Non-declarative memory regroups diverse forms of memory, more or less conscious, corresponding to various aptitudes and conditioned habits. Autobiographic memory corresponds to a part of the episodic memory which only deals with the individual and his or her past experiences (Rubin, 1986; Conway, 1990) excluding episodes concerning others. This memory has a strong cognitive and emotional[15] load and it may play a very significant role upon exposure to messages or stimuli evoking these happy or unpleasant episodes (Baumgartner *et al.*, 1992).

These various types of memory play a fundamental role in the decoding of new stimuli. They provide the individual consumers with cognitive categories and structures, rules and heuristics, and a set of emotions and images linked to past behaviour, which can be used to assimilate stimuli or to generate inferences (Derbaix and Vanden Abeele, 1985; Dick *et al.*, 1990; Meyers-Levy, 1991).

To recognize, identify and judge a stimulus requires that consumers have, beforehand, organized their knowledge to facilitate its use.[16] This organization can take the form of a conceptual taxonomy where the various conceptual categories are hierarchically ordered, starting with basic-level categories (Komatsu, 1992; Howard, 1992; Cordier, 1993) or other forms, such as the network representations used in connectionist models (Nosofsky *et al.*, 1992). Categorization theories have been actively used by consumer researchers in such areas as product judgements (Basu, 1993), attitude towards stores (Ward *et al.*, 1992; Claeys, 1993; Barnes and Ward, 1995), brand extension (Ladwein, 1994; Changeur and Chandon, 1995), comparative advertising (Sujan and Delave, 1987) as well as various other aspects of product categorization (John and Sujan, 1990).

Unlike classical models of categorization (see Smith, 1978) in which category membership is linked to the possession of defining or essential attributes, the theoretical framework used by most researchers (see Ladwein, 1995) is based on the idea that membership is not binary but rather graded.[17] All members of a category do not possess the same degree of membership: some are more representative, more typical of the category than others and can serve as prototypes (Mervis and Rosch, 1981; Kleiber, 1990). This typicality is a function of the structural properties of the category concerned. It is also connected to the 'frequency of instantiation', i.e. the frequency of exposure to the product as well as to the preferences within the product class: the more typical products are in general more appreciated (see Ward et al., 1992). This effect decreases, however, with the level of consumer expertise (Perkins and Ryna, 1990), the extent to which they seek variety (Aurier, 1991; Steenkamp and Baumgartner, 1992; Loewenstein, 1994) and prestige (Ward and Loken, 1988), which seems evident enough. The degree of typicality is finally linked to the objectives pursued by consumers (Barsalou, 1993) and the presence of salient attributes (Loken and Ward, 1990).

In certain cases, however, categories may be represented in a less abstract manner. This is the case when category membership is determined by similarity with category members which are endowed with 'exemplary value' (Smith and Sloman, 1994), essentially for psychological reasons; these exemplars may be, for example, the most used product, the most recently purchased product, the best known product, the most distinctive product, etc. These exemplars may, therefore, reflect important biases, prejudices and errors (Das-Smaal, 1990).

The information stored in memory guides consumers' perceptions and actions and generates expectations (van Raaij, 1991). The probability of this information being used depends on a certain number of factors, the major ones being consumer involvement (Maheswaran and Meyers-Levy, 1990; Heslin and Johnson, 1992; Park and Hastak, 1994), perceived information relevance in relation to the task to be accomplished, consumers' objectives and the degree of risk which they are ready to assume in their decisions (Maheswaran and Sternthal, 1990; Martin and Achee, 1992), information accessibility (Fazio, 1990; Ratneshwar et al., 1990) and finally, the difficulty of the task and the abilities required to achieve it (Anand and Sternthal, 1990). Certain individual variables are also going to play a role, for example, the 'need for cognition' (Cacioppo et al., 1996; Venkatraman et al., 1990; Haugtvedt et al., 1992; Stayman and Kardes, 1992) and more generally speaking the motivation to process the information (Smith and Schaffer, 1991).

As indicated above, the importance of the role played by emotions and moods in consumer behaviour has only recently been fully acknowledged (Sjöberg et al., 1987; Cohen and Areni, 1991). And this, in spite of what common sense suggests and what the specialized literature proposes in terms of empirical findings, concepts, theories and measurement instruments. Research on the affective dimensions of behaviour has focused mainly on the manner in which consumers react to advertising (e.g. Kuykendell and Keating, 1990; MacInnis and Stayman, 1993; Derbaix, 1995; Mooradian, 1996), form product judgements and perceptions (Sjöberg et al., 1987) and react to certain consumption situations (Derbaix and Pham, 1991).

In their response and elaboration processes, consumers will let themselves be guided by a myriad of emotions and images going well beyond the information given. This is why semioticians working on the reception of communication speak of a co-production of meaning (see Fouquier, 1988; Mick and Buhl, 1992). Because they internalize and transform incoming messages, consumers may not be considered to be simple and passive receivers of information.[18]

9. Consumers' imperfect choices

It is well documented in the specialized literature on judgement and decision-making (e.g. Hogarth, 1990; Payne *et al.*, 1992), that individuals are far from being perfect processors of information. When evaluating products or brands, consumers do not really apply rational or quasi-rational rules which would allow them to identify, based on certain constraints, the 'best' possible option. Rather, they allow the expression of an entire range of subjective reactions which result from their (conscious or unconscious) rejection of what reason would dictate, their willingness to be guided by impulsions and personal impressions (Rook, 1987; Dittmar *et al.*, 1995), or even by a desire to, as much as the situation permits, reduce unnecessary stress. Thus at times it appears difficult to speak of a true 'decision-making' process.

Alba and Hutchinson (1987) present an impressive review of the literature bearing on consumer difficulties in acquiring a certain expertise. Choosing among products is made difficult by such factors as the number and types of options offered and the manner in which the information is presented. Tolerance of ambiguity and the level and type of cognitive complexity of consumers are two of the cognitive styles studied by Pinson (1988). Among the other individual variables playing an important role in processing information, one can cite education, age, self-confidence, the sum of experiences accumulated in regard to the product, the aptitude to store information and to access memorized information and, of course, all the emotions and moods which alter the decision-making process. It is well known, for example, that consumers, and individuals in general, have great difficulty in processing adequately any information which carries or generates strongly negative thoughts, emotions or guilty feelings (Krohne, 1993; Coulter and Pinto, 1995). The natural tendency in individuals characterized by a 'repressive coping' type (Clark *et al.*, 1995; Terry, 1994) is to block or suppress these unpleasant evocations instead of dealing with them (Davies and Schwartz, 1990; Miller, 1991).

When the available information is incomplete, which is often the case, the consumer is not always capable or motivated to draw rigorous inferences (Dick *et al.*, 1990; Simmons and Lynch, 1991; Lee and Olshavsky, 1994). Intuition (Broniarczyk and Alba, 1994), information gathered during conversations (Thomas, 1992) can very well suffice. Consumers may alternatively use as an inference base their 'implicit theories' of the product concerned (Pinson, 1986). Mental images[19] evoked by stimuli may also facilitate data processing, serve as a mental model and, therefore, have an impact on consumers' responses (Unnava and Burnkrant, 1991; Bone and Ellen, 1992; Burns *et al.*, 1993; Janiszewski, 1990a). Given that these emotions are 'effortlessly' produced, we can hardly expect consumers to follow rational principles strictly, at least when the products or services in question are poorly differentiated or only imply limited risk. When the decision concerns a product or service that the consumer judges important, he or she will naturally attempt to be 'as rational as possible', so as to reduce the cognitive dissonance, doubt and anxiety which could arise during or after the purchase.

Moschis and Cox (1989) have listed various types of 'deviant' consumer behaviour among which is compulsive purchasing. A given behaviour is defined as 'compulsive' when it corresponds to an irresistible desire or need, to a loss of personal control, or even to a state of dependence leading repeatedly to excessive purchasing and consequences which are disturbing for the individual and eventually for his or her entourage (Glatt and Cook, 1987; Hirschmann, 1992). Compulsive buyers are generally conscious of the uncontrollable and harmful character of their behaviour, and only cede after an anxious, and often very difficult, struggle followed by post-purchasing feelings of guilt, remorse and sometimes real shame. Unlike impulsive buyers, 'compulsive' buyers do not buy in order to possess the desired object, but to liberate themselves from tension and anguish. It is in this sense, that their behaviour is pathological (d'Astous, 1990; Ledoyeux and Adès, 1994). Compulsive buying intervenes against the will of the subject and is accompanied by a strong feeling of distress: because they are conscious of the abnormal character of their compulsion, subjects feel the obligation to resist it, but at the same time the idea of not satisfying it provokes mounting anguish within them. The individual is therefore confronted with a form of 'psychasthenia' or 'aboulia', i.e. a weakening of the will accompanied by doubts, feelings of imperfection and irrational apprehensions.

Researchers who have studied in more detail the antecedents and correlates of compulsive buying (see d'Astous et al., 1990; Hanley and Wilhem, 1992; Nataraajan and Boff, 1992; Fabien and Jolicoeur, 1993) emphasize that this behaviour is linked to personal factors, such as a strong basic anxiety, a negative self-image, a general feeling of boredom, alienation and of bad social integration which results in a strong tendency to fantasize. These individual factors, partly due to family or hereditary causes, are amplified by professional or family stress, adherence to materialistic values, the proliferation of more and more insistent ways to incite consumers to buy (proliferation of stores, direct marketing, TV shopping, etc.).[20]

Procrastination (from the Latin *procrastinare*: put off to later) is another form of deviant behaviour. It is generally defined as the tendency to defer, without valid reason, the accomplishment of a task (Ferrari et al., 1995). Filled with doubt, incapable of settling on choice criteria, a deadline beyond which they consider that they will have sufficiently analyzed the problem, 'procrastinators' delay the moment of making their final decision; or, once having taken it, they 'freeze' the actual act of purchasing and taking possession of the good. Procrastinators 'do not take their time', they delay the execution of it in a way which they will later judge as irrational (Milgram et al., 1992). For an individual to qualify as a procrastinator, it is thus necessary that these deferments, postponements be chronic, unjustified and psychologically disturbing for the subject; nor should they be explained by situational factors (Greenleaf and Lehmann, 1995).[21]

From the main studies carried out on procrastinators (Akerloff, 1991; Ferrari, 1991; Lay et al., 1992; Shouwenburg, 1992; Larrick, 1993) one can obtain a fairly clear psychological profile. Most procrastinators have a low self-image, high social anxiety, diffused identity and a strong degree of perfectionism. They generally lack energy, have a bad sense of organization and usually underestimate the time necessary to accomplish a task. Anxious, they tend to seek more information, which can only increase the difficulty of the task with which they are confronted. Lay et al. (1992) note that procrastinators present this uncommon particularity to take on difficult tasks, or those doomed to failure, rather than those which show promise of succeeding; as if they seek, in advance, to impose themselves with a 'self-handicap' (Higgins et al., 1990) allowing them to justify later the non-accomplishment of the task. This exaggerated risk-taking, this exalted feeling linked to the frenzy of the last moment when the procrastinator forces himself or herself, in spite of everything, to accomplish something before the imposed deadline, has been emphasized by numerous authors (e.g., Ferrari, 1991; Hendricks and Vlek, 1991). Other authors (Burka and Yaen, 1983) have suggested that in delaying the execution of the task, procrastinators have the impression of revolting against a mission which they judge to be unpleasant or imposed on them (Ferrari, 1993; Ferrari and Emmons, 1994). In this sense, procrastination would be a form of sublimated rebellion.

Philosophers and sociologists have grounds for examining the excesses of the 'consumption society', presented as the unrestrained search for the satisfaction of often artificial needs. It is perhaps time that researchers now examine the excesses of the 'buying society'. While the act of consumption can be likened, in most cases, to satisfaction, or even pleasure, this barely holds true for the act of buying, as many purchasers live in a manner which can hardly be called pleasant. The efforts of public authorities, manufacturers, and distributors should be directed towards rendering the act of purchasing as efficient and as stress-free as possible. This double demand represents a real project for all of the economic partners involved.

Notes

1. Given the space constraints of this article, cross-cultural studies of consumer behaviour will not be discussed here. The interested reader is referred to Johansson (1986), McCracken (1986), Dubois (1987), Yang (1989), Lee (1990), Cheng and Swinyard (1991), Valette-Florence (1991), Yau (1994).
2. For an overview of the European consumers' environment, see Leeflang and van Raaij (1995) and the 1995 'European Marketing Data and Statistics' report published by *Euromonitor* (London).
3. In France in 1978, 9.4 per cent of births occurred outside marriage; in 1990 this figure had risen to 30 per cent. Since the early 1980s one out of three marriages in France has ended in divorce, compared to one in six in 1975. By comparison, it is estimated that 50 per cent of marriages in the United States end in divorce, 45 per cent in Sweden, 40 per cent in England, Australia and Denmark. These percentages are lower in southern European countries, where divorce has only recently been legalized.
4. The word *persona* in Latin designates the mask worn by theatre actors (the *prosôpon* of the Greeks). There were a limited number of masks which corresponded to standard characters from which spectators would expect predetermined behaviours.
5. See Digman (1990); Rolland (1990); De Raad (1992); Shmelyov and Pokhilko (1993); Ostendorf and Angleitner (1994); Narayanan *et al.* (1995); Church *et al.* (1996); Saucier and Goldberg (1996).
6. See Kassarjian and Scheffet (1991); also the special issue devoted to this subject by the *European Journal of Personality*, 1992, 6(2), 83–176.
7. See for instance Ashford and Timms (1992), Mermet (1991, 1995), Riffault (1994), as well as the special issue of *Futuribles* 2000, July/August 1995, devoted to the study of the evolution of European values.
8. In addition, Todd distinguishes a fifth, more minor, type: the 'incomplete founder family', which actually practises inequality between sons, although this is contrary to succession customs.
9. The 'stage' concept is dangerous because it could induce the idea that information processing always functions in a sequential order. Some authors (Coles *et al.*, 1986, for instance) propose a model characterized by a continuous flow in which the output of each stage may constitute the input of the following and preceding stages.

10. C. Bonnet (1986) reminds us, among others, that Bouguer, in his *Traité d'Optique sur la Gradua-tion de la Lumière*, as early as 1729, proposed this law. History retained only Weber's name.

11. This constant number would be on average 1/60 when one wants to estimate the luminosity of a lighted room, 1/14 for smell, 1/5 for taste (salinity), and only 1/333 when one wants to estimate the pitch of pure tones (see Bonnet, 1986; Mattin and Foley, 1992). These values are approximate and individuals may, depending on their adaptation level, lower these differential thresholds to adjust to the situation. In practice, one usually retains the liminal perception thresholds obtained for the same person in 50 per cent of the cases.

12. 'Signal Detection Theory' and especially its methodology have been widely applied in areas which go largely beyond the field of sensations and psychophysics, such as selective attention, categorical judgement and memory. It was, for instance, used in marketing to study the recognition of advertising campaigns (see Tashchian *et al.*, 1988). For a discussion of the various issues raised by these extensions, one might refer to Lecocq (1981a and b), Sweets (1986) and Yorelinas (1994).

13. The word 'unconscious' is extremely polysemic and raises a real debate (see Dennet, 1991; Farthing, 1992 and Nelson, 1996).

14. The distinction between automatic and controlled processing is still contentious (Posner and Petersen, 1990). Processing is usually said to be automatic when: (a) it does not correspond to any intention; (b) it is unconscious; (c) it does not dip into the person's attentional resources and capacities. Some processes are automatic because they have been genetically programmated; others become automatic after very long learning periods.

15. Over the last decade, some researchers have demonstrated the fact that carrying out a task increases very much the memorization of this task. This phenomenon can be explained by the fact that the fulfilment of a task is linked to a 'multimodal' experience (bodily activities, hearing, vision, taste, etc.) which leads to a richer episodic integration (Engelkamp and Zimmer, 1994; Bäckman *et al.*, 1991). Denis *et al.* (1991) have shown that memorization of a task can be improved if subjects are asked to imagine themselves doing it.

16. For an overall presentation of the various theories and models related to knowledge structures and categorization processes, see Richard (1991), Dubois (1991) and Smith (1995).

17. Some authors have questioned the idea that class membership is determined on the sole basis of a similarity judgement, while others regret that the concept is not better specified (Barsalou, 1990; Vandierendonck, 1991).

18. Lack of space prevents us from developing these ideas. The reader interested by the semiotic approach to communication may refer to IREP (1976, 1983), Umiker-Sebeok (1988), Pinson (1988), Floch (1990, 1995), Cook (1992).

19. A good review of the literature and controversies on the exact nature of images and their functioning can be found in: Paivio (1991), Tye (1991), Hampson *et al.* (1990), Kosslyn (1994), Denis and De Vega (1993).

20. The compulsive character of individuals can be measured by general scales, for example the Yale-Brown scale (Goodman *et al.*, 1988; Bouvard *et al.*, 1992; Mollard *et al.*, 1989), as well as scales specifically developed for the buying context (Valence *et al.*, 1988; Scherhorn *et al.*, 1990; Faber and O'Guinn, 1992; d'Astous, 1989).

21. The most popular measure of the tendency to procrastinate is the scale developed by Lay (1986); see Ferrari *et al.* (1995) for a presentation of other available instruments.

References

Adler A., *Social Interest: A Challenge to Mankind*, London: Faber, 1938.

Agres S.J., Edell J.A. and Dubitsky T.M. (eds.), *Emotion in Advertising: Theoretical and Practical Explorations*, NY: Westport, 1990.

Ajzen I., 'The theory of planned behavior', *Organizational Behavior and Human Decision Processes*, 1991, **50**, 179–211.

Ajzen I. and Driver B.L., 'Contingent value measurement: On the nature and willingness to pay', *Journal of Consumer Psychology*, 1992, 1(4), 297–316.

Akerloff G.A., 'Procrastination and obedience', *American Economic Review*, 1991, **81**(2), 1–19.

Alba J.W. and Hutchinson J.W., 'Dimensions of consumer expertise', *Journal of Consumer Research*, 1987, **13**(3), 411–54.

Alba J.W., Hutchinson J.W. and Lynch J.G. Jr, 'Memory and decision making', in Robertson T.S. and Kassarjian H.H. (eds.), *Handbook of Consumer Behavior*, Englewood Cliffs, NJ: Prentice-Hall, 1991, 1–49.

Albanese P.J., 'Personality, consumer behavior and marketing research: A new theoretical and empirical research', in Hirschman E.C. (ed.), *Research in Consumer Behavior*, **4**, Greenwich, CT: JAI Press, 1990, 1–49.

Allsopp J.F., 'Personality as a determinant of beer and cider consumption among young men', *Personality and Individual Differences*, 1986a, **7**, 341–7.

Allsopp J.F., 'The distribution of on-licence beer and cider consumption and its personality determinants among young men', *European Journal of Marketing*, 1986b, **30**(3/4), 44–62.

Anand P. and Sternthal B., 'Ease of message processing as a moderator of repetition effects in advertising', *Journal of Marketing Research*, 1990, **27**, 345–53.

Aron A., Aron E.N., Tudor M. and Nelson G., 'Close relationships as including other in the self', *Journal of Personality and Social Psychology*, 1991, **60**(2), 241–53.

Aron A., Aron E.N. and Smollan D., 'Inclusion of other in the self-scale and the structure of interpersonal closeness', *Journal of Personality and Social Psychology*, 1992, **63**(4), 596–612.

Ashford S. and Timms N., *What Europe Thinks: A Study of Western European Values*, Aldershot: Dartmouth, 1992.

Astous A. d', 'An inquiry into the compulsive side of normal consumers', *Journal of Consumer Policy*, 1990, **13**, 15–31.

Astous A. d', Valence G. and Fortier L., 'Conception et validation d'une échelle de mesure de l'achat compulsif', *Recherche et Applications en Marketing*, 1989, **4**(1).

Astous A. d', Malais J. and Roberge C. 'Compulsive buying tendencies of adolescent consumers', *Advances in Consumer Research*, 1990, **17**, 306–12.

Aurier R., 'Recherche de variété: un concept majeur de la théorie en marketing', *Recherche et Applications en Marketing*, 1991, **6**(1), 85–106.

Aurier P. and Jean S., 'L'ensemble de considération du consommateur: une approche personne × objet × situation', *Actes du 12ème Congrès de l'Association Française du Marketing*, Poitiers, 1996, **12**, 599–614.

Aurifeille J.M. and Valette-Florence P., 'An empirical investigation of the predictive validity of micro versus macro approaches in consumer value research', in Grunert K.G. and Fuglede D. (eds.), *Marketing for Europe*, Aarhus: European Marketing Academy, 1992, **1**, 65–81.

Babin B.J., Darden W.R. and Griffin M., 'Work and/or fun: Measuring hedonic and utilitarian shopping value', *Journal of Consumer Research*, 1994, **20**, 644–56.

Bäckman L., Nilsson L.-G., Herlitz A., Nyberg L. and Stigsdotter A., 'A dual conception of the encoding of action events', *Scandinavian Journal of Psychology*, 1991, **32**, 289–99.

Badot O. and Cova B., 'Communauté et consommation: Prospective pour un marketing tribal', *Revue Française du Marketing*, 1995, **151**(1), 5–17.

Bagozzi R.P., 'The role of psychophysiology in consumer research', in Robertson T.S. and Kassarjian H.H. (eds.), *Handbook of Consumer Behavior*, Englewood Cliffs, NJ: Prentice Hall, 1991, 124–60.

Bagozzi R.P., 'On the neglect of volition in consumer research: A critique and proposal', *Psychology and Marketing*, 1993, **10**(3), 215–37.

Bagozzi R.P., Yi Y. and Baumgartner J., 'The level of effort required for behavior as a moderator of the attitude–behaviour relation', *European Journal of Social Psychology*, 1990, **20**, 45–59.

Bagozzi R.P. and Warshaw P.R., 'Trying to consume', *Journal of Consumer Research*, 1990, **17**, 127–140.

Bakhurst D. and Sypnowich C. (eds.), *The Social Self*, London: Sage, 1995.

Ball A.D. and Tasaki L.H., 'The role and measurement of attachment in consumer behavior', *Journal of Consumer Psychology*, 1992, **1**(2), 155–72.

Banaji M.R., 'The self in social contexts', *Annual Review of Psychology*, 1994, **45**, 297–332.

Barak B., 'Cognitive age: A new multidimensional approach to measuring age identity', *The International Journal of Aging and Human Development*, 1987, **25**(2), 109–28.

Barnes J.W. and Ward J.C., 'Typicality as a determinant of affect in retail environments', in Kardes F.R. and Sujan M. (eds.), *Advances in Consumer Research*, 1995, **22**, 204–9.

Barsalou L.W., 'On the indistinguishability of exemplar memory and abstraction in category representation', in Srull T.K. and Wyer R.S. (eds.), *Advances in Social Cognition*, Vol. 3, Hillsdale, NJ: Erlbaum, 1990, 61–88.

Bartoshuk L.M., 'Taste', in Atkinson R.C. *et al.* (eds.), *Stevens' Handbook of Experimental Psychology*, New York: Wiley, 1988, 461–99.

Basden B., Basden D. and Gargano G., 'Directed forgetting in implicit and explicit memory tests: A comparison of methods', *Journal of Experimental Psychology: Learning, Memory and Cognition*, 1993, **19**(3), 603–16.

Batra R., 'Affective advertising: Role, processes and measurement', in Peterson R.A., Hoyer W.D. and Wilson W.R. (eds.), *The Role of Affect in Consumer Behavior: Emerging Theories and Applications*, Lexington, MA: DC Heath, 1984, 53–85.

Baudrillard J., *Le Système des Objets*, Paris: Gallimard, 1968.

Baumgartner H., Sujan M. and Bettman J.R., 'Autobiographical memories, affect and consumer information processing', *Journal of Consumer Psychology*, 1992, **1**, 53–82.

Bearden W.O. and Rose L.R., 'Attention to social comparison information: An individual difference factor affecting consumer conformity', *Journal of Consumer Research*, 1990, **16**, 461–71.

Beatty S.E., Homer P.M. and Kahle L.R., 'Problems with VALS in international marketing research: An example from an application of the empirical mirror technique', *Advances in Consumer Research*, 1988b, **15**, 375–80.

Becker W., 'Consequences of different kinds of parental discipline', in Hoffman M.L. and Hoffman L.W. (eds.), *Review of Child Development Research*, 1964, **1**, 169–204.

Becker G.S., *A Treatise of the Family*, Cambridge, MA: Harvard University Press, 1991.

Béguin P. and Costermans J., 'Le traitement de l'information olfactive', *L'Année Psychologique*, 1994, **94**, 99–122.

Belk R.W., 'Attachment to possessions', in Altman I. and Low S.M. (eds.), *Place Attachment: Human Behavior and Environment*, Vol. 12, New York: Plenum Press, 1992, 37–62.

Ben-Porath Y.S. and Waller N.G., 'Normal personality inventories in clinical assessment: General requirements and the potential for using the NEO personality inventory', *Psychological Assessment*, 1992, **4**, 14–19.

Bénéton P., *Les Classes sociales*, Paris: PUF, 1991.

Bergadaà M. and Roux E., 'L'interaction mère–enfant sur le point de vente: mesure des attitudes et observation des stratégies de négociation', *Actes du 4ème Congrès de l'Association Française du Marketing*, Montpellier, 1988, **4**, 1–15.

Berger I.E., 'The nature of attitude accessibility and attitude confidence: A triangulated experiment', *Journal of Consumer Psychology*, 1992, **1**, 103–123.

Bettman J.R., Johnson E.J. and Payne J.W., 'Consumer decision making', in Robertson T.S. and Kassarjian H.H. (eds.), *Handbook of Consumer Behavior*, Englewood Cliffs, NJ: Prentice-Hall, 1991, 50–84.

Block J., 'A contrarian view of the five-factor approach to personality description', *Psychological Bulletin*, 1995, **117**(2), 187–215.

Böcker F., 'Die Bildung von Präferenzen für langlebige Konsumgüter in Familien', *Marketing*, 1987, **1**, 16–24.

Bone P.F. and Ellen P.S., 'The generation and consequences of communication-evoked imagery', *Journal of Consumer Research*, 1992, **19**, 93–104.

Bonnet C., *Manuel Pratique de Psychophysique*, Paris: Armand Colin, 1986.

Bonnet C., Ghiglione R. and Richard J.F., *Traité de Psychologie Cognitive Vol. 1: Perception, Action, Langage*, Paris: Dunod, 1989.

Borstein R.F., 'Subliminal techniques as propaganda tools: A review and critique', *Journal of Mind and Behavior*, 1989, **10**, 231–62.

Borstein R.F., 'Exposure and affect: Overview and meta-analysis of research, 1968–1987', *Psychological Bulletin*, 1989b, **106**, 265–89.

Borstein R.F., 'Perception without awareness: Retrospect and prospect', in Borstein R.F. and Pitman T.S. (eds.), *Perception without Awareness*, New York: Guilford Press, 1992a, 3–54.

Borstein R.F., 'Subliminal mere exposure effects', in Borstein R.F. and Pitman T.S., *Perception without Awareness*, New York: Guilford Press, 1992b, 192–210.

Borstein R.F. and Pitman, T.S. (eds.), *Perception without Awareness: Cognitive, Clinical and Social Perspective*, New York: Guilford Press, 1992.

Bottomore T., *Classes in Modern Society*, London: HarperCollins Academic, 1991.

Bourdieu P., *La Distinction, Critique sociale du Jugement*, Paris: Editions de Minuit, 1979.

Bouvard M., Sauteraud A., Note I., Bourgeois M., Dirson S. and Cottraux J., 'Etude de validation et analyse factorielle de la version française de l'échelle d'obsession–compulsion de Yale–Brown', *Journal de Thérapie Comportementale et Cognitive*, 1992, **2**(4), 18–22.

Brée J., *Les Enfants, la Consommation et le Marketing*, Paris: PUF, 1993.

Brehmer B., 'The psychology of linear judgment models', *Acta Psychologica*, 1994, **87**, 137–54.

Brewer M.B., 'The social self: On being the same and different at the same time', *Personality and Social Psychological Bulletin*, 1991, **17**(5), 475–82.

Briggs S.R., 'Assessing the five-factor model of personality description', *Journal of Personality*, 1994, **60**, 253–93.

Brisoux J. and Cheron E., 'Brand categorisation and product involvement', *Advances in Consumer Research*, 1990, **17**, 101–9.

Broniarczyk S.M. and Alba J.N., 'The role of consumers' intuitions in inference making', *Journal of Consumer Research*, 1994, **21**, 393–407.

Brown J.J. and Wildt A.R., 'Consideration set measurement', *Journal of the Academy of Marketing Science*, 1992, **20**(3), 235–43.

Burgoyne C.B., 'Money in marriage: How patterns of allocation both reflect and conceal power', *Sociological Review*, 1990, **38**, 634–65.

Burka J.B. and Yuen L.M., *Procrastination: Why you do it, What to do about it*, Reading, MA: Addison-Wesley, 1983.

Burkitt I., *Social Selves*, London: Sage, 1991.

Burns, A.C., Biswas A. and Babin L.A., 'The operation of visual imagery as a mediator of advertising effects', *Journal of Advertising*, 1993, **22**(6), 71–85.

Burt S. and Gabbott M., 'The elderly consumer and non-food purchase behavior', *European Journal of Marketing*, 1995, **29**(2), 43–57.

Buss W.C. and Schaninger C.M., 'An overview of dyadic family behavior and sex roles research: A summary of findings and an agenda for future research', *Review of Marketing*, 1987, 293–324.

Cacioppo J.T., Petty R.E., Feinstein J.A. and Jarvis W.B.G. 'Dispositional differences in cognitive motivation: The life and times of individual varying in need for cognition', *Psychological Bulletin*, 1996, **119**(2), 197–253.

Campbell J.D., Campbell P.D., Heine S.J., Katz I.M., Lavallée L.F. and Lehman D.R., 'Self-concept clarity: Measurement, personality correlates and cultural boundaries', *Journal of Personality and Social Psychology*, 1996, **70**(1), 141–56.

Cantor J., Engle R.W. and Hamilton G., 'Short-term memory, working memory and verbal abilities: How do they relate?' *Intelligence*, 1991, **15**, 229–46.

Carlson L., Grossbart S. and Stuenken J.K., 'The role of parental socialization types on differential family communication patterns regarding consumption', *Journal of Consumer Psychology*, 1992, **1**, 31–52.

Castellan Y., *Psychologie de la Famille*, Toulouse: Privat, 1993.

Cathelat B., *Socio Styles-Système*, Paris: Editions d'Organisation, 1990.

Cattell R.B., *Structural Personality Learning Theory*, New York: Praeger, 1983.

Chandon J.L. and Strazzieri A., 'Une analyse de structure de marché sur la base de la mesure de l'ensemble évoqué', *Recherche et Applications en Marketing*, 1986, **1**, 17–39.

Changeur S. and Chandon J.-L., 'Le territoire-produit: étude des frontières cognitives de la marque', *Recherche et Applications en Marketing*, 1995, **10**(2), 31–51.

Cheng P.S. and Swinyard W.R., 'The influence of cultural dynamics on family purchase roles: Chinese versus American husbands and wives', *Singapore Marketing Review*, 1991(5), 5–18.

Chernatony L. de and Benicio de Mello S.C., 'Predicting brand preferences using self-concept theory', *Journal of Marketing Communications*, 1995, **1**, 121–35.

Chu G.C. and Ju Y., *The Great Wall in Ruins*, Albany, NY: SUNY Press, 1993.

Church A.T., Katigbak M.S. and Reyes J.A.S., 'Toward a taxonomy of trait adjectives in Filipino: Comparing personality lexicons across cultures', *European Journal of Personality*, 1996, **10**, 3–24.

Claeys C., *Vertical and Horizontal Category Structures in Consumer Decision Making. The Nature of Product Hierarchies and the Effect of Brand Typicality*, Doctoral Dissertation, K.U. Leuven Faculteit der Economische en Toegepaste Economische Wetenschappen, Belgium, 1993.

Claeys C., Swinnen A. and Vanden Abeele P., 'Consumers' means–end chains for think and feel products', *International Journal of Research in Marketing*, 1995, **12**(3), 193–208.

Clapier-Valladon S., *Les Théories de la Personnalité*, Paris: PUF, 1991.

Clark K.K., Borman C.A., Cropanzano R.S. and James K., 'Validation evidence for three coping measures', *Journal of Personality Assessment*, 1995, **65**(3), 434–55.

Cohen J.B. and Areni C.S., 'Affect and consumer behavior', in Robertson T.S. and Kassarjian H.H. (eds.), *Handbook of Consumer Behavior*, Englewood Cliffs, NJ: Prentice-Hall, 1991, 188–240.

Coles M.G.H., Donchin E. and Porges S., *Psychophysiology: Systems, Processes and Application*, New York: Academic Press, 1986.

Commaille J., *La Stratégie des Femmes*, Paris: La Découverte, 1992.

Conway M.A., 'Associations between autobiographical memories and concepts', *Journal of Experimental Psychology: Learning, Memory and Cognition*, 1990, **16**, 799–812.

Cook G., *The Discourse of Advertising*, London: Routledge, 1992.

Cordier F., *Les Représentations Privilégiées: Typicalité et Niveau de base*, Lille: Presses Universitaires de Lille, 1993.

Costa P.T.J.R. and McCrea R.R., 'Revised NEO Personality Inventory (NEO PI-R) and NEO Five-Factor Inventory', Professional Manual, Odessa: Fl. Psychological Assessment Resources, 1992a.

Costa P.T.J.R. and McCrea R.R., 'Four ways five factors are basic', *Personality and Individual Differences*, 1992b, **13**(6), 653–65.

Costa P.T.J.R. and McCrea R.R., 'Domains and facets: Hierarchical personality assessment using the revised NEO Personality Inventory', *Journal of Personality Assessment*, 1995, **64**(1), 21–50.

Coulter R.H. and Pinto M.B., 'Guilt appeals in advertising: What are their effects?', *Journal of Applied Psychology*, 1995, **80**(6), 697–705.

Courson J.P. and Saboulin M. de, 'Ménages et familles: vers de nouveaux modes de vie', *Economie et Statistique*, 1985, **175**, 3–20.

Cova B., *Au delà du Marché: Quand le Lien importe plus que le Bien*, Paris: L'Harmattan, 1995.

Cowen N., Wood N.L. and Borne D.N., 'Reconfirmation of the short-term storage concept', *Psychological Science*, 1994, **5**, 103–6.

Cristau C. and Strazzieri A., 'Implication durable et leadership d'opinion: la valeur prédictive de trois échelles d'implication durable', *Actes du 12ème Congrès de l'Association Française du Marketing*, Poitiers, 1996, **12**, 141–58.

Czikszentmihalyi M. and Rochbert-Halton E., *The Meaning of Things*, Cambridge: Cambridge University Press, 1981.

Darmon D., Houriez J.M. and L'Hardy P., 'Consommation: l'effet du vieillissement', *Economie et Statistique*, (1991), **243**(5), 89–104.

Das-Smaal E.A., 'Biases in categorization', in Caverni J.-P., Fabre J.-M. and Gonzalez M. (eds.), *Cognitive Biases*, Amsterdam: Elsevier, 1990, 349–86.

Davies P.J. and Schwartz G.E., 'Repression and the inaccessibility of affective memories', in Singer J.L. (ed.), *Repression and Dissociation*, Chicago: University of Chicago Press, 1990, 387–404.

Day E., Stafford M.R. and Camacho A., 'Opportunities for involvement research: A scale development approach', *Journal of Advertising*, 1995, **24**(3), 69–75.

De Raad B., 'The replicability of the Big Five personality dimensions in three world-classes of the Dutch language', *European Journal of Personality*, 1992, **6**, 15–29.

Debevec K. and Romeo J.B., 'Self-referent processing in perception of verbal and visual commercial information', *Journal of Consumer Psychology*, 1992, **1**, 83–102.

De Gaulejac V. and Aubert N., *Femmes au Singulier ou la Parenté Solitaire*, Paris: Klincksieck, 1990.

Denis M. and De Vega M., 'Modèles mentaux et imagerie mentale', in Ehrlich M.F., Tardieu H. and Cavazza M. (eds.), *Les Modèles Mentaux: Approches Cognitives des Représentations*, Paris: Masson, 1993, 79–100.

Denis M., Engelkamp J. and Mohr G., 'Memory of imagined actions: Imagining oneself or another person', *Psychological Research*, 1991, **53**, 246–50.

Dennet D.C., *Consciousness Explained*, Boston: Little Brown, 1991.

Derbaix C.M., 'L'impact des réactions affectives induites par les messages publicitaires', *Recherche et Applications en Marketing*, 1995, **10**(2), 3–30.

Derbaix C. and Pham M.-T., 'Pour un développement des mesures de l'affectif en marketing: synthèse des prérequis', *Recherche et Applications en Marketing*, 1984, **4**(4), 71–87.

Derbaix C. and Pham M.-T., 'Affective reactions to consumption situations: A pilot investigation', *Journal of Economic Psychology*, 1991, **12**, 325–55.

Derbaix A. and Vanden Abeele P., 'Consumer inferences and consumer preferences. The status of cognition and consciousness in consumer behavior', *International Journal of Research in Marketing*, 1985(2), 157–174.

Desrosières A. and Thévenot L., *Les Catégories Socio-Professionnelles*, Paris: Editions La Découverte, 1988.

Dichter E., *The Strategy of Desire*, New York: Doubleday, 1960.

Dick A, Chakravarti D. and Biehal G., 'Memory-based inferences during consumer choice', *Journal of Consumer Research*, 1990, **17**, 82–93.

Digman J.M., 'Personality structure: Emergence of the five-factor model', *Annual Review of Psychology*, 1990, **41**, 417–40.

Dittmar H., *The Social Psychology of Material Possessions: To Have is to Be*, London: St Martin Press, 1992.

Dittmar H., Beattie J. and Friese S., 'Gender identity and material symbols: Objects and decision consideration in impulse purchases', *Journal of Economic Psychology*, 1995, **16**, 491–511.

Divard R., *Le désaccord et la résolution de conflit dans la prise de décisions d'achat au sein du couple*, Thèse de doctorat ès sciences de gestion, Institut de Gestion de Rennes, 1992.

Divine R.L., 'The influence of price on the relationship between involvement and consideration set', *Marketing Letters*, 1995, **6**(4), 309–19.

Donati P., *Famiglia e Politiche Sociali*, Milano: Franco Angeli, 1985.

Douglas M. and Isherwood B., *The World of Goods*, London: Routledge, 1996.

Doulhitt R.A. and Fedyk J.M., 'The influence of children on family cycle spending behavior: Theory and applications', *Journal of Consumer Affairs*, 1988, **22**, 220–48.

Dubar C., *La Socialisation: Construction des Identités sociales et professionnelles*, Paris: A. Colin, 1991.

Dubois B., 'Culture et marketing', *Recherche et Applications en Marketing*, 1987, **2**(1), 43–64.

Dubois B., *Comprendre le Consommateur*, Paris: Dalloz, 1994.

Dubois B. and Marchetti R.Z., 'Le triangle d'influence: un nouvel outil pour mesurer la répartition des rôles dans les décisions familiales d'achat', *Actes du 8ème Congrès International de l'Association Française du Marketing*, Lyon, 1992, 295–308.

Dubois D., *Sémantiques et Cognition*, Paris: Editions du CNRS, 1991.

Eagly A.H. and Chaiken S., *The Psychology of Attitudes*, Forth Worth, TX: Harcourt Brace Jovanovitch, 1993.

Easterling D., Miller S and Weinberger N., 'Environmental consumerism: A process of children's socialization and families' resocialization', *Psychology and Marketing*, 1995, **12**(6), 531–50.

Edwards K., 'The interplay of affect and cognition in attitude formation and change', *Journal of Personality and Social Psychology*, 1990, **59**(2), 202–16.

Endler N.S. and Parker J.D.A., 'Interactionism revisited: Reflections on the continuing crisis in the personality area', *European Journal of Personality*, 1992, **6**, 177–98.

Engel J.F., Blackwell R.D. and Miniard P.W., *Consumer Behavior*, Hillsdale, IL: Dryden Press, 1995.

Engelkamp J. and Zimmer H.D., *The Human Memory*, Göttingen: Hogrefe and Huber, 1994.

Engen T., *Odor Sensation and Memory*, New York: Praeger, 1991.

Erdelyi M., 'Psychodynamics and the unconscious', *American Psychologist*, 1992, **47**(6), 784–7.

Eriksen C.W., Webb J.M. and Fournier L.R., 'How much processing do non-attended stimuli receive? Apparently very little, but . . .', *Perception and Psychophysics*, 1990, **47**(5), 477–88.

Euromonitor, 'European consumer lifestyle', *Market Research Europe*, 1995, **27**(6), 1–64.

Eysenck H.J., *The Biological Basis of Personality*, Springfield, IL: Charles Thomas, 1967.

Eysenck H.J., 'Four ways five factors are *not* basic', *Personality and Individual Differences*, 1992, **6**, 667–73.

Faber R. 'Compulsive buying: A biopsychosocial perspective', *American Behavioral Scientist*, 1992, **35** (July–August), 809–19.

Faber R.J. and O'Guinn T.C., 'A clinical screener for compulsive buying', *Journal of Consumer Research*, 1992, **19**, 459–69.

Fabien L. and Jolicoeur D., 'Socialization as an etiological factor of compulsive buying behavior among young adult consumers', in van Raaij W.F. and Bamossy G.J. (eds.), *European Advances in Consumer Research*, 1, Provo, UT: Association for Consumer Research, 1993, 262–8.

Farthing G.W., *The Psychology of Consciousness*, Englewood Cliffs, NJ: Prentice Hall, 1992.

Fazio R.H., 'Multiple processes by which attitudes guide behavior: the MODE model as an integrative framework', *Advances in Experimental Social Psychology*, 1990, **23**, 75–109.

Fazio R.H., Powell M.C. and Williams C.J., 'The role of attitude accessibility in the attitude to behavior process', *Journal of Consumer Research*, 1989, **16**, 280–8.

Fechner G.T., *Elements of Psychophysics*, 1860 (translation Adler H.E., New York: Holt, Rinehart and Winston, 1966).

Ferrari J.R., 'Procrastinators and perfect behavior: An explanatory analysis of self-presentation, self-awareness and self-handicapping components', *Journal of Research in Personality*, 1991, **1**, 75–84.

Ferrari J.R., 'Christmas and procrastination: Explaining lack of diligence at a "real-world" task deadline', *Personality and Individual Differences*, 1993, **14**, 25–33.

Ferrari J.R. and Emmons R.A., 'Procrastination as revenge: Do people report using delays as a strategy for vengeance?', *Personality and Individual Differences*, 1994, **15**, 539–44.

Ferrari J.R., Johnson J.L. and McGown W.G., *Procrastination and Task Avoidance: Theory, Research and Treatment*, New York: Plenum Press, 1995.

Filser M., *Le Comportement du Consommateur*, Paris: Dalloz, 1994.

Fiske S.T. and Taylor S.E., *Social Cognition*, New York: McGraw Hill, 1990.

Floch J.M., *Sémiotique, Marketing et Communication*, Paris: PUF, 1990.

Floch J.M., *Identités Visuelles*, Paris: PUF, 1995.

Flynn L.R., Goldsmith R.E. and Eastman J.K., 'Opinion leaders and opinion seekers: Two new measurement scales', *Journal of the Academy of Marketing Science*, 1996, **24**(2), 137–47.

Ford J.B., LaTour M.S. and Henthorne T.L., 'Perception of marital roles in purchase decision processes: A cross-cultural study', *Journal of the Academy of Marketing Science*, 1987, **14**(9), 264–79.

Fosse-Gomez M.-H., 'L'adolescent dans la prise de décision économique de la famille', *Recherche et Applications en Marketing*, 1991, **4**, 100–18.

Fouquier, E., 'Figures of reception: Concepts and rules for a semiotic analysis of mass media reception', *International Journal of Research in Marketing*, 1988, **4**, 331–41.

Fournier S., 'A consumer–brand relationship framework for strategic brand management', Unpublished Ph.D. dissertation, University of Florida, December 1994.

Foxall G.R., 'Consumer innovativeness', in Hirschman E. and Sheth J.N. (eds.), *Research in Consumer Behavior*, Greenwich, CT: Jai Press, 1988, 3, 79–113.

Foxall G.R. and Goldsmith R.E., *Consumer Psychology for Marketing*, London: Routledge, 1994.

Foxman E., Tansuhaj P. and Ekstrom K., 'Family members' perceptions of adolescents' influences in family decision making', *Journal of Consumer Research*, 1989, **15**, 159–72.

Freeman W.J., 'The physiology of perceptions', *Scientific American*, 1991, **264**, 78–84.

Friestad M. and Thorson E., 'Remembering ads: The effects of encoding strategies, retrieval cues and emotional response', *Journal of Consumer Psychology*, 1993, **2**(1), 1–23.

Gardner M.P., 'Mood states and consumer behavior: A critical review', *Journal of Consumer Research*, 1985, **12**, 281–300.

Gemunden H.G., 'Perceived risk and information search: A systematic meta-analysis of the empirical evidence', *International Journal of Research in Marketing*, 1985, **2**(2), 79–100.

Gengler, C. and Reynolds T.J., 'Consumer understanding and advertising strategy: Analysis and strategic translation of laddering data', *Journal of Advertising Research*, 1995 (7–8), 19–33.

Gertzen H., 'Component processes of phased decision strategies', *Acta Psychologica*, 1992, **80**, 229–46.

Giboin A., 'Mémoire épisodique, mémoire sémantique et niveaux de traitement', *L'Année Psychologique*, 1978, **78**, 203–32.

Gilly M.C. and Enis B.M., 'Recycling the family life cycle: A proposal for redefinition', *Advances in Consumer Research*, 1982, **9**, 211–76.

Glatt M. and Cook C., 'Pathological spending as a form of psychological dependence', *British Journal of Addiction*, 1987, **82** (November), 1257–8.

Glaude M. and de Singly F., 'L'organisation domestique: pouvoir et négociation', *Economie et Statistique*, 1986, **187**(4), 3–30.

Goldsmith R.E. and Emmert J., 'Measuring product category involvement: A multitrait-multimethod study', *Journal of Business Research*, 1991, **23**, 363–71.

Goodman W.K., Price L.H., Rasmussen S.A., Mazure C., Fleischmann R.L., Hill C.L., Heninger G.R. and Charney D.S., 'The Yale–Brown Obsessive–Compulsive Scale (Y-BOCS)', *Archives of General Psychology*, 1989, **46**, 1006–16.

Gould S.J., 'Jungian analysis and psychological types: An interpretive approach to consumer choice behavior', *Advances in Consumer Research*, 1991, **18**, 743–8.

Greenleaf E. and Lehmann D., 'Reasons for substantial delay in consumer decision making', *Journal of Consumer Research*, 1995, **22**, 186–99.

Greenwald A.G., 'New Look 3: Unconscious cognition reclaimed', *American Psychologist*, 1992, **47**(6), 766–79.

Greenwald A.G. and Banaji M.R., 'Implicit social cognition: Attitudes, self-esteem and stereotypes', *Psychological Review*, 1995, **102**(1), 4–27.

Greiveldinger J.F., Maisonneuve C. and Lion S., *Le Consommateur âgé et l'Alimentation*, Rapport N° 92, 1990 (12), Paris: Credoc, 1990.

Grønhaug K. and Troye S.V., 'Exploring the content of the evoked set in car buying', *European Research*, 1983 (7), 98–104.

Grønhaug K. and Trapp P.S., 'Perceived social class appeals of branded goods and services', *Journal of Consumer Marketing*, 1989, **6**, 13–18.

Grunert K.G., 'Another attitude on multi-attribute attitude theories', in Grunert K.G. and Ölander F. (eds.), *Understanding Economic Behaviour*, Dordrecht: Kluwer, 1989, 213–30.

Grunert K.G., *Kognitive Structuren in der Konsumforschung*, Heidelberg: Physica, 1990.

Grunert K.G. and Grunert S.C., 'Measuring subjective meaning structures by the laddering method: Theoretical considerations and methodological problems', *International Journal of Research in Marketing*, 1995, **12**, 209–25.

Guérin C., *Papyboom: Le Marketing des Seniors*, Paris: Les Presses du Management, 1995.

Guiot D., 'L'âge cognitif: un concept utile pour le marketing des seniors', *Actes du 12ème Congrès de l'Association Française du Marketing*, Poitiers, 1996, **12**, 45–60.

Gutman J., 'A means–end chain model based on consumer categorization processes', *Journal of Marketing*, 1982, **46**, 60–72.

Guyon F., *La Publicité n'affiche pas la Couleur*, Paris: Denoël, 1984.

Haberstroh J., *Ice Cube Sex: The Truth about Subliminal Advertising*, Notre Dame, IN: Crossroads Books of Cross Cultural Publications, 1994.

Haineault D.M. and Roy J.Y., *L'inconscient qu'on affiche*, Paris: Aubier, 1984.

Hamou-Poline J., *Les stratégies d'influence des enfants et les styles parentaux dans la prise de décision familiale d'achat*. Thèse ès Sciences de Gestion, Université Pierre Mendès-France de Grenoble, 1997.

Hampson P.J., Marks D. and Richardson J.T.E. (eds.), *Imagery: Current Developments*, London: Routledge, 1990.

Hanley A. and Wilhem M.W., 'Compulsive buying: An exploration into self-esteem and money attitudes', *Journal of Economic Psychology*, 1992, **13**, 5–18.

Harte J.M. and Koele P., 'A comparison of different methods for the elicitation of attribute weights: Structural modeling, process tracing and self-reports', *Organizational Behavior and Human Decision Processes*, 1995, **64**(1), 49–64.

Hasson L., 'Monitoring social change', *Journal of the Market Research Society*, 1995, **37**(1), 69–80.

Hasson M. and Ladet M., 'New cultural maps for the '90s: The future axes of consumer needs', *Proceedings of the ESOMAR Congress*, Davos, 1994, 197–207.

Hatie J., *Self-Concept*, Hillsdale, NJ: Erlbaum, 1992.

Haugtvedt C.P., Petty R.E. and Cacioppo J.T., 'Need for cognition and advertising: Understanding the role of personality variables in consumer behavior', *Journal of Consumer Psychology*, 1991, **1**, 239–60.

Heilbrunn B., 'My brand the hero: A semiotic analysis of the consumer brand relationship', Proceedings of the 24th European Marketing Academy Conference, Paris (16–19 May), 1995a, 451–70.

Heilbrunn B., 'Consumption values and brand attachment', 49th ESOMAR Congress (Istanbul), 'Changing Business Dynamics', Amsterdam: ESOMAR, 1996, 122–37.

Heller M.A. and Schiff W. (eds.), *The Psychology of Touch*, Hillsdale, NJ: Erlbaum, 1991.

Hendrickx L. and Vleck C., 'Perceived control, nature of risk information and risk taking', *Journal of Behavioral Decision Making*, 1991, **4**, 235–47.

Herpin N., 'L'habillement, la classe sociale et la mode', *Economie et Statistique*, May 1986, 35–54.

Heslin R. and Johnson R.T., 'Prior involvement and incentives to pay attention to information', *Psychology and Marketing*, 1992, **9**, 209–19.

Heslop L.A. and Marshall J., 'Prise de décision jointe chez les couples âgés: un schéma d'étude', *Recherches et Applications en Marketing*, 1990, **5**(3), 27–52.

Higgins R.L., Snyder C.R. and Berglas S. (eds.), *Self-handicapping: The Paradox that isn't*, New York: Plenum, 1990.

Hirsch I.J. and Watson C.S., 'Auditory psychophysics and perceptions', *Annual Review of Psychology*, 1996, **47**, 461–84.

Hirschman E., 'The consciousness of addiction: Toward a general theory of compulsive consumption', *Journal of Consumer Research*, 1992, **19**, 155–79.

Hoffmann-Nowotny H.J., 'The future of the family', *Congrès Européen de Démographie*, Jyväskylä (Finland), 1987, **1**, 113–200.

Hogarth R.M. (ed.), *Insights in Decision Making: A Tribute to H.J. Einhorn*, Chicago: University of Chicago Press, 1990.

Holbrook M.B., 'The psychoanalytic interpretation of consumer behavior: I am an animal', in Sheth J.N. and Hirschman E.C. (eds.), *Research in Consumer Behavior*, Vol. 3, Greenwich, CT: JAI Press, 1988, 149–78.

Holbrook M.B. and Batra R., 'Assessing the role of emotions as mediators of consumer responses to advertising', *Journal of Consumer Research*, 1987, **14**(12), 404–20.

Hong Y.J., *L'influence des enfants dans la décision d'achat familial: une étude comparative entre la France et la Corée*, Thèse de doctorat, ESA, Université Pierre Mendès-France, Grenoble, 1994.

Horney K., *Neurosis and Human Growth: The Struggle toward Self-Realization*, New York: Norton, 1950.

Howard R.W., 'Classifying types of concepts and conceptual structure: Some taxonomies', *European Journal of Cognitive Psychology*, 1992, **4**, 81–111.

Hyman M.R. and Tansey R., 'A rapprochement between the advertising community and the Jungians', *Current Issues and Research in Advertising*, 1991, **13**, 105–23.

Ichiyama M.A., 'The reflected appraisal process in small-group interaction', *Social Psychology Quarterly*, 1993, **56**(2), 87–99.

IREP, *Apport de la Sémiotique au Marketing et à la Publicité*, Colloque IREP, Paris: IREP, 1976.

IREP, *Sémiotique II*, Colloque IREP, Paris: IREP, 1983.

Irwin D.E., Zacko J.L. and Brown J.S., 'Visual memory and the perception of a stable visual environment', *Perception and Psychophysics*, 1990, **47**, 35–46.

Jacoby L.L., 'A process dissociation framework: Separating automatic from interactional uses of memory', *Journal of Memory and Language*, 1991, **30**, 513–41.

Jacoby L.L., Lindsay D.S. and Toth J.P., 'Unconscious influences revealed: Attention, awareness and control', *American Psychologist*, 1992, **47**(6), 802–9.

Jain K. and Srinivasan N., 'An empirical assessment of multiple operationalizations of involvement', *Advances in Consumer Research*, 1990, **17**, 594–602.

Janiszewski C., 'The influence of print advertisement organization on affect toward a brand name', *Journal of Consumer Research*, 1990a, **17**, 53–65.

Janiszewski C., 'The influence of non-attended material on the processing of advertising claims', *Journal of Marketing Research*, 1990b, **27**, 263–78.

Janiszewski C., 'Pre-attentive mere exposure effects', *Journal of Consumer Research*, 1993, **20**, 376–92.

Johansson J.K., 'Japanese consumers: What foreign marketers should know', *International Marketing Review*, 1986 (Summer), 37–43.

John O.P. and Robins R.W., 'Gordon Allport, father and critic of the Five-Factor Model', in Craik K.H. *et al.*, *Fifty Years of Personality Psychology*, New York: Plenum Press, 1993, 215–49.

Jolibert A. and Baumgartner G., 'Values, motivations and personal goals: A conceptual and empirical analysis', *Proceedings 22nd International Research Seminar in Marketing*, Aix-en-Provence, France, 1995, 312–21.

Jung C.G., *Psychological Types*, Princeton, NJ: Princeton University Press, 1921. Paperback reprint by Princeton University Press, 1976.

Kahle L., Beatty S. and Homer P., 'Alternative measurement approaches to consumer values: The List of Values (LOV) and Values and Life Styles (VALS)', *Journal of Consumer Research*, 1986, **13**, 405–9.

Kamakura W.A. and Novak T.P., 'Value-system segmentation: Exploring the meaning of L.O.V.', *Journal of Consumer Research*, 1992, **19**, 119–32.

Kanwar R. and Pagiavlas N., 'When are higher social class consumers more and less brand loyal than lower social class consumers? The role of mediating variables', *Advances in Consumer Research*, 1992, **19**, 589–95.

Kapferer J.N. and Laurent G., 'Les décalés et les jouisseurs n'ont pas enterré les cadres supérieurs et les cols bleus', *Stratégies*, 1981, **292**, 52–3.

Kapferer J.N. and Laurent G., 'Consumer involvement profiles', *Journal of Advertising Research*, 1986, **25**(6), 48–56.

Kapferer J.N. and Laurent G., 'Further evidence on the consumer involvement profile: Five antecedents of involvement', *Psychology and Marketing*, 1993, **10**, 347–55.

Kassarjian H.H. and Sheffet M.J., 'Personality and consumer behavior: An update', in Kassarjian H.H. and Robertson T.S. (eds.), *Perspectives in Consumer Behavior*, Englewood Cliffs, NJ: Prentice Hall, 1991, 281–303.

Kaufmann J.C., *La Châleur du Foyer: Analyse du Repli domestique*. Paris: Klinsieck, 1988.

Kaufmann J.C., *La Trame conjugale: l'Analyse du Couple par son Linge*, Paris: Nathan, 1992.

Keating N., 'What do I do with him 24 hours a day? Changes in the housewife role at retirement', *The Gerontologist*, 1980, **20**(4), 437–43.

Kellerhals J., 'Les types d'interactions dans la famille', *L'Année Sociologique*, 1987, **37**, 154–79.

Kellerhals J., Perrin J.F., Cresson-Steinauer G., Conèche L. and Wirth G., *Mariages au quotidien*, Lausanne: P.M. Faure, 1982.

Kellerhals J. and Roussel L. (eds.), 'Sociologie de la famille', *L'Année Sociologique* (special issue), 1987, **37**, 8–310.

Kellerhals J. and Troutot P.Y., 'Une construction interactive des types familiaux', *Actes de la Chaire Quételet*, Louvain-la-Neuve, 1986.

Kelter D. and Ekman P., 'Affective intensity and emotional responses', *Cognition and Emotion*, 1996, **10**(3), 323–8.

Kessler D. and Masson A. (eds.), *Cycles de Vie et Générations*, Paris: Economica, 1985.

Kinchla R.A., 'Attention', *Annual Review of Psychology*, 1992, **43**, 711–42.

Kleiber G., *La Sémantique du Prototype*, Paris: PUF, 1990.

Kleine III R.E., 'Mundane consumption and the self: A social identity perspective', *Journal of Consumer Psychology*, 1993, **2**(3), 209–35.

Kleine S.S., Kleine III R.E. and Allen C.T., 'How is a possession "me" or "not me"? Characterizing types and an antecedent of material possession attachment', *Journal of Consumer Research*, 1995, **22**, 327–43.

Komatsu L.K., 'Recent views of conceptual structure', *Psychological Bulletin*, 1992, **112**, 500–26.

Kosslyn S.M, *Image and Brain: The Resolution of the Imagery Debate*, Cambridge, MA: MIT Press, 1994.

Kosslyn S.M. and Koenig O., *Wet Mind, the New Cognitive Neuroscience*, New York: Free Press, 1992.

Kranichfeld M.L., 'Rethinking family power', *Journal of Family Issues*, 1987, **8**, 42–56.

Krebs D. and Schmidt P., *New Directions in Attitude Measurement*, Berlin: De Gruyter, 1993.

Krishnan H.S. and Stewart S., 'Comparing implicit and explicit memory for brand names from advertisement', *Journal of Experimental Psychology, Applied*, 1996, **2**(2), 147–63.

Kroeber-Riel W., 'Activation research: Psychobiological approaches in consumer research', *Journal of Consumer Research*, 1979, **5**, 240–50.

Kroeber-Riel W., *Konsumenten-Verhalten*, 5th edition, Munich: Verlag Vahlen, 1992.

Krohne H.W. (ed.), *Attention and Avoidance*, Göttingen: Hogrefe and Huber, 1993.

Krueger L.E., 'Towards a unified psycho-physical law and beyond', in Bolanowski S.J. and Gescherder G.A. (eds.), *Ratio Scaling of Psychological Magnitude: In Honor of the Memory of S.S. Stevens*, Hillsdale, NJ: Erlbaum, 1991.

Kuhl J., 'A theory of self-regulation: Action versus state orientation, self-discrimination and some applications', *Applied Psychology: An International Review*, 1992, **41**(2), 97–129.

Kuhl J. and Beckmann J. (eds.), *Volition and Personality: Action vs. State Orientation*, Göttingen: Hogrefe and Huber, 1994.

Kuykendell D. and Keating J.P., 'Mood and persuasion: Evidence for the differential influence of positive and negative states', *Psychology and Marketing*, 1990, **7**, 1–9.

Laaksonen P., *Consumer Involvement: Concepts and Research*, London: Routledge, 1994.

LaBerge D.L., 'Attention', *Psychological Science*, 1990, **1**, 156–62.

Labich K., 'Class in America', *Fortune*, 1994, **2**(7), 114–26.

Ladet M., 'RISC: une analyse systémique du changement social pour un marketing stratégique international', *Décisions Marketing*, 1994, **2** (May–August), 73–80.

Ladwein R., 'Le jugement de typicalité dans l'évaluation de l'extension de marque', *Recherche et Applications en Marketing*, 1994, **9**(2), 1–18.

Lapersonne E., Laurent G. and Le Goff J.J., 'Consideration set of size one: An empirical investigation of automobile purchases', *International Journal of Research in Marketing*, 1995, **12**, 55–66.

Larkin J.E., 'The implicit theories approach to the self-monitoring controversy', *European Journal of Personality*, 1991, **5**(1), 15–34.

Larrick R.P., 'Motivational factors in decision theories: The role of self-protection', *Psychological Bulletin*, 1993, **113**(3), 440–50.

Larsen R.J. and Ketelaar T., 'Personality and susceptibility to positive and negative emotional states', *Journal of Personality and Social Psychology*, 1991, **61**(1), 132–40.

Laslett P., 'The family as a knot of individual interests', in McC.Netting R., Wilk R.R. and Arnould E.J. (eds.), *Households: Comparative and Historical Studies of the Domestic Group*, Berkeley: University of California Press, 1984, 353–82.

Laslett P. and Wall R. (eds.), *Household and Family in Past Time*, Cambridge: Cambridge University Press, 1972.

Lastovicka J.L. and Joachimsthaler E.A., 'Improving the detection of personality–behavior relationships in consumer research', *Journal of Consumer Research*, 1988, **14**, 583–7.

Lastovicka J.L., Murray J.P. and Joachimsthaler E.A., 'Evaluating the measurement validity of lifestyle typologies with qualitative measures and multiplicative factoring', *Journal of Marketing Research*, 1990, **27**, 11–23.

Laurent G. and Kapferer J.N., 'Measuring consumer involvement profiles', *Journal of Marketing Research*, 1985, **22**, 41–53.

Laurent G. and Kapferer J.N., 'Les profils d'implication', *Recherche et Applications en Marketing*, 1986, **1**, 41–57.

Lavin M., 'Husband-dominant, wife-dominant, joint: A shopping typology for baby boom couples?', *Journal of Consumer Marketing*, 1993, **10**, 33–42.

Lay C.H., Krish S. and Zanatta C., 'Self-handicappers and procrastinators: A comparison of their practice behavior prior to an evaluation', *Journal of Research in Personality*, 1992, **26**, 242–57.

Lecas J.-C., *L'Attention visuelle: de la Conscience aux Neurosciences*, Liège: Mardaga, 1992.

Lecocq P., 'Les problèmes posés par l'application de la théorie de la détection du signal à la mémoire: 1. Problèmes Théoriques', *Cahiers de Psychologie Cognitive*, 1981(a), **1**(2), 139–72.

Lecocq P., 'Les problèmes posés par l'application de la théorie de la détection du signal à la mémoire: 2. Problèmes Techniques', *Cahiers de Psychologie Cognitive*, 1981(b), **1**(3), 335–70.

Ledoyeux M. and Adès J., 'Les achats pathologiques', *Neuro-Psychologie*, 1994, **9**(1–2), 25–32.

Lee C., 'Modifying an American behavior consumer model for consumers in Confucian culture: The case of Fishbein Behavioral Intention Model', *Journal of International Consumer Marketing*, 1990, **3**(1), 27–50.

Lee D.H. and Olshavsky R.W., 'Toward a predictive model of the consumer inference process: The role of expertise', *Psychology and Marketing*, 1994, **11**(12), 109–27.

Leeflang P.S.H. and van Raaij W.F. (guest editors), 'The changing consumer in the European Union', special issue, *International Journal of Research in Marketing*, 1995, **12**(5), 373–502.

Lemel Y., 'A la recherche de la production domestique', *Sociétés Contemporaines*, 1991, **8**.

Lemel Y., 'Les activités domestiques: qui en fait le plus?', *L'Année Sociologique*, 1993, **43**, 235–52.

Lemel Y., *Stratification et Mobilité sociale*, Paris: A. Colin, 1991.

Lemel Y. and Verger D., 'Composition démographique et cycle de vie', *Revue Française de Sociologie*, 1986, **27**, 273–300.

Lesourne O., *Le grand Fumeur et sa Passion*, Paris: PUF, 1984.

LePlay F., *L'Organisation de la Famille suivant le vrai Modèle signalé par l'Histoire de toutes les Races et de tous les Temps*, Tours: Maine, 1871.

Lewicki P., *Non Conscious Social Information Processing*, New York: Academic Press, 1986.

Lewicki P., Hill P. and Czyzewska, 'Non conscious acquisition of information', *American Psychologist*, 1992, **47**(6), 796–801.

Lockhart R.S. and Craik F.I.M., 'Levels of processing: A prospective commentary on a framework of memory research', *Canadian Journal of Psychology*, 1990, **44**, 87–112.

Loevinger J., 'Has psychology lost its conscience?', *Journal of Personality Assessment*, 1994, **62**, 2–8.

Loewenstein G., 'The psychology of curiosity: A review and re-interpretation', *Psychological Bulletin*, 1994, **116**(1), 75–98.

Loftus G.R., Duncan J. and Gehrig P., 'On the time course of perceptual information that results from a brief visual presentation', *Journal of Experimental Psychology: Human Perception and Performance*, 1992, **18**, 530–49.

Loken B. and Ward J., 'Alternative approaches to understanding the determinants of typicality', *Journal of Consumer Research*, 1990, **17**, 111–26.

MacInnis D.J. and Jaworski J.B., 'Information processing from advertisements: Toward an integrative framework', *Journal of Marketing*, 1989, **53**, 1–23.

MacInnis D.J., Moorman C. and Jaworski B.J., 'Enhancing and measuring consumers' motivation, opportunity and ability to process brand information from ads', *Journal of Marketing*, 1991, **55**, 32–53.

MacInnis D.J. and Price L., 'The role of imagery in information processing: Review and extensions', *Journal of Consumer Research*, 1987, **13**, 473–91.

MacInnis D.J. and Stayman D.M., 'Focal and emotional integration: Constructs, measures and preliminary evidence', *Journal of Advertising*, 1993, **22**(4), 51–66.

MacMillan N.A. and Creelman C.D., *Detection Theory: A User's Guide*, Cambridge: Cambridge University Press, 1991.

Madrigal R. and Miller C.L.M., 'Construct validity of spouses' relative influence measures: An application of the direct product model', *Journal of the Academy of Marketing Science*, 1996, **24**(2), 157–70.

Maffesoli M., *Le Temps des Tribus: le Déclin de l'Individualisme dans les Sociétés de Masse*, Paris: Klincksieck, 1988.

Maheswaran D. and Sternthal B., 'The effects of knowledge, motivation and type of message on ad processing and product judgments', *Journal of Consumer Research*, 1990, **17**, 66–73.

Malhotra N.K., Pinson C. and Jain A.K., 'Accommodative cognitive style differences in consumer reduction of alternatives', *Advances in Consumer Research*, 1980, **7**, 48–51.

Mangleburg T., 'Children's influence in purchase decisions: a review and critique', *Advances in Consumer Research*, 1989, **17**, 813–25.

Manrai A.K. and Manrai L.A., 'A comparative analysis of two models of store preference incorporating the notion of self image: Some empirical results', *Journal of Marketing Channels*, 1995, **4**(3), 33–51.

Marbeau Y., 'Harmonization of demographics in Europe: A State of the Art', *Marketing and Research Today*, 1992(3), 33–40.

Marshall G., Rose D. and Vogler C., *Social Class in Modern Britain*, London: Hutchinson, 1988.

Martin L.L. and Achee J.W., 'Beyond accessibility: The role of processing objectives in judgment', in Martin L.L. and Tesser A. (eds.), *The Construction of Social Judgments*, Hillsdale, NJ: Erlbaum, 1992, 195–216.

Maslow A.H., *Motivation and Personality*, New York: McGraw Hill, 1964.

Mattin M.W. and Foley H.J., *Sensation and Perception*, Boston: Allyn and Bacon, 1992.

Maule A.J., 'A componential investigation of the relation between structural modelling and cognitive accounts of human judgment', *Acta Psychologica*, 1994, **87**, 199–216.

Maurin E., 'Types de pratiques quotidiennes, types de journées et déterminants sociaux de la vie quotidienne', *Economie et Statistique*, July–August, 1989, **223**, 25–46.

McAdams, D.P., 'The Five-Factor Model in personality: A critical appraisal', *Journal of Personality*, 1992, **60**, 329–61.

McAdams S. and Bigand E., *Penser les sons: Psychologie congitive de l'audition*, Paris: PUF, 1994.

McCrea R.R. and John O.P., 'Introduction to the Five-Factor Model and its applications', *Journal of Personality*, 1992, **60**, 175–215.

McCracken G., 'Culture and consumption', *Journal of Consumer Research*, 1986, **13**, 196–213.

McGuire W.J., 'Attitudes and attitude change', in Lindzey G. and Aronson E. (eds.), *Handbook of Social Psychology, Vol. 2*, New York: Random House, 1985, 233–346.

McIntyre R.P., Claxton R.P. and Jones D.B., 'Empirical relationship between cognitive style and LOV: Implications for values and value systems', *Advances in Consumer Research*, 1994, **2**, 141–6.

McLeod P.B. and Ellis J.R., 'Alternative approaches to the family life cycle in the analysis of housing consumption', *Journal of Marriage and the Family*, 1993, **45**(8), 201–10.

McQuarrie E. and Munson J.M., 'A revised product involvement inventory: Improved usability and validity', *Advances in Consumer Research*, 1992, **19**, 109–15.

Mensing J. and Beck C., 'The psychology of fragrance selection', in Toller S.V. and Dodd G.H. (eds.), *Perfumery: The Psychology and Biology of Fragrance*, London: Chapman, 1988, 185–204.

Merikle P.M., 'Perception without awareness: Critical issues', *American Psychologist*, 1992, **47**, 792–5.

Merikle P.M. and Reingold E.M., 'Comparing direct (explicit) and indirect measures to study unconscious memory', *Journal of Experimental Psychology: Learning, Memory and Cognition*, 1991, **17**, 224–33.

Mermet G., *Euroscopie: Les Européens qui sont-ils? Comment vivent-ils?*, Paris: Larousse, 1991.

Mermet G., *Francoscopie*, Paris: Larousse, 1996.

Mervis C.B. and Rosch E., 'Categorization of natural objects', *Annual Review of Psychology*, 1981, **32**, 89–115.

Mick D.G., 'Levels of subjective comprehension in advertising processing and their relations to ad perceptions, attitudes and memory', *Journal of Consumer Research*, 1992, **19**, 317–38.

Mick D.G. and Buhl C., 'A meaning-based model of advertising experiences', *Journal of Consumer Research*, 1992, **19**(12), 317–38.

Milgram N.A., Gehrman T. and Keinan G., 'Procrastination and emotional upset: A typological model', *Personality and Individual Differences*, 1992, **13**(12), 1307–13.

Miller S.M., 'To see or not to see: Cognitive confirmatorial styles in the coping process', in Rosenbaum M. (ed.), *Learned Resourcefulness: on Coping Skills, Self-Regulation and Adaptive Behavior*, New York: Springer, 1991.

Mischel W., 'Personality dispositions revisited and revisited: A view after three decades', in Pervin L.A. (ed.), *Handbook of Personality Theory and Research*, New York: Guilford Press, 1990, 111–34.

Mischel W. and Shoda Y., 'A cognitive-affective system theory of personality: Reconceptualising situations, dispositions, dynamics and invariance in personality structure', *Psychological Review*, 1995, **102**(2), 246–68.

Mittal B., 'A comparative analysis of four scales of consumer involvement', *Psychology and Marketing*, 1995, **12**(7), 663–82.

Moingeon B., 'La sociologie de Pierre Bourdieu et son apport au marketing', *Recherche et Applications en Marketing*, 1993, **2**, 105–23.

Moles A.A., *Théorie des Objets*, Paris: Editions Universitaires, 1972.

Mollard E., Cottraux J. and Bouvard M., 'Version française de l'échelle d'obsession–compulsion de Yale–Brown', *L'Encéphale*, 1989, **15**, 335–41.

Monteil J.M., *Soi et le Contexte*, Paris: Armand Colin, 1993.

Montmollin G. de, *L'Influence sociale*, Paris: PUF, 1977.

Mooradian T.A., 'Personality and ad-evoked feelings: The case for extraversion and neuroticism', *Journal of the Academy of Marketing Science*, 1996, **24**(2), 99–109.

Moschis J.P., *Consumer Socialization: A Life-Cycle Perspective*, Lexington MA: Lexington Books, 1987.

Moschis G.P. and Cox D., 'Deviant consumer behavior', *Advances in Consumer Research*, 1989, **16**, 732–7.

Murphy S.T. and Zajonc R.B., 'Affect, cognition and awareness; Affective priming with optimal and suboptimal stimulus exposures', *Journal of Personality and Social Psychology*, 1993, **64**, 723–9.

Murray J.B., 'Review of research on the Myers-Briggs type indicator', *Perceptual and Motor Skills*, 1990, **70**, 1187–1202.

Näätänen R., *Attention and Brain Functions*, Hillsdale, NJ: Erlbaum, 1992.

Narayanan L., Menon S. and Levine E.L., 'Personality structure: A culture-specific examination of the Five-Factor Model', *Journal of Personality Assessment*, 1995, **64**(1), 51–62.

Natarajan R. and Boff B., 'Manifestations of compulsiveness in the consumer-marketplace domain', *Psychology and Marketing*, 1992, **1**, 31–44.

Nelson T.O., 'Consciousness and metacognition', *American Psychologist*, 1996, **51**(2), 102–6.

Netemeyer R.G. and Bearden W.O., 'A comparison of two models of behavioral intention', *Journal of the Academy of Marketing Science*, 1992, **20**(1), 49–60.

Nicolas S., 'Réflexions autour du concept de mémoire implicite', *L'Année Psychologique*, 1994, **94**, 63–80.

Nosofsky R.M., Kruschke J.K. and McKinley S.C., 'Combining exemplar-based category representations and connectionist learning rules', *Journal of Experimental Psychology: Learning, Memory and Cognition*, 1992, **18**(2), 211–33.

Nöth W., 'The language of commodities', *International Journal of Research in Marketing*, 1988, **3**, 173–86.

Nystedt L., Smari J. and Boman M., 'Self-schemata: Ambiguous operationalizations of an important concept', *European Journal of Personality*, 1991, **5**(1), 1–14.

Oatley K. and Jenkins J.M., 'Human emotions: function and dysfunction', *Annual Review of Psychology*, 1992, **43**, 55–85.

Odin Y., Vinais J.Y. and Valette-Florence P., 'Analyse confirmatoire des domaines motivationnels de Schwartz: une application au domaine des medias', *Actes du 12ème Congrès de l'Association Française du Marketing*, Poitiers, 1996, **12**, 125–39.

Olson D. and McCubbin M.I., *Families: What Makes Them Work*, Beverly Hills, CA: Sage, 1983.

Olson J.C. and Reynolds T.J., 'Understanding consumer cognitive structures: Implications for advertising strategies', in Percy L. and Woodside A.G. (eds.), *Advertising and Consumer Psychology*, Lexington, MA: Lexington Books, 1983, 77–90.

Olson J.M. and Zanna M.P. (eds.), *Self Inference Processes*, Hillsdale, NJ: Erlbaum, 1990.

Olson J.M. and Zanna M.P., 'Attitudes and attitude change', *Annual Review of Psychology*, 1993, **44**, 117–54.

Oppenheimer L. (ed.), *The Self Concept: European Perspectives on its Development, Aspects and Applications*, Berlin: Springer-Verlag, 1990.

Ostendorf F. and Angleitner A., 'A comparison of different instruments proposed to measure the Big Five', *European Review of Applied Psychology*, 1994, **44**(1), 45–53.

Ott N., *Intrafamily Bargaining and Household Decisions*, Berlin: Springer Verlag, 1992.

Packard V., *The Hidden Persuaders*, New York: McKay, 1957.

Pahl J., *Money and Marriage*, London: Macmillan, 1990.

Paivio A., *Images in Mind: The Evolution of a Theory*, New York: Harvester Wheatsheaf, 1991.

Pan Y. and Vanhonacker W.R., 'Chinese ethnicity: Value structure and family orientation. A comparison with American culture', in Bamossy G.J. and van Raaij W.F. (eds.), *European Advances in Consumer Research*, Provo, UT: Association for Consumer Research, 1993, **1**, 222–5.

Park C.W. and Hastak M., 'Memory-based product judgments: Effects of involvement at encoding and retrieval', *Journal of Consumer Research*, 1994, **21**(12), 534–47.

Park C.W. and Mittal B., 'A theory of involvement in consumer behavior: Problems and issues', *Research in Consumer Behavior*, 1985, **1**, 201–31.

Payne J.W., Bettman J.R., Coupey E. and Johnson E.J., 'A constructive process view of decision making: Multiple strategies in judgment and choice', *Acta Psychologica*, 1992, **80**, 107–42.

Payne J.W., Bettman J.R. and Johnson E.J., 'Behavioral decision research: A constructive processing perspective', *Annual Review of Psychology*, 1992, **43**, 87–131.

Payne J.W., Bettman J.R. and Johnson E.J., *The Adaptive Decision Maker*, Cambridge: Cambridge University Press, 1993.

Peracchio L.A., 'How do young children learn to be consumers? A script-processing approach', *Journal of Consumer Research*, 1992, **18**, 425–40.

Perfect T.J. and Askew C., 'Print adverts: Not remembered but memorable', *Applied Cognitive Psychology*, 1994 (8), 693–703.

Perfect T.J. and Heatherley S., 'Implicit memory in print ads', *Admap*, 1996 (1), 41–2.

Perkins W.S. and Reyna V.F., 'The effects of expertise on preference and typicality in investment decision-making', *Advances in Consumer Research*, 1990, **17**, 355–60.

Peterson R.A., Alden D.L., Attir M.O. and Jolibert A., 'Husband–wife report disagreement', *International Journal of Research in Marketing*, 1988, **5**(2), 125–36.

Petty R.E. and Cacioppo J.T., *Communication and Persuasion: Central and Peripheral Routes to Attitude Change*, New York: Springer-Verlag, 1986a.

Petty R.E. and Cacioppo J.T., 'The elaboration likelihood model of persuasion', in Berkowitz L. (ed.), *Advances in Experimental Social Psychology*, 1986b, **19**, 123–205.

Petty R.E., Unnava R. and Strathman A.G., 'Theories of attitude change', in Robertson T.S. and Kassarjian H.H. (eds.), *Handbook of Consumer Behavior*, Englewood Cliffs, NJ: Prentice-Hall, 1991, 241–80.

Pinson C. (guest ed.), 'Semiotics and marketing communications research', *International Journal of Research in Marketing* (special double issue), 1988, **4**(3–4), 165–356.

Pinson C., 'An implicit product theory approach to consumers' inferential judgments about products', *International Journal of Research in Marketing*, 1986, **3**, 19–38.

Pinson C. and Malhotra N.K., 'Styles cognitifs et comportements des consommateurs: illustrations et conclusions provisoires', *Recherche et Applications en Marketing*, 1988, **3**(1), 81–100.

Piolat M., Hurtig M.C. and Pichevin M.F., *Le Soi: Recherches dans le Champ de la Cognition Sociale*, Lausanne: Delachaux et Niestlé, 1992.

Popenoe D., 'American family decline, 1960–1990: A review and appraisal', *Journal of Marriage and the Family*, 1993, **55**, 527–55.

Posner M.I. and Petersen S.E., 'The attention system of the human brain', *Annual Review of Neuroscience*, 1990, **13**, 25–42.

Pratkanis A. and Greenwald A., 'Recent perspectives on unconscious processing: Still no marketing applications', *Psychology and Marketing*, 1988, **5**(4), 337–50.

Quatrezooz J. and Vancraeynest D., 'Using the Esomar harmonized demographics: External and internal validation of the results of the Eurobarometer Test', *Marketing and Research Today*, 1992, **3**, 43–7.

Ratneshwar S., Mick D.G. and Reitinger G., 'Selective attention in consumer information processing: The role of chronically accessible attributes', *Advances in Consumer Research*, 1990, **17**, 547–53.

Reynolds T.J. and Guttman J., 'Laddering theory, method, analysis and interpretation', *Journal of Advertising Research*, 1988, **28**(1), 11–31.

Ribadeau-Dumas M., 'L'influence de la communication familiale sur les savoir faire de consommation de l'enfant: une synthèse', *Actes du 11ème Congrès de l'Association Française du Marketing*, Reims, 1995, **11**, 339–75.

Richard J.-F., 'Les modèles de compréhension basés sur les structures de connaissance', *Psychologie Française*, 1991, **36**(2), 109–17.

Richins M.L., 'Valuing things: The public and private meanings of possession', *Journal of Consumer Research*, 1994, **2**, 522–33.

Riffault H., *Les Valeurs des Français*, Paris: PUF, 1994.

Rimé B. and Le Bon C., 'Le concept de conscience de soi et ses opérationnalisations', *L'Année Psychologique*, 1984, **84**, 535–53.

Robertson T.S. and Kassarjian H.H. (eds.), *Handbook of Consumer Behavior*, Englewood Cliffs, NJ: Prentice Hall, 1991.

Rochefort R., *La Société des Consommateurs*, Paris: Odile Jacob.

Rodgers W.C. and Schneider K.C., 'An empirical evaluation of the Kapferer–Laurent Consumer Involvement Profile Scale', *Psychology and Marketing*, 1993, **10**(4), 333–46.

Roedder-John D. and Cole C.A., 'Age differences in information processing: Understanding deficits in young and elderly consumers', *Journal of Consumer Research*, 1986, **13**(12), 297–315.

Rogers C.R., *On Becoming a Person*, Boston: Houghton Mifflin, 1961.

Rogers S., 'How a publicity blitz created the myth of subliminal advertising', *Public Opinion Quarterly*, 1992–1993 (Winter), **56**(4), 12–17.

Rolland J.P. (ed.), 'Le Modèle de Personnalité des Big Five en Europe', *Revue Européenne de Psychologie Appliquée*, 1994, **44**(1), 1–75.

Rook D.W., 'The buying impulse', *Journal of Consumer Research*, 1987, **14**, 189–99.

Roskos-Ewoldson D.R. and Fazio R.H., 'On the orienting value of attitudes: Attitudes accessibility as a determinant of an object's attraction of visual attention', *Journal of Personality and Social Psychology*, 1992, **63**, 198–211.

Rossides D.W., *Social Stratification*, Englewood Cliffs, NJ: Prentice Hall, 1990.

Roussel L., *La Famille incertaine*, Paris: Odile Jacob, 1989.

Roussel L., 'Les types de famille', in Singly F. de (ed.), *La Famille: l'Etat des Savoirs*, Paris: La Découverte, 1991, 873–94.

Rubin D.C., *Autobiographical Memory*, New York: Cambridge University Press, 1986.

Russo J.E. and Leclerc F., 'An eye-fixation analysis of choice processes for consumer non durables', *Journal of Consumer Research*, 1994, **21**, 274–90.

Sanyal A., 'Priming and implicit memory: A review and synthesis relevant for consumer behavior', *Advances in Consumer Research*, 1992, **19**, 795–805.

Saris W.E., 'Attitude measurement: Is there still hope?', in Krebs D. and Schmidt P. (eds.), *New Directions in Attitude Measurement*, Berlin: Walter de Gruyter, 1993.

Saucier G. and Goldberg L.R., 'Evidence for the Big Five in analyses of familiar English personality adjectives', *European Journal of Personality*, 1996, **10**, 61–77.

Schab F.R., 'Odor memory: Taking stock', *Psychological Bulletin*, 1991, **109**, 242–51.

Schacter D., 'Understanding implicit memory: A cognitive neuroscience approach', *American Psychologist*, 1992, **47**(4), 559–69.

Schacter D.L., Bowers J. and Booker J., 'Intention, awareness and implicit memory: The retrieval intentionality criterion', in Lewandowsky S., Dunn J.C. and Kirsner K. (eds.), *Implicit Memory*, Hillsdale, NJ: Erlbaum, 1989.

Schacter D.L., Chiu C.-Y.P. and Ochsner K.N., 'Implicit memory: A selective review', *Annual Review of Neuroscience*, 1993, **47**, 559–69.

Schaninger C.M. and Danko W.D., 'A conceptual and empirical comparison of alternative household life cycle models', *Journal of Consumer Research*, 1993, **19**(4), 580–94.

Scherhorn G., Reisch L. and Raab, G., 'Addictive buying in West Germany', *Journal of Consumer Policy*, 1990, **13**, 355–88.

Schiffman L.G. and Sherman E., 'Value orientations of new-age elderly: The coming of an ageless market', *Journal of Business Research*, 1991, **22**(2), 187–94.

Schneider W. and Shiffrin R.M., 'Controlled and automatic information processing', *Psychological Review*, 1977, **84**(1), 1–66.

Schwartz O., *Le Monde privé des Ouvriers*, Paris: PUF, 1990.

Schwartz S.H. and Sagiv L., 'Identifying culture-specifics in the content and structure of values', *Journal of Cross-Cultural Psychology*, 1995, **26**(1), 92–116.

Segalen M., *Sociologie de la Famille*, Paris: A. Colin, 1993.

Sekuler R. and Blacke R., *Perception*, New York: McGraw-Hill, 1994.

Semprini A., *L'Objet comme Procès et comme Action*, Paris: L'Harmattan, 1995.

Shmelyov A.G. and Pokhilko V.I., 'A taxonomy-oriented study of Russian personality-trait names', *European Journal of Personality*, 1993, **7**, 1–18.

Shouwenburg H.C., 'Procrastinators and fear of failure: An exploration of reasons for procrastination', *European Journal of Personality*, 1992, **6**, 225–36.

Simmons C.J. and Lynch J.G. Jr, 'Inference effect without inference making? Effects of missing information on discounting and use of presented information', *Journal of Consumer Research*, 1991, **17**, 477–91.

Singly F. de (ed.), *La Famille: l'Etat des Savoirs*, Paris: La Découverte, 1991.

Singly F. de, *Fortune et Infortune de la Femme mariée*, Paris: PUF, 1993a.

Singly, F. de, *Sociologie de la Famille contemporaine*, Paris: Nathan, 1993b.

Sirgy M.J., *Self Concept*, New York: Praeger, 1986.

Sjöberg L., Derbaix C. and Jansson B., 'Preference and similarity: Affective and cognitive judgment?', *Scandinavian Journal of Psychology*, 1987, **28**, 56–68.

Slama M.E. and Tashchian A., 'Selected socio-economic and demographic characteristics associated with purchasing involvement', *Journal of Marketing*, 1985, **49**, 72–82.

Smith E.E., 'Theories of semantic memory', in Estes W.K. (ed.), *Handbook of Learning and Cognitive Processes*, Vol. 6, Hillsdale, NJ: Erlbaum, 1978, 1–56.

Smith E.E., 'Concepts and categorisations', in Smith E.E. and Osherson D.S. (eds.), *An Invitation to Cognitive Science, Vol. 3: Thinking*, Cambridge, MA: MIT Press, 1995, 3–33.

Smith E.E. and Sloman S., 'Similarity vs rule-based categorisation', *Memory and Cognition*, 1994, **22**, 377–86.

Smith K.H. and Rogers M., 'Effectiveness of subliminal messages in television commercials: Two experiments', *Journal of Applied Psychology*, 1994, **79**(6), 866–74.

Smith M.F. and Carsky M.L., 'Grocery shopping behavior: A comparison of involved and uninvolved consumers', *Journal of Retailing and Consumer Services*, 1996, **3**(2), 73–80.

Smith R.E. and Buchholz L.M., 'Multiple resource theory and consumer processing of broadcast advertisements; An involvement perspective', *Journal of Advertising*, 1991, **20**, 1–7.

Smith S.M. and Schaffer D.R., 'The effects of good moods on systematic processing: Willing but not able, or able but not willing', *Motivation and Emotion*, 1991, **15**, 243–79.

Squire L.R., 'Declarative and nondeclarative memory: Multiple brain systems supporting learning and memory', *Journal of Cognitive Neuroscience*, 1992, **4**, 232–43.

Stayman D.M., Alden D.L. and Smith K.H., 'Some effects of schematic processing on consumer expectations and disconfirmation judgments', *Journal of Consumer Research*, 1992, 240–55.

Stayman D.M. and Kardes F.R., 'Spontaneous inference processes in advertising: Effects of need for cognition and self-monitoring on inference generation and utilisation', *Journal of Consumer Psychology*, 1992, **1**, 125–42.

Steenkamp J.B. and Baumgartner H., 'The role of optimum stimulation level in exploration consumer behavior', *Journal of Consumer Research*, 1992, **19**, 434–48.

Stevens S.S. and Stevens G. (eds.), *Psychophysics: Introduction to its Perceptual, Neural and Social Prospects*, New Brunswick: Transaction Publishing, 1975.

Strazzieri A., 'Mesurer l'implication durable vis à vis d'un produit', *Recherche et Applications en Marketing*, 1994, **9**(1), 73–92.

Strazzieri A. and Chandon J.L., 'Categorisator: une analyse panoramique du marché par situations d'usage', *Décisions Marketing*, 1994, **1**, 69–85.

Strazzieri A. and Hadjukowicz-Brisson E., 'Clearing up ambiguity about enduring involvement by opposing appeal involvement to stake involvement', in Jolibert A., Peterson R.A. and Strazzieri A. (eds.), *International Research Seminar in Marketing*, IAE d'Aix-en-Provence, 1995, 471–90.

Swets J.A., 'Indices of discrimination or diagnostic accuracy: Their ROCs and implied models', *Psychological Bulletin*, 1986, **99**(1), 100–17.

Tashchian A., White J.D. and Pak S., 'Signal detection analysis and advertising recognition: An introduction to measurement and interpretation issues', *Journal of Marketing Research*, 1988, **25**(11), 397–404.

Tchernia J.F., 'La recherche dans le domaine des valeurs', *Futuribles*, 1995 (8), 9–24.

Terry D.J., 'Determinants of coping: The role of stable and situational factors', *Journal of Personality and Social Psychology*, 1994, **66**(5), 895–910.

Theeuwes J., 'Endogenous and exogenous control of visual selection', *Perception*, 1994, 429–40.

Theus K.T., 'Subliminal advertising and the psychology of processing unconscious stimuli: A review of research', *Psychology and Marketing*, 1994, **11**(3), 271–90.

Thomas G.P., 'The influence of processing conversational information on inference, argument elaboration and memory', *Journal of Consumer Research*, 1992, **19**, 83–92.

Todd E., *L'Invention de l'Europe*, Paris: Seuil, 1990.

Trafimov D., Triandis H.C. and Goto S.G., 'Some tests of the distinction between the private self and the collective self', *Journal of Personality and Social Psychology*, 1991, **60**(5), 649–55.

Trappey, C., 'A meta-analysis of consumer choice and subliminal advertising', *Psychology and Marketing*, 1996, **13**(5), 517–30.

Treguer J.P., *Le Senior Marketing*, Paris: Dunod, 1994.

Tyagi P.K., 'Validation of the CAD instrument: A replication', *Advances in Consumer Research*, 1983, **10**, 112–18.

Tye M., *The Imagery Debate*, Cambridge, MA: MIT Press, 1991.

Umiker-Sebeok J. (ed.), *Marketing and Semiotics, New Directions in the Study of Signs for Sale*, Berlin: Mouton de Gruyter, 1988.

Unnava H.R. and Burnkrant R.E., 'An imagery-processing view of the role of pictures in print advertisements', *Journal of Marketing Research*, 1991, **28**, 226–31.

Usai M.C., Umiltà C. and Nicoletti R., 'Limits in controlling the focus of attention', *European Journal of Cognitive Psychology*, 1995, **7**(4), 411–39.

Valence G., d'Astous A. and Fortier L., 'Compulsive buying: Concept and measurement', *Journal of Consumer Policy*, 1988, **11**, 419–33.

Valette-Florence P., 'Les démarches de styles de vie: concepts, champs d'investigation et problèmes actuels', *Recherche et Applications en Marketing*, 1986, **11**, 93–110, **12**, 41–8.

Valette-Florence P., 'Conceptualisation et mesure de l'implication', *Recherche et Applications en Marketing*, 1989a, **4**(1), 57–78.

Valette-Florence P., 'Valeurs et marketing: Origine, historique, spécificités et champ d'applications', *Economie et Société*, 1989b, 7–56.

Valette-Florence P., 'Understanding the European consumer: Myth and realities', in Makridakis S.G. (ed.), *Single European Market*, San Francisco: Jossey Bass, 1991, 236–53.

Valette-Florence P., *Les Styles de Vie*, Paris: Nathan, 1994a.

Valette-Florence P., 'Introduction à l'analyse des chaînages cognitifs', *Recherche et Applications en Marketing*, 1994b, **9**(1), 93–118.

Valette-Florence P., Grunert S.C., Grunert K.G. and Beatty S., 'Une comparaison Franco-Allemande de l'adhésion aux valeurs personnelles', *Recherche et Applications en Marketing*, 1991, **6**(3), 5–20.

Valette-Florence P. and Jolibert A., 'Un essai empirique de clarification des approches de styles de vie', *Actes du 1er Congrès de l'Association Française du Marketing*, 1985, **1**, 133–57.

Valette-Florence P. and Jolibert A., 'Social values, A.I.O. and consumption patterns', *Journal of Business Research*, 1990, **20**, 109–22.

van Auken S. and Barry T.E., 'An assessment of the trait validity of cognitive age measures', *Journal of Consumer Psychology*, 1995(2), 107–32.

van Heck G.L., Perugini M., Caprara G.V. and Fröger J., 'The Big Five as tendencies in situations', *Personality and Individual Differences*, 1994, **16**(5), 715–31.

van Raaij F.W., 'The formation and use of expectations in consumer decision making', in Robertson T.S. and Kassarjian H.H. (eds.), *Handbook of Consumer Behavior*, Englewood Cliffs, NJ: Prentice-Hall, 1991, 401–18.

Vandierendonck A., 'Are category membership decisions based on concept gradedness?', *European Journal of Cognitive Psychology*, 1991, **3**, 343–62.

Vanhuele M., 'Mere-exposure and the cognitive affective debate revisited', *Advances in Consumer Research*, 1994, **21**, 264–8.

Venkatraman M.P., 'Opinion leadership, enduring involvement and characteristics of opinion leaders: A moderating or mediating relationship?', *Advances in Consumer Research*, 1990, **17**, 60–7.

Venkatraman M.P., Marlino D., Kardes F.R. and Sklar K.B., 'The interactive effect of message appeal and individual differences in information processing and persuasion', *Psychology and Marketing*, 1990, **7**, 85–96.

Vera L., 'Trouble obsessionnel-compulsif: approche cognitivo-comportementale', *Psychologie Française*, 1993, **34**(3/4), 217–22.

Verger D., 'Avoir des biens durables: une affaire de goûts ou de coûts?', *Consommation*, 1986, **1**, 43–60.

Verhage B.J., Yavas U. and Green R.T., 'Perceived risk: A cross-cultural phenomenon?', *International Journal of Research in Marketing*, 1990, **7**(4), 297–303.

Vincent B., 'La consommation des ménages européens: L'euro-consommateur à l'épreuve d'une analyse statistique comparée, 1980–1988', *Futuribles*, March 1992, 3–34.

Volle P., 'Le concept de risque perçu en psychologie du consommateur: antécédents et statut théorique', *Recherche et Applications en Marketing*, 1995, **10**(1), 39–56.

Voller B. and Winkler A.R., 'European consumers and environmental behavior', *Seminar of the Growing Individualism of Consumer Lifestyles and Demand, How is Marketing Coping With It?*, Amsterdam: ESOMAR, 1991.

von Hippel W., Hawkins C. and Narayan S., 'Personality and perceptual expertise: Individual differences in perceptual identification', *Psychological Science*, 1994, **5**(6), 401–6.

von Keitz B., 'Eye movement research: Do consumers use the information they are offered?', *European Research*, 1988 (11), 217–24.

Ward J.C. and Loken B., 'The generality of typicality effects on preference and comparison: An exploratory test', *Advances in Consumer Research*, 1988, **15**, 55–61.

Ward J.C., Bitner M.J. and Barnes J., 'Measuring the prototypicality and meaning of retail environment', *Journal of Retailing*, 1992, **68**(2), 194–220.

Watson D. and Clark L.A., 'On traits and temperament: General and specific factors of emotional experience and their relation to the Five-Factor Model', *Journal of Personality*, 1992, **60**(6), 441–76.

Weil-Barais A. (ed.), *L'Homme cognitif*, Paris: PUF, 1993.

Weinberger J. and Hardaway R., 'Separating science from myth in subliminal psychodynamic activation', *Clinical Psychology Review*, 1990, **10**, 727–56.

Westen D., 'A model and a method for uncovering the nomothetic from the ideographic: An alternative to the Five-Factor Model?', *Journal of Research in Personality*, 1996, **30**, 400–16.

Westenberg M.R.M. and Koele P., 'Multi-attribute processes: Methodological and conceptual issues', *Acta Psychologica*, 1994, **87**, 65–84.

Wicks A., 'Fashionable myths about the housewife of the eighties', *ADMAP*, 1987 (10), 22–9.

Wiest W.M. and Bell B., 'Stevens's exponent for psychophysical scaling of perceived, remembered and inferred distance', *Psychological Bulletin*, 1985, **98**, 457–70.

Wiggins J.S., 'Have model, will travel', *Journal of Personality*, 1992, **60**, 527–32.

Wiley N., *The Semiotic Self*, Chicago, IL: University of Chicago Press, 1995.

Wilkes R.E., 'A structural modelling approach to the measurement and meaning of cognitive age', *Journal of Consumer Research*, 1992, **19**(2), 292–301.

Wilkes R.E., 'Household life cycles stages, transitions and product expenditures', *Journal of Consumer Research*, 1995, **22**, 27–42.

Wolfe D.B., *Serving the Ageless Market*, New York: McGraw-Hill, 1990.

Yang C.F., 'Une conception du comportement du consommateur Chinois', *Recherche et Applications en Marketing*, 1989, **4**(1), 17–36.

Yau O.H.M., *Consumer Behavior in China. Customer Satisfaction and Cultural Values*, London: Routledge, 1994.

Yonelinas A.P., 'Receiver-operating characteristics in recognition memory: Evidence for a dual-process model', *Journal of Experimental Psychology: Learning, Memory and Cognition*, 1994, **20**(6), 1341–51.

Yost W.A., Popper A.N. and Fay R.R. (eds.), *Human Psychophysics*, New York: Springer-Verlag, 1993.

Zaichkowsky J.L., 'Measuring the involvement construct', *Journal of Consumer Research*, 1985, **12**, 341–52.

Zaichkowsky J.L., 'The personal involvement inventory: Reduction, revision and application to advertising', *Journal of Advertising*, 1994, **23** (December), 59–70.

Zajonc R.B., 'Attitudinal effects of mere exposure', *Journal of Personality and Social Psychology* (monograph suppl.), **9**(2), part 2, 1–27.

Zouaghi-Bensedrine S., *Concept de Soi, Concept de Nous et Comportement du Consommateur*, Thèse ès Sciences de Gestion, Université Paris-Dauphine, 1996.

Zuckerman M., Kuhlman D.M., Joireman J., Teta P. and Kraft M., 'A comparison of three structural models of personality: The Big Three, the Big Five and the Alternative Five', *Journal of Personality and Social Psychology*, 1993, **65**(4), 757–68.

Theories and models of consumer behaviour

2

Ehrenberg, A.S.C., 1991, 'New brands and the existing market', *Journal of the Market Research Society*, **33**(4) (October), 285–99

Ehrenberg, A.S.C., Goodhardt, G.J. and Barwise, T.P., 1990, 'Double jeopardy revisited', *Journal of Marketing*, **54** (July), 82–91

Foxall, G.R., 1992, 'The behavioral perspective model of purchase and consumption: From consumer theory to marketing practice', *Journal of the Academy of Marketing Science*, **20**(2), 189–98

Introduction

One of the most extensive European contributions to the modelling of consumer behaviour is that of Andrew Ehrenberg and his colleagues. Their approach is concerned primarily with observable consumer choice. Their work, basically known as the Dirichlet model (see Goodhardt *et al.*, 1984, for a theoretical account of the model), has been based on descriptions of patterns which exist commonly in consumer markets which have reached a stable state, i.e. there is a slight upward trend in sales in the short to medium term. This represents the vast majority of consumer-type markets, especially for fast-moving groups. A great deal of consumer behaviour is described in terms of a small number of variables: frequency of purchase, penetration level and patterns of multi-brand purchasing. Ehrenberg and his colleagues have established that there are law-like patterns of regularity for brands in markets such as these. Many of these implications are surprising to marketing students brought up on typical textbooks of consumer marketing.

The first article in this chapter presents a practical application of the Dirichlet model to new brand introduction into existing stable markets. It shows that in a particular area of vital importance to marketing management, established brands of packaged grocery products also follow regular and law-like patterns. The import of the article is in its showing that the law-like regularities uncovered by the Dirichlet model can be employed practically in the forecasting of the performance of a new brand in such markets. The underlying philosophy of science adopted by Ehrenberg can be found in a further article not reproduced here (Ehrenberg, 1992). And a comprehensive review of consumer behaviour in 'Dirichlet-type markets' is also available (Ehrenberg and Uncles, 1995).

The second article deals with a very common and widespread phenomenon in branded packaged good markets, that is 'double jeopardy'. This effect relates to the fact that, in any given period, a small brand typically has far fewer buyers than a larger brand, i.e. attracts somewhat less loyalty, and furthermore its buyers tend to buy it less often. One of the most fascinating aspects of this effect is its generalizability from a pragmatic and theoretical point of view. Keng *et al.* (1984) have, for instance, established a double jeopardy effect for smaller supermarket chains, in the sense that they have fewer buyers, and that these buyers tend also to purchase rather less frequently than do the consumers who shop mainly at other supermarkets. These authors also pointed out a consistency among supermarket chains in the degree to which heavy buyers are attracted to them.

The vast number of studies on double jeopardy, such as the present article by Ehrenberg and his colleagues, represent a fascinating discovery, in the sense that it provides marketing practitioners with a pattern that is highly predictable, something which is very seldom to be found in all the marketing literature. Furthermore, by giving convincing explanations for the existence of the 'double jeopardy', the authors provide brand managers with insights on how to adapt their branding strategy in order to deal with this effect.

The third article in this chapter shows how a very different model of consumer behaviour from that assumed in the mainstream consumer research literature can be formulated. Whereas consumer researchers for the most part have been concerned with the development of cognitive models of consumer behaviour, consumer research lacks, above all, a theory of the situational determinants of consumer choice. This article is concerned with showing that it is possible to interpret consumer behaviour comprehensively as a phenomenon determined by environmental considerations – notably the setting in which the behaviour takes place and the pattern of rewards which maintains it, in addition to the consumer's history of reinforcement. The full derivation, application and critique of the Behavioural Perspective Model with which this article is concerned are available elsewhere (Foxall, 1993, 1994). The present exposition specifically applies the model to our understanding of marketing management.

References

Ehrenberg, A.S.C., 1992, *Theory of Well-based Results: Which Comes First?* Paper presented at the EIASM Conference on 'Research Tradition in Marketing', Brussels, 9–10 January.

Ehrenberg, A.S.C. and Uncles, M., 1995, *Dirichlet-Type Markets: A Review*, Working Paper, South Bank Business School, London.

Foxall, G.R., 1993, 'Situated consumer behaviour', *Research in Consumer Behaviour*, 6, 113–42.

Foxall, G.R., 1994, 'Behaviour analysis and consumer psychology', *Journal of Economic Psychology*, 5, 5–91.

Goodhardt, G.J., Ehrenberg, A.S.C. and Chatfield, C., 1984, 'The Dirichlet: A comprehensive model of buying behaviour', *Journal of the Royal Statistical Society*, A147, 621–55.

Keng, Kau Ah and Ehrenberg A.S.C., 1984, 'Patterns of store-choice', *Journal of Marketing Research*, 21 (November), 399–408.

New brands and the existing market

Andrew S.C. Ehrenberg
Research Professor of Marketing, South Bank University, Business School, London

Summary

This paper reports on part of a programme of work at the Centre for Marketing and Communications at the London Business School, supported by some 30 leading companies in the UK and USA. It shows that consumers' buying of established brands of packaged grocery products follow regular and lawlike patterns. These patterns can be used to predict how a new brand will perform once it has settled down.

Developing a new brand is risky. Hence much data about the market, the new brand concept, the product, and its pre-test market and test-market performances are usually pored over. But marketing people cannot easily relate such data to how the new brand will actually perform.

In as far as the brand is new, its ultimate sales performance will naturally be difficult to predict. But for packaged grocery products or 'fmcgs', it is known that the established brands all attract much the same patterns of buyer behaviour (e.g. Ehrenberg, 1972, 1988). As a result, any sales target for the new brand can be translated into predictions about its penetration, repeat-buying rates, and competitive performance for when the new brand has 'settled down' and itself become an established brand. Such fleshing out of a brand's sales target in consumer terms – which is the topic of this paper – provides yardsticks for judging the new brand concept, its proposed marketing support, and its pre-launch and early launch performances.

A successful new brand has usually 'settled down' within a year or so of its launch. This means that its sales level as well as other measures such as its penetration and average buying frequency will have become more or less steady. In this paper we illustrate how one can therefore predict for a particular new brand, X say, that to reach its given sales target of say 4,000 tons a year:

(i) X would have to be bought by about 5% of the population in the year;
(ii) On average somewhat under three times a year;

From the *Journal of the Market Research Society*, 33(4), October 1991, 285–99.

(iii) Half of X's buyers would however buy it only once in the year;

(iv) Few, about one in ten, would be 100%-loyal to it;

(v) X would account for only about a third of its buyers' total requirements of the product-category.

(vi) 40% of X's buyers would also buy the market leader that year, as many as 20% would buy a certain smaller competitive brand with an 8% market share, and so on.

These predictions may not seem very encouraging. But they reflect the patterns for the established brands in that particular market – here instant coffee in the USA. They therefore should serve to provide realistic norms for judging the new brand's prospects and for evaluating its progress.

Apparently regular patterns in a particular product category such as US instant coffee could however be due to any number of *ad hoc* factors to do with the particular brand's product-formulation (e.g. caffeinated versus decaffeinated), price, advertising support, image, distribution, etc. They need therefore not necessarily apply to a new and potentially very different brand. The patterns could even just be temporary in the US instant coffee market itself, and be replaced by others a year or two later.

What matters therefore is that the patterns in this particular market reflect much more general lawlike regularities which have also been found for the different established brands in more than fifty *other* product fields (food, non-food, etc.), in different countries, at different points in time, and using different consumer panel techniques (see Table 10 [page 77]). Different products vary in the total size of the market and the overall degree of brand-switching that occurs. But after allowing for that, the different brands in each category all follow the same predictable patterns. That is why we can make the same predictions for the new brand as well, for when it has settled down. [. . .]

The regularities have been summarized by a theoretical model, the Dirichlet and its predecessors (Goodhardt *et al.*, 1984; Ehrenberg, 1972, 1988), as is outlined in the Appendix. This paper is therefore about a practical application of already well-established theory. The theory does not have to be taken on trust but can always be checked against any available empirical data for the market in question. We will in fact focus here as much on the empirical regularities as on the theory.

The Dirichlet model is very simple in that the only input required about any specific brand is its market share. Thus the regularities in buying patterns which it models have been found to be largely unaffected by differences in the product and the marketing mix. As we will see, these differences typically do not show up by way of major departures from the regular and predictable patterns of buying behaviour.

A major exception, such as that the new brand might turn out to have a repeat-rate as high as six, i.e. twice the predicted value of about three, would be revolutionary. It could only occur if the new brand were to differ more radically from any of the existing brands than *any of these differ from each other*. Despite the hype of some new brand proposals, few new brands or line extensions are however positioned to be *that* different. And if they were, one would know and be able to allow for it.

None of this is to say that differences in product-formulation, promotional support, pricing, etc. do not matter. These marketing-mix factors will have given the established brands their differing market shares. What the observed patterns and models say is only that these marketing factors have little or no effect on brand loyalty beyond their effect on market share. It follows that the lawlike patterns which we will be discussing do not inhibit the marketing manager's choice of product-formulation, price, promotional support, etc. for the new brand X. Anything is possible, just as it was in the past. But if the mix is not right, the brand will not sell and reach its target of 4,000 tons. It will attract far less than the required market penetration of 5% buying it in the year.

Even then the loyalty pattern will be much the same. The brand's few buyers will still buy it somewhat less than three times on average, with just over half in fact buying it only once in the year, less than one in ten will be 100%-loyal to it, and so on. These are the patterns which can be predicted and they are worth knowing. But we stress that it is not at all clear (i.e. 'no one knows') just how the new brand will reach its target market share or required penetration level, and how this can be brought about.

The sales target

The predictions which are discussed in this paper are not about the new brand's ultimate market share or sales level itself. Instead, we are reversing the traditional process of new product prediction by using a targeted market share or sales objective as the starting point. Given such and such a sales target – say 4,000 tons p.a. in the USA (or 1,000 tons in the UK) – what does this mean in consumer terms?

The sales target for the new brand may have been derived by some kind of break-even analysis based on certain (or uncertain) assumptions, or by senior management, or by some new-brand-prediction procedure such as Bases, Microtest, Assessor, Sensor, etc. (see, for example, Narasimhan and Sen 1983; Mahajan and Wind 1986; Shocker and Hall 1986; Research International 1990, for reviews). These procedures are derived in part from earlier new-brand forecasting procedures such as Fourt and Woodlock (1960); Baum and Dennis (1961); Parfitt and Collins (1968).

More than one sales target may even be considered. The chairman may, for instance, want twice the 4,000 tons aimed at by the new product group, whilst the sales director feels that he can only guarantee half of that. But whatever the sales target, the predictions discussed in this paper will flesh it out in consumer terms. How many buyers of X will the target require to get? What will X's repeat-buying rate have to be? How many *heavy* buyers can we get for X, and how many light ones will we be saddled with? Which brands will X be competing with most? And so on. The answers to these questions will help in evaluating not only the new brand, its marketing plan, and its early test data, but also the sales target itself. We now spell out the prediction process more fully in terms of the specific example of a new brand of instant coffee.

Fleshing out the sales target

Suppose that we are developing a new brand or line-extension X in the US instant coffee market. We will no doubt be considering various possible sales targets for when X has settled down. As one example, a particular break-even analysis may have led to an annual target of just over 4,000 tons a year, which is about 2% of the market.

To help us assess the new brand proposal, we can ask what such a level of sales will imply in *consumer terms*. For some 80 million households in the US and a 1lb pack, 4,000 tons boil down to a target of some 12 purchases per 100 households in the population. This level of purchasing can be translated into how many people buy the brand, times how often they buy it, as in the sales equation?

Sales per 100 households = % of households buying *times* the average number of purchases per buyer.

Table 1 shows how the target of 12 purchases per 100 households could then in principle be achieved in very different ways: by as many as 12% of the population buying the brand just once in the year, or by only 1% buying it as often as 12 times, or by any other combination multiplying up to 12. Aiming at relatively many very occasional buyers or at only a few but very frequent buyers has very different marketing implications in terms of product, advertising, pricing and distribution, as well as in designing and later interpreting pre-testing and test-market evaluations: an 'add-on' brand bought for variety perhaps or a classical 'niche' brand. Which is it going to be for brand X – 12% buying once, 1% buying 12 times, or what?

By looking at the *existing* brands in the US instant coffee market we can see that these various possibilities narrow down to just about one. Table 2 shows that the penetrations of the eight leading brands vary from 24% down to 6%. But compared with that, the average number of purchases per buyer varies relatively little, being roughly three for each brand (average 2.8). This is the common pattern for packaged goods: the penetrations vary markedly, but the purchase frequencies much less. And typically, this occurs despite differences in product formulation, price, advertising support, etc.

We can therefore predict that when *X* has settled down to behave like an established brand, its average purchase frequency will also be roughly three. Hence *X*'s target of 12 sales per 100 households can only be met by having about 4% of the population buying it on average about three times per year. Anything radically different (such as 1% buying it 12 times, or 12% buying it once) would be totally out of step with the existing structure of the market. As already stressed in the introduction, such a different

Table 1 A break-even target of twelve purchases per 100 households

% of Households Buying at Least Once	Average Purchases per Buyer					
	1	2	3	4	6	12
1						12
2					12	
3				12		
4			12			
6		12				
12	12					

Table 2   Brand penetration and purchase frequency over twelve months

US Instant Coffee 12 months	Purchases per 100 Households	% Households Buying at Least Once	Average Purchases per Buyer
Maxwell House	86	24	3.6
Sanka	69	21	3.3
Tasters Choice	62	22	2.8
High Point	57	22	2.6
Folgers	49	18	2.7
Nescafé	38	13	2.9
Brim	18	9	2.0
Maxim	16	6	2.6
Brand X	12	5	2.5
Average brand	48	17	2.8

expectation for X would have to be backed by some very exceptional claims, whereas the marketing plan for X probably only said that the new brand's USP would be its better bottle-top.

We can also see from the table that *whatever* the sales target for X – whether it is the chairman's ambitious requirement of, in effect, 24 purchases per 100, or the sales director's cautious guarantee of only six – the new brand will normally be bought on average about three times by its buyers. What will vary mainly is the number of buyers the brand will need to have in order to meet these different sales targets: about 8% of households buying X on average three times for the chairman, and only about 2% buying it about three times for the sales director.

The prediction of an average of three purchases a year per buyer of X can however be refined because there is a 'Double Jeopardy' sub-pattern in Table 2. Brands with few buyers tend typically also to be bought somewhat less frequently by them. This sub-pattern occurs very generally and is also predicted by the theoretical models, as we note in Table 9 later (Ehrenberg, 1972; 1988, Section 10.2; Ehrenberg *et al.*, 1990). Hence a more precise forecast for X is that its average purchase frequency will be about 2.5 in a year as shown in Table 2, and that to reach its target of 12 purchases per 100 it will need to be bought by almost 5% of US households rather than 4%.

The actual average purchase frequency for X may in the end turn out to be a bit more than 2.5 or a bit less, in line with the typically rather small variation for the existing brands in Table 2. (The low value of 2.0 shown by Brim does not always recur in other years – which is the first thing to check with an exception – and is therefore a rather temporary 'lower bound' for any prediction.) Such variations will however be too small to affect the broad marketing plan for brand X, e.g. whether its proposed promotional support will be good enough to attract *about* 5% of the population (i.e. four million US households) who should buy it on average *something* like 2.5 times each year.

The penetration of *X* in shorter time-periods

We have predicted that X will have to have about 5% of the population buying it at least once in the year (on average 2.5 times). But how many customers will brand X be having in a week, a month, or a quarter? This is often very relevant because promotional activities – advertising campaigns and consumer and trade promotions such as price-cuts, in-store displays, coupon-ing, sampling, etc. – generally take place over much shorter periods than a year.

A brand's penetration is always much smaller in shorter periods – for example, only 2% buy the market leader Maxwell House in a typical week, compared with 24% in a year. But the penetration growth of different brands follows a regular, predictable pattern. This is illustrated by the fit of the Dirichlet prediction for typical cases in Table 3. For brand X, with 5% expected to buy it in the year, the theoretical predictions are therefore that only 1% will do so in a month, and 0.3% in a week.

Hence fewer than 300,000 US households will buy X in a typical week once it has settled down, compared with as many as four million in a year. This provides a base-line for judging short-term promotional activities. Normally less than one in ten out of brand X's four million annual customers would buy it in a given week, and only one in five or 50 in a given month.

Light and heavy buyers

Brand X's predicted average purchase frequency of about 2.5 in the year might suggest that people will buy it about every four or five months. Yet most buyers of X will in fact buy it far less often.

Table 4 illustrates this: the frequency distributions of purchase of different brands are all highly skew. Almost 40% of the buyers of Maxwell House buy it only once in the year, and

Table 3 Penetration in different length time-periods (observed values and Dirichlet predictions: selected brands)

		% Households Buying in			
		48 weeks	24 weeks	4 weeks	1 week
Maxwell House	Obs	24	14	8	2.0
	Theo	29	12	6	2.0
Nescafé	Obs	13	7	3	1.0
	Theo	12	6	3	0.7
Maxim	Obs	6	4	2	0.5
	Theo	5	4	1	0.4
Brand X	Theo	5	2	1	0.3

Table 4 Frequent and infrequent buyers in the year (observed values and Dirichlet predictions: selected brands)

12 months		Number of Purchases per Buyer							
		1	2	3	4	5	6	7+	Average
Maxwell House	Obs	38	16	11	8	7	4	15	3.6
	Theo	43	19	11	7	5	2	12	
Nescafé	Obs	46	22	9	7	4	2	10	2.9
	Theo	48	19	10	6	7	3	10	
Maxim	Obs	56	19	6	5	3	1	10	2.6
	Theo	51	19	10	6	4	3	7	
Brand X	Theo	52	19	10	6	4	3	6	2.6

smaller brands like Nescafé and Maxim have even more light buyers. This is in line with their lower average purchase frequencies (the DJ effect again) and is very much as predicted. We can therefore predict correspondingly for brand X itself that as many as half of its expected four million or so annual customers will buy it only once that year. (During X's launch period, i.e. before it has settled down, even higher proportions of once-only buyers can be expected.)

Repeat-buying rates

These large numbers of infrequent buyers imply that the great bulk of brand X's buyers will mostly not be very regular from period to period, even when X has settled down. With 80% of its annual buyers buying X at most three times a year, none of these will buy it every quarter, let alone once a month. Some specific predicted repeat-buying rates for brand X are roughly as follows:

> Week to week: 10%
> Year to year: 70%.

That is, about one in ten of X's buyers in one week will buy it also in the following week. This should not be unexpected – we know that we ourselves do not always buy instant coffee every week, let alone the same brand. But it is worth having this quantified, for use in planning and especially also in evaluating pre-test-market and test-market results.

The year-by-year prediction of only 70% may at first be more surprising. Yet we saw in Table 4 that almost 50% of the buyers of X will normally not buy it a second time that year. It therefore is not so remarkable that 30% of them will not buy it again in the whole of the *following* year.

Competing with the other brands

We can also use the established patterns of buyer behaviour to predict the new brand's competitive situation, once it has settled down (although experience suggests that the predictions will also largely apply during the preceding launch period). We consider three standard aspects that are frequently tabulated from consumer panel data. They are:

1. The proportion of X's buyers who will be 'sole' or 100%-loyal buyers in the period of analysis.
2. How often brand X buyers will also buy *other* brands (in total).
3. Which particular other brands brand X buyers will also buy.

In all cases there are regular patterns, predictable from the Dirichlet or from sub-models, which can be applied also to the new brand X once it has settled down.

Sole buyers

The Dirichlet model predicts, for example, that in a year only about 10% of brand X buyers will satisfy all their instant coffee requirements with X, i.e. be 100%-loyal to it. In longer periods, the proportions of sole buyers will be even lower.

Further, these 100%-loyal consumers will buy X less than three times on average in the year, i.e. much the same rate as the 2.5 purchases predicted for *all* of X's customers, as was shown in Table 2. Hence 100%-loyal buyers of X will not only be few, but they will not even be of any special sales importance.

We can once more make these theoretical predictions with confidence because they are typical for *any* US brand of instant coffee with a comparable market share, and arise also in all the other product categories studied. In more qualitative terms, all the available evidence implies that grocery products do not have a 'hard-core' of loyal buyers. Hence we should not plan for brand X to have such a hard-core either.

Buying other brands

Most of brand X's customers will therefore buy other brands. Or more precisely, brand X being new, its customers will *continue* to buy other brands, rather as they did before. The picture is that people often have one or two favourite brands, but also buy other brands less frequently, but still more or less habitually. Once X has settled down, we can predict that its customers' 'multi-brand buying' will be in line with the pattern for the existing brands.

Thus the Dirichlet predicts that on average buyers of X will make about seven purchases of other brands – a good many more than their average of 2.5 or so purchases of brand X itself. This makes for an annual total of about ten purchases of instant coffee per buyer of X. Table 5 shows how this prediction simply reflects the picture for the existing brands: each accounts for only about a third of its customers' yearly instant coffee requirements – predictably slightly more for the market leaders and slightly less for smaller brands like X (a so-called 'Natural monopoly' effect – see Appendix). We believe that understanding this low degree of loyalty is invaluable for properly interpreting pre-test market and test-market data, and indeed for thinking about the new brand concept itself.

Table 5   Buying the brand and buying any instant coffee (average purchases per buyer of the brand)

12 months		Average Purchases of	
		Brand*	Product
Maxwell House	Obs	4	9
Sanka	Obs	3	9
Tasters Choice	Obs	3	9
High Point	Obs	3	9
Folgers	Obs	3	9
Nescafé	Obs	3	10
Brim	Obs	2	9
Maxim	Obs	2	11
Brand X	Theo	3	10
Average brand	Obs	3	9

* As in Table 2, but rounded.

Which other brands?

A further set of predictions is that buyers of brand X will buy the different competing brands in the market mainly in line with their penetrations or market shares. Table 6 gives the background for the existing market.

Table 6   Brand duplication of purchase

12 months		Maxwell House	Sanka	Tasters Choice	High Point	Folgers	Nescafé	Brim	Maxim	% will Buy Brand X
				% Who Also Bought						
Buyers of										
Maxwell House	%	–	32	29	32	38	26	13	13	8
Sanka	%	36	–	32	40	25	23	20	11	8
Tasters Choice	%	31	32	–	36	28	20	17	14	8
High Point	%	34	38	34	–	31	22	18	10	8
Folgers	%	51	30	35	40	–	25	15	11	8
Nescafé	%	48	39	34	40	34	–	15	8	8
Brim	%	33	45	39	44	27	20	–	15	8
Maxim	%	52	38	51	39	34	17	25	–	8
Average duplication	%	41	35	36	39	31	22	17	12	8

Each column in Table 6 shows the percentage of buyers of the brands listed on the left who also bought the brand in the column heading in that year. Thus Maxwell House was bought by something like 41% of the buyers of each of the other brands in the year (the first column average), Nescafé over to the right by about 22%, and Maxim by some 12%. The individual figures in each column vary somewhat (by a maximum of as much as 20% either way). But the *main* variation is with the column averages.

These in turn are largely in line with the penetrations of each brand, by a proportionality factor of about 1.7. This is shown in Table 7. The pattern is that of the long-established 'Duplication of purchase law' (a simplified approximation to the Dirichlet model). It says that in an unsegmented market the percentage of buyers of one brand who also buy another brand varies in a constant proportion (here 1.7) with the penetration of this other brand.

If there is segmentation or systematic 'partitioning' of the different brands, this will show up as deviations. Some of the variation in the columns of Table 6 could reflect this, although nothing clear-cut has been established in this particular instance. (The first check should again always be whether a deviation occurred also in the previous year, ie whether or not it appears to be at all systematically related to the brand in question.) Clusters which do occur at times would typically be for sub-groupings of brands by product formulation (e.g. caffeinated or decaffeinated, a spray – versus freeze-dried, etc. – but not, in fact, for instant coffee), by price, by retail availability, or by their stemming from the same manufacturer (e.g. Collins, 1971).

In as far as brand X will behave broadly like the existing brands, once it settles down with a 5% expected penetration, the prediction is that about $1.7 \times 5 = 8\%$ of the buyers of each of the existing brands will also buy X in the year, as is shown on the right of Table 6. Given the ±20% limits of variation already noted in the body of Table 6, the actual duplication figures for brand X might vary between extremes of about 6% to 10% rather than all being exactly 8%. But such a degree of variation seems unlikely to affect any marketing decisions or evaluations.

Table 8 shows the predicted annual duplication of purchase for brand X the other way round – what percentage of brand X's expected customers will also be buying the existing brands. The middle row gives the values directly predicted by the Duplication Law, i.e. 1.7 times each brand's annual penetration. The maximum and minimum values correspond to the ±20% maximum observed scatter in the body of Table 8. They are indications of the extreme limits of either closer or weaker substitutability between X and the other brands.

Table 7 The duplication of purchase law (duplication of purchases is proportional to penetration)

		Maxwell House	Sanka	Tasters Choice	High Point	Folgers	Nescafé	Brim	Maxim
		% Who Also Bought							
12 months									
Average duplication	%	41	35	36	39	31	22	17	12
1.7 x penetration	%	41	36	37	37	31	22	15	10
Penetration	%	24	21	22	22	18	13	9	6

Table 8 Predicted brand duplications for brand X (with likely maxima and minima)

12 months			Maxwell House	Sanka	Tasters Choice	High Point	Folgers	Nescafé	Brim	Maxim
					% Who Will Also Buy					
Buyers of										
	Max	%	49	43	44	44	37	26	18	12
Brand X	Pred	%	41	36	37	37	31	22	15	10
	Min	%	38	29	30	30	25	18	12	8

Broadly the picture is that between 30% and 50% of the buyers of X would also buy any one of the four leading brands, some 30% ±5 would buy P&G's Folger (which since then has become joint market leader in the US market), and some 20% or less would buy any one of the three smallest brands shown. The variations within these limits are again unlikely to influence major marketing conclusions about X's predicted competitiveness.

Discussion

This paper has sought to show how the known patterns of buyer behaviour for established brands can be used to predict the corresponding features of a new brand. This is presented as a practical application of known knowledge. The inputs are more or less standard ways of tabulating consumer panel data. But the patterns and their predictability are seldom brought out clearly, or applied to a specific situation such as the development of a new brand or a line extension.

It is currently fashionable to talk of academic research into marketing as 'knowledge generation' (e.g. AMA Task Force, 1988). Here we are concerned with the *use* of such knowledge. There are of course also many uses other than in NPD as here. They range from using the 80:20 implications of the frequency distribution in Table 4 for setting realistic quotas in sampling heavy and light buyers, to using the repeat-buying norms noted in Section 2 when evaluating consumer promotions (e.g. Ehrenberg *et al.*, 1991).

We now briefly discuss three general points which may need special emphasis, namely: (i) that we are not predicting the new brand's ultimate sales level itself, and why not; (ii) that the predictions are for when the new brand has settled down; and (iii) that the main potential for a new brand should lie in exploiting the patterns in the market rather than the deviations.

(i) Brand-share prediction

The predictions in this paper do not include predictions of the new brand's ultimate market share itself. This is the 64 million dollar question. But such predictions – in as far as they can be successfully made – would depend on the *brand-specific* factors in its marketing mix, not on the general structure of markets which we have built on here.

Rather than predicting sales, the predictions discussed in this paper started with a sales target – say 4,000 tons annually or 12 purchases per 100 households – and fleshed this out in customer terms. Thus in Table 1 we noted that this target could in principle be reached by 1% buying the brand 12 times in the year or by 12% buying just once – anything multiplying up to 12. But looking at the structure of the established market, we then learnt that *it would have to be roughly 5% buying on average about 2.5 times*. This seems to us the answer to a 64 *thousand* dollar question and typifies the level of the contributions discussed in this paper.

Forecasts of sales as such have of course to be made, and as noted in the introduction, there are a variety of proprietary procedures on the market (Bases, Microtest, Assessor, Sensor, etc.). The mechanics are broadly: (a) to expose consumers to the new brand concept and/or its advertising or the product itself; (b) give them an opportunity to purchase a sample of the brand or to express a purchase intention; and (c) express a likelihood to repurchase, or make an actual purchase, after an appropriate number of weeks, and also then assess their attitudes. Previous experience of similar tests is used to a greater or lesser extent to calibrate the results or provide interpretative norms. Two major issues are how many initial 'trialists' will convert into 'adopters' (i.e. repurchase *at all*), and how many initial trialists there will be under real-life launch conditions.

A worry about these procedures is that they generally seem to emphasise forecasts of the ultimate repurchase rate at least as much as forecasts of the ultimate penetration. But the ultimate repurchase rate of a new brand is firmly predictable just from the existing market as we have discussed in this paper (e.g. at about 2.5 purchases per buyer for US instant coffee). It is the new brand's ultimate *penetration* (i.e. how many consumers will buy the new instant coffee about 2.5 times) which remains the big 64 million dollar forecasting question.

More generally, the aim of (correctly) forecasting an ultimate share for a new brand may be misplaced. The practicalities are more ones of 'control theory' (e.g. Kalman, 1985; Holly and Hallett, 1989), i.e. to develop a range of possible scenarios with differing levels of sales, and to establish what can and needs to be done to make *each* of them financially and technically feasible (or not), depending on the way the new brand actually develops.

(ii) The steady state

The predictions about the new brand are for when it has become an established brand. Its 'steady state' performance is of interest because that is what matters to the new brand's ultimate profitability.

The new brand's previous performance, during its launch and any earlier test periods, is of only *diagnostic* interest. But the steady-state predictions are of value also in helping to interpret such early results. When judging a test-market for example, it helps to know that buyers of the new brand are expected to buy it ultimately, when it has settled down, about 2.5 times a year on average, that this is part of an average of about 10 purchases of the *product-category* that they will make, and that a very few of the new brand's buyers will be 100%-loyal to it then.

(iii) Following the patterns

The paper has illustrated the degree of variability in the observed patterns on which the predictions are based. Mostly this variation is fairly small – e.g. the ultimate average purchase frequency of brand X can be expected to lie well between 2 and 3, rather than precisely 2.5. This will not radically affect one's marketing strategy or evaluations.

To expect the new brand's performance to lie outside such limits would therefore require very special assumptions. These should not, we believe, be lightly made. Why should the new brand attract exceptional loyalty (e.g. be bought *six* times by its buyers), if the like of that has *never* been observed before?

A consumer orientation in new brand development means trying to 'read the market' and building on its patterns, rather than trying to 'buck the trend' and hoping that the customers will somehow oblige.

Obeying these regular patterns does not imply uniformity: there are already many different kinds of products and brands on the market, and many different marketing practices, and they are there despite all the lawlike patterns described here. Hence there will still be much room for variety in developing new brands also, even within the context of the regular patterns which we have discussed. The pay-off from knowing these patterns is to avoid setting the wrong consumer targets and to avoid costly mistakes.

Technical appendix: the Dirichlet model

The predictions for the new brand of instant coffee in the main paper have been presented as stemming sometimes from a theoretical model like the Dirichlet and sometimes from the observed patterns of the US instant coffee market itself. The two approaches come to much the same thing, since the theoretical model largely summarizes the empirical patterns. The theoretical model is more convenient and powerful to use, but the empirical patterns give more of a 'feel' of the specific market.

The Dirichlet model is a stochastic formulation of buyer behaviour at the individual consumer level in markets which are: (a) stationary; and (b) unsegmented. These are ones where there is: (a) little, or strictly no, variation over time in the different brands' market-shares, or in any other aggregate measures such as penetrations and average purchase frequencies during the time-periods analysed; and (b) little or no tendency for some particular brand or brands to appeal especially to an identifiable subgroup of consumers. Most fmcg markets behave like this to a first degree of approximation in the medium term (e.g. for a year or two), with any strong segmentation being the exception rather than the rule.

The model produces theoretical predictions for key measures of consumer behaviour as discussed in the main paper, dealing both with each brand on its own and with the competitive interaction between the brands.

To use the model one needs to first estimate its parameters. Here the Dirichlet is very parsimonious. It needs as inputs the size of the total market and of each brand or brand-grouping (i.e. its market share), and the diversity of consumers in their rates of purchase of the product-category (the so-called K parameter), and in their propensity to buy each of the brands (the S parameter).

One way of estimating these two parameters K and S is from the penetrations and average purchases, in some chosen base-period, both of the product-category as a whole (which gives a value of K) and of any one or more brands or brand-groupings (which gives a value of S). The mathematics of the calculations is relatively complex (e.g. Ehrenberg, 1988, Appendix C; Goodhardt *et al.*, 1984), but has been greatly eased by available software (Nelson, 1986; Uncles, 1989; Hewitt, 1990), mostly based on programming in the 1970s by Dr Chris Chatfield. The penetrations and purchase frequencies of the individual brands are used in this process, but are then combined into an overall weighted average estimate of S for the product category. The only *brand-specific* input into the model remains therefore the market-shares, as noted in the body of the paper.

The model derives from five distributional assumptions – two concerning purchase incidence, two brand choice, and one their interrelationship. For purchases of the product class, the assumptions are (i) that the purchase incidence for each individual consumer follows a Poisson distribution with (ii) mean rates which vary across consumers according to a Gamma distribution. For brand choice, the assumptions are that (iii) the number of purchases of each brand that an individual makes in a product-buying sequence follows a multinomial distribution, and (iv) the probabilities of choosing the various brands on a given purchase occasion vary across individuals according to a particular type of multivariate Beta distribution known as the Dirichlet distribution. For the relationship between the product-buying and brand-choice distributions, the model assumes that (v) the probabilities of product purchase and brand choice are distributed independently over the population.

In making such assumptions it is not supposed that individual consumers' purchases are made literally at random, but only that they occur so irregularly, when seen across many consumers, that they appear *as if* random. There are also cogent *a priori* theoretical arguments for the specific assumptions (Goodhardt *et al.*, 1984; Ehrenberg, 1988). For example, in an unsegmented market where brand-choice is independent (other than for the constraint that the probabilities have to add to one), it can be shown theoretically that the distribution of brand choice probabilities in (iv) above *must* be a Dirichlet-type multivariate Beta distribution. Again, the assumption of the lack of segmentation itself is close to what is generally observed in most markets.

The ultimate test of the model is how well it reproduces the various observed measures for the individual brands. The observed patterns have already been illustrated here for US instant coffee for some of the measures, in Tables 3, 4 and 6. Table 9 now gives the corresponding predictions for the average frequencies with which buyers of each brand buy the brand (as shown in Table 2) and the product-category (Table 5). The fit is close.

In particular, we may note how the model reproduces both the small 'double jeopardy' trend in the average frequency with which buyers of each brand buy it (from 3.3 for Maxwell House down to 2.6 for Maxim) and the even smaller 'natural monopoly' trend in their frequency of buying the *product* (from 8.6 up to 9.4) even though these patterns (first discussed by McPhee, 1963) were not specified in the model definitions or in the fitting process. They are *real* theoretical predictions.

As noted in the main text, a crucial issue in predicting the new brand's characteristics from the patterns in the US instant coffee market (or a model which represents them) is that these patterns are not some *ad hoc* and possibly ephemeral manifestation of the US

Table 9   Penetration and frequency of purchase: instant coffee (observed 'O' and theoretical Dirichlet predictions 'T')

USA 12 months	Market-share	% Buying at Least Once		Av. Purchases per Buyer of Brand		of Product	
	%	O	T	O	T	O	T
Any instant	100	67	–	–	–	6.7	–
Maxwell House	19	24	28	3.6	3.3	9.3	8.6
Sanka	16	21	23	3.3	3.0	9.2	8.8
Tasters Choice	14	22	20	2.8	2.9	8.8	8.9
High Point	13	22	20	2.6	2.9	8.5	8.9
Folgers	11	18	17	2.7	2.9	9.4	9.1
Nescafé	8	13	13	2.9	2.8	10.3	9.2
Brim	4	9	7	2.0	2.6	9.4	9.4
Maxim	3	6	6	2.6	2.6	11.2	9.4
Other brands	12	20	21	3.0	3.0	9.3	8.9
Average brand	11	17	17	2.8	2.9	9.5	9.0

instant coffee market but apply much more generally. Hence their apparent applicability not only to instant coffee in our illustrative discussion here but also, more importantly, to other product categories altogether.

Table 10 summarizes the wide range of conditions under which the Dirichlet model is in fact so far known to hold for consumers' purchasing behaviour. There are many regularities in our markets and it is up to us to learn how to apply them to an increasingly wide range of practical marketing problems.

Acknowledgement

I am indebted to MRCA for the use of data on the US instant coffee market. Early versions of this paper have been presented at an ESOMAR Seminar and to numerous marketing companies in the USA and Europe.

References

AMA Task Force (1988) 'Developing, disseminating and utilizing market knowledge', *Journal of Marketing* **52**, 4, 1–51.

Baum, J. and Dennis, K.E.R. (1961) 'The estimation of the expected brand share of a new product'. 7th ESOMAR/WAPOR Conferences, Baden-Baden. Amsterdam: ESOMAR.

Ehrenberg, A.S.C. (1959) 'The pattern of consumer purchases', *Applied Statistics* 8, 26–34.

Ehrenberg, A.S.C. (1972, 1988) *Repeat-buying: Facts, Theory and Applications*, 2nd edition. London: Charles Griffin and Co; New York: Oxford University Press.

Ehrenberg, A.S.C., Goodhardt, G.J. and Barwise, T.P. (1990) 'Double jeopardy revisited', *Journal of Marketing* **54**, 82–91.

Table 10 Conditions under which the Dirichlet model holds

Food and drink
Biscuits, breakfast cereals, butter, canned vegetables, cat and dog foods, cigarettes, coffee, confectionery, convenience foods, cooking fats and oil, flour, food drinks, frozen foods, instant potatoes, jams and jellies, margarine, peanut butter/spreads, processed cheese, refrigerated dough, sausages, soft drinks, soup, take-home beer.

Cleaners and personal care products
Cosmetics, deodorants, detergents, disinfectants, disposable nappies, fabric softeners, feminine protection, hair sprays, household soap, household cleaners, paper tissues, polishes, shampoos, toilet paper, toilet soap, toothpaste, washing-up liquids.

Automotive and health
Aviation fuel, motor cars, motor oil, petrol.
OTC medicines, pharmaceutical prescriptions.

Distribution channels
Chains, individual stores, brands within chains.

Time and place
1950 to 1991.
Britain, continental Europe, USA, Japan.
Demographic subgroups.
Analysis periods from one week to two years.

Measures
Recorded and reported buying.

Exceptions or partial exceptions
Restricted distribution (e.g. private labels).
Some submarkets (e.g. spray deodorants).
Special funding (e.g. luxury cars, bribes).

Ehrenberg, A.S.C., Hammond, K. and Goodhardt, G.S. (1991) 'The after-effects of consumer promotions'. London Business School: CMaC Working Paper.

Fourt, L.A. and Woodlock, J.W. (1960) 'Early prediction of market surveys for new grocery products', *Journal of Marketing* **25**, 31–8.

Goodhardt, G.J., Ehrenberg, A.S.C. and Chatfield, C. (1984) 'The Dirichlet: a comprehensive model of buying behaviour', *Journal of the Royal Statistical Society*, **A 147**, 621–55.

Hewitt, J.I. (1990) *DIRPRED: A Programme for Predicting Buyer Behaviour from the Dirichlet Model (version 2.6)*. Port Sunlight: URL Report.

Holly, S. and Hughes Hallett, A. (1989) *Optimal Control, Expectations and Uncertainty*. Cambridge: Cambridge University Press.

Kalman, R.E. (1985) 'System theory'. Lecture at Kyoto Prize Celebration, 11 November 1985.

Mahajan, V. and Wind, Y. (1986) *Innovation Diffusion Models of New Product Acceptance*. Cambridge, Mass: Ballinger.

McPhee, W.N. (1963) *Formal Theories of Mass Behavior*. New York: Free Press.

Narasimhan, C. and Sen, S.K. (1983) 'New product models for test market data', *Journal of Marketing* **47**, 11–24.

Nelson, J.F. (1986) *GAPM*. Niverville, NY: Recurrent Statistics.

Parfitt, J.H. and Collins, B.J.K. (1968) 'The use of consumer panels for brand-share prediction', *Journal of Marketing Research* **51**, 131–46.

Shocker, A.D. and Hall, W.G. (1988) 'Pretest market models: a critical evaluation', *Journal of Product Innovation Management* **3**, 86–107.

Uncles, M.D. (1989) BUYER. London Business School: CMaC Working Paper.

Uncles, M.D. and Ehrenberg, A.S.C. (1985) Buying patterns in the US coffee market. London Business School: CMaC Working Paper.

Wellan, P.M. and Ehrenberg, A.S.C. (1988). 'A successful new brand: Shield', *Journal of the Market Research Society* **30**, 35–44.

Double jeopardy revisited

Andrew S.C. Ehrenberg
Research Professor of Marketing, South Bank University, Business School, London

Gerald J. Goodhardt
Sir John E. Cohen Professor of Consumer Studies and Deputy Dean, City University Business School

T. Patrick Barwise
Professor of Management and Marketing, London Business School

Summary

In any given time period, a small brand typically has far fewer buyers than a larger brand. In addition, its buyers tend to buy it less often. This pattern is an instance of a widespread phenomenon called 'double jeopardy' (DJ). The authors describe the wide range of empirical evidence for DJ, the theories that account for its occurrence, known exceptions and deviations, and practical implications.

In this article, we review a little-known but widely occurring and theoretically supported regularity in competitive markets, namely that small brands generally attract less 'loyalty' among their buyers than large brands do among theirs. Twenty-five years ago the Columbia University sociologist William McPhee (1963) noted this pattern for competitive items such as different comic strips and radio presenters. In comparison with a popular strip, one that was read by fewer people was usually also liked less by those few who read it. McPhee thought it unfair for less popular items to suffer in *two* such ways. Hence he named the phenomenon 'double jeopardy'. Subsequently, this double jeopardy (DJ) pattern was found to occur much more widely – for example, for branded packaged goods, the less popular a brand, the less loyal its buyers tended to be (Ehrenberg, 1972, 1988; Martin, 1973; Shuchman, 1968). The reverse, a small brand having few but exceptionally loyal buyers, has seldom if ever been reported.

Despite increasing empirical evidence and strong theoretical support for DJ, which we review here, DJ is not widely known among marketing scholars and practitioners, nor has it

From the *Journal of Marketing*, **54** (July 1990), 82–91. This article is part of a program of work that was supported by Procter & Gamble, Colgate Palmolive, General Mills, M&M Mars, and the Ogilvy Center in the US and by 35 leading companies in the UK.

featured in most of the literature. Yet anyone who analyzes or models consumer behavior or market structures should presumably seek to recognize and take account of such a regularity. Marketing managers also should be aware of DJ, at least as background to the strategic and especially the more tactical options for increasing or defending sales. In allocating marketing effort it is worth knowing that it is *normal* for a small brand to attract somewhat less 'loyalty' and yet to survive. We return to these issues in the final discussion.

All the general explanations of double jeopardy are statistical, relating to the size structure of the market. Other things being equal, small brands attract less loyalty just because they are small (i.e. have lower market shares). No other marketing mix or consumer variables need to be invoked to explain DJ. McPhee himself outlined this notion in broad terms and it is also common to the later, more detailed models reviewed here.

What, then, is the role of marketing factors such as product formulation, price, distribution, advertising, promotions and market segmentation? The answer seems to be that these factors give brands their different sales levels, which in turn show up in the DJ pattern, *but rarely cause big additional differences in brand loyalty.* Hence competitive brands tend to differ mainly in how many buyers they have rather than in how loyal those buyers are (e.g. Ehrenberg, 1972, 1988). But in as far as they *do* differ in loyalty, the differences contain a systematic DJ trend.

With real-life data there are also many minor deviations from the DJ trend, as well as very occasional exceptions. They mostly reflect specific marketing or segmentation factors (though they are rarely simple to pin down). In principle such factors could be large or even overshadow the DJ trend. One therefore must check the structure of one's own particular market: the DJ pattern is very general, but markets also have their own characteristics. How much these characteristics lead to deviations from DJ should be tested empirically – once – for each market.

After presenting the empirical evidence for DJ, we examine the theories that account for its occurrence. We then discuss the implications of both DJ and the deviations from it.

The empirical evidence for DJ

Double jeopardy trends have been reported for a variety of loyalty or liking measures when customers choose between items that are similar but differ in their popularity. We here briefly illustrate the evidence covering

- brand choice, store choice, and attitudinal measures for packaged goods,
- program choice, channel choice, and audience appreciation in the media (especially TV), and
- isolated instances of brand buying in durable and industrial goods markets.

DJ effects often are observed but not recognized (e.g. Raj, 1985). Even the 40 or so published articles that *do* refer to DJ usually do so only in a limited context and mostly in passing (e.g. just as a footnote in Ehrenberg, 1972). Hence the need for this review.

The most extensive evidence reported for DJ trends in marketing is for repeat buying. It ranges over 50 different frequently bought product categories from breakfast cereals through gasoline to toilet soap, and in Britain, Continental Europe and Japan as well as in the United States.

Table 1 illustrates DJ for the average purchase frequencies of eight leading US brands of instant coffee. The number of households that bought each brand in a year – the annual penetration – varies by a factor of four from 24% to 6%. In contrast, the number of times on average that each brand's buyers bought it in the year varies much less, but also tends to be somewhat lower for the brands with fewer buyers. This is double jeopardy. The correlation between the two variables is 0.65. (The corresponding correlations for 35 Procter & Gamble product categories based on recent IRI scanner-panel data also average about 0.6; Davis *et al.*, 1990).

Deviations from the DJ trend are typified by the rather low purchase frequency of 2.0 for Brim in Table 1, as we discuss subsequently. The remarkable feature is that the deviations are relatively small given how much the brands differ in their product formulation (e.g. caffeinated or decaffeinated, freeze-dried or spray-dried), as well as in their branding and advertising, pricing, packaging, distribution, ownership, maturity, and so on. The correlations here are as low as 0.6, not because the deviations are large but because the average purchase rates per buyer differ little anyway. As stressed in the introduction, the *dominant* finding with packaged goods is that brands do not differ greatly in loyalty.

Similar DJ effects occur also in the context of *media*. One example is for regular TV series. For a high-rating series, 40% to 50% of persons who watch one episode also watch the next; for a low-rating series, the repeat-viewing rate is only 20% to 30% (e.g. Barwise, 1986; Barwise and Ehrenberg, 1988; Goodhardt, Ehrenberg and Collins, 1975).

Another example occurs for national daily newspapers in Britain, a market with very diverse product formulations that is extremely segmented, as shown by the percentages of white-collar readers in Table 2. Yet a strong DJ trend again shows up: the less popular papers are not only read by far fewer people, but also read less frequently by those who do read them. Double jeopardy, as we see shortly, can be expected theoretically for similar items – for example, *within* a market segment – but here it even occurs across very different segments.

Table 1   Brand penetration and average purchase frequency

Brand*	% Buying in Year	Purchases per Buyer
Maxwell House	24	3.6
Sanka	21	3.3
Tasters Choice	22	2.8
High Point	22	2.6
Folgers	18	2.7
Nescafé	13	2.9
Brim	9	2.0
Maxim	6	2.6
Average	17	2.8

* Instant coffee, MRCA, USA, 1981 in market-share order (Uncles, 1985).

Table 2   Double jeopardy despite strong segmentation

Daily Newspapers, UK, 1983	% of Readers Who Are ABCI*	% of Adults Who Read it in a Week	Daily Issues Read per Weekly Reader
Popular			
The Sun	24	45	3.9
Daily Mirror	25	39	3.6
Daily Star	19	20	3.2
Middle			
Daily Express	50	24	3.2
Daily Mail	56	22	3.3
Quality			
Daily Telegraph	83	15	3.1
The Guardian	79	9	2.3
The Times	85	7	2.0
Financial Times	86	6	1.7

* Broadly, 'in white-collar households' (Ehrenberg and Goodhardt, 1988).

A similar DJ effect occurs for repeat purchasing of *automobile makes* (Colombo and Morrison, 1989, Table 2), and DJ has been reported explicitly in an *industrial* market, as in Table 3 for the number of contracts for aviation fuel held by an oil company's airline customers across different airports. This DJ effect has been replicated for Europe (Uncles and Ehrenberg, 1990).

DJ patterns also arise with *channels of distribution*. They occur, for instance, for the repeat buying of a packaged-goods product at small versus large stores or store groups (e.g. Keng

Table 3   Penetration and average number of airline contracts for aviation fuel

Oil Company*	% Airlines That Are Customers	Contracts per Customer
Shell	69	2.4
BP	55	2.3
Mobil	53	2.3
Esso	42	1.7
Total	26	1.1
Texaco	19	1.1
Average	44	1.8

* Africa, 1972 (Ehrenberg, 1975).

and Ehrenberg, 1984; Uncles and Ehrenberg, 1988; Wrigley and Dunn, 1984). For broad-cast TV channels, smaller channels reach fewer viewers who generally view them less. Two quite major exceptions have been reported, however: some Spanish-language and religious stations in the US attract very heavy viewing from their relatively few viewers (Barwise and Ehrenberg, 1984, 1988).

The preceding examples relate to *repeat-choice* measures of loyalty (e.g. repeat buying or repeat viewing). Double jeopardy also occurs for *brand-switching* aspects of brand loyalty, such as the incidence of 100%-loyal or 'sole' buyers of a brand. As illustrated for instant coffee brands in Table 4, only 11% of the 6% who bought Maxim in the year bought only that brand and no others, fewer than for the larger brands.

Finally, DJ effects arise for various *attitudinal* responses, both for brands and for most TV series (e.g. Barwise and Ehrenberg, 1985, 1987, 1988), but with more deviations and exceptions than for behavioral measures of loyalty. The audience appreciation of a low-rating entertainment program among its few viewers tends to be lower than that of a more popular program among the latter's more numerous viewers. The results are akin to McPhee's (1963) original findings for people's liking of comic strips and radio announcers. An exception is that DJ does not seem to arise for the perhaps more varied 'demanding' types of program (Barwise and Ehrenberg, 1987, 1988; Castleberry and Ehrenberg, 1990; Meneer, 1987).

DJ occurs for free-choice measures of consumers' beliefs about specific brand at-tributes for about half the attributes usually covered, such as 'reasonably priced' and 'tastes nice', as in Table 5. For the other attributes, such as 'fun for children to eat' in Table 5, there are major exceptions to an overt DJ trend, with highly brand-specific factors dominating. DJ also seems less marked with forced-choice questioning (Barnard and Ehrenberg, 1990).

Table 4   Incidence of 100%-loyal buyers in a year

Brand*	% Buying in Year	% of Buyers Who Bought Only That Brand
	Obs.	Obs.
Maxwell House	24	20
Sanka	21	20
Tasters Choice	22	24
High Point	22	18
Folgers	18	13
Nescafé	13	15
Brim	9	17
Maxim	6	11

* Instant coffee, MRCA, USA, 1981 (Uncles, 1985).

Table 5 Beliefs about brand attributes: double jeopardy and exceptions

Brand*	% Buying the Brand Regularly	% of Regular Buyers of Brand Who Say it:	
		'Tastes Nice'	'Is Fun for Children to Eat'
Raisin Bran	32	59	11
Cheerios	31	44	35
Corn Flakes	27	47	7
Sugar Frosted Flakes	18	51	36
All Bran	16	20	4
Honey-Nut Cheerios	16	38	39
Froot Loops	15	27	86
Rice Chex	9	37	14
Crispy Wheats N'Raisins	8	32	12
Coco Puffs	5	21	70
Boo Berry	1	10	83

* Breakfast cereals, USA, 1986 (Castleberry and Ehrenberg, 1990).

Theory: Why does DJ occur?

The occurrence of DJ in so many contexts and for so many aspects of liking and loyalty suggests a common underlying causal factor. The alternative would have to be a variety of many different *ad hoc* explanations. For example, in many markets larger brands have more advertising support and possibly also wider distribution, either of which might lead both to more buyers *and* to greater loyalty. But would both factors generalize to *all* such markets? In any case, they would not explain DJ for different network TV programs, say, or for retail channels, which would therefore need different kinds of theoretical explanation.

In contrast, a single parsimonious set of probabilistic arguments shows that unless specific other factors prevail, *double jeopardy will arise whenever competitive items differ in their popularity* (e.g. in their shares of the market). McPhee's original explanation and all subsequent theories have this in common.

McPhee's 'exposure' explanation

McPhee's (1963) theoretical explanation of DJ arose from his noting an asymmetry in people's familiarity with, or exposure to, items that are similar but differ in popularity. For instance, suppose there are just two restaurants in town, one widely known and the other more obscure. Suppose also that people who know both restaurants regard them as being of equal merit (equal in quality, service, value for money, accessibility, etc.). If people are asked which is their favorite, a DJ effect is bound to occur. The reason is that of the many people who know the popular restaurant, most do not know the more obscure one exists and cannot mention it if asked for their favorite. In contrast, of the few people who know the obscure restaurant, most also know the popular one. Hence they will 'split their vote' – they are equally likely to mention either restaurant as their favorite (or say 'undecided') because we have supposed the two restaurants are of equal merit to those who know both. Of the many people who know the popular restaurant, most therefore will rate it their favorite, whereas of the few who know the obscure one, only about half will say that *it* is their favorite. This is a classic double jeopardy effect.

A similar argument applies behaviorally. Not only will fewer people go to eat at the more obscure restaurant, but (unless they eat out often) they will not go there frequently because about half the time they will go to the widely known one (which they regard as of equal merit). In contrast, most of the many who patronize the widely known one will go there relatively often because they do not even know of the obscure one. For DJ effects to develop, one therefore need assume no differences between the two restaurants other than in their overall exposure and resulting popularity – that is, in how widely they happen to be known and therefore patronized.

The paradox, if there is one, is why two restaurants of equal 'merit' should differ in how well they are known. This phenomenon is common in competitive markets – brands may be very similar yet differ dramatically in market share because of what marketers do (or have done in the past). The marketing challenge for the more obscure restaurant is that to increase its sales (without changing its whole nature, e.g. its quality and/or prices), it must not only make itself better known, but also deserve being as well regarded as is the more popular one ('of equal merit') by its new customers, and continue to be so.

Quantitative models

Stochastic models of buying behavior have been developed that predict the size as well as the presence and direction of DJ trends for competitive brands. We outline three models for DJ in buying behavior, in increasing order of sophistication. Each predicts DJ just from the fact that the brands differ in popularity (i.e. market share), using no information about their product positioning, promotional backup, or other factors.

First we give an oversimplified artificial example to provide intuitive insight. All consumers are assumed to be identical. Each buys the product twice a year and each time chooses one of two brands, A and B, with fixed independent probabilities of 0.7 and 0.3. We need to compare how many customers each brand has in the year, and how often they buy it. (The same mathematics applies if consumers can make three or more purchases, or can choose from three or more brands.)

To work out how many consumers buy brand A at least once in a year, it is easiest to calculate first how many do *not* buy the brand in the year. As a consumer's probability of not buying A on a given purchase occasion is $(1 - 0.7) = 0.3$, it is $0.3^2 = 0.09$ for not buying A on either purchase occasion. The proportion of consumers who buy A at least once is therefore 0.91 (91%). But brand A's per capita sales are 1.4 (i.e. 0.7×2). The average purchase frequency per buyer of A is therefore $1.4/0.91 = 1.54$.

The corresponding calculations for brand B show that its per capita sales of 0.6 must be made up of 51% buying it in the year on average 1.18 times. In summary, we have for the year:

	Purchase Prob.	Per Capita Sales	% Buying at Least Once	Av. Purchases Per Buyer of Brand
Brand A	0.7	1.4	91	1.54
Brand B	0.3	0.6	51	1.18

This is the DJ effect: compared with brand A, the smaller brand B has fewer buyers and they buy the brand less often.

The other two models are much more realistic in that they allow for consumer hetero-geneity. One is usually referred to in the literature as $w(1 - b)$ and the other as the Dirichlet. The $w(1 - b)$ model relates b_x (the proportion of consumers buying brand X at least once in the period analyzed) and w_x (how often on average they buy it then) to the corresponding values b_y and w_y for brand Y. It states that $w_x(1 - b_x) = w_y(1 - b_y) = w_o$, where w_o is a constant (estimated as the average value of $w(1 - b)$ for all the itemized brands). The predicted value of w_x for a given b_x is therefore $w_o/(1 - b_x)$. Hence the smaller b, the smaller w must be, which is double jeopardy.

The model follows by simple algebra from two independence assumptions (Ehrenberg, 1972, 1988, Section 11.5; Ehrenberg and Bound, 1990):

1. Buying of different brands is independent across consumers (e.g. the proportion of households that buy brand X in the analysis period is b_x, irrespective of whether or not they also buy brand Y),
2. Brands do not differ in how often their customers on average buy the total product category (i.e. any brand).

Both assumptions hold approximately in real life. Hence the $w(1 - b)$ model itself should do so also.

The third model, the Dirichlet, is more flexible and also much wider ranging (e.g. Chatfield and Goodhardt, 1975; Ehrenberg, 1988; Ehrenberg and Goodhardt, 1976; Good-hardt, Ehrenberg and Chatfield, 1984, who also give other references). First, it relaxes both assumptions 1 and 2. Second, it predicts not only b and w for each brand (with a DJ trend), but also many other aggregate features of buyer behavior such as the incidence of 100%-loyal buyers as shown in Table 4 (again with a DJ trend).

As the model reflects, when a purchase is made and which brand is then chosen generally appear very irregular and can be thought of as occurring 'as if at random' with specified probabilities, even though individual consumers have their varying and probably deterministic reasons for doing what they do. The technicalities are that the Dirichlet model uses four probability distributions to specify the ways individual consumers buy. Two are for *how often* they buy, each consumer buying the product category according to a Poisson distribution, with the long-run average buying rates of different consumers following a Gamma distribu-tion. The third and fourth distributions are of *brand choice*, each consumer buying the different brands according to a multinomial distribution, with the distribution of such probabilities across consumers following a particular 'Dirichlet' type of multivariate beta distribution. The model is for a market that is (a) stationary, with no trends from period to period, and (b) unsegmented, the various distributions being mutually independent. The choice of these distributions is supported both empirically and by statistical theory – for example, given an unsegmented market, the mixing distribution for the brand-choice probabilities *must* be of the 'Dirichlet' type of beta distribution (Mosimann, 1962, 1984). Any segmentation or non-stationarity will show up as deviations from the model's predictions.

The Dirichlet model has only three parameters relating to the product category. One reflects the size of the market. The other two reflect how diverse consumers are in (a) how often they buy, and (b) their choice of brands (i.e. the overall degree of brand switching in the product category). The three parameters can be estimated from the penetration and average purchase frequency of the product category and of each or any of the itemized brands in a chosen base period. This procedure requires heavy arithmetic – there are no closed algebraic formulas – but is much helped by available software (e.g. Nelson, 1986; Uncles, 1989).

The central aspect of the Dirichlet model is that once its three product-category parameters have been estimated, the only brand-specific input required is the individual brands' market shares. The middle part of Table 6 illustrates how the w(1 – b) and Dirichlet models predict the DJ effect for the average frequency of buying each brand in terms of both direction and size, and how the Dirichlet also predicts the DJ effect for the incidence of sole buyers. The correlations with the observed values are about 0.7 or 0.8.

The wider context of DJ

In practice, most buyers of a brand buy some of the competitive brands also and they do so rather often in any period long enough to include several purchases of the product category. For example, buyers of a brand buy instant coffee as a whole (i.e. *any* brand) on average about 9 times in the year, which is more than three times as often as their average of 2.8 purchases of the brand itself. This pattern is both as observed and as predicted by the Dirichlet, as shown in the right columns of Table 6.

It follows that the DJ effect is not due to the buyers of a small brand being light users of the product category as a whole. Instead, buyers of a small brand like Maxim could in principle buy it much more without having to drink more coffee. They simply could buy Maxim more and other brands less and thus counter the DJ trends in Table 6 – but that does not occur. Consumers mostly choose more than one brand in the course of a year. That is, they habitually tend to opt for some variety in their brand choice, even under strictly stationary conditions when there are no special promotions (etc.). The observed data bear out the theory's prediction that they will mostly buy each brand relative infrequently. That is the context in which the double jeopardy trend for smaller brands occurs.

DJ in attitudes and behavior

McPhee's initial explanation of double jeopardy for people's attitudinal responses, as noted before, was in terms of their lower exposure to or familiarity with the less popular items. Links with the preceding *behavioral* DJ patterns also have been developed (e.g. Barwise and Ehrenberg, 1985, 1987, 1988).

Table 6 Observed and predicted rates of buying the brand and the product, and 100%-loyal buyers (rates of buying per buyer of each brand)

Brand*	Observed Share (%)	Observed % Buying	Average Frequency of Buying the Brand			% Buyers Who Are 100% Loyal to the Brand		Average Frequency of Buying the Product	
			Observed	$\dfrac{w_o}{(1-b)}$	Dirichlet	Observed	Dirichlet	Observed	Dirichlet
Maxwell House	19	24	3.6	3.1	3.2	20	18	9.5	9.2
Sanka	15	21	3.3	2.9	3.0	20	17	9.2	9.4
Tasters Choice	14	22	2.8	3.0	2.9	24	16	8.8	9.5
High Point	13	22	2.6	3.0	2.9	18	16	8.5	9.5
Folgers	11	18	2.7	2.8	2.9	13	15	9.4	9.7
Nescafé	8	13	2.9	2.7	2.8	15	14	10.5	9.8
Brim	4	9	2.0	2.5	2.6	17	13	9.4	10.1
Maxim	3	6	2.6	2.5	2.6	11	13	11.2	10.1
Average	11	17	2.8	2.8	2.9	17	15	9.6	9.7

* Instant coffee, MRCA, USA, 1981 (Uncles, 1985).

Thus, in comparison with large brands, low-market-share brands are bought less frequently by their few buyers – the purely behavioral DJ effect. Also, however, infrequent buyers of a brand have been widely found to say they like the brand less than do its more frequent buyers (e.g. they are less likely to give a positive attitudinal or belief response). Because a small brand has a higher proportion of infrequent buyers, it receives less positive average attitudinal responses from its customers than a more popular brand receives from *its* customers. This is the *attitudinal* DJ effect. The same explanatory mechanism applies also to the liking and viewing of regular TV series.

Implications

We have noted the wide occurrence of double jeopardy patterns and that there are parsimonious theories accounting for their presence, direction, and in many cases also their *size*. All these explanations are statistical manifestations of the relative popularity or market shares of the competitive items. There is no need to invoke other marketing factors for explanation (product formulation, advertising, price, etc.). These factors generally would have to act in *ad hoc* ways (e.g. to account for DJ for very different kinds of product categories, and also for store choice, for TV channels and programs, and so on, and not only behaviorally but also for attitudinal responses). These marketing factors do, however, account for the different items' differing popularity, and also may lead to *deviations* from the regular pattern. We now briefly discuss some implications.

Above all, knowing about double jeopardy should simply make practitioners look at their markets differently. They will be more likely to notice any DJ patterns in their own markets. They also will know that these patterns are normal. In particular, they will know that if a brand has a lower repeat-buying level than others, they need not immediately rush into remedial action. Instead, they first can assess whether the low repeat rate is perhaps just normal for a brand of that size.

Market analysts eventually will stop being surprised to find DJ in their data. There will probably also increasingly be counter-examples. We would expect some major exceptions when the competitive items are not similar (perhaps Cadillacs vs. Toyotas – Colombo and Morrison, 1989, p. 89). Theoretically, double jeopardy need not show through in the presence of very marked product differentiation, though in practice it often does.

Theorists of consumer behavior (e.g. Cooper and Nakanishi, 1988) must acknowledge, or at least allow implicitly, that buyers of smaller brands tend to be less loyal. Unless contrary assumptions are imposed deliberately (e.g. in terms of product differentiation or 'added values' for a brand), any theory that involves consumers, such as how pricing or advertising might work, must at least be consistent with the occurrence of DJ effects.

We now consider more specific implications of DJ in the contexts of share-building strategies, new brand introductions, niche brands, and cashing in on deviations.

Share-building

DJ has implications for the way the sales of an established brand can be increased. Common marketing thinking here has been to formalize two extreme options (e.g. Raj, 1985; Wind and Mahajan, 1981):

- *The penetration option:* increasing the number of buyers of the brand, but not how often they buy it.
- *The loyalty option:* increasing how often the brand's present buyers buy it, but not how many of them there are.

Suppose a brand is bought by 10% of the population in a year on average three times and that the aim is to double the brand's sales. The penetration option would be to get twice as many consumers, that is, 20% still buying it three times on average. The loyalty option would be to get the present customers to buy the brand twice as often, that is, 10% buying it on average six times. Innumerable intermediate options also exist in principle to get new buyers *and* more purchases per buyer in some proportion (a popular choice in many marketing plans). None of these options look implausible *a priori*. However, in practice, the DJ pattern implies that, within the limits of approximation that we have illustrated, there is only one single option.

The feasible option is for the penetration of the brand to almost double to about 18%, combined with a slight increase in the average purchase frequency, say to about 3.3 times a year. This outcome would be close to the penetration option. There can be deviations from these targets but, as illustrated in the tables, they would generally be small. To be radically different would mean being almost unique in 'bucking the trend'. This may seem to be just what the enterprising marketing manager should do – but not out of ignorance, especially not when the normal market structure is empirically and theoretically as broadly established as double jeopardy. Anything like the loyalty option would be going right against the grain and correspondingly painful, or risky at best.

We know of no reports of large increases in the average purchase frequency of a brand. In contrast, when Colgate Palmolive's dishwashing liquid doubled its sales in Germany over a period of five years fairly recently, it achieved this gain by a large increase in the average number of purchases per buyer (w), in line with the DJ pattern discussed here (Drehmann, 1987).

The evidence is that in a dynamic situation, when the sales of a brand change, DJ applies both before the change and afterward (i.e. when sales have settled down again). However, little, if anything, is known about the intervening process – for example, to what extent present buyers change their buying patterns and whether some extra buyers come in or drop out, and if so whether they are light or heavy buyers, or both.

More generally, it is instructive to envisage a simple speculative scenario of how sales might increase. Suppose that because of some sales-enhancing advertising, this year's sales have gone up ('Glory be!'). This increase could have resulted from everyone's propensity to buy the brand going up by the same proportion. In a given period such as a year, more people would then buy the brand, and on average would buy it somewhat more often, with the brand 'riding up the DJ curve'.

To illustrate numerically, we can go back to the first oversimplified stochastic model in the last section. Brand B had a 0.3 probability of being bought by each consumer, all of whom made two purchases of the product category in the year. Annual per capita sales of brand B were 0.6 (i.e. 0.3 × 2), made up of 51% buying it on average 1.18 times. Suppose advertising for brand B has now increased everyone's probability of buying B to 0.4, giving it annual per capita sales of 0.8 (= 0.4 × 2). By the same kind of arithmetic as before, we can calculate that these higher sales are due to 64% of consumers now buying B an average of 1.25 times each. Sales of B have increased with more buyers buying more often. Similarly, brand A's probability of being bought must drop from 0.7 to 0.6 because of the failure to defend against B's advertising push: A is now bought by 84% of consumers 1.43 times each. Sales of A have decreased, with fewer buyers buying less often.

	Purchase Prob.	Per Capita Sales	% Buying at Least Once	Av. Purchases Per Buyer of Brand
Before B's Advertising				
Brand A	0.7	1.4	91	1.54
Brand B	0.3	0.6	51	1.18
After B's Advertising				
Brand A	0.6	1.2	84	1.43
Brand B	0.4	0.8	64	1.25

This hypothetical example shows how sales can vary despite the double jeopardy constraint and how the DJ pattern can persist despite the sales changes.

Sometimes marketers try to increase people's frequency of buying their brand by finding and promoting new uses for it (examples are Arm & Hammer baking soda for deodorizing refrigerators, Johnson's baby oil and talc for adults, Schweppes Tonic Water as a straight soft drink, or Vaseline Petroleum Jelly for varied new uses). Such attempts at extended usage are not always successful. But when they do succeed, the new use is likely to carry over to competitive brands. The result is higher purchase frequencies across the board and a reestablished DJ effect. In the same way, seasonal variations in product usage (e.g. Wellan and Ehrenberg, 1990) or differences in consumption levels between large and small households tend to apply across a parent category as a whole without disturbing any DJ patterns.

New brand targets

Double jeopardy also provides some background information for planning new brands (Ehrenberg, 1971, 1990; Wellan and Ehrenberg, 1988). The DJ pattern helps in predicting the repeat-buying target of a new brand once its sales have stabilized.

Table 1, for instance, implies that a new brand of instant coffee, once it is established, will be bought at an average rate of about three times a year by its buyers, however many buyers it may obtain. More precisely – because of DJ – the target would be slightly less than three times if the brand is expected to be a small one. A very different average purchase frequency, such as say six purchases a year, would mean that the new brand has been successfully positioned very differently indeed from all other brands in the market. Few marketing plans attempt as much for their new brands. Even fewer are successful in achieving such a result, let alone in sustaining it.

Niche brands

Some niche brands are thought of as being bought relatively often by relatively few people. This notion raises issues of the definition of market segments. However, within any market that actually includes some non-niche brands, a very heavily bought small brand would be a departure from DJ. Such a situation is possible if the brand's exceptional 'niche' properties specifically or even uniquely fit its particular users or usages. Because the general double jeopardy trend would be in the opposite direction, such cases ought to stand out very clearly as significant exceptions. Other than for the Spanish-language and religious TV channels noted before, no very dramatic evidence has been documented (see Kahn, Kalwani and Morrison, 1988 for some nondramatic empirical analyses).

Counter-examples of niche brands strikingly bucking the trend would be welcome. Current evidence suggests that in practice most niche brands are perhaps just brands with small shares of the market – brands that appeal especially to a small group of consumers or for certain special usage occasions, but are *not* bought exceptionally often by their buyers. This issue could be an area for further research.

Deviations from DJ

Knowing that DJ patterns tend to exist helps in recognizing not only any major exceptions, but also smaller though still sizable deviations. The low purchase frequency of 2.0 for Brim instant coffee in Table 1 (vs. a theoretical 2.6 in Table 6) is an example. Rather than jumping immediately to some brand-specific rationalization (e.g. 'Brim is rather strong; therefore people must be using less'), one first should establish whether the low value of 2.0 occurs consistently for the brand. Table 1 is from MRCA diary-panel data in 1981, and a low purchase frequency for Brim also occurred for IRI scanner-panel data in the same year – but it did *not* recur later (Davis *et al.*, 1990). The low 2.0 therefore may not have been a general characteristic of Brim as such, but a temporary deviation due perhaps to an out-of-stock position in 1981 or to exceptionally heavy sales promotions having attracted incremental light, once-only buyers that year. Typically, much work is usually needed just to diagnose and properly interpret a deviation, quite apart from then establishing how to cash in on it profitably.

An isolated deviation has been found for the sixth largest heart drug in Britain in 1987. This was prescribed on average 10 times that year by those doctors who prescribed it at all, rather than the expected 5 times. This level is quite a market deviation from the general DJ pattern for medical prescriptions (Stern, 1990).

The manufacturer was promoting the drug by supplying a free personal computer to doctors who prescribed it frequently enough (at no financial cost to themselves). The brand was therefore no longer altogether 'similar' to its competitors, in what seemed perhaps a rather tangible way (a free PC). The size of the effect was none the less not dominant (i.e. 10 prescriptions vs. 5 expected), because the prescribing doctors still prescribed *other* drugs for hypertension (the drug's diagnosis category) on average about 50 times in the year. This is in line with the total level of prescriptions for hypertension drugs generally and with the predictable pattern of category usage that is illustrated in Table 6. It seems that the doctors were being influenced only when there was an uncertain choice between the drug and fairly close substitutes or even look-alikes.

One case of deviations that appear systematic has been reported recently, for private label brands in the UK. These brands obtain a somewhat higher average purchase frequency (about 20% or more) than their market shares or penetrations would warrant, in comparison with the w(1 − b) or Dirichlet models (Ellis, 1989). The explanation is not that repeat-buying loyalty for private labels is higher than normal, but that consumers' access to any particular supermarket chain's private label is necessarily restricted. In other words, it seems that the penetration b for private labels in the w(1 − b) model is low rather than that the repeat-buying measure w is high; within their own stores, private label brands tend to have very high market shares.

An occasional deviation seems to occur also for major market leaders. In our consulting experience, some leaders have a somewhat higher than expected level of repeat buying (i.e. they behave like an even bigger brand than they already are), but this deviation does not occur universally.

Summary conclusions

Overall, the message is that frequent-purchase markets almost invariably show a regular or 'lawlike' double jeopardy pattern whereby smaller brands tend to attract somewhat less loyalty, with deviations that are mostly relatively small and so far little understood. Not many such empirically and theoretically based generalizations can be made in marketing (Anderson, 1983; Jacoby, 1978; Leone and Schultz, 1980), though DJ is not the only one even in just the narrow area of buyer behavior (e.g. Ehrenberg, 1990; Keng, Ehrenberg and Barnard, 1990). Both marketing practitioners and scholars of consumer behavior should recognize that their markets contain such a predictable pattern, and why it occurs.

Managers should capitalize on the DJ pattern, mainly in tactical planning and evaluation but also in longer-term considerations of brand equity (e.g. Barwise et al., 1989; Leuthesser, 1988). Trying to buck the DJ trend might look suspiciously like trying to make aeroplanes fly by waiting for breakdowns in the law of gravity. Indeed, people have successfully built very varied aircraft, from gliders to rockets, all using the laws of aerodynamics to cope with the lawlike relationships rather than against it. Marketing history similarly shows that even within the constraint of a regularity such as double jeopardy, marketers can develop highly varied brands and adopt dynamic marketing policies, and can do so successfully.

References

Anderson, Paul F. (1983), 'Marketing, scientific progress, and scientific method', *Journal of Marketing,* **47** (Fall), 18–31.

Barnard, Neil R. and Andrew S.C. Ehrenberg (1990), Robust measures of consumer brand beliefs', *Journal of Marketing Research*, **27** (November), 477–84.

Barwise, T.P. (1986), 'Repeat-viewing of prime-time US programs', *Journal of Advertising Research,* **28** (August–September), 9–14.

Barwise, T.P. and A.S.C. Ehrenberg (1984), 'The reach of TV channels', *International Journal of Research in Marketing,* **1**(1), 37–49.

Barwise, T.P. and A.S.C. Ehrenberg (1985), 'Consumer beliefs and brand usage', *Journal of the Market Research Society,* **27**, 81–93.

Barwise, T.P. and A.S.C. Ehrenberg (1987), 'The liking and viewing of regular TV programs', *Journal of Consumer Research*, **14** (June), 63–70.

Barwise, T.P. and A.S.C. Ehrenberg (1988), *Television and Its Audience*. Newbury Park, CA, and London: Sage Publications, Inc.

Barwise, T.P., C.J. Higson, J.A. Likierman, and P.R. Marsh (1989), *Accounting for Brands*. London: Institute of Chartered Accountants.

Castleberry, S.R. and A.S.C. Ehrenberg (1990), 'Brand usage: A factor in consumer beliefs', *Marketing Research*.

Chatfield, Christopher and Gerald Goodhardt (1975), 'Results concerning brand choice', *Journal of Marketing Research*, **12** (February), 110–13.

Colombo, R.A. and D.E. Morrison (1989), 'A brand switching model with implications for marketing strategies', *Marketing Science*, **8**, 89–106.

Cooper, L.G. and M. Nakanishi (1988), *Market-Share Analysis*. Boston: Kluwer.

Davis, R.E., A.S.C. Ehrenberg, K. Hammond and M.D. Uncles (1990), 'The Dirichlet for 35 product-categories'. London Business School: CMaC Working Paper.

Drehmann, M. (1987), personal communication.

Ehrenberg, A.S.C. (1971), 'Predicting the performance of new brands', *Journal of Advertising Research*, **11** (6), 3–10.

Ehrenberg, A.S.C. (1972, 1988), *Repeat-Buying: Theory and Applications*, 2nd edn. London: Charles Griffin; New York: Oxford University Press.

Ehrenberg, A.S.C. (1975), 'The structure of an industrial market: Aviation fuel contracts', *Industrial Marketing Management*, **4**(5), 273–85.

Ehrenberg, A.S.C. (1990), 'New brands and the existing market'. London Business School: CMaC Working Paper.

Ehrenberg, A.S.C. and J.A. Bound (1990), 'Prediction and predictability: A case discussion'. London Business School: CMaC Working Paper.

Ehrenberg, A.S.C. and G.J. Goodhardt (1976), *Decision Models and Descriptive Models in Marketing*. Cambridge, MA: Marketing Science Institute.

Ehrenberg, A.S.C. and G.J. Goodhardt (1988), 'The double jeopardy effect for UK daily papers'. London Business School: CMaC Working Paper.

Ellis, K. (1989), 'Private label buying behaviour', PhD thesis, London University.

Goodhardt, G.J., A.S.C. Ehrenberg and C. Chatfield (1984), 'The Dirichlet: A comprehensive model of buying behaviour', *Journal of the Royal Statistical Society*, A **147**, 621–55.

Goodhardt, G.J., A.S.C. Ehrenberg and M.A. Collins (1975), *The Television Audience: Patterns of Viewing*. Aldershot, UK: Gower (updated edition 1987).

Jacoby, Jacob (1978), 'Consumer research: State of the art review', *Journal of Marketing*, **42** (April), 87–96.

Kahn, Barbara E., Manohar U. Kalwani, and Donald G. Morrison (1988), 'Niching versus change-of-pace brands', *Journal of Marketing Research*, **25** (November), 384–90.

Keng, Kau Ah and A.S.C. Ehrenberg (1984), 'Patterns of store-choice', *Journal of Marketing Research*, **21** (November), 399–408.

Keng, Kau Ah, A.S.C. Ehrenberg and N.R. Barnard (1990), 'Competitive brand-choice: Japan and the West'. London Business School: CMaC Working Paper.

Leone, Robert P. and Randall L. Schultz (1980), 'A study of marketing generalizations', *Journal of Marketing*, **44** (Winter), 10–18.

Leuthesser, L., ed. (1988), *Defining, Measuring, and Managing Brand Equity*. Cambridge, MA: Marketing Science Institute.

Martin, G.R. (1973), 'The theory of double jeopardy', *Journal of the Academy of Marketing Science*, **1** (Fall), 148–55.

McPhee, W.N. (1963), *Formal Theories of Mass Behavior*. New York: Free Press.

Meneer, P. (1987), 'Audience appreciation – A different story from audience numbers', *Journal of the Market Research Society*, **29**, 241–54.

Mosimann, J.E. (1962), 'On the compound multinomial distribution, the multivariate B-distribution, and correlations among proportions', *Biometrika*, **44**, 65–82.

Mosimann, J.E. (1984), 'Size and shape analysis', in *Encyclopedia of the Statistical Sciences*, S. Kotz and N.L. Johnson, eds. New York: John Wiley.

Nelson, J.F. (1986), *GAPM*. Niverville, NY: Recurrent Statistics.

Raj, S.P. (1985), 'Striking a balance between brand popularity and brand loyalty', *Journal of Marketing*, **49** (Winter), 53–9.

Shuchman, A. (1968), 'Are there laws of consumer behavior?', *Journal of Advertising Research*, **8**(3), 19–28.

Stern, P. (1990), personal communication.

Uncles, M.D. (1985), 'Buying patterns in the US coffee market'. London Business School: CMaC Working Paper.

Uncles, M.D. (1989), 'BUYER: Software for the Dirichlet'. London Business School: CMaC Report.

Uncles, M.D. and A.S.C. Ehrenberg (1988), 'Patterns of store-choice: New evidence from the USA', in *Store Choice, Store Location, and Market Analysis*, N.R. Wrigley, ed. London: Routledge & Kegan Paul.

Uncles, M.D. and A.S.C. Ehrenberg (1990), 'Aviation fuel contracts in Europe', *International Journal of Research in Marketing*.

Wellan, D. and A.S.C. Ehrenberg (1988), 'A successful new brand: Shield', *Journal of the Market Research Society*, **30**, 35–44.

Wellan, D. and A.S.C. Ehrenberg (1990), 'Seasonal segmentation', *Marketing Research*.

Wind, Yoram and Vijay Mahajan (1981), 'Market-share: Concepts, findings and directions for future research', in *Review of Marketing 1981*, Ben Enis and K.J. Roering, eds. Chicago: American Marketing Association.

Wrigley, N.R. and R. Dunn (1984), 'Stochastic panel-data models of urban shopping behaviour', *Environment and Planning A*, **16**, 629–50, 759–78.

The behavioral perspective model of purchase and consumption: From consumer theory to marketing practice

●●●

Gordon R. Foxall
Distinguished Research Professor in Consumer Psychology, Cardiff Business School

Summary

The Behavioral Perspective Model of purchase and consumption (BPM) portrays the rate at which consumer behaviors take place as a function of the relative openness of the setting in which they occur and the informational and hedonic reinforcement available in or promised by the setting. Each of eight combinations of contingencies based on these explanatory variables is uniquely related to a specific mode of observed consumer behavior. By providing an environmental perspective on consumer behavior, the model makes a critical contribution to the development of contemporary consumer research that frequently decontextualizes its subject matter. It also presents an innovative conceptualization of the nature of marketing strategies.

Introduction

No scientific paradigm, taken alone, can provide a comprehensive explanation of so complex a field as consumer behavior. Each perspective presents insights not made available by the others. While recognizing the merits of the prevailing paradigm, still overwhelmingly cognitive, consumer research can benefit from an accurate appreciation of the ontological and methodological concerns of its alternatives.

The Behavioral Perspective Model of purchase and consumption (BPM) derives from a research program that has sought to fix the scope and limits of the contribution of behavior analysis (Skinner, 1953) to consumer research. Assuming that 'the variables of which human behavior is a function lie in the environment' (Skinner, 1977, p. 1), behavior analysis explains the rate at which responses recur by reference to the consequences they have produced in the past. A comprehensive account will eventually incorporate both cognitive and behavioral sources of explanation but, as a prelude to such synthesis, the BPM explores the implications of a radical environmental perspective on choice (Foxall, 1990). This

---

From the *Journal of the Academy of Marketing Science*, **20**(2), 1992, 189–98.

article describes and evaluates the model in the context of micro-positive marketing in profit and not-for-profit sectors (Hunt, 1976).

The BPM contributes to marketing science in two ways. First, it provides a means of conceptualizing situational influences on consumer behavior. Cognitive decision models assume purchasing to be the outcome of goal-directed information processing: the consumer sets objectives, plans their achievement, and intentionally deploys resources to secure desired benefits. None of these models omits external influences on consumer choice, but none stresses them either. In the process, such models tend to decontextualize consumer behavior. In spite of recent interest in the effects of situational variables on consumer choice (reviewed by Troye, 1985), no general conceptual framework has yet emerged. The theoretical contribution of the BPM comprises such a framework.

Second, the BPM suggests a new understanding of marketing strategy. Some consumer researchers have described systems that explain behavior by reference to external stimuli rather than internal states and processes (Berry and Kunkel, 1970; Nord and Peter, 1980; Rothschild and Gaidis, 1981; Foxall, 1986, 1987), thereby opening up the possibility of a balanced perspective. But no model of purchase and consumption has emerged that is both based on empirical principles of human behavior and relevant to marketing management. The applied contribution of the BPM is its elucidation of market behavior.

The behavior analytic approach to consumer choice is first discussed generally, and the derivation of the BPM, based on a critique of modern behavior analysis, is then described. The latter part of the paper pursues the applied goal of the BPM: to understand how marketing strategies increase approach and, where ethically acceptable, reduce escape and avoidance.

Consumer choice in behavioral perspective

Approach and avoidance

Purchasing is approach behavior with both reinforcing and punishing consequences, outcomes likely to increase the probability of its being repeated and others that have an inhibiting effect. Buying a well-known brand is reinforced by acquiring the attributes of the product class and the resulting consumption possibilities. It is simultaneously punished by the surrender of money, depriving the buyer of opportunities to acquire other reinforcers, possibly inviting censure or generating dissonance. The sequence comprises the following behavioral contingencies:

$$S^D \text{———} R \text{———} \begin{cases} S^R \\ S^A \end{cases}$$

where S^D is a discriminative stimulus, an element of the setting in the presence of which the individual emits response R, the consequences of which are a reinforcing stimulus S^R and an aversive or punishing stimulus S^A. The same S^R and S^A are involved in the control of the corresponding escape behavior, non-purchase (which may result in short- or long-term saving and/or the purchase of an alternative brand or product). The contingencies controlling such escape are:

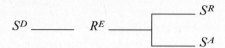

where R^E is the escape behavior, S^R the avoidance of/escape from the aversive consequences of purchasing the target brand, and S^A the loss of reinforcers contingent on purchasing.

The probability of each of these alternative responses – the approach represented by purchase, and the escape/avoidance represented by non-purchase – is a function of the consumer's history of reinforcement. The strength of approach depends on reinforcer effectiveness, the reinforcement schedule in operation, and the quantity and quality of available reinforcers. That of escape is a function of the amount of money purchasing would require the consumer to surrender, his/her access to alternative reinforcers, and the loss of the exchange value represented by money. The probability of purchasing a specific brand can be depicted as the equilibrium point at the interaction of two functions representing the strengths of approach and escape behaviors (Alhadeff, 1982).

An interpretive account

In the context of animal experiments, the basic elements of the 'three-term contingency' – the paradigm's fundamental explanatory mode (Skinner, 1953, p. 110) consisting of antecedent stimulus, behavior and consequences – can be readily identified and the effects of their interrelationships, prescribed by the reinforcement schedule imposed, can be objectively observed. But within the complex situations in which much human social behavior takes place, it is often impossible to isolate the elements and their linkages so unambiguously. However, areas of human behavior that lie beyond the rigorous analysis made possible in laboratory experimentation are open to an interpretation founded on the extension of scientific laws derived from the analysis of the simpler behavior (Skinner, 1969, p. 100). The result is a 'plausible account' of complex actions that is essentially 'an interpretation, not an explanation . . . merely useful, neither true or false' (Skinner, 1988, p. 364).

Such an interpretation must nevertheless take account of the most recent improvements in understanding human economic behavior in relation to the environment in which it occurs. The BPM therefore recognizes two broad deviations from orthodox behavior theory in positing as its independent variables (1) a continuum of relatively open/relatively closed behavior settings and (2) the bifurcation of reinforcement into hedonic and instrumental consequences of behavior. The following account discusses the nature of these variables after briefly describing the model's dependent variable.

Derivation of the behavioral perspective model

Dependent variable: rate of consumer response

A response is behavior that can be related to the environmental contingencies that control its rate of occurrence. The BPM account of purchase and consumption conceptualizes behavior at a more molar level than that of the individual response by considering the whole sequence of pre-purchase, purchase and post-purchase activity as a single unit and by noting the generalization of purchase responses from one retail setting to another or the extension of purchasing in one setting from one to many items. A model of consumer behavior based on operant principles must be able to relate the strengthening or elimination of responses consistently to the environmental consequences that reinforce or punish them. In the case of human behavior in the relatively unrestrained environments characteristic of economic purchase and consumption, the schedules of reinforcement can be no more than inferred from the behavior and its consequences. It is a test of the validity of the model that this process of interpretation can be carried out systematically and consistently with the predictions of a behavioral analysis.

Independent variable: the behavior setting

Relatively closed settings are those in which the contingencies that shape and maintain consumer behavior can be closely and unambiguously specified and controlled by marketers or researchers. The closure of purchase or consumption settings increases as the number of available reinforcers declines and as the control of marketers over deprivation and reinforcement expands (e.g. obtaining the services provided by a postal system that is a public monopoly takes place in such a setting). Relatively open settings are, by contrast, those from which such control is (largely) absent or where the contingencies that control behavior cannot be unambiguously specified by the researcher. In a supermarket, for instance, although some sources of environmental control (such as the physical deployment of point-of-sale advertising and the prominent placing of leading brands at eye level) are in evidence, it may be impossible to specify completely and with finality why a consumer chose a given brand by reference to behavioral criteria alone. It is possible, however, to provide an interpretation of the behavior in these terms, as cognitive psychology would provide another based on the analogy of computer-based information processing.

In sum, the distinction between closed and open behavior settings is based – as far as experimental analysis is concerned – on the relative ease with which behavior can be brought under contingency control and – in the case of an interpretive analysis – on the extent to which the rate of response can be accurately and objectively attributed to environmental influences. Hence in the interpretive account of consumer behavior provided by the BPM, the criteria for the positioning of a given behavior setting on the open–closed continuum are (1) availability of and access to reinforcement, which encompasses three considerations: (i) the number of reinforcers available, (ii) the number of means of obtaining the reinforcers, and (iii) the necessity of performing specific tasks on which the reinforcers are contingent; and (2) the external control of the consumer situation, which rests on three more considerations: (i) whether the marketer or other provider of the product/service controls access to the reinforcers, (ii) whether the contingencies are imposed by agents not themselves subject to them, and (iii) whether there are readily accessible alternatives to being in the situation (Schwartz and Lacey, 1982).

Independent variable: hedonic and informational reinforcement

The reinforcement of human operant behavior plays a broader role than is the case for animals. Reinforcers for human behavior may act informationally as well as hedonically to strengthen behavior. Hedonic reinforcement refers to the strengthening of purchase and consumption behaviors through the generation of fantasies, feelings, fun, amusement, arousal, sensory stimulation and enjoyment (Holbrook and Hirschman, 1982). Hedonic reinforcers are consequences of behavior that are internal to the individual, feelings of pleasure and satisfaction, positive affect and other internal states that are produced by and reward overt actions. They correspond to the affective phenomenology ascribed by some authors to the playful aspects of consumption and may be related to intrinsic motivation (Holbrook, Chestnut, Oliva and Greenleaf, 1984).

However, human operant experiments indicate that the reinforcers employed may be informational rather than hedonic; they signal to subjects the accuracy of their performance or that it has been otherwise satisfactory (Wearden, 1988). It is improbable that the points earned by these subjects and the negligible sums of money for which they are typically exchanged act as reinforcers in the way that food pellets strengthen animal behavior. Such rewards possess little if any intrinsic capacity to reinforce affluent, well-fed humans. Moreover, the operant performance of adult human subjects is disorderly and variable in the absence of performance-related information. Once adequate information (scores or graphs showing relative achievement) is made available, performances become orderly and behavioral change is sensitive to the schedule in operation and more rapid (Wearden, 1988). The points or money are not in themselves a motivating factor and a different kind of reinforcement is apparently operating in these circumstances.

The resulting concept, informational reinforcement, does not refer to the provision of information *per se*: it is specific informational feedback on the individual's performance or achievement that has implications for the rate at which performance continues. The essence of informational reinforcement is that it helps consumers solve problems posed by the web of contingencies to which their learning histories have brought them. It does so by providing precise feedback on the correctness and appropriateness of their performances as consumers, not only in terms of immediate economic rationality, but, more particularly, the wider socio-economic ramifications such as status, prestige and social acceptance. Informational reinforcement is the product of external consequences of behavior, often publicly available and of social significance. It is closely related to the process in which consumers' behavior is governed by rules which they or others have extracted from the contingencies that face them (Hayes, 1989) and may suggest a cognitive dimension.

This bifurcation of the consequences of behavior extends the range of reinforcing agencies with the intention of providing a more comprehensive behavioral interpretation of purchase and consumption. The reality and independence of hedonic and informational sources of reinforcement is empirically supported by a large volume of applied behavior analytic studies of human economic behavior. Field experiments incorporating incentives in the form of monetary rewards, competitions, and social praise (hedonic reinforcement), and performance feedback in the form of records of recent consumption levels (informational reinforcement) indicate the powerful influence of these consequential stimuli in reducing such environmentally-injurious activities as car exhaust pollution, littering and excess fuel consumption (Geller, Winett and Everett, 1982).

The second independent variable incorporated in the BPM is thus hedonic and informational reinforcement. The consumer's unique learning history determines the saliency of the configuration of hedonic and informational reinforcers made available through purchase and/or consumption of the products and services being offered. Hedonic and informational reinforcers are conceptualized as exerting, in each case, a relatively high or low level of control over behavior. High versus low hedonic reinforcement denotes the extent to which the consequences of behavior are affective, emotive, or pleasant. High versus low information reinforcement denotes the extent to which the consequences of behavior provide data that regulate (or allow the individual to regulate through conscious calculation and verbal formulation of contingencies) the rate at which the relevant purchase or consumption responses are emitted. High informational reinforcement infers a great deal of relevant feedback on performance through which further responses can be adjusted or regulated. Low informational reinforcement means a smaller quantity of such information or a lower quality of feedback.

Synthesis: the consumer situation

An account of situated consumer behavior must incorporate variables that refer to differences between environments, which can be specified independently of the person, and variables that refer to differences between persons, which can be specified independently of the environment (Russell and Mehrabian, 1976). In the BPM, the extrapersonal variables refer to the settings in which prepurchase, purchase and postpurchase activities occur (including the relevant elements of the marketing mix). The personal variables derive from the learning history which summarizes the consumer's previous experience. Hence a situation of purchase and consumption is defined by reference to the relative openness of the settings in which these behaviors take place; the nature and relative importance of the hedonic and informational reinforcers that have influenced consumer responses in the past and that are now signalled by the setting stimuli as contingent upon the performance of specific purchase and/or consumption responses; and the unique personal learning history of the consumer.

Much micro-consumer behavior such as store selection or brand choice is a function of the specific contingencies of reinforcement operating in a given setting plus the individual factors brought to the setting by the consumer, his or her prior experience with brands or stores, for instance, which determine the detailed influences of the situation on his or her behavior. It is the combined effect of the personal and environmental factors, and their interrelationships, summarized in the BPM, that transform the general setting into a situation of immediate personal relevance to the consumer. A situation is more specific than a setting; it is defined and circumscribed not only by the setting variables that signal hedonic and informational consequences of behavior, but by the salience of those discriminative stimuli as determined by the consumer's learning history. These consequences are of two kinds: immediate outcomes (finding and acquiring products) of behavior in the current setting (browsing, negotiating, or purchase in a clothes store) and subsequent outcomes of postpurchase activities (e.g. wearing the clothes purchased) delivered later, perhaps in another setting (e.g. a restaurant).

Figure 1 summarizes the BPM account of situated consumer behavior. The consumer situation comprises the current behavior setting and the consumer's history of reinforcement in similar settings. The behavior setting is the set of discriminative stimuli that signal reinforcement contingent on the performance of specified consumer behaviors. Point-of-sale advertising might, for instance, signal the social status that will follow purchase of a particular item of jewelry (informational reinforcement) or the physical well-being that will result from consumption of a course of vitamins (hedonic reinforcement). The salience of these signals for the consumer depends on his/her learning history: whether these or similar behaviors have been so rewarded in the past. The resulting situation determines the rate at which the consumer now responds, if at all. The resulting hedonic and/or information reinforcement (or possibly punishment) modifies his or her learning history and thus alters the probability of performing similar behaviors in the future.

Situational analysis of consumer behavior

An interpretive account of consumer activity should systematically relate known topographies of purchase and consumption to the contingencies on which they are maintained. From the derivation of the BPM described above, there emerge eight distinct categories of contingencies, combinations of setting and reinforcer variables in terms of which such topographies can be described. These situational categories are shown in the BPM Contingency Matrix (Figure 2). The following analysis first identifies the fundamental classes of consumer behavior and the schedules of reinforcement that apparently control them. It then relates them to the situational categories defined in the Contingency Matrix.

Like other behaviors, purchase and consumption can be classified according to the nature of their consequences, the pattern of hedonic and informational reinforcement on which they are maintained. This pattern also involves the schedule of reinforcement in operation, i.e. the frequency with which responses are followed by reinforcers. When a response is reinforced every time it occurs, the procedure is known as continuous reinforcement (CRF). When less than every response is reinforced, the behavior takes longer to learn but extinguishes slowly. Fixed interval (FI) schedules provide reinforcement when a given

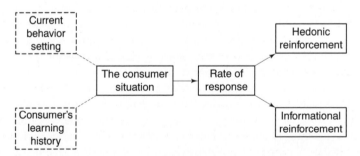

Figure 1   The Behavioural Perspective Model (BPM).

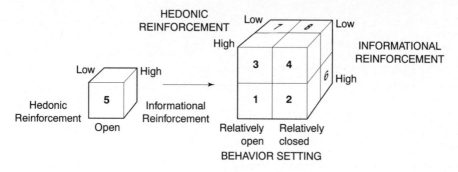

Figure 2   The BPM Contingency Matrix.

period of time has elapsed for a response made after that period; for variable interval (VI) schedules, the period of time that must elapse before a response is reinforced varies from reinforcement to reinforcement. Fixed ratio (FR) schedules provide reinforcement when a specific number of responses has been performed, regardless of the time required, whereas variable ratio (VR) schedules are such that a different number of responses is required to produce reinforcement on each occasion. Ratio schedules maintain a higher rate of responding than interval schedules. Fixed schedules maintain patterns of responding characterized by a pause after each reinforcement, whereas variable schedules maintain a steady rate of responding.

Shaping and maintaining complex behavior may reflect several concurrent reinforcement schedules that exert multiple, complex influences. For this exposition though, consumer behavior can be interpreted in terms of one or another of the familiar schedules. The four classes into which the consequences of consumer behavior are divided are accomplishment, pleasure, accumulation, and maintenance (Figure 3).

Accomplishment refers to social and economic achievement and maintains such behaviors as the acquisition and conspicuous consumption of status symbols, and the activities involved in seeking sensation and excitement or personal fulfilment as long as these acts result in the accumulation of some measure of attainment: points, products, certificates, rites of passage, etc. that mark progress. Accomplishment is the pattern of consequences produced by high levels of both hedonic and informational reinforcement. Behaviors controlled by accomplishment are apparently maintained on a VR schedule. In the case of the open behavior setting (Contingency 1: Extended Consumer Behavior), a typical example is the prepurchase search for and comparative evaluation of information relating to luxuries or discontinuous innovations. In the case of the closed setting (Contingency 2: Excitement and Fulfilment), casino gambling provides a typical instance.

Pleasure is the result of all forms of popular entertainment and of behaviors such as taking medication that are controlled (negatively reinforced) by the alleviation of suffering or displeasure. It is the consequence linked with a high level of hedonic reinforcement but only a low level of informational reinforcement which, nevertheless, is neither absent nor unimportant. These behaviors occur as if maintained by a VI schedule of reinforcement. In the open behavior setting (Contingency 3: Popular Entertainment), an example is the TV

BEHAVIOR SETTING

relatively open ◄────────────► relatively closed

ACCOMPLISHMENT

	CONTINGENCY 1	CONTINGENCY 2	
apparent schedule: VARIABLE RATIO	*Extended Consumer Behavior* – search & evaluation for status symbols (innovations, luxuries) – reading literary novels – watching TV documentaries etc.	*Excitement & Fulfillment* – casino gambling – personal development training (e.g., *est*) – religious training – (e.g., Scientology auditing etc.)	high informational reinforcement

PLEASURE

	CONTINGENCY 3	CONTINGENCY 4	
apparent schedule: VARIABLE INTERVAL	*Popular Entertainment* – watching TV game/variety show or 'happy news' – listening to popular music – watching pop music video etc.	*Inescapable entertainment/ Alleviation of Personal Plan* – watching in-flight movie – taking headache remedy – having hospital treatment etc.	low informational reinforcement

high hedonic reinforcement

ACCUMULATION

	CONTINGENCY 5	CONTINGENCY 6	
apparent schedule: FIXED RATIO	*Collecting* – installment buying – Christmas club saving – collection of coupons or other tokens in connection with promotional deal, etc.	*Token Economy-based Buying* – accumulation of 'airmiles' – purchasing products which confer entitlement to prizes, etc.	high informational reinforcement

MAINTENANCE

	CONTINGENCY 7	CONTINGENCY 8	
apparent schedule: FIXED INTERVAL	*Routine Purchasing of Socialized Economic Necessities* – supermarket grocery shopping – having dental checkup – hairdressing, etc.	*Regular Mandatory Purchase/Consumption* – paying taxes – buying TV license or passport – paying road/vehicle tax, motor insurance premiums, etc.	low informational reinforcement

low hedonic reinforcement

Figure 3 Consumer behaviour and its consequences.

game show, whereas in the closed setting (Contingency 4: Inescapable Entertainment), a typical example would be in-flight consumption of meals or movies.

Accumulation is produced by consumer behaviors involving collecting, saving (notably saving up irregularly to buy something), instalment buying, and responses to promotional deals requiring the accumulation of tokens or coupons. It is the consequence that embodies a high level of informational reinforcement but a low level of hedonic reinforcement, though the latter is neither absent nor, necessarily, unimportant. Such behaviors are apparently maintained on FR schedules. An example of accumulation in an open setting (Contingency 5: Collecting) is collecting packet tops to obtain a fairly trivial free gift. Accumulating airmiles as one uses airline services exemplifies the relevant behavior in a closed setting (Contingency 6: Token-based Buying). The distinction between them and closed settings derives from the inevitability of the ultimate reward. In the case of trivial free gifts, collecting is not enforced and the consumer has a degree of choice. Automatically given tokens leading to more substantial target rewards such as consumer durable products may engender greater compulsion and, by implication, a more closed setting.

Maintenance is the consequence of the activities involved in survival (e.g. regular food purchasing), and the fulfilment of social and cultural obligations of citizenship (e.g. the consumption of public goods for which taxes are paid at regular intervals). Note that maintenance does not refer simply to physical survival and well-being but includes the outcomes of performing the cultural and economic duties of the society, especially as the consumer makes sense of social being through consumption and consumption-related behaviors. These behaviors are seemingly maintained on FI schedules. The routine weekly purchasing of food items and other fast moving consumer goods in a supermarket is an example of the behavior in question in an open behavior setting (Contingency 7: Routine Purchasing of Necessities), whereas mandatory consumption of public goods for which compulsory taxes are levied exemplifies such behavior in a closed setting (Contingency 8: Mandatory Purchase or Consumption).

Consumer theory in marketing strategy

The BPM explicitly recognizes the role of managerial marketing in the manipulation of discriminative stimuli and reinforcers through branding and other forms of differentiation. Marketer action takes two broad forms. The first is the closure of purchase/consumption settings by reducing the probability of escape/avoidance and encouraging specific purchase and consumption approaches; this may be accomplished through the use of merchandising techniques that may bring consumer behavior under stimulus control. The second is the manipulation of hedonic and informational reinforcers to increase the probability of approach purchasing and consumption behaviors. The deliberate use of hedonic and informational reinforcers is effective in increasing the probability of approach behaviors involving purchase and/or consumption while reducing the probability of avoidance and escape responses such as leaving the sales area. Such reinforcers are especially effective when they are linked to established discriminative stimuli. Marketers' techniques for achieving these ends are based on three determinants of response strength: enhancing reinforcer effectiveness, controlling reinforcement schedules, and increasing the quality and quantity of reinforcement.

The following discussion relates these broad strategies to specific contingencies or consumer behavior. There is no simple one-on-one correspondence between marketing strategies and each of the eight contingencies identified above – all market-led organizations can be assumed to pursue constant product development (increasing the quantity and quality of reinforcers), for instance. But it is possible to identify the situations in which particular strategic responses are especially relevant.

Closure of behavior settings

Accomplishment

Such manipulation may involve the closure of sales environments once the customer has tacitly agreed to buy. In departmental stores, for instance, purchase agreements, especially those involving the arrangement of credit for infrequent purchases of luxuries or innovations (Contingency 1: Extended Consumer Behavior), are finalized not in the relatively open store setting in which the merchandise has been inspected and sales claims made, but in separated areas of the store such as offices or corner desks, where behavior not germane to the agreement is discouraged and the customer is less likely to change his/her mind, and from which escape may be accomplished only with difficulty and embarrassment.

Managerial control

Managerial control of the behavior setting is especially apparent in the case of Contingency 2 (Excitement and Fulfilment). In the case of gambling, for instance, access to the casino is strictly determined by its management who pronounce on membership rights and may deny entry on any particular occasion to anyone who does not conform to the required codes of conduct. The casino managers arrange the physical and, to a degree, social environment, within the law, controlling lighting, lack of clocks, the situation of tables, and even the clientele, all of which may be manipulated to ensure the continued presence of the punters where they are most likely to gamble, to the extent of serving drinks and even meals at the table, and providing opportunities to gamble in the restaurants. Although there are such obvious physical encouragements to gamble and movement may be severely restricted on occasion, the most subtle control is social. Quitting, failing to take risks by staking inadequate sums, and so forth evoke social disprobation that makes escape and avoidance less probable. Similar contingencies are maintained in self-improvement programs such as 'est' (Baer and Stolz, 1980).

Pleasure

More closed still is the setting in which many long distance airline passengers find themselves in which meals must be purchased along with travel, and which, like the in-flight movies that follow them, are consumed without alternative (Contingency 4: Inescapable Entertainment). The intended strategy here is the distraction of the consumer from the discomfort of extended travel, a managerial reaction against the closure of the setting, rather than a purposive attempt to close it further. But inasmuch as showing a movie or serving a meal disallows alternative behaviors, such as reading or sleeping, it may have a counter-effect on some passengers.

Maintenance

Often the discriminative and reinforcing stimuli available in stores are so arranged as to maximize consumers' patronage and shape purchase responses. Such manipulation may be the result of modification of the physical or social environment by means of the familiar merchandising techniques that route supermarket shoppers past specific products, juxtapose leading brands with complementary items, or employ point-of-sale advertising to encourage unplanned purchasing (Contingency 7: Routine Purchasing). The physical and social settings in which financial institutions such as banks and insurance companies transact business are such that only the serious business of transacting is encouraged. Extraneous activity that might detract from efficiency is punished, principally by the austere, or at least pointed, behavior of the seller; the environmental stimuli are so arranged as to be sufficiently closed to ensure that the transactions in question are effectively accomplished. However, more subtle means of closing consumer settings are apparent. Sommer (1974) suggests that the seating in airport lounges is deliberately arranged to minimize social interaction and to encourage passengers to visit the profitable concessions such as shops and restaurants provided by airline operators.

Not all consumer behavior in closed settings is controlled by managers of private firms or public corporations. On occasion, consumption is mandatory. Some consumer behavior involves compulsory purchase and consumption of state-enforced escape commodities such as social worker intervention, taxation, and TV licensing (Category 8: Mandatory Purchase). Other consumer behaviors maintained by these contingencies include the purchase of complementary secondary escape commodities such as pension fund membership, or mortgage-related endowment insurance. The product or service is purchased usually as a complement to another item that is the principal source of reinforcement. The secondary commodity is purchased only because its consumption is a prerequisite of more strongly reinforced purchase or consumption. It is often the eventual acquisition of the additional product or service and the reinforcement it confers that reinforces purchase of the secondary escape commodity.

Increasing reinforcer effectiveness

Pleasure

Often the effectiveness of reinforcers is enhanced through deliberate delaying of reinforcement in which the marketer forces the prospective purchaser to wait for the product. It is difficult to effect this in many markets for fast moving consumer goods where competitors are able to step in quickly to provide the item, but it can be achieved in more closed settings, particularly for service products. In cinemas, for example, the entertainment is usually arranged so that the most strongly hyped movie appears only after a B-feature, travelogue, or other short, plus advertisements, have been screened; similarly, in theatres offering variety shows or concerts, the biggest star appears last on the bill (Contingencies 3 and 4: Popular and Inescapable Entertainment). The design and presentation of discriminative stimuli that inform the audience of the eventual appearance of movie or star, and the progressive reinforcement of watching preceding films or acts, becomes a key promotional device in which sustained viewing may come under stimulus control. Consumer behavior is thus shaped or chained by a series of events, each of which acts as both reinforcer of what has transpired and discriminative stimulus for what is to come. Some products and services, such as the inescapable entertainments encountered on long air journeys, are effective reinforcers simply because the closed setting in which they are provided is otherwise boring or uncomfortable. Marketers attempt in these instances to alleviate the temporarily punishing circumstances of consuming the primary product (air travel) by providing more pleasant accompaniments.

Accumulation

A powerful marketing strategy involves the use of token economy principles (Battalio, Kagel, Winkler, Fisher, Basman, and Krasner, 1974) by making additional reinforcers contingent upon prior purchasing. The practice is simply an extension of the familiar prize schemes open to collectors of cigarette cards or trading stamps (Contingencies 5 and 6: Collecting and Token-based Buying). Air-miles earned by frequent flyers on international airlines are informational reinforcers analogous to the tokens earned for prosocial behavior in therapeutic and correctional institutions (Chesanow, 1985). Some hotels also offer gifts to customers who accumulate points by staying frequently. The collection of these tokens is reinforced by gaining additional free air travel or hospitality (an increase in reinforcer quantity) and/or by access to different types of reinforcers such as prizes (an increase in reinforcer quality). Purchase and consumption of the basic product, the air travel or accommodation originally demanded, are maintained by both the intrinsic hedonic reinforcers they embody and the informational consequences of buying and using them. These extrinsic, informational reinforcers also act as discriminative stimuli, directing behavior toward the attainment and consumption of the additional (back-up) reinforcers offered. The use of tokens in this way may not only increase the loyalty of existing consumers but also increase overall demand, at least while the deal is operated.

Maintenance

A similar process is at work in the maintenance of some mandatory or required consumer behaviors (Contingency 8: Mandatory Purchase). Purchase of the (less desired) complementary good (say, life insurance) is reinforced by acquisition of the principally desired product (a mortgage), and marketers may be able to increase sales of the former by making the primary product contingent upon it being made more attractive.

Control of reinforcement schedules

Accomplishment

Marketing strategies that provide Excitement and Fulfilment (Contingency 2) belong here. Casino managers, for instance, have considerable control over access to the informational and hedonic reinforcement represented by winning by virtue of its determining the schedule of reinforcement in operation. (Although the rules of a game like roulette may be said to determine the schedule, the casino may have legal discretion over the favorability of the odds to the house, and over the amounts staked.) Stretching the VR schedule in operation, so that progressively more responses are needed to achieve reinforcement, is a particularly powerful means to affect behavior.

Pleasure

Watching popular television game shows that provide near-constant entertainment, playing Trivial Pursuit, and reading mass fiction that contains a sensation on almost every page, seem to be maintained on VI schedules. Even a short period of attending is reinforced and the consumer is meant to be little more than the passive recipient of transitory thrills. Behavior is often maintained on these schedules for long periods through the mechanisms of variety, pace, and change. Personal cassette players and the viewing of many television shows and movies have replaced for many people the more demanding cultural habits essential to the appreciation of the literary and dramatic art forms. Instead, mass culture presents frequent and predictable, relatively strong and continuous hedonic reinforcements that are not contingent upon long periods of concentrated effort. Competing television channels and other electronic media provide dozens of sources of highly hedonic reinforcement with some informational content. The portable nature of the technologies involved extends the geographical scope of these behaviors.

The consumption behaviors in question are apparently maintained on low VI schedules, though in some instances reinforcement is almost continuous. Mass visual communication presents reinforcers in such a way that the audience's attention is maintained in the face of strong competition from alternative media and pursuits. Although TV advertisements fulfill the primary function of presenting discriminative stimuli that signal the reinforcements contingent upon specified purchase and consumption responses, they also reinforce sustained attention on the part of their viewers. Since they are usually presented in open settings that offer numerous incentives to pursue alternative activities, their use of emotional and social reinforcements is understandable. The constant reduction in consumers' attention spans – evidenced by frequent switching of TV channels and use of split screens to watch two or more programs simultaneously – implies a constant search for reinforcement. In an attempt to overcome this, some television shows incorporate a sustained presentation of reinforcement for very short periods of responding, e.g. the 'happy news' bulletin format in which reports entertain by featuring 'action, pace, [and] an almost dizzy attempt to keep the audience from getting bored' (Tunstall and Walker, 1981, p. 123). News broadcasts feature a series of sensational and entertaining stories, each receiving one or two minutes concentrated coverage in a half-hour bulletin, interrupted by three two-minute commercial breaks and a five-minute weather forecast presented with similar non-stop pace and verve.

Accumulation

Consumer behaviors that require systematic collection or the accumulation of a specified number of tokens before a major reinforcement is provided are apparently maintained on a fixed ratio schedule (Contingency 5: Collecting). These include purchases where payments are made prior to consumption, e.g. the payment of installments for a vacation that can only be taken once the full amount has been paid. Indeed, any saving done with the intention of making a large purchase when a certain amount has accumulated would fall into this category. Promotions requiring the accumulation of coupons or other tokens before a product or service can be obtained also belong here. In both Collecting and Token-based Buying (Contingencies 5 and 6), the effectiveness of the smaller, frequently acquired reinforcers is enhanced by the promise of the ultimate reinforcer that takes the form of a prize, dividend, or additional product or service. The next item in the series is always strongly reinforcing, not through its intrinsic worth but because its acquisition is a measure of the consumer's progress toward the final goal.

Increasing reinforcer quality and quantity

Accomplishment

Marketer activity often involves overcoming the effects of reinforcer delays that are beyond the control of marketer or consumer. The shorter the time between the emission of a response and the presentation of a reinforcer, the greater is the likelihood that the behavior in question will be repeated in the future (Alhadeff, 1982). Reduction of reinforcer delay is, therefore, an integral component of the enhancement of reinforcer quality. Where it is necessary for consumers to await gratification already paid for, e.g. when an expensive exotic vacation that will be taken in August must be paid for some months earlier (Contingency 1: Extended Consumer Behavior), both payment and patient waiting are elicited and maintained by the presentation of reinforcers for intervening acts: letters of acknowledgement and receipt, brochures and books describing the trip, preparatory instructions and meetings or films of the destination, and so on.

Accumulation

The encouragement of approach and the minimization of escape may be simultaneously accomplished through promotions that make an extraordinary reinforcement (such as a prize) contingent upon repeat purchasing (Contingency 5: Collecting). The requirement that the promoted brand be successively purchased before the additional reinforcer is obtained reduces the probability of escape or avoidance such as purchasing an alternative brand. Indeed, products that arrive periodically in parts (such as the weekly and monthly magazines that build into an encyclopedia) are promoted such that non-response (missing even one part) is punished. Missed parts may become available again only after a period of time has elapsed and the series is rerun, or they may be obtained only through additional cost and inconvenience. Competitions and promotions demanding repeat buying to be effective also apparently change the schedule of reinforcement, albeit temporarily, for those customers not already brand loyal.

The benefits of saving and investing are also necessarily delayed; in these cases, the eventual reinforcements on which consumer behavior is to some extent contingent can be described through prompts and vicarious reinforcement relating to the gaining of interest and bonuses, and the future level of consumption that will ensue. All strengthen the responses that add up to sustained saving or investment over many years.

Conclusions

The BPM does more [than] redescribe consumer choice in operant terminology; it organizes well-established and documented patterns of consumer behavior, relating each to unique and appropriate contingencies. The systematic way in which various patterns of consumer behavior have also been related to reinforcement schedules indicates that the BPM interpretation is reliably postulating relationships among its dependent and independent variables.

The BPM presents a behavioral interpretation of purchase and consumption that does not seek to eliminate alternative explanations. The inevitability of a plurality of explanatory mechanisms is in fact central to its approach (Foxall, 1990). Further research should proceed toward the synthesis of environmental and intrapersonal sources of motivation, in which the isolation of the hedonic and informational effects of reinforcement suggests a relationship with affective and cognitive theories of consumer behavior that should be pursued.

The BPM interpretation also elucidates marketing practice. Its explanatory variables and its categorization of the contingencies influencing consumer behavior are centrally relevant to our understanding of the strategic conduct of customer-oriented marketing. This applied emphasis of the model also gives impetus to the development of a synthesis of cognitive and behavioral accounts of consumer choice. In open societies, consumers are seldom so constrained that they cannot escape or avoid aversive contingencies. Further refinements of the model will include an account of consumers' cognitive interpretations, representations, and manipulations of the contingencies that influence their behavior.

References

Alhadeff, David A., 1982, *Microeconomics and Human Behavior*, Berkeley, CA: University of California Press.

Baer, Donald M. and Stephanie B. Stolz, 1978, 'A description of the Erhard seminars training (est) in the terms of behavior analysis', *Behaviorism*, 6 (Spring), 45–70.

Battalio, Raymond C., John H. Kagel, Robin C. Winkler, Edwin B. Fisher, Robert L. Basman, and Leonard Krasner, 1974, 'An experimental investigation of consumer behavior in a controlled environment', *Journal of Consumer Research*, 1 (September), 52–60.

Berry, Leon and John H. Kunkel, 1970, 'In pursuit of consumer theory', *Decision Sciences*, 1(1), 25–39.

Chesanow, N., 1985, 'Prize flights: All about frequent flyer programs', *Savvy*, 6 (June), 67–9.

Feyerabend, Paul, 1975, *Against Method*, London: NLB.

Foxall, Gordon R., 1986, 'Theoretical progress in consumer psychology: The contribution of a behavioral analysis of choice', *Journal of Economic Psychology*, 7 (December), 393–414.

Foxall, Gordon R., 1987, 'Radical behaviorism and consumer choice', *International Journal of Research in Marketing*, 4(2), 111–29.

Foxall, Gordon R., 1990, *Consumer Psychology in Behavioral Perspective*, New York: Routledge.

Geller, E. Scott, Richard A. Winett and Peter B. Everett, 1982, *Preserving the Environment*, New York: Pergamon.

Hayes, Steven C. (ed.), 1989, *Rule-governed Behavior: Cognition, Contingencies and Instructional Control*, New York: Plenum.

Holbrook, Morris B. and Elizabeth C. Hirschman, 1982, 'The experiential aspects of consumption: Consumer fantasies, feelings and fun', *Journal of Consumer Research*, 9 (September), 132–40.

Holbrook, Morris B., Robert W. Chestnut, Terence A. Oliva, and Eric A. Greenleaf, 1984, 'Play as a consumption experience: The roles of emotions, performance, and personality in the enjoyment of games', *Journal of Consumer Research*, **11** (September), 728–39.

Hunt, Shelby D., 1976, 'The nature and scope of marketing', *Journal of Marketing*, **40** (July), 17–28.

Nord, Walter R. and J. Paul Peter, 1980, 'A behavior modification perspective on marketing', *Journal of Marketing*, **44** (Spring), 36–47.

Rothschild, Michael L. and William C. Gaidis, 1981, 'Behavioral learning theory: Its relevance to marketing and promotions', *Journal of Marketing*, **45** (Spring), 70–8.

Russell, James A. and Albert Mehrabian, 1976, 'Environmental variables in consumer research', *Journal of Consumer Research*, **3** (June), 62–3.

Schwartz, Barry and Hugh M. Lacey, 1982, *Behaviorism, Science, and Human Nature*, New York: Norton.

Skinner, B. Frederic, 1953, *Science and Human Behavior*, New York: Macmillan.

Skinner, B. Frederic, 1969, *Contingencies of Reinforcement: A Theoretical Analysis*, New York: Appleton-Century-Crofts.

Skinner, B. Frederic, 1977, 'Why I am not a cognitive psychologist', *Behaviorism*, **5** (Fall), 1–10.

Skinner, B. Frederic, 1988, 'Is behaviorism vacuous?', in *The Selection of Behavior*, A. Charles Catania and Steven Harnad (eds.), Cambridge, MA: Cambridge University Press.

Sommer, R., 1974, *Tight Spaces: Hard Architecture and How to Humanize It*, Englewood Cliffs, NJ: Prentice-Hall.

Troye, S.V., 1985, 'Situationist theory and consumer behavior', in *Research in Consumer Behavior*, Volume 3, Jagdish N. Sheth (ed.), Greenwich, CT: JAI Press, 285–321.

Tunstall, Jeremy and David Walker, 1981, *Media Made in California*. New York: Oxford University Press.

Wearden, John H., 1988, 'Some neglected problems in the analysis of human operant behavior', in *Human Operant Conditioning and Behavior Modification*, Graham C.L. Davey and Christopher Cullen (eds.), Chichester: John Wiley.

Part II

individual
processes

The consumer: Identification and measurement

3

Bon, J. and Pras, B., 1984, 'Dissociation of the roles of buyer, payer and consumer', *International Journal of Research in Marketing*, **1**, 7–16

Foxall, G.R. and Goldsmith, R.E., 1988, 'Personality and consumer research: Another look', *Journal of the Market Research Society*, **30**(2), 111–25

Derbaix, C. and Pham, M.T., 1989, 'For the development of measures of emotion in marketing: Summary of prerequisites', *Recherche et Applications en Marketing*, **4**(4), 71–87

Introduction

This third chapter refers to the methodologies and concepts related to the study of the consumer as an individual. Three topics of importance have been selected to represent this very wide research area, namely the consumers' roles, the importance of personality and the importance of emotions.

The first article by Bon and Pras analyzes the interfaces between the roles of consumers, buyers and payers. Traditionally, most studies on consumer behaviour focus either on the consumer or on the buyer. The interface between both roles has very seldom been explored because most studies are based on situations in which the buyer, the payer and the consumer roles are played by different persons. What the authors suggest is that the understanding of the various roles played by an individual in the buying and consumption process (be it an individual or an organizational process) may be enlarged by examining the basic roles of buyer, payer and consumer when held by separate individuals or by one single person. Thus the study aims at testing if role dissociation (the buyer-consumer is not the payer) versus role association (the buyer-consumer is also the payer) has an effect on buying behaviour; this led the authors to investigate the effect of the paying situation (payer versus non payer) on buying behaviour. Then the study analyzes in the case of role dissociation the influence of the relationships between the buyer and the payer on the buying decisions. They point out the fact that the buyer's decisions (when he or she is not the payer) are related both to the degree to which he or she takes into consideration the payer's preferences versus his or her own preferences, and to situational variables. A conceptual framework is then developed whose interest lies in the fact that it might be easily generalized to other situations than those specifically mentioned in the study (the restaurant and hotel sector).

Together with the role played by the individual in the decision process, personality has a strong influence on consumer attitudes and decision-making. This aspect is largely developed by Foxall and Goldsmith in the second article of this chapter. Traditional studies on personality investigate the links between consumers' personalities and their consumption habits. Classic studies which go back to as early as 1959 (see Evans) deal with the relationships existing between personality traits or types and product ownership (see Foxall and Goldsmith, 1994, for a review). The interest of this article is to investigate the links between personality and innovativeness. The article discusses the empirical use of a personality-related measure of cognitive style, which is the famous KAI (Kirton Adaptation-Innovation Inventory) in the context of consumers' innovative purchasing of food brands and products. The concept of cognitive style is essentially based on the fact that individuals differ in the way they seek and process information. It therefore presupposes that differences between consumers' acquisition and processing of information are relatively permanent, in the sense that these cognitive characteristics should be similar in various areas and situations of choice.[1] The study shows a relevant qualitative difference between purchasers of contrasting cognitive styles, a result which is of important value for marketing managers as regards the launch of new products (and how they will be perceived by consumers) and the management of efficient marketing communication programmes.

Another stream of research developed in this chapter relates to the importance of affective versus cognitive factors in consumer choices. There is a long tradition both in Europe and in North America to consider that cognitive processes are essential to the understanding of human behaviour. Until the late 1970s most studies in the area of consumer behaviour were essentially driven by a cognitive approach, which largely neglected the influence of emotional factors in consumers' attitudes and decision-making process.

One of the most intriguing facets of consumer research in the 1970s had been the relationship between consumers' attitudes (mainly cognitive), especially towards brands, and their purchase behaviour patterns. After the advent of the theory of reasoned action (Fishbein and Ajzen, 1975), the problem appeared to have been solved: attitudes towards the act of purchase and the social normative influences to buy a particular brand appear to determine consumers' intentions which are approximately equated with their brand purchase behaviour. In this perspective, intentions are said to be largely determined by conscious cognitive processes.

The model of attitude formation and modification designed by Fishbein and Ajzen has nevertheless since been seriously questioned, because it does not take into sufficient consideration the influence of affective factors on decision-making processes. A given behaviour is in fact always simultaneously determined by cognitive, affective and conative factors. Another criticism often levelled against this model is that decision-making is not solely influenced by conscious factors but is also largely determined by affective factors, which often lie beyond the conscious level of perception.

In the third article, Derbaix and Pham remind us that affective dimensions play a very important role in most consumer decision-making, hence the crucial necessity for marketers to understand these emotional reactions, but also to design tools in order to measure them. This article is extremely interesting for several reasons. First, it proposes a systematic and conceptual typology of affective reactions based on the distinction of seven types of affective reactions, namely shock emotion, feeling, mood, temperament, preference, attitude and appreciation. Second, the article stresses the specificities of affect measurement and provides perceptive remarks which should contribute significantly to both the understanding and the measurement of affective reactions.

Note

1. For a review on cognitive styles see C. Pinson, N.K. Malhotra and A.K. Jain, 1988, 'Les styles cognitifs des consommateurs', *Recherche et Applications en Marketing*, 3(1), 53–73.

References

Evans, F., 1959, 'Psychological and objective factors in the prediction of brand choice', *Journal of Business*, **32**, 340–69.

Fishbein, M. and Ajzen, I., 1975, *Beliefs, Attitudes, Intention and Behavior: An introduction to theory and research*, Reading, MA: Addison-Wesley.

Foxall, G. and Goldsmith, R., 1994, *Consumer Psychology for Marketing*, London: Routledge.

Dissociation of the roles of buyer, payer and consumer

●●●

Jérôme Bon
Associate Professor, Ecole Supérieure de Commerce de Paris

Bernard Pras
Professor, University of Paris X and Ecole Supérieure des Sciences Economiques et Commerciales

Summary

Focusing on role dissociation, this article hypothesizes that the relationship between buyer, payer and consumer is an important explanatory factor of individual buying behavior and illustrates this through a choice of hotels and restaurants by salesmen with travel expense accounts reimbursed by their company.

1. Introduction

In the field of consumer behavior, research has primarily been focused on the individual buyer, and then on family and organizational buying. Within these broad categories largely studied these days, specific situations such as gift purchasing (Mauss, 1950; Belk, 1976), buying for someone else and purchasing something paid for or reimbursed by a third party have received very little attention, although they can be expected to have a strong influence on buying behavior (Bon, 1978).

These specific situations are typical of role dissociation in consumer behavior since in the first case (gift purchasing) the buyer and the payer are usually one person but the consumer another, in the second case (buying product reimbursed), the buyer and the consumer are generally one person, the payer another. A promising approach to study role dissociation would consist in examining the basic roles of buyer, payer and consumer when held by separate individuals or by one single person.

2. Role specialization within groups

Roles are relatively stable social positions held by individuals; for example, the role of the wife, the child within the family, the engineer, the production manager within the firm, the

From the *International Journal of Research in Marketing*, 1 (1984), 7–16.

medical doctor in society. The concept can also be used to describe what is expected from someone holding a position he obtained in a group, e.g. leader, observer, follower, or a position derived from an activity (Goffman, 1972). Similarly, it can be said that someone has the role of user, purchaser, decision-maker in the 'buying center' of an organization for the purchase of a specific product (Webster and Wind, 1972).

In group purchasing, buying is complex because the persons involved in the process may have conflicting objectives. Role specialization among members of the 'buying center' provides a way to avoid or limit conflicts (Davis, 1970; Webster and Wind, 1972). Role specialization will vary according to the type of product under study and the stage of the buying process considered.

Product specialization occurs in the family: the husband dominates the purchasing of some goods or services, such as insurance; the wife dominates the purchasing of clothing or food (Cunningham and Green, 1974; Davis, 1971). Specialization at the different stages of the buying process for a specific product also occurs: the wife may play an important part in identifying needs; the husband may be dominant at the evaluation stage, and the final decision may be syncretic (Davis and Rigaux, 1974). Specialization still occurs within the evaluation stage since the wife is generally said to consider mainly expressive aspects of the product while the husband attaches more importance to instrumental criteria (Sheth, 1974).

Examples can also be suggested in industrial buying. It has been shown that the weight in the decision process of various employees varies according to the technological complexity and commercial risk of the product considered. When considering the user, purchaser, decision-maker, it appears that their influence on the decision process varies at different stages; the user defines the product needs and specifications and the purchaser searches for information (Haymann, 1973). At the evaluation stage, differences can be observed too; users may attach more importance to quality and technological criteria, while purchasers will mainly consider price (Wind, 1966, 1970; Scott and Wright, 1976).

These investigations of complex buying have generally dealt with the family and the organization. They start from given situations, analyze the roles and relate them to the buying process. Another approach would be to begin with basic roles to derive buying situations and implications.

In the buying process, one can define three basic functions: buying, paying, consuming; the buyer being the one who makes the purchase, the payer the one who finances it, the consumer the one who uses or consumes the product or service. Table 1 presents the possible allocation of roles (corresponding to these functions: buyer, payer, consumer); one can create five possible theoretical situations in which different buying situations can be positioned such as industrial buying, family buying, invitations, mandated buying, company gift, personal gift, medical care expenses when reimbursed, business purchases on expense accounts, etc.

The choice of the buyer will depend upon the situation – of the five mentioned above – in which he is involved. The consumer-payer-buyer will probably not have the same priorities as the non-consuming or the non-paying buyer. For example, the self-centered non-paying buyer may not care much about price, the self-centered non-consumer-buyer would not care much about quality since he is not directly concerned with this aspect of the product. But in most cases, the buyer is not indifferent to the payer's or to the consumer's

Table 1   Examples of the possible relationships between participants in the buying process

Differentiation of functions	Buyer's role	Payer's role	Consumer's role
1. The three functions are held by the same person	←————————————individual buyer————————————→		
2. Each of the three functions is held by a specific person	organizational buyer	financial manager in an organization	users or consumers in an organization
3. One person is both the payer and the buyer. Another person is the consumer	← – family buyer – gift purchaser – intermediate goods purchase – host →		– consumers in the family – gift receiver – invited person or guests
4. One person is both the buyer and the consumer. Another person is the payer	– buyer-consumer of free or reimbursed services – invited person choosing the meal without paying	– supplier of free services – reimburser of services – host	– buyer consumer of free or reimbursed services – invited person
5. One person is the buyer. Another is both payer and consumer	mandated	←————————mandator————————→	

preferences and the choice is influenced by a second element; the level to which the buyer integrates the perceived preferences of his buying partners, if any. For example, gift purchasers do take into account the preferences of the person to whom they offer the gift and do pay attention to quality (Belk, 1976). In the field of industrial buying it has been shown (Wind, 1966) that purchasers give more consideration either to price or to quality or delay depending upon the structure of the firm (centralized or decentralized) and from whom they expect organizational rewards (purchasing manager or engineers).

This article focuses on two aspects: first, the behavior of the payer versus the non-payer; second, the differences in buying behavior among non-payers.

3. Non-paying buying behavior: a conceptual framework

When a consumer-buyer and a payer are involved in a purchase, they may have conflicting preferences. The consumer-buyer may be attracted by the high quality, the accessibility of products or services which generally cost rather more, and the payer will, in most cases, set up some price range for the expense or even prefer low priced products or services. The supposed conflict can be solved in various ways (Simon, 1955; Davis, 1976) according to what degree the buyer takes the payer's preferences into consideration versus his own.

Following the classification of Thomas (1975) four types of conflict resolution may occur.

1. *Domination.* If the consumer-buyer takes little account of the payer's preferences but attaches great importance to his own preferences, then he can be expected to choose quality and ease of access whatever the price.
2. *Negligence.* The consumer-buyer takes little account of the payer's preferences and of his own preferences. He will choose the first item or service he finds whatever the price or the quality.
3. *Appeasement.* The consumer-buyer attaches great importance to the interests of the payer and takes little account of his own preferences. He will choose low priced products or services if he perceives this to be what the payer will prefer.
4. *Integration.* The buyer attaches great importance both to his own preferences and to those of the payer. In this case, he will look for a good price–quality ratio.

Some of these conflict resolution situations have been theoretically and empirically studied for joint decisions. For example, Curry and Menasco (1979) analyze the effects on post-choice satisfaction or 'family utility' of two types of decision rules: capitulation (= appeasement) and compromise (= integration) between husband and wife,[1] and they demonstrate that capitulation results in less total utility than compromise.

Focusing on the purchase decision of a specific actor (the non-paying buyer-consumer) and not on joint decisions, it may be said that the non-paying buyer-consumer will select the product or service which maximizes his global utility. His global utility depends on his direct utility for the object and on the utility he derives from the satisfaction or dissatisfaction of the payer when he (the buyer-consumer) buys the object, both weighted by the importance the buyer gives to his own preferences and to the payer's preferences (Figure 1).

Obviously, situational, social, and supply variables also play an important part. For example, even a businessman who is refunded by his company may pick out a second-rate restaurant if it is the only one open late at night, when he arrives in a town. Nevertheless, according to the conceptual framework developed, major determinants of buying-behavior can be expected to be whether the consumer-buyer is also the payer and the degree to which the non-payer buyer integrates the perceived preferences of the payer. If the buyer and the payer are very close, we may expect a high level of integration of the payer constraints. Research on restaurant menu preferences by Green and Wind (1973) supports this hypothesis.[2]

4. An empirical example

4.1 Field of study

Among paying versus non-paying situations the above framework has been applied to the study of salesmen's buying behavior of hotel and restaurant services in France.[3] For a given meal and a known quality, payers can be expected to be negatively sensitive to price.[4] But, in the case of hotel and restaurant services, one can reasonably assume price to be important

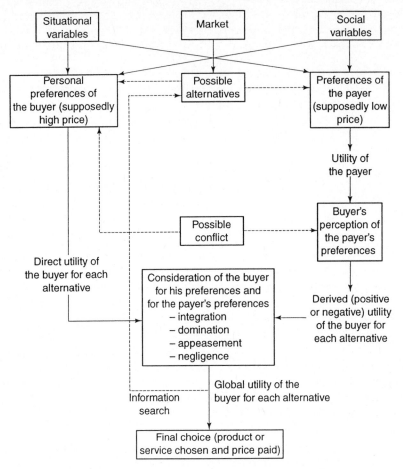

Figure 1   Non-paying buyer consumer choice.

in another way since in this area it is difficult to evaluate quality beforehand, and price therefore comes to serve as an indicator of quality. Further, the reimbursement policies of companies differ, so comparative analyses can be made. In France, we can broadly define three types of policies:

(a) the 'real expense' reimbursement system by which salesmen are repaid on presentation of their bills. They can be considered non-paying buyers–consumers.

(b) the 'per diem allowance' reimbursement whereby salesmen are paid a fixed allowance per day or meal even if they do not spend anything. In this situation, one can assume they will act as if they were payers-buyers because their expenses affect their own budget.

(c) the 'limited real expense' reimbursement according to which salesmen are repaid on presentation of their bills up to a fixed amount per day or per meal. In this case, the salespersons are partly payers.

4.2   Hypotheses

The empirical study has two objectives. The first is to test if role dissociation (versus role association) has an effect on buying behavior, that is, to test the effect of the paying situation (payer versus non-payer) on buying behavior. The second, focusing on role dissociation (case where the buyer-consumer is not the payer), is to examine the influence of the relationships between the buyer and the payer on the buying decisions.

The variables used to represent salesmen's buying decisions are the prices paid for meals in restaurants and rooms at hotels. The explanatory variables whose influences are tested are: first, the paying situation (payer or partial payer versus non-payer situations) resulting from the reimbursement policy ('per diem allowance', 'limited real expense' or 'real expense'), and, second, the salesmen–company relationship (domination, negligence, integration, appeasement). The salesperson can be considered as a payer when on a 'per diem allowance' system, a partial payer when on a 'limited real expense' system, and a non-payer when on a 'real expense' system. For the non-payer's case, hypotheses about the price level are formulated for the domination, integration, and appeasement categories. None is suggested for the negligence category since the salesperson will then choose on the basis of convenience, not price, which means that the price paid can be high or low. The hypotheses derived are as follows:

1. The price paid per meal and per hotel by a buyer non-payer (salesman on 'real expense') is higher than the price paid by a buyer partly-payer (salesman on 'limited real expense'), which in its turn is higher than the price paid by a buyer–payer (salesman on a 'per diem allowance').
2. The price paid by a non-payer (salesman on 'real expense') is higher when he has an attitude of domination towards the payers than when he has an attitude of integration. In the latter case, the price paid per meal and per hotel will be higher than when he has an attitude of appeasement.

5. Methodology

5.1   Sample

The sample consisted of 126 salespersons selected on an availability basis. One salesman per company was interviewed during international fairs in Paris and Bordeaux. In order to have a homogeneous sample, that is composed only of salespersons who were actually travelling during the fair, we had to eliminate, first, companies which had only permanent salesmen in the city at the fair – frequently the case for large companies – and second, companies represented only by their marketing managers – frequently the case in very small companies. This led to an over-representation of medium sized companies, but offered the advantage of a homogeneous situation since the salespersons had the same set of choices for lodging and meals. Further, data collection during the fair provided a large sample of subjects on whom information could be gathered easily and with a minimum time lag.

5.2 Questionnaire, operationalization and measure of variables

A structured questionnaire was used to obtain data on the different variables: prices, buyer–payer relationship, system of reimbursement.

- Prices were the exact amount of expenses for hotel and for the last five dinners during the fair.
- The buyer–payer (salesman–company) relationship illustrated in Table 2 results from the consideration of the salesperson for himself or the importance he attaches to the choice of restaurants and hotels and from his consideration for the company or the importance he attaches to the satisfaction of the payer's preferences in terms of travel expenditures (the combination of these two variables as components of the buyer–payer relationship is presented in Table 2).

Since salespeople may be eager to present a good, socially acceptable image of themselves, someone who receives a large allowance for meals may, for example, overestimate the

Table 2 Attitudes resulting from consideration of one's own preferences and for the payer's preferences[a, b, c]

Consideration for one's own preferences

Question: Is the satisfaction of your own preferences very important to you when you choose a hotel/restaurant, or are you indifferent to them?[d]	6 5 4	Domination[e] $n_H = 10$ $n_R = 11$	Integration $n_H = 29$ $n_R = 26$
	3 2 1	Negligence $n_H = 0$ $n_R = 1$	Appeasement $n_H = 6$ $n_R = 10$
		1 2 3	4 5 6

Consideration for the payer's preferences
Question: Is it important to you to satisfy the preferences of the payer (reimbursement officer) or are you indifferent to them when you choose a hotel or restaurant?

a. Considerations for one's own preferences and for the payer's preferences are rated on ordinal scales going from 1 to 6, where 1 = completely indifferent, 2 = indifferent, 3 = rather indifferent, 4 = rather important, 5 = important, 6 = very important.
b. We refer only to salespersons on 'real expense' since in this case there may be a conflict between the preferences of the buyer and those of the payer. Some salespersons did not answer the questions, especially the one concerning the 'consideration for the payer's preferences'. We classified them as 'no answer'.
c. The classification used in this table fits in with the four conflict resolution categories from Thomas (1975).
d. Separate questions for hotels and for restaurants.
e. In each category (domination, integration, negligence, appeasement) the number of subjects is indicated (n_H = number of subjects responding to the questions on hotels; n_R = number of subjects responding to the questions on restaurants).

price he pays to hide the fact that he keeps most of his allowance as a benefit. This bias was limited by asking questions on prices paid before the respondent knew there were also questions about the amount he was reimbursed.

5.3   Data analysis

The goodness of fit tests are one-way analyses of variance (SPSS, ANOVA program), the dependent variable being the price paid for hotels and restaurants.

For the first hypothesis, the analyses of variance are used to test whether or not the effect of the reimbursement system is statistically significant at $p \leq 0.05$ in the case of hotels ($n = 103$) and restaurants ($n = 106$). The three levels of the factor are: 'per diem allowance', 'limited real expense', 'real expense'.

Then, focusing on the non-payer's case ('real expense'), the analyses test the significance of the effect of the buyer–payer relationship on the price paid for hotels ($n = 45$) and restaurants ($n = 47$). The three levels of the relationship to be tested are: appeasement, integration, domination. But it might be questionable to use an analysis of variance when the number of subjects is less than 30 and when the hypothesis of equal variances is rejected at $p \leq 0.05$ as is the case with domination versus appeasement and integration for restaurants. Therefore, a U–Mann Whitney test is appropriate and computed in this case.

6. Results

The first hypothesis is supported by the data. The prices paid for meals and hotels are much higher when the salespersons are on a 'real expense' system than when they are on 'limited real expense' or a 'per diem allowance' system of reimbursement, as Table 3 and Figure 2 show.

The data also strongly support the second hypothesis, that non-payers' behavior depends on the buyer–payer relationship, i.e. on the attitude of salesmen considering their preferences and the payer's perceived preferences. The group of salesmen adopting what was called an attitude of domination spend more than the group whose attitude is one of integration and this group spends more than the one with an attitude of appeasement (Table 4 and Figure 3).

Table 3   Analysis of variance. Effects of the systems of reimbursement on price

Hotels Source	df	SS	MS	F	Restaurants Source	df	SS	MS	F
Explained	2	15796	7898	8.31[a]	Explained	2	2210	1105	4.01[b]
Residual	100	95008	950		Residual	103	28341	275	
Total	102	110804	1086		Total	105	30552	290	

[a] Significant at $p \leq 0.001$.
[b] Significant at $p = 0.02$.

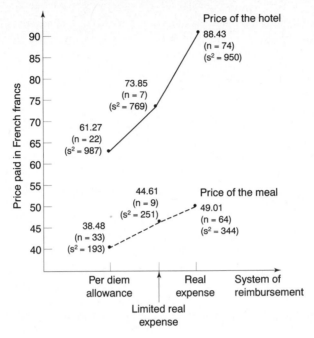

Figure 2　Price of the hotel and average price of the restaurant with respect to the system of reimbursement (number of subjects and variance).

7. Conclusion and implications

The buyer's decisions appear to be related when he is reimbursed, both to the degree to which he takes into consideration the payer's preferences versus his own preferences, and to situational variables such as the system of reimbursement.

Table 4　Analysis of variance. Effects of the buyer-payer relationship on price

Hotels Source	df	SS	MS	F	Restaurants[a] Source	df	SS	MS	F
Explained	2	6338	3269	4.25[b]	Explained	2	1844	922	2.44[c]
Residual	42	31293	745		Residual	44	16602	377	
Total	44	37631	855		Total	46	18447	401	

[a] For restaurants, in the case of domination versus appeasement and integration, the number of subjects is less than 30 and the hypothesis of equal variances is rejected at $p < 0.05$. We must therefore use a U-Mann-Whitney test:
Domination versus Appeasement U = 2.22 significant at $p \leq 0.05$;
Domination versus Integration U = 1.76 significant at $p \leq 0.05$;
Integration versus Appeasement t = 2.24 significant at $p \leq 0.05$.
[b] Significant at $p = 0.02$.
[c] Significant at $p = 0.098$.

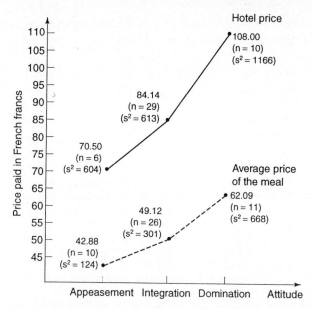

Figure 3   Price of the hotel and average price of the restaurant with respect to the buyer–payer relationship (number of subjects and variance).

As to restaurants and hotels, they could segment their market according to the systems of reimbursement. For example, offering a wide range of products and services (haircut, shopping, movie theater) is good for their business when their customers are refunded on a 'real expense' basis, since all these services will be on the final global bill. Moreover, customers on a 'real expense' system are ready to pay and spend more when they have an attitude of domination, and this may be a function of the size of the firm, of the revenue of the customer, etc. as our preliminary results suggest; this is useful for a marketing segmented approach. These strategies can be applied to various cases. For example airlines can differentiate rates and services according to the type of passenger (on 'expense' or not); they can also reward heavy flyers (usually on expense accounts) with 'free' tickets for personal use.

For employers, the choice of reimbursement system may be important. The 'real expense' system might be more costly than a 'fixed allowance' system. But companies may offer generous expense accounts in lieu of salary to help their salesmen to 'live well'. This can also be good advertising for the company and signify such attributes as financial stability, 'status', care, etc. The 'fixed allowance' system, however, may be an incentive for the traveling businessman since he has the possibility of not spending it all and such a fringe benefit is free of tax.

The conceptual framework that we have developed for the non-paying buyer's behavior can be used and tested in many other situations; for example, in cases where co-insurance (health care, automobiles, etc.) is an important issue (Arrow, 1970). Should insured persons be completely refunded in case of a car crash for which they are partly or totally responsible, or is it an incentive to better driving to have part of the repair costs paid by the insured client? Should people pay a significant part of health care expenditures in order to avoid overconsumption?

The general framework differentiating buyer, consumer and payer can be applied and tested in all situations mentioned in Table 1, taking into account the buyer's attitudes of domination, integration, negligence or appeasement with respect to his other partners (consumer, payer) when they are different persons.

Notes

1. Curry and Menasco use the following definitions of capitulation and compromise: '*Capitulation*: The husband/wife uses his/her spouse's weights for the decision' (p. 197); '*Compromise*: The weights used for the decision are the arithmetic average for the husband and wife' (p. 196).
2. Green and Wind asked their subjects to evaluate restaurant menus and to indicate their preferences under different conditions. In one phase, the subjects had 'to imagine that they were responsible for purchasing their own meal'; in another phase, they had 'to imagine that they had been invited out to dinner by a friend'. Since, in the second situation, the subjects were close to the payer (who was a friend), it could be expected that evaluations and preferences would be rather stable under the two conditions, which was the case.
3. The meals taken with a client or the boss were not considered because they may have special significance (Halvorson and Rudelius, 1977).
4. In their research on restaurant-type menus, Green and Wind (1973) showed that, for a given menu, the utility declined as price increased; the subject did consider price as important when he paid or was invited by a friend.

References

Arrow, K.J. (1970), *Essays in the Theory of Risk Bearing*. London and Amsterdam: North-Holland.

Belk, R.W. (1976), 'It's a thought that counts: A signed diagraph analysis of gift giving', *Journal of Consumer Research* 3, 155–162.

Bon, J. (1978), *Le comportement de l'acheteur non payeur*. Unpublished doctoral dissertation, University of Aix Marseille III, France.

Bon, J. and Pras, B. (1983), 'The buying behavior of the non paying consumer: A role dissociation approach', *Proceedings*, 12th Annual Conference of the European Marketing Academy, Grenoble, 13–15 April, 1983, pp. 65–81.

Cunningham, I.C.M. and Green, R.T. (1974), 'Purchasing roles in the U.S. family, 1955–1973', *Journal of Marketing* 38, 61–64.

Curry, D.J. and Menasco, M.B. (1979), 'Some effects of differing information processing on husband–wife joint decisions', *Journal of Consumer Research* 6, 192–203.

Davis, H.L. (1970), 'Dimension of marital roles in consumer decision making', *Journal of Marketing Research* 7, 168–177.

Davis, H.L. (1971), 'Measurement of husband–wife influence in consumer purchase decisions', *Journal of Marketing Research* 8, 305–312.

Davis, H.L. (1976), 'Decision making within the household', *Journal of Consumer Research* 2, 241–260.

Davis, H.L. and Rigaux, B.P. (1974), 'Perception of marital roles in decision processes', *Journal of Consumer Research* 2, 51–62.

Goffman, E. (1972), *Encounters: Two studies in the sociology of interaction*. Harmondsworth: Penguin.

Green, P.E. and Wind, Y. (1973), 'Consumer evaluation of restaurant menus', in *Multiattribute decisions in marketing: A measurement approach*, 159–185. Hillsdale, IL: The Dryden Press.

Halvorson, P.J. and Rudelius, W. (1977), 'Is there a free lunch?', *Journal of Marketing* **41**, 44–99.

Haymann, P. (1973), 'Qui décide des achats industriels?', *Le Management*, 57–63.

Mauss, M. (1950), 'Essai sur le don', in *Sociologie et anthropologie*. Paris: PUF.

Scott, J.E. and Wright, P. (1976), 'Modeling an organizational buyer's product evaluation strategy: Validity and procedural considerations', *Journal of Marketing Research* **13**, 211–224.

Sheth, N. (1974), 'A theory of family buying decisions', in Jadgish N. Sheth (ed.), *Models of buyer behavior: Conceptual, quantitative and empirical*, 17–33. New York: Harper and Row.

Simon, H.A. (1955), 'A behavioral model of rational choice', *Quarterly Journal of Economics* **1**, 99–118.

Thomas, K. (1975), 'Conflict and conflict management', in Marvin D. Dunette (ed.), *Handbook of Industrial and Organizational Psychology*. Chicago: Rand-McNally.

Webster, F.E. and Wind, Y. (1972), *Organizational Buying Behavior*. Englewood Cliffs, NJ: Prentice Hall.

Wind, Y. (1966), *Industrial Buying Behavior: Source loyalty in the purchase of industrial components*. Unpublished doctoral dissertation, Stanford University.

Wind, Y. (1970), 'Industrial source loyalty', *Journal of Marketing Research* **7**, 450–457.

Personality and consumer research: Another look

● ●

Gordon R. Foxall
Distinguished Research Professor in Consumer Psychology, Cardiff Business School

Ronald E. Goldsmith
Associate Professor of Marketing, Florida State University

Summary

The proposition that individual differences in personality may lead to variations in buying behaviour was responsible during the 1960s for a considerable volume of marketing research. The results were, at best, highly equivocal and devastating critiques brought much of this stream of research to a halt in the 1970s. More recently, researchers have again taken up the study of personality in consumer behaviour, avoiding this time many of the mistakes of the past and utilising the insights of recent developments in personality theory and measurement. The paper discusses the empirical use of a personality-related measure of cognitive style, the Kirton Adaptation–Innovation Inventory, in the context of consumers' innovative purchasing of food brands and products. It concludes that careful investigation of consumer choice by means of appropriate psychometric tests may yet have much to offer marketing research and management.

1. Introduction

The 1950s witnessed a revolutionary transformation in the way managers, especially in marketing and advertising, viewed their relationship with their customers, actual and potential. An increasing imbalance between the excess supply of goods and services over primary demand, coupled with rising levels of education, affluence and exposure to the mass media, transformed the competitive environment, making it far more intensive than that which most businessmen were then accustomed to. How to cope with the constantly changing markets and intensive competitive pressures became a matter of crucial concern. The behavioural sciences seemed to many to present a path out of the confusion of this new business environment. As a result, the theories, techniques and attitudes of the scientist began to infiltrate the boardroom and advertising agency.

From the *Journal of the Market Research Society*, **30**(2), 1988, 111–25.

This interest in behavioural science and 'human engineering' is typified in a series of articles appearing in 1954 in *Business Week* (14, 21 and 28 August) which sought to introduce readers to some of the new concepts and the people who were struggling to bring the insights of social science to bear on a variety of business problems. Whilst not promising sure-fire, fail-safe solutions, the pioneers of this era were able to show that marginal efficiencies in sales and profits could be achieved by spending a portion of the budget along lines suggested by systematic marketing or advertising research directed to answering the fundamental questions about the why and how of consumer purchasing.

One idea in particular which seemed to capture the attention of marketers and advertisers was the concept that personality might play a role in product purchase. This was most likely because, of all the ideas available in the array of psychological theories, personality – the basic notion that individuals differ from one another in systematic and stable patterns of behaviour and attitude – is both intuitively appealing and very familiar to most observers. Scientific concepts and measures of personality developed in order to account for consistencies in behaviour across situations and behavioural scientists employing such ideas confirmed what was anyway a widespread belief that patterns of behaviour were due to internal motives, needs, beliefs and traits. The possibility that markets could be segmented psychographically, on the basis of groupings of consumers who shared determinative personality traits that could be related to purchase and consumption loomed large.

During the 1940s, the clinical psychologist Ernest Dichter had argued that marketers and advertisers were neglecting the psychological aspects of consumption which play a decisive role in product and brand preferences (Dichter, 1949). The 1950s saw a headlong rush into the use of psychological concepts in the design of marketing and advertising strategies. A prime example of this trend is Sidney Levy's classic 1959 *Harvard Business Review* article, 'Symbols for sale' which provided a broad summary of the rapidly spreading ideas that consumers bought products for many reasons other than to obtain the functional benefits they represented. So popular was the notion that marketers could identify and manipulate the psychological precursors of consumer behaviour that Vance Packard's thesis that the unscrupulous use of *The hidden persuaders* (1957) to deprive consumers of their freedom of choice in the marketplace gained widespread currency.

From today's perspective, both positions seem naive and unwarranted. Competitive action soon erodes any benefit conferred by the application of behavioural science and consumers have proved remarkably resistant to the efforts of marketers and advertisers to influence them. Far less real power accrued to the users of the psychoanalytically-derived tools on which so-called motivation research was founded than many feared at the time and, whilst they still play a part (e.g. Heylen), their influence has long since waned.

However, much of the criticism of the psycho-dynamically-based study of consumer choice stems from the fact that these techniques were frequently misapplied in the marketing context. Different researchers could, moreover, disagree on the interpretation of a single consumer in-depth interview, projective test, or whatever and this led to a lack of reliable findings that could be consistently applied. Since only one consumer could be interviewed at a time, the approach was also time-consuming and expensive (Wells and Beard, 1973). In order to enable marketing managers to derive information on target segments, representative samples of large mass markets had to be obtained through survey techniques.

Personality and consumer research

Hard on the heels of the clinically-based motivation researchers came psychologists armed with a different approach to personality assessment, based this time on multiple-item, self-report, pencil-and-paper inventories. Psychologists and market researchers alike sought to apply various standardised personality tests, such as the Edwards Personal Preference Schedule and the Minnesota Multiphasic Personality Inventory to the problems of explaining media use and brand choice in psychological terms.

Typical of the studies conducted at the time was Evans' (1959) use of the Edwards Personal Preference Schedule and Westfall's (1962) use of the Thurstone Temperament Schedule to try to distinguish Ford from Chevrolet owners. Although each of these cars had been given a distinctive 'personality' by advertising, neither study produced evidence to suggest that systematic personality differences accounted for brand choice on the part of consumers. Tucker and Painter (1961) used the Gordon Personal Profile to measure 'ascendancy', 'responsibility', 'emotional stability' and 'sociability', finding statistically significant but weak correlations with purchase or use of some consumer products.

Literally hundreds of such studies were conducted during the 1960s and early 1970s, each seeking to explain differences in product or brand selection by means of scores on standard personality trait measures; few found anything more interesting than those cited above. Those studies that yielded significant findings were limited in generality to a single brand or product class or by the social or economic composition of the study's sample, and as a practical matter the trait measures usually 'explained' less than 10% of the variance in the dependent variables. No other behavioural science concept was so decisively written off by both academic and commercial consumer researchers by the mid-1970s (Foxall, 1980).

Several reasons have been offered to explain the general failure to marry personality psychology with marketing via the trait approach (Kassarjian, 1971; Kassarjian and Sheffet, 1981; Wells and Beard, 1973).

First, the tests have inherently low predictive power. In their clinical application, the tests do not explain large proportions of variance in criterion variables; the consumer researchers had unrealistic expectations of how they would perform in market research.

Secondly, the tests were inappropriate. The personality inventories used to study consumers had been developed by psychologists for clinical and other purposes which usually involved abnormal behaviour, making them inapplicable to the study of consumer choice. While they had been validated for the situations in which they had been developed, the assumption that they would transfer directly to other contexts was naive.

Thirdly, marketing researchers neglected to consider the conditions under which the tests were administered. The subjects in consumer studies, students or otherwise, may have reacted to the clinical tests in ways that confounded the results, acquiescing or giving socially desirable responses that the researchers failed to foresee or control for.

Fourthly, the tests were used indiscriminately. That is, many researchers chose to use conveniently administered and scored tests without carefully developing a theoretical rationale as to why the traits measured by a particular inventory could be expected to relate to consumption.

Fifthly, the reliability (consistency) of the dependent variables was typically low or unknown. Many studies used single instances of behaviour or single-item measures for dependent variables. These are inherently of low or unknown reliability, a factor which places low upper-limits on the size of any relationship with independent variables such as the scores on personality tests.

And, finally, personality tests are general in that they apply to global views of behaviour. Pencil-and-paper personality tests are designed to cover as wide a scope of behaviour as possible, while the consumption behaviour of interest to market researchers is at a very specific level (sometimes individual brands were used). For accurate measurement of the association of two variables, both need to be conceptualised and measured at the same level of generality/specificity.

New approaches

As has been noted, the cumulative effect of much of the early research on the relationship between personality and consumption, especially in the wake of Kassarjian's (1971; Kassarjian and Sheffet, 1981) damaging critique, was to dampen enthusiasm for this area of study among both managers and academic researchers (Arndt, 1986). Recent studies, however, seeking to avoid past mistakes and to benefit from current theory development have begun to reintroduce personality research into consumer behaviour.

The newer studies have used more specific measures of more precisely defined personality traits and types which are theoretically relevant to economic behaviour rather than relying on post hoc explanations to justify findings from shotgun-type, general scales (e.g. Allsopp, 1986a). More stress is being placed on verifying the reliability and validity of both independent and dependent variables. Where possible, researchers seek to use multiple measures of behaviour rather than single indicators or one-off instances of behaviour to enhance dependent variable reliability through aggregation (Epstein, 1986). The personality scales being used are less confined to clinical applications and more relevant to the analysis of everyday behaviours including economic actions and choices. Consumer researchers have more modest expectations of the effects that personality factors will have on consumer choice, and they see personality traits and types as offering only partial explanations interacting with social, cultural and economic moderator variables to yield distinctive patterns of buying behaviour (Punj and Stewart, 1983).

Several successful examples of recent studies of personality and consumer choice deserve mention. Using the well-established, theoretically-grounded and widely-validated measures of second-order personality types developed by Eysenck (Eysenck and Eysenck, 1969, 1975), Allsopp (1986b) found significant positive correlations of scores on measures of extraversion, emotionalism, tough-mindedness and impulsiveness with alcoholic beverage consumption among 18–21-year-old males. On the basis of patterns of personality test responses (high scorers on three or four of the scales had consumption levels several times greater than high scorers on none), he was able to suggest marketing strategies for pubs based on psychographic segmentation.

Becherer and Richard (1978) and Snyder and DeBono (1985) have shown that individual differences in self-monitoring, the tendency to observe and control expressive behaviour and self-presentation to match social surroundings, may moderate the relationship between certain personality traits and consumption behaviours and influence individual reception of advertisements. Goldsmith (1987) suggests that high self-monitoring may be linked to willingness to try innovations. Other studies indicate that venturesomeness and novelty-seeking may explain individual differences in learning about the trial of new products (McAlister and Pessemier, 1982; Raju, 1980).

Foxall (1988) and Goldsmith (1983) both offer evidence from independent studies that individual differences in problem-solving and decision-making of a global nature find expression in variations in the purchases of new brands and products which are relevant to the establishment of segmentation criteria and the pre-launch development of innovations. In these studies, scores on the Kirton Adaptation-Innovation Inventory (Kirton, 1976), a self-report measure of individual preferences for styles of intellectual processing are related to awareness and purchase of new grocery items. Studies such as these are giving substance to the hope that careful use of appropriate tests, the examination of more sophisticated hypotheses, and sophisticated analysis would result in better explanations and applicable findings. The following discussion describes an exemplar of the new approach.

Personality and innovative consumer choice

Early identification of consumer innovators is of strategic importance in new product development since it assists in the process of tailoring each element of the marketing mix to the requirements and probable behaviours of those buyers who initiate markets and without whom the social comparison that leads to diffusion would often not occur. New brands and products which do not appeal to this group are unlikely to find a mass market and it has been argued that innovative buyers should be represented disproportionately in concept and product testing (Midgley, 1977). The social and economic characteristics of innovators are known in general terms but a means of psychometric assessment which allowed an early, quick, accurate, sensitive and inexpensive identification would be more valuable since it could be employed in the initial stages of new product development prior to major invest-ment in plant and marketing. In view of the history of personality research in marketing, a measure was sought which had been validated over a wide range of behaviours and situa-tions and which, in particular, had relevance to economic problem solving and decision-making.

The KAI is a measure of cognitive style which possesses attractive psychometric proper-ties and which has been shown to have a high degree of validity in the sphere of economic behaviour, particularly in organisational contexts (Kirton, 1987). In addition, KAI scores correlate with numerous measures of personality traits whose validity and reliability are well established. The adaptation-innovation theory from which the test derives posits that individuals consistently display one or other of two styles of problem-solving and decision-making. At one pole of this continuum, the (extreme) Adaptor confines his or her problem-solving to the frame of reference within which the problem has arisen. Adaptors aim to produce better ways of accomplishing familiar tasks and, in organisational and other social milieux, their solutions can usually be implemented without disrupting established working patterns or networks of interaction. The (extreme) Innovator, by contrast, is far less likely to seek solutions that can be readily incorporated within existing systems. His or her underlying approach to problem-solving is much more likely to result in a complete re-evaluation of the entire frame of reference within which the problem has arisen and, in seeking solutions, the Innovator may redefine not only the problem but the context. As a result, Innovators produce different ways of meeting needs and solving problems. (In order to prevent confusion with consumer innovators, i.e. the first buyers of a new brand or product, Adaptors and Innovators are identified in this paper with capital initial letters.)

The personality traits associated with these styles of information processing have been confirmed by research conducted by some twenty investigators in eight countries, using two dozen or more psychological tests to produce over sixty correlations. Adaptors have been shown to be more controlled, systematic, consistent, steady, reliable, prudent, sensitive, realistic, efficient and orderly than Innovators. Innovators tend to be more extravert, less dogmatic, more tolerant of ambiguity, radical, flexible, assertive, expedient, undisciplined and sensation-seeking than Adaptors (Kirton, 1987; Goldsmith, 1984). In summary, 'A consistent picture emerges of the intuitive-innovator who pays little attention to routine details, welcomes the new and different, and generates many novel ideas, contrasted with the equally-creative sensing-adaptor, who watches the details, works routinely and steadily, preferring standard solutions to problems' (Goldsmith, 1985, p. 103).

The KAI was administered to two quota samples of female supermarket shoppers: members of the first sample had purchased at least one of thirteen innovative brands of food products launched within three to four months of the research; all but four members of the second had purchased at least one of twenty-six food products recently introduced by supermarkets and promoted as conducive to 'healthy eating'. (Research method and findings are only summarised here; for additional details, see Foxall and Haskins, 1986, 1987.) The expectation that guided the research was that these consumer innovators would tend to prefer Innovative approaches to problem-solving and decision-making: the diffusion literature suggests that relative to later adopters, consumer innovators are less dogmatic, more able to cope with abstractions, ambiguity and uncertainty, less fatalistic (and thus presumably more flexible, self-controlled and unsubjugated) and high in achievement motivation and aspiration (Rogers, 1983). Furthermore, many marketing studies have indicated (albeit on the basis of numerous small but positive correlations between personality measures and consumers' innovative choices) that consumer innovators are risk-takers, impulsive, active, dominant, inner-directed and self-reliant (Midgley, 1977; Foxall, 1984).

In view of this, the results of the investigations are surprising. There is some tendency for the consumer innovators in both samples to be Innovative: the KAI means of respondents in both cases show them to be significantly more Innovative than members of the female general population. However, whilst both samples contained more Innovators than Adaptors, both cognitive styles were substantially represented in each instance: both samples contained Adaptors and Innovators in the ratio of approximately 40:60, indicating that both cognitive styles and their accompanying personality traits are to be found among the earliest buyers of new brands and products. The small, positive correlations typical of earlier research are, therefore, explicable in that investigators appear to have been concerned with only one set of personality traits, those of Innovators, and have ignored the role of Adaptive consumer innovators.

Also contrary to the expectations that guided the planning of the research, Innovators were not responsible for purchasing a larger volume of new brands or products than Adaptors. In both cases, whilst the mean KAI score of purchasers of the fewest innovations was Adaptive, purchasers of intermediate numbers of brands or products were (in terms of mean KAI score) distinctly Innovative. However, purchasers of the largest volumes of brands or products were not, as anticipated, even more Innovative: they were clearly Adaptive. Whilst this is contrary to the weak evidence provided by both diffusion and marketing studies, it is quite readily explicable in terms of adaption-innovation theory. It is well known that many consumer innovators exhibit little or no loyalty, trying novel brands and products frequently but moving on to other innovations and abandoning at least for the time being, the items that initially attracted them (e.g. Pymont *et al.*, 1988). Consumer innovators whose cognitive style is predominantly Innovative conform to this stereotype by purchasing a reasonable but intermediate number of innovations, while purchasers of just a few, if any, innovations are predictably unadventurous, sound, steady Adaptors. However, the theory proposes that those individuals who decide firmly upon a different lifestyle (such as one that includes a 'healthy' diet) are more likely to be Adaptors, who will thoroughly, patiently and assiduously target and seek out not a few but as many relevant products as possible (Kirton, 1987, and personal communication).

A practically relevant qualitative difference between purchasers of contrasting cognitive styles also emerged from the research. Three categories of brands/products emerged from each of the investigations: first, a small number of innovations for each of which purchasers' mean KAI scores were significantly more Innovative than non-purchasers'; secondly, a larger group in which purchasers' mean scores were significantly more Adaptive than non-purchasers'; and, thirdly, another relatively large group for which purchasers' means were more Innovative than those of non-purchasers', though the difference did not reach the conventional level of statistical significance. An *ad hoc* qualitative evaluation of the brands by an independent panel of consumers suggested that the first of these groups might be the more discontinuous of the innovations surveyed, i.e. those most disruptive of established patterns of consumption, whilst the second 'group were the more continuous, and third 'dynamically-continuous' (Robertson, 1967). Food innovations rarely exhibit large discontinuities, however (as consumer durables and some fashion items often do) and this suggestion requires replicative studies to be undertaken before it can be strongly asserted. Nevertheless, the differences among brands and among products are indicative of an opportunity to segment markets for innovations, either directly or as part of a broader approach to lifestyle targeting.

Theoretical implications of this research have been rehearsed elsewhere (Foxall, 1988) and only the potentially managerially-relevant aspects will be discussed here. Data analysis for each investigation revealed small, non-significant correlations between Innovativeness (as measured by the KAI) and the volume of innovative purchasing reported by respondents and this is entirely in line with the many previous, disappointing studies of personality in marketing. Yet careful further analysis of the data, based on expectations of relatively complex interactions between consumers' personalities and brand/product continuity/discontinuity, indicate more subtle relationships and suggest that the adaptive-innovative dimension of cognitive style and the personality traits associated with it can provide a basis for market segmentation based on both the quantity and quality of innovations purchased. It is particularly interesting that cognitive decision processes can be detected so obviously in innovative consumers of food items, a sphere of purchasing which is often assumed to entail low involvement (Lastovicka and Bonfield, 1982).

Differences between purchasers of different qualitatively defined groups of innovations were greater in the case of the brands investigated (where Innovators were disproportionately responsible for buying apparently discontinuous items), whereas quantitative differences, reflecting the number of innovations purchased, were more obvious for products (where Adaptors were disproportionately responsible for purchasing the largest quantities). This is consistent with the amount of brand differentiation produced by manufacturers of the innovative brands (all of which bore prominent trade names). Two substantial possibilities emerge. First, the opportunity to identify consumer innovators, particularly for essentially discontinuous brands and products, offers a means of overcoming problems of product design and customer acceptance. And, secondly, there is the possibility of employing the adaptor-innovator continuum in lifestyle segmentation and market targeting. Both illustrate the relevance of personality testing to consumer research.

Summary and conclusions

Early studies of personality and consumer behaviour were characterised by an atheoretical clinical orientation dominated by subjectivity and eccentricity in interpretation. Later trait-based studies were often naive in their assumption that so broad a measure of an individual as personality would be consistently related to so narrow a behavioural criterion as brand or even product choice. In more recent years, several researchers have attempted to revive the analysis of consumer choice in terms of personality variables by correcting mistakes of the past and by using newer theories of personality. Theory-grounded typologies of the higher-order factors which organise series of traits into dominant personality or cognitive styles appear more successful in making sense of consumer decision-making than the simple, single-trait studies pursued in the 1960s. Judicious use of personality theory and measures is also capable of showing why earlier research failed to find managerially useful associations, e.g. in the search for the innovative consumer.

References

Allsopp, J.F. (1986a), 'Personality as a determinant of beer and cider consumption among young men', *Personality and Individual Differences*, 7, 341–347.

Allsopp, J.F. (1986b), 'The distribution of on-licence beer and cider consumption and its personality determinants among young men', *European Journal of Marketing*, 20(3), 44–62.

Arndt, J. (1986), 'Paradigms in consumer research: a review of perspectives and approaches', *European Journal of Marketing*, 20(8), 23–40.

Becherer, R.C. and Richard, L.M. (1978), 'Self-monitoring as a moderating variable in consumer behaviour', *Journal of Consumer Research*, 5, December, 159–162.

Dichter, E. (1949), 'A psychological view of advertising effectiveness', *Journal of Marketing*, 14, July, 61–66.

Epstein, S. (1986), 'Does aggregation produce spuriously high estimates of behaviour stability?', *Journal of Personality and Social Psychology*, 50, 1119–1210.

Evans, F.B. (1959), 'Psychological and objective factors in the prediction of brand choice', *Journal of Business*, **32**, October, 340–369.

Eysenck, H.J. and Eysenck, S.B.G. (1969), *Personality Structure and Measurement*. London: Routledge and Kegan Paul.

Eysenck, H.J. and Eysenck, S.B.G. (1975), *Manual of the Eysenck Personality Questionnaire*. London: Hodder and Stoughton.

Foxall, G.R. (1980), *Consumer Behaviour: A Practical Guide*. London: Croom Helm; New York: Wiley.

Foxall, G.R. (1984), *Corporate Innovation: Marketing and Strategy*. London: Croom Helm; New York: St Martin's Press.

Foxall, G.R. (1988), 'Consumer innovativeness: novelty-seeking, creativity and cognitive style', in *Research in Consumer Behaviour*, E.C. Hirschmann (Ed), 3. Greenwich, CT: JAI Press.

Foxall, G.R. and Haskins, C.G. (1986), 'Cognitive style and consumer innovativeness: an empirical test of Kirton's adaptation-innovation theory in the context of food purchasing', *European Journal of Marketing*, **20**(3), 63–80.

Foxall, G.R. and Haskins, C.G. (1987), 'Cognitive style and discontinuous consumption', *Food Marketing*, **3**(2), 19–32.

Goldsmith, R.E. (1983), 'Dimensions of consumer innovativeness: an empirical study of open processing', PhD dissertation, University of Alabama.

Goldsmith, R.E. (1984), 'Personality characteristics associated with adaption-innovation', *Journal of Psychology*, **117**, 159–165.

Goldsmith, R.E. (1985), 'Personality and adaptive-innovative problem solving', *Journal of Social Behavior and Personality*, **1**, 95–106.

Goldsmith, R.E. (1987), 'Self-monitoring and innovativeness', *Psychological Reports*, **60**, 1017–1018.

Heylen, P. (nd), *Libido als drijfveer van het konsumentengedrag*. Antwerp: Instituut voor Marketing-Diagnostiek.

Kassarjian, H.H. (1971), 'Personality and consumer behaviour: a review', *Journal of Marketing Research*, **8**, November, 409–418.

Kassarjian, H.H. and Sheffet, M.J. (1981), 'Personality and consumer behaviour: an update', in *Perspectives in Consumer Behavior*, H.H. Kassarjian and T.S. Robertson (eds). Glenview, IL: Scott Foresman, pp. 160–180.

Kirton, M.J. (1976), 'Adaptors and innovators: a description and measure', *Journal of Applied Psychology*, **61**, 622–629.

Kirton, M.J. (1987), *KAI Manual* (2nd edn). Hatfield: Occupational Research Centre.

Lastovicka, J.L. and Bonfield, E.H. (1982), 'Do consumers have brand attitudes?', *Journal of Economic Psychology*, **2**, 57–75.

Levy, S.J. (1959), 'Symbols for sale', *Harvard Business Review*, **37**(3), 117–124.

McAlister, L. and Pessemier, E. (1982), 'Variety seeking behavior: an interdisciplinary review', *Journal of Consumer Research*, **9**, December, 311–322.

Midgley, D.F. (1977), *Innovation and New Product Marketing*. London: Croom Helm.

Packard, V. (1957), *The Hidden Persuaders*. New York: David McKay.

Punj, G.N. and Stewart, D.W. (1983), 'An interaction framework of consumer decision making', *Journal of Consumer Research*, **10**, September, 181–196.

Pymont, B.C., Morgan, R.P. and Bond, J.R. (1988), 'The application of micro-modelling to predict total market mix potential', *Journal of Marketing Management*, **3**(3), 278–295.

Raju, P.S. (1980), 'Optimum stimulation level: its relationship to personality, demographics, and exploratory behavior', *Journal of Consumer Research*, **7**, December, 272–282.

Robertson, T.S. (1967), 'The process of innovation and the diffusion of innovation', *Journal of Marketing* **31**, January, 14–19.

Rogers, E.M. (1983), *Diffusion of Innovations* (3rd edn). New York: The Free Press.

Snyder, M. and DeBono, K.G. (1985), 'Appeals to image and claims quality: understanding the psychology of advertising', *Journal of Personality and Social Psychology*, **49**(3), 586–597.

Tucker, W.T. and Painter, J. (1961), 'Personality and product use', *Journal of Applied Psychology*, **45**, October, 325–329.

Wells, W.D. and Beard, A.D. (1973), 'Personality and consumer behavior', in *Consumer Behavior: Theoretical Sources*, S. Ward and T.S. Robertson (eds). Englewood Cliffs, NJ: Prentice-Hall, pp. 141–199.

Westfall, R. (1962), 'Psychological factors predicting product choice', *Journal of Marketing*, **26**, April, 34–40.

For the development of measures of emotion in marketing: Summary of prerequisites

● ●

Christian Derbaix and Michelle T. Pham
Marketing Department, Facultés Universitaires Catholiques de Mons, Belgium

Summary

This article is organized around three themes, beginning with the necessity of studying emotional reactions in marketing, and concluding with a demonstration of the peculiarities of their measurement.

It begins by pointing out that an affective dimension is present in nearly every example of consumer behavior. Next, using a more conceptual approach, the authors stress the need to define and characterize emotional reactions, and propose a marketing-oriented typology. The third and final point concerns the need for a multi-method approach in measuring the various dimensions of emotional reactions. The authors conclude by recommending the use of the study of surprise as a starting point.

> The affect system is . . . the primary motivational system because without its amplification, nothing else matters, and with its amplification, anything else *can* matter.
> It thus combines urgency and generality. It lends its power to memory, to perception, to thought and to action no less than to the drives.
>
> *(Silvan Tomkins, 1984, p. 164)*

I. The affective approach and consumer behavior

Contemporary psychology is basically detached from the affect. Words such as affective, emotion or feeling rarely appear in important studies in this discipline, which is essentially cognitive.

From *Recherche et Applications en Marketing*, 4(4), 1989, 71–87.

Ever since motivational research was abandoned by academics studying consumer behavior, relatively little quantitative empirical work has examined the affective facets of consumer experience.

At least three factors explain this long-term neglect:

1. The fact that emotion was often studied in the context of mental illness or behavioral problems apparently dampened the enthusiasm of marketing researchers more concerned with positive aspects of emotion.
2. The non-verbal tools currently available for the study of emotional reactions can 'detect' the 'intensity' dimension, sometimes the 'direction', but never the 'content' of these reactions.
3. The 'seriousness' and apparent 'thoroughness' of the cognitive approach, fashionable in the 1960s and especially the 1970s.

Following this long dry spell, and beginning with Zajonc's controversial article (1980), a new school of consumer behavior analysis has taken form, which considers that understanding the consumer's emotions and feelings is as important as understanding his or her thoughts (Edell and Burke, 1987).

It should be recalled that the 1970s were dominated by what has been called the *cognitive approach* to consumer behavior. In tracing the consumer's reasoning and in dissecting the decision process, this approach no doubt focused too strongly on perception, memorization, comprehension, reasoning, and considered decision-making, at the expense of the affective dimension, that is, of feelings and emotions.

As a reminder, the three essential steps, from the cognitive perspective, of consumer behavior are (Olshavsky and Granbois, 1979):

1. In general, the consumer is faced with several options (brands, models . . .) which could satisfy her [or his] needs/desires. The existence of multiple options forces the consumer to carry out a decision-making process leading to the selection of a single option.
2. Evaluation criteria on which [she or] he informs [her or] himself will facilitate the choice of one brand/option over the others.
3. This option/brand will be chosen through an evaluation procedure characterized by a decision rule (either the best-choice rule, in which the brand to which the evaluation procedure assigns the highest grade is chosen, or the first-choice rule, in which the first brand to obtain a predetermined grade is chosen).

This approach assumes that people are active, conscious of all their actions, that they establish goals, seek information, deliberate on the basis of this information, and choose.

Research on persuasive communications carried out over thirty years ago at Yale under the direction of C. Hovland, the model of the hierarchy of effects (particularly in its 'learning' version), McGuire's (1974) information processing model, which states explicitly that 'the consumer solves problems', have all contributed to the emergence of this highly cognitive approach, centered on the consumer's information processing behavior.

It was, however, Fishbein and Ajzen's (1975) model of attitude forming and modification, and perhaps even more the linear compensatory model stemming from Fishbein and Rosenberg's work, which popularized this approach involving voluntaristic models of the 'expectation-value' type, described and criticized recently in this same periodical (Derbaix, 1987).

Preference ('the classic affective measure in marketing') is presented in this type of approach as resulting from considerable conscious cognitive activity. Thus, the consumer, who has access to information (in the form of grades, for example) regarding the characteristics he sees as pertinent, combines this information through a sort of mental gymnastics in order to assign a grade to each brand; the one receiving the highest grade will have the consumer's preference. Entire publications (culminating with that of Bettman, 1979) have been dedicated to this cognitive approach, which also affected the chronology of data collection in market studies. Thus, these studies traditionally begin with questions about notoriety, go on to preferential classifications, the importance of the selection criteria, and lastly the evaluation of the brands according to the criteria, and in this way provide the perfect raw material for application of these models.

Among the main criticisms of this approach, aside from the absence of truly affective components, are the following:

1. In some cases, the direction of causality between attitude (which takes the form of preference in the cognitive approach described above) and cognition (beliefs in the form of grades) can be reversed. Thus an impression or general reaction can be formed first, which will then influence the consumer's evaluation of various dimensions through a halo affect. The halo effect implies that this general impression 'rubs off' onto the specific evaluations of each dimension. Concretely, this leads to the following scenario: 'What a fabulous car!' (first general affective reaction), only after which the evaluation of various characteristics is carried out (outstanding comfort, well-priced, exceptional traction, mileage for this type of car is fairly good . . .). Holbrook (1986) has demonstrated that the paradigm used in the cognitive approach is far from able to account for all the paths of reasoning which may be carried out by the consumer.

2. In studying attitude, researchers (Bagozzi, 1978; Bagozzi et al., 1979; Ray and Batra, 1983) have recently brought two components to the fore:
   – a utilitarian, voluntary component which can be broken down into attributes. This utilitarian component seems to be rooted in the instrumental value of the product, measured according to its various attributes. It is the component described by the cognitive approach;
   – a more involuntary component, which cannot be broken down into these same attributes and which is linked to an affective, hedonistic reaction reflecting a feeling of attraction or repulsion vis-à-vis the considered option.

Certain cognitivists did, none the less, realize that their information processing models did not fit all types of behavior, and therefore proposed a model labeled *emotional attachment* (Wright, 1975). This variant is applicable in cases where people express only a general evaluation, giving no other reasons for their choice than 'I like it', 'It's not bad' . . ., that is, vague or even tautological commentaries. No cognitive antecedents in the form of evaluation of the various pertinent criteria can be found. Traditionally, *emotional attachment* has usually been associated with situations in which the consumer is not prepared to make an effort (minimal investment situations) or did so long ago and has forgotten all but an overall impression. The concept of emotional attachment has also been referred to when analyzing studies involving children, who often have circular and redundant responses: 'why do you like this?', 'because I like it', 'yes, but why?', 'because it's something I like' . . .

Katz (1968) stated in this context that the affect is a residue of cognition, but that, in certain cases, it is not possible to find the cognitive antecedents. Those who subscribe to the views of Zajonc and Markus (1982) go further, and believe that in certain circumstances, emotions may be independent of cognition and/or dominate it considerably.

It is clear that, in order to explain consumer behavior, the affective processes deserve *specific study*, in terms of their *essential complementary role* (Batra, 1986) in relation to cognitive processes.

Before moving on, two points should be highlighted:

(a) The fact that no selection process exists in certain cases (as shown by Kassarjian, 1982, for example), does not automatically imply that emotions, rather than cognitive thought, directed the acquisition or the choice of certain goods. For example, in hospitals, retirement homes, prisons . . ., discretionary behavior cannot often find expression.

   In addition, an individual may be a consumer-buyer without being the payer, and thus be obligated, for example, to go to a given restaurant.

(b) *Impulsive* purchases have long attracted the attention of researchers (West, 1951; Stern, 1962). These purchases are by definition more spontaneous, less controlled, more emotional than rational, and are almost always linked to emotional comments ('isn't this crazy?', 'I feel guilty', 'it's wrong').

   Rook (1987) states that, when talking about their impulsive purchases, the majority of respondents say these purchases make them 'happy', 'lighthearted' . . ., or else they express regret, post-buying stress, guilt. While impulsive behavior can be considered a *prototype* of *emotional* behavior, set off by the affective attraction of situational factors, our goal here is to **stress** that the affective component is present in many other types of behavior.

This affective component may have multiple origins, such as: affective conditioning by advertising, repeated exposure to commercial stimuli, important non-utilitarian effects of consumption and product use (Zajonc and Wilson, 1974; Holbrook and Hirschman, 1982). It could be viewed in terms of 'emotional benefits' which help in deciding between different options of equal instrumental (or functional) value (Havlena and Holbrook, 1986).

II. Proposal for a typology of affective reaction

The need for progress in the study of the affect having been thus demonstrated, the first step is no doubt to specify the type of affect in question.

Currently, the terms 'affect' and emotion are often used interchangeably in the literature. Thus, when we proceed to describe below the various theories of 'emotion', this term is understood in its broadest sense. In a later section, however, we will distinguish between different types of affective states, of which emotion – understood here in a limited sense – is one subcategory.

1. The theories of emotion

There are nearly as many classifications of emotions as there are theoretical perspectives on them. Thus, Kemper (1987) distinguishes seven approaches to the study of emotions:

- *evolutionary* approaches based on the adaptive function of emotions (Plutchik [1980]);
- *neural* approaches which attribute primary emotions to certain properties of neural circuits (Tomkins, 1962);
- *psychoanalytic* approaches based especially on concepts elaborated by Freud (ego, libido, anxiety, etc.) (Brenner, 1980);
- *autonomic* approaches which relate emotions to various organic processes following activation of the peripheral nervous system (Fromme and O'Brien, 1982);
- approaches based on the *facial expressions* of emotional states (Ekman, 1973);
- *empirical* classifications aimed at isolating various emotions from subjective verbal reports (Fehr and Russell, 1984);
- and approaches centered on babies' and children's *development* of emotions (Emde, 1980).

Holbrook (1986) suggests classifying typologies of emotion according to two dimensions underpinning their construction (Table 1). The first distinguishes *conceptual* from *empirical* typologies, the second contrasts *systematic* typologies with those which are not. However, as noted by Strongman (1978), it is difficult to class theories of emotion according to their approach (cognitive, physiological, behaviorist, etc.), because some are unclear and thus hard to categorize, and others accord equal importance to several facets of the subject.

There is none the less a consensus around the fact that emotion is a multidimensional construct whose principal dimensions are intensity, polarity (direction) and content. Emotion in addition has various components, each necessitating appropriate measurement methods. One component is neurophysiological and biochemical, another is expressive, and another subjective and 'experiential' (Izard, 1979). Buck (1984) proposed that these components be called Emotion I, II and III, respectively.

Emotion I concerns mechanisms for homeostatic adaptation and maintenance via the endocrine system and the autonomic nervous system. Emotion II concerns the spontaneous expression of an emotional state, and may be measured by the observation and analysis of facial or vocal expressions and body movements. Emotion III concerns the direct subjective

Table 1 Classification of typologies of emotion		
	Conceptual	**Empirical**
Non-systematic	Enumeration (Descartes, Spinoza)	Data reduction (Nowlis, 1970; Mehrabian and Russell, 1974)
Systematic	Logical derivation (Arnold, 1960; de Rivera, 1977)	Theoretical development and testing (Plutchik, 1980)

experience of the state of certain neurochemical systems. It may be observed through verbal reports.

2. Proposal for a typology of affective reactions

As noted by Simon (1982), the 'affect' is an imprecise word used in often related but rarely synonymous manners. It is a generic term used to designate emotions, moods, feelings, drives (Batra and Ray, 1986), attitudes, preferences and evaluations (Pieters and Van Raaij, 1988).

Distinguishing between these different types of 'affect' (we will adopt the term 'affective reaction' below) is often confusing in English language literature, as shown in the following excerpt:

> moods are a subcategory of feeling states. The phrase 'feeling state' will be used to refer to an affective state that is general and pervasive . . . These states can be contrasted with feelings directed towards specific objects, e.g., the affective component of brand attitude. (Gardner, 1985, p. 282)

Therefore, we propose what we consider to be a *systematic* and *conceptual* typology, as understood by Holbrook, that is, one which presents all the major dimensions underlying affective reactions. In Table 2, seven types of affective reactions are distinguished: shock emotion (the most 'affective' of reactions), feeling, mood, temperament, preference, attitude and appreciation (the most 'cognitive' of these reactions) (see Table 2).

The following paragraphs elaborate on each line of the table.

One of the characteristics which helps in distinguishing different types of affective reactions is the *degree of specificity of the stimulus* which provokes it, *or of the target* at which it is directed. Pieters and Van Raaij (1988) point out that certain affective reactions, such as preference, attitude and appreciation, refer to evaluations of objects, ideas, behaviors or persons. Thus, they are directed at a specific target. Other reactions, such as emotion, feelings, moods and temperament, are more strongly linked to the person. Emotion and feelings are provoked by a specific stimulus, even if the stimulus is not always identified (Zajonc, 1980). Mood and temperament, on the other hand, are neither directed at a *specific* target nor provoked by a *specific* stimulus (Pieters and Van Raaij, 1988).

Affective reactions may also be distinguished according to their *intensity*. Thus, emotions differ from feelings by their extreme, even explosive character (Pradines, 1958). They are accompanied by a high degree of endocrine and autonomic system reaction. Preference intensity is generally average, but dependent on the targets at which the preference is directed (preferring one child over another is very different from preferring a given brand of consumer product).

The *duration* of an affective reaction is also a discriminating feature. Passion, which is a feeling, is close to emotion in intensity, but differs in that it is longer-lasting than a shock-emotion. Some emotions such as surprise and disgust are so brief that they have been qualified as reflexes (Kemper, 1987). In addition, it is the permanence (duration) and stability of moods which distinguish them from temperaments (Gardner, 1985).

Directly correlated to the intensity of affective reactions is another characteristic, the *frequency of the accompanying somatic (and autonomic) experiences*. Appreciation of

Table 2 Proposal for a typology of affective reactions

Affect types Characteristics	Emotion (shock)	Feeling	Mood	Temperament	Preference	Attitude	Appreciation
Examples	Surprise Fear	Pride Jealousy	Melancholy Joy	Optimism Pessimism	Stimulus classification	Predispositions	Candidate evaluation
Target or Stimulus	Specific stimulus	Specific stimulus	Non-specific target and stimulus	Non-specific target and stimulus	Specific target	Specific target	Specific target
Somatic (and Autonomic) Intensity	Strong	Average	Weak to average	Weak to average	Average (function of target)	Weak	Weak
Duration	Very brief	Average	Average	Long	Average	Average	Brief
Frequency of Somatic (and Autonomic) Experiences	Always	Sometimes to often	Sometimes to often	Often	Sometimes	Rarely	Rarely
Frequency of Somatic Expression	Often	Function of social constraints	Function of social constraints	Often	Sometimes	Rarely	Rarely
Desire to Control Expression (Deception)	May be strong, especially if the affective states are negative	May be strong, whether feelings are positive or negative	May be strong, especially if the affective states are negative	Fairly weak	May be strong, depending on targets	May be strong	May be strong

Table 2 (continued)

Affect types Characteristics	Emotion (shock)	Feeling	Mood	Temperament	Preference	Attitude	Appreciation
Possibility (Ease) of Expression Control (Deception)	Weak	Fairly weak due to duration[a] and intensity	Fairly weak due to duration[a]	Fairly weak due to duration[a]	May be weak if the targets are important and/ or the situations permanent	High	High
Probability of Subjective Elementary Experience	High	Fairly high	Low	Average	High (consciousness)	Average	High (consciousness)
Importance of Cognitive Antecedents	Very weak	Strong	Average	Average	Weak to average	Strong	Very strong
Subsequent Cognitive Processes	Sometimes to often	Often	Often[b] (in the form of reinforcement and justification)	Often[b]	Often	Considerable in cases of cognitive dissonance	Often (and in correlation with the cognitive antecedents)

a. The more long-lasting the affective reaction, the more difficult it is to permanently control its expression.
b. Information processing can be modified. Halo effects may be expected in the form of positive contamination of attributional dimensions by optimists and negative contamination of dimensions by pessimists.

individuals and objects (as well as attitudes held towards them) is rarely accompanied by such experiences. However, emotion is always linked to somatic (and autonomic) experiences.

Somatic experiences are not, however, necessarily accompanied by *somatic expression* (facial or body language). There is a fundamental difference between experiencing and *expressing* an affective state. It is possible to have one feeling (being disappointed by a gift) while showing another (simulating pleasure at receiving it). The experience of an affective state may differ according to its expression, in terms of its magnitude (restraining one's happiness, limiting the expression of a bad mood), as well as its nature (pretending indifference to someone). Somatic expressions of mood and feelings, and their frequency, are thus influenced by social pressure. According to Buck (1984), this pressure is exercised through *symbolic rules of conduct*, which can be defined as the cultural rules or expectations about the expression of affective states. Buck uses the term 'deception' to designate the voluntary modification of affective expression due to rules of conduct.[1]

The *desire and possibility to control* expression also differs according to the type of affective reaction. A person may desire to control his or her expression of surprise or fear, for example, but given that these are shock emotions, the possibility of doing so is limited. This can be explained by the fact that the brevity of this type of affective reaction precludes the cognitive processes necessary for deception. At the opposite end of the continuum, the desire and possibility to control the expression of an appreciation are much greater.

The probability of *elementary subjective experience*, i.e. of an individual being conscious of his affective state, is generally considered to be high for shock emotions (Gardner, 1985), as well as for preferences and appreciations. Often, however, a subject may need the intervention of a third party to become aware of an attitude, a temperament, or *above all* a mood.

Lastly, concerning *previous cognitive processes*, the analyses developed by Zajonc (for emotion and preference), by Fishbein and Ajzen (for attitudes and appreciations), and by Pieters and Van Raaij (for moods), as well as certain standard definitions (cf. Thines and Lempereur, 1984), justify the modalities shown in line 10 of Table 2.

The frequency of subsequent cognitive processes (shown in the last line of the table) is generally high, given the rationalizations, justifications and research for psychological balance which characterize most adult consumers.

III. Specificities of affect measurement

To progress in perfecting tools for measuring affective reactions, four aspects should be examined:

1. their intensity;
2. their direction;
3. their content, that is, the three dimensions mentioned above; as well as
4. the individual's consciousness of them.

No single method is currently able adequately to cover these four aspects. For example, in terms of psychobiological measurements aimed at recording physiological manifestations (heart rate, pupil dilation, the skin's electrical conductance), the only certainty is that we can measure the intensity of these reactions, but not their content, and only rarely their direction (Cacioppo *et al.*, 1986).

Thus, combining several methods seems the best way to progress. One could, in this manner, combine an electrodermic response (showing intensity) with a record of facial (or body) expressions showing direction and occasionally content. Electrodermic response would show the *internal aspect* of the affective reaction, while the facial and/or body expression (which Buck calls 'spontaneous emotional communication') would show the *external aspect*. Prideaux (1920) declared over sixty years ago that 'at the most, emotional signs are visible, and at the least we can record a response with the galvanometer'.

In this context, it should be noted in relation to what was mentioned above in section II, that deception increases with age and that a child is thus more 'revealing' (on the exterior) than an adult. Moreover, children can be expected to exhibit a greater magnitude in the expression of emotion – in terms of the external, but sometimes also the 'internal' aspects; more spontaneous and less 'reserved', they are more likely to give themselves over to emotions.

The preceding points tend to support the need for a *multimethod approach*, which could be developed from three classic methods, corresponding to the three components of affective reactions:

(a) *Psychobiological measurements* (heart rate, blood pressure, muscle reactions, electrodermic reactions, electro–encephalograms . . .).

(b) *Subjective reports*. We can distinguish between non-verbal methods (pushing a button, choosing a picture . . .) and verbal methods, such as the use of a differential semantic scale. These scales traditionally take the form of an adjective and its opposite, separated by a certain number of steps (sweet — — — sour). However, those used in measuring affective reactions often have a positive and a negative pole (attractive $-3 -2 -1\ 0 +1 +2 +3$ repulsive) (cf. for example Mehrabian and Russell, 1974; Russell, 1979). This second format shows that the level 0, which represents a lack of phenomenon in *ratio* scales, does not have the same meaning in measuring affect. In relation to stimuli in general, no universally accepted scale exists to show that a statement has no emotional content. While null factual content exists (cf. Resnik and Stern, 1977), null emotional content most certainly does not.

(c) Observation of motor behavior (facial expressions, body movements . . .). The rapid facial signals of Ekman and Friesen's classification (1978) are of import here in recording facial expression, as they reveal spontaneous manifestations of emotions. No perfect isomorphism exists . . . between different facial expressions and different affective reactions. Thus, a single facial expression may represent different affective reactions. Knitting one's brows can, for example, be a sign of anger, disgust or intense concentration. Reductionist logic should therefore be avoided in the study of emotion, as affect is not limited to a single manifestation, be it corporal, verbal or somatic.

Lastly – and in further support of a multimethod approach – some facial changes are not visible and others are too subtle to recognize reliably, as Ekman and Friesen acknowledge.

It could be tempting to transpose methods which have been successful in cognitive studies to the study of affect (paper and pencil). However, it is clear that affective reaction is difficult to verbalize. Many people are unable to explain why they prefer a given thing or person. The researcher's desire for rational and detailed explanations, which leads to influencing the consumer being questioned by providing possible reasons to justify his or her affective reactions, must therefore be avoided.

It would thus be a mistake to use the classic cognitive approach of the survey. Moreover, consumers will not tend to reveal their feelings and emotions to a stranger (the person conducting the survey). Table 3 summarizes the main advantages and drawbacks of verbal reports.

It is clear from Table 3 that experimentation is far preferable to the survey method. It is necessary in this context to emphasize the non-verbal, as suggested by Kroeber-Riel (1979). According to this author, in the study of non-verbal behavior, subjects must not have the time to rationalize their answers. The practice of impulse measurement has the dual advantage of making the subject conscious of his or her behavior, while minimizing rationalization, by interrupting the behavioral sequence. This implies rapid measurement-taking, in order to favor the occurrence of affective responses. As emotional response to a given stimulus varies not only from one person to another, but over time for the same person, it is important to measure affective reactions in real time, at the moment they occur. This objective, and those discussed in the above paragraphs, can be pursued through laboratory experiments.

It is advisable to use a proper sample during the development phase of the measurement tools. Reliable manipulations of affective reaction will be ensured by such an environment (laboratory + proper sample). As pointed out by Gorn (1982), the cost with this type of procedure in terms of external validity is secondary during this stage of perfecting a measurement instrument.

Table 3 Verbal reports of affective reactions

Advantages	Drawbacks
• Highly adaptable to the range of affective reactions under study.	• Problems of retrospection.
• Anonymity easily ensured (compared to laboratory experiments), and minimization of reactive effects if the researcher is not present (as an investigator's presence likely has a negative impact on emotional expressiveness).	• Danger of 'false' cognitive processes being declared, e.g. for reasons of social acceptability.
• Does not necessitate special equipment.	• Improper translation (deliberate or not: possibility of deception) of the perceived affective tone.
• Representative samples due to ease of data collection.	• Impossible to collect supplementary information, as anonymity prevents subjects from being recontacted.
• Direction and content of emotions can be evaluated.	• Centered only on subjective experience of the affective reaction (type III emotion according to Ross Buck).

Certain necessary precautions must, nonetheless, be taken when using an experimental approach. First, certain limits must be respected in terms of manipulation and treatment in the area of affect. In cognitive studies, indefinitely increasing the information content in a message, in order to see when the consumer is saturated or no longer understands, is basically without risk. In the affective domain, however, and particularly for shock emotions, certain doses may be dangerous to participants' health. Injecting too much emotion may provoke malaise.

In addition, it should be noted that most affective reactions in marketing, including emotions, are fairly moderate. Rage, hatred or euphoria are rarely exhibited. Thus, the planned magnitude of instruments, while larger than for cognitive measurements, should nonetheless be limited.

IV. Final remarks and an invitation to measurement

A five-step procedure seems advisable for the improvement of affective reaction measurement, consisting in:

a. Focus on *one* affective reaction.
b. Review the relevant literature and adopt *one definition* based on its conceptual and operational value.
c. Suggest *one theory* based on the above point, which refers to an explicit typology similar to that detailed in section II of this article.
d. Select *one procedure* for measurement development based on the theory and the arguments developed in section III, above.
e. Carry out *experimental validation* in order to offer convincing arguments to those who will not fail to suggest counter-proposals.

Where to begin?

Priority should probably not be given to the three final columns of Table 2, as a great deal of empirical research and methodological advice already exists on preferences, attitudes and appreciations.

Surprise is unquestionably one of the first affective reactions to be measured, as it is a preferred means used by advertising agencies for capturing consumer attention in markets saturated with products and publicity. Even passive, television-watching consumers, those often characterized by minimal involvement, can be reached through surprise effects. In addition, surprise is not only an important aspect affecting communication, it is also often present in sales situations, before, during and after.

Aside from its practical implications, the study of surprise is interesting in both the conceptual and the methodological domains. Surprise is included in all major emotion typologies (Plutchik, 1980; Izard, 1977; Emde, 1980). Izard defines it as a 'pleasant and transitory feeling of uncertainty provoked by a sudden and unexpected event'. However, surprise is not always a pleasant affective reaction. In a study comparing Mehrabian and Russell's dimensional typology (1974) with Plutchik's categorical typology (1980), Havlena and Holbrook (1986) highlight the negative tone which sometimes characterizes surprise.

Therefore, before elaborating a standard of measurement for surprise, a definition should be developed which reflects its capacity to be intense or weak, pleasant or unpleasant, according to the nature of the stimulus. The definition and theory chosen should also be carefully situated in relation to others with which they could be confused. Thus, a theory of surprise should be clearly distinguished from reflex theory or from Pavlov's orienting response theory dating back to the beginning of the century.[2]

Surprise also has particular methodological interest, as a range of different types of measurement can be used in studying it (cf. section III, above). Physiological measurements (electrodermic response, heartbeat, electroencephalogram, salivation, etc.) can capture its adaptive and homeostatic components (Kroeber-Riel, 1979).

The expressive component of surprise, i.e. spontaneous emotional expression (Buck, 1984), can be studied through observation of accompanying facial expressions, as this type of affective reaction, especially shock emotion, is characterized by a low capacity for control and deception. This method implies either assigning a specific emotional state to observed configurations of the entire face and its different areas, or systematically recording and measuring all signal-carrying facial movements, as in Ekman and Friesen's FACS (Facial Action Coding System, 1978).

Lastly, surprise may be measured by subjective reports, as the probability of subjective elementary experience (emotion III, as defined by Buck, 1984) is high. Subjects can be verbally questioned about the emotional state they have just experienced.

In short, we have briefly presented some initial thoughts which may help in developing a non-verbal measurement of surprise. Churchill's eight-step procedure (1979), aimed at maximizing validity and reliability, could easily contribute to its development. Rather than presenting it here, we invite the reader to refer to Laurent and Kapferer's study on the measurement of involvement (1986), an example of the success of this paradigm.

The preceding lines – advocating the measurement of surprise – should not distract others in their operationalization of moods, feelings, or temperament.

Nowlis's work (1965), already a reference in measuring mood, has been followed up and adapted by others (Sjöberg, Svensson and Persson, 1979). Managerial issues in the study of mood were illustrated by Goldberg and Gorn (1987), for example, who demonstrated how the mood provoked by a television show affects the memory and evaluation of advertising broadcast during it. Their results have obvious implications for the selection of programs in which to insert commercials.

Managerial interest in distinguishing optimistic from pessimistic temperaments is evident: each should be offered differing 'risk reducers' (money-back guarantees, tests carried out . . .) both in nature and in quantity. In addition, different advertising arguments need to be presented both before and after the purchase (to reduce possible cognitive dissonance) when addressing optimists – more inclined to discretionary spending – as opposed to pessimists.

Lastly, feelings most certainly also deserve study. Pride, for example, is unquestionably linked to ostentatious buying. Also, feelings (friendship, love, tenderness . . .) often represent an important element of the advertising 'context'.

Conclusions

The aim of this article is to provide a conceptual and methodological summary which may be useful in developing measurement tools for affective reactions in marketing.

A given behavior is always simultaneously cognitive, affective and behavioral, but the second component of this triptych (whose elements are, in reality, inseparable) is the most difficult to measure. We hope the preceding pages will entice specialists in the field of consumer behavior research to deal precisely and empirically with affective components of consumer behavior.

Translated from the French by Joy Gehner

Notes

1. Besides deception, there exists a process of inhibition through which a mitigation of the magnitude of affective expression can be observed. According to Pavlov, this mitigation is essentially a function of the 'strength' of the individual's nervous system, and is independent of his will and/or of social pressure.
2. The most recent and talked-about theory concerning the Orienting Response is that of Ohman (1979).

References

Ajzen, I. and Fishbein, M. (1980), *Understanding Attitude and Predicting Social Behavior*, Englewood Cliffs, NJ: Prentice Hall.

Arnold, M.B. (1960), *Emotion and Personality*, New York: Columbia University Press.

Bagozzi, R.P. (1978), 'The construct validity of the affective, behavioral and cognitive components of attitudes by the analysis of covariance structures', *Multivariate Behavioral Research*, 13, 9–31.

Bagozzi, R.P. *et al.* (1979), 'The construct validity, of the tripartite classification of attitudes', *Journal of Marketing Research*, 16, 88–95.

Batra, R. (1986), 'Affective advertising: role, processes and measurement', in *The Role of Affect in Consumer Behavior*, R.A. Peterson, W.D. Hoyer and W.R. Wilson (eds), Lexington, MA: D.C. Heath, 53–85.

Batra, R. and Ray, M.L. (1986), 'Affective responses mediating acceptance of advertising', *Journal of Consumer Research*, 13, 234–249.

Bettmann, J.R. (1979), *An Information Processing Theory of Consumer Choice*, Reading, MA: Addison-Wesley.

Brenner, C. (1980), 'A psychoanalytic theory of affects', in *Emotion: Theory, Research and Experience*, vol. 1, R. Plutchik and H. Kellerman (eds), New York: Academic Press, 341–348.

Buck, R. (1984), *The Communication of Emotion*, New York: The Guilford Press.

Cacioppo, J.T. *et al.* (1986), 'Properties of affect and affect-laden information processing as viewed through the facial response system', in *The Role of Affect in Consumer Behavior*, R.A. Peterson, W.D. Hoyer and W.R. Wilson (eds), Lexington, MA: D.C. Heath, 87–118.

Churchill, G.A. (1979), 'A paradigm for developing better measures of marketing constructs', *Journal of Marketing Research*, 14, 64–73.

Derbaix, C. (1987), 'Le comportement de l'acheteur. Voies d'études pour les années à venir', *Recherche et Applications en Marketing*, II(2), 81–92.

de Rivera, J. (1977), *A Structural Theory of the Emotions*, New York: International Universities Press.

Edell, J.A. and Burke, M.C. (1987), 'The power of feelings in understanding advertising effects', *Journal of Consumer Research*, 14, 421–433.

Ekman, P. (1973), 'Cross-cultural studies of facial expression', in *Darwin and Facial Expressions*, P. Ekman (ed.), New York: Academic Press, 169–222.

Ekman, P. and Friesen, W.V. (1978), *Facial Coding Action System (FACS): A Technique for the Measurement of Facial Actions*, Palo Alto, CA: Consulting Psychologists Press.

Emde, R.N. (1980), 'Levels of meaning for infant emotions: A biosocial view', in *Development of Cognition, Affect, and Social Relations: The Minnesota Symposium of Child Psychology*, Vol. 13, W.A. Collins (ed.), Hillsdale, NJ: Erlbaum, 1–37.

Fehr, B. and Russell, J.A. (1984), 'Concept of emotion viewed from a prototype perspective', *Journal of Experimental Psychology: General*, **13**, 464–468.

Fishbein, M. and Ajzen, I. (1975), *Belief Attitude, Intention, and Behavior. An Introduction to Theory and Research*, Reading, MA: Addison-Wesley.

Fromme, D.K. and O'Brien, C.S. (1982), 'A dimensional approach to the circular ordering of emotions', *Motivation and Emotion*, **6**, 337–363.

Gardner, M.P. (1985), 'Mood states and consumer behavior: A critical review', *Journal of Consumer Research*, **12**, 281–300.

Gardner, M.P. and Rock, D. (1988), 'Effects of impulse purchases on consumers' affective states', *Advances in Consumer Research*, **XV**, 127–130.

Goldberg, M. and Gorn, G. (1987), 'Happy and sad TV programs: How they affect reactions to commercials', *Journal of Consumer Research*, **14**, 387–403.

Gorn, G. (1982), 'The effect of music in advertising on choice behavior: A classical conditioning approach', *Journal of Marketing*, **46**, 94–101.

Havlena, W.J. and Holbrook, M.B. (1986), 'The varieties of consumption experience: Comparing two typologies of emotion in consumer behavior', *Journal of Consumer Research*, **13**, 394–404.

Hess, E.H. (1965), 'Attitude and pupil size', *The Scientific American*, **112**(4), 46–54.

Holbrook, M.B. (1986), 'Emotion in the consumption experience: Toward a new model of human consumer', in *The Role of Affect in Consumer Behavior*, R.A.Peterson, W.D. Hoyer and W.R. Wilson (eds), Lexington, MA: D.C. Heath, 17–52.

Holbrook, M.B. and Hirschman, E.C. (1982), 'The experiential aspects of consumption: Consumer fantasies, feelings and fun', *Journal of Consumer Research*, **9**, 132–140.

Hovland, C., Lumsdaine, A. and Sheffield, F.D. (1949), *Experiments on Mass Communication*, Princeton, NJ: Princeton University Press.

Izard, C.E. (1977), *Human Emotions*, New York: Plenum Press.

Izard, C.E. (1979), *Emotions in Personality and Psychopathology*, New York: Plenum Press.

Kassarjian, H.H. (1982), 'Consumer psychology', *Annual Review of Psychology*, **33**, 619–649.

Katz, E. (1968), 'On reopening the question of selectivity in exposure to mass communications', in *Theories of Cognitive Consistency: A Source Book*, R.P. Abelson *et al.* (eds), Chicago, IL: Rand-McNally.

Kemper, I.D. (1987), 'How many emotions are there? Wedding the social and the autonomy components', *American Journal of Sociology*, **93**(2), 263–289.

Kroeber-Riel, W. (1979), 'Activation research: Psychobiological approaches in consumer research', *Journal of Consumer Research*, **5**, 240–250.

Laurent, G. and Kapferer, J.N. (1986), 'Les profils d'implication', *Recherche et Applications en Marketing*, **1**, 41–57.

McGuire, W.J. (1974), 'An information-processing approach to advertising effectiveness', in *The Behavioral and Management Sciences in Marketing*, H. Davis and A. Silk (eds), New York: Ronald Press.

Mandler, G. (1975), *Mind and Emotion*, New York: Wiley.

Mehrabian, A. and Russell, J. (1974), *An Approach to Environmental Psychology*, Cambridge, MA: MIT Press.

Nowlis, V. (1965), 'Research with the mood adjective check list', in *Affect, Cognition and Personality: Empirical Studies*, S. Tomkins and C. Izard (eds), New York: Springer-Verlag, 352–389.

Nowlis, V. (1970), Mood: Behavior and experience', in *Feelings and Emotions*, M. Arnold (ed.), New York: Academic Press, 261–277.

Ohman, A. (1979), 'The orienting response, attention, and learning: An information-processing perspective', in H.D. Kimmel (ed.), *The Orienting Reflex in Humans*, Hillsdale, NJ: Lawrence Erlbaum.

Olshavsky, R.W. and Granbois, D.H. (1979), 'Consumer decision making: Fact or fiction?', *Journal of Consumer Research*, **6**, 93–100.

Pieters, R.G.M. and Van Raaij, W.F. (1988), 'Functions and management of affect: Applications to economic behavior', *Journal of Economic Psychology*, **9**, 251–282.

Plutchik, R. (1980), *Emotion: A Psychoevolutionary Synthesis*. New York: Harper & Row.

Pradines, M. (1958), *Traité de Psychologie*, Vol. I, 6th edn, Paris: PUF.

Prideaux, E. (1920), 'The psychogalvanic reflex: A review', *Brain*, **43**, 50–73.

Ray, M.L. and Batra, R. (1983), 'Emotion and persuasion in advertising: What we know and don't know about affect', in *Advances in Consumer Research*, vol. X, R.P. Bagozzi and A.M. Tybout (eds), Ann Arbor, MI: Association for Consumer Research, 543–548.

Resnik, A. and Stern, B.L. (1977), 'An analysis of information content in television advertising', *Journal of Marketing*, **41**, 50–53.

Rook, D.W. (1987), 'The buying impulse', *Journal of Consumer Research*, **14**, 189–199.

Rosenberg, M.J. (1956), 'Cognitive structure and attitudinal effect', *Journal of Abnormal and Social Psychology*, **53**, 367–372.

Russell, J.A. (1979), 'Affective space is bipolar', *Journal of Personality and Social Psychology*, **37**, 345–356.

Simon, H.A. (1982), 'Affect and cognition: comments', in *Affect and Cognition*, M.S. Clark and S.T. Fiske (eds), Hillsdale, NJ: Lawrence Erlbaum Associates, 333–342.

Sjöberg, L., Svensson, E. and Persson, L.-O. (1979), 'The measurement of mood', *Scandinavian Journal of Psychology*, **20**, 118.

Stern, H. (1962), 'The significance of impulse buying today', *Journal of Marketing*, 26 April, 59–62.

Strongman, K.T. (1978), *The Psychology of Emotion*, New York: John Wiley.

Thines, G. and Lempereur, A. (1984), *Dictionnaire général des Sciences humaines*, GIACCO Edn.

Tomkins, S.S. (1962), *Affect, Imagery, Consciousness*, Vol. 1, New York: Springer.

Tomkins, S.S. (1984), 'Affect theory', in *Approaches to Emotion*, K.R. Scherer and P. Ekman (eds), Hillsdale, NJ: Lawrence Erlbaum, 163–196.

West, J. (1951), 'Results of two years of study into impulse buying', *Journal of Marketing*, **15** (January), 362–363.

Wright, P. (1975), 'Consumer choice strategies simplifying vs optimizing', *Journal of Marketing Research*, **12**, 60–67.

Zajonc, R.B. (1980), 'Feeling and thinking preferences need no inferences', *American Psychologist*, **35**, 151–175.

Zajonc, R.B. (1981), 'A one-factor mind about mind and emotion', *American Psychology*, **36**, 102–103.

Zajonc, R.B. (1984), 'On the primary of affect', *American Psychologist*, **39**, 117–123.

Zajonc, R.B. and Markus, H. (1982), 'Affective and cognitive factors in preferences', *Journal of Consumer Research*, **9**, 123–131.

Zajonc, R.B. and Wilson, W.R. (1974), 'Exposure, object preference, and distress in the domestic chick', *Journal of Comparative and Physiological Psychology*, **86**, 581–585.

Attitudes and decision processes

4

Laurent, G. and Kapferer, J.-N., 1985, 'Measuring consumer involvement profiles', *Journal of Marketing Research,* **22** (February), 41–53

Pinson, C., 1986, 'An implicit product theory approach to consumers' inferential judgments about products', *International Journal of Research in Marketing,* **3,** 19–38

Derbaix, C. and Vanden Abeele, P., 1985, 'Consumer inferences and consumer preferences. The status of cognition and consciousness in consumer behavior theory', *International Journal of Research in Marketing,* **2,** 157–74

Introduction

The study of consumer decision processes is central to consumer behaviour research. It is important for product producers and service providers to know which alternative products and brands consumers consider, how they compare these alternatives, and how they select the brand or product they want to buy. Not only for marketing purposes, but also for consumer education and protection it is relevant to know how consumers go about selecting products.

In this perspective, the European approach to studying consumer decision processes is not significantly different from the North American approach. One reason might be that consumer decision processes seem to be a culturally universal phenomenon. Except for some minor differences in perspective, most researchers agree implicitly that these processes are the same for all consumers. However, in East Asian and other countries with less individualistic values and behaviours, consumer decision processes are likely to differ from the Anglo-Saxon 'standards' we are accustomed to in the scientific journals.

This chapter assumes that in Europe, North America and other parts of the world, there is a common understanding about the relevance of this topic and how consumer decision processes should be studied. However, the European view differs in a few aspects from the typical North American approach.

Three areas have been chosen to represent the contributions of European research to the study of attitudes and decision processes: involvement, inferential judgements and affects.

The first article, by Laurent and Kapferer, has come to be considered a classic in the sense that it significantly enlarged our understanding of the involvement concept. Traditionally, involvement had been studied mainly through its relationships to advertising strategy; the level of involvement was said to affect both the decision process of consumers and their attitude towards advertising; second, involvement was essentially seen as a single construct, with measures differing from one study to another. The reason the involvement profiles scale designed by Laurent and Kapferer became so widely used by researchers is that it largely contributed to the redefinition of the concept of involvement on a multi-dimensional basis, and that it proposed a very reliable and at the same time convenient scale to predict it. Involvement, they suggest, cannot be based on a single indicator, but refers to antecedents, which they call the facets of involvement; these facets include the perceived importance of the product, the perceived risks associated with the product purchase, the symbolic value and the hedonic value. Thus the meanings of involvement derive from differences in the antecedent conditions producing it, and therefore, the involvement cannot be approached as a single construct because all the facets must be taken into consideration simultaneously to be able to predict behaviour. It is further proposed to substitute for the general concept of 'involvement' an analytical distinction between the facets (hence the concept of involvement profile), in the sense that a behavioural outcome might be dependent on some facets of involvement and not others.

The second article by Pinson is a brilliant and innovative application of a very important psychological theory: the implicit personality theory. This theory, mainly developed in the field of social psychology, refers to a tendency to assume inferential relationships among traits or attributes of people; hence it holds that individuals tend to believe that certain characteristics occur jointly in other persons. The article applies this theory to the area of consumer behaviour by extending it analogically to consumers' inferential judgements about products – hence a theory called 'implicit product theory'. Pinson suggests that individuals store product attribute relationships in memory in the same way as they store human relationships. He therefore suggests that despite individual differences in the types of relationships stored, there are a number of common intrinsic and extrinsic cues which consumers use to infer product attributes. The article provides perceptive examples of inferential judgements on product attributes (or cues) such as odour, colour, sound, product design, etc. Even though the article constitutes more a theoretical orientation than a theory of implicit product *per se*, it provides a very useful framework for studying consumer product cue utilization behaviour.

The third article deals with the status of cognition in consumer choices. Cognitive psychology has had the most wide-reaching effect on consumer research of any contemporary psychological paradigm. The cognitive approach to consumer decision-making was established in the 1960s, a time when cognitive psychology was in the ascendancy in behavioural sciences generally. It is no surprise, therefore, that consumer researchers conceived of the individual consumer as making goal-oriented decisions via a process of information sequencing and handling which resulted in attitudes, intentions and finally purchase. It was inevitable that this paradigm would eventually come under fire. In the third article in this chapter, Derbaix and Vanden Abeele examine the so-called 'non-cognitive' turn in consumer behaviour theory. The authors conclude that a more sophistic-ated approach to non-cognitive processes is required. Cognition, emotion and conation often overlap, despite the usefulness of distinguishing them at a conceptual level. Rather than concentrate on cognitive versus non-cognitive processes, they argue that it is more valuable for consumer researchers to examine the distinction between conscious and auto-matic processing.

In the future, research on consumer attitudes and decision processes is likely to include more emotional factors, habits like brand loyalty, social and reference group influences and 'sign values'. The latter refers to consumption as a form of communication of values and lifestyles to other consumers. Consumption is not only about the physical product attributes but also the psycho-social aspects of brands, products and services. This is discussed in Chapters 5, 6 and 8.

Measuring consumer involvement profiles

••

Gilles Laurent and Jean-Noël Kapferer

Professors of Marketing, Ecole des Hautes Etudes Commerciales and Institut Supérieur des Affaires, France

Summary

There is more than one kind of consumer involvement. Depending on the antecedents of involvement (e.g. the product's pleasure value, the product's sign or symbolic value, risk importance and probability of purchase error), consequences on consumer behavior differ. The authors therefore recommend measuring an involvement profile, rather than a single involvement level. These conclusions are based on an empirical analysis of 14 product categories.

The degree of consumer involvement in a product category is now widely recognized as a major variable relevant to advertising strategy (Ray, 1982; Rothschild, 1979; Vaughn, 1980). Depending on their level of involvement, individual consumers differ in the extent of their decision process and their search for information. Depending on their level of involvement, consumers may be passive or active when they receive advertising communication, and limit or extend their processing of this communication. To adapt to these differences, advertisers may consider a number of operational variables such as the type of media, the degree of repetition, the length of the message, the tone of the message, and the quantity of information (Tyebjee, 1979). In practice, however, one question arises frequently: how can we know whether a specific group of consumers is indeed highly involved in some product category?

Today, this question generally receives qualitative assessment from advertising and product managers. When quantitative indicators of involvement are used, the instruments often boil down to a single scale (Vaughn, 1980) or to a single-item measure of perceived importance (Agostini, 1978; Hupfer and Gardner, 1971; Lastovicka and Bonfield, 1982; Traylor, 1981). Should involvement be reduced to a single dimension? Does 'perceived importance' alone capture all the richness of the involvement concept? Is it sufficient to classify people in terms of a single involvement indicator or should involvement be analyzed in terms of multiple facets, which need to be measured simultaneously if one wants to provide managers with a full picture of the type of involvement of a specific target group?

From the *Journal of Marketing Research*, **22** (February 1985), 41–53.

Fifteen years ago, in their extensive review of the involvement concept, Kiesler, Collins and Miller (1969) called it a pot-pourri concept which may encompass several independent elements. More recently Rothschild (1979) concluded that no *single* indicator of involvement could satisfactorily describe, explain or predict involvement. In line with these remarks, we suggest that marketing researchers stop thinking in terms of single indicators of the involvement level and instead use an 'involvement profile' to specify more fully the nature of the relationship between a consumer and a product category.

Our objective is to provide marketing and advertising managers with a scale of specifying the nature and level of consumer involvement that is reliable and valid but also convenient. Satisfying the convenience criterion implies that the items should make sense for any product class – from yogurt to bras, from color TV sets to detergents – and that the total number of items allows the scale to be inserted at little extra cost in a usage and attitude survey.

In the next section we review the uses of the involvement concept, as revealed by the literature and managers' interviews with the authors. This review suggests that consumers differ not only in level of involvement, but also in type of involvement. Then we describe a method by which indicators can be developed for each type of involvement. Finally, data analysis provides evidence about the reliability and validity of the indicators as well as the usefulness of thinking in terms of involvement profile to predict selected aspects of consumers' decision-processes and receptivity to advertising.

Involvement or involvements?

Research on consumer involvement goes back to Sherif and Cantril's (1947) early work. Many authors have reviewed this field of consumer research and theory (Arora, 1982; Assael, 1981; De Bruicker, 1979; Engel and Blackwell, 1982; Ray, 1973; Robertson, 1976). It is not our objective here to add another review, but to focus on *different* facets or types of involvement.

In theory, involvement is considered an individual difference variable. It is a causal or motivating variable with a number of consequences on the consumer's purchase and communication behavior. Thus, depending on their level of involvement, consumers will differ greatly in the extensiveness of their purchase decision process (indicated by the number of attributes used to compare brands, the length of the choice process and the willingness to reach a maximum or a threshold level of satisfaction) or in their processing of communications (indicated for instance by the extent of information search, receptivity to advertising, and the number and type of cognitive responses generated during exposure) (Krugman, 1965, 1967).

The involvement literature and in-depth interviews with advertising managers suggest that the hypothetical construct 'involvement' is not a unitary one. There are different views of involvement as revealed by the uses of the concept and the conditions imposed by different researchers to manipulate and measure it.

The uses of the concept

Researchers and practitioners tend not to use the word 'involvement' alone, but rather imply a distinction between types of involvement. For example, Houston and Rothschild

(1977) make a distinction between enduring involvement and situational involvement. The latter reflects concern with a specific situation such as a purchase occasion or election. The former, stemming from the individual, reflects a general and permanent concern with the product class. The crucial difference between these two types of involvement is suggested by Rothschild (1979, p. 77): an individual might usually purchase various low-price brands of liquor in a stochastic manner because of low enduring involvement; on the occasion of a visit by the boss, however, a high involvement decision would be made to purchase a specific brand. Enduring involvement derives from the perception that the product is related to centrally held values (Arora, 1982), those defining one's singularity and identity, one's ego (Ostrom and Brock, 1968; Rokeach, 1968). Situational involvement is heightened when the consumer perceives risk in a specific situation.

Another differentiation is subsumed by the practitioners' tendency to speak of 'emotional involvement' (Vaughn, 1980). Such a qualification supposes a contrario that there could be a non-emotional involvement, such as what French sociologist Chombart de Lauwe (1979) calls 'rational involvement' devoid of any affect. For instance, confronting a choice of steam irons, the consumer would merely try to optimize a cost–benefit ratio, with no emotion or interest toward the product category. Pleasure is absent. This would not be the case for the choice of a restaurant (Hirschman and Holbrook, 1982).

A final differentiation is highlighted by authors who speak of 'personal involvement' as though there were another, impersonal, kind of involvement. For instance, French semiologist Baudrillard (1968, 1970) posits that 'there is involvement only when there is sign'. Looking at some product alternatives, the consumer looks for the difference that corresponds to his or her own identity, or ego. When product choice is perceived as the sign of oneself, involvement is present. In their early work, Sherif and Cantril (1947) made a similar restriction. They spoke of 'ego involvement' to emphasize the personal and emotional nature of involvement. Greenwald (1965) proposes the term 'solution involvement' to denote the commitment of the consumer in the search for the right solution to a problem, and views this form of involvement as independent of ego involvement stemming from the individual's very personal and central values.

The antecedents of involvement

As a hypothetical construct, involvement cannot be measured directly. Looking at empirical research, one finds a great diversity in the operational indicators of involvement – further reflecting the differences in meaning of the construct for different researchers.

Sherif and Hovland (1961) typically recruited their 'highly involved' subjects among WCTU women, emphasizing three possible antecedents of their involvement. Involvement could stem from the 'intrinsic importance' of an issue, its 'personal meaning' (Sherif and Hovland, 1961, p. 197), a public stand taken or strong affect *vis-à-vis* an issue (Kiesler, Collins and Miller, 1969).

Working in the cognitive dissonance paradigm, Zimbardo (1960) experimentally manipulated involvement. In choice or attitude change experiments 'highly involved' subjects were led to believe that they would have to make a public stand on their opinion in front of a group of spectators. 'Low involved' subjects, on the contrary, perceived their choice or opinions as inconsequential. Such an operationalization typically manipulated a perceived risk antecedent of involvement (Chaffee and McLeod, 1973) and specially a psychological risk related to the image one might project.

In marketing, price is probably the most commonly used indicator of involvement. Because the risks of a mispurchase are high when price is high, consumers are likely to be involved (Rothschild, 1979). Durable goods also have been used to create conditions of high involvement because, in case of mispurchase, one is stuck with a poor product for a long time. Among those goods, dresses are generally considered as extremely ego-involving because of their symbolic meaning *vis-à-vis* relevant others, their capacity to express one's lifestyle or personality (Levy, 1959), or their hedonic character (Hirschman and Holbrook, 1982).

Empirical data

Empirical data also highlight the necessity of thinking in terms of different types of involvement. For example, Lastovicka and Gardner (1979) asked their subjects to evaluate 14 products on a series of items measuring importance, commitment and affect. Their analysis revealed three types of product: low involvement, high involvement and special interest or enthusiast products (products expressing one's hobby). The difference between the two last types lay in the presence of affect and hedonic character in the latter case.

To summarize, our review of uses and indicators of involvement and of empirical research suggests that the (permanent or situational) state of 'involvement' may stem from different types of antecedent. Frequent use of the word 'involvement' with a qualifier (*personal* involvement, *emotional* involvement, etc.) suggests that the source of involvement is important information and that researchers or managers should not be content with knowing only that an individual is or is not involved. Knowing the level of involvement offers a static description. Understanding of the sources of involvement provides a dynamic picture of the consumer's subjective situation and gives clues as to what appeals should be used in communicating with consumers.

Beyond controversies over definitions of involvement, our review of current research and practices indicates five antecedents, or facets, of involvement:

1. The perceived importance of the product (its personal meaning).
2. The perceived risk associated with the product purchase, which in turn has two facets (Bauer, 1967):
   - the perceived importance of negative consequences in case of poor choice and
   - the perceived probability of making such a mistake.
3. The symbolic or sign value attributed by the consumer to the product, its purchase, or its consumption. This differentiates functional risk from psychosocial risk (Bauer, 1967).
4. The hedonic value of the product, its emotional appeal, its ability to provide pleasure and affect.

Instead of developing a composite of items tapping these different sources to obtain a single index of involvement level, it seems essential to keep the full picture of the nature of

consumer involvement by measuring the consumers' position on each of these five facets –
thus providing their involvement profile.

Before turning to the proposed measurement method, we should note that there is not a
one-to-one correspondence between the facets of the involvement profile and Houston and
Rothschild's distinction between enduring and situational involvement. Two facets of the
involvement profile correspond to enduring, nonsituational, aspects of the consumer's
relationship to a product: the perceived importance of the product and its hedonic value.
Two other facets, however, are more difficult to classify: the perceived risk associated with
the product and the sign value attributed to the product. Certain products entail a risk in all
circumstances (e.g. a vacuum cleaner), whereas for other products the risk depends on the
situation (e.g. a wine to be drunk alone or with the boss). The former case could be
described as enduring involvement, the latter as situational involvement. Similarly, certain
products may have an enduring symbolic value, whereas other products may have a symbolic value only in the presence of *relevant others*.

Method

Our objective was to create a reliable and valid measure for each of the facets of involvement. Following Churchill's (1979) suggestions, once the facets were identified, we generated a pool of items for each facet. Sources of these items were twofold, a literature review
and in-depth interviews of a sample of housewives. Three surveys were necessary to purify
the measures and obtain five scales that would be satisfactory psychometrically but also
short enough to be of practical use. Two preliminary data collection waves were completed
with samples of about 100 housewives, each person being asked about several products. The
results reported hereafter are based on the third wave, for which a sample of 207 housewives
was recruited on the basis of age and socio-economic quotas. Face-to-face interviewing was
done at home. Each housewife was interviewed on two product categories, with a systematic
rotation of product categories by interviewee. Thus, the data analysis was based on 414
cases. Fourteen product categories were studied. To be qualified for the interview, in
addition to meeting the socio-demographic criteria of the quotas, the housewife had to be a
consumer of the two products.

Each facet of involvement was measured by a multi-item scale with a 5-point Likert-type
response format (fully disagree to fully agree). Table 1 lists some items corresponding to
each facet that were used in the third and final data collection.

In creating conditions whereby the facets could appear independent if such were the case,
the selection of the stimulus products was crucial. Fourteen products were selected to
represent contrasting profiles on the dimensions of perceived sign value, perceived hedonic
value, perceived risk and perceived importance. These products were suggested by qualitative in-depth interviewing of housewives; for each dimension, the housewives were asked
what typical product came to mind among four categories (food, durables, textile and
drugs). For instance, TV sets, washing machines, dresses and bras were mentioned as high-
risk products (the consequences of a mispurchase are great). Low-price frequently purchased items were at the other extreme. When asked what products were devoid of any
hedonic character, the housewives mentioned detergents, vacuum cleaners and irons. For

Table 1 Measurement of the presumed facets (translated from the original French items)

Facet	Number of Items	Code Name	Examples of Items
Product perceived importance	4	Importance	_____ is very important to me For me _____ does not matter
Perceived importance of negative consequences of a mispurchase	3	Risk importance	When you get a _____, it's not a big deal if you make a mistake
Subjective probability of a mispurchase	3	Risk probability	When you get a _____, it's hard to make a bad choice
Hedonic value of the product class	5	Pleasure	I can't say that I particularly like _____
Perceived sign value of the product class	4	Sign	You can really tell about a person by the _____ she picks out

the housewives these products are tied to household chores. At the other extreme (high hedonic character), many food items came to mind (wine, chocolate, yogurt, jams, etc.) as well as perfumes and dresses. In terms of sign value, dresses, bras, jeans, wines, perfumes and cars were mentioned spontaneously.

A choice had to be made among all the mentioned products. In this selection process we dropped products lacking substantial penetration (e.g. only a minority of housewives wear jeans) and products which presumably were high (or low) on all facets (cars, perfume, paper towels): such products would prevent the facets from appearing distinct. Finally, we did not retain products purchased essentially by the husband (cars). The final list of products consists of washing machines, vacuum cleaners, irons, TV sets, dresses, bras, detergents, shampoo, facial soaps, toothpaste, oil, yogurt, chocolate and champagne. As we show subsequently (Table 3), mean scores of each product category for each facet showed high correspondence with the *a priori* judgements.

Empirical analysis of the facets

We first examine the quality of each scale. Discriminant validity also is assessed. Then special emphasis is given to the analysis of the relationships between facets. Finally, we look at predictive validity by focusing on the relationships of the facets to consumers' decision processes and communication receptivity.

Evaluation of the quality of each scale

Two criteria were used to evaluate each scale, multiproduct fit and reliability. The first criterion is very important if one wants to build a tool appropriate for any product. Unfortunately, many items that would fit well in the case of, say, washing machines are found silly by the interviewee when applied to yogurt, and vice versa. Consequently two surveys were necessary to prune a large initial item base. Items were rejected if they had a significant number of nonresponses or don't know answers (and after negative feedback from the field team about the interviewees' actual reaction to them). At the third data collection phase, all items met the first criterion. The second criterion is Cronbach's alpha measure of internal consistency of a scale (Carmines and Zeller, 1979). To make the full instrument easy to use in commercial market studies, we limited each scale to no more than five items; for reliability purposes, each scale had no less than three items. Despite the small number of items per scale, the Cronbach's alpha values proved satisfactory – importance 0.80, sign 0.90, pleasure 0.88, risk importance 0.82, and risk probability 0.72.

Trait and discriminant validity

Campbell (1960) and Nunnally (1978) suggest that each scale should measure a single dimension if it is considered to have 'trait validity'. Discriminant validity of each scale represents the distinctiveness of each scale *vis-à-vis* others. It might be possible – despite different names and items and good alpha values – for two scales to be so correlated that they cannot be considered as measuring different concepts. They would lack discriminant validity (Campbell, 1960). To test simultaneously trait and discriminant validity, we undertook a factor analysis of the items using all 414 observations. To have trait validity, a scale should load on one and only one factor. To have discriminant validity, a scale should not load on the same factor as another scale.

Because the scales tap different facets of the same concept, the factors should not be expected *a priori* to be orthogonal. With this in mind, we use an oblique factor analysis. The eigenvalue criterion leads to four significant factors, reproducing 66% of the total variance. Table 2 reports the loadings of the items.

The loading patterns show that each scale is single-factored (trait validity). As predicted by theory (Bauer, 1967), each dimension of perceived risk loads on a factor. However, 'perceived importance of the product' and the first dimension of risk do not display discriminant validity, but instead load on the same factor. Therefore, in further analyses, these items are merged to form a single scale of seven items (resulting in a Cronbach's alpha of 0.87). Its code name is 'imporisk' – denoting that for consumers to deem a product important is akin to feeling that a mispurchase would have high negative consequences.

From this data analysis, we conclude that the involvement profile should have four distinct facets:

1. Imporisk (the perceived importance of the product and the perceived importance of the consequences of a mispurchase).
2. The subjective probability of a mispurchase.

Table 2 Oblique factor analysis of the items of the involvement facets*

	Factor 1	Factor 2	Factor 3	Factor 4
Importance 1	0.59			
Importance 2	0.56			
Importance 3	0.62			
Importance 4	0.74			
Pleasure 1		–0.73		
Pleasure 2		–0.68		
Pleasure 3		–0.82		
Pleasure 4		–0.67		
Pleasure 5		–0.58		
Sign 1			0.78	
Sign 2			0.94	
Sign 3			0.73	
Sign 4			0.77	
Risk importance 1	0.62			
Risk importance 2	0.74			
Risk importance 3	0.74			
Risk probability 1				0.76
Risk probability 2				0.64
Risk probability 3				0.50

* Omitted loadings are less than 0.25.

3. The hedonic value of the product class.
4. The perceived sign value of the product class.

It appears that involvement cannot simply be equated with perceived risk. Our results provide a direct and positive response to Chaffee and McLeod's (1973) conclusion after their literature review: 'Although perceived risk appears clearly a sufficient condition for involvement, it is problematic whether it is a necessary one. There would seem to be a number of more positive sources of involvement, such as rewards inherent in the product after purchase' (p. 389).

What are the relationships between facets?

Oblique factors are not expected to be independent because the facets belong to the same construct. The following table is the matrix of the correlations between facets, computed over all 414 observations (each facet score is measured by the scale described before).

	Imporisk	Risk Probability	Sign
Imporisk			
Risk probability	0.47		
Sign	0.40	0.16	
Pleasure	0.46	0.15	0.53

A relationship does exist between facets. However, the correlations indicate that one facet cannot be fully predicted by another. It is not possible to pick up a single index, for no single facet alone catches the richness of the relationship between a consumer and a product class. The extent of correlations warns that a consumer may be high on one facet but low on another. Two scatterplots illustrate the relationships between facets of involvement. Figure 1 shows how the perceived sign value varies with the perceived importance of consequences (imporisk). Each point corresponds to the average scale scores of a product category, computed over all respondents interrogated on that product category. We see that, despite their visible covariation, one facet cannot be fully predicted by the other. For example, though they have similar sign values, chocolate and irons are perceived differently in terms of the importance of consequences. Figure 2 illustrates the relationship between perceived sign value and perceived pleasure value, using average scale scores of each product category.

These scatterplots suggest the desirability of measuring the full *involvement profile* of a consumer in a product category because no facet alone summarizes consumers' relationships to products. Table 3 describes the average profiles of the product categories on the four facets. There is a good correspondence between empirical data and the *a priori* judgments

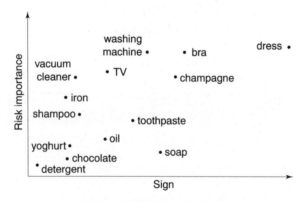

Figure 1   Relationship between facets of involvement: risk importance/sign.

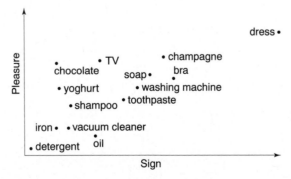

Figure 2   Relationship between facets of involvement: pleasure/sign.

that led to the selection of this product sample. However, the profiles of some products warrant a comment. The involvement profile of washing machines differs from that of vacuum cleaners or irons. There is pleasure value in purchasing a washing machine for it liberates the housewives by giving them free time, whereas the latter products necessitate the housewives' presence and evoke 'bondage' to household chores. Devoid of any hedonic or sign value, vacuum cleaners create risk involvement. A vacuum cleaner is an expensive durable product and in case of a poor choice one is stuck with it for many years. Furthermore, there are many different features on the various brands and the consumer may not feel at all assured of making a good choice. Her subjective probability of mispurchase is high. Facial soap position mirrors soap advertising appeals. There is no mention any more of the washing power, but rather the fragrance and the physical and psychological sensations. Facial soap advertising is now very similar to perfume advertising. Marketers have prevented soap from becoming a low involvement product by playing on two conditions of involvement: pleasure and sign value.

Naturally, the figures are averages for each product category, based on small samples. Consumers do vary in their perceptions. Intraproduct typologies are recommended to isolate the groups of consumers with homogeneous involvement profiles.

Some consequences of the involvement profile

Theory predicts that involvement exerts a strong influence on consumers' decision processes and information search. Because involvement is captured better when all its

Table 3   Involvement profiles*

	Importance of Negative Consequences	Subjective Probability of Mispurchase	Pleasure Value	Sign Value
Dresses	121	112	147	181
Bras	117	115	106	130
Washing machines	118	109	106	111
TV sets	112	100	122	95
Vacuum cleaners	110	112	70	78
Irons	103	95	72	76
Champagne	109	120	125	125
Oil	89	97	65	92
Yogurt	86	83	106	78
Chocolate	80	89	123	75
Shampoo	96	103	90	81
Toothpaste	95	95	94	105
Facial soap	82	90	114	118
Detergents	79	82	56	63

* Average product score = 100.

antecedent conditions (facets) are taken into account, it is useful to investigate the influence of these facets on consumer behavior.

The behavioral consequences of involvement have been reviewed often (Assael, 1981; Engel and Blackwell, 1982; Finn, 1982; Robertson, 1976). Traditional views hold that highly involved consumers (Assael, 1981, p. 84):

- seek to maximize expected satisfaction from their brand choice through an extensive choice process (Chaiken, 1980), e.g., comparing many brands, spending time, using multiple attributes,
- are information seekers, actively looking for information from alternative sources,
- are more likely to be influenced by reference groups,
- are more likely to express their lifestyle and personality characteristics in their brand choice, and
- process communication cognitively by going through stages of awareness, comprehension, attitude, and behavior (Krugman, 1965; Rothschild, 1969).

In the context of our study, we selected the first two behavioral consequences to assess the contribution of measuring the full involvement profile instead of a single indicator of involvement level. A scale of extensiveness of choice process was built with three self-perception Likert-type items (number of attributes used in comparing brands, amount of time spent, degree of attention exerted during choice). This 3-item scale resulted in a high reliability coefficient (Cronbach's alpha = 0.80). Information seeking was operationalized by three self-perception items measuring the tendency to keep permanently informed about the product class, interest for articles and TV programs about the product, and propensity to look at advertising in the product class. The reliability coefficient (0.60) indicated that these three items did not actually constitute a scale. Thus subsequent analyses were done on each item separately.

To hypothesize that involvement has an influence on certain aspects of consumer behavior does not imply that these aspects depend from involvement alone. Other explanatory variables may be at work. For this reason, in this section on predictive validity, we take into account variables other than involvement that may be expected to influence the two consequences of interest: extensiveness of the choice process and information seeking. Omitting these variables would result in specification error. A review of previous empirical research suggested the inclusion of two other variables, perceived differences between alternatives and price. Perceived differences act as a major stimulus of choice and search behavior (Assael, 1981; Claxton, Fry and Portis, 1974; De Bruicker, 1979; Ray, 1973; Rothschild, 1979). When price is high, the expectation of obtaining a better price justifies spending more time in the choice process and actively searching for information (Dommermuth and Cundiff, 1967; Kiel and Layton, 1981; Newman and Staelin, 1972). A 3-item scale measured the perceived differentiation variable (Cronbach's alpha = 0.71). Price was measured by the index of average retail prices of the product category. We used the logarithm of the price to reduce the skewness of the variable. Because we had four separate dependent variables, we ran four separate regressions on all 414 observations.

Table 4 reports the results of the regressions. A major conclusion of the analysis is that the facets of the involvement profile have different influences on the dependent variables. Sometimes one facet is determinant and sometimes another facet exerts the major influence.

Analysis of the standardized regression weights shows that the extensiveness of the decision process is influenced above all by the perceived importance of the product and by the negative consequences of a mispurchase. The second variable influencing extensiveness is the degree of perceived difference between alternatives. Consumers have a tendency to keep permanently informed when they perceive the product category as important, or when it has sign value or pleasure value. Consumers take an interest in articles and programs when the product has pleasure value and sign value. Propensity to expose oneself to advertising is dependent on the pleasure value of the product class.

Interestingly, the importance facet does not affect all aspects of communication behavior. The pleasure facet influences communication behavior but has no influence on the extensiveness of the choice process. The perceived probability of making a mispurchase exerts a small positive influence on the extensiveness of the decision process, but has no influence on the other dependent variables.

Figures 3 through 6 are graphic illustrations of these results. Each of them shows, on the basis of average product scores, the influence of one facet of involvement (abscissa) on a possible consequence (ordinate). They suggest that the extensiveness of the decision process is weakly influenced by a product's pleasure value (Figure 3), but strongly influenced by risk importance (Figure 4). In contrast, propensity to exposure to advertising does not depend much on risk importance (Figure 5), but derives mainly from the product's pleasure value (Figure 6).

Discussion and conclusions

Looking at consumer behavior textbooks (Assael, 1981; Engel and Blackwell, 1982), one sees that involvement theory makes rather simple predictions on the effects of involvement

Table 4   Influence of the involvement facets (standardized regression weights)

	Risk (Importance)	Sign Value	Pleasure Value	Risk (Probability)	Price	Perceived Differentiation	R^2
Extensive decision process	0.61[a]	0.10[b]	0.00	0.06[c]	0.10[b]	0.17[a]	0.71
Keeping permanently informed	0.27[a]	0.18[a]	0.15[b]	0.08	–0.08	0.05	0.28
Interest in articles and TV programs	0.13	0.14[b]	0.28[a]	0.01	0.03	0.00	0.20
Looking at advertising	0.05	0.06	0.37[a]	–0.04	0.01	0.00	0.17

a. $p < 0.001$.
b. $p < 0.01$.
c. $p < 0.05$.

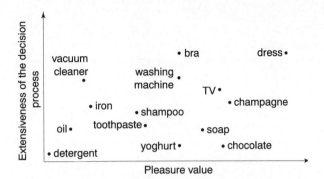

Figure 3   Relationship between a facet of involvement (pleasure value) and a consequence (extensiveness of the decision process).

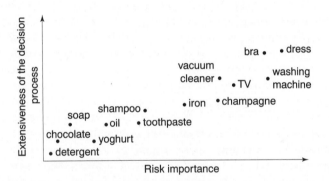

Figure 4   Relationship between a facet of involvement (risk importance) and a consequence (extensiveness of the decision process).

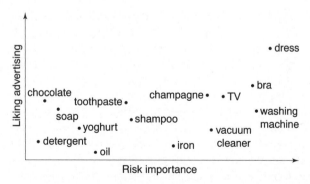

Figure 5   Relationship between a facet of involvement (risk importance) and a consequence (liking advertising).

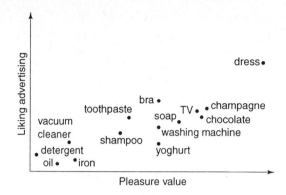

Figure 6   Relationship between a facet of involvement (pleasure value) and a consequence (liking advertising).

on consumer behavior. Typically, when consumers are involved, they should engage in a number of behaviors (active search, extensive choice process, active information processing, etc.); when consumers are not involved, they should not engage in these behaviors. Knowing the conditions that gave rise to involvement has no role in the theory. Prediction of behaviors entails knowing only the consumer's level of involvement. In contrast, our research was prompted by the fact that managers and researchers use the word 'involvement' with a qualifier, implying that the term used alone is too imprecise unless one specifies what kind of involvement is concerned. Here, we propose that the nuances in meanings of involvement derive from differences in the antecedent conditions producing involvement. The literature review suggested five such antecedent conditions of involvement – perceived importance of the product or the situation, perceived sign value, perceived pleasure value and perceived risk (itself divided in two subcomponents). A factor analysis indicated that though they were correlated, each facet of involvement brought some specific information. One could not capture the consumer's involvement through a single index: all facets of the involvement profile must be taken into account simultaneously.

Regression analyses showed that all facets contributed to the prediction of behavior. Also, some facets influence specific behaviors but not other behaviors. Therefore no precise prediction on the consequences of involvement could be made unless the antecedent conditions were specified. Knowing the involvement level on one facet (e.g. perceived importance, the classical indicator of involvement) is not sufficient. The full profile must be known because different facets have different influences on selected aspects of consumer behavior.

On practical grounds, the involvement profile can be used to segment the market. Rather than merely indicating high–low involvement divisions of the market, the profile allows identification of consumers high on some facets but low on others. Moreover, the involvement profile affords a better understanding of the dynamics of consumer involvement. Looking at the facets, one may understand better where involvement originates, which provides clues as to what types of appeals should be used in communication for each segment.

How does the involvement profile compare with FCB's advertising planning matrix (Vaughn, 1980)? FCB's approach is based on the plotting of products or people or situations in two dimensions, involvement and think–feel (whether the decision is based more on facts or more on feeling). Because the items used to build the involvement index have not been published, it is difficult to assess whether FCB's involvement represents one of our facets or a mix of them. The think–feel dimension is related to the weight of the sign and pleasure value facets within the involvement profile. When one of these two facets is strongly present, people should engage more in 'feel' decisions than in 'think' decisions. However, the think–feel dimension confounds these two determinants, thus providing fewer clues to advertising managers looking for a clear picture of the involvement dynamics.

On theoretical grounds, Rothschild (1979) spoke of involvement as 'a vague concept' (p. 78) and Kiesler, Collins and Miller (1969) called it 'a pot-pourri concept' (p. 279). Our results strongly suggest that, as it stands now, involvement theory may be oversimplified. Involvement does not systematically lead to the expected differences in behavior. They depend on the antecedents of involvement, as measured here by the involvement profile. Some consequences depend on certain facets but not on others. Therefore at a meta-theoretical level, if prediction of specific behavioral outcomes depends on knowledge of the specific facets (risk, sign, pleasure, importance), one may question the utility of thinking of the gross concept called 'involvement' and instead substitute an analytical distinction between the facets.

References

Agostini, J.M. (1978), 'Communication publicitaire et implication du consommateur. Conséquences pratiques pour la conception des messages et le choix des media', IREP, Proceedings of the 18th Annual Conference, 79–86.
Arora, R. (1982), 'Validation of an S-O-R model for situation, enduring, and response components of involvement', *Journal of Marketing Research*, **19** (November), 505–16.
Assael, H. (1981), *Consumer Behavior*. New York: Wadsworth.
Baudrillard, J. (1968), *Le Système des Objets*. Paris: Gallimard, Collection Tel.
Baudrillard, J. (1970), *La Société de Consommation*. Paris: SGPP.
Bauer, R.A. (1967), 'Consumer behavior as risk taking', in *Risk Taking and Information Handling in Consumer Behavior*, D.F. Cox, ed. Boston: Harvard University Press. Division of Research, Graduate School of Business Administration. Harvard University, 23–33.
Campbell, D.T. (1960), 'Recommendations for APA Test Standards regarding construct, trait and discriminant validity', *American Psychologist*, **15**, 546–53.
Carmines, E.G. and R.A. Zeller (1979), 'Reliability and Validity Assessment', Sage University Paper.
Chaffee, S.H. and J.M. McLeod (1973), 'Consumer decisions and information use', in *Consumer Behavior: Theoretical Sources*, S. Ward and T.S. Robertson, eds. Englewood Cliffs, NJ: Prentice-Hall, 385–415.
Chaiken, S. (1980), 'Heuristic versus systematic information processing and the use of source versus message cues in persuasion', *Journal of Personality and Social Psychology*, **39**(5), 752–66.
Chombart de Lauwe, M.J. (1979), *Un monde autre: l'Enfance*. Paris: Payot.
Churchill, G.A., Jr. (1979), 'A paradigm for developing better measures of marketing constructs', *Journal of Marketing Research*, **16** (February), 64–73.
Claxton, J.D., J.N. Fry and B. Portis (1974), 'A taxonomy of prepurchase information gathering patterns', *Journal of Consumer Research*, **1** (December), 35–42.
De Bruicker, F.S. (1979), 'An appraisal of low-involvement consumer information processing', in *Attitude Research Plays for High Stakes*, J.C. Maloney and B. Silverman, eds. Chicago: American Marketing Association, 112–30.

Dommermuth, W.P. and E.W. Cundiff (1967), 'Shopping goods, shopping centers and selling strategies', *Journal of Marketing*, **31** (October), 32–6.

Engel, F. and R.D. Blackwell (1982), *Consumer Behavior*, 4th edn. New York: The Dryden Press.

Finn, W.F. (1982), 'It is time to lay the low-involvement hierarchy to rest', in *Proceedings of the Association for Consumer Research*, 13th Conference, 99–102.

Greenwald, H.S. (1965), 'The involvement controversy in persuasion research', unpublished manuscript, Columbia University.

Hirschman, E.C. and M.B. Holbrook (1982), 'Hedonic consumption: Emerging concepts, methods and propositions', *Journal of Marketing*, **46** (Summer), 92–101.

Houston, M.J. and M.L. Rothschild (1977), 'A paradigm for research on consumer involvement', Working Paper 11-77-46, University of Wisconsin-Madison.

Hupfer, N.T. and D.M. Gardner (1971), 'Differential involvement with products and issues: An exploratory study', in *Proceedings of the Association for Consumer Research*, 2nd Conference, D.M. Gardner, ed. College Park, MD, 262–70.

Kiel, G.C. and R.A. Layton (1981), 'Dimensions of consumer information seeking behavior', *Journal of Marketing Research*, **18** (May), 223–9.

Kiesler, C.A., B.E. Collins, and N. Miller (1969), *Attitude Change*. New York: John Wiley.

Krugman, H.E. (1965), 'The impact of television advertising: Learning without involvement', *Public Opinion Quarterly*, **29** (Fall), 349–56.

Krugman, H.E. (1967), 'The measurement of advertising involvement', *Public Opinion Quarterly*, **30** (Winter), 583–96.

Lastovicka, J.L. and E.H. Bonfield (1982), 'Do consumers have brand attitudes?', *Journal of Economic Psychology*, **2**, 57–75.

Lastovicka, J.L. and D.M. Gardner (1979), 'Components of involvement', in *Attitude Research Plays for High Stakes*, J.C. Maloney and B. Silverman, eds. Chicago: American Marketing Association, 53–73.

Levy, S.J. (1959), 'Symbols for sale', *Harvard Business Review*, **37** (July–August), 117–19.

Newman, J.W. and R. Staelin (1972), 'Prepurchase information seeking for new cars and major household appliances', *Journal of Marketing Research*, **9** (August), 249–57.

Nunnally, J.C. (1978), *Psychometric Theory*. New York: McGraw-Hill.

Ostrom, I.M. and T.C. Brock (1968), 'A cognitive model of attitudinal involvement', in *Theories of Cognitive Consistency*, R.P. Abelson *et al.*, eds. New York: Rand-McNally.

Ray, M.L. (1973), 'Marketing communication and the hierarchy of effects', in *Sage Annual Reviews in Communication Research*, F. Gerald Kline and P. Clark, eds. Beverly Hills, CA: Sage.

Ray, M.L. (1982), *Advertising and Communication Management*. Englewood Cliffs, NJ: Prentice-Hall.

Robertson, T.S. (1976), 'Low-commitment consumer behavior', *Journal of Advertising Research*, **16** (April), 19–24.

Rokeach, M. (1968), *Belief, Attitudes and Values*. San Francisco: Jossey-Bass.

Rothschild, M.L. (1979), 'Advertising strategies for high and low involvement situations', in *Attitude Research Plays for High Stakes*, J.C. Maloney and B. Silverman, eds. Chicago: American Marketing Association, 74–93.

Sherif, M. and H. Cantril (1947), *The Psychology of Ego-Involvement*. New York: John Wiley.

Sherif, M. and C.L. Hovland (1961), *Social Judgment: Assimilation and Constrasts Effects in Communication and Attitude Change*, New Haven, CT: Yale University Press.

Traylor, M.B. (1981), 'Product involvement and brand commitment', *Journal of Advertising Research*, **21** (December), 27–33.

Tyebjee, T.T. (1979), 'Refinement of the involvement concept: An advertising planning point of view', in *Attitude Research Plays for High Stakes*, J.C. Maloney and B. Silverman, eds. Chicago: American Marketing Association, 94–111.

Vaughn, R. (1980), 'How advertising works: A planning model', *Journal of Advertising Research*, **20** (October), 27–33.

Zimbardo, P.G. (1960), 'Involvement and communication discrepancy as determinants of opinion conformity', *Journal of Abnormal and Social Psychology*, **60**, 86–94.

An implicit product theory approach to consumers' inferential judgments about products

Christian Pinson
Associate Professor of Marketing, INSEAD and Affiliate Professor, Université Paris-Dauphine, France

Summary

This article builds on the idea that consumers use (possibly unconscious) expected relationships between product attributes when they have to draw inferences about uncertain product characteristics. These individuals' expectancies regarding the way product attributes are related are conceived of as composing implicit product theories. The paper illustrates the existence of these implicit product theories and addresses some of the key methodological and conceptual issues that deserve future attention within the suggested paradigm.

1. Introduction

When making judgments about products, consumers often need to go beyond the information immediately available to them at the time their judgment is made. Using Nelson's work (1974), the FTC distinguishes three types of product qualities: 'search qualities' (e.g. the color of a product) which can be determined by consumers before purchase; 'experience qualities' (e.g. the taste of a product) which can be assessed only on the basis of actual experience with the product, and finally 'credence qualities' relating to qualities that consumers cannot usually evaluate for themselves (e.g. the robustness of a set of shelves). Although the FTC classification is useful, it does not explicitly address the issue of how consumers may react to missing information.

When a consumer attends to product qualities for which information is not externally available, several reactions may occur. First, the incomplete information may not be noticed, or, if it is noticed, the consumer may not find it important enough to search for additional information. A second alternative could be that the missing information is retrieved from memory or obtained from other individuals. When information is not

From the *International Journal of Research in Marketing*, 3 (1986), 19–38.

available from memory or others, consumers may postpone their product judgment. Alternatively, they may form an inference about the missing information. This inference is then integrated with the information available in the environment. This paper will focus as this final option.

Past research on consumer cue-utilization (e.g. Cohen, 1972; Cox, 1967; Lutz, 1976; Mitchell and Olson, 1981; Olson, 1978, 1980) has shown that a variety of accessed product attributes and product-related attributes often serve as cues to infer other non-accessed product attribute levels. Huber and McCann (1982) have demonstrated that these inferred attributes' values have considerable influence on consumers' product evaluations and purchase intentions. These authors further suggest three conditions which can lead to inference formation: (a) there must be a high ecological correlation between the consumer's perception of the accessed and non-accessed attributes' values; (b) the non-accessed product attribute must be judged important, and (c) certain (unspecified) situational conditions must be met.

The work of Huber and McCann, as well as a related paper by Hansen and Zinkham (1984), is a useful starting point for theoretical development. However, in developing a more complete theoretical model of how and when product inferences are formed, additional factors must be taken into account. With respect to the high ecological correlation or more broadly speaking 'connecting' condition, there is ample evidence that consumers may be influenced by various inferential biases (e.g. Bettman, John and Scott, 1984; Crocker, 1984; Ofir and Lynch, 1984; Tybout and Scott, 1983) and that they often hold and use inferential beliefs which are not necessarily warranted by the information available to them. For example, in their investigation of the causal determinants of consumer attitude formation and change, Mitchell and Olson (1981) discovered that subjects seemed to use visual information that was not directly related to the product to make inference about the product's characteristics. A second factor is that inferential judgments need not be restricted to 'important' non-accessed product attributes (Deighton, 1983). Even for complex products, consumer inferences may involve unimportant attributes. In many instances, they also may rest on highly spontaneous or even unconscious processes (see Winter and Uleman, 1984).

A first objective of this article is thus to show that, in their use of cues, consumers frequently resort to using a kind of lay, or implicit, theory about the underlying structure or internal organization of product attributes. As a quick review of cue utilization studies will show, these relationships need not be logical, and their selection and use may be totally unconscious. A second objective is to explain the cognitive role played by implicit product theories and to suggest how they can be measured. Finally, the issue of their integration into a fully developed conceptualization of consumer inferential judgments is addressed.

2. Consumer use of implicit product theories

The idea that people store information in their memory and use it when confronted with uncertainty is not new. An adequate model of the product judgment process must account for the influence of beliefs about expected relations among known and unknown product attributes. Because they are very similar to the personality trait relationships described in implicit personality theories, the expression 'implicit product theory' is proposed to refer to those subjective networks of relationships among product characteristics which presumably play an important role in mediating product inferential judgments. Therefore, the focus of this paper will be on a *consumer*'s theory of products rather than on a *researcher*'s theory of the way consumers make judgments about products.

The term 'implicit personality theory' was originated by Bruner and Tagiuri (1954). It refers to the fact that people tend to believe that certain characteristics occur jointly in other persons. The theory is called implicit because it is inferred from a person's judgments rather than being presented explicitly by him or her, as a set of conscious and organized beliefs. 'Implicit personality' research (see Schneider, 1973; and Tzeng, 1981) stresses the idea that judgments made about others involve inferences based on trait implicative relationships and that an understanding of these often unconscious judgments is of importance.

One cannot fail to see the similarity between these implicit personality theories and what is termed – by analogy – *implicit product theories*. The term 'theories' is used to indicate that different consumers may hold different implicit product theories, albeit with some common elements and relationships. According to this view, common or general implicit product theory is the reflection of the general, perceived distribution of *attributes* in products, while individual differences represent the effects of idiosyncratic experience coding and retrieval. Individuals may differ (a) in the particular kinds of product attribute inter-relationships that they hold; (b) in the formats and structure used to store these inter-relationships in memory, and (c) in the consciousness and readiness with which the constructs are used in making inferences.

It is through experience and training that people learn to select the right cues and ignore irrelevant cues. Maratsos (1974) provides an amusing example in the genetic psychology area. He found that 'top point' (defined as the distance of an object's top from the base-line) tends to be the key defining characteristic used by pre-operational children to judge how 'tall', 'high' and 'big' an object (or individual) is. Thus a child standing on a chair will be judged 'taller' than an adult who is squatting. The same learning process obviously occurs in the product evaluation area (e.g. Fox and Kehret-Ward, 1985). The consumer slowly builds expertise in discovering the best indicators of the unknown product attributes and developing appropriate knowledge structures (John, 1985).

Information about consumers' implicit product theories might be quite relevant for marketing managers as well as for public policy makers. Marketing managers must determine what might be called the 'cue-mix' of the firm's products. They need to know which cues can be used to reinforce the idea that a product exhibits the desirable characteristics. Consider some of the basic questions about consumers that managers often ask:

- product: what is the psychological meaning of the raw materials that might be used? What would be the consumer's interpretation of the various shapes, textures, sizes, colors . . . that the product could be given?
- branding: will a certain brand name improve or damage the product image?
- pricing: would a certain price be interpreted as a sign of high quality, newness . . .?
- copy research: what are the product characteristics that could be best used to suggest other features of the product?

Public policy makers are interested in providing consumers with better information about products. This requires knowledge of existing inferential practices with a special attention being given to those factors which explains why consumers' inferences are often inaccurate. Consumers are said (Norman and Bobrow, 1975) to be 'data-limited' when the information available to them in their buying environment does not allow sound inferences and decisions. Available information may be inappropriate, insufficient or even in certain cases consciously or unconsciously biased by unethical sellers, e.g. through the use of non-verbal (Cohen, 1972) or emotional cues (Kroeber-Riel, 1984). Such abuse is most likely to occur in low-involvement purchase situations (see Olshavsky and Granbois, 1979), i.e. when consumers are often totally unaware of, and uninterested in their inference processes.[1] Even when the natural consumer environment is not data-limited, consumers' inferences are limited by such individual processing resources as effort, memory capacity and the existence of very subjective beliefs. Thus, the simplifying inferential strategies used by consumers need to be studied – and possibly corrected – by policy makers. A selective survey of the types of intrinsic and extrinsic cues[2] frequently used by consumers follows.

Odor

The original idea for adding fragrance to certain products was to cover foul odors inherent in the materials. Now some manufacturers are using scents to create subconscious impressions of 'newness', 'prestige', 'antiqueness', 'freshness' and so forth. For example, some sellers are reported (Winter, 1976) to spray 'new car smell' (a blending of oil, leather and metal scents) on used cars to make them smell 'new'. In a test (*Women's Wear Daily*, 1961), women perceived stockings with an orange aroma to be of better quality than unscented yet identical stockings. Petroleum companies must inspect gasoline to make sure that it 'smells like gasoline' (Kernan *et al.*, 1970: 146), although the actual odor of gasoline after processing can be very different from the smell consumers are used to.

Noise

The noise made by a product may evoke certain product attributes. The typical automobile buyer is known to use the sound of the door of a car being closed as a cue to quality (Markin, 1974; 223). A new noiseless mixer failed to gain consumer acceptance because 'it didn't seem to have any power . . . it didn't make enough noise' (Froman, 1953). The noise made by the cap of a fountain pen or a lighter being closed, by the shutter of a camera are also used by certain consumers to judge product quality (Yokota, 1983). Cohen (1981: 180) cites several advertising campaigns where sound was used to discriminate food products (cereal, corn chips, tomato juice) from their competition.

Color

The great majority of people are not conscious of the effect[3] a color combination has on them, and yet the fact that color can be effectively used to suggest certain product characteristics is well documented in marketing (e.g. Birren, 1956; Cheskin, 1954; Danger, 1968; Deribéré, 1969; Favre, 1969; Margulies, 1970). For example, reds make the product appear warmer to the individuals whereas greens and blues make the product appear cooler. Several researchers have reported data which suggest that most individuals infer decreasing apparent weight from increasing color lightness. Black boxes usually look heaviest, followed by red and blue, which in turn are followed by yellow and white. Cooper (*Marketing News*, 1983a) reports that Hoover and General Electric went for light colors when they discovered that light weight was valued over strength in a vacuum cleaner, and in an iron, respectively. One of the most persistent findings of the Color Research Institute and of other researchers is that the color of a detergent and its package is a cue often used to judge strength. In one study, the color of a tranquilizer package was found to be associated with the tranquilizing action that people expected from the drug (Dichter, 1971). Frank Perdue – a chicken producer – discovered that in the northeastern regions of the USA, yellow-skinned poultry is better received than the typical white-skinned poultry found in supermarkets. To capitalize on this, he decided to produce yellow chickens by feeding them large quantities of corn and marigold petals (cited by McNeal, 1982: 220).

The meaning of these findings is clear; the color of a product or of its package may set up expectations about the characteristics of this product. Are these perceived associations general? Most probably not. Rather, the effect of color appears to be dependent upon the nature of the product, the particular consumer, and the context.[4] It also varies according to the cultural context. For the Djukas – a black tribe living in Surinam – 'black is a color symbolic of happiness, while white is considered a color of deep mourning' (*Newsweek*, 1974: 30). Red connotes bad luck, death or witchcraft in certain African countries (*Business America*, 1979: 6), whereas it has very positive associations in Asian countries, except those where it is associated with communism and blood. Carson (1967) cites the case of a manufacturer of water recreation products who belatedly discovered that his green emblem was negatively associated in Malaysia with the dangers and diseases of the jungle.

Packaging, product design and brand name

Most marketers agree that product packaging is more than 'just a container'. It is an important communication vehicle: shapes, symbols, colors and designs are vital cues about the contents (Margulies, 1970; Dichter, 1971; Sacharow, 1982). Various combinations of shape, typography, packaging materials, texture, color and illustration may make the product appear expensive or inexpensive, old-fashioned or modern, and so forth. For example, form is said to have an influence on the perceived volume and heaviness of objects (Holmberg, 1983). Shapes are also known to influence the perceived effectiveness of certain products (Dichter, 1971; McNeal, 1982: 223–7). People tend to associate squareness and neatness in the surface design or in the wrapping with solidity and effectiveness. Other associations include sweetness with roundness and bitterness with triangular shapes. A sphere is viewed as being more feminine and delicate whereas a pyramid is masculine. Sacharow (1982) gives the following example:

> The bottle used in Canada for La Batt's beer is short, squat, and brown; however, La Batt market researchers found out that a premium imported beer image can only be projected by a long slender green bottle. The net result was two different shapes: one short Canadian bottle and one long slender green bottle designed for American distribution. (Sacharow, 1982: 42)

Among the other elements that play a decisive role as cues to certain product attributes are labels, brands, logos and other types of symbols (Beraud, 1981). In 1974 United Airlines repainted its entire 367-plane fleet in bold red, white, and orange colors and wide stripes (*Newsweek*, 1974: 70). Its planes had been painted red, white and blue and had featured four official looking stars on the tail and fuselage. This combination was believed to have created in the public the false impression that the company was connected with the military, an impression that United officials were eager to correct, given the prevailing attitude toward the government at the time. Because two elephants symbolize bad luck in Africa, Carlsberg was forced to add a third elephant to its well-known label for one of its major export products (McConnel, 1971).

Another illustration of the power of design as a vehicle is reported by Cheskin (1972: 23–4). In connection with interviews about a problem in interior design, several hundred women were given two jars of cold cream. Both jars contained the same product and were identical in all respects except for the fact that one jar had a cap with a design of two triangles whereas the other jar had a cap with a design of two circles. The women were asked to use both cold creams. Two weeks later, when the interviewer returned he told the women that he would give them a new jar of the one cream that they liked better. More than 80% of the participants asked for the cream in the jar with the circles because 'it was finer in quality', 'the consistency was better' and 'it was easier to apply'. This example illustrates what Cheskin calls 'sensation transference', i.e. consumers transfer the sensation produced by the package to the contents in the package.

Words used in the product or on the package can, too, have connotative meanings. They can connote certain shape, size, sex, age, color, weight and so forth. The interested reader is referred to McNeal (1982: 228–30) for a more detailed presentation of word symbolism. Stauder (1973) and Calder (*Marketing News*, 1983b: 3) give some revealing examples of the way brand name can influence the perceived quality of products. Another related, general point which emerges from several studies (see Cattin *et al.*, 1982) is that the little phrase 'Made in . . .' can have a strong influence on the evaluation of products by consumers.

Other physical attributes

Finally, other physical attributes can be used as cues. One researcher discovered a relationship between the amount of pickup drivers perceived in a car and the amount of tension in the spring controlling the accelerator pedal (Politz, 1957). One detergent manufacturer used the weight of a package in advertising to suggest that Dash is concentrated. Levy (1973: 7) advises against round tables in banks because '. . . there is some indication that people feel round tables create ambiguity about one's proper place at it and reduce the sense of privacy that is preferred while filling out forms'.

Price

Numerous studies have shown that consumers use price as an important cue for the quality of products (Helgeson and Beatly, 1985; Jacoby and Olson, 1977). In spite of the abundance of studies, the exact form of the relationship between price and quality remains unclear (Zeithaml, 1984). There is some evidence that price may be a cue for quality only within certain upper and lower limits (e.g. Wheatley and Chiu, 1977). Several researchers have found that price had a more limited influence on perceived quality when other cues were available such as 'brand-related knowledge', 'reports of product tests', 'perceived market share', 'store image' and 'product composition' (e.g. Monroe *et al.*, 1977; Berkowitz and Walton, 1980; Park and Lessig, 1981). The phenomenon of judging quality by price seems to occur more frequently when quality is difficult to judge on the basis of other quality-connoting criteria and when there are perceived variations of quality among brands. The importance of price as a cue, however, is underscored by the fact that many consumers do not perceive price correctly. Consumers tend to rely more on the price ranges of different stores than on the prices of single products, particularly when such price comparisons are inconvenient, confusing or rendered more difficult (Zeithaml, 1982).

Although the foregoing review is not exhaustive, it presents a representative picture of the cue utilization literature, both in terms of direction and scope. One of the major problems with these studies is that they tend to be anecdotal and quite product-specific. Also, most of them deal with bivariate associations involving a single cue and a single attribute to be inferred. Therefore it is suggested that instead of examining the manner in which certain cues are used to form an inference, a more reasonable and fruitful approach would be to move to a more abstract level of analysis and to explicitly consider the structure of product-related information as stored in memory.

The prime focus of this paper is on describing the structure of knowledge representations for a product as corresponding to each consumer's implicit theory of how product attributes are related to each other. This view of consumer inferential judgments is quite compatible with a good deal of consumer information processing research. It is believed to offer a parsimonious model (if not a theory) of some of the constructs and processes at work in consumer inferential judgments.

3. The notion of implicit product schemata

In stressing that individuals evaluate products by placing their own cognitive construction over them, implicit product theory establishes an absolute necessity for studying consumers' idiosyncratic, and often very subjective viewpoints. An adequate model of the products judgment process must account for the influence of all (accurate or inaccurate) beliefs about the implicit structure of the product being judged. These assumed associations among product attributes we call *implicit product schemata*. Consumers can form a judgment on the basis of their implicit product schemata whenever information on product attributes is missing or incomplete. The whole set of implicit product schemata relating to the various attributes of a given product constitutes the implicit product theory held by the consumer regarding the particular product under judgment.

The notion of implicit product schemata has its roots in such earlier expressions as 'inferential beliefs' (Fishbein and Ajzen, 1975; Olson, 1978, 1980; Dover, 1982), and 'implicational molecules' (Abelson and Reich, 1969). The main reason for adding yet another term is to integrate these concepts within the current terminology of cognitive psychology and artificial intelligence research, where information coding, storing, and retrieval are usually studied within the memory schemata paradigm (Alba and Hasker, 1983). The use of the term schemata (singular: schema) stresses the filtering function of the anticipated relationships between product attributes and the nature of the internal representation (Taylor and Crocker, 1981). The term schema, as it is used in cognitive psychology and artificial intelligence, refers to 'a framework for tying together the information about a given concept or even with specifications about the types of inter-relations and restrictions upon the way things fit together' (Norman and Bobrow, 1975a: 125). Other authors such as Rumelhart (1977) and Thorndyke and Hayes-Roth (1979) give somewhat similar definitions.

Implicit product schemata have three functions: (a) they produce an organization of information to be encoded; (b) they create expectations about what to look for and direct attention and selection from the many cues presented by the environment, and (c) they permit making an inference as to the signification of the ambiguous elements of the inference-object. This paper focuses on the third function.

Implicit product schemata may be at varying levels of abstractness and generality. Consider, for example, the semantic statement: 'Speed is dangerous'. This statement is very general in that it does not refer to a product class in particular but rather applies to any circumstance involving speed. 'Driving fast is dangerous' would be a subschema of the above general schema. It explicitly refers to an action (driving) but the entities to which the statement refers are left undetermined – it could be any vehicle or any missile. Now consider the following statement:

> 'I would not want to drive a care like that' (the customer points to a small BMW car in the parking lot). 'I know it is a good German car but I would not feel secure inside it. It is really a sports car, you know. Look! I am not a Grand Prix champion . . . Small cars are dangerous, any way. The crash tests the government runs proves that . . . My secretary's boyfriend has an Audi Quattro (also a German car). He gave me a ride one day. It was the sort of experience I will never forget!'

This statement refers to a particular product (a car) and involves at least four products cues: the size (small), the brand (BMW), the type (a sports car) and the country of origin (Germany). In inferring that the car is likely to be unsafe, the consumer explicitly also uses an external cue (the tests run by the government) and alludes to his own driving habits and skills. He also extracts from his episodic memory a particularly unpleasant experience involving another individual (his secretary's boyfriend). The schemata retrieved by this consumer to infer the safety of the car involve more than one cue and are much more specific than the ones mentioned earlier.[5]

4. Development of implicit product schemata

At least two reasons can be given for the existence of a given product schema. First of all, it may be based on the individual's (or someone else's) experience of 'past regularities' of the relationships between the various phenomena of interest (e.g. the known and to-be-inferred product attributes). For example, the size and price of cars are reasonably well correlated with each other. The assumption here is that certain attributes tend to co-exist in products and that the consumer, consciously or not, is able to store information about these relationships.[6]

Attribute relationships may be interpreted in at least two ways: (a) as an indication of synonymity or semantic substitutability (e.g. 'robust' and 'sturdy'), and (b) as an indication of co-existence e.g. 'expensive' and 'robust', that is the degree to which the two attributes are perceived as occurring in the same product. For purposes here, co-existences are more appropriate.

The most important feature of the relationship between the uncertain properties of products and the cues available in the consumer environment is its lack of univocality. Cues provide only a hint as to the true nature of the unknown product attribute. To illustrate, the size–price schema mentioned earlier will obviously provide a wrong inference if the consumer is comparing a standard Chevrolet station wagon with the latest Porsche model. Brunswik (1955) suggested that the individual behaves much like an 'intuitive statistician'. Because the environment does not provide totally reliable cues, the individual will cope with such a semi-erratic information base by a process of 'vicarious functioning', that is, by accumulating and combining cues. When a cue, which is ordinarily depended upon for information is unavailable, a second cue which is believed to be highly correlated with the missing cue can be substituted.

Secondly, some more subjective processes seem to accompany the learning and transmission of past regularities. Certain cues seem to take an *eindringlich* (i.e. 'impressive') quality which means that they are used more than their 'ecological' validity (in Brunswik's sense) warrants. A cue is said to have high predictive value when there is, *a priori*, a high perceived probability that it will lead to a correct inference regarding the unknown product attribute, if correctly used. Confidence value refers to the individual's perceived probability of correctly using the cue. Past research shows that people often do not hesitate to use weak cues, i.e. cues with low predictive value but with reasonable confidence value (for a review of this literature see Schellinck, 1980). This mixture of statistical analytic analysis, intuitive thinking and personal 'resonance' (Duncker, 1945) is very close to what has been called 'quasi-rationality' by Hammond and Brehmer (1973).

That man is an imperfect information processor has been amply documented in the psychological literature (e.g. Hogarth, 1975; Nisbett and Ross, 1980; Hogarth and Makridakis, 1981; Kahneman *et al.*, 1982), as well as in consumer research studies (e.g. Wright, 1975; Bettman, 1979; Henry, 1980). Individuals are not only biased in the way they *acquire* information, but also in the way they *process* information.

Individuals tend to acquire information on the basis of their own experience, i.e. in a selective way. For example, a number of researchers have shown that covariation may go undetected when subjects do not expect covariation, and conversely, that individuals may perceive covariation where there is none if they hold beliefs leading them to expect it (see Bettman, John and Scott, 1984).

People are conservative in processing information. For example, research on subjective probability assessment has consistently found that subjects fail to revise their opinions on receipt of new information to the same extent as Bayes' theorem. Typically, the new data have less impact on the subjects' estimates than the formula warrants. Attribution biases (Kelley and Michela, 1980) can also be viewed as a form of information processing conservatism or inertia: individuals tend to attribute information conflicting with past inferential judgments to external or random factors. Base-rate fallacy research (Bar-Hillel, 1980; Dickson, 1982; Tybout and Scott, 1983) shows that judgments tend to be dominated by case (singular) information rather than by base-rate (distributional) information.

Hutchinson (1983) has shown that judgment of an object is affected by characteristics of accompanying objects to be judged concurrently. Related to this is the well-known problem of halo effect (for an excellent review of the phenomenon and of potential solutions, see Holbrook, 1983; and Dillon et al., 1984). This effect is genuinely defined as a global, general impression that seeps into the individual perceptions of the attributes of an entity. Whether due to conscious or subconscious mechanisms (Nisbett and Wilson, 1977a), this effect corresponds to a perceptual/cognitive distortion; unless of course the individual and global perceptions are truly correlated (Cooper, 1981). This error is usually attributable to the individuals' insufficient effort or motivation to fully sample the available information and to their lack of sensitivity to the coloring impact of their overall impressions. Research by Beckwick and Lehmann (1975) suggests that stimulus ambiguity increases the likelihood of halo effect. Forcing subjects to rate non-salient product attributes is also believed (e.g. Mitchell and Olson, 1981) to encourage the development of halo effects. Such moderating effect is of great potential importance in the study of inferential judgment, which by definition involves considerable stimulus ambiguity.

5. Storage of implicit product schemata

Faced with a complex information environment (Wright, 1974) and to simplify past data encoding and later inferential tasks, consumers may not store implicit product schemata in the form of propositional systems. Rather, they could conveniently store implicit product schemata in the form of 'exemplars' (Ebbesen and Allen, 1979) or 'typical instances' (Bruner et al., 1956: 64), i.e. instances which are seen as prototypical of the product category. When asked to make an inference, consumers may retrieve one or more instances which possess the known product attributes (cues) and examine whether they also possess the attribute(s) to be inferred (see Schneider and Blankmeyer, 1983). For example, one may access the reliability of a microcomputer by recalling the types of microcomputers used by one's acquaintances and the types of problems associated with them; poor reliability will appear probable if problems are prevalent among the cases which are retrieved in this manner. Prototype-based inference will of course be totally inaccurate if the typical instances retrieved do not actually 'represent' the category they are supposed to be prototypes of. Use of non-representative instances is not uncommon. Research on social inferences has shown that subjects may solve a particular inference task by way of analogy with some entities they feel particularly comfortable with. Secord and Jonrard (1956) show that individuals use their mothers as frames of reference when asked to rate young women. Another example of prototype-like instances is the self. Self schemata (Markus, 1980) are constructed from information about specific events and situations involving the individual and from the invariances that people have discovered in their own past behavior. A series of experiments by Kuiper and Rogers (1979) suggest that the 'self' can be viewed as a prototype-like instance that the individual is using – mainly in the absence of other types of information – to make inferences about others.

Similarly one can conjecture that consumers may assign a prototype-like function to the product most easily 'available', the product they are the most familiar with, the 'best' product they have experienced (Nedungadi and Hutchinson, 1985) or more generally speaking the product most 'concrete', 'salient' or 'vivid' (Nisbett and Ross, 1980; Taylor and Thomson, 1982; Ajzen and Fishbein, 1983). The presence of idiosyncracies in consumer implicit product theories may thus be attributed – at least in some cases – to a particularly interesting or marking past encounter with an instance of the product class. For example, the cues '1972 vintage' and 'Bordeaux red wine' are more likely to be vividly remembered as being negatively associated with 'below average quality' if the consumer, claiming to be a wine connoisseur, went through the socially embarrassing experience of presenting such a bottle as 'outstanding'. The concreteness and proximity/directness of this episode involving one particular instance (one 1972 red Bordeaux bottle), and the resulting involuntary imagery are expected to contribute substantially to its emotional impact and possibly to the extension of the found relationship to say, all 1972 French wines (clearly a mistake if applied to some Rhone red wines). In contrast, when reading the same information in a specialized magazine, it seems to be one of those things that is relevant but does not necessarily get stored in memory as a vivid experience. Consequently, the tendency to give excessive weight to vivid, episodic or case-history information and to partly disregard pallid, statistical or abstract information can result in drastic distortions of reality. Implicit product theories may thus involve stereotypic views of products, when consumers indulge in too much biased selection and assimilation of evidence (Grant and Holmes, 1981). We turn now to the issue of how to measure consumers' implicit product theories.

6. Measurement of product implicit theories

The literature on implicit personality theory suggests a variety of methods to measure consumers' implicit product theories. In the following we consider two distinct steps in the research procedure: (a) the measurement of product attribute relationships, and (b) the representation and interpretation of these relationships.

Product attribute relationships can be generated *directly* by presenting subjects with a set of product attributes pre-selected by the investigator on the basis of prior experience with the stimulus domain. In some way, subjects are asked to assess rather directly the perceived relationships among product attributes. The various ways of obtaining the data are briefly described.

In the check list method, subjects are given a list of adjectives (or expressions) describing product attributes and asked to check those adjectives that best correspond to some stimulus-products. Alternatively, product profile data can be obtained by using rating or semantic differential scales. Correlations among product attributes can be calculated across stimulus products (or across subjects) and the matrix of product interrelationships can be reduced – usually through some form of factor analysis (for a recent application, see Van der Kloot and

Kroonenberg, 1982). In traditional trait-inference studies (e.g. Warr and Knapper, 1968), subjects are presented with (personality) trait-names as descriptive of some hypothetical individual and then asked to make inferences about the presence of other traits in that individual. In the product judgment area, the typical question would have the following form: 'Given that product P possesses attribute X, how likely is it that it has attribute Y?'.

Alternative methods are available. For example, subjects can be asked to rate how similar or dissimilar pairs of attributes are, given one or more stimulus domains (e.g. Girard and Cliff, 1973). Another approach, the trait sorting method was first used in implicit personality research by Rosenberg *et al.* (1968). In their study, subjects were asked to describe several persons of their own choice by sorting personality trait names into different groups, each group representing a different person. Subjects were free to distribute the traits given to them among the persons they had in mind in any way they wished. In addition, those traits which did not seem to go together with others could be put in a 'miscellaneous' category.

As noted by Schneider (1973: 297), the major advantage of methods which focus on correlations between attributes actually assigned to stimulus products is that they are more natural hence less subjective and potentially biased than methods where subjects are asked to explicitly state perceived inter-relationships among more abstract product attributes. A limitation of correlational measures[7] however, is that they do not allow for the study of asymmetrical relationships. A number of empirical studies make the assumption of symmetry questionable. Within the field of person perception, several researchers have often found marked asymmetries (e.g. Hendrick, 1969). For example, 'being cynical' implied 'being precise', but 'being precise' did not imply 'being cynical'. If the inference task – 'does X imply Y?' – is solved by examining an imaginal or analog representation of the product (for possible co-occurrence of X and Y within this representation), then one would probably expect to find a symmetric $X - Y$ association. Use of a propositional code or (mental) examination of several instances of the product class would allow more clearly for the existence of an asymmetric association. Although intuitively appealing, such an hypothesis can only be speculative, given the absence of empirical evidence.

All the direct methods described above assume that the investigator is able to collect a representative sample of all the important (conscious and unconscious) factors underlying the 'gestalt' of the product(s) considered. If this condition is not met, the basic factors obtained will not reflect the true implicit product theories but rather the investigator's product attribute sampling biases. This limitation is particularly severe for product judgment situations where it is believed that cue selection and inferences may operate unconsciously. Those product attribute interrelationships that are perceived to be illogical by the investigator are particularly likely to be excluded, hence eliminating the possibility of identifying certain subjects' idiosyncrasies. One partial solution to this problem is the use of a *free-response approach* as advocated by Rosenberg and his co-workers (e.g. Rosenberg and Sedlak, 1972; Kim and Rosenberg, 1980).

In this approach, subjects are asked to describe in their own terms a set of persons they know. The subjects' data are then aggregated to obtain a profile distance measure (δ) that reflects the direct and indirect co-occurrence of the traits in the free response protocols. The profile distance measure (δ_{ij}) is given by the following formula:

$$\delta_{ij} = \sum_{k \in T} (s_{ik} - s_{jk})^2,$$

where T is the set of traits; i, j and k are traits, and s is the 'disagreement score' between any two traits. It is obtained for each pair of traits by counting the number of subjects who assigned the two traits to two different persons they had in mind. For example, if n of the N subjects assign two given traits to the same person, the 'disagreement score' will be $N - n$. As explained by the authors, the main rationale for using the δ-measure rather than simply the s-measure is that the δ-measure provides a measure of *direct* trait co-occurrence (the s-measure) plus a measure of *indirect* trait co-occurrence. The concept of indirect trait co-occurrence refers to instances where traits i and k co-occur in one description, j and k co-occur in another description, and i and j do not occur in either description. As noted by Rosenberg (1977), indirect co-occurrences allow to capture certain perceived covariations that subjects may not be willing to acknowledge directly.[8] The trait structures obtained from aggregated free-response data however yield less stable measures of trait relatedness and do not permit a reliable ascertainment of individual differences (Rosenberg, 1977).

Finally, *naturalistic* descriptions or data have also been recently used. A naturalistic description is a description 'that is not in response to any contrived arrangement between subject and investigator' (Rosenberg, 1977). For example Rosenberg and Jones (1972) used Theodore Dreiser's *A gallery of women* to study his implicit personality theory. Terms and phrases referring to traits were extracted from Dreiser's descriptions of 15 women. A measure of trait co-occurrence for each pair of traits, based on the proportion of times the two traits were actually ascribed to the same characters relative to the total usage of the two terms, was used as input. Whereas naturalistic descriptions of this type may prove impossible to obtain for consumer products, they might be somewhat easier to extend to industrial products, where written documents might be found and analyzed. One should acknowledge however, that such opportunities are likely to be extremely rare and that such an approach is likely to be economically prohibitive.

In conclusion, consumer protocol data, at least those generated in response to an arrangement between an investigator and a set of subjects (e.g., free elicitation) might be a satisfactory compromise[9] between fixed format and totally naturalistic methods (Rosenberg, 1977). Protocol methods have already been frequently used in consumer research (see Marks and Olson, 1981; Lynch and Srull, 1982). Admittedly, they are time-consuming and subjects are obviously selective in what they report. First, there is no guarantee that people are fully conscious of all their implicit product schemata nor are they able to express them (Nisbett and Wilson, 1977b; Peterson and Kerin, 1981). A problem is that some elements of implicit product schemata may be withheld because they are perceived to be irrelevant, unimportant, illogical or embarrassing. Also the act of reporting schemata may positively or negatively affect its strength in subsequent inferences. Still protocol approaches provide a potentially useful way to uncover the type of subject's idiosyncracies that a fixed format method would find difficult to either incorporate in its instructions or to extract from the data gathered. The research program undertaken by Olson and his co-workers on consumer cognitive structures (e.g. Kanwar *et al.*, 1981; see also Dover, 1982) provides encouraging evidence that protocol and protocol-type methods can indeed be used, at least in the research exploratory stages. In later stages, more structured methods such as the ones described earlier can be fruitfully used.[10]

The attribute co–occurrence matrix[11] can be analyzed by employing multidimensional scaling techniques (see Rosenberg *et al.*, 1968; Chan and Jackson, 1979). The application of MDS allows one to represent attributes as a set of points in a space of reduced dimensionality. Points close together in the configuration represent highly 'related' attributes, and points distant from one another represent highly 'unrelated' attributes. The paper by Green (1974) constitutes a pioneering but unfortunately isolated attempt to extend the MDS analysis of personality traits to the production of spatial representation of product features configurations. His 'product feature model' was not thought of in implicit product theory terms, but it is an excellent illustration of the paradigm presented here. Cluster analysis provides a complement to multidimensional scaling. The application of a clustering routine to attribute co–occurrences effectively reduces the entire set of terms to a small set of meaningful clusters. These clusters can be viewed as more or less distinct product types. The usual limitations of data analysis methods apply here. For example, MDS and cluster analysis procedures often fail to adequately represent small, highly meaningful clusters of attributes, at least when they are isolated (i.e. in the minority) in large protocol data (Rosenberg, 1976).

7. Research issues

The central idea which has been developed in the preceding pages is that in judging products, consumers often tend to form overall, very subjective impressions that extend beyond the limited information available to them. Of particular interest to the present article was the consumers' predispositions to use certain cues on the basis of pre-existing assumptions about the way product attributes are inter-related. These anticipated inter-relations were labeled 'implicit product schemata'. The set of implicit product schemata constitutes the implicit product theory held by a consumer or group of consumers regarding a given product.

The conceptualization suggested is believed to provide a useful framework for studying consumer product cue utilization behavior. The ideas developed in this paper do not constitute a theory of implicit product theories but rather a theoretical orientation that requires more conceptual and empirical research. At this point, there is insufficient evidence for predicting which implicit product schemata may exist and which ones are apt to be brought to bear on judgments in a given situation. In the following, some of the research issues which need to be addressed are briefly mentioned.

Measure validation

The various methods available to measure implicit product schemata need to be contrasted in terms of their appropriateness for extracting the actual implicit product schemata. Subjects are very often unable (or unwilling) to report the factors that actually prompted their behavior. This suggests that the correctness of the implicit product schemata extracted by traditional methods may have to be controlled by using some form of probing (Lynch and Srull, 1982); by identifying and eliminating all social desirability factors, and by checking the data obtained through a multi-method approach. For a step in this direction, see Kim and Rosenberg, 1980; Powell and Jühnke, 1983.

Cue configurality

Conceivably the types of cue patterns that consumers use need not be linear. Rather they may be configural. 'Configurality' means that the individual's interpretation or weighing of a cue varies according to the nature of other available information. A study by Holbrook and Moore (1981) strongly suggests that product feature interactions may be encouraged by pictoral stimulus presentations. Also configurality is more likely to occur when subjects evaluate products on the basis of very subjective criteria such as sensory experience, symbolic or aesthetic value. One can further hypothesize that a similar tendency to rely on configural cue patterns should characterize those individuals who tend to rely on imaginal or analog representations of products when making inferential judgments; as opposed to propositional representations, within which interaction effects might be more difficult to store. At this point, such an idea is purely speculative and requires empirical testing.

Format of implicit product schemata

Another critical issue which needs to be raised concerns the exact format used by consumers for encoding and retrieving implicit product schemata. The position adopted in this paper is that consumers are capable of using different forms of representation. Consumers can retain information about product attribute interrelationships in the form of specific semantic statements of varying generality. Alternatively they can store implicit product schemata as images corresponding to 'proto-typical', 'typical' or 'impressive' instances.

The exact format in which implicit product schemata are encoded will be affected by the individual's idiosyncratic characteristics and experiences. Encoding is also likely to be influenced by the feeling states and the subjective perspective adopted by the individual at the time the information is initially received and organized (Bower, 1981). For example, it seems reasonable to postulate that consumers probably encode only those aspects that they believe sufficient for making future decisions. If later, information about the missing attribute is not contained in the propositional memory files, the individual might be able to retrieve an image of a prototypical product and to inspect it to find an answer (Kosslyn, 1975). This suggests several research questions. First, under what conditions is an image more likely to be used to encode an implicit product schema rather than a propositional code? Paivio (1971) suggests that the concreteness and vividness of the stimulus-object will encourage the differential formation of an image, and hence its potential utilization (see also Lutz and Lutz, 1977). Are there other factors, and if yes, which ones? Second, it would be of vital importance for consumer researchers and managers to identify the factors that lead to the conscious or unconscious selection of a particular product as a 'proto-typical' or 'impressive' instance. Third, when using an image or a propositional system to answer an inferential task, subjects may be unable to extract from it the relevant information. They may have to resort to the simplifying heuristic of 'filling in' the missing details in a manner consistent with other schemata. What are the mechanisms underlying this 'filling in' process? What are the factors influencing which additional schemata will be elicited and at the exclusion of others? These are important questions for future research to address.

Structural properties of implicit product theories

Procedures are potentially available for measuring such structural properties of implicit product theories as their abstraction, complexity, centralization and consistency (Scott *et al.*, 1979). These procedures cannot be described in this paper but the reader will find an early use of some of them, although in a slightly different conceptual context, in a study by Kanwar *et al.* (1981). Such an approach would allow the investigator to study the possible existence of structural differences in the various implicit product theories held by consumers. If found, these differences could be investigated and their origins traced to individual and/or situational factors. For example, one can speculate that the complexity of a given individual's implicit product theory will be a function of certain personal, cognitive and personality traits as well as the expression of such situational variables as the familiarity with, and involvement in, the product class (Park and Lessig, 1981; Conover, 1982).

Changing implicit product schemata

Implicit product schemata need to be studied on three dimensions: *veridicality*, *stability* and *generality* (Hogarth, 1980). A *veridical* implicit product schema accurately represents reality. A *stable* implicit product schema is one that is not likely to change. A *general* product implicit schema is one that applies to a wide range of products. There is no doubt that the generality of the implicit product schemata is of great interest to marketing people. Do certain groups of consumers share the same implicit product schemata? Are these schemata generalizable across products? At this point in time, the above issues have to be left unanswered. In the following, we briefly address the general issue of the modification of consumers' implicit product schemata.

As indicated earlier, certain subjective processes can lead consumers to hold implicit theories that are premature or even erroneous: this is all the more important since several researchers (see Wyer *et al.*, 1984) have shown that with the passing of time schemata tend to replace the original information or experience on which they are based. An optimistic expectation is that consumers would be able and willing to change their beliefs, if presented with disconfirming evidence. Research on belief perseverance and change (e.g. Weber and Crocker, 1983) indicates that modification of implicit product schemata may require either massive amounts of disconfirming evidence or vivid and dramatic experience. Suppose that a consumer has been transmitted the stereotypic belief – still common in some European countries – that cars 'with an automatic transmission' are 'unsafe' because they lack the type of quick acceleration response necessary to escape from a dangerous situation. Next, assume that a close relative of this individual gets severely hurt in a car accident which is partly or totally attributed to the type of car and (automatic) transmission used. Such an event would be so unique that provision of massive statistical evidence is unlikely to eliminate the memory trace of the dramatic and therefore immediately 'available' event. Concrete, imagery-inducing scenes such as difficult and dangerous pursuits involving well known racing drivers, policemen or stunt men might have more impact over time.

More generally, the present paper suggests the following question: Should and can consumers be trained to become more competent 'intuitive statisticians'? To be effective, debiasing programs would require a substantial change in the individual's perception and attitude towards the inferential task (Fischoff, 1982; Nisbett *et al.*, 1982: 12). The perceived nature of product evaluations – expressed in perceived interest, importance, risk and so forth – must justify the extra effort of producing an improved inference.

A second difficulty is that even the so-called experts often lack the 'correct' inferential rules or heuristics to apply to what can be called 'ill-defined' inferential tasks, i.e. situations in which no fixed criteria are available for deciding the extent to which a product does have a certain attribute or combination of attributes. One should therefore acknowledge that in certain cases, eliminating or reducing subjective and symbolic processes will not necessarily be possible or desirable, as most consumers appear to require some minimum level of symbolic interpretation of the goods and services they purchase and consume (Belk *et al.*, 1982). The fact that *some* inferential judgments are very subjective and may be highly unstable in the face of changing experiences and choice environments should not however discourage consumer researchers from studying their genesis and evolution. Not *all* consumers are *all* the time behaving in a purely subjective manner!

8. Conclusion

The issue of how prior knowledge about a product affects product judgments has been of growing importance in consumer research. Because consumers often make judgments on the basis of information that is not directly present at the time of judgment, much more research needs to be conducted on consumer inference processes.

Instead of trying to develop a researcher's theory of the way consumers judge products, the paper stressed the importance of better understanding consumers' implicit theories about products, i.e. the set of product attribute relationships (logical and illogical) that the consumer (consciously or unconsciously) stores in, and retrieves from memory when inferring missing product attributes. Although some of these implicit product theories may be poor representations of reality, they serve the function of providing simple and quick heuristics for solving a variety of inferential tasks. This function is particularly significant in those situations where consumers do not engage in formal decision making but rather evaluate products in an intuitive, global, involuntary or unconscious fashion (Olshavsky and Granbois, 1979).

This has implications for both private and public policy makers. It is worthwhile for marketing managers to further explore the conditions under which recipients of product related persuasive messages may engage in heuristic information processing (Chaiken, 1980) and to explore more systematically the kinds of mental constructs and processes that underlie product evaluations. On the other hand, public policy makers should recognize that consumers are often guided by goals that are quite distant from those guiding rational or scientific inferences. Whether the consumer will find it advisable to substitute more rational strategies for heuristic ones will most probably be a matter of relative costs and benefits (Shugan, 1980).

Like many new conceptualizations, the present paper generates more questions than it answers. The paper's basic value is probably in raising the issue of how consumers' expected product relationships – and particularly those which seem 'odd' to observers, should be treated as a construct in consumer behavior theory and practice. We believe that the literature reviewed and the ideas introduced in this paper are sufficiently interesting to warrant further investigation.

Notes

1. In the field of advertising, Coleman (1983) provides an extremely interesting description of how consumers are frequently manipulated through the use of semantic and prosodic cues. The other chapters in Part III of the same volume offer a stimulating presentation of other forms of deceptive communication.
2. Although situational variables (Belk, 1975) are appropriately excluded from the definition of the implicit product theory held by consumers, this should not be construed to mean that they cannot be used as cues to judge certain unknown product attributes. Kotler (1973–74) coined the term 'atmospherics' to describe the conscious designing of space to create certain effects in buyers (see also Donovan and Rossiter, 1982). The major dimensions of an atmosphere are the visual dimension (color, brightness, size, shape); the aural dimension (volume, pitch), and the tactile dimension (softness, smoothness, temperature). Other features of the buying environment such as location, store layout and display, and characteristics of sales personnel also may provide consumers with cues as to the types and quality of products being carried by the store.
3. Consumers' responses to colors can be explained by a combination of rather general physiological factors and of certain traditional uses. For example, red is known to have arousing effects on behavior in comparison to green, which is said to be 'restful' (e.g. Bellizi et al., 1983). Although subjects may differ in their color preferences and in their reactions to different colors, lists of general affective and semantic associations with colors are available for a variety of countries (e.g. Oyama et al., 1962; Winick, 1963; Osgood et al., 1975; Sivik, 1975; Dumaurier, 1980–81).
4. Color associations may undergo drastic changes over time. For example, yellow and green were the official colors of European court fools and a symbol of folly during the Middle Ages. Today, they have more positive associations.
5. Russo and Johnson (1980) offer an interesting study of how consumer knowledge is organized by inferential level.
6. One should note that self perceptions are themselves inferences.
7. Moreover, correlations reflect only covariations, whereas distance measures reflect means and variance as well as covariances.
8. In contrast with this, the trait sorting approach often assumes mutually exclusive categories, i.e. mutually exclusive attribute possession.
9. This is not to say that other traditional methods such as experimentation should not be used. The method developed by Lynch and Shoben (see Lynch and Srull, 1982: 28) is a good illustration of the usefulness of the experimental paradigm in understanding inference processes.
10. There are other problems associated with the various data gathering techniques suggested here but they are not specific to measurement of implicit product theories. Rather they can be found in a variety of consumer research contexts.
11. One could also think of covariation type measures, where high or low levels of given attributes are perceived to coincide with high or low levels of other attributes.

References

Abelson, R.P. and C.M. Reich (1969), 'Implicational molecules: A method for extracting meaning from input sentences', *Proceedings of the International Joint Conference on Artificial Intelligence.* Washington, DC: A.C.M.

Ajzen, I. and M. Fishbein (1975), 'A Bayesian analysis of attribution processes', *Psychological Bulletin*, 82, 261–277.

Ajzen, I. and M. Fishbein (1983), 'Relevance and availability in the attribution process', in J. Jaspars, F.D. Fincham and M. Hewstone (eds.), *Attribution Theory and Research: Conceptual Developmental and Social Dimensions*, London: Academic Press, 63–89.

Alba, J.W. and L. Hasker (1983), 'Is memory schematic?', *Psychological Bulletin*, 93, 203–231.

Bar-Hillel, M. (1980), 'The base rate fallacy in probability judgments', *Acta Psychologica*, 44, 211–233.

Beckwith, N.E. and D.R. Lehmann (1975), 'The importance of halo effects in multi-attribute attitude models', *Journal of Marketing Research*, 12, 265–275.

Belk, R.W. (1975), 'Situational variables and consumer research', *Journal of Consumer Research*, 2, 157–164.

Belk, R.W., K.D. Bahn and R.N. Mayer (1982), 'Developmental recognition of consumption symbolism', *Journal of Consumer Research*, 9, 4–17.

Bellizzi, J.A., A.E. Crowley and R.W. Hasty (1983), 'The effects of color in store design', *Journal of Retailing*, 59, 21–45.

Beraud, R. (1981), 'Le bestiaire des marques', *Revue Française du Marketing*, Cahier 86, 3–35.

Berkowitz, E.N. and J.R. Walton (1980), 'Contextual influences on consumer price responses: An experimental analysis', *Journal of Marketing Research*, 17, 349–358.

Bettman, J.R. (1979), *An Information Processing Theory of Consumer Choice*. Reading, MA: Addison-Wesley.

Bettman, J.R., D.R. John and C.A. Scott (1984), 'Consumers' assessment of covariation', in T.C. Kinnear (ed.), *Advances in Consumer Research*, Vol. 11, Ann Arbor, MI: ACR, 466–471.

Birren, F. (1956), *Selling Color to People*. New York: University Books.

Bower, G.H. (1981), 'Mood and memory', *American Psychologist*, 36, 129–148.

Bruner, J.S., J.J. Goodnow and G.A. Austin (1956), *A Study of Thinking*. New York: Wiley.

Bruner, J.S. and R. Tagiuri (1954), 'The perception of people', in G. Lindzey (ed.), *Handbook of Social Psychology*, Vol. 2, Cambridge, MA: Addison-Wesley, 634–654.

Brunswik, E. (1955), 'Representative design and probabilistic theory', *Psychological Review*, 62, 193–217.

Business America (1979), 'Adapting export packaging to cultural differences', 3 December, 3–7.

Capon, N. and R. Lutz (1979), 'A model and methodology for the development of consumer information programs', *Journal of Marketing*, 43, 58–67.

Carson, D. (1967), *International Marketing: A comparative approach*. New York: Wiley.

Cattin, P., A. Jolibert and C. Lohnes (1982), 'A cross-cultural study of "made in" concepts', *Journal of International Business Studies*, 13, 131–141.

Chaiken, S. (1980), Heuristic vs. systematic information processes, and the use of source versus message cues in persuasion', *Journal of Personality and Social Psychology*, 39, 752–766.

Chan, D.W. and D.N. Jackson (1979), 'Implicit theory of psychopathology', *Multivariate Behavioral Research*, 14, 3–19.

Cheskin, L. (1954), *Color Guide for Marketing Media*. New York: Macmillan.

Cheskin, L. (1972), *Marketing Success: How to Achieve It*. Boston, MA: Cahners Books.

Cohen, D. (1972), 'Surrogate indicators and deception in advertising', *Journal of Marketing*, 36, 10–15.

Cohen, D. (1981). *Consumer Behavior*. New York: Random House.

Coleman, L. (1983), 'Semantic and prosodic manipulation in advertising', in R.J. Harris (ed.), *Information Processing Research in Advertising*. Hillsdale, NJ: Erlbaum, 217–240.

Cooper, W.H. (1981), 'Ubiquitous halo', *Psychological Bulletin*, 90, 218–224.

Conover, J.N. (1982), 'Familiarity and the structure of product knowledge', in A.A. Mitchell (ed.), *Advances in Consumer Research*, Vol. 9, Ann Arbor, MI: ACR, 494–498.

Cox, D.F. (1967), 'The sorting rule model of the consumer product evaluation process', in D.F. Fox (ed.), *Risk Taking and Information Handling in Consumer Behavior*. Boston, MA: Graduate School of Business Administration, Harvard University, 34–81.

Crocker, J. (1981), 'Judgment of covariation by social perceivers', *Psychological Bulletin*, **90**, 272–292.

Crocker, J. (1984), 'A schematic approach to changing consumers' beliefs', in T.C. Kinnear (ed.), *Advances in Consumer Research*, Vol. 11, Ann Arbor, MI: ACR, 472–477.

Danger, E.P. (1968), *Using Colour to Sell*. London: Gower.

Deighton, J. (1983), 'How to solve problems that don't matter: Some heuristics for uninvolved thinking', in R.P. Bagozzi and A.M. Tybout (eds), *Advances in Consumer Research*, Vol. 10, Ann Arbor, MI: ACR, 314–319.

Deribéré, M. (1969), *La Couleur dans la Publicité et la Vente*. Paris: Dunod.

Dichter, E. (1971), 'The strategy of selling with packaging', *Package Engineering Magazine* (July), 16a–16c.

Dickson, P.R. (1982), 'The impact of enriching case', *Journal of Consumer Research*, **8**, 398–406.

Dillon, W.R., N. Mulani and D.G. Frederick (1984), 'Removing perceptual distortions in product space analysis', *Journal of Marketing Research*, **21**, 184–193.

Donovan, R.J. (1982), 'Store atmosphere: an environmental psychology approach', *Journal of Retailing*, **58**, 34–57.

Dover, P. (1982), 'Inferential belief formation: an overlooked concept in information processing research', in A.A. Mitchell (ed.), *Advances in Consumer Research*, Vol. 9, Ann Arbor, MI: ACR, 187–189.

Dumaurier, E. (1980–81), 'La représentation imagée de la couleur', *Bulletin de Psychologie*, **34**(348), 51–56.

Duncker, K.A. (1945), *On Problem-solving*. Psychological monographs, No. 270.

Ebbesen, E.B. and R.B. Allen (1979), 'Cognitive processes in implicit personality trait inferences', *Journal of Personality and Social Psychology*, **37**, 471–487.

Favre, J.P. (1969), *Richtige Farbe Erfolgreiche Packung*. Zurich: ABC Verlag.

Fishbein, M. and I. Ajzen (1975), *Belief, Attitude and Behavior: An introduction to theory and research*. Reading, MA: Addison-Wesley.

Fischhoff, B. (1982), 'Debiasing', in D. Kahneman, P. Slovic and A. Tversky (eds.), *Judgment under Uncertainty: Heuristics and Biases*. Cambridge: Cambridge University Press.

Fox, K.F.A. and T. Kehrey-Ward (1985), 'Theories of value and understanding of price: A developmental perspective', in E.C. Hirschman and M.B. Holbrook (eds.), *Advances in Consumer Research*, Vol. 12, Ann Arbor, MI: ACR, 79–84.

Froman, R. (1953), 'Marketing research, you get what you want', in J.H. Westin (ed.), *Readings in Marketing*. New York: Prentice-Hall.

Gara, M.A. and S. Rosenberg (1981), 'Linguistic factors in implicit personality theory', *Journal of Personality and Social Psychology*, **41**, 450–457.

Girard, R. and N. Cliff (1973), 'A comparison of methods for judging the similarity of personality inventory items', *Multivariate Behavioral Research*, **8**, 71–87.

Grant, P.R. and J.G. Holmes (1981), 'The integration of implicit personality theory, schemas and stereotypes images', *Social Psychology Quarterly*, **44**, 107–115.

Green, P.E. (1974), 'A multidimensional model of product-features association', *Journal of Business Research*, **2**, 107–118.

Hamilton, D.L. and R.K. Gifford (1976), 'Illusory correlation in interpersonal perception: A cognitive basis of stereotypic judgment', *Journal of Experimental Social Psychology*, **12**, 392–407.

Hammond, K.R. and B. Brehmer (1973), 'Quasi-rationality and distrust: implications for international conflict', in L. Rappoport and D.A. Summers (eds.), *Human Judgment and Social Interaction*, New York: Holt, Rinehart and Winston, 338–391.

Hansen, C.J. and G.M. Zinkham (1984), 'When do consumers infer product attribute values?', in T.C. Kinnear (ed.), *Advances in Consumer Research*, Vol. 11, Ann Arbor, MI: ACR, 187–192.

Helgeson, J.G. and S.E. Beatley (1985), 'An information processing perspective on the internalization of price stimuli', in E.C. Hirschman and M.B. Holbrook (eds.), *Advances in Consumer Research*, Vol. 12, Ann Arbor, MI: ACR, 91–96.

Hendrick, C. (1969), 'Asymmetry of the trait inference process in impression formation', *Perceptual and Motor Skills*, **28**, 715–720.

Henry, W.A. (1980), 'The effect of information-processing ability on processing accuracy', *Journal of Consumer Research*, **7**, 42–48.

Hoch, S.J. (1984), 'Hypothesis testing and consumer behavior', in T.C. Kinnear (ed.), *Advances in Consumer Research*, Vol. 11, Ann Arbor, MI: ACR, 478–483.

Hogarth, R.M. (1975), 'Cognitive processes and the assessment of subjective probability distributions', *Journal of the American Statistical Association*, **70**(350), 271–294.

Hogarth, R.M. (1980), *Judgment and Choice: The Psychology of Prediction*. Chichester, Wiley.

Hogarth, R.M. and S. Makridakis (1981), 'Forecasting and planning: an evaluation', *Management Science*, **27**, 10–20.

Holbrook, M.B. (1983), 'Using a structural model of halo effect to assess perceptual distortion due to affective overtones', *Journal of Consumer Research*, **10**, 247–252.

Holbrook, M.B. and W.L. Moore (1981), 'Feature interactions in consumer judgments of verbal versus pictorial presentations', *Journal of Consumer Research*, **8**, 103–113.

Holmberg, L. (1983), 'The effect of form on the perceived volume and heaviness of objects', *Psychological Research Bulletin*, **20**, 15.

Huber, J. and J. McCann (1982), 'The impact of inferential beliefs on product evaluations', *Journal of Marketing Research*, **19**, 324–333.

Hutchinson, J.W. (1983), 'On the locus of range effects in judgment and choice', in R.P. Bagozzi and A.M. Tybout (eds.), *Advances in Consumer Research*, Vol. 10, Ann Arbor, MI: Association of Consumer Research, 305–308.

Jacoby, J. and J.C. Olson (1977), 'Consumer response to price: An attitudinal, information processing perspective', in Y. Wind and M.G. Greenberg (eds), *Moving Ahead with Attitude Research*, Chicago, IL: American Marketing Association, 73–86.

John, D.R. (1985), 'The development of knowledge structures in children', in E.C. Hirschman and M. Holbrook (eds), *Advances in Consumer Research*, Vol. 12, Ann Arbor, MI: ACR, 329–333.

Kahneman, D. and A. Tversky (1972), 'Subjective probability: A judgment of representativeness', *Cognitive Psychology*, **3**, 430–454.

Kahneman, D., P. Slovic and A. Tversky, eds. (1982), *Judgment under Uncertainty: Heuristics and Biases*. Cambridge: Cambridge University Press.

Kanwar, R., J.C. Olson and L. Sims (1981), 'Toward conceptualizing and measuring cognitive structures', in K.B. Monroe (ed.), *Advances in Consumer Research*, Vol. 8, Ann Arbor, MI: ACR, 122–127.

Kelley, H.H. and J.L. Michela (1980), 'Attribution theory and research', *Annual Review of Psychology*, **31**, 457–501.

Kernan, J.B., W.P. Dommermuth and M.S. Sommers (1970), *Promotion: An Introductory Analysis*. New York: McGraw-Hill.

Kim, M.P. and S. Rosenberg (1980), 'Comparison of two structural models of implicit personality theory', *Journal of Personality and Social Psychology*, **38**, 375–389.

Kotler, P. (1973–74), 'Atmospherics as a marketing tool', *Journal of Retailing*, **49**, 48–64.

Kosslyn, S.M. (1975), 'Information representation in visual images', *Cognitive Psychology*, **7**, 341–370.

Kroeber-Riel, W. (1984), 'Emotional product differentiation by classical conditioning', in T.C. Kinnear (ed.), *Advances in Consumer Research*, Vol. 11, Ann Arbor, MI: ACR, 538–543.

Kuiper, N.A. and T.B. Rogers (1979), 'Encoding of personal information: self–other differences', *Journal of Personality and Social Psychology*, **37**, 499–514.

Levy, S.J. (1973), 'Consumer views of bank services'. A paper presented at the Research Conference on Bank Planning, 20–21 March. Evanston, IL: Northwestern University.

Lutz, R.J. (1976), 'First-order and second-order cognitive effects in attitude change', in M.L. Ray and S. Ward (eds.), *Communicating with Consumers*, Beverly Hills, CA: Sage Publications, 101–112.

Lutz, K.A. and R.J. Lutz (1977), 'Effects of interactive imagery on learning: application to advertising', *Journal of Applied Psychology*, **62**, 493–498.

Lynch, J.G. and T.K. Srull (1982), 'Memory and attentional factors in consumer choice: concepts and research methods', *Journal of Consumer Research*, **9**, 18–37.

Maratsos, P.M. (1974), 'When is a high thing the big one?', *Developmental Psychology*, **10**, 367–375.

Margulies, W.P. (1970), *Packaging Power*. New York: World Publishing.

Marketing News (1983a), 'Color needs to be integrated in marketing plans'. 11 November, 3.

Marketing News (1983b), 'Packaging remains an underdeveloped element in pushing consumer's buttons'. 14 October, 3.

Markin, R.J. (1974), *Consumer Behavior: A Cognitive Orientation*. New York: Macmillan.

Marks, L.J. and J.C. Olson (1981), 'Toward a cognitive structure conceptualization of product familiarity', in *Advances in Consumer Research*, Vol. 8, Ann Arbor, MI: ACR, 145–150.

Markus, H. (1980), 'Self reference in thought and memory', in D. Wegner and R. Vallacher (eds.), *The Self in Social Psychology*, New York: Oxford University Press, 102–130.

McConnel, F.J.D. (1971), 'The economics of behavior factors in the multi-national corporation', in F.C. Allvine (ed.), *Relevance in Marketing: Problems, Research Action*. Chicago, IL: AMA, 261–266.

McNeal, J.U. (1982), *Consumer Behavior: An Integrative Approach*. Boston, MA: Little, Brown.

Mitchell, A.A. and J.C. Olson (1981), 'Are product attribute beliefs the only mediator of advertising effects on brand attitude?', *Journal of Marketing Research*, **18**, 318–332.

Monroe, K.B., A.J. Della Bitta and S.L. Downey (1977), 'Contextual influences on subjective price perceptions', *Journal of Business Research*, **5**, 277–291.

Nedungadi, P. and J.W. Hutchinson (1985), 'The prototypicality of brands relationships with brand awareness, preference and usage', in E.C. Hirschman and M.B. Holbrook (eds.), *Advances in Consumer Research*, Vol. 12, Ann Arbor, MI: ACR, 498–503.

Nelson, P. (1974), 'Advertising as information', *Journal of Political Economy*, **82**, 729–754.

Newsweek (1974), 'The missing link', 9 September, 30.

Nisbett, R.E. and T.D. Wilson (1977a), 'The halo effect: Evidence for unconscious alteration of judgments', *Journal of Personality and Social Psychology*, **35**(4), 250-256.

Nisbett, R.E. and T.D. Wilson (1977b), 'Telling more than we can know: verbal reports on mental processes', *Psychological Review*, **84**, 231–259.

Nisbett, R.E. and L. Ross (1980), *Human Inference: Strategies and Shortcomings of Social Judgment*. Englewood Cliffs, NJ: Prentice-Hall.

Nisbett, R.E., D. Krantz, C. Jepson and G.T. Fong (1982), 'Improving inductive inference', in D. Kahneman, P. Slovic and A. Tversky (eds.), *Judgment under Uncertainty: Heuristics and Biases*. Cambridge: Cambridge University Press, 445–459.

Norman, D.A. and D.G. Bobrow (1975a), 'On the role of active memory processes in perception and cognition', in C.N. Cofer (ed.), *The Structure of Human Memory*. San Francisco, CA: W.H. Freeman, 114–132.

Norman, D.A. and D.G. Bobrow (1975b), 'On data-limited and resource-limited processes', *Cognitive Psychology*, **7**, 44–64.

Ofir, C. and J.C. Lynch (1984), 'Context effects on judgment under uncertainty', *Journal of Consumer Research*, **11**, 668–679.

Olshavsky, R.W. and D.H. Granbois (1979), 'Consumer decision making: Fact or fiction?', *Journal of Consumer Research*, **6**, 93–100.

Olson, J.C. (1978), 'Inferential belief formation in the cue utilization process', in H.K. Hunt (ed.), *Advances in Consumer Research*, Vol. 5. Chicago, IL: ACR, 706–713.

Olson, J.C. (1980), 'Encoding processes: levels of processing and existing knowledge structures', in Jerry C. Olson (ed.), *Advances in Consumer Research*, Vol. 7. Ann Arbor, MI: ACR, 154–160.

Osgood, C.E., W.H. May and M.S. Miron (1975), *Cross-cultural Universals of Affective Meaning*. Urbana, IL: University of Illinois Press.

Oyama, T., Y. Tanaka and Y. Chiba (1962), 'Affective dimensions of colors: A cross-cultural study'. *Japanese Psychological Research*, **34**, 78–91.

Paivio, A. (1971), *Imagery and Verbal Processes*. New York: Holt, Rinehart and Winston.

Park, C.W. and V.P. Lessig (1981), 'Familiarity and its impact on consumer decision biases and heuristics', *Journal of Consumer Research*, **8**, 223–230.

Peterson, R.A. and R.A. Kerin (1981), 'The quality of self report data: Review and synthesis', in B.M. Enis and K.J. Roering (eds.), *Review of Marketing*. Chicago, IL: AMA, 5–20.

Politz, A. (1957), 'Science and truth in marketing research', *Harvard Business Review*, **35**(1), 117–126.

Powell, R.S. and R.G. Jühnke (1983), 'Statistical models of implicit personality theory: A comparison', *Journal of Personality and Social Psychology*, **44**, 911–922.

Rosenberg, S. (1977), 'New approaches to the analysis of personal constructs in person perception', *Nebraska Symposium on Motivation*, **24**, 179–242.

Rosenberg, S. and R.A. Jones (1972), 'A method for investigating and representing a person's implicit theory of personality: Theodore Dreiser's view of people', *Journal of Personality and Social Psychology*, **22**, 372–386.

Rosenberg, S., C. Nelson and P.S. Vivekananthan (1968), 'A multidimensional approach to the structure of personality impressions', *Journal of Personality and Social Psychology*, **9**, 283–294.

Rosenberg, S. and A. Sedlak (1972), 'Structural representations of implicit personality theory', in L. Berkowitz (ed.), *Advances in Experimental Social Psychology*, Vol. 6. New York: Academic Press, 235–297.

Ross, L. and C. Anderson (1982), 'Shortcomings in the attribution process: on the origins and maintenance of erroneous social assessments', in D. Kahneman, P. Slovic and A. Tversky (eds.), *Judgment under Uncertainty: Heuristics and Biases*. Cambridge: Cambridge University Press, 129–160.

Rumelhart, D.E. (1977), *Introduction to Human Information Processing*. New York: Wiley.

Russo, J.E. and E.J. Johnson (1980), 'What do consumers know about familiar products?', in J.C. Olson (ed.), *Advances in Consumer Research*, Vol. 7, Ann Arbor, MI: ACR, 417–423.

Sacharow, S. (1982), *The Package as a Marketing Tool*. Radnor, PA: Chilton Book.

Schellinck, D.A. (1980), 'Determinants of cue choice behavior', University of Illinois (unpublished doctoral dissertation).

Schneider, D.J. (1973), 'Implicit personality theory: A review', *Psychological Bulletin*, **79**, 294–309.

Schneider, D.J. and B.L. Blankmeyer (1983), 'Prototype salience and implicit personality theories', *Journal of Personality and Social Psychology*, **44**, 712–722.

Scott, W.A., D.W. Osgood and C. Peterson (1979), *Cognitive Structure*. New York: Wiley.

Secord, P.F. and S.M. Jonrard (1956), 'Mother-concepts and judgments of young women's faces', *Journal of Abnormal and Social Psychology*, **52**, 246–250.

Shugan, S.M. (1980), 'The cost of thinking', *Journal of Consumer Research*, **7**, 99–111.

Sivik, L. (1975), 'Studies of color meaning', *Man–Environment Systems*, **5**, 155–160.

Stauder, D.M. (1973), 'Testing new product ideas in an "Archie Bunker" world', *Marketing News*, **15**, 1, 4, 5 and 12.

Taylor, S.E. and J. Crocker (1981), 'Schematic basis of social information processing', in E. Higgins, C. Herman and M. Zanna (eds.), *Social Cognition: The Ontario Symposium*, Vol. 1, Hillsdale, NJ: Erlbaum, 89–134.

Taylor, S.E. and S.C. Thompson (1982), 'Stalking the elusive vividness effect', *Psychological Review*, **89**, 155–181.

Thorndyke, P.N. and B. Hayes-Roth (1979), 'The use of schemata in the acquisition and the transfer of knowledge', *Cognitive Psychology*, **11**, 82–106.

Tversky, A. and D. Kahneman (1973), 'Availability: A heuristic for judging frequency and probability', *Cognitive Psychology*, **5**, 207–232.

Tversky, A. and D. Kahneman (1979), 'Causal schemata in judgments under uncertainty', in M. Fishbein (ed.), *Progress in Social Psychology*. Hillsdale, NJ: Erlbaum, 49–72.

Tybout, A.M. and C.A. Scott (1983), 'Some indirect effects of cas vs. base-rate data on information processing strategies', in R. Bagozzi and A.M. Tybout (eds.), *Advances in Consumer Research*, Vol. 10, Ann Arbor, MI: Association for Consumer Research, 161–170.

Tzeng, O.C. (1981), *Implicit Personality Theory: A Comparative Review of the Issues*. West Lafayette, IN. Purdue University, Psychology Department.

Van der Kloot, W.A. and P.M. Kroonenberg (1982), 'Group and individual implicit theories of personality: an application of three-mode principal component analysis', *Multivariate Behavioral Research*, **17**, 471–491.

Warr, B. and C. Knapper (1968), *The Perception of People and Events*. London: Wiley.

Weber, R. and J. Crocker (1983), 'Cognitive processes in the revision of stereotypic beliefs', *Journal of Personality and Social Psychology*, **45**, 961–977.

Wheatley, J.J. and J.S.Y. Chiu (1977), 'The effect of price, store image, and product and respondent characteristics on perceptions of quality', *Journal of Marketing Research*, **14**, 181–186.

Winick, C. (1963), 'Taboo and disapproved colors and symbols in various foreign countries', *Journal of Social Psychology*, **59**, 361–368.

Winter, L. and J.S. Uleman (1984), 'When are social judgments made? Evidence for the spontaneousness of trait inferences', *Journal of Personality and Social Psychology*, **47**, 237–252.

Winter, R. (1976), *The Smell Book*. New York: Lippincott.

Women's Wear Daily (1961), 28 January, 15.

Wright, P.L. (1974), 'The harassed decision maker: time pressures, distractions, and the use of evidence', *Journal of Applied Psychology*, **59**, 555–561.

Wright, P.L. (1975), 'Consumer choice strategies: simplifying vs optimizing', *Journal of Marketing Research*, **11**, 60–67.

Wright, P.L. and B. Weitz (1977), 'Time horizon effects on product evaluation strategies', *Journal of Marketing Research*, **14**, 429–443.

Wyer, R.S., T.K. Srull and S. Gordon (1984), 'The effects of predicting a person's behavior on subsequent trait judgments', *Journal of Experimental Social Psychology*, **20**, 29–46.

Yokota, J. (1983), Personal communication to the author.

Zeithaml, V.A. (1982), 'Consumer responses to in-store price information environment', *Journal of Consumer Research*, **8**, 357–369.

Zeithaml, V.A. (1984), 'Issues in conceptualizing and measuring consumer response to price', in T.C. Kinnear (ed.), *Advances in Consumer Research*, Vol. 11, Ann Arbor, MI: ACR, 612–616.

Consumer inferences and consumer preferences. The status of cognition and consciousness in consumer behavior theory

●●

Christian Derbaix
Associate Professor of Marketing, Facultés Universitaires Catholiques de Mons, Belgium

Piet Vanden Abeele
Professor of Marketing, Katholieke Universiteit Leuven, Belgium

Summary

This conceptual paper discusses the so-called 'non-cognitive' revolution in modern Consumer Behavior Theory. We argue that this new emphasis is not a radical departure when viewed from the vantage point of cognitive psychology. Cognitive psychology has become a way of studying many, if not most, forms of behavior: as it grows and expands, it becomes less correct to equate it with the study of only some forms of behavior (cognition). It is often the case that consumer researchers associate the term 'cognitive' with the conscious, the rational, the verbal and, by implication, call non-cognitive the unconscious, subconscious or non-verbal phenomena. However, many findings on 'non-cognitive' processes are the result of research in cognitive psychology. Our paper therefore starts out by discussing the nature of the cognitive Consumer Research Tradition. It points out that the distinction between conscious and automatic processes is more fruitful than that between cognitive and non-cognitive ones. The recent emphasis on emotional processes and direct behavior manipulation is discussed in this light. Implications of the distinction for consumer and marketing research are mentioned in a concluding section.

1. Introduction

Consumer research, a multidisciplinary and applied field, reflects the shifting emphasis in the disciplines from which it borrows. Following a decade of consumer studies inspired by

From the *International Journal of Research in Marketing*, **2** (1985), 157–74.

199

remarkable advances in cognitive psychology, present-day consumer research echoes the attention paid by psychologists to the limitations of conscious human information processing and to the non-cognitive determinants of action (Kassarjian, 1982). The focus on emotion or on behavior is not new for consumer research: thirty years ago motivation research stressed the subconscious emotional foundations of behavior (Dichter, 1964); twenty years ago, the fashion was to model choice in a behavioristic way (Massy, Morrison and Montgomery, 1970). Have we then come full circle? While there is an inevitable swing of the pendulum, we argue that the movement is evolutionary. We return to our old interests enriched with the knowledge acquired during the previous 'excursions'. Since the field of consumer research is noted for embracing new approaches with zeal and for burning the bridges left behind, this paper pleads for continuity.

Such continuity is apparent from our acceptance, in the first paragraph, of the time-honoured distinction between the cognitive, the affective and the conative aspects of behavior. This distinction is deemed useful, even though purely conceptual. The problem of understanding behavior then appears as that of the determination of these aspects and of their interrelationships. A paragraph is devoted to the presentation of conscious and of automatic processes as the two (extreme) types of the determination of behavior. Cognition has been closely linked to conscious processes in consumer research. The too restrictive conscious cognitive approach is detailed and its ecological validity is questioned. The importance of less conscious cognitive processes is simultaneously stressed.

The three next paragraphs are devoted to affect and conation which have again moved to the fore since Zajonc's seminal paper (1980). A last paragraph draws conclusions for the field of Consumer Behavior Research, both in terms of its theory and of its methods.

The main purpose of this paper is to bring the various facets of consumer behavior (cognitive, affective, conative; conscious and unconscious) in better perspective. As a consequence, we argue that more attention needs to be given to the non-cognitive and to the less conscious aspects of consumer behavior than before. But this shift in attention should not lead to the banishment of that which is cognitive and conscious in its object, theory or method. The cognitivistic excursion has taught us much about consumer behavior and allows a better study of 'non-cognitive' determinants than before.

2. Cognition, emotion and conation: putting Humpty Dumpty back together

Psychology attempts to describe and explain individual behavior. In scientific work it is useful to make conceptual distinctions between aspects, components of the object under study. In our case, the time-honoured distinction is between the cognitive (knowing), the affective (feeling) and the conative (acting) aspects of behavior. These concepts are inferences drawn from the same, holistic, observable behavior; such constructs exist in the eye of the beholder only as distinct abstractions from the phenomena. Scientific inquiry is furthered by this conceptual separation, but difficulties arise when it becomes necessary to integrate the constructs, e.g., for applied research or practice. The problem has been referred to as that of 'putting Humpty Dumpty back together' (Coyne, 1982). The integration is rendered even more difficult by our natural tendency to equate the constructs with physiological functions and processes (Ryan, 1982) or with their measurement operationalization.

Supposedly, the most adequate definition of concepts such as cognition, emotion and conation can be found in psychological encyclopedias. Yet, the definitions found in some respected dictionaries of psychological terms[1] do not always succeed in giving mutually exclusive descriptions of these constructs. A reason for this finding is that the definitions are of constructs which belong to an integrated structure; as we have just remarked, conceptual distinctions are not usually suited to express integration. Once in a while, scientists have to frame a neologism in order to overcome the limitations built in their categories, e.g. the recent concepts of cold and hot cognitions. The idea of integrated response units of knowledge, feeling and action tendency, which are internally coherent but may externally co-exist in relative isolation is of course quite old (Ajzen and Fishbein, 1980). The tricomponent view has dominated most marketing thinking about attitude-structure, -formation and -change (Day, 1973). More significant, insight-stimulating and newer for consumer research is the demonstration that such response units can act or be acted upon unconsciously, i.e. outside of focal attention, automatically. Indeed, evidence of various sorts is available for unconscious phenomena such as:

- Unconscious meaning effects on automatic response, where unattended stimuli have an impact on emotion through their meaning, e.g. psychogalvanic response to unattended or to subliminally presented conditioned stimuli (Corteen and Wood, 1972).
- Unconscious activation of motor responses as the result of mental or of emotional processes, e.g. the production of facial expression, of covert myographic activity related to thought of associated motor activity (Caccioppo and Petty, 1981), and the production of involuntary behavior in general states of absorption such as watching a dramatic production (Natsoulas, 1981).
- Unconscious activation of evaluation through motor behavior as, e.g., in the Wells and Petty (1980) headphone experiment.
- Unconscious activation of meaning, whereby unattended stimuli seem to prime related meaning nodes in long term memory, e.g. the Stroop effect, the disambiguation of words or sentences with multiple meanings through unattended disambiguating stimuli (Marcel, 1980).

This array of findings on unconscious effects is not presented here in order to reject the view of the conscious and cognitive consumer in favor of a view where he is mindlessly driven by subconscious emotions. Rather, the significant conclusions are (1) that behavior is always cognitive-affective-conative instead of exclusively cognitive, or emotional, or conative, and (2) that behavior can be so at the conscious but also at the unconscious level. The first conclusion thus does not lead to the rejection of the cognitive approach, but embeds it in a broader perspective. The second conclusion allows a better discussion of what has come to be known as 'low involvement consumer behavior' (Houston and Rothschild, 1978). The concept of involvement however has proven elusive to define and measure. The artificial dichotomy between low and high involvement is related to that between the two basic modes of consciousness mentioned by Hilgard (1980): the passive receptive states, reminiscent of Krugman's description of a passive consumer watching an active medium (TV), and the active productive mental activities illustrated by the (active) reader of a newspaper (passive medium) looking for specific information. The distinction between automatic and controlled processes made in psychology can also be of help in this respect.

3. Automatic and controlled processes

Recent advances in cognitive psychology provide better insight in the nature of, and distinction between, the conscious and unconscious modes of functioning of the consumer. The distinction between automatic and control processing is conceptual, an abstraction (it will lead to a new Humpty Dumpty Problem in due time).[2]

Several authors venture descriptions of automatic and of control processes in terms of multiple characterizations (Vandenbergh and Eelen, 1983; Schneider *et al.*, 1984). Control processes are those where we are conscious, aware or attentive. They are flexible, conditional. They seem to require capacities which are of limited availability and thus cannot easily be carried out in parallel.

Automatic processes are unconscious, unaware (even though some of them, e.g. car driving, can be brought to awareness). They are unconditional inflexible, rigid. They can be likened to computer subroutines, blindly executed when called upon by the main program. They occur without intention with high efficiency and are resistant to modification. They are thought to occur without capacity limitations (e.g. to occur in parallel along multiple modes without mutual interference). A number of comments are in order concerning the distinction between automatic and controlled processes:

1. The distinction is between response units (of cognition-emotion-conation). It is important not to equate controlled processes with cognition only (as, e.g., in the Theory of Reasoned Action (Ajzen and Fishbein, 1980)), and automatic processes with emotion or with action habits only. There can also be cognitive automatisms, e.g. schemata or scripts (Abelson, 1976) or consciously controlled emotions, as for instance in the voluntary control of automatic functions through bio-feedback.

Table 1 Characterization of controlled and of automatic processes

Controlled Process	Automatic Process
Genuine decisions, original	Habitual, routine
Volitional	Spontaneous
Aware, conscious	Unaware, unconscious
Attentive	Unattentive
Flexible	Rigid
Conditional	Unconditional
Capacity constrained	Capacity unconstrained
Divisible	Indivisible, unitary
Much effort	Effortless
High involvement	Low involvement

2. The automatic-controlled distinction is not absolute. Kahneman and Treisman (1984) talk of strong, semi-strong and of weak automatisms. Both processes are complementary: controlled processes call up automatic ones to efficiently carry out behavioral sequences; automatic processes may forcefully mobilize controlled ones, e.g. the involuntary mobilization of attention. An example of this can be given in the case of supermarket shopping. The shopper plans his shopping sequence in a controlled way, partial shopping tasks (e.g. steering the cart) being delegated to automatisms. Unattentive shopping can be brought under controlled processing when an unusual deal is identified.

3. Since controlled processing requires mental capacity which is in limited availability, it is efficient for the actor to delegate the execution of a multitude of behaviors to automatic control. In view of the multiplicity of consumption tasks facing the consumer, it is to be expected that in consumption, as in other walks of life, automatic processes will be the rule and controlled ones the exception. Much, if not most, of our consumption-related acts occur outside of conscious deliberation. While many of these behaviors have been under conscious control at some point, they have become overlearned to the point of being strong or semi-strong automatisms.

4. While the emission of habitual behavior belongs to the class of automatic behaviors, the latter also encompasses automatisms in the acquisition and processing of information. Automatisms prevail at the input side as well as at the output side of behavior.

   – Unattentive processing of perceptual information can lead to automatic analysis of stimuli of considerable complexity without awareness, eventually eliciting seemingly unrelated overt responses. According to some views, in unattentive processing all possible meanings of a perceptual input are jointly activated in long term memory (Dixon, 1981). Conscious representation is constructed out of one of the primed meanings in consciousness. This is achieved through the inhibition of other meanings which were also activated. An unattentively processed ad for a food product, showing a lovely face, may unconsciously prime the meaning for make-up, facilitating a subsequent cosmetics purchase.

   – Automatic vs. controlled processing at the input side of behavior is related to the 'levels-of-processing' framework which has been applied to consumer behavior (Olson, 1979). The framework contrasts rather superficial, shallow processing with deep processing of incoming information. Shallow processing results from the analysis of only superficial, directly available properties of the stimulus, as for instance its physical properties and relies predominantly on inborn or on overlearned analytical skills. Deep processing considers the semantic, meaning aspects of the percept and will obtain especially if it relates the perceived stimulus to the personal experiences of the subject. The latter is reminiscent of Krugman's connection concept (Krugman, 1965). Deep processing embeds the stimulus in richer associative networks in memory; the deeper and more elaborate the processing, the stronger apparently the memory trace. While deep processing is clearly the appropriate mode for correctly identifying and analyzing incoming stimuli, it may overload the information processing capacity if each object is to be thoroughly analyzed (Jacoby, 1976). Semi-strong automatisms under the form of schemata or chunks are then available as shortcuts for identification or analysis, as means for easily finding or completing the meaning of stimuli (Bettman, 1979).

– The automatic vs. controlled distinction also holds for the processing of information related more directly to the activation of a course of action. A novel situation is likely to engage the individual in conscious cognitive processing in order to decide on the appropriate course of action. Upon each repetition, less information is processed until the actions are guided by contextual cues (shallow processing) with only minimal information processed. New goal-relevant information may then even be ignored (Langer *et al.*, 1978). With repetition, the situational cues may ultimately be reduced to the superficial properties of the situation rather than to its essential meaning. The consumer's supermarket shopping routine is an example of a script which, after some trials, can proceed with only minimal meaning analysis.

While limited processing is typical for repetitive situations, it may also occur with novel information that appears irrelevant to the subject. In such situations of latent or individual learning, there is no reason for the subject to critically examine the stimulus, as the scarce conscious cognitive capacities can better be used elsewhere. In abstaining from a critical examination, the subject may prematurely commit himself to the script or schema inherent in the information. The person is prepared with one response and does not consider alternatives (Langer and Chanowitz, 1981). Advertisements attended to without concurrent product interest may thus shape knowledge or behavior for future purchase by default.

We conclude that there are two basic types of functioning for the consumer, namely the controlled and the automatic processing mode. Both modes are relevant for the various stages in consumer 'decision making'. Expediency and pleasure dictate that the consumer most often functions in the automatic processing mode and only occasionally in the deliberative optimizing mode. The relevance of both modes also appears from the discussion of the cognitive approach to consumer behavior in the next paragraph.

4. The cognitive approach to the consumer

If the cognitive approach to the consumer can be defined as the application to consumer behavior of the theories and methods of cognitive psychology, then this approach appears as differentiated as cognitive psychology itself. It studies phenomena such as the search and acquisition of information, its analysis and encoding, its storage, structure and transformation in memory, its retrieval or reprocessing from memory and its use for control of behavior (Bettman, 1979). As Table 2 shows, the theories applied are as variegated as the aspects of consumer behavior investigated.

From Table 2 the following comments are warranted. First, the 'cognitive approach' to the consumer is not a monolithic theory, susceptible to falsification as a whole. New approaches, e.g. those emphasizing emotional processes in the consumer can at best replace or complement some of its components. Second, the cognitive consumer approach is not exclusively that of the consciously functioning consumer; it encompasses many other facets than only the formation of preferences and choices in the multi-attribute cognitive algebra

Table 2 Topics and theories in cognitive consumer studies

Topics	Theories
Search for external information	Perceived risk Optimal arousal Adaptation level
Interpretation of external information	Attribution Self-perception
Analysis/coding of information	Dual coding Levels of processing
Formation of inferences	Attribution Self-perception Associative networks
Structure of knowledge in memory	Associative networks Prototypes Semantic memory Episodic memory Chunking
Concept formation/categorization	Anticipatory schemata Associative networks Template matching
Preference formation/choice	Information integration Reasoned action Expectancy-value Attitudinal hierarchies Social judgment
Retrieval of information	Associative networks Attentive processing Early vs. late filtering

framework. Yet, it is the latter Conscious Cognitive Processing (CCP) approach which has dominated cognitively oriented consumer studies and can be typified as follows:

> . . . we make the assumption that most actions of social relevance are under volitional control . . . we argue that people consider the implications of their actions before they decide to engage or not to engage in a given behavior . . . (Ajzen and Fishbein, 1980)

> [the cognitive processing view] depicts the individual as one who is cognitively aware most of the time, and who consciously, constantly and systematically applies 'rules' to incoming information about the environment in order to formulate interpretations and courses of action. (Langer, 1978)

In the consumer behavior literature the CCP view of the consumer often implies some of the following assumptions:

1. The hierarchy of attitudinal effects is characterized by a cognition-affect-conation pro-gression which can be seen as a causal sequence.
2. Except for those variables which affect purchase outcomes rather than behavior, the effect of all determinants is mediated by the cognitive component of the response unit.
3. Affect and behavioral intention are the result of conscious higher-order processing of beliefs.
4. The choice object/alternatives are known to the consumer as a vector of beliefs or of expectancies provided by the external environment or residing in long term memory; this knowledge is of semantic-analytical nature.
5. The consumer is conscious of a decision situation between competing behaviors or choice tendencies.

Our deliberately extreme depiction of the assumptions underlying the CCP model of consumer choice leads to the consideration of three questions: (1) is this model valid for most consumer choice processes; (2) if not, is it a valid representation for at least some consumer choice processes, and (3) do we need it to account for consumer choices anyway?

5. The validity of the CCP model for consumer choice behavior

Even if deliberate, mindful behavior and the assorted cognitive algebra occur in some instances, one may doubt that it will be a valid representation of most consumer choice processes. Deliberate, mindful behavior is effortful and capacity-constrained and will thus be the exception. Behavioral automatisms, motor habits, direct affect referral and cognitive habits (scripts, schemata) rule over much consumer behavior as they free our conscious cognitive functions for more important tasks and organize his behavior efficiently under normal circumstances. As a result, not all consumer behavior will belong to the 'mindless' variety. Consumers will engage in deliberative thought, in reasoned action primarily when they have no script or schema or when these appear inadequate or cannot be enacted. More specifically, mindful processes are expected (Langer, 1978):

1. When facing a new, involving situation for which, by definition, there is no available script or schema, e.g. when confronted with a discontinuously innovative product.
2. When enacting the scripted behavior becomes effortful, e.g. when significantly more of the scripted behavior is demanded by the situation. For the shopper who routinely checks the deals available in local stores in the newspaper, the script may become effortful if several more outlets start advertising in the local paper.
3. When enacting scripted behavior is interrupted by external factors that do not allow for its completion, e.g. when the habitual brand is not available or in case of a new layout of the habitual supermarket.
4. When experiencing a negative or positive consequence sufficiently discrepant with the consequences of prior enactments, e.g. in case of dissatisfaction with the habitual brand.
5. When the enactment of scripted behavior becomes aversive, e.g. when getting bored with the shopping routine in the habitual supermarket.

The above conditions are usually not met and behavior of some automaticity prevails. We now discuss some departures from the conditions.

As mentioned at length in the literature on attitudinal change hierarchies (Ray, 1973), the causal chain does not always follow the progression from cognition to affect and then to behavioral intention. Also, the consumer often does not experience a conscious conflict between competing behavior tendencies likely to mobilize deliberative thought, especially with merely differentiated brands within a product class. Not all models of cognitive algebra are equally demanding of attentive processing capacity (Wright, 1974). The mental arithmetic of a linear compensatory rule appears more demanding than that of sequential and/or of satisficing rules. Some such rules reduce the processing tasks to the point of allowing them to be carried out under virtually automatic control. Certainly, the consumer is not likely to measure up to the data quality requirements implicit in the linear compensatory model (Bultez and Derbaix, 1982).

The acquisition of information from the environment is often not an attentive quest for knowledge but the outcome of incidental learning, of unattentive processes of attribution, self-attribution or proprioception. As a result, the knowledge can be less semantic and more directly associated with emotional or with motor responses. In particular, much stored consumer knowledge will be of the episodic variety. Certainly, the content and structure of consumer knowledge in long-term memory is unlikely to allow a complete analogy with information display boards. This 'knowledge' may contain episodic as well as emotional or motor nodes. The structure may depart from the Cartesian grid representation (two-dimensional matrix of brands by attributes); hierarchial structures are possible as e.g. when conceptual chunks (Bettman, 1979) replace more detailed knowledge.

These criticisms do not lead to a rejection of the CCP model. Rather, it will be applicable only at some times or in some respects. But even where the consumer deliberately attempts to operate in the CCP mode, he may be hindered in his pursuit of rationality by the intrusion of largely automatic and unconscious processes. The literature argues that these automatic processes serve us well in ordinary behavior, but that they occasionally lead us astray when we are engaged in tasks requiring a novel perspective, a restructuration of the field (Katona, 1975; Nisbett and Wilson, 1977; Nisbett and Ross, 1980). The consumer who sets out to act rationally may thus end up making suboptimal decisions without becoming aware of this. Nisbett and Ross (1980) provide ample evidence of the shortcomings of the human mind when it comes to (1) observing, categorizing and describing events; (2) drawing samples of observations; (3) making inferences; (4) detecting covariation and assessing causality; (5) making predictions; (6) testing and revising conceptions, and (7) making decisions. In fact, if this were not so, the human mind would practice science and statistics intuitively. Nisbett and Ross's arguments give us reason to doubt the easy attainability of the CCP mode as a norm for the consumer. The knowledge he acquires and encodes will be heavily influenced by preconceptions (any Volkswagen is somehow small), be based on limited samples (judging Spain from a single vacation experience), and be influenced by the vividness of the information (stronger impact, of a neighbor's comments than of Consumer Report statistics). The inferences will also be influenced by the representativeness and availability heuristics, by the tendency to attribute dispositionally as well as by the inability to observe the real degree of covariation (BMW buyers are of a particular life style category). Such inferences are judgments that will prove remarkably resistant to further information, to alternative modes of reasoning and to logical or evidential challenges (Consumer Report statistics can hardly correct the attitude developed on the basis of a single negative experience with a brand). Finally, problems occur in decision making. Human judges are known to make less accurate predictions than do formulas; non-diagnostic information dilutes the effect of more diagnostic data, recency effect influences evaluation, etc. The literature on information load (Jacoby, 1976) shows that excessive amounts of information impede optimal choice without the decision maker becoming aware.

6. On the predictive validity of the CCP model

We have argued that the CCP model may not be applicable to, or attainable by, the consumer. In contrast with this assertion is the observation that the model has proven useful and predictive in many consumer studies over a protracted time period. How can the model be predictive when its validity is in doubt?

The CCP model of reasoned action is structurally virtually indistinguishable from the micro-economic model of consumer choice, especially in its Abstract Mode formulation (Ratchford, 1975). Both see utility as an idiosyncratically weighted function of multiple characteristics. But the micro-economic model dispenses with the necessity to assume thoughtful, rational deliberation. It requires rationality only in the sense of consistency of preferences. The predictive or explanatory power of demand functions does not require the assumption of conscious deliberation, of attentive optimization. The micro-economic model allows one to post a variety of functions for the formation of utility (attitude). These models are not intended as representations of mental processes and indeed only their ordinal properties matter; many functions which differ in their interval properties will be obser-vationally equivalent for the economist as they result in the same ranking of the alternatives.

This leads us to conclude that the Theory of Reasoned Action makes some assumptions which are not necessary (reasoned choice, the occurrence of cognitive algebra), or proposes a framework which is needlessly restrictive (different models of cognitive algebra). Reas-oned action and the assorted cognitive algebra may occur in reality, but this fact may be irrelevant if the purpose is to predict behavior. The result is a rather paradoxical situation between consumption economics and consumer psychology. The latter field often sets out by noting that the rationality required by the microeconomic model is irrealistic and that some psycho-logical realism should be brought in. All things considered, the CCP 'realism' which psychologists brought to economics derives from a rationalist view of man.

If the CCP view is superfluous or mistaken, then how can consumer psychologists uphold it for so long? First of all, the CCP view may be an adequate, but less parsimonious explanation of behavior; while it cannot be proven wrong, it will have contending hypoth-eses that obtain the same results with fewer assumptions. Second, the cognitive approach has resulted in the development of an extensive methodology; inadvertent application of these methods to automatic processes may yield interpretations cast in the model of thoughtful behavior. Third, the cognitive approach has restored introspection as an accept-able method to access thought. The introspective methodology is particularly susceptible to the bias of rationalization, and the bias is likely to be in favor of the script of thoughtful behavior. It occurs often that different models are proposed which are observationally equivalent. Only under extreme conditions will some of the models be falsified. There are many possible reasons why choice under automatic control can be confused with that under conscious control:

- The external environment (markets, suppliers) may confront us only with those choice alternatives which we would choose deliberately. This hypothesis of selectivity, reflected and enforced by the social environment is known from the studies on selective exposure (Katz, 1968). A well-functioning market can be trusted to present the alternatives preferred by specific publics to those same publics. The result would be that the consumers are provided with optimal 'choice' without any need to think.
- Routine response tendencies may develop from original thoughtful behavior and remain adequate as long as the situation remains unchanged: Affect Referral may become the automatic process after a number of repetitions, yet produce the same behavior as would reasoned action.
- Preferences may result from mindless trial-and-error learning, leading to the development of habits indistinguishable from the behavior dictated by conscious 'optimization' (Rothschild and Gaidis, 1981).
- Preferences and habits can be forced directly as the result of socialization processes; such preferences will be consistent with 'thoughtful' preferences if the collective, socializing mind is consistent with them.

In the last two paragraphs we attempted to provide an answer to three questions relative to the validity of the CCP model in a consumer behavior framework. A recapitulation of the answers is in order. First, the CCP model's predictive validity may be due as much to its intrinsic validity as to the fact that it produces the same results as contending plausible hypotheses. Second, the area of applications where the model has intrinsic validity, is likely to be fairly restricted. Finally, this intrinsic validity, where it can occur, is always in the nature of an ideal to strive for, that will never be fully attained.

7. The primacy of emotion and consumer behavior

The previous paragraphs put an emphasis on unconscious cognitive processes and their effects. In many overt or covert reactions of an emotional nature, cognition figures as an important prerequisite. In his seminal paper Zajonc (1980), however, posits that in some situations the dominant processes or those appearing first are affective. This primary or dominant affective response, 'love at first sight', is supported by a number of well known findings. First, in ontogeny (the development of the person), affective responses tend to occur prior to cognitive ones; very young babies laugh to a face before being able to discriminate between faces (Izard, 1978). Second, emotions are expressed without a conscious or unconscious construction of meaning for the stimuli that elicit them.[3] Extreme cold applied to the body provokes an immediate affective expression, as may an unidentified loud voice of a particular kind of music in an unattended commercial. Subliminally presented advertisements could potentially evoke an affective response even though there is no empirical documentation for stronger effects, such as inducing behaviors or changing motivation (Moore, 1982). *A posteriori* questioning about the reason for the reaction – in a more or less reactive way – may often yield justifications rather than substantial explanations. Third, the original cognitive bases of certain emotions or preferences can become forgotten or dissociated from their affective expression (functional autonomy). Thus affect referral (Wright, 1973) is often proposed as an explanation for the basis of consumer choice. The Litman and Manning (1954) study on cigarette preference and recognition shows that smokers can identify their favorite brand in terms of preference (affect) but not in terms of recognition. Zajonc's mere exposure research shows a link of repetition to affect in the absence of stimulus recognition.

The dominance or precedence of affect discussed here does not contradict the tri-component approach to attitudes presented above. When emotions are manifestly the dominant or leading response, this does not rule out the presence of conscious or of unconscious cognitive and conative reactions. Consumers have limited capacities to explicitate the reasons for their (affective) responses however, and presently available measurement tools tap mainly the conscious facets of the tri-component unit. The limited informational value of introspective reports is due a.o. to the fact that the processes to which we might have direct access are very complex and are constantly variable (Natsoulas, 1981: 150). In this sense, we agree with Vandenbergh and Eelen (1983) when they rephrase Zajonc's 'preferences need no inferences' into 'conscious preferences need no conscious inferences' in order to resolve the conflict between Zajonc and Mandler (1982).

Further evidence is available for a different basis of affect and cognition. The latent structure behind stimuli seems to differ depending on whether it is inferred from affective (preference) judgments or from cognitive ones (perceived similarity judgments). Zajonc mentions the studies by Nakashima (1909) and by Cooper (1973) in this context. Nakashima found that judgments of pleasantness of sensory stimuli were unrelated to their (conscious) sensory qualities. The affective evaluation appeared as a spontaneous and independent dimension. Cooper attempted to recover the same perceptual configurations (except for attribute weights) for soft drinks based on preference and on similarity judgments, but failed. Preference judgments tended to reveal more subjective dimensions, unrelated to the product's objective characteristics. In the same area, Derbaix, Sjoeberg and Jansson (Sjoeberg *et al.*, 1984) conducted a further study. They had male and female respondents evaluate famous movie actors of both sexes for preference and similarity. The latent structures recovered from preference judgments revealed different and simpler structures than those obtained with perceptual data. The discrimination between the stimuli (actors) was more pronounced on affective evaluation scales than on (unidimensional) cognitive judgment scales. The preference judgments also appeared more stable and were performed with more confidence by the subjects. An additional finding was that female respondents, as evidenced by concurrently administered mood scales (Green and Nowlis, 1957), reacted more negatively to the perceptual similarity tasks than males. Could this be evidence in favor of the stereotype which makes emotion a female and cognition a male mode of response?

8. The properties of affective responses

Although we have recently recorded a flow of theories of emotion,[4] the knowledge presently available regarding the nature of the affective response is meagre. If the consumer sometimes reacts primarily by way of emotion, it matters to know these properties in order to conduct research. With logical arguments, but sometimes with limited empirical support Zajonc (1980: 151, 156, 157, 168, 169) stressed that the affective response can be said to be pre-cognitive, primary, basic, instantaneous, dominant, automatic, partly independent of cognition, inescapable, effortless, irrevocable, holistic, more difficult to verbalize, yet easy to communicate and understand.

Some of these properties have particular relevance for consumer behavior research:

Pre-cognitive and primary; instantaneous

If the leading reaction in the behavioral chain is affective, this opens the possibility for attitudinal change hierarchies where affective change precedes and colors subsequent conative/cognitive changes. Such an 'affective' hierarchy is proposed for children by Derbaix (1982) and cannot be ruled out for adults.

Irrevocable; inescapable

'Deep in one's heart' one knows what is right. Emotions cannot somehow be 'wrong'. As a result, consumer affect will be hard to change if it is primary; rather, it may lead to a search for supportive cognitive elements in order to rationalize or justify itself. Consumers will easily state their preference for a product and refuse to admit that the cognitive bases for it are mistaken or not applicable anymore. The same will hold even more strongly for political or ideological preferences. The expression of emotion can sometimes be controlled, but not the experience of it. This opens the possibility for a discrepancy between what is experienced and what is expressed.

Difficult to verbalize

Descriptions and explanation of affect often yield only vague and tautological verbalizations. Methods to tap the intensity, direction and content of affect which are less verbal in nature seem to be required in order to conduct methodologically unbiased studies.

Easy to communicate and understand

Understanding and communication of feelings are easy at the spontaneous, intuitive and non-verbal level. Emotions however defy verbal expression to some extent; problems are encountered if one attempts to register them by means of classical 'paper and pencil' methods. On the other hand, categories and instruments to record objectively affective experience are still relatively undeveloped, despite the efforts of some researchers, e.g. Kroeber-Riel (1982), Russo (1978).

Holistic and global

This refers to the relatively integrated, undifferentiated nature of emotions, at least at the present state of our knowledge. As discussed above, for instance, preference data, in comparison with perceptual similarity data, uncover relatively simple, low-dimensional stimuli-spaces (Derbaix, 1978; Giorgi and Derbaix, 1981).

A few more characteristics of emotions could be added. The experience of emotions seems to be accompanied by somatic changes, hence the tendency to use biopsychological methods to record them. Further, emotions perhaps involve different processes and are stored separately from cognitions. Kahneman and Treisman (1984) put forward a challenging hypothesis about the integration and interaction of psychological functions in the individual. Their idea is that the organism and especially the brain should be compared to an organization, where some things are known to, or experienced by, some components without the other components sharing directly in this knowledge or experience. The hemispheral lateralization view (Hansen, 1981) espouses this logic to some extent, by placing the locus of semantic-analytic processes in the left brain and of the more analog and direct experience processes in the right brain. Krugman (1977) relates this left/right brain distinction to the concepts of recall and of recognition and to those of high/low involvement in communication effects. Recall would be the province of semantic memory, recognition more of episodic memory. Recall of imagery, of picture memory is difficult; 'there is no recall because we have had only right-brain involvement'.

As a last property, one may mention that affect can be short-lived, episodic. Emotions 'wax and wane in the course of particular experiences, rather than being necessarily present on demand at the moment of questioning' (Abelson et al., 1982).

When asked 'are you angry at the President?', it might be reasonable to answer 'not today'. Such an answer would be less reasonable to the question whether one thinks the President is an able politician. If emotions are ephemeral, positive and negative affect (mixed feelings) could occur simultaneously.

The characterization given of emotions implies that the measurement of affect which is not based on inferences confronts one with novel problems. Fishbein, Ajzen, Rosenberg and their many marketing disciples conceptualized preferences as a weighted sum of cognitions. The allied measurement methodology allows one to bypass the direct measurement of affect itself. The cognitive elements, in this conception, are not only the mediators between the stimulus and the affective response, they are the atoms of the preference molecule itself. In the non-cognitive approach to affect, specific tools need to be devised in order to apprehend the occurrence, the intensity and content of the affective response. An excellent survey of appropriate observation instruments is given by Kroeber-Riel (1983).

9. Modifying attitudes involving little or no cognitive support

Modifying affect which is not cognitively based may require rather different methods from those used to change an attitude founded on cognition. It is possible that attitudes having a firm emotional basis without cognitive elaboration can be changed only by methods that have a direct emotional influence, thus bypassing unimportant cognitive elements. In a clinical context, the relative independence of the cognitive and affective systems may help to account for the 'irrationality' of fear and for other forms of abnormal experiences and hence for the notable resistance to cognitively induced changes that give rise to the need for therapies and therapists (Rachman, 1981).

In the advertising context, more appropriate models of presenting material to the visual system have to be devised. Visual materials, the use of imagery and of musical stimulation may lead directly and efficiently to affect modification (Gorn, 1982). Paivio (1978) has argued that affective judgments are more closely associated with the imagery system than with the verbal system. He has also proposed that visual and verbal material are organized and processed separately. In this respect we are convinced that our visual representation of products, stores, services, etc. is much more suited to generate hypotheses about them than the semantic definitions we have for those same objects. It is relevant that Paivio found that reaction times for pleasant–unpleasant ratings were longer for words than for pictures. He commented on this result as follows: 'The analog information involved in pleasantness and value judgments is more closely associated with the image system than with the verbal system' (Paivio, 1978: 207).

It is our conviction that marketing practice has much to learn from the scientific results obtained in this area. This knowledge will be gained through experimental rather than through survey research. It is much easier to find ways to manipulate the 'factual' content of an ad than to manipulate its 'affective' content. A communication can be 'objectively' content-analyzed in terms of the information it will deliver (e.g. using the method proposed by Resnik and Stern, 1977). This is harder from the point of view of the affect it will induce, if only because of the very subjective nature of the affective response. The importance of experimental approaches is clear here.

We have not yet mentioned the conative component of the response unit as a pathway to the manipulation of affect. In the associative network view, the induction of acts will also activate meaning and emotion, as the Wells and Petty (1981) headphone experiment demonstrates. This reverses the usual order of causality between changes in cognition, affect and behavior. As Zajonc and Markus (1982) point out, 'affect can be acquired through habituation, familiarization and positive reinforcement'.

The preceding suggests at least three things from the perspective of behavior modification:

1. It is not always necessary to use factual or rational communication. The propaganda of the thirties based its success on methods designed to appeal directly to emotion, with an impressive behavioral effect.
2. The way to changing behavior may be shorter or less arduous if affect and cognition are dissociated.
3. New tools and means are needed in order to measure and to modify attitudes.

These points assume that it is necessary to modify affect in order to influence behavior. In addition, situations can be envisioned where cognitions directly induce behavioral change; knowing what to do, and doing it, is very well possible without involving affect. Let us not forget, finally, that affective processes or states may cause or enhance cognitive effects, in the sense that the one who 'loves the most' also 'understands the best'.

The three preceding paragraphs discussed the revival of psychological theories focused on direct emotional, or even on direct conative responses. When we reflect on the nature of emotions, we become aware that these are still ill-defined and, as a result, very hard to measure. When reflecting, in addition, on behavior manipulation, we must further admit that little is known still on ways to modify affect that do not operate through the cognitive components.

10. Implications for the field of consumer research

The preceding sections drew heavily on contributions from psychology. What are the more concrete implications for the field of Consumer Research? We see specific repercussions in the areas of theories/models, of research methods and of marketing practice. Rather than summing up detailed opportunities, we shall indicate interesting areas for new contributions in the domains of theories and of methods.

In terms of theory, the area of low involvement consumer behavior is to benefit from the insights expounded above. Low involvement has been an elusive concept to define and measure. The distinction between automatic and controlled processing as well as the conditions for the occurrence of either are contributions from cognitive psychology which will help to clarify the concept of low involvement. But further, low involvement is hardly more than a concept in consumer theory. There are few models that detail low involvement behavior beyond Krugman's low involvement attitudinal hierarchy (Krugman, 1965); this leads to a pressing need for models of the formation, change and structure of low involvement cognition, affect and conation. Alternatives for the multi-dimensional expectancy-value conceptions are available in terms of consumer scripts and schemata, of associative network structures, of analog representations, etc.

The area of Consumer Research contains two dormant streams of research, the one non-cognitive, the other non-conscious in orientation; both are worth reactivating within the present, enriched framework. The non-cognitive area of routine choice behavior, of brand loyalty and stochastic brand choice models should be revised and extended in its scope to other behavioral habits than brand choice or even to cognitive habits; this will help to make the concept of routinized consumer response more meaningful. The non-conscious stream of research in Consumer Psychology has been the province of Motivation Research. This orientation, while pronounced dead by theoreticians, is alive and well in the world of marketing practitioners. Motivation Research drew its inspiration from the psychology of the subconscious, while its intent mostly was to explain unconscious effects, which we would now associate with automatic processing and with mindless behavior. The results of present-day cognitive psychology allow us to draw more, better founded and more refined conclusions in this area. This is the case a.o. in the field of subliminal stimulation (Moore, 1982) where we are now able to state which effects can be expected under what circumstances.

Beyond low involvement effects, psychology offers interesting contributions in the areas of the primacy of emotions and of behavior manipulation. Both have received relatively less attention in consumer psychology so that an influx of theories, models and methods is to be expected and welcomed.

In terms of methods, new developments should take into account that consumers are often unaware of some states or processes and barely aware of others. Moreover, their cognitions may be of a nonverbal nature and/or do not conform to the structure or content required by CCP models. This recommendation is not new. Every market research handbook warns of the drawbacks of structured undisguised questionnaire studies, suggests alternative methods but usually fails to make these very operational or to provide a framework for their application. Verbal self-reports assume a respondent who is able and willing to provide valid answers. Nisbett and Wilson (1977) alert us to instances where the ability to report introspectively is attenuated, namely:

– when the event and the report are removed in time,
– when the behavior is caused by contextual effects,
– when the behavior is due to the mechanics of judgment,
– when the behavior is due to the nonoccurrence, rather than the occurrence of events,
– when the determinants of behavior are rather nonverbal, and
– when there is a discrepancy between the nature or magnitude of determinants and of events.

In addition, the type of verbal questions asked can be misleading in suggesting the desirable content or structure of the replies.

In view of these difficulties, one avenue is to avoid the verbal self-report. The conscious cognitive contents could be elicited directly in an appropriate nonverbal mode. Direct magnitude scaling (Behrens, 1983) in nonverbal modes can rely on well-established findings in psychophysiology. Even if reports cannot be given directly in the corresponding sensory mode, human synaesthetic capacities may allow better expression in other than verbal modes. The Program Analyzer methodology, as a specific example, adds the advantage of continuous, almost concurrent and therefore more spontaneous response registration.

Other principles of measurement avoiding the verbal self-report rely on the registration of manifest or of nonmanifest behavior. Manifest behavior often is the ultimate decision criterion. Experimental research using manifest behavior as the dependent variable offers the advantage of strong internal validity and of higher external validity than studies taking intermediate variables as their dependent variable. Unfortunately, experiments tend to be obtrusive, and the question of reactivity looms large in marketing studies, where it is often hard to develop a suitable disguise. In addition to manifest behavior, there are innumerable kinds of less manifest bodily processes which are concomitants of psychological states or processes. On the somewhat manifest side, nonverbal behaviors (bodily posture, facial expression) are available as dependent variables or as indicators of intervening variables (Kroeber-Riel, 1983; Weinberg, 1983). Less manifest are physiological changes (EDR, heart-rhythm, blood pressure, eye movements), which presently allow vastly better measurement, encoding and analysis due to the progress in digital equipment. The progress in measurement ability is not, at present, matched by an equal proficiency in the validation of such measures. In particular, the danger is real that such measurements are too easily equated with direct observations of specific abstractions (e.g. 'EDR measures emotion') and uncritically applied in a consumer research context. This observation methodology can yield its full potential only in well planned research which specifies its hypotheses *a priori* and selects the operationalizations in function of the hypotheses.

The former research methods allow the study of unconscious processes and states as well as of the barely or fully conscious ones. In the latter cases, we recommend to apply them in addition to verbal self-reports, as suggested by the Multimethod-Multitrait approach.

The barely conscious contents could, in principle, also be revealed by verbal self-reports. Care should then be taken to avoid contamination of the verbalizations by conscious and rather verbal intervening processes. The principles for the elicitation of the barely conscious will mainly involve (1) methods to heighten the consciousness of what was till then barely conscious; (2) the concurrent or almost concurrent elicitation of verbal reports with the processes under investigation, and (3) the facilitation of the expression by means of projective materials (Kroeber-Riel, 1983).

Conscious cognitive content suited for verbal expression, finally, lends itself to elicitation through self-report measures. The danger of contamination through the reporting process can be minimized by applying unstructured spontaneous elicitation formats. The analysis of the content of its structure, however, puts more of a burden on the investigator. He should take appropriate measures in order not to contaminate the data by his interpretation (Leigh and Rethans, 1983; Dillon, 1982).

11. Conclusions

Our introductory comment stated that the present 'non-cognitive' revolution in consumer research is reminiscent of previous episodes in the field, where behavioristic and emotional or motivational concerns were in their heyday. We also argued that we are not witnessing a simple return to the old approaches, but that the cognitivistic research line had deepened our understanding and prepared us for a better study of the 'non-cognitive' processes. Two major insights seem to be especially relevant. First, the distinction between cognition, emotion and conation is an artificial one, even though it is often useful. The recent cognitive research tradition has made us attentive to the fact that these constructs cannot be sharply distinguished from one another and that they interrelate in often subtle ways. It has also emphasized the distinction between conscious and pre-conscious processes. In particular, the automatic tendency to equate cognition with conscious phenomena and emotion with unconscious ones is shown to be counterproductive.

As a result, consumer research findings made a long time ago are again opened for investigation. In 1961, D.F. Cox, in his classical text on communication principles in advertising stated that the connection between a person's knowledge and his attitudes and between the latter and his behavior were not necessarily direct, one-to-one. In the same year, Bauer and Bauer wrote that one of the major ways in which mass media influence public attitudes is via the second order effect of having first elicited behavior based on other existing attitudes. These and other similar effects are now again fashionable study objects. While a substantial body of theoretical insight has diffused from psychology to consumer behavior research, this theory will now have to be translated and adapted to the consumption field. More in particular, the methodology of this research will need to be adopted, adapted and developed.

Notes

1. In Wolman (1973) we find the following definitions: Cognition: (1) a general term for any process which allows an organism to know and be aware; it includes perceiving, reasoning, conceiving, judging; and (2) a postulated stimulus-stimulus association or perceptual organization thought to account for expectancies of an organism. Emotion: A complex reaction, consisting of a

physiological change from the homeostatic state, subjectively experienced as feeling and manifested in bodily changes which are preparatory to overt action. Conation: The aspect of personality characterized by conscious, willing strong and purposive action. Other definitions are found, e.g. in Eysenck, Arnold and Meili (1982): Cognition: Every process by which a living creature obtains knowledge of some object or becomes aware of its environment (perception, discovery, recognition, imagining, judging, memorizing, learning, thinking); knowing, as distinct from volitional or emotional processes; the product of cognizing or knowing. Emotion: A complex state involving heightened perception of an object or situation, widespread bodily changes, an appraisal of felt attraction or repulsion, and behavior organized toward approach or withdrawal. Conation: A term for purposive mental drive or striving toward action; conative forces can appear as 'blind impulse' or as purposeful effort.

2. While the existence of automatic processes is generally accepted, their nature and the limit between automatic and controlled processing is subject to discussion. The debate can be followed e.g., between Kahneman and Shiffrin/Schneider (Kahneman and Treisman, 1984). The former, while accepting the idea of automaticity in principle, seems to argue that attentive processes are too easily discounted in favor of unattentive ones and that our models of attention, perception and memory are still inadequate.

3. The experience of emotion, contrary to the expression of it, cannot occur without some form of cognition.

4. These can be categorized under: Cognitive theories of emotion, where cognitive processes constitute necessary elements and lead to the explication of emotional experience (Mandler, 1975; Lazarus, 1966; Schachter and Singer, 1962) and somatic theories of emotion, essentially focused on the expression of emotion (Izard, 1978; Leventhal, 1980; Tomkins, 1981).

References

Abelson, R.P. (1976), 'Script processing in attitude formation and decision making', in J.S. Carroll and J.W. Payne (eds), *Cognition and Social Behavior*. Hillsdale, NJ: Erlbaum.

Abelson, R.P., D.R. Kinder, M.D. Peters and S.T. Fiske (1982), 'Affective and semantic components in political person perception', *Journal of Personality and Social Psychology*, **42**, 619–630.

Ajzen, I. and M. Fishbein (1980), *Understanding Attitudes and Predicting Social-Behavior*. Englewood Cliffs, NJ: Prentice-Hall.

Batra, R. and M.L. Ray (1983), 'Operationalizing involvement as depth and quality of cognitive responses', in R.P. Bagozzi and A.M. Tybout (eds.), *ACR Proceedings*, Vol. 10, Association for Consumer Research, 309–313.

Bauer, R. and A. Bauer (1961), 'America, mass society and mass media', *Journal of Social Issues*, Vol. 16(3), 3–66.

Behrens, G. (1983), 'Magnitudekalierung', in *Forschungsgruppe Konsum und Verhalten. Innovative Marktforschung*. Würzburg: Physica Verlag.

Bettman, J.R. (1979), *An Information Processing Theory of Consumer Choice*. Reading, MA: Addison Wesley.

Bower, G.H. (1983), 'Affect and cognition'. *Proceedings of the Royal Society of London*.

Bultez, A. and C. Derbaix (1982), 'La validation des modèles multi-attributs décrivant les préférences du consummateur individuel'. *Annales de Sciences Economiques Appliquées*, **38**(1), 149–170.

Caccioppo, J.T. and R.E. Petty (1981), 'Electromyograms as measures of extent and affectivity of information processing', *American Psychologist*, **36**, 441–456.

Childers, T.L. and M.J. Houston (1983), 'Imagery paradigms for consumer research: Alternative perspectives from cognitive psychology', in R.P. Bagozzi and A.M. Tybout (eds.), *ACR Proceedings*, Vol. 10. Association for Consumer Research, 59–64.

Cooper, L.G. (1973), 'A multivariate investigation of preferences', *Multivariate Behavioral Research*, **8**, 253–272.

Corteen, R.S. and B. Wood (1972), 'Autonomic responses to shock-associated words in an unattended channel', *Journal of Experimental Psychology*, **94**, 308–313.

Cox, D.F. (1961), 'Clues for advertising strategists: II', *Harvard Business Review*, **39**, 160–182.

Coyne, J. (1982), 'Putting Humpty Dumpty back together: Cognition emotion and motivation reconsidered', in A. Mitchell (ed.), *ACR Proceedings*, Vol. 9, Association for Consumer Research, 153–155.

Day, G.S. (1973), 'Theories of attitude structure and change', in S. Ward and T.S. Robertson (eds.), *Consumer Behavior: Theoretical Sources*. Englewood Cliffs, NJ: Prentice Hall.

Derbaix, C. and M. Giorgi (1980), 'L'apport des échelles unidimensionelles dans l'étude de l'image de marque', *Annales de Sciences Economiques Appliquées*, **36**(4), 61–68.

Derbaix, C. (1978), *Pour un meilleur contenu publicitaire*. Université de Catholique de Louvain. (Ph D Dissertation.)

Derbaix, C. (1982), 'L'enfant, la communication publicitaire et la hiérarchie des effets', *Revue Française du Marketing*, **2**, 31–47.

Dichter, E. (1964), *Handbook of Consumer Motivations*. New York: McGraw-Hill.

Dillon, W.R. *et al.* (1982), 'An approach to measuring thought patterns and gauging causal schemata', in A. Mitchell (ed.), *ACR Proceedings*, Vol. 9, Association for Consumer Research, 181–186.

Dixon, N.F. (1981), *Preconscious Processing*. New York: Wiley.

Dover, P.A. (1982), 'Inferential belief formation: An overlooked concept in information processing research', in A. Mitchell (ed.), *ACR Proceedings*, Vol. 9, Association for Consumer Research, 187–189.

Eysenck, H.J., W. Arnold and R. Meili (1982), *Encyclopedia of Psychology*. London: Search Press.

Gorn, G. (1982), 'The effects of music in advertising on choice behavior: A classical conditioning approach', *Journal of Marketing*, **46**, 94–101.

Green, E. and V. Nowlis (1957), *A Factor Analytic Study of the Domain of Mood with Independent Experimental Validation of the Factors*. Technical Report 4, Office of Naval Research.

Hansen, F. (1981), 'Hemispherical lateralization: Implications for understanding consumer behavior', *Journal of Consumer Research*, **8**, 23–36.

Hansen, F. (1983), *An Alternative Theory of the Advertising Communication Process*. Copenhagen School of Economics and Business Administration. (Mimeo.)

Hilgard, E.R. (1980), 'Consciousness in contemporary psychology' *Annual Review of Psychology*, **31**, 1–26.

Houston, M.J. and M.L. Rothschild (1978), Conceptual and methodological perspectives on involvement', in S.C. Jain (ed.), *Research Frontiers in Marketing Dialogues and Directors*. Chicago, IL: American Marketing Association, 184–187.

Izard, C.E. (1978), 'On the development of emotions and emotion–cognition relationship in infancy', in M. Lewis and L. Rosenblum (eds.), *The Development of Affect*. New York: Plenum Press.

Jacoby, J. (1976), 'Consumer psychology: An octennium', *Annual Review of Psychology*, 331–358.

Kahneman, D. and A. Treisman (1984), 'Changing views of attention and automaticity', in R. Parasuraman and D.R. Davies (eds.), *Varieties of Attention*. New York: Academic Press.

Kassarjian, H.H. (1982), 'Consumer psychology', *Annual Review of Psychology*, **33**, 619–649.

Katona, G. (1975), *Psychological Economics*. Amsterdam: Elsevier Science Publishers.

Katz, E. (1968), 'On reopening the question of selectivity in exposure to mass communications', in R.P. Abelson *et al.* (eds), *Theories of Cognitive Consistency: A Source Book*. Chicago, IL: Rand-McNally.

Kroeber-Riel, W. (1979), 'Activation research: Psychological approaches in consumer research', *Journal of Consumer Research*, **5**, 240–250.

Kroeber-Riel, W. (1983), 'Analyse des nicht-kognitiven Konsumentenverhaltens', in W. Kroeber-Riel (ed.), *Forschungsgruppe Konsum und Verhalten: Innovative Marktforschung*. Würzburg: Physica Verlag.

Krugman, H.E. (1965), 'The impact of television advertising: Learning without involvement', *Public Opinion Quarterly*, **29**, 344–356.

Krugman, H.E. (1977), 'Memory without recall, exposure without perception', *Journal of Advertising Research*, **17**(4), 7–12.

Langer, E., A. Blank and B. Chanowitz (1978), 'The mindlessness of ostensibly thoughtful action', *Journal of Personality and Social Psychology*, **36**(6), 635–642.

Langer, E. and B. Chanowitz (1981), 'Premature cognitive commitment', *Journal of Personality and Social Psychology*, **41**(6), 1051–1063.

Lazarus, R.S. (1981), 'A cognitivist's reply to Zajonc on emotion and cognition', *American Psychologist*, **36**, 222–223.

Leigh, T.W. and A.J. Rethans (1983), 'Experiences with script elicitation within consumer decision making context', in R.P. Bagozzi and A.M. Tybout (eds.), *ACR Proceedings*, Vol. 10, Association for Consumer Research, 667–672.

Leventhal, H. (1980), 'Toward a comprehensive theory of emotion', in L. Berkowitz (ed.), *Advances in Experimental Social Psychology*, Vol. 13, New York: Academic Press.

Littman, R.A. and H.M. Manning (1954), 'A methodological study of cigarette brand discrimination', *Journal of Applied Psychology*, **38**, 185–190.

Mandler, G. (1975), *Mind and Emotion*. New York: Wiley.

Marcel, A. (1980), 'Explaining selective effects of prior context on perception: The need to distinguish conscious and preconscious processes in word recognition', in R. Vickerson (ed), *Attention and Performance*. Hillsdale, NJ: Erlbaum.

Massy, W.F., D.B. Montgomery and D.G. Morrison (1970), *Stochastic Models of Buyer Behavior*. Cambridge, MA: MIT.

Meyer-Hentschel, G. (1983), *Aktivierungswirkung von Anzeigen*. Würzburg: Physica Verlag.

Mitchell, A. (1982), 'Models of memory: Implications for measuring knowledge structures', in A. Mitchell (ed.), *ACR Proceedings*, Vol. 9, Association for Consumer Research, 45–51.

Moore, T. (1982), 'Subliminal advertising: What you see is what you get', *Journal of Marketing*, **46**, 94–101.

Nakashima, T. (1909), 'Contribution of the study of affective processes', *American Journal of Psychology*, **20**, 157–193.

Natsoulas, T. (1981), 'Basic problems of consciousness', *Journal of Personality and Social Psychology*, **41**(1), 132–178.

Nisbett, R.E. and D.T. Wilson (1977), 'Telling more than we can know: Verbal reports on mental processes', *Psychological Review*, **84**, 231–259.

Nisbett, R.E. and L. Ross (1980), *Human Inference Strategies and Shortcomings of Social Judgment*. Englewood Cliffs, NJ: Prentice Hall.

Olshavsky, R.W. and D.H. Granbois (1980), 'Consumer decision making: Fact or fiction?', *Journal of Consumer Research*, **6**, 93–100.

Olson, J.C. (1980), 'Encoding processes: Levels of processing and existing knowledge structures', in J.C. Olson (ed.), *Advances in Consumer Research*, Vol. VII. Ann Arbor, MI: Association for Consumer Research.

Paivio, A. (1978), 'Mental comparisons involving abstract attributes', *Memory and Cognition*, **3**, 199–208.

Raaij, W.F. van (1983), 'Affectieve en cognitieve reacties of reclame and voorlichting', Erasmus University Rotterdam (mimeo).

Rachman, S. (1981), 'The primacy of affect: Some theoretical implications', *Behavior Research and Therapy*, **19**, 279–290.

Ratchford, B.T. (1975), 'The new economic theory of consumer behavior: An interpretive essay', *Journal of Consumer Research*, **2**(2), 65–75.

Ray, M.L. and E. Batra (1983), 'Emotion and persuasion in advertising: What we know and what we don't know about effect', in R.P. Bagozzi and A.M. Tybout (eds.), *ACR Proceedings*, Vol. 9, Association for Consumer Research, 543–548.

Rossiter, J. (1982), 'Visual imagery: Applications to advertising', in A. Mitchell (ed.), *ACR Proceedings*, Vol. 9, Association for Consumer Research, 101–106.

Rothschild, M.L. and W.C. Gaidis (1981), 'Behavioural learning theory: Its relevance to marketing and promotions', *Journal of Marketing*, **45**, 70–78.

Russo, J.E. (1978), 'Eye fixations can save the world: A critical evaluation and a comparison between eye fixation and other information processing methodologies', in H.K. Hunt (ed.), *ACR Proceedings*, Vol. 5, Association for Consumer Research, 561–570.

Ryan, M. (1982), 'Achieving correspondence among cognitive processes and physiological measures', in A. Mitchell (ed.), *ACR Proceedings*, Vol. 9, Association for Consumer Research, 170–172.

Schachter, S. and J. Singer (1962), 'Cognitive, social and physiological determinants of emotional state', *Psychological Review*, **69**(5), 379–399.

Scheurin, H. and S. Dickman (1980), 'The psychological unconscious', *American Psychologist*, **35**, 421–434.

Schneider, W., S.T. Dumais and R.M. Shiffrin (1984), 'Automatic and control processing and attention', in R. Parasuraman and D.R. Davies (eds.), *Varieties of Attention*. New York: Academic Press.

Shiffrin, R.N. and W. Schneider (1977), 'Controlled and automatic human information processing', *Psychological Review*, 127–190.

Sjoberg, L., C. Derbaix and B. Jansson (1984), *Preference and Similarity: Affective and Cognitive Judgment?* Technical Report, Department of Psychology, University of Göteborg.

Srull, R.K. (1983), 'Affect and memory: The impact of affective reactions in advertising on the representation of product information in memory', in R.P. Bagozzi and A.M. Tybout (eds.), *ACR Proceedings*, Vol. 10, Association for Consumer Research, 520–525.

Tomkins, S.S. (1962), *Affect Imagery and Consciousness*, Vol. 1. New York: Springer.

Vandenberg, O. and P. Eelen (1983), *Unconscious Processing and Emotions*. Dept. of Psychology, University of Leuven.

Watson, P.J. and R.J. Gatchel (1979), 'Autonomic measures of advertising', *Journal of Advertising Research*, **19**, 15–20.

Weinberg, P. (1983), 'Beobachtung des emotionalen Verhaltens', in P. Weinberg (ed.), *Forschungsgruppe Konsum und Verhalten: Innovative Marktforschung*. Würzburg: Physica Verlag.

Wells, G.L. and R.E. Petty (1980), 'The effects of overt head movement on persuasion: Compatibility and incompatibility or responses', *Basic and Applied Social Psychology*, **1**, 219–230.

Wolman, R.B. (ed.) (1973), *Dictionary of Behavioral Science*. London: Macmillan.

Wright, P.L. (1975), 'Consumer choice strategies: Simplifying vs. optimizing', *Journal of Marketing Research*, **12**, 60–67.

Zajonc, R.B. (1980), 'Feeling and thinking: Preferences need no inferences', *American Psychologist*, **35**, 151–175.

Zajonc, R.B. and H. Markus (1982), 'Affective and cognitive factors in preferences', *Journal of Consumer Research*, **9**, 123–131.

Part III

societal influences

Socialization and lifestyles

5

Webley, P. and Lea, S.E.G., 1993, 'Towards a more realistic psychology of economic socialization', *Journal of Economic Psychology*, **14**(3), 461–72
Böcker, F., 1992, 'Preference-forming for durable goods within families', *Recherche et Applications en Marketing*, **7**(2), 51–66

Introduction

Even though consumption decision processes have traditionally been studied at the individual level, it is now widely acknowledged that consumption is essentially a societal process. After looking at the consumer at an individual level, the next two chapters consider the societal interactions involved in any consumption action. Broadly speaking, two main types of societal influences can be outlined: (1) social interactions which derive from the socialization process and the way the individual is integrated in a community which dictates rules and norms as to how to consume, and (2) cultural influences which are more implicit and diffuse, and thus harder to grasp.

For a long time, the sociological approach to consumption has been subordinated to the mere study of the role of products and brands in building status symbols for consumers. Consistent with the concept of conspicuous consumption proposed by Veblen as early as 1899, the sociological approach to goods has long been associated with the connotative powers of objects and their ability to communicate a given social status. Having moved away from the naivety underlying the concept of status symbols, the sociology of consumption has acquired a new legitimacy (Fabris, 1990) by developing new fields of research, such as the role of socialization in the consumption process, the division of roles and decisions within the family, the study of lifestyles or the way rumours get developed, amplified, distorted and propagated.

The first article is concerned with the role of children as socialization agents and more specifically with childhood consumer socialization, that is, how children gradually acquire the knowledge, skills, values and attitudes which allow them to act as consumers in the marketplace. This topic is of interest because companies now consider children as real economic agents *per se* with a strong economic and prescriptive power. Children (as well as teenagers, single people and seniors) have also become new target groups and represent profitable segments which need to be marketed specifically and appropriately. Hence the need to investigate how children acquire economic ideas. Most of the studies undertaken in this field have been very much influenced by the works of Jean Piaget who pioneered the field of psychological research on children's cognitive development.

The article by Webley and Lea considers the economic behaviour of children not in a cognitive perspective, as is usually the case, but rather by describing ethnologically the way children solve the economic problems they are faced with. Acting as ethnographers, the authors investigate such behaviours as swapping or bartering, which can be found among children in all school playgrounds. They point out the fact that several types of rituals and plainly economic behaviours are linked to children's games, such as marbles.

The second article, by Böcker, deals with another type of social interaction by looking at the way purchase decisions are made within the family. The focus is laid on durable goods which represent an interesting product category because they reflect consumer lifestyles and they indicate a necessary interaction phenomenon, in the sense that the decision to buy such products is always influenced by several members within the family. The author considers the buying decision of such goods not as a homogeneous process, but on the contrary, as emerging from a partialized decision process; some family members might, for instance, influence the choice of a product, whereas others might influence the choice of a specific brand. This type of analysis is shown to be relevant for the purchase of a car. The author then acknowledges that the complexity of decision processes within the family is increased by the fact that they involve several phases and participants, thus often being multidimensional. A valuable theoretical framework is proposed to assess with clarity and pertinence the various forms of influences within the family group, but also to visualize the decision stages (image creation of the product, pre-selection of acceptable products, choice of preferred product).

This article thus provides an interesting model of social interactions involved in the buying decision of durable goods. It gives a good overview of the role of children and women in the family decision process, a role that is usually underestimated. The traditional idea that there exist masculine products exclusively bought by men and feminine products exclusively bought by women, is seriously questioned by showing that most decisions are in fact jointly made.

References

Fabris, G., 1990, 'Consumer studies: New perspectives', *Marketing and Research Today*, June, 67–73.
Shields, R. (ed.), 1992, *Lifestyle Shopping. The Subject of Consumption*, London: Routledge.
Veblen, T., 1899, *The Theory of the Leisure Class*, London: Macmillan.

Towards a more realistic psychology of economic socialization

●●●

Paul Webley and Stephen E.G. Lea
Department of Psychology, Washington Singer Laboratories, University of Exeter

Summary

In this paper we argue that current research into economic socialization is unsatisfactory for two main reasons. Most researchers have tended to regard the meaning of the term 'economic' as static and given and so have taken an adult-centred view of the child's world and investigated only those domains which are obviously economic (working, spending, borrowing, saving etc.). Secondly, researchers have concentrated almost exclusively on the question of cognitive development and so have asked 'how do children come to understand the economic world of grown-ups?' and not 'how do children solve the economic problems they are faced with?'. We propose that researchers should be more concerned with the real economic world of childhood and we describe a few investigations that we have done in the style we favour. We conclude by discussing the implications of this approach for the future of economic psychology.

1. Introduction

When we wrote *The Individual in the Economy* (Lea *et al.*, 1987) we commented on the lack of work on economic socialization and its neglect by economic psychologists. Times have certainly changed: there have been well-attended symposia on economic socialization at most recent conferences of the International Association for Research in Economic Psychology (IAREP) and not very long ago there was a special issue of the *Journal of Economic Psychology* devoted solely to this topic (Leiser *et al.*, 1990a). So you might expect us to be well pleased. To a certain extent we are but our pleasure is tinged with regret that our specific suggestions for future research in the field have been generally ignored. In our conclusions we suggested (p. 398) that

> a truly developmental economic psychology seems to us to require empirical and
> theoretical progress in two directions. The first . . . involves relating the economic

From *Journal of Economic Psychology*, **14**(3), 1993, 461–72.

structure of a society to the economic ideas and behavior that its youngest members develop. The second . . . [is] that we should examine the economic world that children are constructing themselves.

There has been definite progress in the first direction (e.g. Dittmar, 1992; Leiser *et al.*, 1990b) but, other than the work described below, none that we have been able to trace in the second. The bulk of the recent research in economic socialization has continued along existing lines; it can perhaps be well characterized as 'more of the same'. There would be nothing wrong with this, of course, if the existing lines were satisfactory, but in our view they are not.

We find current research in economic socialization unsatisfying in two main ways. First, researchers in this field have not thought deeply enough about the defining characteristics of economic behaviour. For the most part they have tended to regard the meaning of the term 'economic' as static and given; the term has simply served as a label for the concepts associated with the social world related to the acquisition, management and distribution of wealth. So developmental researchers have applied themselves to conventional economic behaviours: working and spending, borrowing and lending, investing and saving. Treating the meaning of the term 'economic' as given is not unique to developmentalists (it is an issue throughout economic psychology) but it is a particular problem for those studying children. We cannot rely on shared assumptions between researchers and the researched and since children do not in general use the word 'economic' we cannot simply ask them to tell us what is and what is not economic behaviour in their eyes.

The second reason why we find current research in economic socialization unsatisfactory is that it has concentrated almost exclusively on the question of cognitive development, and its implications for the child's understanding of the economic world of grown-ups. This Piagetian approach is not useless: it has produced some valuable results, for example those of Berti and Bombi (1988) and that reported in the *Journal of Economic Psychology* special issue on 'Economic Socialization' (e.g. Leiser *et al.*, 1990b) and for the most part, researchers in this tradition are anyway primarily interested in the nature and development of social thinking rather than economic socialization. But it has looked on economic socialization as a monotonic process of adaptation to the economic behaviour and concepts of adults. The question researchers have been concerned with has been 'how do children come to understand the economic world of grown-ups?' and not 'how do children understand and solve the economic problems they are faced with?'.

Although we have identified two reasons why we feel current research in this field is unsatisfactory, there are actually three issues here; the question of what the 'economic' in economic socialization refers to, the question of whether we should focus on economic behaviour rather than economic cognition, and a concern that we should investigate things that matter to children. We will deal with each in turn.

Above we criticized researchers for taking the definition of economic behaviour for granted. But what are the alternatives? One possibility would be to investigate only those behaviours that involve maximizing utility or optimization. This has the merit of directing our attention to real problems that matter to people, but since any behaviour that is consistent can be described as maximizing something (Rachlin, 1980), by this definition economic behaviour would include nearly all behaviour. Though it is possible to conceive of a research programme based on this assumption (which, in essence, asks the two questions 'when do children begin to act like economists with regard to their use of time, with regard to their relationships etc.?' and 'what are they maximizing when they do so?'), the fact that virtually all behaviours would be grist to its mill makes this approach unmanageable. This problem could perhaps be resolved if we used the idea that economic behaviour involves action where an individual intends to maximize. However, this probably raises more problems than it solves; identifying when children's intentions [are] to maximize is hardly straightforward, and anyway many behaviours that are not obviously economic are none the less planned. Another option is to define as economic behaviours those that are generally considered economic (the approach that has usually been followed). This has the advantage of including behaviours that by any definition would be economic (e.g. buying sweets in a shop), but it begs the question 'generally considered by whom?'. The answer can only be 'adults in our society', and that exposes two serious problems. First, it is adult-centred; adults may well agree that putting money in a savings account is an economic act and feel that swapping in the playground is just playing – to the child, however, the first may be a meaningless routine and the second a vibrant economic negotiation. Secondly, the concept of economic behaviour is culturally and historically determined, a fact that inevitably has implications for the future of economic psychology in general, which we will discuss later.

Having been critical of existing definitions the reader may be expecting us to put forward our own. But we have no intention of so doing. Definitions, as such, do not matter; good definitions are to be read from right to left and not from left to right (see Popper, 1966), so a term like economic behaviour is just a shorthand way of saying something like 'those behaviours concerned with the acquisition, management and distribution of wealth'. It is theories that matter. Thus it is the implicit theory embodied in the use of a conventional definition of economic behaviour by researchers in economic socialization that is misguided, rather than the definition *per se*. The implicit theory is that the roots of adult economic behaviour are to be found in children's understanding of that behaviour. This is not to say that researchers in economic socialization would *claim* that adult saving has its origins in children's understanding of the functioning of banks, their understanding of interest, and their use of savings accounts but that their approach implies this. We, on the other hand, believe that some of the precursors of adult economic behaviour are to be found in the real economic behaviour of children and the economic world that children are constructing for themselves. In the case of saving this implies that it is saving up to buy gifts and the use of money boxes that are likely to be much more important – together, perhaps, with other behaviour (such as forming a collection of marbles) that do not look 'economic' at all to conventional eyes.

This brings us to the second issue. Most research in economic socialization to date has been concerned with economic thought rather than economic action. We are not taking a behaviourist position, and we recognize that there are good reasons for the dominance of work on economic cognition. The Piagetian tradition from which it springs offers a paradigm for exploring children's understanding, within which research on economic concepts can be seen alongside comparable work on many related areas. But there is a problem. Thought may be a cause, a consequence or independent from behaviour; only systematic investigation will tell us which. Research on moral development illustrates how important it is to realize this. Once it had been grasped, studies of moral thought could be seen in their proper perspective as necessary but not sufficient (Tomlinson, 1980). Similarly in the economic field; given the dominance of studies of cognition it is appropriate to redress the balance by being more concerned with the economic behaviour of children. And the recent history of economic psychology in general suggests that moving away from an exclusively cognitive approach will bring other gains (Foxall, 1990; Lea, 1992).

Finally, the economic behaviour that we study must be behaviour that matters to the children concerned. Just because we are engaged in developmental research, it is a non-trivial problem to identify behaviour that matters. The amount of money involved, for example, may be no guide at all to a behaviour's importance to a child who has not yet adapted the economic attitudes and behaviour of a grown-up. Only a determined effort of observation, empathy and imagination will enable us to enter children's own economic world and assess the relative importance of the events that happen in it.

This third issue offers the key to the other two. If we make the effort to carry out research into the economic world of children and young people, and to start our research at the points that are important to its inhabitants, we are inevitably drawn to look at behaviour as well as thought. And through looking within that world, we will be led to an effective definition of the 'economic' – one that groups together behaviours and concepts that are related in practice, and so ought to be related in the implicit theory that a definition enshrines. That, at least, is our claim; so let us now attempt to justify it by describing some research into the economic world of young people.

2. The economic world of childhood

In this section we describe a few investigations that have sprung from our wish for a 'truly developmental economic psychology' (Lea *et al.*, 1987). A comment about methodology is appropriate at the outset. L.P. Hartley began *The Go-Between*, a novel essentially about childhood, with the phrase, 'The past is a foreign country: they do things differently there'. Developmental research has much in common with ethnography. Since it is likely that there will be considerable variability in the forms of 'indigenous' economic culture found among children, it is essential that investigations are grounded in a firm knowledge of the particular culture. For example, one of the fields we shall report on below is inter-child bartering, or 'swopping'. This is banned at some schools, and where it is allowed, what is swapped depends to a certain extent on what is the current 'craze'. Like ethnographers, if we are not to make elementary mistakes of interpretation, we need local informants (and not mere 'subjects' or 'respondents'); in other words child collaborators are vital.

2.1 Playground games: The marble economy

Games with marbles are very popular among English school children, though their popularity is very seasonal; there are marble 'crazes' during which the school playground is full of children playing marbles and nothing else, followed by periods when no marbles are seen. Marble playing is unusual in that it is enjoyed by both sexes across a reasonable age range, although this has not always been the case: Sutton-Smith (1982) shows that a hundred years ago marble games were played mainly by boys. Marbles come in a wide variety of colour and size combinations, which cost different amounts in the shops but, more importantly, have different values in the playground. These two scales of values do not correspond; the playground value is the number of 'goes' that a player can have in the various marble games. A 'miniature jinks' (a small plain marble all of one colour), for example, is worth 3 goes in one Exeter school.

Games of marbles also come in a variety of forms. As well as the standard game (where the aim is to hit a target marble by rolling a marble from a distance) there are a number of others (e.g. where the aim is to pass between the gap between two marbles). What is interesting about these variants is that it is possible to win marbles even if one lacks technical skill. Whatever variant is being played usually two children play and at the end of the game the winner wins one or more marbles. Thus the child has the chance to win or lose property which thereafter really belongs to him or her. We have found that several plainly economic behaviours are linked to such games (more details can be found in Webley and Webley, 1990; and Webley, [1996]). For example:

(i)   One child may 'work for' another. In this situation there is a 'capitalist' who owns plenty of marbles, and a 'worker' who is an expert player; the capitalist provides the marbles, the worker plays the games, and they share the proceeds. The interesting question is how the winnings are shared. If an adult researcher puts this question to the children, the modal answer is that the winnings should be divided equally, with a distribution of 30/70 with the owner taking the greater share being the second most common answer. However, when a child researcher (in this case the daughter of the first author) was asked to help, the answer was rather different: she reported that despite the rhetoric of equality, in practice the marble capitalist *always* took a bigger share than the marble worker. Whilst the idea of working for someone is presumably a straight copy from the adult world, the distribution rules are not. It is also evident that there are clear economic lessons to be drawn from the experience of being a worker (or a capitalist).

(ii) What determines the value of marbles? A good deal of swapping of marbles goes on. But there isn't a one-to-one correspondence between the price of marbles in the shops and their 'price' in the playground, which is a function of local supply and demand. In the playground, children seem to understand supply and demand; they can explain why they have to give their common-or-garden marbles to get one attractive one; they understand it much better than they do if we ask them questions about the 'real' (but for them less salient) world of the adult economy.

(iii) Lastly there is the phenomenon of Scrambling – which appears to be a true potlatch (Codere, 1950). A child who has plenty of marbles, throws them all up in the air and shouts, 'Scramble!' The other children run after them, and can keep any they find. Scrambling remains something of a puzzle; though it may be a reputation-enhancing act obviously a variety of motives are implicated. As one respondent commented, watching children rushing for marbles he had just thrown in the air was 'really funny'. What is involved here is the use of one's own economic power to make others ridiculous by their own materialism, as Terry Southern's 'Magic Christian' Guy Grand did by leaving a million dollars in a bath of hot manure on a street corner.

The marble economy seems to be a genuinely autonomous economic world with its own norms and rules, though clearly these are in some cases derived from the adult economic world. In all three examples the idea of exchange is involved: the use of marbles for expertise at play; one marble for another (or several others); giving away marbles for social 'credit'. We suspect that the heart of the childhood economic world is in exchange, rather than, say, production or distribution, things which children can rarely control.

2.2 Swapping

It is not only marbles that are swapped. Swapping is a very common activity in middle childhood and has been investigated by two of our students, Bardill (1985) and Traub (1991). Based on their studies it appears that swapping peaks at age 9 or 10 and is in sharp decline by age 12. Children swap items of low value such as pencils, toys, erasers, stickers, football cards and food (sweets and crisps) and most of these swaps take place at school. The children's accounts of why they swapped were of three kinds; economic, social and intrinsic (done for fun). Sometimes the economic motive was boldly stated ('get rid of rubbish and get other things free') but more commonly swapping was felt to be an enjoyable social activity. Even when its motive is primarily social, however, swapping involves a fairly exact sense of the relative values of the objects swapped. Children make 'good swaps' and 'bad swaps' as well as fair ones, but they know the difference. Unequal swaps are made for specific purposes; for example, a child may make a bad swap (a good swap for the other person) with a new member of a school class, as a gesture of friendship. It is possible that this is a precursor of the 'hidden economy' of part-time trading, which also has an ambiguous character, part economic and part social (Henry, 1978). Henry describes two kinds of social rewards in trading, 'competitive play' and 'reciprocal favours'. Competitive play is concerned with beating the system and perhaps has parallels with children's acquisition of things through swapping that they could otherwise not get hold of. A girl who is not allowed sweets by her parents, for example, can easily get hold of them at school through swapping. The idea of reciprocal favours captures the notion that part-time trading is governed by the norms and expectations of friendly relationships – it is not appropriate to strive for economic advantage or to 'put one over' a customer who is only a part-time customer but a full-time friend. The parallels with childhood swapping are clear. Though the evidence is not overwhelming, it is at least arguable that swapping is essentially an act with an economic content but a social function.

2.3 Experimental economies

Our last example is a bit different. In several studies, we have constructed artificial economies for children, within which they can work and earn tokens which they can then save or spend (Sonuga-Barke and Webley, 1993; Webley et al., 1991). Using these techniques, we have obtained interesting results on a number of questions concerned with self-control and saving. But there is one unexpected result that recurs in most studies: there are always some children who break out of the rules of the game, and start to negotiate with the experimenter, trying to get better conditions, to have their chosen toy even though they have saved less than the designated price and so on. Should we regard such children as 'failures', as evidence that the experimental situation has failed? On the contrary, they are the touchstone of its success. When children stay within the 'rules of the game' in an experiment, they may well be treating it as just that – a game: a situation in which reality, and real goals, are suspended, and the artificial goal of 'winning' or 'succeeding' within the rules takes over. The child who refuses to suspend disbelief, on the other hand, is taking the artificial world of the experiment and making it real. That is not to say that the child who stays within the 'game' is not showing us real behaviour. We all know the intensity with which children (and not only children) can be involved in games. But this occasional leakage from the game into real life allows the child participants to demonstrate some real economic sophistication, where prices and tasks are subject to negotiation and do not have to be taken as given.

That ends our brief review. We want to conclude from it that it is possible to explore the economic world of childhood. Childhood may be a foreign country, but it does not have to remain an unknown world.

3. Implications for the future of economic psychology

What has all of this to do with the future of economic psychology? The reader may accept that researchers in economic socialization have neglected playground economics but believe that this is a minor issue, of concern only to developmental researchers. We think not. We believe that there are four lessons or implications for economic psychology in general in what we have discussed.

First, our argument about the importance of studying real behaviour can be extended to adult economic behaviour. We said earlier that researchers into economic socialization have generally taken an implicit definition of economic behaviour for granted, and the chapter headings in our textbook (work, buying, saving money, taxation and so on) are an obvious example. Clearly economic psychology should be concerned with these topics, but should not be restricted to these issues and we need to ask with open minds how adults try to solve affairs of practical importance in their own lives. Even within these categories care is needed to avoid too narrow a definition; recall Scitovsky's (1976) calculation that only 61 per cent of the work done in the US economy goes through the marketplace. But we need to broaden our view about the kinds of behaviours that might be economic. What behaviours might be grist for our economic psychological mill? Van Veldhoven's work provides a good example; at a conference a few years ago he described a fascinating study of shoplifting (Van Veldhoven, 1987) – which is clearly economic but not something economic psychologists would normally think of studying. We have recently completed a study of the norms governing neighbourly help (Webley and Lea, 1993) which is outside the cash economy but again clearly economic. And we can look at real behaviour in another sense; one of our students reported a variety of practical ways in which people partition their money between different budget headings: some kept it in jam-jars, some distributed it around a variety of pockets while one carried it around in plastic bags (Hussein, 1985).

Second, the fact that the concept of economic behaviour is culturally and historically determined has implications for how any research in economic psychology is conducted, not just developmental research. It suggests that we should not just be concerned with the here and now. Take again the example of saving. We could not understand the importance of the thrift ethic, the exalting of the virtues of patience and forbearance typified by the Victorian self-help ideas of Samuel Smiles (Smiles, 1875) without understanding how changes in religious thought contributed to the emergence of a spirit of rationalism. To understand the decay of this ethic (and its possible replacement with a 'debt culture': Lea *et al.*, 1993) we also need to look at things historically, and consider the institutional and legal changes that have made credit easily available, and the political changes that have distributed income away from the poor in most 'western' societies.

Third, we would want to argue that one way of using the real economic life of people is to make use of games, both the games that people play spontaneously (like Monopoly) and experimental 'games' (though we do not like the term) that can be devised for investigative purposes, such as those that have been used to look at tax evasion (e.g. Webley *et al.*, 1992). A game provides a situation where people can take risks, where their behaviour is important to them, but where they are protected from the consequences of ill-advised actions. So we have a paradox: it is perhaps via economic games that we can learn about economic reality (for an extended discussion of this issue, see Webley *et al.*, 1992).

The last lesson that general economic psychology can learn from this discussion of economic socialization research is the most obvious. Maital (1982) described economic man as an obstetric marvel, who leapt fully formed from the womb. Economic man may be capable of such acrobatic feats but we know this is not the case for humans as conceived of by economic psychologists. If we want to understand any economic behaviour, we need to know something of its origins. So to come to grips with the forms and functions of saving that Van Veldhoven and Groenland describe in this issue, it is evident that we need to know something about how time-perspective develops and how children deal with situations involving delay of gratification. In other words, in order to better understand the economic world of grown-ups, we ourselves need to find our way back into the economic world of childhood.

References

Bardill, J. (1985), 'Swopping'. Unpublished BSc Project, University of Exeter, Department of Psychology.

Berti, A. and A. Bombi (1988), *The Child's Construction of Economics*. Cambridge: Cambridge University Press.

Codere, H. (1950), *Fighting with Property: A Study of Kwakiutl Potlatch and Warfare 1792–1930*. New York: J.J. Augustin.

Dittmar, H. (1992), *The Social Psychology of Material Possessions*. Brighton: Harvester Wheatsheaf.

Foxall, G. (1990), *Consumer Psychology in Behavioural Perspective*. London: Routledge.

Henry, S. (1978), *The Hidden Economy*. Oxford: Martin Robertson.

Hussein, G. (1985), 'An examination of the psychological aspects of money', Unpublished M. Phil. thesis, University of Exeter.

Lea, S.E.G. (1992), 'Assessing the psychology of economic behaviour and cognition', in G.M. Breakwell (ed.), *The Social Psychology of Political and Economic Cognition* (pp. 161–183). Guildford: Surrey University Press.

Lea, S.E.G., R.M. Tarpy and P. Webley (1987), *The Individual in the Economy*. Cambridge: Cambridge University Press.

Lea, S.E.G., P. Webley and R.M. Levine (1993), 'The economic psychology of consumer debt', *Journal of Economic Psychology*, **14**, 85–119.

Leiser, D., C. Roland-Lévy and G. Sevón (1990a), 'Introduction – Special issue on "Economic Socialization"'. *Journal of Economic Psychology*, **11**, 467–468.

Leiser, D., G. Sevón and D. Lévy (1990b), 'Children's economic socialization: Summarizing the cross-cultural comparisons of ten countries', *Journal of Economic Psychology*, **11**, 591–614.

Maital, S. (1982), *Minds, Markets and Money*. New York: Basic Books.

Popper, K. (1966), *The Open Society and its Enemies*, 5th edn. London: Routledge and Kegan Paul.

Rachlin, H. (1980), 'Economics and behavioral psychology', in J.E.R. Staddon (ed.), *Limits to Action* (pp. 205–236). New York: Academic Press.

Scitovsky, T. (1976), *The Joyless Economy*. Oxford: Oxford University Press.

Smiles, S. (1875), *Thrift*. London: Murray.

Sonuga-Barke, E.J.S. and P. Webley (1993), *Children's Saving*. Brighton: Erlbaum.

Sutton-Smith, B. (1982), 'Sixty years of historical change in the game preferences of American children', in R.E. Herron and B. Sutton-Smith (eds.), *Child's Play*. Malabar, FA: Krieger.

Tomlinson, P. (1980), 'Moral judgement and moral psychology: Piaget, Kohlberg and beyond', in S. Modgil and C. Modgil (eds.), *Toward a Theory of Psychological Development* (pp. 303–366). Windsor: NFER.

Traub, A. (1991), 'A study of children's swopping'. Unpublished Testamur project, Department of Psychology, University of Exeter.

Van Veldhoven, G.M. (1987), 'Attributional aspects in the evaluation of shoplifting', in F. Ölander and K.G. Grunert (eds.), *Understanding Economic Behaviour* (pp. 731–740). Århus: Handelshøjskolen.

Van Veldhoven, G.M. and E.A.G. Groenland (1993), 'Exploring saving behaviour: A framework and a research agenda', *Journal of Economic Psychology*, **14**, 507–522 (this issue).

Webley, P. (1996), 'Playing the market: The autonomous economic world of children', in A. Furnham and P. Lunt (eds.), *The Economic Beliefs and Behaviours of Young Children*. Brookfield, VT: E. Elgar.

Webley, P. and S.E.G. Lea (1993), 'The partial unacceptability of money as repayment for neighbourly help', *Human Relations*, **46**, 65–76.

Webley, P., R.M. Levine and A. Lewis (1991), 'A study in economic psychology: Children's saving in a play economy', *Human Relations*, **44**, 127–146.

Webley, P., H.S.J. Robben, H. Elffers and D.J. Hessing (1992), *Tax Evasion: An Experimental Approach*. Cambridge: Cambridge University Press.

Webley, P. and E. Webley (1990), 'The playground economy', in S.E.G. Lea, P. Webley and B.M. Young (eds.), *Applied Economic Psychology in the 1990s* (pp. 1082–1087). Exeter: Washington Singer Press.

Preference-forming for durable goods within families

•••

Franz Böcker
Professor of Marketing, University of Regensburg

Summary

Buying decisions for consumer goods are based to a great extent on processes of influence and voting within families. The multiplicity of participants involved in the buying process has long been neglected in marketing planning, due to a lack of relevant information. This article presents a measurement method for detailed observation of complex purchasing decisions within households, to better enable a marketing plan to exploit these processes. This empirical study was carried out using a sample of 973 people and concerns automobiles, dishwashers and video-tape recorders. Its results are surprising in that they reveal that a large proportion of decisions are made jointly.

1. Families, the locus of buying decisions

For most people, the family is the most important social environment. Most of their life is spent in the family, which strongly influences their view of the world and their consumption behavior. Most purchasing decisions are made within the family circle. Despite this fact, current marketing strategies are devised and implemented from measurements relative to individuals. Almost no notice is taken of the integration of the family unit.

Current marketing thought is based on preconceptions such as:

— cars are purchased exclusively by men. Given this definition of the segment, cars are almost never advertised in women's magazines;
— kitchen appliances are only advertised in women's magazines;
— according to our planners' accepted ideas, pre-cooked dinners and most food products can only be sold to women. Thus they are only present in women's magazines or similar supports.

As a result of our planners' preconceptions, products are designated as masculine or feminine, and as such seem to be designed for the one or the other half of the population,

---

From *Recherche et Applications en Marketing,* 7(2), 1992, 51–66.

but are actually wanted, purchased and utilized by either 53% of the female population or 47% of the male population. It is clear that this vision does not correspond to reality. Its predominance as a practical approach can only be explained by a lack of precise information about real behavior.

2. Possession and purchase of durable goods

Durable goods largely determine the lifestyle of individuals and households (cf. Kroeber-Riel, 1984, p. 432; Valette-Florence, 1986). Lifestyle is evaluated less by the possession of a given product, than by the possession of a certain brand or type of product. Cars and clothing are particularly significant examples of this phenomenon. Durable goods, however, not only reflect the lifestyle of an individual or group of individuals, but also absorb a large portion of a household's budget, as shown in Table 1.

Daily experience shows that many buying decisions and most uses of durable goods are not isolated decisions or uses, but rather indicate a certain *social integration*.

3. Buying decisions for durable goods within families

Given their cost and their significance in determining lifestyle, durable goods are not used or bought by a single individual. Faced with diverse modes of joint decision-making and phenomena of unilateral and reciprocal influence, marketing experts must learn about family decision-making processes (that is, decisions made within the family). With this goal in mind, we will first present examples of results of traditional research on family behavior, before proposing and validating a differentiated model for decision-making processes within families.

Table 1   Share of private spending on durable goods

| | Proportion of Total Consumer Spending for Households of: | | | |
| | 4 People with Average Income | | 4 People with High Income | |
Categories of Durable Goods	1981	1984	1981	1984
Clothing/shoes	9.2	8.1	9.0	8.9
Furniture	3.4	3.0	4.0	4.0
Small appliances	2.6	2.2	2.3	2.3
Vehicles	11.5	13.1	12.8	12.3
Hi-fi/TV	1.2	1.2	1.1	1.1
All the above-mentioned consumer goods	27.9	27.6	29.2	28.6

Source: Bundesamt Statistics (1985), 458–459.

3.1 The traditional approach to spouses' influence on buying decisions within the family

Until the late 1960s, empirical marketing research was almost exclusively focused on individual decision-making processes. Only later was better knowledge of multiple-participant decision-making processes seen as necessary to marketing planning, along with the need to move away from qualitative data towards sufficiently precise quantitative measurements.

The first attempt to quantify, on a theoretical basis, the influence of wives and husbands on family buying decisions for durable goods, was in research by Davis and Rigaux (1974). Fishbein's previously presented expanded model (Ajzen and Fishbein, 1973) is merely a theoretical framework lacking the component quantification necessary for use in marketing planning. Davis and Rigaux's results have been reproduced repeatedly and have considerably influenced later studies (cf., for example, Kroeber-Riel, 1984, p. 457). The authors took into account both the relative influence of each spouse, and their desire to make decisions together.

The starting point for this study, and others which followed, is the idea that something resembling a joint and single decision exists for a given product, this decision being more or less influenced by each partner (only couples were observed in these studies).

The idea of a quasi-homogeneous buying decision has been progressively replaced by partialized analysis of the decision process (*partialisierte Kaufentscheidungsprozesse*, Böcker, 1987). One aspect of partialization which was recognized early on is the distinction between the choice of a product and that of a brand. Product choice is the decision to buy or not to buy a given product, while brand choice is the selection of specific brands (or sorts/types of products). This partialized approach is especially relevant to buying decisions within a family: on the one hand, the head of the family (= the man) is 'traditionally' in charge of long-term financial planning and therefore decides if a product will be purchased or not. In addition, as the 'technical expert', he notices, for example, when it is necessary to replace a vehicle. The woman intervenes above all in the choice of type, additional features, etc.

A very thorough empirical study taking this distinction into account, was carried out by the Burda publishing group in 1983 (Burda, 1983). Some data significant to the automobile sector are shown in Table 2.

These results clearly show that wives' influence on the purchase of a second car is significantly greater than on the purchase of a first car; that wives of a certain educational level, who earn their own living and who live in small households have greater influence than other women; that product choice is more strongly influenced by wives than brand choice. No doubt the man's greater technical competence comes into play in this latter decision.

Distinctions of this type, based on characteristics of buying decisions and of the people involved, provide considerably more relevant marketing information in influence analysis than Davis and Rigaux's results. However, this approach does not provide precise data for the definition of a sales policy, as the source and forms of influence are not indicated. Such information is none the less necessary in defining a strategic communications policy.

| Table 2 | Wives' influence on automobile purchases | | | | | |

| | Index of Wife's Influence (%) on the Purchase | | | | | |
| Sample: | of an Automobile | | of the First Car | | of the Second Car | |
Women aged 18–69	Choice of Product	Choice of Brand	Choice of Product	Choice of Brand	Choice of Product	Choice of Brand
Total	0.42	0.40	0.40	0.38	0.50	0.45
Education:						
primary school	0.40	0.37	0.38	0.36	0.47	0.39
secondary school	0.45	0.41	0.42	0.38	0.52	0.48
high school graduate/ university	0.50	0.51	0.49	0.50	0.55*	0.54*
Employment:						
active/in training	0.47	0.45	0.45	0.44	0.53	0.47
inactive/retired	0.38	0.35	0.36	0.33	0.47	0.42
Income:						
DM 0	0.37	0.34	0.35	0.32	0.45	0.41
up to 1000 DM	0.44	0.41	0.42	0.39	0.51*	0.42*
from 1000 to 1500 DM	0.45	0.43	0.45	0.46	0.49*	0.35*
over 1500 DM	0.55	0.56	0.50	0.53	0.63	0.61
Household size:						
2 people	0.48	0.45	0.45	0.43	0.63	0.57
3 people	0.41	0.39	0.40	0.39	0.45	0.37
4 people	0.41	0.38	0.38	0.34	0.50	0.48
5 or more people	0.39	0.36	0.36	0.35	0.47	0.40
City size:						
up to 20,000 inhabitants	0.40	0.38	0.39	0.39	0.40	0.32
20,000 to 499,999 inhabitants	0.44	0.40	0.42	0.39	0.55	0.48
over 500,000 inhabitants	0.43	0.40	0.39	0.37	0.54	0.52

* These numbers are barely significant due to the small sample size; cf. Burda (1983, pp. 38–47).

3.2 A theoretical model of preferences in buying decisions for durable goods within families

Buying decisions for durable or industrial goods frequently involve complex processes, which are not only multidimensional, like all preference-forming processes, but may also be broken down into different phases concerning several individuals (cf. Böcker, 1986, and its references).

An automobile example can illustrate the *multidimensionality, multiple phases and multiple participants* of the preference-forming process, and thus of a buying decision: an Opel

Corsa, for example, will be chosen not for a fixed set of characteristics, but because it offers the desired level of economic performance, ease of handling and comfort (multidimensionality of the buying decision). The decision is made in multiple phases, as the selection of the Opel Corsa does not result from a decision made at one given moment, but from a process occurring over several stages. Thus, the decision to consider only mid-sized cars, given the household's budget, could be made long before the decision to buy. Later, personal experience or advice from others may reduce the set of cars considered to Opel Corsa, Peugeot 104 and VW Polo models. The decision to buy a specific type of car is made only after this step.

In general, two phases in the buying decision can be distinguished: a first phase where the acceptable options are distinguished from those which are less acceptable, and a second phase where one option is actually chosen. Annex 1 details the characteristics of these two phases (pre-choice and final choice).

In choosing a vacation destination, for example, those options retained at the end of phase 1 will either be within a certain price range, or have good sports facilities, or be easy to travel to. During phase 2, the sites seen as acceptable during phase 1 will be examined in more detail: thus, the object finally chosen will, following this procedure, be one of those that was present in phase 1.

The image creation process (cf. Böcker, 1986, pp. 554–6), seen as the cognitive reality of a product universe ('perception-forming process', Böcker, 1986, p. 552), takes place before preference-forming. During the image creation process, products to be evaluated are identified, perceived in a certain way, and classified. The results of these mental operations constitute the starting point for human decision-making, as humans do not decide in terms of real data but rather of their perceptions of reality. It has been repeatedly shown that considerable differences may exist between these two realities. The complete process for decisions involving several participants within one family is described in Annex 2. This graphic representation of real family buying behavior is the basis for the empirical research described below, and significantly enriches our knowledge and perception of traditional issues.

Preference-forming Phase	Products to be Evaluated	Selection Process	Result
Pre-choice of acceptable products	All products for which information is available	Verification, for each product, of minimum levels of each pre-choice criterion	Products classified as: • acceptable products • unacceptable products • insufficiently known products
Selection of preferred product	All products classed as acceptable	Evaluation of each product's advantages and drawbacks on selection criteria	Ordering of products according to evaluations

Annex 1   The two phases of a buying decision.

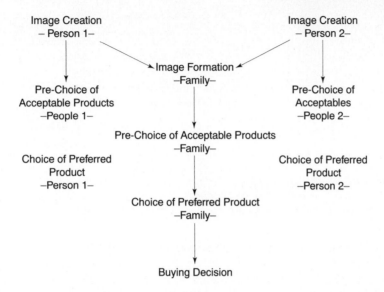

Annex 2   The multiple-phase buying decision process involving several people.

4. One individual's influence on the preference of a group of individuals

4.1 Theoretical measurement

Research to date has measured the influence of one person on the buying decision of another person or of a group of people, seen as a whole (or divided into phases of product and brand selection) and *ex post*. The measurement model below presents the influence phenomenon in detail.

The quantification of influence after the fact ('influence from memory') should be considered with suspicion. Differentiating between influence on another person and influence on a group of people (a group decision) is not possible with this approach, because both cases involve compromise, with the sole difference that this compromise is communicated by a single person in the first case, collectively in the second.

Influence is a highly ambiguous notion which may be interpreted in various ways (cf. for example Zelger, 1975; Gaski and Nevin, 1985). These different possible interpretations must be considered when quantifying the concept of influence. We can, for example, enumerate the various forms which influence can take in a two–person decision, questioning both whether or not there is influence, and whether or not the influence is recognized as such. The four types of influence which result are described in Annex 3.

Customarily, when we speak of influence we are referring to direct influence, which is only one of the four types of influence. Socialization is, for example, a type of influence exercised by parents (or society) on young people. All four types of influence shown in Annex 3 are operational from a marketing standpoint. While direct influence can be

		The other person is identified as influential	
		YES	NO

The other person	YES		Direct influence*	Manipulation**
exercises influence	NO		Anticipated influence*	Assimilation*** Socialization

    *   Zone of influence announced by the influencer
   **   Zone of influence announced by the influencee
 *** Zone of influence recognized by observation in the context of an experiment

Annex 3   Forms of influence between two people.

exercised on a short term basis, assimilation necessitates a longer period to be set in motion.

Clearly, the term influence is understood in different ways according to the people questioned. If the influenced person is questioned, he or she will measure real influence by adding together direct and anticipated influence. The influencer will, on the other hand, refer to influence as the sum of direct influence and manipulation.

Neither one will speak of influence through assimilation. Only when influence is defined through observation within the context of an experiment, rather than through direct questioning, can all types of influence be recognized.

Lastly, influence through assimilation occurring over a longer period of time cannot be measured by experimentation over a short period.

Influence measurements have traditionally (Burda, 1983; Davis and Rigaux, 1974) been based on questionnaires. This implies, besides the usual problems involved in constructing a reliable questionnaire, additional problems of content (differing perceptions of influence), as seen in Annex 3. It is not surprising that empirical studies measuring respective influence within a couple usually do not come to similar conclusions, which is a factor in the empirical approach's loss of credibility (Silk and Kalwani, 1982).

Using the principles thus defined, we carried out an influence study using a realistic experiment. The procedure consisted in first isolating family members, then reuniting them in order to reach a decision concerning a given problem. Factors indicating intensity of influence could easily be distinguished by comparing results from the different levels of individual and group decisions (details in Hubel, 1986).

Reciprocal vectors of influence exist in families for nearly all products, although less important for low-value products designed for personal use than for more expensive products for shared consumption. There are two main explanations for the lower degree of influence in the case of products destined for individual use:

— Person A has less influence on person B's buying decision because A's opinion is not taken into account, even though the decision was jointly discussed. This is defined as reaction influence (*Wirkung*). The corresponding measurement is the *reaction index* (*Wirkungsindex*).

— Person A can have no influence on person B because he is not involved in the buying decision process. The corresponding index is the *involvement index (Beteiligungsindex)*.

The basic formula for influence measurement is thus: Involvement index × reaction index = influence index.

Influence vectors thus result from involvement which may be observed through participation in processes taking place over time, and from reactions which may be identified through questioning in the framework of an experiment.

4.2 Study procedure and objectives

Each individual's influence on his or her own family's preferences was studied for the three types of durable good.

Unlike analyses of processes of influence already carried out in the past, our study innovated by including not only couples, but also younger members of families.

In collaboration with the companies which financed the study, the following products were considered:

— automobiles
— dishwashers
— video-tape recorders

The survey was carried out using a sample of 396 nationally dispersed households, of which 215 consisted of two people and 181 of three people. The results for automobiles concern 202 households with a total of 499 people questioned, those for dishwashers concern 98 households with a total of 236 people questioned, and results for video-tape recorders concern 96 households and 238 people questioned.

It seemed advisable to structure the questionnaire like a game, given the quantity of information sought. The first step in the study was to establish lists of attributes and types corresponding to each brand, with the help of specialists. Only objective attributes, controllable by management, were considered.

Participants made their choices using cards on which the attributes or types were written. They first were asked to choose the attributes and models which best suited themselves or their family, and then to classify the chosen types in order of preference.

The questionnaires were perceived almost as games, and were easy to administer.

4.3 A few study results

We will begin with a rapid description of individual and family behavior in the context of buying decisions, before describing the structure and sources of influences within families. By comparing the two structures, we can then deduce the influence of individuals.

4.3.1 The structure of individual and family preferences

One task for the people questioned was to select those models they saw as suitable choices from the 65 automobiles offered. On average, 6.6 automobiles were chosen by individuals and 4.6 by families. That is, an average of 90% of the proposed cars were considered inadequate in the prechoice phase. This 'scrap' percentage was higher for collective than for individual decisions, which is easily explained by the fact that more people have veto rights.

A move towards simplification of decision behavior was made through a consideration of the attributes which were used for evaluation. The number of criteria used in decision-making varied between 8 and 11 (from 22 available), depending on whether the decision was collective or individual, and whether it was made during the prechoice phase or at final selection.

Even in choosing complex and much discussed products like automobiles, only 10 criteria were retained on the average. During preselection, where unacceptable alternatives are eliminated, families unsurprisingly used more criteria than individuals. In the final selection phase, however, where the advantages and drawbacks of different models are compared, families use fewer criteria than individuals, to increase simplicity.

Concerning the nature of the attributes evaluated in each decision phase, Table 3 shows that during preselection, the highly dependent criteria of price and manufacturer are prioritized, while criteria of reliability, security and gas mileage are important in the final selection phase.

Table 4 shows the criteria used in purchasing decisions for dishwashers and video-tape recorders by order of importance, using only data relative to families as a whole.

In addition to ordering pertinent attributes by their importance in the prechoice and selection phases (Tables 3 and 4), it is necessary to consider the number of types retained (Tables 5 and 6).

It is interesting to note that the number of attributes retained is usually significantly higher than the 4–7 habitually quoted.

Table 3   Ranking of criteria during preselection and final selection

Phase	Decision type	Criteria Ranking 1	2	3	4	5
Preselection	Man	Manufacturer	Price	Rust	Resale value	Maintenance costs
	Woman	Price	Manufacturer	The look	Maintenance costs	Gas mileage
	Family	Manufacturer	Price	Rust	The look	Security
Final selection	Man	Reliability	Security	Price	Gas mileage	Wear
	Woman	Price	Security	Reliability	Gas mileage	Rust
	Family	Reliability	Price	Security	Gas mileage	Wear

Table 4   Ranking of criteria for dishwashers and video-tape recorders during preselection and final selection phases

| | | Criteria Ranking | | | | |
		1	2	3	4	5
Dishwashers	Preselection	Water consumption	Energy consumption	Price	Manufacturer	Customer service
	Final selection	Energy consumption	Price	Number of programs	Reliability	Cleaning efficiency
Video-tape recorders	Preselection	System	Manufacturer	Price	Image quality	Sound quality
	Final selection	Image quality	System	Sound quality	Price	Guarantee

Table 5   Average number of attributes considered, according to the decision phase and the decider

| | Decision Phase and Decider | | | |
| | Preselection | | Final Selection | |
Product	Individuals	Family	Individuals	Family
Automobiles	8.2	10.1	10.7	9.7
Dishwashers	5.1	6.1	8.3	7.7
Video-tape recorders	4.9	6.2	10.4	10.3

Table 6   Average number of types/models retained according to the decision-maker

| | Decision-Maker | |
Product	Individuals	Family
Automobiles	6.6	5.6
Dishwashers	5.7	5.1
Video-tape recorders	6.9	6.1

Individuals consistently retain a smaller number of attributes than families during pre-selection, while the reverse is true during the final selection phase. This confirms the following hypotheses (cf. Böcker, 1986, pp. 566–8):

— during preselection, individuals choose according to attributes which are important to them;
— during final selection, groups retain the attributes which are seen as important by all.

Table 6 illustrates the practical significance of the preselection phase. In selecting an automobile, 6 models are retained from 65, for dishwashers, 5–6 from 25, and 6–7 video-tape recorders from 32.

The hypothesis of a 'Relevant Set' which usually varies from 4 to 7 objects is thus confirmed (Schobert, 1979, pp. 55–64 and the related references).

4.3.2 Family members' influence on family preferences

The question of individual influence on collective decisions is immediately raised, given the sizeable differences between the various individual and collective patterns. In the following, we consider only data concerning automobiles, men and women, excluding adolescents (12–18 years).

In order for an individual to influence a purchasing decision process, he or she must naturally participate in this process. The degree of participation depends on the type of product. Degrees of participation for the three products tested are shown in Table 7.

A person's influence has been defined as the product of the indices of involvement and reaction. The reaction index (*Wirkungsindex*) merely indicates the influence of a person involved in the decision process. The influence index of each individual is thus determined by the involvement and reaction indices.

Influence indices for the three product categories are shown in Table 8.

The results in Table 8 are easy to interpret: in families of two people, males are responsible for 68% of image-forming for automobiles, and are the decision-makers in 61% of model choices and 71% of final decisions.

The same table shows that women and adolescents together represent in general approximately 50% of the preference, and that women's position is relatively strong in the selection of acceptable car models (no sports cars!), etc., while adolescents have a relatively strong influence on image-forming, undoubtedly due to intensive information-seeking.

The structure of the buying decision process can be deduced from these results, with significant male influence on automobile purchases, a slight advantage for the woman in dishwasher purchase, and joint influence by men and adolescents on the purchase of video-tape recorders.

4.3.3 Men's and women's influence by segments

When explaining an individual's influence on family preference, sex and age variables are undeniably easy to analyze. However, these 'visible' factors for measuring influence are

Table 7 Individuals' participation (in %) in family buying decisions for three product categories

Product	2-person Household			3-person Household			
	Man	Woman	Friends	Man	Woman	Adolescent	Friends
Automobile	91	76	52	96	83	75	50
Dishwasher	67	89	67	71	86	29	64
Video-tape recorder	69	54	92	73	36	73	40

Table 8   Family member influence on family preference

| | Product | 2-person Household | | 3-person Household | | |
		Man	Woman	Man	Woman	Adolescent
Image	A	0.68	0.32	0.45	0.28	0.27
	D	0.44	0.56	0.38	0.50	0.12
	V	0.65	0.35	0.39	0.20	0.41
Preselection	A	0.61	0.39	0.49	0.30	0.21
	D	0.48	0.52	0.42	0.46	0.12
	V	0.67	0.33	0.44	0.40	0.16
Final Selection	A	0.71	0.29	0.50	0.26	0.24
	D	0.46	0.54	0.44	0.44	0.12
	V	0.69	0.32	0.46	0.16	0.38

A = automobile, D = dishwasher, V = video-tape recorder.

secondary to factors of a psychological nature, or 'deeper' factors such as the legitimacy, likableness, capacity to reward, or ability to communicate of the people concerned.

These variables were recognized in the theory of social power (French and Raven, 1959) as determinants of interpersonal influence. The conclusions of these studies will not, however, be presented here (cf. Hubel, 1986, pp. 190, 196). We are far more interested in the segmentation of groups according to their similarities in terms of influence structures.

The starting point of this cluster analysis is the man's degree of influence during each phase, for each household studied (values for the men in three-person households were first standardized so that the sum of the influence of the man and the woman was equal to 1). We have used a hierarchical and agglomerative data analysis method based on the 'average linkage' principle (Steinhausen and Langer, 1977). Degrees of influence in the various segments are given in Table 9. The smallest segments are not included in this table.

As shown in Table 9, there is a small segment (3), representing close to one eighth of the population, in which the final buying decision for automobiles as well as their preselection are dominated by women.

This segment contains more women with higher-than-average job levels and academic qualifications. It was not possible within the framework of the present study to determine whether the decision principally concerned the purchase of a second car.

Similarly, in one segment (3), male influence on the purchase of dishwashers is dominant. This is also true in the video-tape recorder category.

5. Family preference-forming and marketing planning

The results of the empirical study shown in the various tables and annexes above, provide a large amount of information which may be used in the framework of a *targeted marketing policy*. The following points should especially be taken into account:

Table 9 Men's and women's degrees of influence on family preference, by segment: segments are specific to product category

Product category		Segment 1		Segment 2		Segment 3		Segment 4	
		Man	Woman	Man	Woman	Man	Woman	Man	Woman
Automobiles	Image formation	0.69	0.31	0.63	0.37	0.65	0.35	0.62	0.38
	Pre-choice	0.68	0.32	0.60	0.40	0.55	0.45	0.62	0.38
	Final choice	0.92	0.08	0.57	0.43	0.13	0.87	0.66	0.34
% of the total		0.46		0.33		0.12		1.00	
Dishwashers	Image formation	0.35	0.65	0.38	0.62	0.68	0.32	0.41	0.59
	Pre-choice	0.36	0.64	0.65	0.35	0.50	0.50	0.45	0.55
	Final choice	0.28	0.72	0.84	0.16	0.88	0.12	0.48	0.52
% of the total		0.53		0.22		0.18		1.00	
Video-tape recorders	Image formation	0.74	0.26	0.53	0.47			0.69	0.31
	Pre-choice	0.76	0.24	0.64	0.36			0.70	0.30
	Final choice	0.82	0.18	0.20	0.80			0.74	0.26
% of the total		0.82		0.17				1.00	

— Segmentation into masculine/feminine products is inadequate. *Women have a relatively strong influence* on the decision-making process and on the decision itself for *masculine products*, and *vice versa*.

— Not only the multiplicity of participants, but also the *different phases of the decision process* should be taken into account. Specifically, the prechoice phase merits closer attention from marketing specialists, given that 90% of products are eliminated during this phase, and only the remaining 10% are considered during final selection.

— The role of the wife and children is significantly greater within the context of a family buying decision than was traditionally believed, particularly during information collection (image-forming) and preselection.

— Average influence indices hide important differences in interpersonal influence. Thus in a small segment of families, women clearly have their say, even in automobile purchases which are traditionally dominated by men.

— Information targeted at each household member has an effect on the entire household's decision. Following the results of this study, for example, automobile advertising in the general media, important during the preselection phase, should take the form of institutional advertising concerning, above all, brand and overall quality.

Details on price/quality relationships and reliability, in contrast, should be contained in detailed sales brochures. In addition, when purchasing an automobile, women are apparently more sensitive to price than men.

— A large proportion of buying decisions for durable goods are made jointly, even if each participant (man, woman, acquaintances, friends, adolescents) makes his or her own evaluation with its own results. Women are less important than men as participants in the decision-making process, but in a market segment representing approximately 15% of observed couples, the women's influence was significantly dominant.

— Lastly, adolescents constitute a particularly attractive marketing target, as they are especially open to information, easily influenced, and yet have considerable influence on decisions.

Translated from the French by Joy Gehner

References

Ajzen I. and Fishbein M. (1973), 'Attitudinal and normative variables as predictors of specific behavior', *Journal of Personality and Social Psychology*, pp. 41–57.

Burda GmbH (ed.) (1983), *Kaufeinflüsse '83 – PKW und Zubehör*, Offenburg.

Burda GmbH (ed.) (1984), *Zeitreihen ausgewählter Wirtschaftsdaten*, Offenburg.

Böcker F. (1986), Präferenzforschung als Mittel marktorientierter Unternehmensführung, *Zeitschrift für betriebswirtschaftliche Forschung*, pp. 543–574.

Böcker F. (1987), *Marketing*, 2nd edition, Stuttgart, New York.

Davis H.L. and Rigaux B.P. (1974), 'Perception of marital roles in decision processes', *Journal of Consumer Research*, pp. 51–61.

French J.R.P. and Raven B.H. (1959), 'The bases of social power', in D. Cartwright (ed.), *Studies in Social Power*, Ann Arbor, pp. 150–167.

Gaski J.P. and Nevin J.R. (1985), 'The differential effects of exercised and unexercised power sources in a marketing channel', *Journal of Marketing Research*, pp. 130–142.

Hubel W. (1986), *Der Einfluß der Familienmitglieder auf gemeinsame Kaufentscheidungen*, Berlin.

Kroeber-Riel W. (1984), *Konsumentenverhalten*, 3rd edition, Munich.

Schobert R. (1979), *Die Dynamisierung komplexer Marktmodelle mit Hilfe von Verfahren der Mehrdimensionallen Skalierung*, Berlin.

Silk A.J. and Kalwani M.U. (1982), 'Measuring influence in organizational purchase decisions', *Journal of Marketing Research*, pp. 165–182.

Statistisches Bundesamt (ed.) (1985), *Statistisches Jahrbuch*, Stuttgart, Mainz.

Steinhausen D. and Langer K. (1977), *Clusteranalyse*, Berlin, New York.

Valette-Florence P. (1986), 'Les démarches des styles de vie: Concepts, chemins d'investigation des problèmes actuels', *Recherche et Applications en Marketing*, pp. 93–109.

Zelger, J. (1975), *Konzepte zur Messung von Macht*, Berlin.

Cultural perspectives

6

● ●

Featherstone, M., 1990, 'Perspectives on consumer culture',
Sociology, **24**(1) (February), 5–22
van Raaij, W.F., 1993, 'Postmodern consumption', *Journal of
Economic Psychology*, **14**(3), 541–63
Schwartz, S.H. and Bilsky, W., 1990, 'Toward a theory of the universal
content and structure of values: Extensions and cross-cultural
replications', *Journal of Personality and Social Psychology*, **58**(5),
878–91

Introduction

The second type of external influence exerted on the consumer is culture. Although this concept is widely used in the literature, culture is very often quite loosely defined. It usually refers to a set of attitudes, values and beliefs shared by a group of individuals, which guide and influence behaviours and reactions to various stimuli, and are usually expressed through rituals and symbols used to express these values and beliefs. Culture also explains how these mental construct behaviours are acquired and transmitted through socialization.

The first two articles analyze the meaning of consumption in contemporary Western societies dominated by the postmodern paradigm. The first clarifies what is really meant by the concept of consumer culture by reference to an impressive body of literature as well as a subtle and sophisticated analysis. The argument made by Featherstone is that consumption has gained autonomy so as to emerge as an autonomous culture which can thus no longer be understood as being derived from the production sphere. First, in line with Baudrillard's work, it is argued that consumption is mainly related to a manipulation of signs. In consumption culture, goods are semantized and commodified, that is they only exist through their immersion into a symbolic system. Because of the ever more rapid circulation of commodities linked to an over-manipulation of signs, distinction rapidly becomes blurred between images and reality. It becomes harder for the consumer to distinguish between what the commodities stand for and the way they are symbolically decoded as commodity signs. In other words, signs are able to 'float free from objects', hence a sort of 'depthless culture' which characterizes the postmodern era and which leads to a loss of stable meaning in the commodity system. As signs have essentially become 'detached', consumption goods can no longer be permanently tied to a stable set of associations in the sense that these symbolic associations may be permanently renegotiated. Objects in contemporary societies have gradually become emptied of both symbolic and material content because what is increasingly produced are more and more signs rather than material objects (Lash and Urry, 1994, p. 15). The tendency towards an ever-changing flow of commodities, which characterizes contemporary Western societies, raises the problem of the ability of goods to play their anthropological role of markers and, for instance, to help read the status of the commodity bearer. Thus the thesis of the postmodern political economy is one of the ever-more rapid circulation of both subjects and objects, linked to a subsequent 'emptying out' of objects (Lash and Urry, 1994, p. 13). A phenomenon of time and space distanciation gradually led to the fact that individuals have become disembedded from concrete time and space, which have themselves become more abstract. This essential process of spatio-temporal disembedding has been analyzed by both Durkheim and Mauss as the main difference between tribal and modern societies. For them modernization goes together with an emptying out of the categories by which people inhabit the world by classifying it (see Lash and Urry, 1994, pp. 13–15). As pointed out by Baudrillard, postmodern societies hence explode the epistemology by creating a situation in which subjects lose contact with the real, and themselves fragment and dissolve (Kellner, 1994, p. 9).

Nevertheless, as illustrated by the French sociologist Pierre Bourdieu, consumption acts as a system of classification in the sense that it involves discriminatory judgements which identify our own judgement of taste to others. Certain consumption practices are intimately connected to specific occupations or class categories. What is important in this respect is not only access to the economic capital but also access to cultural capital, which helps to decode the symbolic relationships involved in the commodity system. This area of research, which has gained increasing attention, builds upon the familiar lifestyle approach. Broadly speaking, lifestyles can be defined as shared values, tastes, opinions, interests and ways of behaviour, especially as they are expressed through consumption practices. Largely influenced by Pierre Bourdieu, whose study entitled *The Distinction* (published in 1979) provided an important methodological framework for the analysis of the relations existing between social status and consumption practices, the concept of lifestyle can be viewed as an interaction of three levels (social values, activities and attitudes, and consumption practices) so as to express analogous behaviour modes within a group of individuals. The lifestyle approach should also be read in the light of postmodern consumption. Some authors have argued that the lifestyle approach implies an *a priori* segmentation of individuals, which in some ways contradicts new forms of affiliation and grouping. It might, for instance, contradict the rise of individualism characteristic of European societies, but also the need for individuals to find a sense of identity through their affiliation to local tribes (Maffesoli, 1988) which are not constituted by fixed rules, being more in *statu nascendi* than in *statu essendi*[1] (Bauman, 1992).

Another tendency which represents the postmodern era, raised by Featherstone and further developed by van Raaij (1993), is the blurring of genres and a deconstruction of symbolic hierarchies. The best example is the shift of art into industry, which leads to a collapse of the boundaries between art and everyday life correlated to an expansion of the role of art within consumer culture. This led to the famous 'aestheticization' of everyday life promulgated by Featherstone (1991) and others (Maffesoli, 1990; Morace, 1990). In this perspective, consumption becomes a flow of dream-like perceptions, sensory overload and a permanent aesthetic immersion experienced by decentred subjects who may have lost a sense of their identity. Consumers can thus be regarded as 'agents who engage in (. . .) the elaboration of a "personal practice" of the self through (. . .) the appropriation of symbolic commodities' (Shields, 1992, p. 6). Hence postmodernism is very much related to such practices as 'paradoxical combinations', or more generally the refusal to consider any fashion as dominant or prescriptive in the sense that 'no major fashion, but all combinations are allowed'. The idea of paradoxical combination infuses fashion but also has some implications for discourse in the sense that 'irony and double meaning' become legitimized. Individuals have lost a sense of identification to stable groups, hence the phenomenon of severe individualism, but also a subtle recomposition of society around tribes. The individual consumer exists as a mutable self through his or her multiple identifications in a series of specific tribes (Maffesoli, 1988, 1992). This multifaceted subjectivity led to the presentation of everyday life as a series of masks of a postmodern *persona* (Shields, 1992). The individual is transformed into a *persona*, that is, according to the Latin etymology of the word, into a mask. This, for instance, questions the pertinence and validity of the lifestyle approach in the sense that a given lifestyle no longer requires inner coherence and because within these new and local forms of grouping and identification, tribes have no fixed and stable rules, but rather are created and maintained through shared emotions, values, and consumption practices.

This leads to new forms of consumption such as *flânerie*, browsing, sampling and non-rational, spontaneous purchases which indicate behaviours of individuals looking for a sense of identity through their consumption practices. Consuming becomes more than the mere acquisition, possession and use of things; it becomes an essential way for individuals to create an identity for themselves but also for the commodity world that surrounds them. Consumption may be seen in an anthropological perspective as a *bricolage* of signs effected by the consumer to regain a sense of identity by projecting onto them a subjective meaning. Consumption is no longer a deconstruction or use of things but rather a construction of the self.

The second article, by van Raaij, concentrates on specific aspects of contemporary postmodern culture and analyzes their impacts on consumption. The first merit of this article is to explicate with great clarity a concept, that of postmodernism, which has been widespread among a plethora of articles and books in the field of cultural studies over the last fifteen years, without a clear consensus on what it exactly means. It is important to remind ourselves that the concept of postmodernity was largely initiated and developed in Europe by Jean-François Lyotard in a book first published in 1979 called *La Condition humaine* (Lyotard, 1979, 1984). What Lyotard calls the 'postmodern condition' is the desperate search for meaning in a disintegrating social order resulting from a societal fragmentation which can be characterized by the loss of community and the gradual emptying of our 'selves'. Thus the main thesis of postmodernism is the evermore rapid circulation of subjects and objects which leads to the 'emptying out' of both objects and subjects (see Lash and Urry, 1994). The postmodern approach also aimed at redefining the conditions of production of knowledge. Lyotard sees a danger in the presupposition that some 'Grand Narratives' of Western culture, like the rationalistic bias, 'offers a solution that remains neutral and uncontaminated by the interest of domination' (Kearney and Rainwater, 1996, p. 426). Postmodernity aims at rejecting such fictitious 'Grand Narratives', to replace them by less ambitious *petits récits* ('little narratives') that resist closure and totality, stressing the singularity, the particularity and the irreducibility of every event (Kearney and Rainwater, 1996, p. 426). The underlying hypothesis is that knowledge strongly resists global categorization and conformity, a bias which implies a necessity for the postmodern approach to redefine new ways of considering knowledge as well as new stylistic forms, as was magnificently illustrated by Stephen Brown in his very postmodern book on *Postmodern Marketing* (1995).

Another important element to be stressed is that the postmodern concept does not imply, as is often believed, a linear temporal sequence, which would place 'postmodernity' after 'modernity'. As Kearney and Rainwater remind us, 'the postmodern is already implied by the modern because modernity, by its very nature, is continuously thrusting ahead of itself to become other than itself' (1996, p. 426).

Postmodernity has been widely used to describe the evolution of social practices and van Raaij successfully draws a parallel between the meaning of postmodernity in such fields as architecture, literature,[2] and its very particular meaning in the field of consumption. In the postmodern condition, consumption becomes a way for the individual to construct a self by ingesting products and rebuilding signs of identity. Postmodernity sets new conditions to the understanding and the description of consumption practices by proposing paradigms such as fragmentation of experiences, hyperreality and the confusion of subject and object. This sets out new perspectives in the role of consumption's key role in giving meaning to life.

The influence of culture on consumption is analyzed in a very different manner in the third article, which presents a quantitatively based investigation on the extent to which values are universal across cultures. The field of research in the area of cultural values is very large and therefore it is important to consider studies which attempt to define, measure and validate values or value structures across cultures.

The study of cultural values in the field of consumption is traditionally based on the works developed in psychology and sociology in the 1950s and the 1960s. The major paradigm is that there is a common list of needs (Maslow, 1954) or values (Rokeach, 1960, 1968; Kahle *et al.*, 1986) which are organized in a hierarchical way depending on the cultural environment. Culture is thus said to have a strong influence on the way these values and beliefs are prioritized for any individual.

Based on the fundamental philosophical hypothesis that, for any individual, values are prioritized through adjectival and terminal values (Lovejoy, 1950), the most successful model used to segment consumers on the basis of values is the list of values worked out by the psycho-sociologist Milton Rokeach (1960, 1968), a former student of Abraham Maslow, who distinguished two types of values: (1) terminal (or means) values, which are beliefs individuals have about the goals or end-states for which they strive; and (2) instrumental values, which refer to beliefs about desirable ways of behaving to help them attain the terminal values. This system, which has informed all consumer textbooks, has nevertheless been severely criticized because of an ethnocentric bias, that is, some values were not considered to be ever valid outside the American cultural system.

The article by Schwartz and Bilsky is important in this respect because it proposes a way to validate the universal aspect of the inventory proposed by Rokeach. It confirms the universal theory proposed earlier (Schwartz and Bilsky, 1987) about the psychological content and structure of human values. It can be noted that this study was further developed in an inventory of 56 values proposed by Schwartz (1992), whose universality has been successfully tested in more than twenty countries.

Notes

1. This idea is further developed in the introduction to chapter 6.
2. Lyotard, for instance, once said that Don Quixote could be considered as a typical postmodern man.

References

Bauman, Z. (1992), 'A sociological theory of postmodernity', in P. Beilharz, G. Robinson and J. Rundell (eds.), *Between Totalitarianism and Postmodernity*, Cambridge, MA: MIT Press, 149–62.

Bourdieu, P. (1979), *La Distinction*, Paris: Editions de Minuit; English translation: *Distinction: A Social Critique of the Judgement of Taste*, 1984, London: Routledge.

Brown, S. (1995), *Postmodern Marketing*, London: Routledge.

Featherstone, M. (1991), *Consumer Culture and Postmodernism*, London: Sage.

Kahle, L.R., Beatty, S.E. and Homer, P. (1986), 'Alternative measurement approaches to consumer values: The list of values (LOV) and values lifestyles (VALS)', *Journal of Consumer Research*, **13**, 405–9.

Kearney, R. and Rainwater M. (eds.) (1996), *The Continental Philosophy Reader*, London: Routledge.

Kellner, D. (1994), 'Introduction: Jean Baudrillard in fin-de-millennium', in D. Kellner, *Baudrillard. A Critical Reader*, Oxford: Basil Blackwell, 1–23.

Lash, S. and Urry, J. (1994), *Economies of Signs and Space*, London: Sage.

Lovejoy, A. (1950), 'Terminal and adjectival values', *The Journal of Philosophy*, **47**(21) (12 October), 593–608.

Lyotard, J.-F. (1979), *La Condition postmoderne. Rapport sur le savoir*, Paris: Editions de Minuit; English translation, *The Postmodern Condition: A Report on Knowledge*, 1984, Manchester: Manchester University Press.

Maffesoli, M. (1988), *Le Temps des tribus: le déclin de l'individualisme dans les sociétés de masse*, Paris: Méridiens Klincksieck.

Maffesoli, M. (1990), *Au Creux des apparences: pour une éthique de l'esthétique*, Paris: Plon.

Maffesoli, M. (1992), *La Transfiguration du politique: la tribalisation du monde*, Paris: Grasset.

Maslow, A. (1954), *Motivation and Personality*, New York: Harper.

Morace, F. (1990), *Controtendenze: una nuova cultura del consumo*, Milan: Domus Academy.

Rokeach, M. (1960), *The Open and Closed Mind: Investigations into the Nature of Beliefs Systems and Personality Systems*, New York: Basic Books.

Rokeach, M. (1968), *Beliefs, Attitudes and Values*, New York: Jossey-Bass.

Schwartz, S.H. (1992), 'Universals in the content and structure of values: Theoretical advances and empirical tests in 20 countries', in M. Zanna, *Advances in Experimental Social Psychology*, **25**, 1–65.

Schwartz, S.H. and Bilsky, W. (1987), 'Toward a psychological structure of human values', *Journal of Personality and Social Psychology*, **54**, 550–62.

Shields, R. (1992), 'Spaces for the subject of consumption', in R. Shields (ed.), *Lifestyle Shopping. The Subject of Consumption*, London: Routledge, 1–20.

van Raaij, W.F. (1993), 'Postmodern consumption', *Journal of Economic Psychology*, **14**, 541–63.

Perspectives on consumer culture

●●

Mike Featherstone
Professor of Psychology and Communications, TCS Centre, Nottingham Trent University

Summary

Three accounts of consumer culture are discussed in this paper. The first one, the production of consumption perspective, presents the culture which develops around the accumulation of commodities as leading to greater manipulation and control. The second, the mode of consumption perspective, focuses upon the way in which goods are variably used to create distinctions and reinforce social relationships. The third perspective examines the emotional and aesthetic pleasures, the desires and dreams generated within particular sites of consumption and by consumer culture and imagery. In addition the paper discusses the alleged tendencies towards cultural disorder and de-classification within consumer culture which some refer to as postmodernism.

Introduction

This paper identifies three main perspectives on consumer culture. First is the view that consumer culture is premised upon the expansion of capitalist commodity production which has given rise to a vast accumulation of material culture in the form of consumer goods and sites for purchase and consumption. This has resulted in the growing salience of leisure and consumption activities in contemporary Western societies which although greeted as leading to greater egalitarianism and individual freedom by some, is regarded as increasing the capacity for ideological manipulation and 'seductive' containment of the population from some alternative set of 'better' social relations, by others. Second, there is the more strictly sociological view, that the satisfaction derived from goods relates to their socially structured access in a zero sum game in which satisfaction and status depends upon displaying and sustaining differences within conditions of inflation. The focus here is upon the different ways in which people use goods to create social bonds or distinctions. Third, there is the question of the emotional pleasures of consumption, the dreams and desires which become celebrated in consumer cultural imagery and particular sites of consumption which variously generate direct bodily excitement and aesthetic pleasures.

From *Sociology*, **24**(1), February 1990, 5–22.

This paper argues that it is important to focus on the question of the growing prominence of the *culture* of consumption and not merely regard consumption as derived unproblematically from production. The current phase of over-supply of symbolic goods in contemporary Western societies and the tendencies towards cultural disorder and declassification (which some label as post-modernism) is therefore bringing cultural questions to the fore and has wider implications for our conceptualisation of the relationship between culture, economy and society. This has also led to an increasing interest in conceptualising questions of desire and pleasure, the emotional and aesthetic satisfactions derived from consumer experiences, not merely in terms of some logic of psychological manipulation. Rather sociology should seek to move beyond the negative evaluation of consumer pleasures inherited from mass culture theory. We should endeavour to account for these emergent tendencies in a more detached sociological manner, which should not merely entail a reverse populist celebration of mass pleasures and cultural disorder.

The production of consumption

If from the perspectives of classical economics the object of all production is consumption with individuals maximising their satisfactions through purchasing from an ever-expanding range of goods, then from the perspective of some twentieth-century neo-Marxists this development is regarded as producing greater opportunities for controlled and manipulated consumption. The expansion of capitalist production, especially after the boost received from scientific management and 'Fordism' around the turn of the century, it is held, necessitated the construction of new markets and the 'education' of publics to become consumers through advertising and other media (Ewen, 1976). This approach, traceable back to Lukács's (1971) Marx–Weber synthesis with his theory of reification, has been developed most prominently in the writings of Horkheimer and Adorno (1972), Marcuse (1964) and Lefebvre (1971). Horkheimer and Adorno, for example, argue that the same commodity logic and instrumental rationality manifest in the sphere of production is noticeable in the sphere of consumption. Leisure-time pursuits, the arts and culture in general become filtered through the culture industry; reception becomes dictated by exchange value as the higher purposes and values of culture succumb to the logic of the production process and the market. Traditional forms of association in the family and private life as well as the promise of happiness and fulfilment, the 'yearning for a totally different other' which the best products of high culture strove for, are presented as yielding to an atomised, manipulated mass who participate in an *ersatz* mass-produced commodity culture targeted at the lowest common denominator.

From this perspective it could, for example, be argued that the accumulation of goods has resulted in the triumph of exchange-value, that the instrumental rational calculation of all aspects of life becomes possible in which all essential differences, cultural traditions and qualities become transformed into quantities. Yet while this utilisation of capital logic can account for the progressive calculability and destruction of residues of traditional culture and high culture – in the sense that the logic of capitalist modernisation is such to make 'all that is solid melt into air' – there is the problem of the 'new' culture, the culture of capitalist modernity. Is it to be merely a culture of exchange value and instrumental rational calculation – something which might be referred to as a 'non-culture' or a 'post-culture'?[1] This is one tendency within the work of the Frankfurt School, but there is another. Adorno, for example, speaks of how once the dominance of exchange-value has managed to obliterate the memory of the original use-value of goods, the commodity becomes free to take up a secondary or *ersatz* use-value (Rose, 1978: 25). Commodities hence become free to take on a wide range of cultural associations and illusions. Advertising in particular is able to exploit this and attach images of romance, exotica, desire, beauty, fulfilment, communality, scientific progress and the good life to mundane consumer goods such as soap, washing machines, motor cars and alcoholic drinks.

A similar emphasis upon the relentless logic of the commodity is to be found in the work of Jean Baudrillard who also draws upon the commodification theory of Lukács (1971) and Lefebvre (1971) to reach similar conclusions to Adorno. The major addition to Baudrillard's (1970) theory is to draw on semiology to argue that consumption entails the active manipulation of signs. This becomes central to late capitalist society where sign and commodity have come together to produce the 'commodity-sign'. The autonomy of the signifier, through, for example, the manipulation of signs in the media and advertising, means that signs are able to float free from objects and are available for use in a multiplicity of associative relations. Baudrillard's semiological development for commodity logic, entails for some an idealistic deflection of Marx's theory and movement from a materialist emphasis to a cultural emphasis (Preteceille and Terrail, 1985). This becomes more noticeable in Baudrillard's (1983a, 1983b) later writings where the emphasis shifts from production to reproduction, to the endless reduplication of signs, images and simulations through the media which effaces the distinction between the image and reality. Hence the consumer society becomes essentially cultural as social life becomes deregulated and social relationships become more variable and less structured by stable norms. The overproduction of signs and reproduction of images and simulations leads to a loss of stable meaning, and an aestheticisation of reality in which the masses become fascinated by the endless flow of bizarre juxtapositions which takes the viewer beyond stable sense.

This is the postmodern, 'depthless culture' of which Jameson (1984, 1985) speaks. Jameson's conception of postmodern culture is strongly influenced by Baudrillard's work (see Jameson, 1979). He also sees postmodern culture as the culture of the consumer society, the post-Second World War stage of late capitalism. In this society culture is given a new significance through the saturation of signs and messages to the extent that 'everything in social life can be said to have become cultural' (Jameson, 1984: 87). This 'liquefaction of signs and images' is also held to entail an effacement of the distinction between high mass culture (Jameson, 1985: 112): an acceptance of the equal validity of Las Vegas strip pop culture, alongside 'serious' high culture. At this point we should note the assumption that the immanent logic of the consumer capitalist society leads towards postmodernism. We will return to this question later to discuss images, desires and the aesthetic dimension of consumer culture.

It is clear that the production of consumption approach has difficulty in addressing the actual practices and experiences of consumption. The Frankfurt School's tendency to regard the culture industries as producing a homogeneous mass culture which threatens individuality and creativity[2] has been criticised for its elitism and inability to examine actual processes of consumption which reveal complex differentiated audience responses and uses of goods (Swingewood, 1977; Bennett *et al.*, 1977; Gellner, 1979; Turner, 1988; Stauth and Turner, 1988).

Modes of consumption

If it is possible to claim the operation of a 'capital logic' deriving from production, it may also be possible to claim a 'consumption logic' which points to the socially structured ways in which goods are used to demarcate social relationships. To speak of the consumption of goods immediately hides the wide range of goods which are consumed or purchased when more and more aspects of free time (which includes everyday routine maintenance activities as well as leisure) are mediated by the purchase of commodities. It also hides the need to differentiate between consumer durables (goods we use in maintenance and leisure, e.g. refrigerators, cars, hi-fis, cameras) and consumer non-durables (food, drink, clothing, body care products) and the shift over time in the proportion of income spent on each sector (Hirschman, 1982: chapter 2; Leiss, Kline and Jhally, 1986: 260). We also need to pay attention to the ways in which some goods can move in and out of commodity status and the different length of life enjoyed by commodities as they move from production to consumption. Food and drink usually have a short life, although this is not always the case; for example a bottle of vintage port may enjoy a prestige and exclusivity which means that it is never actually consumed (opened and drunk) although it may be consumed symbolically (gazed at, dreamt about, talked about, photographed, and handled) in various ways which produce a great deal of satisfaction. It is in this sense that we can refer to the *doubly* symbolic aspect of goods in contemporary Western societies: symbolism is not only evident in the design and imagery of the production and marketing processes, the symbolic associations of goods may be utilised and renegotiated to emphasise differences in lifestyles which demarcate social relationships (Leiss, 1978: 19).

In some cases the object of purchasing may be to gain prestige through high exchange value (the price of the bottle of port becomes constantly mentioned), especially the case within societies where the aristocracy and old rich have been forced to yield social power to the new rich (e.g. Veblen's 'conspicuous consumption'). The opposite situation can also be envisaged in which a former commodity becomes stripped of its commodity status. Hence gifts and inherited objects may become decommodified on reception and become literally 'priceless' (in the sense that it is extreme bad taste to consider selling them or to attempt to fix a price on them) in their ability to symbolise intense personal relationships and their capacity to invoke memories of loved ones (Rochberg-Halton, 1986: 176). Art objects, or objects produced for ritual, and hence given a particular symbolic charge, tend often to be ones excluded from exchange, or not permitted to remain in the commodity status for long. At the same time their professed sacred status and denial of the profane market and commodity exchange may paradoxically raise their value. Their lack of availability and 'pricelessness' raises their price and desirability. For example, Willis's (1978) description of the way bike boys make sacred the original '78' records of Buddy Holly and Elvis Presley and refuse to use compilation albums which may have better reproduction, illustrates this process of the decommodification of a mass object.

Hence while there is the capacity for commodities to break down social barriers, to dissolve the long-established links between persons and things, there is also the counter-tendency, the movement towards decommodification, to restrict, control and channel the exchange of goods. In some societies stable status systems are protected and reproduced by restricting possibilities for exchange, or for the supply of new goods. In other societies there is an ever-changing supply of commodities which gives the illusion of complete changeability of goods and unrestricted access to them; yet here, legitimate *taste*, knowledge of the principles of classification, hierarchy and appropriateness is restricted, as is the case in fashion systems. An intermediate stage would be *sumptuary* laws, which act as consumption-regulating devices, prescribing which groups can consume which goods and wear types of clothing in a context where a previous stable status system is under strong threat from a major upsurge in the number and availability of commodities – the case in late pre-modern Europe (Appadurai, 1986: 25).

In contemporary Western societies the tendency is towards the second case mentioned, with an ever-changing flow of commodities making the problem of reading the status or rank of the bearer or the commodities more complex. It is in this context that taste, the discriminatory judgement, the knowledge or culture capital, which enables the particular groups or categories of people to understand and classify new goods appropriately and how to use them, becomes important. Here we can turn to the work of Bourdieu (1984) and Douglas and Isherwood (1980) who examine the ways goods are used to mark social differences and act as communicators.

Douglas and Isherwood's (1980) work is particularly important in this respect because of their emphasis on the way in which goods are used to draw the lines of social relationships. Our enjoyment of goods, they argue, is only partly related to their physical consumption, being also crucially linked to their use as markers; we enjoy, for example, sharing the names of goods with others (the sports fan or the wine connoisseur). In addition the mastery of the cultural person entails a seemingly 'natural' mastery not only of information (the autodidact 'memory man') but also of how to use and consume appropriately and with natural ease in every situation. In this sense the consumption of high cultural goods (art, novels, opera, philosophy) must be related to the ways in which other more mundane cultural goods (clothing, food, drink, leisure pursuits) are handled and consumed, and high culture must be inscribed into the same social space as everyday cultural consumption. In Douglas and Isherwood's (1980: 176ff) discussion consumption classes are defined in relation to the consumption of three sets of goods: a staple set corresponding to the primary production sector (e.g. food); a technology set corresponding to the secondary production sector (travel and consumer's capital equipment); and an information set corresponding to tertiary production (information goods, education, arts, cultural and leisure pursuits). At the lower end of the social structure the poor are restricted to the staple set and have more time on their hands, while those in the top consumption class not only require a higher level of earnings, but also a competence in judging information goods and services in order to provide the feedback necessary from consumption to employment, which becomes itself a qualification for employment. This entails a lifelong investment in cultural and symbolic capital and in time invested in maintaining consumption activities. Douglas and Isherwood (1980: 180) also remind us that ethnographic evidence suggests that the competition to acquire goods in the information class generates high admission barriers and effective techniques of exclusion.

The phasing, duration and intensity of time invested in acquiring competences for handling information, goods, and services as well as the day-to-day practice, conservation and maintenance of these competences, is, as Halbwachs reminds us, a useful criterion of social class. Our use of time in consumption practices conforms to our class habitus and therefore conveys an accurate idea of our class status (see the discussion of Halbwachs in Preteceille and Terrail, 1985: 23). This points us towards the need for detailed time-budget research (see, for example, Gershuny and Jones, 1987). Such research, however, rarely incorporates, or is incorporated into, a theoretical framework drawing attention to patterns of investment over the life course which make such class-related differentiation of time-use possible. The chances, for example, of encountering and making sense (i.e. knowing how to enjoy and/or use the information in conversational practices) of a Godard film, the pile of bricks in the Tate Gallery, a book by Pynchon or Derrida, reflect different long-term investments in informational acquisition and cultural capital.

Such research has, however, been carried out in detail by Pierre Bourdieu and his associates (Bourdieu et al., 1965; Bourdieu et al., 1969; Bourdieu and Passeron, 1971; Bourdieu, 1984). For Bourdieu (1984), 'taste classifies and classifies the classifier'. Consumption and lifestyle preferences involve discriminatory judgements which at the same time identify and render classifiable our own particular judgement of taste to others. Particular constellations of taste, consumption preferences and lifestyle practices are associated with specific occupation and class fractions, making it possible to map out the universe of taste and lifestyles with its structured oppositions and finely graded distinctions which operate within a particular society at a particular point in history. One important factor influencing the use of marker goods within capitalist societies is that the rate of production of new goods means that the struggle to obtain 'positional goods' (Hirsch, 1975), goods which define social status in the upper reaches of society, is a relative one. The constant supply of new, fashionably desirable goods, or the usurpation of existing marker goods by lower groups, produces a paper-chase effect in which those above will have to invest in new (informational) goods in order to re-establish the original social distance.

In this context knowledge becomes important: knowledge of new goods, their social and cultural value, and how to use them appropriately. This is particularly the case with aspiring groups who adopt a learning mode towards consumption and the cultivation of a lifestyle. It is for groups such as the new middle class, the new working class and the new rich or upper class, that the consumer culture magazines, newspapers, books, television and radio programmes which stress self-improvement, self-development, personal transformation, how to manage property, relationships and ambition, how to construct a fulfilling lifestyle, are most relevant. Here one may find most frequently the self-consciousness of the autodidact who is concerned to convey the appropriate and legitimate signals through his/her consumption activities. This may be particularly the case with the group Bourdieu (1984) refers to as 'the new cultural intermediaries', i.e. those in media, design, fashion, advertising, and 'para' intellectual information occupations, whose jobs entail performing services and the production, marketing and dissemination of symbolic goods. Given conditions of an increasing supply of symbolic goods (Touraine, 1985), demand grows for cultural specialists and intermediaries, who have the capacity to ransack various traditions and cultures in order to produce new symbolic goods, and in addition provide the necessary interpretations on their use. Their habitus, dispositions and lifestyle preferences are such that they identify with artists and intellectuals, yet under conditions of the demonopolisation of artistic and intellectual commodity enclaves they have the apparent contradictory interests of sustaining the prestige and cultural capital of these enclaves, while at the same time popularising and making them more accessible to wider audiences.

It should be apparent that the problems of inflation produced by an over-supply and rapid circulation of symbolic goods and consumer commodities have the danger of threatening the readability of goods used as signs of social status. Within a context of the erosion of the bounded state-society as part of a process of the globalisation of markets and culture, it may be more difficult to stabilise appropriate marker goods. This would threaten the cultural logic of differences in which taste in cultural and consumer goods and lifestyle activities are held to be oppositionally structured (see the chart in which they are mapped out in Bourdieu, 1984: 128–9). This threat of disorder to the field or system would exist even if one accepts the premises derived from structuralism that culture itself is subject to a differential logic of opposition. To detect and establish such structured oppositions that enable groups to use symbolic goods to establish differences, thus would work best in relatively stable, closed and integrated societies in which the leakages and potential disorder from reading goods through inappropriate codes is restricted. There is the further question of whether there are relatively stable sets of classificatory principles and dispositions, i.e. the habitus, which are socially recognisable and operate to establish the boundaries between groups. The examples of cultural disorder, the overwhelming flood of signs and images which Baudrillard (1983a) argues is pushing us beyond the social, are usually taken from the media with television, rock videos and MTV (music television) cited as examples of pastiche, eclectic mixing of codes, bizarre juxtapositions and unchained signifiers which defy meaning and readability.

On the other hand, if one 'descends' to the everyday practices of embodied persons held together in webs of interdependencies and power balances with other people, it can be argued that the need to glean cues and information about the other's power potential, status and social standing by reading the other person's demeanour will continue. The different styles and labels of fashionable clothing and goods, however much they are subject to change, imitation and copying, are one such set of clues which are used in the act of classifying others. Yet as Bourdieu (1984) reminds us with his concept of symbolic capital, the signs of the dispositions and classificatory schemes which betray one's origins and trajectory through life are also manifest in body shape, size, weight, stance, walk, demeanour, tone of voice, style of speaking, sense of ease or discomfort with one's body, etc. Hence culture is incorporated, and it is not just a question of what clothes are worn, but how they are worn. Advice books on manners, taste and etiquette from Erasmus down to Nancy Mitford's 'U' and Non 'U', only impress their subjects with the need to naturalise dispositions and manners, to be completely at home with them as second nature, and also make clear that this entails the capacity to spot imposters. In this sense the newly-arrived, the autodidact, will unavoidably give away signs of the burden of attainment and incompleteness of his/her cultural competence. Hence the new rich who may adopt conspicuous consumption strategies are recognisable and assigned their place in the social space. Their cultural practices are always in danger of being dismissed as vulgar and tasteless by the established upper class, aristocracy and those 'rich in cultural capital'.

We therefore need to consider the pressures which threaten to produce an over-supply of cultural and consumer goods and relate this to more general processes of cultural de-classification (DiMaggio, 1987). We also need to consider those pressures which could act towards the deformation of habitus, the locus of taste and classificatory choices. It may be that there are different modes of identity and habitus formation and deformation emerging which make the significance of taste and lifestyle choices more blurred – if not throughout the social structure, at least within certain sectors, for instance the young and fractions of the new middle class. We have also to consider that the much talked about cultural ferment and disorder, often labelled as postmodernism, may not be the result of a total absence of controls, a genuine disorder, but merely point to a more deeply embedded integrative principle. Hence there may be 'rules of disorder' which act to permit more easily controlled swings – between order and disorder, status consciousness and the play of fantasy and desire, emotional control and de-control, instrumental calculation and hedonism – which were formerly threatening to the imperative to uphold a consistent identity structure and deny transgressions.

Consuming dreams, images and pleasure

As Raymond Williams (1976: 68) points out, one of the earliest uses of the term consume meant 'to destroy, to use up, to waste, to exhaust'. In this sense, consumption as waste, excess and spending represents a paradoxical presence within the productionist emphasis of capitalist and state socialist societies which must somehow be controlled and channelled. The notion of economic value as linked to scarcity, and the promise that the discipline and sacrifices necessitated by the drive to accumulate within the production process will lead to the eventual overcoming of scarcity, as consumer needs and pleasures are met, has been a strong cultural image and motivating force within capitalist and socialist societies alike. At the same time within the middle class, and especially within traditional economic special-ists, we have the persistence of the notion of disciplined hard work, the 'inner worldly ascetic conduct' celebrated in nineteenth-century 'self-help' individualism and later twentieth-century Thatcherism. Here consumption is an auxiliary to work, and retains many of the displaced orientations from production. It is presented as orderly, respectable and conserving: old or traditional petit-bourgeois values which sit uneasily alongside new petit-bourgeois notions of leisure as creative play, 'narcissistic' emotional exploration and relationship building (cf. Bell's, 1976 discussion of the paradox of modern consumer so-cieties: to be a 'Puritan by day and a playboy by night'). This fraction within the new middle class, the cultural specialists and intermediaries we have already referred to (which also includes those from the counterculture who have survived from the 1960s and those who have taken up elements of their cultural imagery in different contexts), represent a disturbing group to the old petit-bourgeois virtues and the cultural mission of Thatcherism. This is because they have the capacity to broaden and question the prevalent notions of consumption, to circulate images of consumption suggesting alternative pleasures and desires, consumption as excess, waste and disorder.[3] This occurs within a society where, as we have emphasised, a good deal of production is targeted at consumption, leisure and services and where there is the increasing salience of the production of symbolic goods, images and information. It is therefore more difficult to harness the productive efforts of this expanding group of cultural specialists and intermediaries to the production of a particularly narrow message of traditional petit bourgeois virtues and cultural order.

From this perspective we should pay attention to the persistence, displacements and transformation of the notion of culture as waste, squandering and excess. According to Bataille's (1988; Millot, 1988: 681ff) notion of general economy, economic production should not be linked to scarcity, but to *excess*. In effect the aim of production becomes destruction, and the key problem becomes what to do with *la part maudite*, the accursed share, the excess of energy translated into an excess of product and goods, a process of growth which reaches its limits in entropy and anomie. To control growth effectively and manage the surplus the only solution is to destroy or squander the excess in the form of games, religion, art, wars, death. This is carried out through gifts, potlatch, consumption tournaments, carnivals and conspicuous consumption. According to Bataille, capitalist societies attempt to channel the *part maudite* into full economic growth, to produce growth without end. Yet it can be argued that on a number of levels there are losses and leakages which persist, and, in terms of the argument just mentioned, capitalism also produces (one is tempted to follow the postmodernist rhetoric and say 'overproduces') images and sites of consumption which endorse the pleasures of excess. Those images and sites also favour blurring of the boundary between art and everyday life. Hence we need to investigate: (1) the persistence within consumer culture of elements of the pre-industrial carnivalesque tradition; (2) the transformation and displacement of the carnivalesque, into media images, design, advertising, rock videos, the cinema; (3) the persistence and transformation of elements of the carnivalesque within certain sites of consumption: holiday resorts, sports stadia, theme parks, department stores and shopping centres; (4) its displacement and incorporation into conspicuous consumption by states and corporations, either in the form of 'prestige' spectacles for wider publics, and/ or privileged upper management and officialdom.

In contrast to those, largely late nineteenth-century theories, inspired by notions of the rationalisation, commodification and modernisation of culture, which exhibit a nostalgic *Kulturpessimismus*, it is important to emphasise the tradition within popular culture of transgression, protest, the carnivalesque and liminal excesses (Easton *et al.*, 1988). The popular tradition of carnivals, fairs and festivals provided symbolic inversions and transgressions of the official 'civilised' culture and favoured excitement, uncontrolled emotions and the direct and vulgar grotesque bodily pleasures of fattening food, intoxicating drink and sexual promiscuity (Bakhtin, 1968; Stallybrass and White, 1986). These were *liminal* spaces, in which the everyday world was turned upside down and in which the tabooed and fantastic were possible, in which impossible dreams could be expressed. The liminal, according to Victor Turner (1969; see also Martin, 1981, chapter 3), points to the emphasis within these essentially delimited transitional or threshold phases upon *anti-structure* and *communitas*, the generation of a sense of unmediated community, emotional fusion and ecstatic oneness. It should be apparent that these enclaved liminal moments of ordered disorder were not completely integrated by the state or the emerging consumer culture industries and 'civilising processes' in eighteenth- and nineteenth-century Britain.

To take the example of fairs: fairs have long held a dual role as local markets and as sites of pleasure. They were not only sites where commodities were exchanged, they entailed the display of exotic and strange commodities from various parts of the world in a festive atmosphere (see Stallybrass and White, 1986; Featherstone, 1990a). Like the experience of the city, fairs offered spectacular imagery, bizarre juxtapositions, confusions of boundaries and an immersion in a mêlée of strange sounds, motions, images, people, animals and things. For those people, especially in the middle classes, who were developing bodily and emotional controls as part of civilising processes (Elias, 1978, 1982), sites of cultural disorder such as fairs, the city, the slum, the seaside resort, become the source of fascina-tion, longing and nostalgia (Mercer, 1983; Shields, 1990). In a displaced form this became a central theme in art, literature and popular entertainment such as the music hall (Bailey, 1986). It can also be argued that those institutions which came to dominate the urban marketplace, the department stores (Chaney, 1983; Williams, 1982) plus the new national and international exhibitions (Bennett, 1988), both developed in the second half of the nineteenth century, and other twentieth-century sites such as theme parks (Urry, 1988) provided sites of ordered disorder which summoned up elements of the carnivalesque tradition in their displays, imagery and simulations of exotic locations and lavish spectacles.

For Walter Benjamin (1983) the new department stores and arcades, which emerged in Paris and subsequently other large cities from the mid-nineteenth century onwards, were effectively 'dream worlds'. The vast phantasmagoria of commodities on display, constantly renewed as part of the capitalist and modernist drive for novelty, was the source of dream images which summoned up associations and half-forgotten illusions – Benjamin referred to them as *allegories*. Here Benjamin uses the term allegory not to point to the unity or coherence of the double-coded message which is occluded, as in traditional allegories such as *Pilgrim's Progress*, but to the way a stable hierarchically ordered meaning is dissolved and the allegory points only to kaleidoscopic fragments which resist any coherent notion of what it stands for (see Wolin, 1982; Spencer, 1985). In this aestheticised commodity world the department stores, arcades, trams, trains, streets and fabric of buildings and the goods on display, as well as the people who stroll through these spaces, summon up half-forgotten dreams, as the curiosity and memory of the stroller is fed by the ever-changing landscape in which objects appear divorced from their context and subject to mysterious connections which are read on the surface of things. The everyday life of the big cities becomes aestheticised. The new industrial processes provided the opportunity for art to shift into industry, which saw an expansion of occupations in advertising, marketing, industrial design and commercial display to produce the new aestheticised urban landscape (Buck-Morss, 1983). The growth of the mass media in the twentieth century with the proliferation of photographic images heightened the tendencies of which Benjamin talks. Indeed the unacknowledged impact of Benjamin's theory can be detected in some of the theorisations of postmodernism, such as those by Baudrillard (1983a) and Jameson (1984, 1985). Here the emphasis is on immediacies, intensities, sensory overload, disorientation, the mêlée or liquefaction of signs and images, the mixing of codes, the unchained or floating signifiers of the postmodern 'depthless' consumer culture where art and reality have switched places in an 'aesthetic hallucination of the real'. Clearly these quantities cannot be claimed to be unique to postmodernism and have a much longer genealogy, suggesting continuities between the modern and postmodern, and indeed, the pre-modern (Featherstone, 1990a, 1990b).

There is a strong populist strand in the writings of Benjamin which is usually contrasted to the alleged elitism of Horkheimer and Adorno. Benjamin emphasised the utopian, or positive moment in the mass-produced consumer commodities which liberated creativity from art and allowed it to migrate into the multiplicity of mass-produced everyday objects (the influence of surrealism on Benjamin's theoretical framework is evident here). This celebration of the aesthetic potential of mass culture and the aestheticised perceptions of the people who stroll through the urban spaces of the large cities has been taken up by commentators who emphasise the transgressive and playful potential of postmodernism (Hebdige, 1988; Chambers, 1986, 1987). Here the perceptions of Benjamin and Baudrillard are accepted to point to the enhanced role of culture in contemporary Western cities, increasingly centres of not only everyday consumption but also of a wider range of symbolic goods and experiences produced by the culture industries (the arts, entertainment, tourism, heritage sectors). Within these 'postmodern cities' (Harvey, 1988) people are held to engage in a complex sign play which resonates with the proliferation of signs in the built environment and urban fabric. The contemporary urban *flâneurs*, or strollers, play with and celebrate the artificiality, randomness and superficiality of the fantastic mélange of fictions and strange values which are to be found in the fashions and popular cultures of cities (Chambers, 1987; Calefato, 1988). It is also argued that this represents a movement beyond individualism with a heightened emphasis upon the affectual and empathy, a new 'aesthetic paradigm' in which masses of people come together temporarily in fluid 'postmodern tribes' (Maffesoli, 1988).

While there is a strong emphasis in such writings upon the sensory overload, the aesthetic immersion, dreamlike perceptions of de-centred subjects, in which people open themselves up to a wider range of sensations and emotional experiences, it is important to stress that this does not represent the eclipse of controls. It needs discipline and control to stroll through goods on display, to look and not snatch, to move casually without interrupting the flow, to gaze with controlled enthusiasm and a blasé outlook, to observe others without being seen, to tolerate the close proximity of bodies without feeling threatened. It also requires the capacity to manage swings between intense involvement and more distanced aesthetic detachment. In short to move through urban spaces, or to experience the spectacles of the theme park and heritage museums, demands a 'controlled de-control of the emotions' (Wouters, 1986). The imagery may summon up pleasure, excitement, the carnivalesque and disorder, yet to experience them requires self-control and for those who lack such control there lurks in the background surveillance by security guards and remote-control cameras.

These tendencies towards the aestheticisation of everyday life relate to the distinction between high and mass culture. A dual movement has suggested the collapse of some of the boundaries between art and everyday life and the erosion of the special protected status of art as an enclaved commodity. In the first place there is the migration of art into industrial design, advertising, and associated symbolic and image production industries we have mentioned. Secondly, there has been the internal avant-gardist dynamic within the arts which in the form of Dada and surrealism in the 1920s (Bürger, 1984) and in the form of postmodernism in the 1960s sought to show that any everyday object could be aestheticised (Featherstone, 1989a, 1989b). The 1960s Pop Art and postmodernism entail a focus upon everyday commodities as art (Warhol's Campbell's soup cans), an ironic playing back of consumer culture on itself, and an anti-museum and academy stance in performance and body art. The expansion of the art market and increase in working artists and ancillary occupations, especially in metropolitan centres, plus the use of art as a vehicle for public relations by large corporations and the state, have resulted in significant changes in the artist's role (see Zukin, 1982).

It has been argued that it is no longer useful to speak of an artistic avant-garde in the sense of a group of artists who reject both popular culture and the middle-class lifestyle (Crane, 1987). While the artist's lifestyle may still have an attractive romantic ambience for those engaged in the gentrification of inner city areas and for members of the middle class in general who increasingly value the role of culture in lifestyle construction (Zukin, 1988), many artists have relinquished their commitment to high culture and avant-gardism and have adopted an increasingly open attitude towards consumer culture and now show a willingness to truck with other cultural intermediaries, image-makers, audiences and publics. Hence, with the parallel processes of the expansion of the role of art within consumer culture and the deformation of enclaved art with its separate prestige structure and lifestyle, a blurring of genres and the tendencies towards the deconstruction of symbolic hierarchies has occurred. This entails a pluralistic stance towards the variability of taste, a process of cultural de-classification which has undermined the basis of high culture/mass culture distinctions. It is in this context that we get not just scepticism towards advertising's effectiveness, in that its capacity to persuade people to purchase new products – or indoctrinate – is questioned (Schudson, 1986), but a celebration of its aesthetic pedigree. Design and advertising thus become not only confused with art, but are celebrated and museumified as art. As Stephen Bayley (1979, p. 10) remarks, 'industrial design is the art of the twentieth century' (quoted in Forty, 1986, p. 7).

The attractions of the romantic-bohemian lifestyle with the artist presented as an expressive rebel and stylistic hero has been a strong theme, particularly with respect to popular and rock music, in Britain in the post-war era. Frith and Horne (1987) document this particular injection of art into popular culture which also helped to deconstruct the distinction between high and popular culture. In addition it can be seen as furthering the process of a controlled de-control of the emotions we have spoken of, with jazz, blues, rock and black music presented as forms of direct emotional expression which were regarded as both more pleasurable, involved and authentic by predominantly young audiences, and as dangerously threatening, uncontrolled, 'devil's music' to predominantly older, adult audiences used to more controlled and formal patterns of public behaviour and emotional restraint (Stratton, 1989). Yet there is also a sense in which despite the popularity of artistic lifestyles and the various neo-dandyist transformations of making life a work of art, this project implies a degree of integration and unity of purpose which is becoming increasingly obsolete, despite the compelling nature of some of the symbols of these lifestyles. There is less interest in constructing a coherent style than in playing with, and expanding, the range of familiar styles. The term style suggests coherence and hierarchical ordering of elements, some inner form and expressiveness (Schapiro, 1961). It has often been argued by twentieth-century commentators that our age lacks a distinctive style. Simmel (1979), for example, refers to the age of 'no style' and Malraux (1967) remarked that our culture is 'a museum without walls' (see Roberts, 1988), perceptions which become heightened in postmodernism with its emphasis upon pastiche, 'retro', the collapse of symbolic hierarchies, and the playback of cultures.

A similar argument can be made with reference to the term lifestyle, that the tendency within consumer culture is to present lifestyles as no longer requiring inner coherence. The new cultural intermediaries, an expanding faction within the new middle class, therefore, while well disposed to the lifestyle of artists and cultural specialists, do not seek to promote a single lifestyle, but rather to cater for and expand the range of styles and lifestyles available to audiences and consumers (Featherstone, 1987).

Conclusion

In his book *All Consuming Images*, Stuart Ewen (1988) discusses an advertisement for Neiman-Marcus, a fashionable [US] department store, which seemingly combines a unity of opposites. It juxtaposes two photographs of the same woman. The first presents an image of an upper-class woman dressed in Parisian *haute couture*; the text beneath the image stresses that *Attitude* is 'disposition with regard to people', 'wearing the correct thing at the correct hour', 'exactly sized', 'a mode', 'dressing to please someone else', 'evaluation', 'strolling the avenue'. The second photograph is of a brooding Semitic woman dressed in a Palestinian scarf and desert caftan. In graffiti style typeface the text emphasises that *Latitude* is 'freedom from narrow restrictions', 'changing the structure of a garment when the mood hits', 'whatever feels comfortable', 'a mood', 'dressing to please yourself', 'evolution', 'loving the street life'. Within contemporary culture women and men are asked not to choose, but to incorporate both options. To regard their dress and consumer goods as communicators, as 'symbols of class status' (Goffman, 1951), demands appropriate conduct and demeanour on the part of the wearer/user in order to further the visible classification of the social world into categories of persons. In this sense, within consumer culture there still persist prestige economies, with scarce goods demanding considerable investment in time, money and knowledge to attain and handle appropriately. Such goods can be read and used to classify the status of their bearer. At the same time consumer culture uses images, signs and symbolic goods which summon up dreams, desires and fantasies which suggest romantic authenticity and emotional fulfilment in narcissistically pleasing oneself, instead of others. Contemporary consumer culture seems to be widening the range of contexts and situations in which such behaviour is deemed appropriate and acceptable. It is, therefore, not a question of a choice between these two options presented as alternatives; rather it is *both*. Today's consumer culture represents neither a lapse of control nor the institution of more rigid controls, but rather their underpinning by a flexible underlying generative structure which can both handle formal control and de-control and facilitate an easy change of gears between them.

Notes

1. This approach is one which has a long history within German sociology and reveals a distaste for rationalised *Gesellschaft* and a nostalgia for *Gemeinschaft* (see Liebersohn, 1988; Turner, 1987; Stauth and Turner, 1988). It also has been sustained in critical theory down to the work of Habermas (1984, 1987) in his distinction between system and life-world in which the commodification and instrumental rationalisation imperatives of the technio–economic–administrative system threaten the uncoerced communicative actions of the lifeworld, and hence impoverish the cultural sphere.
2. Not all the Frankfurt School followed this position. Lowenthal (1961) stressed the democratic potential of mass-marketed books in the eighteenth century. Swingewood (1977) has developed this argument into a strong critique of mass culture theory.
3. It is noticeable in the books with titles such as: *Objects of Desire* (Forty, 1986), *Channels of Desire* (Ewen and Ewen, 1982), *Consuming Passions* (Williamson, 1986), *Dream Worlds* (Williams, 1982). Campbell (1987) also deals extensively with the historic genesis of desire for consumer goods. For a critique of the psychological as opposed to sociological grounding of his approach, see Featherstone (1990b). It should be added that the recent upsurge of interest in the sociology of the emotions (see Denzin, 1984; Hochschild, 1983; Elias, 1987; Wouters, 1989) would suggest that we are at last moving towards a sociological framework for understanding the emotions.

References

Adorno, T.W. and Horkheimer, M. (1971). *Dialectic of Enlightenment*. New York: Herder & Herder.
Appadurai, A. (1986). 'Introduction' to Appadurai, A. (ed.), *The Social Life of Things*. Cambridge: Cambridge University Press.
Bailey, P. (1986). *The Music Hall: the Business of Pleasure*. Milton Keynes: Open University Press.
Bakhtin, M. (1986). *Rabelais and His World*. Cambridge, MA: MIT Press.
Bataille, G. (1988). *The Accursed Share*. Volume I. New York: Zone Books.
Baudrillard, J. (1970). *La Société de consommation*. Paris: Gallimard.
Baudrillard, J. (1983a). *Simulations*. New York: Semiotext(e).
Baudrillard, J. (1983b). *In the Shadow of the Silent Majorities*. New York: Semiotext(e).
Baudrillard, J. (1985). 'The ecstasy of communication', in H. Foster (ed.) *Postmodern Culture*. London: Pluto Press.
Bell, D. (1976). *The Cultural Contradictions of Capitalism*. London: Heinemann.
Benjamin, W. (1983). *Das Passagen-Werk*. Frankfurt: Suhrkamp.
Bennett, T. *et al.* (1977). *The Study of Culture*. Milton Keynes: Open University.
Bennett, T. (1988). 'The exhibitionary complex'. *New Formations*, 4.
Berman, M. (1983). *All That is Solid Melts into Air*. New York: Simon & Schuster.
Bourdieu, P. (1984). *Distinction*. London: Routledge.
Bourdieu, P. , Boltanski, L., Castel, R. and Chamboredon, J.C. (1965). *Un Art Moyen*. Paris: Minuit.
Bourdieu, P. and Passeron, J. (1971). *Reproduction in Education Society and Culture*. London: Sage.
Buck-Morss, S. (1986). 'Benjamin's Passagen-Werk', *New German Critique*, 39.
Bürger, P. (1986). *The Theory of the Avant-Garde*. Manchester: Manchester University Press.
Calefato, P. (1988). 'Fashion, the passage, the body', *Cultural Studies* 2: 2.
Campbell, C. (1987). *The Romantic Ethic and the Spirit of Modern Consumerism*. Oxford: Blackwell.
Chambers, I. (1986). *Popular Culture: The Metropolitan Experience*. London: Methuen.
Chambers, I. (1987). 'Maps for the metropolis', *Cultural Studies* 1: 1.
Chaney, D. (1983). 'The department store as a cultural form', *Theory Culture and Society*, 3: 1.
Crane, D. (1987). *The Transformation of the Avant-Garde*. Chicago: University of Chicago Press.
Denzin, N. (1984). *On Understanding Emotion*. San Francisco: Jossey-Bass.
DiMaggio, P. (1987). 'Classification in art'. *American Sociological Review*, **52**: 4.
Douglas, M. and Isherwood, B. (1980). *The World of Goods*. Harmondsworth: Penguin.
Easton, S., Hawkins, A., Laing, S. and Walker, A. (1988). *Disorder and Discipline*. London: Temple Smith.

Elias, N. (1978). *The Civilizing Process, Volume I*. Oxford: Blackwell.

Elias, N. (1982). *The Civilizing Process, Volume II*. Oxford: Blackwell.

Elias, N. (1983). *The Court Society*. Oxford: Blackwell.

Elias, N. (1987). 'On human beings and their emotions', *Theory Culture and Society*, 4: 2–3.

Ewen, S. (1976). *Captains of Consciousness: Advertising and the Social Roots of the Consumer Culture*. New York: McGraw-Hill.

Ewen, S. (1988). *All Consuming Images*. New York: Basic.

Ewen, S. and Ewen, E. (1982). *Channels of Desire*. New York: McGraw-Hill.

Featherstone, M. (1987). 'Lifestyle and consumer culture'. *Theory Culture and Society*, 4: 1.

Featherstone, M. (1989a). 'Towards a sociology of postmodern culture', in H. Haferkamp (ed.), *Some Structure and Culture*. Berlin and New York: de Gruyter.

Featherstone, M. (1989b). 'Postmodernism, cultural change and social practice', in D. Kellner (ed.) *Postmodernism/Jameson/Critique*, Washington, DC: Maisoneuvre Press.

Featherstone, M. (1990a). 'Postmodernism and the aestheticization of everyday life', in J. Friedman and S. Lash (eds.) *Modernity and Identity*. Oxford: Blackwell.

Featherstone, M. (1990b). 'Consumer culture, postmodernism and global disorder', in W.R. Garrett and R. Robertson (eds.) *Religion and the Global Order*. New York: Paragon House.

Forty, A. (1986). *Objects of Desire*. London: Thames & Hudson.

Frith, S. and Horne, H. (1987). *Art into Pop*. London: Methuen.

Goffman, E. (1951). 'Systems of class status', *British Journal of Sociology*, 2.

Habermas, J. (1984). *Theory of Communicative Action Vol. I*. London: Heinemann.

Habermas, J. (1987). *Theory of Communicative Action Vol. II*. Oxford: Polity.

Harvey, D. (1988). 'Voodoo cities', *New Statesman and Society*.

Hebdige, D. (1988). *Hiding in the Light*. London: Routledge.

Hirsh, F. (1976). *The Social Limits to Growth*. Cambridge: Cambridge University Press.

Hirshman, A. (1982). *Shifting Involvements*. Oxford: Blackwell.

Hochschild, A. (1983). *The Managed Heart*. Berkeley: University of California Press.

Jameson, F. (1979). 'Reification and Utopia in mass culture'. *Social Text*, 1: 1.

Jameson, F. (1984). 'Postmodernism: Or the cultural logic of late capitalism', *New Left Review*, **146**.

Jameson, F. (1985). 'Postmodernism and the consumer society', in H. Foster (ed.) *Postmodern Culture*. London: Pluto Press.

Lefebvre, H. (1971). *Everyday Life in the Modern World*. Harmondsworth: Allen Lane.

Leiss, W. (1978). *The Limits of Satisfaction*. London: M. Boyars.

Leiss, W., Kline, S. and Jhally, S. (1986). *Social Communication in Advertising*. New York: Macmillan.

Liebersohn, H. (1988). *Fate and Utopia in German Sociology*. Cambridge, MA: MIT Press.

Linder, S. (1970). *The Harried Leisure Class*. New York: Columbia University Press.

Lowenthal, L. (1961). *Literature, Popular Culture and Society*. San Francisco: Pacific Books.

Lukács, G. (1971). *History and Class Consciousness*. London: New Left Books.

Maravall, J.A. (1986). *The Culture of the Baroque*. Manchester: Manchester University Press.

Maffesoli, M. (1988). 'Affectual postmodernism and the megapolis'. *Threshold* IV 1.

Marcuse, H. (1964). *One Dimensional Man*. London: Routledge.

Martin, B. (1981). *A Sociology of Contemporary Cultural Change*. Oxford: Blackwell.

Mercer, C. (1983). 'A poverty of desire: Pleasure and popular politics', in T. Bennett *et al.* (eds.), *Formations of Pleasure*. London: Routledge.

Millot, B. (1988). 'Symbol, desire and power'. *Theory Culture and Society*, 5: 4.

Preteceille, E. and Terrail, J.P. (1985). *Capitalism, Consumption and Needs*. Oxford: Blackwell.

Roberts, D. (1988). 'The museum and montage', *Theory Culture and Society*, 5: 2–3.

Rochberg-Halton, E. (1986). *Meaning and Modernity*. Chicago: University of Chicago Press.

Rose, G. (1978). *The Melancholy Science: an Introduction to the Thought of Theodor W. Adorno*. London: Macmillan.

Schapiro, M. (1961). 'Style', in M. Phillipson (ed.), *Aesthetics Today*. London: Meridian Books.

Schudson, M. (1986). *Advertising: The Uneasy Persuasion*. New York: Harper.

Shields, R. (1990). 'The system of pleasure: Liminality and the carnivalesque in Brighton', *Theory Culture and Society*, 7: 1.

Simmel, G. (1978). *The Philosophy of Money*. London: Routledge.

Spencer, L. (1985). 'Allegory in the world of the commodity', *New German Critique*, **34**.

Stallybrass, P. and White, A. (1986). *The Politics of Transgression*. London: Routledge.

Stauth, G. and Turner, B.S. (1988). 'Nostalgia, postmodernism and mass culture', *Theory Culture and Society*, **5**: 2–3.

Stratton, J. (1989). 'Postmodernism and popular music', *Theory Culture and Society*, **6**: 1.

Swingewood, A. (1977). *The Myth of Mass Culture*. London: Macmillan.

Touraine, A. 1985. 'An introduction to the study of social movements', *Social Research*, **52**: 4.

Turner, B.S. (1987). 'A note on nostalgia', *Theory Culture and Society*, **4**: 1.

Turner, B.S. (1988). *Status*. Milton Keynes: Open University Press.

Turner, V.W. (1969). *The Ritual Process: Structure and Anti-Structure*. Harmondsworth: Allen Lane.

Turner, V.W. (1974). *Dramas, Fields and Metaphors*. Ithaca, NY: Cornell University Press.

Urry, J. (1988). 'Cultural change and contemporary holiday-making', *Theory Culture and Society*, **5**: 1.

Williams, Raymond (1970). *Keywords*. London: Fontana.

Williams, Rosalind (1982). *Dream Worlds*. Los Angeles: University of California Press.

Williamson, J. (1986). *Consuming Passions*. London: Marion Boyars.

Willis, P. (1978). *Profane Culture*. London: Routledge.

Wolin, R. (1982). *Walter Benjamin*. New York: Columbia University Press.

Wouters, C. (1986). 'Formalization and informalization: Changing tension balances in civilizing processes', *Theory Culture and Society*, **3**: 2.

Wouters, C. (1989). 'The sociology of emotions and flight attendants: Hochschild's managed heart', *Theory Culture and Society*, **6**: 2.

Zukin, S. (1982). 'Art in the arms of power', *Theory and Society*, **11**.

Zukin, S. (1988). *Loft Living* (second edition). London: Radius/Hutchinson.

Postmodern consumption

● ●

W. Fred van Raaij
Professor of Marketing, Erasmus University, Rotterdam

Summary

We live in a period of transition from the modern to the postmodern period. Postmodern elements can be traced in architecture, art, literature, music, cinema, and consumption. The postmodern period is an era without a dominant ideology but with a pluralism of styles. Social and technological changes create four dominant postmodern conditions related to fragmentation of markets and experiences, hyper-reality of products and services, value realization later in the consumption cycle, and paradoxical juxtapositions of opposites. These trends will be more and more reflected in consumer behavior, advertising, product development and introduction. It is obvious that these changed conditions are relevant for economic psychology. In this article, the relevance of postmodernism for consumption and consumer behavior is sketched.

1. Introduction

> It is the emptiness that fascinates me. People collect altars, statues, paintings, chairs, carpets, and books, and then comes a time of joyful relief and they throw it all out like so much refuse from yesterday's dinner table.
>
> *(Milan Kundera, 1984, p. 109)*

Western societies are in a process of 'modernization' or better, 'postmodernization'. According to sociological theory, three independent trends can be observed: societal differentiation, secularization and individualization (Naumann and Hufner, 1985). Taken to its extreme, these trends lead to societal fragmentation, loss of identities and social structures. These processes are not characteristic of the modern era, as some sociologists would argue, but of the postmodern era.

It is extremely difficult to observe trends and trend disruptions of the present period. It is much easier to review the past and to discern past trends and fashions. Nevertheless, many

From the *Journal of Economic Psychology*, **14**(3), 1993, 541–63.

signs tell us that we are passing from the modern into the postmodern era. The modern era was the period of industrialization, rigid structural differences, ideology, nationalism, and mass culture. It brought us wars and material well-being, and sharp economic distinctions between classes and nations.

The postmodern era is the period of information, office workers, differentiated structures, globalism and fragmented culture. It is also the era of the lost Utopias, the end of dominant ideologies. It is a time of incessant choosing. No orthodoxy can be adopted without self-consciousness and irony. All traditions seem to have some validity. Pluralism is both a great problem and a great opportunity. Many people in the West became liberated from oppressing ideologies and became cosmopolitans. Pragmatic political parties with acceptable solutions to societal problems gain voters' support, whereas traditional ideology-based political parties tend to lose voters' interest.

Ihab Hassan (1980) became the self-proclaimed spokesman of postmodernism and he tied this label to the ideas of experimentation in the arts, architecture and technology. For Hassan, postmodernism is 'discontinuity, indeterminacy, immanence'. Harvey (1990) explores the link between economic and cultural transformations. Bauman (1992) is the sociologist of postmodernity.

For many philosophers, a rejection of logical positivism makes one a postmodern thinker. For many consumer researchers, nonconventional research approaches and alternative ways of knowing are labeled postmodern (Sherry, 1991). Postmodernism encourages pluralism, sensitivity to differences and tolerance of the incommensurable (Lyotard, 1984 [1979]).

In this article, an attempt is made to link postmodern developments in art and architecture to consumer behavior. The challenge of the postmodern consumer is an *embarras de richesses* and an *embarras des choix*, to choose among traditions, styles, products and services from the past and the present. Eclecticism and pragmatism are the key-words. Cultural, social and technological changes create new options for experiences and self-expression in consumption. We should be aware that modern theories and models may no longer apply in the postmodern period.

2. Three waves

Alvin Toffler (1980) was one of the first to popularize three waves or periods in the history of civilization: the agricultural, industrial and informational revolution. We are now on the edge of the third wave with its demassification or fragmentation of production, media, styles, ideologies, and even societies. The three waves are summarized in Table 1.

The *pre-modern period* is characterized by its local and agricultural orientation. Hunting tribes settled down and engaged in agriculture. The ruling class consisted of kings, warlords and priests. Most people worked in agriculture, often not owning the land they worked on. Culture was aristocratic. Ordinary people had no time, education, and opportunity to participate in cultural events, except for the church and occasional local fairs.

During the *modern period* (circa 1450–1960) industrial production developed. In the nineteenth century, work became more and more concentrated in factories, and the method became mass production under a strict division of labour and a strict separation of the

Table 1 Characteristics of the premodern, modern and postmodern periods

	Premodern 1000 BC–circa 1450	Modern circa 1450–1960	Postmodern circa 1960–present
Production	Neolithic revolution Agriculture Handwork, artisan Dispersed	Industrial revolution Factory Mass production Centralized	Information revolution Office Segmented production Decentralized
Society	Tribal/feudal Ruling class of kings, priests, and military Peasants	Capitalist Owning class of bourgeoisie Factory workers	Global Para-class of cognitariat Office workers
Time	Slow changing Cyclical	Linear	Fast changing Fragmented
Orientation	Local/city Agrarian	Nationalist Rationalization of business Exclusive	Global/local Multinational Pluralist, eclectic Inclusive
Culture	Aristocratic Integrated style	Bourgeois Mass-culture reigning style	Taste culture Many genres

Source: Adapted from Jencks (1987).

capitalist owners and the working class. Charlie Chaplin in *Modern Times* exemplified the alienation of factory work. These distinctions created the political ideologies of liberalism and socialism. Religion and science split sharply during this period, but Christianity kept its important role in Western society (Berman, 1981).

The modern period is a period of mass production and consumption. It is also a period of utopianism and the 'grand ideologies'. In the Western world, the ideology of progress and welfare through material goods and the nuclear family as the cornerstone of society is dominant. In the Communist world, the idea of 'socialist man' and the collectivization of work, living and free time are promoted, actually separating parents from their children by leaving their education in the hands of specialists, and employing both parents in the development of the socialist society.

In 1956 for the first time in the USA the number of white-collar workers outnumbered blue-collar workers, and by the late 1970s America had made the shift to an information society with relatively few people involved in the manufacture of goods. Most workers (60%) were engaged in the 'manufacture' of information. Whereas a modern, industrialized society depends on the mass-production of objects in a factory, the postmodern society, to exaggerate the contrast, depends on the segmented production of ideas and images in an office.

The transition from the modern to the *postmodern period* was and is not without turbulence. During the second part of the 1960s student revolts and protest, such as in Paris in May 1968 and in other cities, were a sign of a cultural shift from 'materialistic' to 'post-materialistic' values (Inglehart, 1977, 1989). Materialistic values of the older generation emphasize the possession of material goods, law and order, authority, elitism and rigid structures. Postmaterialistic values of the younger generation are related to freedom of speech, self-expression, experiences, tolerance, and harmony. March (1975), however, finds opposing evidence that materialistic values did not decrease in Britain. The transition from the modern to the postmodern period is a gradual shift, not a schism. For some people and in some domains this shift is more prominent than for other segments and domains. The year 1960 is thus only an indication of the time of this transition.

In the postmodern world, there is a revolutionary growth of jobs that create, transform and disseminate information. The proletariat of factory workers is almost replaced by the cognitariat of office workers. These workers are neither working, lower nor middle class, but rather para-class. Most of them are clerks, secretaries, teachers, students, managers, researchers, advertising people, writers, bureaucrats, technicians, bankers, insurance people, stockbrokers, accountants, lawyers, programmers, all handling information. Postmodernism is thus largely a Western, first-world phenomenon.

Jean-François Lyotard (1984) is mostly concerned with knowledge in this scientific age, in particular the way knowledge is legitimized through the 'grand narratives', such as liberation of humanity, equality, progress, the emancipation of the proletariat and increased power. These grand narratives, such as religion, nation-state and the destiny of the West, have largely become non-credible. In his book *The Postmodern Condition* he states: 'The object of this study is the condition of knowledge in the most highly developed societies. I have decided to use the word postmodern to describe that condition . . . I define *postmodern* as incredulity toward meta-narratives . . . Our working hypothesis is that the status of knowledge is altered as societies enter what is known as the post-industrial age, and cultures enter what is known as the postmodern age' (Lyotard, 1984, pp. xxiii–xxiv, 3).

The dominant ideologies of the modern era, liberalism, anarchism, socialism and feminism, have either achieved their goals or became outdated (Bell, 1962; Van Gennep, 1990). Some elements are kept, such as the emphasis in the feministic and liberal ideologies on individual and non-sexist responsibilities. Fukuyama (1992) claims the 'end of history' in postmodern times and states that a dominant liberal-democratic model has become the dominant model in Western societies. Most fascist and communist totalitarian states have collapsed and a liberal form of capitalism has survived. If these liberal democracies guarantee human rights, dignity, freedom, a certain equality, a satisfactory consumption level and avoid military wars (but allow economic wars), the stable situation of the 'end of history' has been reached (Fukuyama, 1992). We cannot expect significant changes in the future.

The end of ideology does not mean the end of styles. On the contrary, the ideological freedom creates a large variety of styles and genres. First, postmodern developments in architecture and art will be described. The scope of this article does not allow a discussion of postmodern literature, cinema, and music. Then, the postmodern impact on consumption and consumer behavior will be discussed.

3. Postmodern architecture

Modernist architectural styles are characterized by their ideology. They have a message to the world. The dominant idea might be minimalism, functionalism, aestheticism, constructivism or even elitism or dogmatism. Often, a technical solution is given to social problems. 'Garden cities', such as the Bijlmer in South-East Amsterdam, are designed to separate pedestrians from car traffic, and to create a park environment around immense apartment buildings. Modernist architects, such as Le Corbusier, were popular in the communist countries and were imitated by Soviet architects. Le Corbusier's largest building is the Tsentrosojuz building, the Central Union of Consumer Cooperations at Moscow, built in 1936. The Soviet architect Nikolaj Kuzmin, for instance, had explicit ideas about the 'new man'. The population should be divided into age categories, and men, women and children should be housed separately. No family life was planned. Private rooms were not planned either; six people of the same sex living in communities slept in sleeping rooms and met in recreation rooms. At ten in the evening, lights would be turned off and at six in the morning, people awake to have their communal breakfast and to go to their factory or office work. Kuzmin even planned how many minutes were needed for exercise, shower, breakfast, etc. The communist paradise was obviously very similar to jail. Modernist architects were the 'executives' of the socialist ideology. Modernist style fits very well in social engineering, systemization, collectivization and homogenization approaches, reducing the differences between the city and the countryside, employed in Ceauşescu's Romania.

A specific style, such as De Stijl or Bauhaus, dictates its followers their designs and restricts their freedom of designs. Pure aestheticism is a *l'art pour l'art* in architecture. The International Style of concrete, glass and steel is the dominating style of late modernism. This is still a popular style, although it is alienating for those who live and work in these buildings.

Modernist architects and designers, such as Le Corbusier, Raymond Loewy and Mies van der Rohe, hold the values of 'truth to materials', 'logical consistency', 'straightforwardness' and 'simplicity'. Late modernist buildings, such as the Centre Pompidou in Paris, communicate the ultimate functionalism of truth to materials and construction. They emphasize structure, circulation, open space, industrial detailing and abstraction.

Postmodernism started in architecture. Most postmodern architects have their education and roots in modernism. There is no sudden rupture. Postmodernism is both the continuation and the transcendence of modernism. Jencks (1987, p. 14) defines postmodernism as: 'Double coding: the combination of modern techniques with something else (usually traditional building) in order for architecture to communicate with the public and a concerned minority, usually other architects'. Double coding, irony, parody, lost innocence, pastiche, hyperreality and hybrid language are the key words.

Double coding means establishing links between the present and the past, between new techniques and old patterns, between the elite and the popular. It has always been the task of architecture to fit new buildings into old structures and thus relate the present to the past. Robert Venturi and Denise Scott Brown integrated Franklin's house at Philadelphia with other buildings and 'ghosted' this house in a stainless steel construction on Franklin Square.

4. Postmodern art

Many of the points made for architecture, could be made for art as well. The modern painter Pablo Picasso became history, inspiring admiration like Rembrandt but no longer opposition. Since 1960, a number of departures from modernism have been given names: pop art, hyperrealism, photo realism, allegorical and political realism, new image painting, 'La Transavanguardia', 'die neue Wilde' (the New Savages) and neo-expressionism. The international media and the art market exerted a pressure to produce new labels and schools. Pop artists in the 1960s, such as Andy Warhol, claimed that they were lending respectability to the images they borrowed from mass culture through an artistic revision (Honnef, 1988). There remains a distinction between art and mass culture, but a painted Campbell soup tin or Coca Cola bottle became works of art. In this way, art relates to consumption (Mamiya, 1992). As traditional art used images from the past, from religion, the ancient Greeks, and from nature, postmodern art borrows images from consumption and our material world. Avantgardism still maintained traditional values to some extent. Transavantgardism, originating in Italy, found elements of mass culture suitable means to express their emotions.

Postmodern art, transavantgardism or neo-expressionism, is influenced by the 'global village' (McLuhan, 1964) and shows an ironic cosmopolitanism. The Italian postmodernist painters Carlo Maria Mariani, Sandro Chia, and Mimmo Paladino are both Italian and international. Their 'Italianness' is between quotation marks. They live in the U.S. and borrow freely from Mediterranean traditions to create secondary meanings. Postmodern artists are not only painters, but painters and performers, photographers, architects, designers, and sculptors. Transavantgarde art adds up to a multimedia display.

Postmodern art is characterized by its layers of meanings. The surface may be quasi-classicistic. It can be enjoyed by different publics for different reasons. It is enigmatic and poses questions to the audience. Mythology, allegory, and narrative are characteristic of postmodern art. There is more concern for content, subject matter, symbolism, and meaning. While late modernists emphasized the esthetic dimension, postmodernists emphasize semantics.

Postmodern art shows an unrestrained use of colour, forms, shapes and styles, a wealth of imagination, and a carelessness towards orthodox artistic conformity. Elements of 'higher art' are freely intermingled with lesser forms of art. It gives the impression of a stylistic hotchpotch, an artistic supermarket, a collage or pastiche. Playfulness co-exists with cynicism. Attitudes range from irony to sarcasm. 'Lack of respect toward any convention' may be the best way of describing the attitude of transavantgarde artists.

According to Huyssen contemporary art is currently in the midst of a transition: 'Postmodern art of the eighties is marked by tension between tradition and innovation, conservatism and progressiveness, mass culture and serious culture. However, the latter is no longer given a privileged position over the former, and the old dichotomies and categories no longer function in the same old reliable way, e.g., progress versus reaction, left versus right, rationalism versus the irrational, future versus past, modernism versus realism, abstraction versus representation, avant-garde versus cheap rubbish' (Honnef, 1988, pp. 39–40).

5. Postmodern consumption

Although architecture and art are 'consumed' by people, and are thus examples of consumer behavior, we will now turn to the consumption of other products and services in the marketplace.

The main characteristics of the postmodern wave according to Toffler (1970) are: de-massification, fragmentation, individualization, and an increasing speed of change. Firat (1993) discerns five categories of the postmodern condition: hyperreality, fragmentation, reversal or production and consumption, decentering of the subject, and paradoxical juxtaposition of opposites. Some of Firat's categories will be followed but given a somewhat different meaning and interpretation. New categories will be added. It is obvious that these characteristics of postmodernity are just one attempt to chart recent cultural developments. Others may observe other trends or evaluate these trends differently. A postmodern attitude of pluralism and tolerance is really needed here.

The major causes of postmodern change are social and technological. Among the social changes may be mentioned: individualization, fragmentation, and paradoxical juxtapositions. Among technological changes, we will discuss: hyperreality, complexity, and value realization.

5.1 Social change

Individualization is a major trend. The 'postmodern household' has fewer members and the proportion of one-person households is increasing. More consumers will decide on their own consumption and more products are used individually. Many 'family consumer goods' become 'individual goods' (Sheth, 1983). Advertising has to follow the changed role patterns of the working woman and the househusband. Two-car families are no longer exceptional. Radios have become a personal medium; for example the Walkman and the car stereo. Many children possess their own hi-fi and television sets in their rooms.

Another social change is fragmentation with its many meanings. First, as dominant ideologies and value systems tend to disappear and are replaced by a plurality of values and norms, market segmentation can no longer be based on lifestyles that are valid over a number of product categories. Fragmentation also refers to the disjointed experiences with products, television programmes, commercials, and shopping malls. A bloody murder is followed by a candybar commercial, soap opera sex by a religious revival. The shopping mall contains a variety of stores: a bank office next to a porno shop, a singles bar close to an interfaith chapel (Kowinski, 1985, p. 72). There is little or no integration. In postmodern terms, this leads to more acceptance of strange combinations, paradoxical juxtapositions of opposites.

5.2 Technological change

New developments in electronic information processing and satellite transmission create possibilities for long-distance news films, simulation of reality on the computer and in the IMAX theater. News and events from the other side of the world reach us in almost real time. Media provide us with fantasy, fiction and non-fiction as entertainment and they blur the boundaries between these genres. The hyperreality of the media and the simulations partly replace 'actual reality' (whatever this may be).

Products become more complex. Video cassette recorders possess many functions. Personal computers and word processing programs require training courses to use them effectively. Cooking and heating food with the microwave oven requires other skills. Although consumers have higher education levels than ever before, they often feel that they are being the servants of their products 'following the instructions'. In postmodern terms, this is called the decentering of the subject.

Finally, the emphasis shifts from the technological production to the usage of goods. Not until consumers use products do they acquire the meanings and values they convey. Postmodernists call this the reversal of production and consumption (Firat, 1993). The impressive or expressive values are 'bought' with the acquisition of the goods, but actually manifested with the consumption of the product. Many products and brands possess an inherent 'packaged' hyperreality. This hyperreality is transferred to the user. It is the easy way of acquiring 'packaged meaning'. Toffler (1970) states that production and consumption coincide: prosumption. Value is produced when consumers add effort and appropriate meaning to the products they buy. A dinner at home is produced with purchased ingredients, some with 'packaged meaning and hyperreality', time, effort, skills and rituals of the consumer added.

6. Fragmentation

In modern times centralized authority is common; the postmodern era is the time of a decentralized pluralism and fragmentation. The lack of a central ideology or a small set of ideologies leads to a variety of norms, values and lifestyles adhered to by 'individualistic individuals'. Some media seem to have adapted to this pluralism by offering fragmented experiences and brief flashes of music, information and entertainment. MTV's program 'Postmodern' is a case in point. Some companies offer a variety of types and 'personalized versions' of their products and services as well. The fragmentation is thus not only on the demand but also on the supply side in the form of product differentiation.

The grand religious and political values and narratives lost their credibility. Authorities connected to these narratives lost their authority as well. The postmodern era is the time of secularization, scepticism and irony, disenchantment (as Max Weber called this) and a plurality of beliefs.

As the single ideology lost its dominance, so did the single lifestyle. Consumers adopt a certain lifestyle depending on the product domain (Van Raaij and Verhallen, 1992). Some authors even go further and state that consumers live by the moment, by their state-of-mind and mood, and should be segmented according to their momentary state. This is playfully called 'market sentimentation' (Michiels, 1992).

In fact, in the postmodern era all styles are permitted. No central authority dictates the style for the next season. No Parisian *haute couture*, but a variety of designers in London, Milan, New York, Paris and Tokyo propose their designs. Subcultures especially have an important impact on the introduction of new trends. Multiculturalism is accepted by many people. Fashion specialists have a hard time explaining which is the dominant style and which will be the dominant styles for the next season. Sometimes this is explained as a *fin de siècle* phenomenon, with the expectation that a new dominant style will develop during the next century. Pluralism will, however, not be temporary but is a permanent characteristic of the postmodern era.

The transition is from few styles to many genres. Not long ago, only one or two styles were dominant at a time. Either you were for Gothic revival or a hopeless pagan. Fashions, moral arguments, and conventions forced you into one camp or another. Now, scepticism is replacing dogmatism. The velocity of change is now much faster. Almost any style can be revived. Electicism is the buzzword. Superabundant choice and widespread pluralism force us to reassert a freedom of choice and comparative judgement. Combinations and oppositions create new alternative genres.

6.1 Disjointed experiences

The fragmentation of the information supply is mirrored by the fragmentation of experiences. Products, services and brands represent disconnected experiences, without linkages, contexts and historical roots (decontextualization). Postmodern consumers are encouraged by marketing messages and images to play a game of 'image switching'. They play the roles of the caring mother, the efficient manager, the loving partner, and the gourmet cook. Self-monitoring is on the increase (Snyder, 1987). Postmodern consumers seem not to possess one self-image but have many self-images adapted to the requirements of the situation. People are playful and serially promiscuous. The 'real self' is hidden behind many situational, role-played selves, if a real self still exists at all. Cindy Sherman and Madonna have multiple disguises.

The hyperrealistic collage leads to disjointed experiences and moments of excitement. But these experiences are basically 'light and empty' (Kundera, 1984). No central meaning, or historical or contextual connection provides integration and background. The Balinese culture became disconnected from its Hindu religious background and became a marketable commodity and a tourist spectacle. Many tourists, alienated from their religious background, visit churches as tourist attractions without understanding the meaning of the paintings and symbols. Beauty is a world betrayed (Urry, 1990). In the world of pastiche and collage, immediate sensory gratification is greatly enjoyed. Consumers watch short commercials, see flashes of billboards, numerous brands in the supermarket and department store, advertorials and infomercials. One wonders how consumers process these flashes, let alone integrate them.

Postmodernity means a freedom from constraints and conventions. Brand loyalty may decrease and fragment (Ogilvy, 1990). Attention to stimuli is not warranted. Each communication must attract attention for its own sake, must be exciting to the senses to be effective. Interest, attention and retention cannot be expected on the basis of relevance, context, linkages or connected representations.

6.2 Segmented production

In the modern era, mass production meant an endless repetition of the same products. Economies of scale were achieved by producing more of the same. In the postmodern era, mass-production is not necessarily producing more of the same, but more of different varieties and 'personalized versions' of a product (product differentiation). A Ford Sierra has now so many varieties in colors, accessories, engine types that one will seldom see two identical cars. The system can even be reversed: the buying decision comes before the production. Rather than producing and stocking a large variety of automobiles, customers may compose their own car (with engine types, accessories, colors and interiors) on a computer screen, and then order it as they like it. It will then be mass-produced upon customer's specification.

Products become isolated from their contexts and even from their original functions. Consumers, however, may attribute values and meanings to them independently of their original functions. This may go as far as 'sacralization' of products, such as collectors' items, dolls, automobiles, antiques, and 'cult items' (Belk *et al.*, 1989). Marketing practice is to glorify products and brands, and to represent them as independent representations of images. The 'Just do it!' ad for Nike shoes promotes liberation from traditional patterns. The brand is the image and the product user is the hero. Benetton became famous, and for some others notorious, for its anti-traditional and anti-racist advertising, promoting world harmony and tolerance. Benetton advertising became more and more detached from its clothing products.

The postmodern era is characterized by individualization, and initially individualization of inequality (Naumann and Hufner, 1985). Traditional social organizations of inequality, such as the family, social class, and trade union, may finally vanish. The father figure as the representative of social roles and conventions is lost. Individuals become their own 'identity managers' in the decisions to work or to study, to marry or to stay single, to take children or not, to adopt one lifestyle or another. As a consequence, there is a continuous search for styles and genres, for personal and collective identities (Harvey, 1990; Korthals, 1991).

Traditional values and norms are based on principles about society and men's relation to God. Postmodern values are less or non-principled. The new values seem to be: irreverence, nonconformity, noncommitment, detachment, anti-elitism, pragmatism, eclecticism, and tolerance.

6.3 Segmented media

Mass media are products of the modern era. Newspapers, magazines, and television channels are losing their large audiences. In 1973 US newspapers reached their peak with a circulation of 63 million copies daily. Since then, the newspapers are gradually losing their readership, not only to television, but also to local and specialized dailies and weeklies. *USA Today* and *Europe Today* represent a countertrend, largely due to their TV-style layout and information and their wide availability. Newspapers with a political ideology are most severely hit. Major general interest magazines, *Life*, *Look* and *Saturday Evening Post*, each went to its grave, and returned later in a more segmented version (Toffler, 1980).

At the same time, we witness a growth of special interest magazines, related to sports, hobbies, geography, gossip, health and fitness, for target groups as diverse as teenagers, retired people, hunters, scuba divers, and minorities. The number of radio and television channels is increasing as well, for local communities and for specific segments in society.

Between 1950 and 1970 the number of radio stations in the US doubled, whereas the population increased by 35%. Instead of one station for every 65,000 Americans, there is now a station for every 38,000. Broadcasting becomes narrowcasting. The segments in society receive tailored information from their own media. A diversity of media means a diversity of opinions and probably less consensus.

But the media are not perfectly segmented. We receive a diversity of often contradictory information. An exhaustive synthesis seems to be untenable. At best we receive 'video clips' of shattered information. Rather than receiving organized strings of information, we receive short, modular 'blips': ads, commands, theories, opinions, news flashes, that do not easily fall into pre-set categories and schemas. The postmodern man digests a 90-second news clip with a 30-second commercial, a headline, a cartoon, part of a song (Toffler, 1980, p. 166), and it is up to the receiver to make sense out of this, to connect and to categorize this overload of fragmented information. Journalists and advertisers alike have to attract the attention of consumers by providing 'exciting' and 'sensational' stimulation from amongst a clutter of others with similar stimulation. Madonna is a good example. She provokes, elicits protests and gets admiration, but remains a postmodern goddess with a detached attitude. In her film *Truth or Dare* she says: 'I do not endorse any lifestyle, I only describe one.'

7. Hyperreality

Simulations of the reality or hypes may become 'hyperreality'. According to semiotic analysis, simulations are signifiers referring to a signified reality (Eco, 1986). A documentary movie is a hyperreality, as it is referring to the 'objective' reality. Fiction may be called hyperreality, because there exists no corresponding reality. Signifiers may become detached from their signified reality and may become 'free floating'. Meaning structure analysis may explain the same phenomenon. Toothpaste is originally connected with the mundane reality of brushing your teeth. Brushing with a certain brand of toothpaste leads to the consequence of having white teeth, fresh breath, and finally to values such as attractiveness, sexiness, self-esteem, security and happiness. These values may be added to the brand over time through advertising. These new meanings (images) signify a new reality. This reality, when believed by the users of the brand feeling more sexy, secure and happy, becomes a hyperreality for them. In postmodern terms, the image does not only represent the product, but the product represents the image.

The reality thus created is 'hyper', because it is beyond the utilitarian and economic reality of modern times. It is a psychological and social reality for the brand users who feel this reality, communicate it to others through their usage behavior, and are judged by others in terms of this reality. Advertising is a powerful tool to add hyperreality to mundane products and brands. Advertising becomes part of the hyperreality. Advertising may even influence the experience of brand usage. Through advertising, *After Eight* acquired the hyperreality of an 'upper-class' mint chocolate. People may even evaluate the quality of *After Eight* as higher than other mint chocolates, although there may be no objective product differences.

As advertising adds hyperreality to products and services, it is difficult to define the concept of misleading advertising any more. The benefits of the product are not only physical/functional but psychosocial as well. Advertising is not only technical information about the product. Transformational advertising is 'potential experience' as part of the product. The 'augmented product' cannot exist without the hyperreality created and reinforced by advertising. The truthfulness of advertising can only be assessed after the experience of the product, in which the consumer is an important part of the experience. If the consumer believes the hyperreality of the advertising, the suggested reality may become self-fulfilling and thus 'true' (Postman, 1985).

Postmodernists often mention show business, Las Vegas, the Disney worlds and other fantasy and magic worlds as examples of hyperreality. Shopping malls like the ones in Edmonton (Alberta, Canada) and Bloomington (Minnesota) offer all the sights of IMAX and more. Many vacation and recreation parks possess hyperrealistic elements and non-authentic attractions, e.g. a 'tropical swimming park' with palm trees while it is freezing outside. The spectacle and the spectacular often are hyperreal: 'staged authenticity'. 'Escape' magazines, such as *Playboy*, and movies, such as James Bond, produce a hyper-reality for their watchers and readers. Numerous tourists visit the IMAX theater as they visit the Grand Canyon to 'really experience the Canyon'. Cities renovate the wharf and city center as images of the past. The 'Boston tea party' is simulated for tourists almost daily. *Son et lumière* shows conjure up the past and create a hyperreality.

In these examples a 'virtual reality' is created or enhanced with the help of media and theater, in order to provide the desired experiences to the audience. Computer simulation such as Cyberspace creates a virtual reality of buildings and scenery that may be used by architects and town planners to 'walk' through a not yet created built environment. Flight simulators are just a first step into cyberspace. The futuristic idea in the movie *Total Recall* may become true. A travel agency delivers a dream tour, realized in cyberspace without transporting the tourist over long distances. Media experiences thus compete with real experiences.

It may be expected that 'virtual reality' will become a new and exciting product/service. Through computer simulation, virtual realities may be created for the visual, auditory and even kinesthetic senses. How does it feel to fly at sound speed or to raft on a wild river? People no longer have to travel to distant sightseeing objects, but may experience being at the Great Wall of China or the Amazon river, while actually being at their local 'Omniver-sum' (Woolley, 1992).

Although hyperreality may have started as a 'rich and thick' meaning structure, the meaning may have become detached from the object ('free floating' as semioticians would say) and become only 'surface without substance'. Implications of hyperreality are thus: lack of context and loss of history. Hyperreality may consequently become a set of disjointed experiences. Examples are seen on television: news flashes, videoclips, superimposed images, animations, and 10-second commercials which create a visual image, pastiche and collage. Younger generations are more accustomed to television and movies than to print media, and thus more to visual rather than to textual information processing. The print media have become more pictorial and thus visual. Through media sponsorship and the merging of the editorial and advertising content of media brand names become an important part of this collage. Voyeuristic exposure to the spectacle seems to have become the cultural pastime. The duality of the appearance (surface) and the essence (substance) is largely dead in postmodernity. The surface is the essence and the medium is the 'message' (McLuhan, 1964).

8. Value realization

It is traditional rhetoric that value is created in the production of goods and destroyed in consumption. Later economists stated that value is created in the exchange of goods. Jean Baudrillard (1975, 1981) argues that value is sign-value, created during consumption. During consumption the image belonging to the product or brand is recreated as a benefit for the consumer. Marketing, emphasizing the satisfaction of needs, has always been postmodern in defending the belief that consumption is the end of production, both in the sense of the goal and the final state. But marketing is often focused on the act of purchasing rather than usage. Personal identity is created and recreated on the basis of usage rather than on the basis of production or purchase. Consumption becomes more important. Many people identify and communicate themselves by their consumptive activities, their sports, hobbies, or music preferences rather than their jobs.

In modern times, the image represents the product. But value is no longer a property of the product, but a property of the image. The product represents the image and the image is the reason of the consumer to buy and to use the product.

8.1 Confusion of subject and object

Toffler (1980) predicts the rise of the prosumer, a combination of producer and consumer. This is not a new phenomenon, because almost all services and products require an active input and participation of the consumer to enjoy the benefits. What is a restaurant dinner without the good mood and positive participation of the customers? The benefits of a novel are only enjoyed by reading it. A dinner at home requires ingredients from the marketplace and a lot of household production of preparing and cooking to obtain the pleasure of the meal. Do-it-yourself home maintenance, medical self-care, and 'distance education' are prosumptive activities on the increase.

In traditional rhetoric, the subject is the agent that acts through objects and situations to produce certain benefits and value realizations. Knowledge and independent behavior is possible through the Cartesian idea of the separation of mind and body. People are able to distance themselves from the experience of 'being' (the state most animals are in) to observe themselves and to develop a state of 'knowing'. The products of modernity are thus under the control and in the service of consumers in order to create benefits for themselves. Products are there to allow the achievement of human goals.

A postmodern decentering of the subject may be observed. Production and consumption are parts of the same cycle. Consumption choices and experiences tend to determine one's taste, values, lifestyle, skills, and ability for future behavior. Traditionally, individuals are the producers of benefits with the help of products as commodities. In postmodern terms, commodities seem to become the producers of benefits for individuals who follow the instructions correctly. There is confusion as to whether the subject or the object is in control (Hassan, 1980). The objects seem to determine the conditions and procedures of consumption. Consumers have to follow instructions in order to obtain the benefits and to avoid problems. Imagine the joy of the 'possessor' of a new telefax machine or personal computer after a troublesome series of trials and tribulations: 'It works!' Mastery of some products is only realized after a trial and training period. In an ironical way, one could state that consumers are there to allow products to achieve their functions.

'Being in control' is a major goal of postmodern consumers realizing that their hi-fi equipment, their fax and washing machines, VCRs, and personal computers, are often too complex to be mastered completely. Consumers often only use a limited set of the possible product functions, feel uneasy about the latent options and happy with at least the functions they actively master.

The confusion of subject and object is also present in the 'self-packaging' and 'self-marketing' of individuals. Consumers may perceive themselves as marketable items and manage their images as perceived by others, both in the job and in the social environment. This is described by the concept of self-monitoring (Snyder, 1987). Fashion becomes the metaphor for culture. Objectification and commodification of one's own body and self allows people 'to be consumed' by others, just like products fulfilling functions in the market place (Goffman, 1973; Hirschman, 1987). Individuals such as hostesses, reception-ists and television presenters become objects in expositions, offices, and shows. This com-modification of selves leads to beauty contests and, in the extreme case, to prostitution.

9. Paradoxical juxtapositions

The major characteristic of postmodern culture is its paradoxical nature. Anything may be combined with and juxtaposed to anything else. Creativity defined as the original combina-tion of elements is very postmodern. Even oppositional and contradictory emotions (love with hate) and cognitions (reverence with ridicule) can be expected. Irony and double meaning may be observed in art, architecture, music, products and advertising. In the UK, a brand of cigarettes became popular which was sold in a black package with a skull and the brand name Death. All warnings are clearly printed on the package including the message: '10 percent of profits donated to Cancer Research'.

Postmodern advertising is shocking for some and liberating for others. Ads show a newborn baby or a dying Aids patient with the United Colors of Benetton. Many ads show no product at all but attract attention with a bizarre combination of visuals and impressions. The pastiche of flashes seems to be basically unrelated to the product or the brand, although the ads may elicit positive sensations and emotions without any deep meaning.

The modern era was a time of rigid structures and consistency. The postmodern era requires a kaleidoscopic sensibility and tolerance. It brings a taste for variety, incongruity, heterogeneity, irony, double meaning, and paradox. Daily newspapers bring us a strange variety of 'news'. News-stands are overloaded with special-interest magazines. In the films of Federico Fellini, a mad competition of opposite tastes create hilarious misunderstandings and sadness. Not everyone likes this kaleidoscope of pluralism. Most people make their choice and restrict themselves to one or two genres. This loyalism makes the plurality work coherently. But even if everybody is limited to a few minority taste cultures, there remains a residual taste for pluralism.

As a dominant ideology or style is absent, there is a demand in the public sphere for lifestyle and identity information. People and media provide information and demonstrations of how to behave, how to talk, and what should be done and avoided. People, television programmes, popular magazines and advertising tell us what is 'in' and what is 'absolutely impossible'. Television is very appropriate for communication on lifestyle. It tells intimate stories of how people give sense to their lives and solve life problems. Behaviour and language of actors and pop singers can easily be imitated.

Most characteristic of the postmodern era is its openness. We are informed about conflicts, viewpoints, styles, and opinions from all over the world. Emancipation of women and homosexuals created a pluralism accepted by many. A cosmopolitan attitude leads to more acceptance of differences: from exclusion to inclusion. In the postmodern era we look to the past and to other cultures with irony and displacement. We may return to 'modern times', if we want or if we need. It is not a disruption. Previous conditions are included in the present, postmodern condition.

Anything is at once acceptable and suspect. On the one hand, postmodernism is liberating, on the other hand, it is frustrating for persons seeking radical transformation of society, since nothing is sufficiently credible to merit commitment. In a fragmented culture, organized action for political and social change is almost impossible. This makes the market the dominant domain of legitimation. Anything can be tried and dropped. No emotional or cognitive commitment beyond a single purchase or trial is needed. Consumers are immersed in a sea of impressions and experiences but are not taken seriously if they oppose this immersion. The market becomes the great assimilator (Firat, 1993). The market absorbs all kinds of protest and rebellion. Punk protest becomes emptied and commodified as a fashion.

The media become dominated by the 'market'. Editors agree that their articles are sponsored by advertisers. The newsworthiness of events is determined by the market. News programmes on commercial television, the covers and articles of magazines are designed to attract audiences and buyers. Voters become buyers of carefully 'designed' political candidates rather than political programs. The American presidential elections are built on, often commercial, campaign funds, advertising, and the 'right' issues at the 'right' time. Poll taking and market research have very similar functions. The roles of citizen and consumer become similar and seem to merge. Marketing becomes an imperialistic art and science, dominating Western culture and society at the 'end of history' (Fukuyama, 1992).

10. Conclusions and discussion

Postmodernism is not a single cultural style and thus not an '-ism' but an increasing pluralism of styles and genres. The absence of a dominant ideology is liberating on the one side but creates insecurity and an *embarras des choix* on the other side. This pluralism is reflected in architecture, art, literature, music and consumption. In this paper, the major postmodern conditions in consumption are: fragmentation, hyperreality, value realization later in the consumption cycle, and paradoxical juxtapositions of opposites. Research methodology has to adapt to the changed conditions, emphasizing naturalistic observation, contextualization, maximized comparisons and sensitized concepts.

The consequences for consumer research, marketing, and consumer policy are manifold. For some postmodernism is something to be 'against'. For others it is something to be 'celebrated'. Consumer policy may set itself the goal of warning consumers of this postmodern nonsense or it may include postmodernity in its policy.

In postmodern societies, marketing may play a key role in giving meaning to life through consumption. Is marketing with its value realization replacing ideologies and religion? And is this a good thing for mankind? Value realization through consumption may be practical and utilitarian. In this sense it is not replacing ideology. Value realization may be hedonic and momentary and is thus often superficial and ego-centered. Self-marketing is mostly self-centered, as it is concerned with improving one's own position and welfare among others. Although marketing may induce people to donate money to 'good causes', such as the Red Cross and Greenpeace, by appealing to their guilt feelings, it is certainly not enough to give 'real' meaning to one's life. Dostoevsky's sinister warning may apply: 'If there is no God, everything is permissible.' Or Durkheim's: 'If the normative grip of society slackens, the moral order will collapse' (Bauman, 1992). A return of the 'lost father' (Van Gennep, 1989) of ideology or religion may be expected to fill the gap of values not really realized by brands and their marketing.

References

Baudrillard, J. (1975). *The Mirror of Production*. St Louis, MO: Telos.

Baudrillard, J. (1981). *For a Critique of the Political Economy of the Sign*. St Louis, MO: Telos.

Bauman, Z. (1992). *Intimations of Postmodernity*. London & New York: Routledge.

Belk, R.W., M. Wallendorf and J.F. Sherry Jr. (1989). 'The sacred and the profane in consumer behavior: Theodicy on the Odyssey', *Journal of Consumer Research*, **16**, 1–38.

Bell, D. (1962). *The End of Ideology. On the Exhaustion of Political Ideas in the Fifties*. New York: Free Press (revised edn.).

Berman, M. (1981). *The Reenchantment of the World*. Ithaca, NY: Cornell University Press.

Chambers, I. (1990). *Border Dialogues. Journeys in Postmodernity*. Comedia Book, London & New York: Routledge.

Eco, U. (1986). *Travels in Hyperreality*. San Diego, CA: Harcourt Brace Jovanovich [translation from Italian].

Firat, A.F. (1993). 'Postmodernity: A marketing age'. *Journal of Marketing*.

Fukuyama, F. (1992). *The End of History and the Last Man*. New York: Free Press.

Goffman, E. (1973). *The Presentation of the Self in Everyday Life*. Woodstock, NY: Overlook Press.

Harvey, D. (1990). *The Condition of Postmodernity*. Oxford: Basil Blackwell.

Hassan, I. (1980). 'The question of postmodernism', in H.R. Garvin (ed.), *Romanticism, Modernism, Postmodernism* (pp. 117–126). Lewisberg, PA: Bucknell University Press.

Hirschman, E.C. (1987). 'People as products: Analysis of a complex marketing exchange', *Journal of Marketing*, **51**, 98–108.

Honnef, K. (1988). *Contemporary Art*. Cologne: Taschen.

Inglehart, R. (1977). *The Silent Revolution. Changing Values and Political Styles among Western Publics*. Princeton, NJ: Princeton University Press.

Inglehart, R. (1989). *Culture Shift in Advanced Industrial Society*. Princeton, NJ: Princeton University Press.

Jencks, C. (1987). *What is Post-Modernism?* New York: Academy Editions (second printing).

Korthals, M. (1991). 'Mass media and lifestyle rationalization', *Massacommunicatie*, **19**, 291–301.

Kowinski, W.S. (1985). *The Malling of America: An Inside Look at the Great Consumer Paradise*. New York: William Morrow.

Kundera, M. (1984). *The Unbearable Lightness of Being*. London: Faber & Faber.

Lyotard, J.-F. (1984). *The Postmodern Condition: A Report on Knowledge*. Manchester: Manchester University Press (original in French: 1979).

Lyotard, J.-F. (1986). *L'Enthousiasme. La critique Kantienne de l'histoire* [*Enthusiasm. The Kantian Critique of History*]. Paris: Editions Galilée.

Mamiya, C.J. (1992). *Pop Art and Consumer Culture: American Supermarket*. Austin, TX: University of Texas Press.

March, A. (1975). 'The "silent revolution" value priorities and quality of life in Britain', *American Political Science Review*, **69**, 21–30.

McLuhan, M. (1964). *Understanding Media*. London: Routledge & Kegan Paul.

Michiels, T. (1992). *Individu – moment en mediaselectie* [*Individual – moment and media selection*]. Blad/ Dossier, No. 4.

Naumann, J. and K. Hufner (1985). 'Evolutionary aspects of individual and social development', in J. Naumann and K. Hufner (eds.), *Individual Development and Social Change*. New York: Academic Press.

Ogilvy, J. (1990). 'This postmodern business', *Marketing and Research Today*, **18**, 4–21.

Postman, N. (1985). *Amusing Ourselves to Death: Public Discourse in the Age of Show Business*. New York: Penguin Books.

Sherry, J.F., Jr. (1991). 'Postmodern alternatives: The interpretive turn in consumer research', in T.S. Robertson and H.H. Kassarjian (eds.), *Handbook of Consumer Behavior* (pp. 548–591). Englewood Cliffs, NJ: Prentice-Hall.

Sheth, J.N. (1983). 'Emerging trends in the retailing industry', *Journal of Retailing*, **59** (Fall), 5–18.

Snyder, M. (1987). *Public Appearances. Private Realities*. New York: Freeman.

Toffler, A. (1970). *Future Shock*. Toronto: Bantam Books.

Toffler, A. (1980). *The Third Wave*. Toronto: Bantam Books.

Urry, J. (1990). *The Tourist Gaze: Leisure and Travel in Contemporary Societies*. London: Sage.

Van Gennep, F.O. (1990). *De Terugkeer van de Verloren Vader* [*The Return of the Lost Father*]. Baarn: Ten Have (fourth printing).

Van Raaij, W.F. and T.M.M. Verhallen (1992). 'Domain-specific market segmentation', *Papers on Economic Psychology*, **93**, Erasmus University, Rotterdam.

Woolley, B. (1992). *Virtual Worlds. A Journey in Hype and Hyperreality*. Oxford: Blackwell.

Toward a theory of the universal content and structure of values: Extensions and cross-cultural replications

● ●

Shalom H. Schwartz
The Hebrew University of Jerusalem

Wolfgang Bilsky
Kriminologisches Forschungsinstitut Niedersachsen e. V., Hanover

Summary

The universality of Schwartz and Bilsky's (1987) theory of the psychological content and structure of human values was examined with data from Australia, Finland, Hong Kong, Spain, and the United States. Smallest space analyses of the importance ratings that individuals assigned to values revealed the same 7 distinct motivational types of values in each sample as had emerged earlier in samples from Germany and Israel: achievement, enjoyment, maturity, prosocial, restrictive conformity, security, self-direction. Social power, studied only in Hong Kong, also emerged. The structural relations among the value types suggest that the motivational dynamics underlying people's value priorities are similar across the societies studied, with an exception in Hong Kong. The interests that values serve (individual vs. collective) and their goal type (instrumental vs. terminal) also distinguish values in all samples.

Recently, we proposed a theory of a universal psychological structure of human values (Schwartz and Bilsky, 1987). This theory identifies the facets necessary to define human values and specifies the types of value contents (called *motivational domains*) that people from all cultures are likely to distinguish (e.g. achievement, security). The theory derives these types from a set of universal human requirements. The theory is not merely a typology; rather, it develops rationales for dynamic relations among value priorities. It suggests which types of values fit together compatibly (e.g. prosocial and security) and which are opposed (self-direction and restrictive conformity). To support the theory, we presented data on the values of Israeli teachers and German college students.

Theories that aspire to universality, like this one, must be tested in numerous, culturally diverse samples. The current research examines data from a set of five societies

From the *Journal of Personality and Social Psychology*, 58(5), 1990, 878–91.

characterized by substantial socioeconomic, cultural, linguistic, and geographical diversity (that of Australia, the United States, Hong Kong, Spain, and Finland). Theory testing was strengthened by using different methods to measure values and by studying groups of differing educational levels. In addition to replicating the Israeli and German analyses, we seek to refine and extend elements of the theory by examining questions about the basic dimensions of values. To place these questions in perspective, we develop them in the course of an overview of the original theory.

Theory and questions

In Schwartz and Bilsky (1987), we generated a conceptual definition of values that incorporated five formal features that recurred in relevant literature. Values (a) are concepts or beliefs, (b) pertain to desirable end states or behaviors, (c) transcend specific situations, (d) guide selection or evaluation of behavior and events, and (e) are ordered by relative importance.

We then derived a comprehensive typology of the content domains of values on the basis of the following reasoning. There are three universal human requirements to which all individuals and societies must be responsive: needs of individuals as biological organisms, requisites of coordinated social interaction, and survival and welfare needs of groups. These requirements must be represented cognitively, taking the form of values. Through socialization and cognitive development, individuals learn to represent the requirements as conscious goals and values, to use culturally shared terms to communicate about these goals and values, and to attribute varying degrees of importance to them.

Goal type

The first facet in the definition of values, specified by the theory, is their classification as representing either *terminal goals* (end states; e.g. equality, wisdom) or *instrumental goals* (modes of behavior; e.g. capable, obedient). This classification is a common feature of value definitions (Lovejoy, 1950; Rescher, 1969; Rokeach, 1973) and of scales that operationalize values (Braithwaite and Law, 1985; Levy, 1985; Rokeach, 1973). This facet received empirical support in analyses of the importance ratings of values from the Rokeach value lists in both the Israeli and the German data (Schwartz and Bilsky, 1987). That is, terminal and instrumental values were easily distinguished as occupying different regions in a two-dimensional projection of the multidimensional space that represented the correlations among all the values.

This support notwithstanding, we question the need for a terminal/instrumental facet in a refined theory. Consider the grounds for this question. Conceptually, the distinction between ends and means is not clear-cut; an end can easily become a means and vice versa (Dewey, 1957). Terminal values (e.g. pleasure) sometimes serve as instrumental for promoting other terminal values (e.g. happiness), and instrumental values (helpful) can become ends to be promoted by other instrumental values (self-controlled; Rokeach, 1973). Moreover, people given the terminal/instrumental conceptual distinction and asked to sort values into these two categories did not distinguish clearly between them (Heath and Fogel, 1978).

Why then were terminal and instrumental values discriminated empirically in the Israeli and German analyses? Consider two alternatives to viewing this discrimination as evidence that the facet is conceptually meaningful. First, the two types of values appeared on separate lists and on different pages, so discrimination may have been an artifact of location. Item locations can influence responses so as to produce distinguishable regions in multi-dimensional space (L. Guttman, personal communication, 14 June 1987). Second, a formal, grammatical feature of the values may explain the discrimination. Terminal values are phrased as nouns, and instrumental values are phrased as adjectives, completely confounding the conceptual and grammatical distinctions.

The grammatical phrasing of values did not vary in two current samples. Hence, we can test the confounded conceptual/grammatical explanation against the location explanation. In Finland, instrumental values were transformed into terminal values (ambitious to ambition, honest to honesty), so that all values were phrased as nouns. In Hong Kong, the terminal/instrumental distinction was indeterminate, because Chinese is a pictographic language that does not distinguish nouns from adjectives. However, in both these samples, the values usually phrased as terminal were located first in the questionnaire, and those usually phrased as instrumental followed. Clear terminal and instrumental regions in the Finnish and Hong Kong data would point to location rather than to conceptual/grammatical distinctiveness as the cause of past empirical evidence for this discrimination. The failure of such regions to emerge would support a conceptual/grammatical explanation of past findings.

Interests served

In our definition of values, the second facet (which is based on the idea that values are goals) is the designation of whose interests the attainment of each value serves. Values may serve individualistic interests (e.g. pleasure, independent), collective interests (e.g. equality, responsible), or both types of interests (e.g. wisdom). Individualism/collectivism is a major dimension of value differentiation at both societal levels (Hofstede, 1980; Mead, 1967) and individual levels (Schwartz, in press; Triandis, 1987; Triandis, Bontempo, Villareal, Asai and Lucca, 1988).

The idea that the interests that values serve systematically influence the importance people attribute to them received strong support in analyses of the German and Israeli data (Schwartz and Bilsky, 1987). One two-dimensional projection of the multidimensional space that represented the correlations among all the values could be partitioned into separate collective, individualistic, and combined regions in both samples. Moreover, 34 of 36 values fell in the interests region predicted for them.

Societies vary substantially in the emphasis their members give to individualism versus collectivism (Hofstede, 1980). This may affect which interests individuals believe that particular values serve and even the very notion that interests are a defining characteristic of values. It is therefore important to investigate this facet in societies that vary across the full range of individualism/collectivism. Germany and Israel are quite similar on this dimension, according to Hofstede's data. Of 40 nations ranked for their emphasis on individualism, Germany was 16th and Israel was 20th.

The societies in the current study differed much more in Hofstede's analysis. They held ranks: 1 (United States), 2 (Australia), 18 (Finland), 21 (Spain), and 32 (Hong Kong). Other studies also indicated that the United States is near the individualism extreme and Hong Kong is near the collectivism extreme, with the other countries spread between them (Chinese Culture Connection, 1987; Leung, 1987; Triandis, 1987). Moghaddam (1987; cf. Yang and Yue, 1988) challenged the view that individualism and collectivism are opposite poles of a single dimension. He suggested that they may be polarized only in Western societies, which makes it crucial to study this facet in an Eastern country like Hong Kong.

We address the following questions: Do values emerge in distinctive regions that reflect the interests they serve, regardless of societal emphases on individualism/collectivism? Assuming that type of interest does generate distinctive value regions, are there systematic departures from the expected locations of particular values? This would indicate the impact of individualism/collectivism emphases on how societal members understand particular values.

Motivational domains: content

The third, and to us the most interesting, facet in the definition of values is the motivational domains: the universal types of motivational concern that values express. Earlier (Schwartz and Bilsky, 1987), we derived seven distinct motivational domains from three universal human requirements. The motivational domain *security* was derived, for example, from the basic need of organisms and of groups to protect themselves against threats to their integrity. *Restrictive conformity* was derived from the prerequisite of smooth interaction and group survival that individuals restrain impulses and inhibit actions that might hurt others. We also pointed to motivational concepts in the social science literature that these domains subsume, and we specified values from the Rokeach lists that might serve as markers for each domain.

The following are capsule definitions of the motivational domains, each definition specifying the goal that the domain represents. This will enable readers to assess whether the values emerge in appropriate domains in the cultures studied here.

Prosocial. Active protection or enhancement of the welfare of others.
Restrictive conformity. Restraint of actions and impulses likely to harm others and to violate sanctioned norms.
Enjoyment. Pleasure, sensuous and emotional gratification.
Achievement. Personal success through demonstrated competence.
Maturity. Appreciation, understanding, and acceptance of oneself, others, and the surrounding world.
Self-direction. Independent thought and action – choosing, creating, exploring.
Security. Safety, harmony, and stability of society, of groups with whom one identifies, of relationships, and of self.

The theoretical claim that people's values are organized by these seven types of motivation received strong support in the empirical analyses. In both samples, the seven motivational domains were readily identifiable in 1 two-dimensional projection of the multidimensional space that represented the correlations among all the values. The domains formed seven wedge-shaped regions emerging from a common origin (cf. Figure 1), and almost all of the marker values fell into regions corresponding with their predicted motivational domain.

Regarding the seven motivational domains of values, we ask, Are all of them present in all the cultures? Do the same specific values constitute each motivational domain in all of the cultures?[1] On the basis of the conceptual definitions of the motivational domains and of the specific values, we hypothesized that each value is located in the domain listed next to it in the first column of Table 1. Because these values were not selected to represent pure motivational domains, some relate conceptually to more than one domain, as indicated.

Variation in the domain location of a particular value suggests nonequivalence in the meaning of that value across cultures. Knowledge about each culture can be used to interpret such variations. Restraint must be exercised in interpreting unique variations, however, because we expect some chance errors when distributing 36 values into seven domains.

We further ask, do additional motivational domains emerge in any of the cultures? That is, are the values arrayed in space in a manner that reveals a new interpretable region? We anticipate no new motivational domains in the four samples where the same 36 values studied previously were used. However, in the Hong Kong data, where four values (from Ng et al., 1982) were added, we hypothesize that a power domain will appear.

We derived a power domain earlier (Schwartz and Bilsky, 1987) but were unable to study it because the Rokeach (1973) lists lacked appropriate marker values. The motivational goal of power is social status and prestige, control and dominance over people and resources. Values added in Hong Kong that could serve as markers (each with the parenthetical

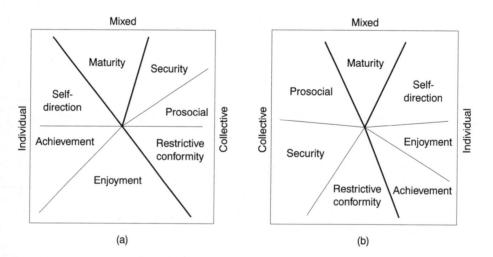

(a) (b)

Figure 1 Structural relations among motivational domains of values from smallest space analysis: (a) observed for an Israeli sample and hypothesized as a general model; (b) observed for a German sample.

explanation that accompanied it) were *power* (position of authority and importance), *self-determination* (ability to determine one's destiny), and *equity* (each person rewarded according to how much contribution he or she has made). Valuing equity signifies a desire for status and control because it implies that effort should lead to differential, not to equal, reward and hence to the accumulation of status and power. A fourth added value, *social justice* (fairness, no discrimination), should emerge in the prosocial domain.

Motivational domains: structure

The final set of hypotheses generated from the theory specifies dynamic relations among the motivational domains of values. We theorize that the psychological, practical, and social consequences of pursuing or expressing values from the different domains organize people's value preferences. For example, actions intended to foster equality (a prosocial value) are likely to conflict with actions intended to pursue a comfortable life (enjoyment). On the other hand, actions that express wisdom (maturity) are compatible with actions that express independence (self-direction).

Briefly, we reason that simultaneous pursuit of values from the following sets of domains is compatible: (a) prosocial, restrictive conformity, and security – because all support smooth social relations, (b) achievement and enjoyment – because both are concerned with self-enhancement, and (c) maturity and self-direction – because both express comfort with or reliance on one's unique experience and capacities. Consequently, we hypothesize that the domains in each of these sets are contiguous in the empirical mapping of motivational domains. This was confirmed in both earlier samples. The schematic mapping in Figure 1 shows the arrangement of domains corresponding to the Israeli and German results.

We further reason that simultaneous pursuit of values in the following sets of domains is contradictory: (a) self-direction versus restrictive conformity – emphasizing own independent thought and action contradicts conforming self-restraint, (b) prosocial versus achievement – emphasizing concern for others interferes with pursuing personal success, (c) enjoyment versus prosocial – emphasizing own pleasure and comfort contradicts devoting oneself to others' welfare, (d) achievement versus security – emphasizing pursuit of success is likely to upset harmonious social relations. These hypothesized oppositions were confirmed in the empirical mappings of the regions occupied by the motivational domains in both earlier samples. Each domain emerged from the common origin in a direction opposed to that of the domains whose pursuit was postulated to conflict with it (cf. Figure 1), though (c) was weak in the Israeli sample and (d) was weak in the German sample.

As noted earlier, the interests that values serve are also expected to structure their relations. By definition, achievement, enjoyment, and self-direction values serve individualistic interests; prosocial and restrictive conformity values serve collective interest. Maturity values are mixed. Security values serve collective interests, but one individualistic value (inner harmony) is also included in this domain. We therefore hypothesize that the domains are grouped empirically by interest, just as they were in both earlier samples (cf. Figure 1).

Our key question regarding value structure is: Are the dynamics of conflict and compatibility among the motivational domains similar across cultures? If so, this would imply that the major social and psychological processes that structure value systems are

Table 1 Predicted and observed locations of values in motivational domains

Value	Predicted	Australia	United States	Hong Kong[a]	Spain	Finland[a]	Germany	Israel
				Terminal				
Comfortable life	ENJ	ENJ	ENJ	ENJ	ENJ	ENJ	ENJ	ENJ
Exciting life	ACH/SD	SD	ACH	ACH	ACH	ACH	SD	ACH
A sense of accomplishment	ACH/SD	ACH	SD	ACH	MAT	ENJ	ACH	SD
A world at peace	PS/SEC	PS (sec)	PS	SEC	PS	PS (sec)	PS	SEC (ps)
A world of beauty	MAT	MAT	MAT	MAT	MAT	PS	MAT	MAT
Equality	PS	PS	PS	PS	PS	PS	PS	PS
Family security	SEC	SEC	SEC	SEC	SEC	SEC	SEC	SEC
Freedom	SD/SEC	SD	SEC	ACH	MAT	SD	SD	SEC
Happiness	ENJ	ENJ	ENJ	ENJ	ENJ	ENJ	ENJ	ENJ
Inner harmony	SEC/MAT	SEC	SEC	SEC	MAT	MAT	MAT	SEC (mat)
Mature love	MAT	MAT	MAT	SEC	MAT	MAT	MAT	MAT
National security	SEC	RC / ENJ	SEC	SEC	RC / ENJ	SEC	SEC	SEC
Pleasure	ENJ	ENJ	ENJ	ENJ	PS	ENJ	ENJ	ENJ
Salvation (belief in God)	PS/SEC	SEC (ps)	PS	PS		PS	PS	PS
Self-respect	MAT/SD	ACH	MAT	SD (mat)	MAT	MAT	MAT	SD
Social recognition	ACH	ACH	ACH	ACH	ACH	ACH	ACH	ACH
True friendship	PS/SEC	SEC	PS	SEC	PS	PS	PS	MAT
Wisdom	MAT	MAT	MAT	MAT	MAT	MAT	MAT	MAT

Table 1 (continued)

Value	Predicted	Australia	United States	Hong Kong[a]	Spain	Finland[a]	Germany	Israel
			Instrumental					
Ambitious	ACH	ACH	ACH	ACH	ACH	ACH	ACH	ACH
Broadminded	SD/MAT	SD (mat)	SD (mat)	MAT (sd)	MAT	SD	MAT	SD
Capable	ACH	ACH	ACH	ACH	ACH	ACH	_SD_	ACH
Cheerful	ENJ	ENJ	ENJ	ENJ	ENJ	_MAT_	_ENJ_	ENJ
Clean	RC	RC	RC	PS/_MAT_	RC	_RC_	RC	RC
Courageous	MAT	MAT	MAT	_MAT_	MAT		MAT	MAT
Forgiving	PS	PS	PS	PS	PS	_SD_/PS	PS	PS
Helpful	PS	PS	PS	PS	PS	PS	PS	PS
Honest	PS	_SEC_/SD	PS	PS	PS	PS	PS	PS
Imaginative	SD	SD	SD	SD	SD	SD	SD	SD
Independent	SD	SD	SD	SD	SD	SD	SD	SD
Intellectual	SD	SD	SD	SD	SD	SD	SD	SD
Logical	SD	SD	SD	SD	_ACH_/PS	_ACH_/PS	SD	SD
Loving	PS	PS	PS	PS	PS	PS	_SD_/RC	PS
Obedient	RC	RC	RC	RC	RC	RC	RC	RC
Polite	RC	RC	RC	RC	RC	RC	RC	RC
Responsible	SEC/RC	RC	SEC	RC	SEC	PS	SEC	SEC
Self-controlled	RC	RC	_SEC_	RC	RC	PS/_ENJ_	RC	RC

Note. Capital letters indicate unequivocal placement; underlined letters indicate placements that do not fit predictions; lowercase letters in parentheses indicate borderline placement in which a priori expectations suggest that the value may belong in the parenthetical motivational domain. ENJ = enjoyment; ACH = achievement; SD = self-direction; MAT = maturity; PS = prosocial; SEC = security; RC = restrictive conformity.

[a] In Hong Kong and Finland, there was no terminal/instrumental distinction in phrasing of the values (see text).

universal. Operationally, the question is, Do the observed sets of opposing and contiguous domains replicate in five more cultures? Because societies differ in socialization patterns, in prevailing norms, and in the organization of basic social units, one might expect differences in the values whose pursuit is experienced as compatible or contradictory. For example, some descriptions of Chinese culture suggest that achievement is often viewed as serving the collectivity (Hsu, 1981; but cf. King and Bond, 1985). Achievement might therefore be compatible with and promote prosocial and security goals in the Hong Kong sample.

Though not predicted, an opposition between maturity and restrictive conformity values was observed in the Israeli and German samples. We now hypothesize that this opposition will replicate in other cultures. We base this on reasoning that the emphasis on self-restraint and self-abnegation inherent in valuing restrictive conformity contradicts the open acceptance of self, others, and the world that characterizes maturity values.

Last, we hypothesize that power, studied for the first time in the Hong Kong sample, is an individualistic domain located next to achievement, which it most resembles in content. We also hypothesize that the power region is located in a direction opposed to the prosocial region, because an emphasis on dominating others conflicts with a concern for their well-being. Although power may be used for collective welfare (King and Bond, 1985), we postulate that its basic goal is self-serving, even in so-called collectivist cultures. Compatible with this hypothesis, Bond (1988) found a bipolar factor opposing power and achievement values to interpersonal prosocial values, even though most of the cultures in his pancultural analysis were collectivist.

Method

We compared the findings and drew conclusions from data for seven countries, including the earlier German and Israeli samples. We therefore describe the methods used in the latter as well.

Samples

Germany

In 1984, 331 students from five colleges and teachers' seminaries completed a German version of the survey in group sessions. Of these, 176 were students of administration, and 155 were preparing to become teachers. The median age was 22, and 66% were female.

Israel

In 1983–84, 455 6th- through 9th-grade teachers from 22 urban public schools completed a Hebrew version of the survey during staff meetings. Of these, 276 completed the full 36-value survey, and the remainder ranked only the 18 terminal values. Correlations are based on all those who ranked a given pair of values. The median age was 35, and 84% were female.

Australia

In 1969, 479 first-year undergraduate students of diverse majors at Flinders University completed the English version of the survey in group sessions. We estimate the median age to be 19 and the percentage of women to be 40. The data were gathered by Norman Feather and described in Feather (1975) and in Feather and Peay (1975).

United States

In 1968, a representative national sample of 1,409 adults individually completed the English version of the survey. The median age was 45, and 53% were female. The data were gathered by the National Opinion Research Center (NORC) and published in Rokeach (1973).

Hong Kong

During 1983–84, 424 undergraduate students of diverse majors at the Chinese University of Hong Kong completed a Chinese version of the survey in group sessions. The median age was the early 20s, and about half were female. Michael Bond gathered and provided the data.

Spain

During 1984–85, 441 undergraduate students of diverse majors at the University of Barcelona completed a Spanish version of the survey in group sessions. The median age was the early 20s, and about half were female. Frederico Javaloy gathered and provided the data.

Finland

In 1982, a sample of 184 adult residents of a small coastal village, with occupational and educational distributions representative of the country, individually completed a Finnish version of the survey. The median age was 38, and about 46% were female. Klaus Helkama and Antti Uutela gathered and provided the data.

Procedure

All of the survey forms were based on the original Rokeach (1973) 36-value English version. The values were presented in alphabetical order. Translations were prepared locally. Aspects of the procedures that varied across samples are relevant for assessing the robustness of the theory; thus they are described in the next paragraphs.

Ranking versus rating

In the United States, Australia, Spain and Finland, respondents first ranked the 18 terminal values from most to least important and then ranked the 18 instrumental values in the same way. In Germany and Israel, after ranking the values in a list, respondents compared each adjacent pair of values and indicated on a 7-point scale how much more important was each value than the value ranked immediately below it. Value importance ratings were computed for each person by scoring the value ranked least important as 1 and assigning to each higher ranked value a score consisting of the sum of all the value comparison scores for the values below it plus 1. Ratings ranged from 1 to 104. In Hong Kong, respondents rated each of their values on a 9-point scale ranging from (1) *no importance for me at all* to (9) *supreme importance for me*.

Criterion

The criterion of evaluation in all samples but Hong Kong was the importance of the values 'as a guiding principle in my life'. In Hong Kong, values were rated for their importance 'to me personally'.

Format

In the United States, Germany, and Israel, values were printed on gummed labels that respondents arranged in order of importance. In Australia, Spain, Finland, and Hong Kong, respondents wrote numbers next to the values to indicate their importance.

Distinctiveness of terminal and instrumental values

In all samples but Finland and Hong Kong, the terminal values appeared on a first list, and the instrumental values appeared on a second, separate list. The former were phrased as nouns; the latter were phrased as adjectives. In Finland, values were also presented on two lists, but the values in the second list were phrased as nouns. Thus, the usual instrumental values were transformed into terminal values. In Hong Kong, all values were presented in a single list. The four new values were added in Positions 19, 20, 21, and 40. Moreover, terminal values were not differentiated from instrumental values by phrasing, because Chinese does not distinguish nouns from adjectives.

Analysis

In all samples but the Australian sample, the analyses were based on an intercorrelation matrix of Pearson product–moment correlations between the importance rankings or ratings of the values. In Australia, Spearman rho correlations were used. The intercorrelation matrixes were analyzed with the Guttman–Lingoes Smallest Space Analysis (SSA; Guttman, 1968). This is one of a variety of nonmetric multidimensional scaling (MDS) techniques for structural analysis of similarity data (Davison, 1983; Guttman, 1968; see Canter, 1985, for an introduction to SSA and for applications). Three- and four-dimensional solutions were specified in advance on theoretical grounds: the hypothesized terminal/instrumental distinction implies a projection on two axes, and the hypothesized interests-served and motivational domains facets imply a second projection on other axes.

When more than two dimensions are specified, MDS programs generate a series of two-dimensional projections of the multidimensional space. Our application of the SSA is what Davison (1983) called 'configural verification'. That is, our hypotheses specify the number of dimensions and the configuration that should be formed by the stimulus points on the two-dimensional projections. The MDS axes are not assumed to have substantive meaning because they are arbitrary. Rather, we interpret the regions formed by groupings of substantively related points and the ordering of these regions. The *a priori*, theoretical specification of the items expected to constitute the contents of each region makes it possible to draw boundaries among the points that fill the two-dimensional space.

Regions are generally not clusters discernible by empty space around them. The content universe is conceived as a geometrical space in which the specific values are but a sample of all conceivable values comprising the total space with points everywhere. This means that some values at the edge of one region may correlate less with other values of the same region than they do with certain values on the edge of neighboring regions. Partition lines may be straight or curved, as long as they yield regions having continuous boundaries that do not intersect with the boundaries of other regions (Lingoes, 1977, 1981). For discussions of the interpretation of SSA and comparisons of MDS techniques with factor and cluster analysis, see Guttman (1977, 1982), Canter (1985), Davison (1983), and Shye (1985, 1988).

We accomplished the division into meaningful regions in our data by drawing partition lines according to the facets used to define and specify the types of values. According to our hypotheses, the space of one projection should be partitionable into regions that represent terminal versus instrumental values, and the space of another projection should be partitionable into wedge-shaped regions representing motivational domains.

Results

For testing the hypotheses, the four-dimensional solution of the SSA proved adequate in all samples (excluding Australia)[2] according to two criteria. First, the coefficient of alienation for this solution indicated a reasonable fit (<0.13 in five samples and <0.17 in Finland) that was little improved in a five-dimensional solution. Second, visual inspection revealed that projections of this solution were clearly interpretable using our substantive theory. The slightly poorer fit in Finland is probably due to the relatively small size and high no response rate (20% vs. the usual 1–3%) of that sample, which yielded less reliable correlations and less valid measurement of values.

Goal type

Maps of the projections relevant to the terminal/instrumental type of goal facet are presented in Figure 2. For clarity of presentation, we outlined the regions occupied by values classified *a priori* as terminal or instrumental, showing specific locations only where terminal (T) or instrumental (I) values were out of place. All five maps can be partitioned into nonoverlapping terminal and instrumental regions with at most 4 errors out of 36.[3]

Interests served

The distribution of values into regions representing the interests they serve corresponds to their distribution into motivational domains, as noted earlier. Figure 3 presents maps of the

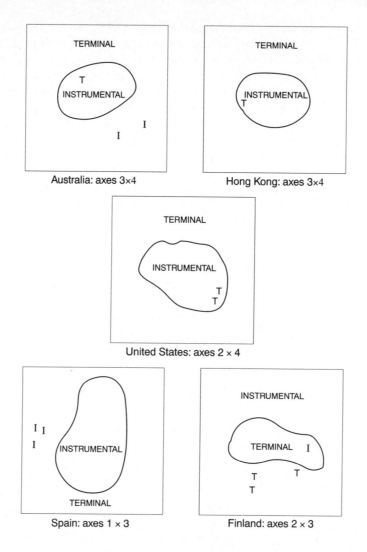

Figure 2   Projections of goal-type facet for 36 values from smallest space analysis in five countries (errors of placement for terminal (T) and instrumental (I) values are indicated).

value projections relevant to the interests served and motivational domain facets. These maps reflect the exact locations of the 36 values on 1 two–dimensional projection of the value space. Partition lines to delineate the motivational domains are drawn according to the *a priori* assignment of specific values to each motivational domain. For the moment, we focus on the regions that represent interests served. These are bordered by the heavy partition lines that group the domains presumed to serve each type of interest.

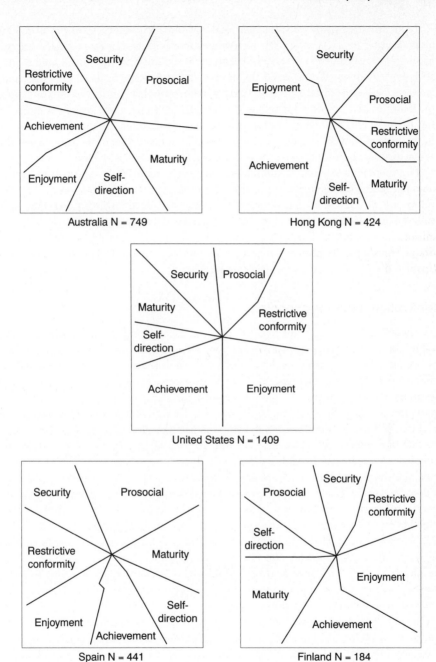

Figure 3 Projections of interests served and motivational domains facets of values from smallest space analysis in five countries.

Recall that enjoyment, achievement and self-direction values were postulated to serve individualistic interests; prosocial, restrictive conformity and security values (except inner harmony) were postulated to serve collective interests; and maturity values were postulated to serve both interests. We expected the three individualistic domains to form one contiguous interests region, the three collective domains to form another contiguous interests region, and the maturity domain to be located on the boundary between these regions. Figure 3 reveals this to be the case in all five samples, as it was in the two earlier samples, with one exception. In the Finnish sample, maturity is one position out of place. It appears between self-direction and achievement rather than on the collective/individualistic boundary.

The consistent location of the motivational domains in their expected interest regions does not mean that all single values also fall in their expected interest regions. Some single values are mislocated in motivational domains (see the following paragraphs), so these values might also be mislocated across the interests boundaries. In fact, however, few such mislocations occurred. There were none in the Hong Kong sample, one each in the United States (freedom), Australian (honest), and Finnish (cheerful) samples, and two in the Spanish sample (freedom, sense of accomplishment).

Motivational domains: content

As shown in Figure 3, in all five samples, the seven predicted motivational domains of values form distinct regions that emerge from a common origin.[4] The empirical locations of the single values in motivational domains are given in columns 2–6 of Table 1. We include the previous data from Germany and Israel in columns 7 and 8 for comparison. Underlined locations indicate placements that do not fit predictions. A second placement is added in parentheses when the value might fit conceptually in either of two motivational domains and its empirical location permits drawing the partition line to place it in either one.

The percentages of values that fall into regions on the maps corresponding to their predicted motivational domains are Australia, 92%; United States, 97%; Hong Kong, 92%; Spain, 89%; Finland, 81%; (Germany, 94%; and Israel, 97%). By considering only those values assigned *a priori* to a single motivational domain, one can count the proportion of correct placements within each domain summed across the seven samples. These are enjoyment 27:28, restrictive conformity 20:21, prosocial 27:28, security 12:14, maturity 25:28, self-direction 26:28, and achievement 21:21. Thus, accuracy of placement was high in every one of the domains. No exact probability level can be computed for this set of results. The high 'hit' (accuracy) rates within samples and within domains, however, and the replication across samples from varied cultures make it hard to believe that these motivational domains emerged by chance.

No additional motivational domains are needed to account for the spatial distribution of the 36 values in any of the samples. The predicted power domain emerged, however, when the four values added to the Hong Kong survey were included in the analysis for that sample. This motivational domain included the added values expected to constitute it (social power, self-determination, and equity) as well as two others (social recognition and freedom). The grouping of these five values suggests that for the Hong Kong sample, the motivational goal of power emphasizes status and dominance that provide both control over others and freedom from others' control over self. The fourth added value, social justice, falls in the prosocial domain, as expected.

Motivational domains: structure

Hypotheses regarding the dynamic relations among the motivational domains were based on the assumption that people's value preferences are organized by the psychological, practical, and social consequences of pursuing or expressing values from the different domains simultaneously. We have seen that the interests that motivational domains serve are indeed one basis for their structural organization. Three additional hypotheses about compatibilities among motivational domains were proposed, as were five hypotheses about conflicts between pairs of motivational domains. Results relevant to these partially redundant hypotheses are presented in Table 2.

The hypothesized compatibilities were confirmed in all five new samples, as they had been in the German and Israeli samples. The three types of values that support smooth social relations (restrictive conformity, prosocial, security) form a single adjacent set. The two types of values that express comfort with or reliance on one's unique experiences and

Table 2 Structural relations among motivational domains of value

Hypothesized	Observed						
	Hong Kong	Australia	United States	Spain	Finland	Germany	Israel
Compatibilities							
Security, prosocial, and restrictive conformity	Y	Y	Y	Y	Y	Y	Y
Achievement and enjoyment	Y	Y	Y	Y	Y	Y	Y
Maturity and self-direction	Y	Y	Y	Y	Y	Y	Y
Conflicts							
Self-direction vs. restrictive conformity	?	Y	Y	Y	Y	Y	Y
Prosocial vs. achievement	Y	Y	Y	Y	Y	Y	Y
Enjoyment vs. prosocial	?	Y	?	Y	Y	Y	?
Achievement vs. security	?	?	Y	Y	Y	?	Y
Restrictive conformity vs. maturity	N	Y	Y	Y	Y	Y	Y

Y = confirmation: For compatibility, domains are adjacent; for conflict, domains are separated by two other domains. ? = indeterminate: Domains are separated by one other domain. N = rejection: Domains are adjacent.

capacities (maturity, self-direction) are in adjacent regions. The two types of values concerned with self-enhancement (achievement, enjoyment) are also adjacent. When the power domain is included in the Hong Kong analysis, this third self-enhancing domain falls between achievement and enjoyment, as predicted (not shown).

The following criteria were developed to evaluate the hypothesized conflicts between motivational domains. In a random ordering of seven domains around a circle, the expected separation between any pair of domains is one other domain. Separation by two other domains in both directions around the circle is the maximum separation possible. This, therefore, is our criterion for the existence of a conflict between two motivational domains. There is no conflict between motivational domains if they occupy adjacent regions. If they are separated by only one other domain, evidence for conflict is questionable. We will call such a finding indeterminate.

Only the opposition between prosocial and achievement values holds across all seven samples (see Table 2). The oppositions between self-direction and restrictive conformity values and between restrictive conformity and maturity values both appear in all the samples but Hong Kong. The oppositions between enjoyment and prosocial values and between achievement and security values each appear in four samples, but they are indeterminate in three. In no instance, however, do these presumably opposed pairs of motivational domains emerge adjacent to one another.

Only in the Hong Kong sample is any hypothesized opposition rejected outright. In each of the other samples, at least seven of the eight motivational dynamics postulated to organize value preferences hold true. As hypothesized, the power domain studied in the Hong Kong sample directly opposes the prosocial domain (not shown). Power values are also opposed, not surprisingly, to restrictive conformity values.

Discussion

Goal type

Distinct regions, occupied almost exclusively by terminal or by instrumental values, emerged in all seven samples studied. Do these results support the hypothesis that people universally distinguish values according to the conceptual terminal/instrumental classification? The results are compatible with this hypothesis, but the fact that Finnish and Hong Kong data also yielded distinct goal type regions supports an alternative explanation. The location of the values in the questionnaire may account for their empirical separation in these samples, because there was no difference in the phrasing of terminal and instrumental values. That is, the empirical distinction may be an artifact of locating the two types of values in serial order in the questionnaire.

Future studies of this distinction might benefit from exploiting the possibility of transforming values from terminal to instrumental and vice versa by rephrasing. If the goal-type distinction is important, the same basic value concept, presented either as a terminal or instrumental value, would show different relations to behavioral and background criteria. Both Rokeach (1973) and Feather (1975) have argued that terminal and instrumental values have different impacts on judgement and behavior: terminal value priorities influence the valences associated with situational outcomes; instrumental value priorities influence the valences associated with courses of action. Data to support this argument would support the conceptual distinction between goal types also. Such data are still very meagre, however.

Interests served

The societies investigated differ substantially in the emphasis their members give to individualism versus collectivism (Hofstede, 1980). Nonetheless, the *a priori* designation of values as serving individualistic, collective, and mixed interests, which was based on our Western perspective, was strongly supported in all seven societies. This was so even in more collectivist societies like Hong Kong and Spain, where one might think that achievement values would be seen as serving collective interests too. In the samples from both these societies, the achievement values were embedded in the individualistic region. They were separated by at least one other individualistic motivational domain from the collectivist and maturity (mixed interests) values. Perhaps, in collectivist societies, achievement standards are more likely to be defined collectively (Yang and Yue, 1988), but even there the primary goal of achievement seekers may be to attain recognition for themselves.

These findings suggest that the discrimination between values as serving the individual's own interests or those of the collectivity is universally meaningful. Moreover, the particular motivational domains understood as individualistic or collective may also be universal. Because of this cross-cultural consensus, it is legitimate to compare the importance of collective versus individualistic values across cultures. Such comparisons typically reveal substantial differences in priorities. We can now say that these differences probably reflect real differences in emphasis on individualistic versus collective interests, rather than differences on how respondents understand these interests.

Motivational domains: content

The cross-cultural evidence clearly supports the universal existence of the seven basic motivational domains tested. The predicted values defined each domain across all samples, and no unexpected values were consistently located among them. Thus, the definitions of the domains and their operationalizations were apparently quite accurate. The emergence of distinct regions for the motivational domains and for the interests cannot be attributed to the sequence of item presentation. Each region included values from locations spread throughout the questionnaire. Moreover, recent analyses, with different item orders, also yielded these seven motivational domains (Schwartz, 1988). The seven postulated domains were sufficient to capture the motivational distinctions among the 36 values. There was also initial evidence in the Hong Kong data for a power domain when appropriate values were included. The universality of this domain remains to be studied.

The content of each domain was also well defined in each sample, despite some errors of value placement. These may be random errors, but they may also reflect cultural differences in the meanings of these values. In Finland, for example, the pro-social region contained eight expected values and two others (responsible and a world of beauty). For the Finns, *responsible* may mean behaving reliably to promote others' interests rather than to restrain own irresponsible inclinations; *a world of beauty* may mean active concern for preserving nature rather than merely appreciating it. These meanings would explain the emergence of these values in the prosocial region. One could easily speculate about the different cultural meanings of values that would explain the other unique empirical placements as well. It is probably wiser to refrain from interpretation, however, until it is clear whether these unusual placements replicate in other samples from the same culture.

The meanings of single values for respondents are reflected in their patterns of association with other values, that is, in their domain placement. For 20 of the 36 values, there was complete consensus across samples, locating them in the *a priori* motivational domains. For 11 other values, there was consensus in six of seven samples. The motivational significance of these 31 values is apparently widely shared.

The remaining five values had consensual locations corresponding to the meanings we attributed to them *a priori* in five of seven samples. For values having two different nonconsensual locations (freedom, a sense of accomplishment, self-controlled), inferring clear additional meanings is difficult. Interestingly, our data bear out Kluckhohn's (1951) speculation that freedom has different meanings in different cultures.

The two consistent misplacements may merit interpretation. National security appeared in the restrictive conformity region in Australia and Spain and bordered on this region in Germany and Finland. Moreover, emphasizing national security and restrictive conformity values is associated with conservative political and social views (Feather, 1979; Rokeach, 1973). These structural and correlational findings suggest that valuing national security sometimes signifies patriotic concern with conformity and order in the service of security. Logical appeared in the achievement region in Spain and Finland and near the achievement border in Israel. We had assumed that valuing logic signifies valuing one's capacity for self-directed decision making. Apparently, logic is also valued as a basis for competent achievement in some cultures.

The 10 values assumed *a priori* to contain elements from two motivational domains did indeed emerge empirically in both domains across the samples. (See the values predicted to be located in two domains, Table 1, column 1, and their observed locations, columns 2–8.) These values obviously have multiple meanings, so they cannot easily be used when constructing indexes of the importance of each motivational domain. Not surprisingly, these complex values are among the most interesting and important (e.g. freedom, responsible).

Motivational domains: structure

There was strong evidence for the universality of the principles of mutually compatible motivations we proposed. All three of the predicted compatibilities appeared in all samples. People tended to give high or low priority to values as a function of whether the values support smooth social relations (restrictive conformity, prosocial, security), express comfort with or reliance on one's unique experiences and capacities (maturity, self-direction), or promote self-enhancement (achievement, enjoyment and perhaps power).

The principles of motivational conflict also received substantial support, but only one held across all samples. This value conflict, between concern for the welfare of others and pursuit of task achievement (prosocial versus achievement), may be universal. Interestingly, this was the one value conflict that we had speculated might not apply in collectivist societies (Hsu, 1981).

The value conflict between emphasizing independent thought and action and restraint of own impulses (self-direction vs. restrictive conformity) appears to have organized value priorities in all samples except Hong Kong. This was true as well for the conflict between emphasizing self-restraint/abnegation and emphasizing open acceptance of self, others, and the world (restrictive conformity vs. maturity).

The remaining two principles of motivational conflict received clear-cut support in four samples, were rejected in none, and were indeterminate in three. The value conflict between emphasizing success or harmonious social relations (achievement vs. security) is apparently not a strong motivational dynamic across all cultures. Nor is the conflict between emphasizing own pleasure and comfort, and devoting oneself to others' welfare a strong motivational dynamic across all cultures. Intuitively, a value conflict between hedonism and altruism seems more plausible. Perhaps our test was weak because the enjoyment domain included happiness and cheerful, values that do not strictly represent hedonism. Future research on this value conflict should use values that define a clear hedonism domain.

Next, consider the applicability of the set of structuring principles within each sample. In Finland and Spain, all principles applied. In Australia, the United States, Israel, and Germany, there was a question about one principle only, and none were rejected. Thus, the postulated dynamics of value conflict and compatibility held quite well in samples from six societies. Hong Kong stands out as markedly different. There, one principle was rejected, and three principles were indeterminate. Both the rejected principle and one indeterminate principle involved restrictive conformity, which was adjacent to maturity and quite close to self-direction. This suggests that self-restraint is compatible with open acceptance of self and the world and with independent thought and action in this society.

The nature of Confucianist thought, which has a strong influence in Hong Kong, may explain these findings. Confucianism teaches that because of human frailty and fallibility, self-development and growth toward wisdom can be achieved only if accompanied by the self-regulation that permits social harmony (Marsella, DeVos and Hsu, 1985, pp. 18–19). These teachings appear to be reflected in the unique structure on motivational domains linking self-direction and maturity to restrictive conformity in the Hong Kong sample. Iwao (1988) described self-restriction and control as necessary to maturity in Japanese culture as well. Hence, the observed pattern may replicate in other samples influenced by Eastern thought – evidence that restrictive conformity values have different motivational dynamics in East and West.

The power region was located opposite the prosocial and restrictive conformity regions in the Hong Kong sample. This supports our assumption that an emphasis on status and dominance conflicts both with a concern for others' well-being and with restraining oneself so as not to harm them. In Confucianism, as in Western thought, pursuing power is disruptive of social harmony. Future research will assess whether the motivational dynamics involving power hold across societies.

Conclusions

Generality of findings

This research tested the universality of elements of a theory of the content and structure of human values. Universality can be established definitively only by studying all cultures. However, the diversity of the samples studied and the variation in methods induce considerable confidence in the universality of results that replicated. Ranking and rating formats of the survey were administered in six different languages, by many researchers, to individuals and groups over a 17-year time span. The samples varied in race, religion, nationality, age, socioeconomic level, educational level, and so forth. Of course, samples from other societies (Communist, Islamic, less developed, etc.) might yield different results.

An alternative explanation

We assume that the empirical mappings of relations among values represent the conceptual structure of values as criteria of importance that people use to evaluate and select behavior and events. Alternatively, the maps might simply represent the semantic similarities and differences among value words. Recent findings reinforce the two reasons, proposed and documented in Schwartz and Bilsky (1987), for rejecting this alternative.

First, were we merely dealing with semantic similarities, we would not expect that the importance people attribute to values would predict their overt behavior. Adding to numerous past studies, however, recent published and unpublished data from the United States, Israel, and Finland show that shopping selections (Homer and Kahle, 1988), weight loss (Schwartz and Inbar-Saban, 1988), choice of college major and political party affiliation (Uutela, 1988), and religious involvement (Gumbo and Schwartz, 1989) are predicted by the importance ratings of values. Future research must examine whether the relations of values to behavior, attitudes, and social structure depend on cultural context.

Second, in the data from each of the five new samples studied here, as in the earlier German and Israeli data, values located within the same motivational domain are frequently not similar to each other in importance. For example, obedient is usually rated low in importance, but self-controlled (also in the restrictive conformity domain) is rated quite important; happiness is rated important, but pleasure (also in the enjoyment domain) is rated unimportant.

Assessing the facets of values

Central to the theory tested here is the conceptual definition of values as characterized by three facets of content: type of goal, interests served, and motivational concern. The spatial representations of the associations among values in all seven samples could be partitioned into regions corresponding to the elements in these facets, that is, to the different types of goals, interests, and motivational concerns specified in the theory. It thus appears that members of very different groups are influenced by these three content distinctions in assigning importance to their values. Absent evidence to the contrary, these three facets may be viewed as possible universals.

Additional conceptual facets may also characterize values universally. For example, the importance people attribute to values may depend on the extent to which the values serve other values or on the extent to which they relate to past, present, or future concerns. Theorizing about how such facets organize relations among values could suggest testable regional hypotheses for future research.[5]

Each of the current facets requires further study. The goal-type facet emerges empirically in structural analyses, but this may reflect noncontent features, notably, grammatical form or location in the questionnaire. Evidence that values relate differently to external criteria, depending on whether they are terminal or instrumental, is crucial for establishing the significance of this facet.

The interests-served facet subsumes the more detailed motivational domains facet. Any hypothesis involving interests served is also a hypothesis about the set of motivational domains serving that same interest. Is there any advantage to working at the more detailed level? Research on individualism/collectivism is at the general level. It has provided numerous insights into cultural and individual differences related to social structure and individual behavior (e.g. Hofstede, 1980; Leung, 1987; Triandis *et al.*, 1988). Moreover, parsimony favors using two interests rather than seven or more motivational domains.

The crucial question, however, is how much information is lost by working only with the interests facet. Is giving priority to one motivational domain that serves a particular interest associated with social or behavioral variables in the same way as giving priority to the other motivational domains that serve the same interest? Published data from studies using the 36 Rokeach values reveal that this is often not the case.[6] Hence, although the less refined interests facet may suffer for some hypotheses, differences at the level of motivational domains should be examined as well.

The emergence of the seven motivational domains in all samples speaks strongly for our assumption that they derive from universal human requirements – from needs of individuals as biological organisms, requisites of coordinated social interaction, and survival and welfare needs of groups. Are other motivational domains also derivable from these universal sources? In addition to power, we are investigating two other domains in our current research: tradition and stimulation. The motivational goal of tradition is respect and commitment to the customs and ideas promulgated by one's cultural or religious group. This domain derives from survival needs of groups (Durkheim, [1912] 1954; Parsons, 1957). It formed one pole of the first bipolar factor in the Chinese Value Survey (Bond, 1988). The motivational goal of stimulation is excitement, novelty, and challenge. It derives from a presumed organismic need for variety and stimulation in order to maintain an optimal level of activation (Berlyne, 1960; Houston and Mednick, 1963; Maddi, 1961).

To investigate the expanded set of motivational domains and to examine the earlier domains more adequately requires a survey instrument that systematically samples values matched to the definitions of the domains. The instrument we are currently refining asks respondents to rate, rather than to rank, value importance. This modification allows respondents to express opposition to values. It also gives researchers the option of adding to the survey values whose cultural uniqueness or whose match with universal domains they wish to study.

The addition of such values by researchers with different perspectives increases the chances of discovering culture-specific or universal domains we may have overlooked.

Past research on value priorities has focused on identifying specific values that correlate between groups. Our findings demonstrate that specific values fall into clearly defined motivational categories. It is therefore possible to construct multi-item indexes of the importance of each motivational domain, using the mean importance score of the several values that constitute the domain. Importance scores for domains are more reliable, more parsimonious, and less ambiguous in meaning than are single value scores. They may therefore predict and discriminate more consistently, contributing more effectively to theory development.

The motivational structure of value domains

The organization of motivational domains according to principles of value compatibility and conflict was consistent across the range of Western countries, and it corresponded well with *a priori* hypotheses. This suggests that the dynamic psychological and social processes that shape value systems are widely shared in Western societies. The deviation from this structure in the Hong Kong sample indicates that these motivational patterns are not universal, however.

Note that according to the content analyses, the meanings of the values and domains were not different for the Hong Kong sample. What differed was the perception of domains as compatible or in conflict. Value domains seen as incompatible in the West (e.g. restrictive conformity and maturity) were seen as compatible in Hong Kong. We have proposed an explanation for these differences that is based on contrasts between Confucianist and Western thought. Replications in Chinese cultures, and studies in Islamic, Buddhist, and other cultures should clarify whether and how cultures differ in the dynamic organization of value conflicts and compatibilities. Analysis of distinctive aspects of the world views of different cultures could suggest hypotheses about the dynamic structuring of motivational domains in these cultures.

Context and meaning

The data point to numerous possible differences in the meaning of specific values as a function of cultural context, though perhaps fewer than one might expect. The meaning of values might also be influenced by two other types of context: the context of other values included in the list of analyzed values and the concrete context of value application. Consider these contextual effects in turn.

Because the meanings of values are represented by their patterns of relations with other values, any change in the values included in the total list might affect the meaning of each particular value. If the values selected for study are a narrow sampling of the universe of value contents, changing the context of values included is liable to produce substantial meaning change. There are reasons to believe, however, that the meanings identified here are fairly reliable.

First, the Rokeach (1973) lists we used were the product of careful efforts to attain comprehensiveness. Braithwaite and Law (1985) found that most types of values mentioned spontaneously by respondents in another Western society were present in the Rokeach lists. Second, adding 4 new values in our Hong Kong analysis yielded an added motivational domain (power), but it had almost no effect on the patterns of relations among the original 36 values. Third is evidence from current research. Using 56 values, including 21 of the original 36 values, we replicated the seven motivational domains in several more samples and identified three or four new domains. Despite the large context change, however, none of the 21 original values showed a significant change in meaning. Thus, although the issue deserves systematic investigation, studies using comprehensive value lists seem unlikely to suggest major revisions in the conclusions about value meanings and structures reached here.

The format used here presents values free of any everyday context: equality as an abstraction rather than in a political or economic relationship, honest as an abstract quality rather than in a school or family setting. This method follows from our definition of values as transituational and permits studying values from all domains together. Studies of values in context would doubtless be interesting and yield somewhat different results. Moreover, there is evidence that asking people to think about self or about attributes in the abstract versus in concrete contexts of daily life produces marked differences in response across cultures (Bond and Tak-sing, 1983; Cousins, 1989; Miller, 1984; Schweder and Bourne, 1984). This may be so with values, too. Hence, cross-cultural studies with values embedded in concrete contexts should be pursued.

Choice of methods

The regional partitioning of the SSA yielded consistent and readily interpretable findings across seven samples in this research. To compare the findings, we performed principal-components factor analyses with varimax rotation on the data from five of these countries (Finland, Israel, Hong Kong, Germany, and the United States). In each sample, the factor analysis yielded a few bipolar factors that were related to pairs of motivational domains. In a pancultural factor analysis of combined data from student samples in nine countries, Bond (1988) also found factors whose poles related to the motivational domains. Overall, however, there was less consistency across samples in the items that defined the factors than in the items that constituted the SSA regions. Lower stability of conceptual categories in factor analysis is the usual outcome of comparisons (Shye, 1988).

In our experience, rotated factors typically represent the elements in only one major facet. This was the case here, too: the factor analyses had no representations of the goal type and interests facets. Furthermore, because the rotated factors were orthogonal, the factor analyses were unsuited to test the hypothesized adjacencies. Finally, the factor analyses did not reveal oppositions between motivational concerns with the clarity and consistency found in the SSA configurations.

This is not the place to explain why MDS techniques like SSA are more appropriate than factor analysis for testing our configurational hypotheses (see Guttman, 1968, 1977, 1982; Lingoes, 1977; Shye, 1988), but a few words to encourage use of SSA may be in order. This method represents proximity data (correlations, similarity matrixes) in multidimensional spatial distance models. The difficult step is to interpret the two-dimensional projections obtained, that is, to identify meaningful regions consisting of substantively related variables. An *a priori* theory of the structure of the variables greatly facilitates interpretation.

The theory presented here – which specifies the facets defining values, the motivational domains, and the relations among them – is a general theory of value structure not limited to the Rokeach lists of values. Rather, it can be used to classify value items from any data-gathering approach into meaningful categories. Equipped with such an *a priori* classification, it is not difficult to find regions in the two-dimensional projections that correspond to these categories, if they are present. Unclassifiable values may suggest new categories within our facets, or even new facets. Perhaps the example of the current research will encourage others to learn this method of analysis and thereby promote progress in values research.

Notes

1. This is a more stringent test of the universality of value types than the pancultural factor analysis in Bond (1988). Bond removed all culturally idiosyncratic patterns of relationships among values before performing his analysis. The common factor structure that emerged does not represent value relations within any particular cultural sample, hence it does not address our question of whether each culture has the same structure of values.
2. For the Australian sample, the analysis began with the published loadings of the values on five dimensions that were obtained in a varimax rotation of a nonmetric multidimensional scaling analysis (Torgerson TORSCA; Feather and Peay, 1975, p. 159). The TORSCA and the SSA 'yield spatial representations that are typically indistinguishable, for practical purposes, when applied to the same matrix of data' (Shepard, 1972, p. 22). Thus, the Australian analysis parallels the others except for the use of a five-dimensional solution. We constructed two-dimensional projections of the value space by graphing the loadings of the values on each pair of dimensions.
3. The errors of placement showed no apparent pattern. They were a world of beauty, cheerful, and loving for Australia; inner harmony and wisdom for the United States; self-respect for Hong Kong; loving, broad minded, and cheerful for Spain; and wisdom, family security, true friendship, and responsible for Finland. The distinct instrumental and terminal regions had different shapes in different countries. We have no clear interpretation for these differences.
4. Separate analyses of the terminal and the instrumental value sets yield similar distinct regions for those motivational domains that are represented by three or more marker values in the set analyzed.
5. For example, the more values there are that serve a given value, the more highly correlated with many other values that value should be. Hence, the extent to which values are served by other values may have a modulating function in the spatial projection: values served by many others would be more central in the space, and those served by few others would be more peripheral.
6. For example, in an Australian study (Ellerman, 1975), student activists and a control group of students attributed equal importance to collectivist values. However, this overall interests comparison obscures the fact that the activists ranked restrictive conformity and security values less important, and they ranked prosocial values more important. Or consider a comparison between American priests and service station dealers (data from Rokeach, 1973, pp. 153–8). Service station dealers ranked individualistic values much higher overall. This reflected the higher ranks they gave to enjoyment and achievement values; but they attributed less importance than did priests to self-direction values. See Schwartz (1988) for greater detail and other examples.

References

Berlyne, D.E. (1960). *Conflict, Arousal and Curiosity*. New York: McGraw-Hill.
Bond, M. (1988). 'Finding universal dimensions of individual variation in multicultural studies of values: The Rokeach and Chinese Value Surveys', *Journal of Personality and Social Psychology*, **55**, 1009–1015.

Bond, M. and Tak-sing, C. (1983). 'College-students' spontaneous self-concept: The effect of culture among respondents in Hong Kong, Japan and the United States', *Journal of Cross-Cultural Psychology*, **14**, 153–171.

Braithwaite, V.A. and Law, H.G (1985). 'Structure of human values: Testing the adequacy of the Rokeach Value Survey', *Journal of Personality and Social Psychology*, **49**, 250–263.

Canter, D. (Ed.) (1985). *Facet Theory: Approaches to Social Research*. New York: Springer-Verlag.

Chinese Culture Connection (1987). 'Chinese values and the search for culture-free dimensions of culture', *Journal of Cross-Cultural Psychology*, **18**, 143–164.

Cousins, S.D. (1989). 'Culture and self-perception in Japan and the United States', *Journal of Personality and Social Psychology*, **56**, 124–131.

Davison, M. (1983). *Multidimensional Scaling*. New York: Wiley.

Dewey, J. (1957). *Human Nature and Conduct*. New York: Modern Library.

Durkheim, E. (1954). *The Elementary Forms of Religious Life* (J.W. Swain, trans.). New York: Free Press of Glencoe. (Original work published 1912.)

Ellerman, D.A. (1975). *Australian Student Activists: Some Social Psychological Characteristics*. Unpublished master's thesis, Flinders University of South Australia, Bedford Park. (Cited in Feather, 1975, op. cit. pp. 162–163.)

Feather, N.T. (1975). *Values in Education and Society*. New York: Free Press.

Feather, N.T. (1979). 'Value correlates of conservatism', *Journal of Personality and Social Psychology*, **37**, 1617–1630.

Feather, N.T. and Peay, E.R. (1975). 'The structure of terminal and instrumental values: Dimensions and clusters', *Australian Journal of Psychology*, **27**, 157–164.

Gumbo, R. and Schwartz, S.H. (1989). 'Ma'arehet ha'arahim shel tzi'irot datiot-harediot b'perspectiva hashvaatit' [The system of ultra-orthodox young women in comparative perspective]. *Megamot*, **32**, 332–360.

Guttman, L. (1968). 'A general nonmetric technique for finding the smallest coordinate space for a configuration of points', *Psychometrica*, **33**, 469–506.

Guttman, L. (1977). 'What is not what in statistics', *The Statistician*, **26**, 81–107.

Guttman, L. (1982). 'Facet theory, smallest space analysis and factor analysis', *Perceptual and Motor Skills*, **54**, 491–493.

Heath, R.L. and Fogel, D.S. (1978). 'Terminal and instrumental? An inquiry into Rokeach's value survey', *Psychological Reports*, **42**, 1147–1154.

Hofstede, G. (1980). *Culture's Consequences: International Differences in Work-related Values*. Beverly Hills, CA: Sage.

Homer, P.M. and Kahle, L.R. (1988). 'A structural equation test of the value–attitude–behavior hierarchy', *Journal of Personality and Social Psychology*, **54**, 638–646.

Houston, J.P. and Mednick, S.A. (1963). 'Creativity and the need for novelty', *Journal of Abnormal and Social Psychology*, **66**, 137–141.

Hsu, F.L.K. (1981). *American and Chinese: Passage to Differences* (3rd edn.). Honolulu: University of Hawaii Press.

Iwao, S. (1988, August). *Social Psychology's Models of Man: Isn't it Time for East to meet West?* Paper presented at the XXIV International Congress of Psychology, Sydney, New South Wales, Australia.

King, A.Y.C. and Bond, M.H. (1985). 'The Confucian paradigm of man: A sociological view', in W.S. Tseng and D.Y.H. Wu (eds.), *Chinese Culture and Mental Health* (pp. 29–46). Orlando, FL: Academic Press.

Kluckhohn, C. (1951). 'Values and value-orientations in the theory of action: An exploration in definition and classification', in T. Parsons and E. Shils (eds.), *Toward a General Theory of Action* (pp. 388–433). Cambridge, MA: Harvard University Press.

Leung, K. (1987). 'Some determinants of reactions to procedural models for conflict resolution: A cross-national study', *Journal of Personality and Social Psychology*, **53**, 898–908.

Levy, S. (1985). 'Lawful roles of facets in social theories', in D. Canter (ed.), *The Facet Approach to Social Research* (pp. 59–96). New York: Springer-Verlag.

Lingoes, J.C. (1977). *Geometric Representations of Relational Data*. Ann Arbor, MI: Mathesis.

Lingoes, J.C. (1981). 'Testing regional hypotheses in multidimensional scaling', in I. Borg (ed.), *Multidimensional Data Representations: When and Why* (pp. 280–310). Ann Arbor, MI: Mathesis.

Lovejoy, A.O. (1950). 'Terminal and adjectival values', *The Journal of Philosophy*, **47**, 593–608.

Maddi, S.R. (1961). 'Exploratory behavior and variation-seeking in man', in D.W. Fiske and S.R. Maddi (eds.), *Functions of Varied Experience* (pp. 253–277). Homewood, IL: Dorsey.

Marsella, A.J., DeVos, G. and Hsu, F.L.K. (1985). *Culture and Self: Asian and Western Perspectives*. London: Tavistock.

Mead, M. (1967). *Cooperation and Competition among Primitive Peoples*. Boston: Beacon Press.

Miller, J.G. (1984). 'Culture and the development of everyday social explanation', *Journal of Personality and Social Psychology*, **46**, 961–978.

Moghaddam, F.M. (1987). 'Psychology in three worlds: As reflected by the crisis in social psychology and the move toward indigenous third-world psychology', *American Psychologist*, **42**, 912–920.

Ng, S.H., Akhtar-Hossain, A.B.M., Ball, P., Bond, M.H., Hayashi, K., Lim, S.P., O'Driscoll, M.P., Sinha, D. and Yang, K.S. (1982). 'Values in nine countries', in R. Rath, H.S. Asthana and J.B.H. Sinha (eds.), *Diversity and Unity in Cross-cultural Psychology* (pp. 196–205). Lisse, The Netherlands: Swets & Zeitlinger.

Parsons, T. (1957). *The Social System*. New York: Free Press.

Rescher, N. (1969). *Introduction to Value Theory*. Englewood Cliffs, NJ: Prentice-Hall.

Rokeach, M. (1973). *The Nature of Human Values*. New York: Free Press.

Schwartz, S.H. (1988, August). *Value Types and Structure: Universal and Culture-specific Aspects*. Paper presented at the Ninth Congress of the International Association for Cross-Cultural Psychology, Newcastle, New South Wales, Australia.

Schwartz, S.H. (in press). 'Individualism–collectivism: Critique and proposed refinements', *Journal of Cross-Cultural Psychology*.

Schwartz, S.H. and Bilsky, W. (1987). 'Toward a psychological structure of human values', *Journal of Personality and Social Psychology*, **53**, 550–562.

Schwartz, S.H. and Inbar-Saban, N. (1988). 'Value self-confrontation as a method to aid in weight loss', *Journal of Personality and Social Psychology*, **54**, 396–404.

Schweder, R.A. and Bourne, E.J. (1984). 'Does the concept of the person vary cross-culturally?', in R.A. Schweder and R.A. LeVine (eds.), *Culture Theory: Essays on Mind, Self and Emotion* (pp. 158–199). New York: Cambridge University Press.

Shepard, R.N. (1972). 'A taxonomy of some principal types of data and of multidimensional methods for their analysis', in R.N. Shepard, A.K. Romney and S.B. Nerlove (eds.), *Multidimensional Scaling: Theory and Applications in the Behavioral Sciences: Vol. 1. Theory*. New York: Seminar Press.

Shye, S. (1985). 'Nonmetric multivariate models for behavioral action systems', in D. Canter (ed.), *The Facet Approach to Social Research* (pp. 97–148). New York: Springer-Verlag.

Shye, S. (1988). 'Inductive and deductive reasoning: A structural reanalysis of ability tests', *Journal of Applied Psychology*, **73**, 308–311.

Triandis, H.C. (1987). 'Collectivism vs. individualism: A reconceptualization of a basic concept on cross-cultural psychology', in C. Bagley and G.K. Verma (eds.), *Personality, Cognition, and Values: Crosscultural Perspectives on Childhood and Adolescence*. London: Macmillan.

Triandis, H.C., Bontempo, R., Villareal, M.J., Asai, M. and Lucca, N. (1988). 'Individualism and collectivism: Cross-cultural perspectives on self–ingroup relationships', *Journal of Personality and Social Psychology*, **54**, 323–338.

Uutela, A. (1988, August). *Value, Structures and Priorities of Finnish Students*. Paper presented at the Ninth Congress of the International Association for Cross-Cultural Psychology, Newcastle, New South Wales, Australia.

Yang, K.S. and Yue, A.B. (1988, August). *Social-oriented and Individual-oriented Achievement Motives: Conceptualization and Measurement*. Paper presented at the XXIV International Congress of Psychology, Sydney, New South Wales, Australia.

Part IV

alternative
perspectives

Economic psychology

7

Antonides, G., 1989, 'An attempt at integration of economic and psychological theories of consumption', *Journal of Economic Psychology*, **10**(1), 77–99
van Raaij, W.F., 1984, 'Micro and macro economic psychology', *Journal of Economic Psychology*, **5**(4), 385–401

Introduction

Economic psychology is largely a European invention and tradition. The Frenchman Gabriel Tarde was the first to use this term some 100 years ago in a study on consumer imitation. It was picked up by the Hungarian George Katona. Katona, as the associate editor of *Der deutsche Volkswirt*, studied hyperinflation in the 1920s in Germany. He was interested in the 'real behaviour' of consumers and businesspeople, in empirical data, and the influence of economic expectations on consumer spending, saving and borrowing. Thus economic psychology became the study of the impact of psychological factors, especially expectations, on consumer behaviour at the macro level (spending on categories, saving and borrowing, rather than brands). When Hitler came to power, Katona emigrated to the United States and continued his work at the University of Michigan at Ann Arbor.

In the 1970s economic psychology was again alive in Europe: Pierre-Louis Reynaud in Strasbourg (France), Karl-Erik Wärneryd at Stockholm (Sweden) and Gery Veldhoven at Tilburg (The Netherlands). The International Association for Research in Economic Psychology (IAREP) was established with annual conferences and workshops, as well as the *Journal of Economic Psychology* in 1981.

What is economic psychology? For Americans, it is still the study of consumer expectations at the macro level. For Europeans, it has become the study of economic and psychological factors on economic behaviour, i.e. all behaviour involving scarce resources such as money, time and effort. In this definition, most human behaviour will be part of economic psychology. Economic psychology is thus more than consumer behaviour in a marketing context. It involves tax behaviour, how people react to inflation, the perception and experience of unemployment, social security benefits, decisions on family size and consumer socialization.

In this chapter only a few economic-psychological topics can be elaborated. Browsing through the sixteen volumes of the *Journal of Economic Psychology* will provide a more comprehensive idea of what topics interest economic psychologists (and behavioural economists alike). Gerrit Antonides compares in his paper economic and psychological concepts such as utility and attitude, and tries to integrate these approaches, whereas Fred van Raaij distinguishes between micro and macro approaches in economic psychology and describes interactions between these levels of analysis.

Other interesting economic-psychological papers discuss such important issues as the management of affect and the importance of emotional factors on consumer decision making, or the relationships between consumers' confidence and their willingness to buy, to save or to borrow (van Raaij and Gianotten, 1990). Pieters and van Raaij (1989) have, for instance, shown that people try to manage their feelings, try to stay in a positive mood and try to avoid negative emotions. This affects their perception and decision making.

In Europe, economic psychologists cover the study of consumer behaviour both in a marketing and in a broader context. This broader context includes the government, macro trends and developments, human conditions, socialization, and cultural differences. This enriches the approaches to describe and to understand consumers and increases the value of these studies. American research is often detailed and based on students as respondents. European research is often broader and based on 'real people', other than students.

References

Katona, G. (1951), *Psychological Analysis of Economic Behavior*, New York: McGraw-Hill.

Katona, G. (1975), *Psychological Economics*, New York: Elsevier.

Pieters, R.G.M. and van Raaij, W.F. (1989), 'Functions and management of affect: Applications to economic psychology', *Journal of Economic Psychology*, 9(2), 251–82.

Reynaud, P.-L. (1981), *Economic Psychology*, New York: Praeger.

Tarde, G. (1890), *The Laws of Imitation* (reprint: 1903, New York: Holt).

Tarde, G. (1902), *La Psychologie économique*, Paris: Alcan (2 volumes).

van Raaij, W.F. (1981), 'Economic psychology', *Journal of Economic Psychology*, 1, 1–24.

van Raaij, W.F. and Gianotten, H.J. (1990), 'Consumer confidence, expenditure, saving, and credit', *Journal of Economic Psychology*, 11(2), 269–90.

Wärneryd, K.-E. (1988), 'Economic psychology as a field of study', in W.F. van Raaij *et al.*, *Handbook of Economic Psychology*, Dordrecht: Kluwer Academic Publishers, 3–41.

An attempt at integration of economic and psychological theories of consumption

● ●

Gerrit Antonides
Erasmus University, Rotterdam

Summary

An attempt has been made to combine the economic theory of demand and the psychological theory of attitude with respect to consumption. It consists of three parts. In the first part, the concepts of utility and attitude are compared. Similarities in meaning, development and specification of the concepts are noted as well as differences with respect to their place in theory, the explanation of behavior and the object of study. In the second part, three different approaches to consumption are considered. Consumer behavior theories in marketing, in economics, and in psychology are summarized and briefly commented upon. In the third part, an attempt is made at integration of theories, the main ingredients of which are utility maximization in economics, the theory of attitudes in social psychology, and psychophysics.

1. Introduction

In the psychological study of economic behavior the concept of attitude has been frequently applied (e.g. by Katona, 1975; Fishbein and Ajzen, 1975) to explain choice in consumer decision making. In economics, consumption is explained by the maximization of utility subject to restrictions, whereas the explanation of utility itself has been of little interest (see Tobin, 1975; Meyer, 1982). This article aims at integrating these two approaches on three levels: conceptual (regarding the definition of two important concepts), theoretical (relating the concepts to behavior) and operational.

Section 2 deals with the relations between two central concepts, utility and attitude. Similarities in meaning, development and application (the explanation of behavior) form a basis for an integration of knowledge of consumer behavior.

Section 3 summarizes how consumer behavior is explained in marketing in economics, and in psychology.

From the *Journal of Economic Psychology*, **10**(1), 1989, 77–99.

Section 4 attempts to integrate the economic and psychological approaches in the explanation of demand. This attempt includes the substitution of social psychological attitudes and psychophysical sensations of stimuli for economic utility. Furthermore, two-stage budgeting is applied to create the framework for the integration.

2. Utility and attitude

The concepts of utility and attitude stem from different disciplines, utility mainly having its roots in economics, while attitude has been developed in psychology. However, interesting similarities in conceptual content seem to exist as well as parallel lines of development of the concepts in each discipline. This section starts with a comparison of conceptual contents (section 2.1), then gives an overview of the main theoretical developments of utility in economics (section 2.2), and attitude in psychology (section 2.3), and describes some ideas about the relation between the constructs (section 2.4).

2.1 Conceptual content

Scientific concepts tend to change over time in definition and operationalization. Without pretension to give an account of the history of utility and attitude, we first look at the meaning of these concepts as given by some authors working relatively early in these fields.

To start with utility, Von Neumann and Morgenstern (1944: 16) state:

> It is clear that every measurement – or rather every claim of measurability – must ultimately be based on some immediate sensation, which possibly cannot and certainly need not be analyzed any further. In the case of utility the immediate sensation of preference – of one object or aggregate of objects as against another – provides this basis.

The kind of sensation, however, they leave unspecified, but the notion of preference indicates consequences for behavior. Indeed, Mosteller and Nogee (1951: 371) state:

> The notion of utility is roughly this: individuals behave as if they had a subjective scale of values for assessing the worth *to them* of different amounts of commodities . . .

So utility is the subjective value of something, related to preference and behavior.
Attitude has been defined by Allport (1935: 8) as follows:

> An attitude is a mental and neural state of readiness, organized through experience, exerting a directive or dynamic influence upon the individual's response to all objects and situations with which it is related.

Allport leaves the 'state of readiness' unspecified, as well as the kind of experience, but the implications for behavior are stressed.

At this early stage of development of the concepts, both disciplines attach a common meaning to an unobserved phenomenon, supposed to influence behavior. Both distinguish relations between the concept and real objects, between sensation or experiences, preference or readiness and relations with behavior. Both lack differentiation of the quality of sensations and readiness, so the concepts can be characterized as unidimensional, referring to one object at a time. In the following sections, differentiation of the concepts and relations with behavior will be considered.

2.2   Utility

Bentham (in Stigler, 1950) has proposed the derivation of utility from the pain or pleasure giving properties of something and so implied a link with emotion and feeling. Bentham has also made some propositions on the degree of utility derived from certain amounts of things, for example the principle of diminishing marginal utility. Bentham says (in Stigler 1950: 59):

> the quantity of happiness produced by a particle of wealth (each particle being of the same magnitude) will be less and less at every particle.

Gossen (in Stigler, 1950: 67) elaborates upon marginal utility:

> A person maximizes his utility when he distributes his available money among the various goods so that he obtains the same amount of satisfaction from the last unit of money spent upon each commodity.

Several authors have tried to define a unit or measure of utility or marginal utility, which implies at least direct intrapersonal comparability of utility. Bentham suggests the faintest distinguishable pleasure as a unit of utility.[1] Walras assumes the existence of a unit of utility and associates a certain level of utility with an absolute magnitude. Fisher has suggested an arbitrary quantity of a certain commodity as a unit of utility. Any other commodity could then be represented by a number of utility units of the reference commodity. Later, it has been shown that the maximization of an ordinal utility function, i.e. without a 'unit of utility', implies the same behavioral consequences as a cardinal utility function.

All economists in Stigler's article ascribe utility to the consumption of commodities. This situation changes drastically with Lancaster's (1966) introduction of characteristics as objective, universal properties of goods (cf. Deaton and Muellbauer, 1980: 243–72). Several goods may contain the same characteristics and Lancaster specifies a linear product technology to relate products to characteristics:[2]

$$z = Bx \tag{1}$$

with z a vector of characteristics, x a vector of goods and B a matrix of coefficients that quantify how much of a characteristic is contained in a good. Lancaster views goods as inputs with characteristics being outputs. Yet something seems missing, because consumers want services from goods. So services are outputs with characteristics as inputs.

> Product characteristics are of interest to the consumer only in that they combine to produce the consumption services from which consumers obtain utility. (Cude, 1980: 111)

Ladd and Zober (1977) assume a functional relationship between the amount of the k-th consumption service, obtained from good i, s_{ik}, and z_{ij}, the total amount of characteristic j a consumer obtains from consumption of good i. A linear specification yields:

$$s_{ik} = \sum_{j=1}^{J} \alpha_{jk} z_{ij}, \tag{2}$$

with parameters α_{jk}. In this framework characteristics can no longer be viewed as outputs, but rather as technical product specifications like the amount of vitamin or sugar in an item of food. The services in this example might be activity arousal in the organism and a taste of sweetness by consuming the item, respectively. By definition, characteristics can be described objectively, whereas services are described in subjective terms.

Traditional utility theory has been concerned with utility derived from commodities as such. The new theory specifies characteristics (or services) that give rise to utility. The number of characteristics may be large, but Lancaster (1979) provides some rules for selecting the relevant ones for explaining behavior, some resulting from his distinction of commodity groups, some resulting from the nature of utility, i.e. whether or not characteristics appear in consumers' preference functions. For the sake of saving space we shall not elaborate upon these rules here.

Another deviation from the idea that commodities directly product utility has been stated by Becker (1965), who combines goods and time inputs of the household into more basic commodities that enter the utility function.

2.3 Attitude

Since Allport (1935) and Thurstone (1932), among others, the attitude concept has been defined in various ways. Berkowitz (1980) distinguishes three main classes of definitions of attitude. The first one is attitude as an evaluation or emotional reaction, the second one is attitude as a readiness to respond in a particular way, the third is attitude as a constellation of cognitive, affective, and conative components. Many authors seem to agree with a three-component attitude structure consisting of cognitive, affective and behavioral elements (e.g. Triandis, 1971; Katz and Stotland, 1959; Tolman, 1959).

The structure of attitude seems to have been developed along two parallel lines in different fields of psychology. In cognitive (Lewin, 1938; Tolman, 1951, 1959) and in social psychology (Rosenberg, 1956; Fishbein, 1966; Triandis, 1971; Fishbein and Ajzen, 1975) attitude has been related to a number of different aspects of the evaluated object. The specification of attitude determines whether the resulting total evaluation is unidimensional or multidimensional.[3]

Lewin (1938) describes the life-space of individuals in which the psychological determination of behavior is described in rather qualitative terms. Later, Tolman (1951, 1959) elaborates upon the psychological structure underlying actions. According to Tolman, people make cognitive distinctions which are valued by the actor, according to their relevance for satisfying personal needs. An inner psychological structure is assumed, organized as a matrix of beliefs and evaluations, which determine selection of (preference for) possible behavior. Tolman goes one step further than Lewin, in differentiating situational aspects. Beliefs and values no longer concern situations (or objects) but involve particular aspects of them, for example the food, the service, the price of food in a restaurant instead of one evaluation of the restaurant as a whole.

Rosenberg (1956) seems to pick up Tolman's ideas and tries to operationalize beliefs and values in order to detect and distinguish the concepts empirically. Evidence has been found of an individual organization of affective and cognitive responses which are congruent with a more global attitude measure about some issue. The affective responses indicate the importance of values for the individual, the cognitive responses reflect the potency of the object for achieving or blocking the realization of these values (perceived instrumentality). Rosenberg's specification of attitudinal organization is:

$$A = \sum_{k=1}^{K} c_k w_k, \qquad (3)$$

with A global attitude, c perceived instrumentalities (beliefs), w the importance of values (evaluations) and K the number of values under consideration. Rosenberg recommends the exclusive use of salient values, but leaves the selection of values as an empirical question. Since the perceived instrumentalities are subjective, these appear to be more closely related to the goods' services than to their characteristics. The relation between perceived services and characteristics will be considered in section 3.3.2.

Fishbein (1966) and Fishbein and Ajzen (1975) point to the conditions under which attitude corresponds to behavior and they suggest to formulate beliefs and evaluation statements with respect to the behavior in question so as to achieve high correspondence of individual statements and individual behavior.

A number of different expectancy-value models of attitude seem to exist (see, for example, Van Raaij, 1977) which have given rise to a number of experiments and problems with respect to specification, operationalization, scaling, and saliency (see, for example, Wilkie and Pessemier, 1973; Ajzen and Fishbein, 1977; for a comparison of models see Mazis *et al.*, 1975; Raju *et al.*, 1975). In contemporary developments of attitude theory, unidimensional specifications of attitude are out-favored by (less restrictive) multidimensional specifications (see, for example, Bagozzi, 1981a,b; Bagozzi and Burnkrant, 1979; Bentler and Speckart, 1979).

Some beliefs are dealing with a restricted range of aspects of an object, for example expenditures on an object (restricted by income), time involved in behavior with respect to the object. Beliefs about this type of aspects of an object should especially be distinguished from other beliefs (a similar view is held by Stroebe and Frey, 1980), so a unidimensional specification of attitude including such beliefs seems inappropriate.

2.4 The relation between utility and attitude

In this section we point to the relation between the constructs of utility and attitude, and consider some differences which may be valuable for further elaboration of, and experimentation with the constructs.

2.4.1 Conceptual content

Both utility and attitude refer to the want- or need-satisfying properties of objects or issues, both are supposed to represent preferences and to influence behavior. In recent developments, both involve (implicit or explicit) cognitive and affective components. Cognitive components deal with the perception and comparison of objects and characteristics. Affective components deal with the evaluation or weighing of objects and characteristics.

In current attitude research (although not all attitude theorists agree) cognitive beliefs, based on perception and/or thinking, and evaluative factors, weights derived from need states, are formulated and measured directly.[4] In economic research, utility has been measured indirectly or not measured at all; however, some economists measure utility concepts directly, for example Van Praag (1968), and Kapteyn and Wansbeek (1985) with respect to income, Kapteyn *et al.* (1979) with respect to durable goods, Hauser and Urban (1979), Ratchford (1979), and Maynes (1976) with respect to goods characteristics. We think that using direct measurements in testing for utility maximizing behavior could help understand the nature of utility functions.

2.4.2 Development

Both the concepts of utility and attitude increasingly refer to characteristics instead of goods. Another parallel lies in the empirical measures of utility and attitude. Etter (1975) notes similarities between the concept of expected utility and the attitude concept.

2.4.3 Specification

In section 2.2 we have already seen that the mathematical form of the utility function has not been tested by means of direct measurement in economics. A number of specifications of utility, based on expenditures or on characteristics of goods, have emerged in demand theory. In psychology, too, attitude frequently has been related to characteristics of objects. In attitude theory, linear forms, including factor-analysis (Bagozzi, 1981a,b), have been the most popular ones, although also interactive (Carmone and Green, 1981; Green and Devita, 1975), and nonlinear (Pras and Summers, 1975) models have been investigated by means of direct measurement. In conjoint analysis (Green and Srinivasan, 1978), too, attitudes are related to product attributes via linear or nonlinear models of preference. The linear attitude model may be considered as a utility model, based on additively separable preferences. In specifying and operationalizing utility models, economics could draw from contemporary models of direct attitude measurement and vice versa. Actually, in marketing and in transportation economics (McFadden, 1974) these models are applied in explaining and predicting consumer choice. In section 4, some ideas about this are presented.

2.4.4 Prediction

A frequently applied economic assumption is utility maximization under an income constraint. When income would not be part of the model, one could hardly explain why people do not always buy the best goods, choose the best service, or buy a new car every week. Economics has found a way to deal with restrictions upon behavior, whereas it appears that psychology has not. Although most research in psychology has not been performed in the area of consumption (where money seems to be a 'natural' restriction), in other areas restrictions exist as well (see Lesourne, 1977; and Frey and Foppa, 1986). Most attitude models, however, have no options to deal with them.[5]

One way to obtain a better correspondence between attitude and behavior has been proposed by Ajzen and Fishbein (1977). They suggest formulating attitude statements in terms of the action under investigation. For example, behavior with respect to donations to the church should not be explained by attitudes towards the church but by attitudes towards donating to the church. Likewise, visiting the church should be explained by attitudes towards visiting the church. We think that, at last, one ends up with such specific attitudes that one should rather speak of intentions towards behavior. Also these 'attitudes' don't explain behavior any more, they have become trivial. Rather, in this case, we should take measures of attitude towards the church (not stated in terms of behavior, however), then define the appropriate restrictions and explain/forecast behavior. Clearly, restrictions differ in the examples mentioned, donating being restricted by one's financial situation, church visiting being restricted by available time and mobility. This, we think, is a more fruitful theoretical approach and it may clear the ground for an integration of economics and psychology in the area of utility and attitude.

3. Consumer choice behavior

Several disciplines have tried to tackle different kinds of problems with consumption. In this section we give a brief overview of the marketing approach of consumer behavior (section 3.1), economic theory (section 3.2), and psychological theory (section 3.3).

3.1 Consumer behavior theory in marketing

Several theoretical consumption models have been developed, including the well-known models of Nicosia (1966), Howard and Sheth (1969) and Engel and Blackwell (1982). These models, comprehensively presented as flow charts of consumption processes, have structured the complex field of determining and mediating factors of consumption. The components of these large models deal with cultural, household, personal and economic conditions and expectations, learning processes (preference formation), information, choice or buying behavior, feedback (satisfaction), etc. These models are able to cope with a number of consumption problems, however in a highly general and non-specific way. Foxall (1980) evaluates the above-mentioned marketing models as pre-scientific and untestable and advocates limited models that allow for empirical testing and falsification.[6]

More limited, but yet quite general models have been developed by Pickering (1981) and Winer (1985) with respect to durable purchases, Andreasen (1984) by means of consumer segmentation, Van Raaij (1979) with respect to budget allocation. The scope of these models has been limited to a specific type of problems that are described by a smaller number of variables. To which degree these models will stand to empirical tests remains an open question. Here, we shall not deal with general consumption models in marketing.

3.2   Economic theory

Economic theory traditionally assumes the maximization of utility derived from the total consumption spectrum of goods, subject to a budget restriction determined from income and wealth. Now consider the demand q_i for the i-th good or service. Utility being functionally related to q_i by

$$U = f(q_1, ..., q_i, ..., q_I),\qquad(4)$$

(see section 2.2). The budget restriction is commonly specified linearly:

$$\sum_{i=1}^{I} p_i q_i \le M,\qquad(5)$$

M being total assets, p_i the price of the i-th good. Now, assuming that consumers are fully informed, basic economic theory derives demand for goods and services from the maximization of the utility function (4) subject to the budget restriction (5). Rational behavior implies that consumers choose consumption alternatives that provide the greatest benefits, given their budget.

The assumption of rationality has often been regarded as unrealistic. According to the assumption, consumers should take each alternative way of spending money into consideration simultaneously. Van Praag (1968) calls this an 'irrational rationality assumption'. Some alternative hypotheses have been proposed. Van Raaij and Wandwossen (1978) suggest a sequential decision-making process. They distinguish generic decisions, in which spending or saving on certain categories is determined, modal decisions, which determine spending on subcategories of product classes, and specific decisions in which specific product choice is made. This suggestion is very similar to the concepts of a utility tree and two-stage budgeting in economics. The utility function of commodities is assumed to be a function of a limited number of 'sub-utility functions' defined on groups of commodities. In the first stage, expenditures are allocated to commodity groups, maximizing the overall utility function subject to the income constraint. In the second stage, expenditures are allocated to commodities within each group, maximizing the sub-utility function subject to restriction of the group budget, allocated in the first stage. Frey and Foppa (1986) also consider a two-stage decision process. In their first stage, constraints narrow the choice set. In the second stage, individuals choose among the (few) alternatives left. Simon (1955) proposes satisficing behavior to simplify the decision process, in which consumers set an aspiration level to guide the search for satisfactory choice alternatives. Kapteyn et al. (1979) find evidence for satisficing behavior with respect to intended expenditures on durables.

The idea of an aspiration level resembles Ironmonger's (1972) assumption of a satiation level for each want. Both of these assumptions tend to reduce the number of desired alternatives, although the aspiration and satiation levels may result from different psychological processes. The aspiration level may be conceived of as a reservation utility (Ratchford, 1982), above which any utility would be acceptable. As soon as a choice alternative is found, yielding the reservation utility or a higher level, the search for alternatives is terminated.

3.3   Psychological theory

Historically, psychology has not been particularly concerned with consumption, but with individual or (small) group behavior in many areas. When applied to marketing theory (section 3.1), a good deal of psychological theories may fit well into the complex schemes of these consumption paradigms. Many theories exist next to each other. Here, we shall discuss social psychological theory (section 3.3.1) and psychophysics (section 3.3.2), where integration with economic theory is considered.

3.3.1   Social psychological theory

In section 2.3, we have discussed the concept of attitude, so we shall not repeat this here. In marketing research, where attitude theories tend to be applied to consumption problems, preference and/or choice seems to be related to attitude, ignoring any restrictions on behavior.[7] Examples of these studies are the multi-attribute studies on movies preference (Humphreys and Humphreys, 1975), food preferences (Green and Devita, 1975), and preferences for toothpaste, automobiles and cigarettes (Mazis *et al.*, 1975). Several studies have included some type of cost variable however.

Gardiner and Edwards (1975) state that, in the absence of a budget constraint, price may be regarded simply as another characteristic of an object. When a budget restriction exists, they recommend choice on the basis of benefit/cost ratios until the budget has been exhausted. This assumption seems correct in case of separability of utility, derived from the object and from the remaining goods and expenditures, and a budget constraint for one good or service. However, this implies only specific consumption where generic and/or modal choice (see section 3.2) has already been made.

Raju *et al.* (1975) include opinions on expensiveness and durability as attributes in an attitude model explaining preferences for cars. Berkowitz *et al.* (1977) include 'value for money' as an attribute in their attitude model explaining choice of cars. Berkowitz and Haines (1980) compare two models of attitude with respect to preferences for heating modes, one includes and the other excludes cost characteristics. Correspondence between preferred heating mode and predicted preference for that mode by the attitude models has been determined by the percentage of respondents for whom both preferences agree. For two heating modes (oil and gas), the model including costs performs significantly better than the model excluding costs, for electric heating the reverse is true, for solar heating the correspondence is not affected by inclusion of costs. The quantitative effect of costs, however, has not been determined. So, in attitude research with respect to consumption, the notion and handling of (financial) restrictions have not been as sophisticated as in the economic theory of consumption. Meyer (1982) also asserts that attitude measures do not seem to catch the opportunity costs of an action.

Nevertheless, we think multi-attribute utility models may be adapted to fit in economic models that take into account the proper restrictions.

3.3.2   Psychophysics

In the linear attitude model (section 2.3), attitude is related to subjective evaluations and beliefs. The subjective beliefs may be considered as perceived services of goods, where services are a function of objective characteristics (see section 2.2). In psychophysics, the relation between subjective sensations (opinions) and objective stimuli has been empirically investigated.

Stevens (1957) has proposed the power law to capture relationships between objective stimuli and subjective sensations of these stimuli. The power law states that the subjective sensation, ψ, depends on the objective value, ϕ, of the stimulus as follows:

$$\psi = c\phi^b, \tag{6}$$

with c and b constants. The power law, relating objective stimuli to beliefs, may be used as an alternative to the linear relation between characteristics and services stated in (2).

The power law has also been found to provide a reasonable description of the relation of attitudes to social stimuli. Hamblin (1973) presents evidence in favor of the power law for relations between, *inter alia*, status and income, status and education, power and per capita military budget, dislike of self and pounds overweight, poverty and income. The social stimuli are all provided on ratio scales, such as dollars of income, years of education, etc. Strictly, these kinds of stimuli and sensations do not belong to Stevens' objective stimuli, but these experiments seem legitimate to find out if more complex concepts obey the same laws as psychophysical ones.

Hamblin (1973) also extends these relationships to attitudes (A) and multiple stimuli (ϕ_k) such as between social status and income, occupational and educational status:

$$A = b \prod_{k=1}^{K} \phi_k^{c_k}, \tag{7}$$

b and c_k being constants and K the number of stimuli. Eq. (7) implies a multiplicative composite of subjective sensations, explaining the attitude, whereas the attitude model in section 2.3 assumes a linear relation. Saris *et al.* (1977) compare the multiplicative form (7) with the additive form:

$$A = w_0 + \sum_{k=1}^{K} w_k \phi_k^{c_k}. \tag{8}$$

They find evidence for composite power functions with several types of stimuli and sensations. The linear form (8) performs better than the multiplicative one (7); adding a scaling parameter to ϕ increases the significance of the estimated relationships further.

The psychology of perception and its extension to stimuli of a social kind may be applied to attitudes based on perceived characteristics and services (see section 2.3) and utility functions based on objective characteristics (see section 2.2).

4. Integration of theories

In economics, attempts to relax the rationality assumption have led to different approaches than in psychology. In economics the assumption of simultaneous maximization has been relaxed by introducing two-stage budgeting models. Psychology usually has been concerned with specific choice, neglecting total consumption. A combination of the two approaches is obtained by separating goods into two groups, satisfying different wants. One group contains goods between which a specific choice is made, the other group is a composite of all other goods. This grouping of commodities seems to be relevant when information about all individual expenditures is lacking. Moreover, it is useful in the study of choice between varieties of a good on the basis of perceived characteristics. The utility function is stated as:

$$U = f[h_1(q_1), h_2(q_2)], \tag{9}$$

with q_1 a vector of quantities of R varieties of the good, q_2 the quantity of the composite. The budget restriction is:

$$\sum_{r=1}^{R} p_{1r}q_{1r} + p_2q_2 \leq M, \tag{10}$$

with p denoting price and M denoting total assets. In psychology, usually individual discrete choice between varieties of a good has been studied, implying at most one of the q_{1r} equals one, while the other $R-1$ are zero. The price of the composite can arbitrarily be set to one (unit of M).

Since many goods are indivisible, discrete choice is implied each time a purchase of such a good is made. Deaton and Muellbauer (1980) give a model for discrete choice including product specifications and household characteristics. The household utility function is suggested to be:

$$U = f[h(\sum_{r=1}^{R} \theta_r q_{1r}), q_2, ..., q_I], \tag{11}$$

with one of the q_{1r} equal to one and the remaining q_{1r} equal to zero, q_i $(i = 2, ..., I)$ are quantities of other goods, R the number of varieties of the first good, θ_r a quality parameter which determines the relative quality of the r-th variety. The function h specifies the utility of the first good. Deaton and Muellbauer (1980) give an example of a function h in the case of two varieties, depending on z (a vector of product characteristics) and a (a vector of household characteristics) as follows:

$$h = \theta_1(z_1, a, \varepsilon_1)q_{11} + \theta_2(z_2, a, \varepsilon_2)q_{12}, \tag{12}$$

where the quality parameter has been made dependent on z, a, and ε, the latter being an error term capturing unobserved elements in z, a, or both. The variety which yields highest marginal utility is chosen, so if $\theta_1/p_{11} > \theta_2/p_{12}$ variety 1 is chosen (p_{1r} being the price of the r-th variety of the first good). Under certain assumptions regarding θ and ε, the model of the choice process turns out to be multinomial logit. When θ_r is specified such that $\log \theta_r = \log \theta^0(z_r, a) + \varepsilon_r$, then variety 1 is chosen if

$$\varepsilon_1 - \varepsilon_2 > [\log \theta_2^0(z_2, a) - \log p_{12}] - [\log \theta_1^0(z_1, a) - \log p_{11}] = v_2 - v_1. \tag{13}$$

Furthermore assuming that ε_r follows a Weibull distribution with parameter α_r, the probability of (13) is given by the Luce model:[8]

$$\text{Prob}(\varepsilon_1 - \varepsilon_2 > v_2 - v_1) = e^{v_1 - \alpha_1} / \sum_{r=1}^{2} e^{v_r - \alpha_r}. \tag{14}$$

We note that the parameter θ^0 has not been specified, but that it specifies utility of product characteristics z for households with characteristics a. We have already mentioned the desirability of transformation rules between characteristics, services and utilities. These rules have been considered in section 3.3.2. In (14), υ may be modelled such as to comprise total utility (11), and a budget constraint (see, for example, McFadden, 1973; and Hensher and Johnson, 1981).

McFadden (1976) considers the binary probit model, dating back to Thurstone, in which the choice probabilities may also depend on attributes of alternatives. The discrete choice model appears to be able to explain choice from the utility or attitude with respect to the choice alternatives. Obviously, this is a desirable property of the discrete choice model in the integration of economic and psychological models of consumer choice.

The economic model assumes a constant utility function, at least for groups of individuals. Psychological models account for the individual differences in utility functions, and thus may provide a more realistic explanation of behavior in micro-economic research. A natural integration of these types of models is accomplished by the use of direct measurement of individual utilities, given that the choice occurs. The alternative, yielding the highest measured utility then has the greatest probability of being chosen by the individual. These utilities can be measured in various ways to be considered below.

Eq. (9) plays a central role in our integrative approach. The function h_1 may be specified by means of a flexible economic model like (12), based on objective characteristics. However, h_1 alternatively may be specified by means of a social psychological model like (3), or a psychophysical model like (8), based on perceived characteristics or objective services of goods, respectively.

Apart from characteristics and services, h_1 may be considered as a global attitude or emotional reaction to a variety of a good. Measurements of this include the Semantic Differential, Thurstone and Likert scales (see Fishbein and Ajzen, 1975), and various psychophysiological measurements, like the Galvanic Skin Response, eye dilation measurements, etc.

The function h_2 also may be specified by means of a psychophysical model like (6), or alternative models like (15) or (17). Most of these specifications are suited to capture subjective information, obtained directly from consumers. In section 2 the rationales for interchange of utility and attitude have been considered, thus providing the basis for integration at the operational level.

Two obvious specifications of (9) are addition and multiplication of h_1 and h_2.[9] A specification of h_1 has been considered in section 3.2.1, where h_1 contains characteristics of goods and of households. For example, h_1 may be specified as a multi-attribute utility function with weights differing between household characteristics. This specification has been proposed by Ratchford (1979):

$$U = \sum_{k=1}^{K} w_k z_k + w_{k+1} y, \tag{15}$$

with z characteristics and y the quantity of a composite of other goods. Without loss of generality, y may be expressed in units of money spent on the other goods. The z_k, according to Lancaster (1966), are related to goods via the product technology matrix in (1). The coefficients of this matrix are objective and universal in Lancaster (1966), but may be subjective in Ratchford (1979). A subjective operationalization is common is psychology, where even the w_k are measured directly. Alternatively, the z_k in (15) may depend on objective characteristics via psychophysical relations like the power function in (6). In this case the utility function takes the form:

$$U = \sum_{k=1}^{K} c_k \phi_k^{b_k} + c_{K+1} \phi_K^{b_{K+1}}, \tag{16}$$

with ϕ_k the objective value of characteristic k. In many applications it is easier to state (16) in multiplicative form (like in (8)), since the logarithmic transformation then yields a function linear with respect to its parameters (see fn. 9).

In (15), the utility of the composite good is a very simple function of the quantity y. Here, too, psychophysical functions may be applied instead. Since the price of y may be set to one, the utility of the composite good may be specified in terms of expenditures made on it. The idea of evaluation of money amounts spent on goods has been developed by Van Praag (1968). Since goods are assumed to possess a large number of characteristics and consumers are able to evaluate any bundle of characteristics on a [0,1] scale, Van Praag (1968) establishes an isomorphism between probability theory and utility. Invoking a few additional assumptions, the utility of broad commodity groups is approximated by a multi-variate lognormal distribution function. Relevant to our discussion is the case of two commodity groups. Van Praag (1975) assumes that, each time consumers make a buying decision, they partition the commodity set in two: a set of relevant commodities with respect to which they feel unsatisfied, and a composite group of commodities with respect to which they feel no need for the moment. Assuming separable utility, the utility function takes the form:

$$U = \Lambda (y_i; \mu_i, \sigma_i) \Lambda (y^i; \mu^i, \sigma^i), \tag{17}$$

with y_i expenditures on the i-th good, and y^i expenditures on the composite of all other goods, such that $y_i + y^i = M$. $\Lambda (y; \mu, \sigma)$ denotes the lognormal distribution function with parameters μ and σ. We remark that (17) can be considered as a multiplicative specification of (9), where the quantities are expressed in units of money spent, and the functions h are specified as lognormal distribution functions. For operationalization of (17) by direct measurement we refer to Kapteyn et al. (1978) and Kapteyn and Wansbeek (1985). The choice of a lognormal function of expenditures is based on theoretical considerations, however many alternatives are available, for instance the power function used in psychophysics. In Kapteyn and Van Herwaarden (1980), a number of alternative utility functions of income have been tested, of which the lognormal and logarithmic turned out to perform best.

Again, the first part of (17) could be replaced by alternative specifications of utility or attitude, either in terms of global evaluations, or in terms of evaluations of characteristics. This would be preferred when evaluation based on money amounts poses problems, e.g. in utility of used goods, where estimation of the money value corresponding with the quality of the good is troublesome, or where the price–quality relation is imperfect (see Assum and Maynes, 1979; and Maynes, 1980).

In the case of discrete choice, utility functions (15)–(17), or alternative specifications of (9) may be substituted for the v_r in (14). In Antonides (1985), these kinds of ideas have been applied to the discrete choice of disposing of a good or repairing it, in case of a defect. In Ratchford (1979), it has been applied to automobile choice. In McFadden (1974), it has been applied to transportation economics. Probably, numerous other applications are possible, e.g. in marketing, micro-economics and public choice.

5. Conclusion

The economic construct of utility and the psychological attitude refer to the same subjective property of an economic good or service. The relation between the objective quantities of goods or characteristics and the perceived quantities has been specified and tested empirically in psychophysics. In social psychology, marketing and psychophysics, the attitude has been specified either as a global emotional reaction or as a weighted function of (perceived) attributes.

Generally, in psychology, consumption has not been considered as a system dealing with the total budget of the consumer. Usually, a set of discrete choice alternatives (e.g. varieties of a good), concerning a part of the budget, has been studied. The integration of economic and psychological theory may be accomplished by separating preferences for varieties of a good and for a composite of other goods, thus maintaining the systems approach. The psychological methods of direct measurement offer fruitful opportunities for the explanation and prediction of consumer behavior at the micro-level. Some economic examples of this approach already indicate close resemblance with psychological theory, but we contend psychology may contribute much more to the detailed understanding of consumption than it currently does.

Notes

1. This unit of utility resembles the absolute threshold in psychophysics. The faintest distinguishable marginal utility resembles the difference threshold, or just noticeable difference.
2. The linear production model has been introduced earlier by Stigler (1945) and Gorman (1956) (cf. Deaton and Muellbauer, 1980: 250).
3. A unidimensional specification is one that results in a single measure of the attitude, for example as in (3). A multidimensional specification yields a measure of each different aspect (dimension) of the attitude. For example, in the case of household appliances, functional and esthetic qualities might be distinguished giving rise to two different dimensions of the attitude, as opposed to a global measure of the attitude or a summary measure of a number of aspects.
4. Direct measurement refers to obtaining information (e.g. about utility or attitude) directly from a source (consumers), for example, by questioning. Indirect measurement refers to deriving the measure from related information (e.g. from behavior). For example, the estimated coefficients of a regression of behavioral intention on attribute beliefs can be considered as indirect measurements of attribute weights.
5. Although belief and evaluation with respect to price of an object refer, in a sense, to a financial restriction, formally in this case income (or total assets) forms the restriction on expenditures.
6. Some attempts have been made to test general models, however. For example Farley et al. (1974), Laroche and Howard (1980), and Goldberger and Lee (1962).
7. One could, however, take social norms (Fishbein, 1966; Triandis, 1971) and habits (Triandis, 1971) as restrictions on behavior, although these authors view them merely as additional explanatory variables. However, Warner and DeFleur (1969) consider concepts like norms, roles, reference groups, etc. as conditions, modifying the relationship between attitudes and action.

8. In McFadden (1973) it has been pointed out that a necessary and sufficient condition for the Luce model to be consistent with the random utility model is that the ε_r in (14) are Weibull distributed.
9. In utility maximization problems, any order preserving transformation of utility yields the same optimal consumer choice. However, given the (measured) utility components, the explanation and prediction of behavior is affected by the choice of the additive or multiplicative specification.

References

Ajzen, I. and M. Fishbein (1977), 'Attitude–behavior relations: A theoretical analysis and review of empirical research', *Psychological Bulletin*, **84**, 888–918.

Allport, G.W. (1935), 'Attitudes'. Excerpted from C. Murchison (ed.), *Handbook of Social Psychology*. Worchester: Clark University Press. In: M. Fishbein (ed.), 1967. *Readings in Attitude Theory and Measurement*. New York: Wiley.

Andreasen, A.R. (1984), 'Life status changes and changes in consumer preferences and satisfaction', *Journal of Consumer Research*, **11**, 784–794.

Antonides, G. (1985), 'Disposition of a durable consumption good', in H. Brandstätter and E. Kirchler (eds.), *Economic Psychology*. Linz: Rudolf Trauner Verlag, pp. 269–280.

Assum, T. and E.S. Maynes (1979), 'Perceived vs. actual price dispersion (quality constant): A new dimension of informationally imperfect markets', *Proceedings of the American Council of Consumer Interests*, 27–44.

Bagozzi, R.P. (1981a), 'Attitudes, intentions and behavior: A test of some key hypotheses', *Journal of Personality and Social Psychology*, **41**, 607–627.

Bagozzi, R.P. (1981b), 'An examination of the validity of two models of attitude', *Multivariate Behavioral Research*, **16**, 323–359.

Bagozzi, R.P. and R.E. Burnkrant (1979), 'Single component versus multicomponent models of attitude: Some cautions and contingencies for their use', *Advances in Consumer Research*, **6**, 339–344.

Becker, G.S. (1965), 'A theory of the allocation of time', *The Economic Journal*, **75**, 493–517.

Bentler, P.M. and G. Speckart (1979), 'Models of attitude–behavior relations', *Psychological Review*, **86**, 452–464.

Berkowitz, L. (1980), *A Survey of Social Psychology*. New York: Holt, Rinehart and Winston.

Berkowitz, M.K. and G.H. Haines (1980), 'A multi-attribute analysis of consumer attitudes towards alternative space heating modes', Working paper, University of Toronto.

Berkowitz, E.N., J.L. Ginter and W.W. Talarzyk (1977), 'An investigation of the effects of specific usage situations on the prediction of consumer choice behavior', *Proceedings of the American Marketing Association*, 90–93.

Carmone, F.J. and P.E. Green (1981), 'Model misspecification in multi-attribute parameter estimation', *Journal of Marketing Research*, **18**, 87–93.

Cude, B.J. (1980), 'An objective method of determining the relevancy of product characteristics', *Proceedings of the American Council of Consumer Interests*, 111–116.

Deaton, A. and J. Muellbauer (1980), *Economics and Consumer Behaviour*. Cambridge: Cambridge University Press.

Engel, J.F. and R.D. Blackwell (1982), *Consumer Behaviour* (4th edition). New York: Holt Saunders.

Etter, W.L. (1975), 'Attitude theory and decision theory: Where is the common ground?', *Journal of Marketing Research*, **12**, 481–483.

Farley, J.U., J.A. Howard and L.W. Ring (1974), *Consumer Behaviour: Theory and Application*. Boston, MA: Allyn & Bacon.

Fishbein, M. (1966), 'The relationships between beliefs, attitudes and behavior', in S. Feldman (ed.), *Cognitive Consistency*. New York: Academic Press.

Fishbein, M. and I. Ajzen (1975), *Belief, Attitude, Intention and Behaviour: An Introduction to Theory and Research*. Reading, MA: Addison-Wesley.

Foxall, G.R. (1980), 'Marketing models of buyer behaviour: A critical view', *European Research*, **8**, 195–206.

Frey, B.S. and K. Foppa (1986), 'Human behavior: Possibilities explain action', *Journal of Economic Psychology*, **7**, 137–160.

Gardiner, P.C. and W. Edwards (1975), 'Public values: Multi-attribute utility measurement for social decision making', in M.F. Kaplan and S. Schwartz (eds.), *Human Judgment and Decision Processes*. New York: Academic Press.

Goldberger, A.S. and M.L. Lee (1962), 'Toward a microanalytic model of the household sector', *American Economic Review*, **52**, 241–251.

Gorman, W.M. (1956), 'A possible procedure for analysing quality differentials in the egg market'. Ames, IA: Iowa State College, mimeo. (Reissued as Discussion Paper No. B4, London School of Economics Econometrics Program, London, 1976.)

Green, P.E. and M.T. Devita (1975), 'An interaction model of consumer utility', *Journal of Consumer Research*, **2**, 146–153.

Green, P.E. and V. Srinivasan (1978), 'Conjoint analysis in consumer research: Issues and outlook', *Journal of Consumer Research*, **5**, 103–123.

Hamblin, R.L. (1973), 'Social attitudes: Magnitude measurement and theory', in H.M. Blalock, Jr. (ed.), *Measurement in the Social Sciences*. London: Macmillan, pp. 61–121.

Hauser, J.R. and G.L. Urban (1979), 'Assessment of attribute importances and consumer utility functions: von Neumann-Morgenstern theory applied to consumer behavior', *Journal of Consumer Research*, **5**, 251–262.

Hensher, D.A. and L.W. Johnson (1981), *Applied Discrete Choice Modelling*. New York: Halsted Press.

Howard, J.A. and J.N. Sheth (1969), *The Theory of Consumer Behaviour*. New York: Wiley.

Humphreys, P. and A. Humphreys (1975), 'An investigation of subjective preference orderings for multi-attributed alternatives', in C. Wendt and C. Vlek (eds.), *Utility, Probability and Human Decision Making*. Dordrecht: Reidel, pp. 119–133.

Ironmonger, D. (1972), *New Commodities and Consumer Behavior*. Cambridge: Cambridge University Press.

Kapteyn, A. and F.G. van Herwaarden (1980), 'Interdependent welfare functions and optimal income distribution', *Journal of Public Economics*, **14**, 375–397.

Kapteyn, A. and T. Wansbeek (1985), 'The individual welfare function: A review', *Journal of Economic Psychology*, **6**, 333–363.

Kapteyn, A., F.G. van Herwaarden and B.M.S. van Praag (1978), 'Direct measurement of welfare functions: Methods and results', *Report 77.02*. Leyden: The Economic Institute of Leyden University.

Kapteyn, A., T. Wansbeek and J. Buyze (1979), 'Maximizing or satisficing?', *The Review of Economics and Statistics*, **61**, 549–563.

Katona, G. (1975), *Psychological Economics*. New York: Elsevier.

Katz, D. and E. Stotland (1959), 'A preliminary statement to a theory of attitude structure and change', in Koch, S. (ed.), *Psychology: A Study of a Science*, Vol. 3. New York: McGraw-Hill.

Ladd, G.W. and M. Zober (1977), 'Model of consumer reaction to product characteristics', *Journal of Consumer Research*, **4**, 89–101.

Lancaster, K.J. (1966), 'A new approach to consumer theory', *Journal of Political Economy*, **74**, 132–157.

Lancaster, K.J. (1979), *Variety, Equity and Efficiency*. New York: Columbia University Press.

Laroche, M. and J.A. Howard (1980), 'Nonlinear relations in a complex model of buyer behavior', *Journal of Consumer Research*, **6**, 377–388.

Lesourne, J. (1977), *A Theory of the Individual for Economic Analysis*. Amsterdam: North-Holland.

Lewin, K. (1938), *The Conceptual Representation and the Measurement of Psychological Forces*. Durham, NC: Duke University Press.

McFadden, D. (1973), 'Conditional logit analysis of qualitative choice behavior', in P. Zarembka (ed.), *Frontiers in Econometrics*. New York: Academic Press.

McFadden, D. (1974), 'The measurement of urban travel demand', *Journal of Public Economics*, **3**, 303–328.

McFadden, D. (1976), 'Quantal choice analysis: A survey', *Annals of Economic and Social Measurement*, **5**, 363–390.

Maynes, E.S. (1976), *Decision-making for Consumers*. New York: Macmillan.

Maynes, E.S. (1980), 'Informationally imperfect markets: The consumer's underrecognized problem', Paper, New York: Cornell University.

Mazis, M.B., O.T. Ahtola and R.E. Klippel (1975), 'A comparison of four multi-attribute models in the prediction of consumer attitudes', *Journal of Consumer Research*, **2**, 38–52.

Meyer, W. (1982), 'The research programme of economics and the relevance of psychology', *British Journal of Social Psychology*, **21**, 81–91.

Mosteller, F. and P. Nogee (1951), 'An experimental measurement of utility', *Journal of Political Economy*, **59**, 371–404.

Nicosia, F.M. (1966), *Consumer Decision Processes: Marketing and Advertising Implications*. Englewood Cliffs, NJ: Prentice-Hall.

Pickering, J.F. (1981), 'A behavioural model of the demand for consumer durables', *Journal of Economic Psychology*, **1**, 59–77.

Pras, B. and J. Summers (1975), 'A comparison of linear and nonlinear evaluation process models', *Journal of Marketing Research*, **12**, 276–281.

Raju, P.S., R.S. Bhagat and J.N. Sheth (1975), 'Predictive validation and cross-validation of the Fishbein, Rosenberg and Sheth models of attitudes', *Advances in Consumer Research*, **2**, 405–425.

Ratchford, B.T. (1979), 'Operationalizing economic models of demand for product characteristics', *Journal of Consumer Research*, **6**, 76–85.

Ratchford, B.T. (1982), 'Cost–benefit models for explaining consumer choice and information seeking behavior', *Management Science*, **28**, 197–212.

Rosenberg, M.J. (1956), 'Cognitive structure and attitudinal effect', *Journal of Abnormal and Social Psychology*, **53**, 367–372.

Saris, W.E., C. Bruinsma, W. Schoots and C. Vermeulen (1977), 'The use of magnitude estimation in large scale survey research', *Mens en Maatschappij*, **52**, 369–395.

Simon, H.A. (1955), 'A behavioral model of rational choice', *Quarterly Journal of Economics*, **69**, 99–118.

Stevens, S.S. (1957), 'On the psychophysical law', *Psychological Review*, **64**, 153–181.

Stigler, G.J. (1950), 'The development of utility theory', *Journal of Political Economy*. Reprinted in A.N. Page (ed.), *Utility: A Book of Readings*. New York: Wiley.

Stroebe, W. and Frey, B.S. (1980), 'In defense of economic man: Towards an integration of economics and psychology', *Zeitschrift für Volkswirtschaft und Statistik*, **116**, 119–148.

Thurstone, L.L. (1932), 'The measurement of social attitudes', *Journal of Abnormal and Social Psychology*, **26**, 249–269.

Tobin, J. (1975), 'On the relevance of psychology to economic theory and research', Chapter 37 in *Essays in Economics. Vol 2: Consumption and Econometrics*. Amsterdam: North-Holland.

Tolman, E.C. (1951), 'A psychological model', in T. Parsons and E.A. Shills (eds.), *Toward a General Theory of Action*. Cambridge, MA: Harvard University Press.

Tolman, E.C. (1959), 'Principles of purposive behavior', in S. Koch (ed.), *Psychology: A Study of Science*. New York: McGraw-Hill.

Triandis, H.C. (1971), *Attitude and Attitude Change*. New York: Wiley.

Van Praag, B.M.S. (1968), *Individual Welfare Functions and Consumer Behaviour*. Amsterdam: North-Holland.

Van Praag, B.M.S. (1975), 'Utility, welfare and probability: An unorthodox economist's view', in D. Wendt and C. Vlek (eds.), *Utility, Probability and Human Decision Making*. Dordrecht: Reidel, pp. 279–295.

Van Raaij, W.F. (1977), 'Consumer choice behavior: An information processing approach', Dissertation, Tilburg.

Van Raaij, W.F. (1979), 'Research on household budget allocation', Papers on Economic Psychology, Erasmus University, Rotterdam.

Van Raaij, W.F. and K. Wandwossen (1978), 'Motivation–need theories and consumer behavior', in H.K. Hunt (ed.), *Advances in Consumer Research*. Ann Arbor, MI: Association for Consumer Research, pp. 590–595.

Von Neumann, J. and O. Morgenstern (1944), *Theory of Games and Economic Behavior* (3rd edn, 1967). Princeton, NJ: Princeton University Press.

Warner, L.G. and M.L. DeFleur (1969), 'Attitude as an interactional concept: Social constraints and social distance as intervening variables between attitudes and action', *American Sociological Review*, **34**, 153–169.

Wilkie, W.L. and E.A. Pessemier (1973), 'Issues in marketing's use of multi-attribute attitude models', *Journal of Marketing Research*, **10**, 428–441.

Winer, R.S. (1985), 'A revised behavioral model of consumer durable demand', *Journal of Economic Psychology*, **6**, 175–184.

Micro and macro economic psychology

●●

W. Fred van Raaij
Professor of Marketing, Erasmus University, Rotterdam

Summary

Four types of data are distinguished, based on individual (micro) *vs* aggregate (macro) level, and on cross-section *vs* time-series. Analytical properties of collectives may be formed through aggregation, while structural and integral properties of collectives have no individual-level counterpart.

Aggregation is not simply a summation of individual properties. People take the behavior of others into account and adapt their own behavior.

Time-series are different from cross-sections in many ways. While at the cross-sectional level buying intentions are predictive, attitudes are better predictors in time-series data.

We come to the conclusion that time-series data are superior to cross-sectional data for estimating a regression coefficient. Cross-sectional data (Type 1) are largely confounded by individual differences, while time-series data (Type 4) provide a better estimate for the relevant effect. Individual panel data (Type 3) combine the good characteristics of Type 4 and Type 1 data, especially if treated in a time-series fashion.

Introduction

In economic psychology, we are often measuring individual behavior in order to test hypotheses on general phenomena. Individuals, thus, are sampled from a population in order to reach conclusions on that population. We define a population or a collective as a set of elements with at least one common property, e.g. the population of car-owners or the collective of law-school graduates.

Not only individuals are members of a collective; in the same way households, organizations, precincts or cities [are] elements of collectives. An individual is a member of a household; a household [is a] member of a precinct; precincts are members of a county or a city; cities are members of a province; provinces are members of a nation, and so on.

From the *Journal of Economic Psychology*, 5(4), 1984, 385–401.

Lazarsfeld and Menzel (1961) give the following illustration of a research proposition using elements and collectives: 'Children of rich parents go to college in greater proportion than do children of poor parents.'

(a) Two collectives are distinguished: children of rich and of poor parents (which income boundaries?).
(b) Children are the elements of both collectives.
(c) Children have the binary property of going or not going to college.
(d) Proportions of college-going children in both collectives are compared (research proposition).

An alternative research proposition is to compare the average or median income of parents of children going and not going to college.

Lazarsfeld and Menzel (1961) distinguish three types of properties that describe collectives:

1. *Analytical properties* are based on individual properties of the members, e.g. average income or proportion of college-going children. The standard deviation of income, and the correlation between educational level and income in a certain collective are also analytical properties. Note that there is a parallel meaning of individual and average income. A proportion, standard deviation, or correlation has no individual parallel meaning. The standard deviation of incomes in a city denotes something quite different – lack of homogeneity or inequality – from individual income, from which it is computed.
2. *Structural properties* are based on the relationships among members. Group cohesiveness and preference relationships among individuals are structural characteristics of the group, without a parallel meaning for the individual members. A research proposition might be: The diffusion of an innovation will be faster in an integrated neighborhood as compared with a non-integrated neighborhood. The degree of integration is a structural property of the neighborhood.
3. *Integral properties* are not based on individual members or their relationships but are absolute properties of the collective as a whole. Integral properties may be obtained from documents in the history or present time of the community (content analysis). The frequency of 'achievement themes' in folk tales, art and literature is an indication for the 'achievement motive' of a tribe, a nation, or other collective (McClelland, 1960). The number of doctors per 1000 inhabitants may be an index for the welfare of a country. Delinquency rate may be an index for 'alienation', in a similar way.

We add to the relationships between individuals and collectives a *time* dimension. In a cross-sectional study we collect data on individual or collective properties at one point in time; in a time-series approach we collect data at a number of points in time, either at the individual or at the collective level. In a panel study, we monitor a number of individuals or households over a period of time. The other time-series approach is to have repeated samples and to develop a series of collective properties from these samples. Adams (1965) finds that a cross-section study on the predictive value of consumer confidence gives results different from a time-series study: the cross-sections *vs* time-series paradox.

The two dimensions, individual *vs* collective and cross–section *vs* time–series, suggest that four types of data are relevant in economic psychology (Figure 1). Adams (1965) compares data of Type 1 and Type 4 in his cross–section *vs* time–series paradox. Here we will describe each of the four types of data with their advantages and disadvantages for economic–psychological research.

Four types of data

Type 1 data (Figure 1) are the common type of data collected in economic psychology. In order to test a specific hypothesis data are collected from a sample of the relevant population or collective. The research hypotheses for Type 1 data will be stated in analytical properties of the individuals. For instance, one wants to study the proposition that there is a positive correlation between household income and the degree of investment in home insulation. The analytical properties of households are income and degree of investment in home insulation.

The basic characteristic of Type 1 data is the parallel meaning of the relationship on the individual and the aggregate level, which allows us to predict home insulation investments for specific households based on their income level.

Structural, integral, and most analytical properties of a collective are meaningless without a comparison with another collective. Knowing that 40% of the members of a consumer organization have a high degree of 'social consciousness' is meaningless, unless we know the percentage of social consciousness of the non-members.

For *Type 2* data we need at least to compare two collectives, for instance the degree of integration of precincts, with the hypothesis that we expect a higher degree of integration in a rural precinct as compared with an inner-city precinct. In Type 2 data, a parallel meaning at the individual and the collective level is not necessary. Prediction at the individual level is no longer possible; we now predict the degree of integration of a precinct based on the level of urbanization, in our example.

The time dimension enters in *Type 3* data. Here, we collect data of individuals at different points in time. This allows us to study sequential processes, such as vacation decision-making or travel behavior. A source of bias in Type 3 or panel data may be the effects of earlier responses. Individuals may try to be consistent with earlier responses, especially with attitudinal and life-style questions.

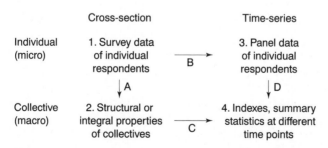

Figure 1   Four types of data in economic psychology.

An example is the foot-in-the-door approach, in which earlier requests influence the response of the individual on a later request (Freedman and Fraser, 1966).

An advantage of Type 3 data is the possibility to test causal effects: the proposition that a stimulus at time t_1 should influence a dependent variable at time t_2. We may even control for external causal factors by comparing the test group with a control group.

Type 4 data are the aggregate level, repeated observations over time, Katona's (1975) Index of Consumer Sentiment (ICS) is an example of this type of data. The ICS is computed from quarterly sample data in the U.S.A. and used to predict discretionary expenditure, credit, and saving. Each sample is drawn from the population, independent of earlier samples. Causal effects can be tested at the aggregate level, for instance an increase of unemployment at time t_1 leads to a decline of consumer sentiment at time t_2 and this causes a decrease in consumer expenditure at time t_3. We should be aware that also external causal factors may have caused the effect on the dependent variables.

Interrelations between types of data

In Figure 1, the *relations* A, B, C, and D between the four types of data are given. The direction of the arrows shows the common type of aggregation or transformation applied to the data.

Relation A is a type of aggregation from individual to collective analytical properties. Computing a proportion, mean, standard deviation, or correlation means that we transform individual analytical data into collective data. Counting relationships between individuals, we arrive at structural properties of the collective. Classifying the content of written documents and folk tales, we may arrive at integral properties of the collective.

In the sociological discussion on atomism *vs* holism, in relation A starting with atomistic observations holistic properties are developed. The holistic properties may become elements in a structuralist approach. However, even the most structuralist sociologist should admit that many structuralistic relations have been developed from individual observations. Moving up from individual data to collective properties and propositions involves the possibility of 'fallacies of aggregation', which means the aggregation of heterogeneous individual data may lead to a misleading 'average', not representative for the population. *Vice versa*, the ecological fallacy is to conclude individual relationships from an aggregate relationship, if the population is heterogeneous or even if the distribution of the population is bimodal.

In *Relation B* several observations over time of one individual are connected. Individual change measures are relevant here. Under influence of which conditions or stimuli do individuals change their behavior or their attitudes? A longitudinal design provides a possibility for correcting measurement errors that cannot be corrected in a one-time cross-section (De Jonge and Oppedijk van Veen, 1982, 1983). Relation B is mainly the process of computing change scores and correcting inconsistencies in the data of the panel members.

Having computed an analytical, structural, or integral property of a collective or population at time t_1, we may repeat this procedure with another sample at time t_2. *Relation C* is the comparison of these properties (indexes or other summary statistics) over time. Econometric time-series studies are mainly of this type. Katona (1975) and Mueller (1963) describe the use of the ICS in explaining consumer expenditure, using a time–series of observations from different samples. Comparison of the results of analyses of Type 1 and Type 4 data led to the cross-section *vs* time-series paradox (Adams, 1965). Relation C caused quite a controversy in the literature on the predictive value of consumer attitudes and purchase intentions (Adams, 1964, 1965; Adams and Green, 1965; Bouwen and van den Abeele, 1979).

In *Relation D*, panel data are aggregated into proportions, means, and standard deviations, which is normally done with panel data. These aggregate properties do no longer reflect individual but collective properties. Collective properties are a net effect of individual properties, both positive and negative. The net collective change may be the result of different constellations of individual changes. An example of this is shown below. At time t_1 we observe a 50:50 distribution of respondents: a proportion of 50 per cent expecting an increase of personal income (+) and 50 per cent expecting an equal or a declining income (–). At time t_2, the proportions are 70% and 30%, respectively. This means an increase of positive income expectations, at least as seen as Type 4 data. However, as Type 3 data, we look for the change pattern of individuals (Table 1).

In pattern I, 80% of the respondents are in the same categories at t_1 and t_2, while 20% change from negative to positive. In pattern II, only 20% of the respondents are in the same category at t_1 and t_2, while 50% change from negative to positive and 30% from positive to negative.

In pattern I, all changers follow the general trend. In pattern II, 50% follow the general trend and 30% swim against the current. While the net result is the same, pattern II is clearly more volatile and unstable. An advantage of Relation D over Relation C is the possibility of studying the change pattern, and, thus, the 'volatility' of the change. The volatility of change may also be a relevant aggregate property (Katona, 1979).

From micro to macro

Relations A and D (Figure 1) are relations from micro to macro phenomena, from individual to collective properties. Somermeyer (1967) asserts that a macro-economic model for a collective should be derived from a micro model for the individual members of the collective through the method of aggregation. Economic theory pertains 'au fond' to individual units (persons, households, nations) and not to aggregates of these individual units. Somermeyer (1967) even asserts that an economic macro-theory that has not been derived from a

Table 1   Change patterns (relation D) between measurements t_1 and t_2

Pattern I	t_2 +	t_2 –	Total	Pattern II	t_2 +	t_2 –	Total
t_1				t_1			
+	50	0	50	+	20	30	50
–	20	30	50	–	50	0	50
Total	70	30	100	Total	70	30	100

micro-theory, cannot be valid. This strong assertion may apply to analytical properties but certainly not to structural or integral properties. Katona (1979), on the other hand, states that 'regularities of economic attitudes, expectations, and behaviors are demonstrated on the aggregate or macro level, whereas attitudes, intentions, and behavior are shown to fluctuate to a much greater extent and to be subject to considerable noise'. Katona (1975) finds strong relationship between attitudes and behavior at the macro level but not at the micro level. He advocates to develop a 'macro-psychology' dealing with aggregate measures of confidence, optimism/pessimism, uncertainty. A parallel relationship of these macro concepts at the individual level is not required.

In marketing research, the prediction of the quantity of grocery products purchased by individual households yields low proportions of explained variance, when the independent variables (in multiple regression analysis) are socioeconomic (Frank, 1967). It is concluded from these studies that socioeconomic characteristics are not particularly effective bases for market segmentation. However, this conclusion is based on individual data (Type 1), while the implementation of a market segmentation strategy involves 'postulates about the characteristics and the behavior of groups, not persons' (Bass *et al.*, 1968). If it is the behavior of groups, not persons, that is relevant, the absence of a satisfactory explanation of individual behavior does not necessarily imply the absence of valid relationships of group characteristics (Type 2 data). Variables may indicate large differences in average purchase rates, while individual relationships, as in multiple regression analysis, have a low proportion of explained variance.

Kramer (1981) states that aggregate data in economics are considered to be inferior to individual-level data. Empirical results based solely on aggregate-level analysis are normally regarded with due caution until confirmed by a proper individual-level study. It is known as the 'fallacy of ecological inference' (Robinson, 1950) to base inferences about individual behavior on aggregate data. An example is that based on time-series analysis of aggregate data (Type 4) an association has been found between macro-economic conditions and election outcomes. However, no such association could be obtained in survey-based studies (Type 1) between personal economic circumstances and voting behavior.

In a similar way, buying intentions predict purchase behavior in panel-based studies (Type 3) but aggregate measures of buying intentions do not predict aggregate purchases (Type 4). The QSI (Quarterly Survey of Buying Intentions) had a low predictive value (Type 4 data), although a test of the QSI at the individual level (Type 3 data) proved to be successful (McNeil, 1974).

The QSI experience has shown that micro findings do not always give parallel results at the macro level, and vice versa, findings at the aggregate level do not necessarily have a parallel meaning at the individual level. In this regard, Katona's (1979) plea for a macro-psychology as distinct from individual-based psychology can be understood. It reaches too far to say that micro and macro are different worlds, but macro-phenomena are not simply additive effects of micro-phenomena.

Schelling (1978) puts the micro/macro relationship in another perspective in his book *Micromotives and Macrobehavior*. Individuals do not act independently from each other. My choice of a recreation area depends on other people's choices, both if I prefer a silent or a lively place. There is an *interaction* between the individual and other individuals and between the individual and the collectivity. The aggregate outcome will be different from a summation of individual decisions. The price a farmer gets for his potatoes depends on how many other farmers want to sell potatoes: 'The market works', and an equilibrium price for potatoes will be reached.

Individual behavior depends on how many others are behaving that way. Coming to the beach for sunbathing and swimming, you may discover that too many others had the same idea, and you may decide to go home again. Driving on a highway is a comfortable and a fast way of travelling, unless too many others want to do the same. Individual advantages turn into disadvantages after a critical number has been surpassed. Other examples in the literature are the 'tragedy of the commons' (Hardin, 1968) and the 'prisoners' dilemma'. These examples show that the aggregate result of persons striving for their self-interest is not in the collective interest, and thus their self-interest in the long run.

The aggregate effect of individual behavior may be different from a simple summation in many ways.

Schelling (1978) distinguishes:

Self-fulfilling expectations: The more people expect that the bank will fail, the more urgent it is to withdraw your funds before the failure.
Self-displacing expectations: Some people want to pay a little more at an auction, and if more people share this behavior, prices will go up.
Self-negating expectations: The more people expect that the beach will be crowded (and stay home), the less crowded the beach will be.
Self-equilibrating expectations: The first time we all bring drinks and no food to a picnic; next time we all bring food and no drinks. Gradually we will bring reasonable amounts of food and drinks (or we make arrangements, who will bring food and who will bring drinks).
Self-confirming expectations: If smokers come to expect that menthol cigarettes are in blue-green packages, all manufacturers may find it advantageous to put menthol cigarettes in packages of this color. Blue-green becomes a signal for menthol cigarettes.

We want to show with the above examples that the aggregate effect is not simply a summation of individual expectations. People take each other's expectations into account and change their own expectations accordingly. Barton (1968) gives similar arguments, why analytical characteristics of individuals cannot be summated to obtain a collective characteristic. 'Other people' or 'individual perceptions of collective characteristics' intervene [in] this summation.

Cross-section *vs* time-series

Adams was the first to formulate the time-series *vs* cross-section paradox in consumer anticipations studies. 'In aggregative time series, measures of attitudes have been found to be significant predictors of consumer expenditure for durable goods.' It has not been possible to show an analogous relationship in the cross-section. 'A parallel but reverse phenomenon can be observed in the case of consumer buying plans. The time-series effect of buying plans is negligible, whereas in the cross-section their effect is readily apparent' (Adams, 1965: 367).

Bouwen and van den Abeele (1979) describe the different results of cross-sectional and time-series data on consumer expectations. Van Raaij (1980) summarizes the differences between cross-section and time-series as represented in Table 2. Note that these cross-section data have one reinterview to check the predictive value of intentions at the individual level. We still consider this as Type 1 data, although it goes in the direction of Type 3.

In cross-section studies, the variability of individuals and collectives dominates. Individuals and collectives are taken as replications to establish the relationships between variables. In time-series studies, the variability over time dominates, while differences between individuals or collectives are removed by an averaging process. Occasions over time are taken as replications to establish the relationships between variables. In time-series studies, changes in the economic conditions have a strong impact. While a cross-section study is static (one occasion), a time-series study is dynamic (many occasions). How to explain that different types of variables are effective in the cross-section and in a time-series study? Okun suggests the following example: 'Suppose Asian flu is a contagious disease which is known to spread gradually. Suppose that the individuals are polled regularly on their expectation of catching the disease. Now, when a few advance cases appear, the polls will record an increase in expectations and these expectations are fulfilled in the aggregate as the disease gradually spreads. Yet, a cross-section study would show that individuals who expressed a high expectation are no more prone to catch the disease than those who expressed low expectations' (1960: 423). In this example, Type 4 data show a predictive value of the expectations. If persons know their own susceptibility to catch the Asian flu and persons with a high susceptibility express higher expectations than persons with a low susceptibility, Type 1 data will also show a predictive value of the expectations. Okun's example shows that persons may base their expectations on general developments not taking personal susceptibility into account (only an aggregative effect in Type 4 data), or stressing personal susceptibiility (also an individual effect in Type 1 data).

Table 2 Differences between cross-section and time-series

Cross-section	Time-series
Data of Type 1 and 2	Data of Type 3 and 4
Interindividual variability Intercollective variability	Intertemporal variability (repeated observations)
Static (picture)	Dynamic (film)
Effect of socioeconomic characteristics of units	Effect of economic events during period of observation
Buying intentions are predictive	Expectations (attitudes) are predictive
Low explained variance with principal component analysis: 3 components explain 50–60%	High explained variance with principal component analysis: 3 components explain 80–90%
Long-term and short-term effects, but unstable	Short-term effects

In Okun's example, we see that expectations may consist of two components, a general one, e_g, based on developments in society, and a personal one, e_p, based on personal susceptibility. In a similar way, one may argue that some persons have always a pessimistic view of life, while others have a more optimistic disposition. To these long-term optimistic or pessimistic expectations, short-term optimistic or pessimistic reactions to economic events are superimposed. An individual i's expectations can thus be partitioned into a long-term component e_{pi} and a short-term component e_{gi}. The long-term component will be stable over time, so that in a time-series study only the short-term component e_g has an effect. In a cross-section study, both e_g and e_p have an effect, if both differ between individuals. If e_g is small relative to e_p, cross-section results will largely capitalize on e_p individual differences in expectations. In Type 1 data, both short-term and long-term effects are present. In Type 3 data, the long-term effect can be differenced out, as we look in panel data for changes over time.

Expectations are measured on a limited discrete scale with upper and lower limits. This means that expectational change may be imperfectly measured and, secondly, that we may expect a negative correlation between e_p and e_g. A person with a high e_p score (an optimist) has less scope in an upward direction and more scope downward. A pessimist (with a low e_p score) has more scope in an upward direction and less scope downward. This is known as the *restriction of range* phenomenon.

In time-series data, we are able to separate the short-term from the long-term component, while in cross-section data both components are confounded. In this sense, time-series data are superior to cross-section data to study the effect of consumer expectations on spending and saving (Gianotten and van Raaij, 1982; van Raaij and Gianotten, 1982). Kramer (1981) even states that the aggregate time-series evidence yields valid inferences about the underlying individual behavioral effects, even better than cross-sectional data can yield. An example is shown in Figure 2a and 2b, derived from Kramer (1981). In a 'normal' situation, positive expectations coincide with more consumer expenditure. In a 'recession' situation, negative expectations coincide with less consumer expenditure.

However, in cross-section studies we probably will not discover this, whereas the cross-sectional regression line may have a zero or even a negative slope (Figure 2b). In a cross-section study, persons with more negative expectations are not necessarily the ones with low expenditure. (Remember the negative correlation between e_p and e_g.)

In a time-series study, we find a regression line with a positive slope. In Figure 2b, the ● signs are the means of the nine observations. Not the shapes of the scatterplots but the overall shift of the scatterplot is the main effect we are concerned with.

The time-series approach aggregates over individual differences, although we may investigate the regression lines for high-, medium- and low-income respondents, or old and young respondents. The time-series approach is also feasible for subgroups or segments of respondents, if the sample sizes are large enough we expect meaningful differences.

The effect of additional and lagged variables

In the above section, the total score of an individual is partitioned into a permanent component e_p and a transitory component e_g. Cross-section data are sensitive to individual

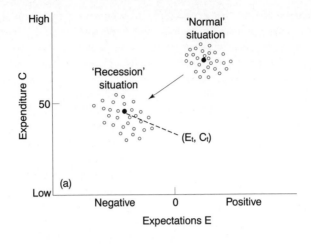

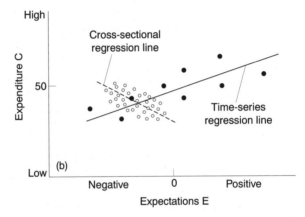

Figure 2   Relationship between expectations E and expenditure C. (a) Two cross-sections in a 'normal' and a 'recession' situation; (b) A cross-section and a time-series regression line.

differences and especially the permanent component. In time-series data, the individual differences are cancelled out; time-series data are especially sensitive to the transitory component. As the correlation between e_p and e_g might be negative, Type 1 and Type 4 data may yield different results.

Another explanation is provided by Simon (1974: Appendix A) in his study on the effects of income on fertility. Simon argues that there is no real statistical contradiction between the evidence from cross-section and time-series data. The various estimation techniques yield different images because they take pictures from different perspectives. An example may illustrate the different perspectives.

If expenditure C is a function of income Y and expectations E:

$$C = f(Y, \text{E}).\tag{1}$$

Let us assume that the direct effect of income on expenditure is positive, and that a number of lagged effects are added in a linear way,

$$C_t = b_0 Y_t + b_1 Y_{t-1} + \ldots + b_n Y_{t-n} \pm c_1 E_{t-1} \pm c_2 E_{t-2} \pm \ldots \pm c_n E_{t-n}. \quad (2)$$

Assume that expectations are a positive function of income:

$$E_{t-n} = m \cdot Y_{t-n}. \quad (3)$$

It means that persons with a higher income have generally more optimistic expectations (van Raaij and Gianotten, 1982). Substituting (3) in (2), one obtains (4):

$$C_t = b_0 Y_t + \ldots + b_n Y_{t-n} \pm c_1 m Y_{t-1} \pm \ldots \pm c_n m Y_{t-n}. \quad (4)$$

The total effect of income on expenditure can be positive or negative, depending upon the relative weights and signs of the various coefficients.

Aigner and Simon (1970) have shown that

$$\hat{b} = b_0 + r_{Y_t Y_{t-1}} b_1 + \ldots + r_{Y_t Y_{t-n}} b_n \pm r_{Y_t Y_{t-1}} c_1 m \pm \ldots \pm t_{Y_t Y_{t-n}} c_n m, \quad (5)$$

in which $\hat{b}$ is the observed coefficient in the contemporaneous cross-section and $r_{Y_t Y_{t-n}}$ is the correlation coefficient between the incomes of individuals in period t and in period $t - n$. This means that the extent to which $\hat{b}$, the estimated mean coefficient, differs from b_0, the 'true' mean coefficient for the current period, is a function of the relative sizes of the coefficients b_n, c_n and m, and the correlations between the sets of independent variables in each pair of the periods. If these correlations are high and if the lagged effect is substantial, $\hat{b}$ differs greatly from b_0. A cross-section according to formula (5) can even yield a negative $\hat{b}$.

In a time-series regression analysis, however, fluctuations of income over time are high and thus the correlation coefficients $r_{Y_t Y_{t-n}}$ may differ greatly. There may be even positive and negative correlation coefficients, cancelling out the effect of the lagged variables. This means that the difference of $\hat{b}$ and b_0 will be smaller. The time-series $\hat{b}$ comes closer to the 'true' mean coefficient. In time-series data, the relationship of income and expenditure will be positive, while in cross-section data one might accidentally obtain a negative relationship.

In addition, Simon (1974) states that long-run secular time-series might be negative over the course of the development. In such long series, not common in economic psychology, the $r_{Y_t Y_{t-n}}$ will be positive and quite high, because the year-to-year changes, as studied in the business cycle, are small relative to the long secular trend. The relationship of income and expenditure might be negative, if $c_n m$ is relatively large and if the time lag is considerable.

Conclusions

The assertion that the micro and macro relationships constitute two 'separate worlds' cannot be maintained. No separate macro-psychology should be developed, although it is true that some relationships obtained in a cross-section cannot be found in time-series, and vice versa. Even with the same independent variables, time-series and cross-section data may lead to different results. If the phenomenon under study is largely a chance phenomenon, as in Okun's (1960) Asian flu example, an aggregate time-series model (Type phenomenon, as in Okun's (1960) Asian flu example, an aggregate time-series model (Type 4) is superior to an individual cross-section model (Type 1). Some variables may be important in time-series research, e.g. attitudes and expectations, while other variables are relevant in individual cross-section data (with one reinterview), e.g. buying intentions.

Time-series data are generally superior to cross-section data, because of the possibility to remove the permanent component e_p and to relate the transitory component e_g to the changing economic conditions. In time-series data of the business cycle, the effect of the lagged variables will generally cancel out, leaving the 'true' effect to be more accurate. Cross-section data are more affected by individual differences, the e_p component, which is not a problem when the researcher is interested in individual differences, but may be a problem when the researcher is interested in the effects of income, economic conditions, and expectations on change in expenditure or savings.

Type 3 data have most possibilities but are generally more expensive and time-consuming to be collected. Type 3 data may be aggregated to Type 4, losing the possibility of tracking persons or households over time. Type 1 or 2 data may be misleading, if used in a 'pilot study' before establishing a panel study. They might even give the wrong sign of the relationship or deviate greatly from the 'true' relationship we seek.

References

Adams, F.G. (1964), 'Consumer attitudes, buying plans, and purchases of durable goods: a principal components, time series approach', *Review of Economics and Statistics*, 46, 347–355.

Adams, F.G. (1965), 'Prediction with consumer attitudes: The time-series cross-section paradox', *Review of Economics and Statistics*, 47, 367–378.

Adams, F.G. and E.W. Green (1965), 'Explaining and predicting aggregative consumer attitudes', *International Economic Review*, 6, 275–293.

Aigner, D.J. and J.L. Simon (1970), 'A specification bias interpretation of cross section vs. time series parameter estimates', *Western Economic Journal*, 8, 144–161.

Barton, A.H. (1968), 'Bringing society back in. Survey research and macro methodology', *American Behavioral Scientist*, 12, 1–9.

Bass, F.M., D.J. Tigert and R.T. Lonsdale (1968), 'Market segmentation: group versus individual behavior', *Journal of Marketing Research*, 5, 264–270.

Bouwen, R. and P. van den Abeele (1979), 'Crisis in het consumentenvertrouwen? Enkele vaststellingen en vragen voor verder onderzoek', in *Jaarboek van de Nederlandse Vereniging van Marktonderzoekers*, pp. 83–91.

De Jonge, L. and W.M. Oppedijk van Veen (1982), 'The prospective buyer of consumer durables', Dissertation, University of Groningen.

De Jonge, L. and W.M. Oppedijk van Veen (1983), 'Accounting for data inconsistencies in a longitudinal mail survey', *Journal of Economic Psychology*, 4, 377–400.

Frank, R.E. (1976), 'Market segmentation research: findings and implications', in F.M. Bass, C.W. King and E.A. Pessemier (eds.), *Applications of the Sciences in Marketing Management*. New York: Wiley.

Freedman, J.L. and S.C. Fraser (1966), 'Compliance without pressure: The foot-in-the-door technique', *Journal of Personality and Social Psychology*, 4, 195–202.

Gianotten, H.J. and W.F. van Raaij (1982), 'Consumer credit and savings as a function of income and confidence', *Papers on Economic Psychology*, no. 17. Rotterdam: Erasmus University.

Hardin, G. (1968), 'The tragedy of the commons', *Science*, 162, 1243–1248.

Katona, G. (1975), *Psychological Economics*. New York: Elsevier.

Katona, G. (1979), 'Toward a macropsychology', *American Psychologist*, 34, 118–126.

Kramer, G. (1981), 'The ecological fallacy revisited: aggregate- versus individual-level findings on economics and elections, and sociotropic voting', *Social Science Working Paper 424*. Pasadena, CA: California Institute of Technology.

Lazarsfeld, P.F. and H. Menzel (1961), 'On the relation between individual and collective properties', in A. Etzioni (ed.), *Complex Organizations: A Sociological Reader*. New York: Holt, Rinehart & Winston, pp. 499–516.

McClelland, D. (1960), 'The achievement motive: how it is measured and its possible economic effects', in *The Achieving Society*. New York: Van Nostrand, ch. 2.

McNeil, J. (1974), 'Federal programs to measure consumer purchase expectations, 1946–1973: A post-mortem', *Journal of Consumer Research*, 1, 1–10.

Mueller, E. (1963), 'Ten years of consumer attitude surveys: their forecasting record', *Journal of the American Statistical Association*, 58, 899–917.

Okun, A.M. (1960), 'The value of anticipations data in forecasting national product', in National Bureau of Economic Research, *The Quality and Economic Significance of Anticipation Data*. Princeton, NJ: NBER.

Robinson, W.S. (1950), 'Ecological correlation and the behavior of individuals', *American Sociological Review*, 15, 351–357.

Schelling, T.C. (1978), *Micromotives and Macrobehavior*. New York: Norton.

Simon, J.L. (1974), *The Effects of Income on Fertility*. Chapel Hill, NC: University of North Carolina, Carolina Population Center.

Somermeyer, W.H. (1967), 'Specificatie van economische relaties', *De Economist*, 115, 1–26.

Van Raaij, W.F. (1980), *Consumentenvertrouwen en -verwachtingen in een periode van recessie*. Rotterdam: Erasmus University.

Van Raaij, W.F. and H.J. Gianotten (1982) 'Consumer expenditure as a function of income and willingness to buy', *Papers on Economic Psychology*, no. 14. Rotterdam: Erasmus University.

Semiotics of
consumption

8

●●

Nöth, W., 1988, 'The language of commodities: Groundwork for a semiotics of consumer goods', *International Journal of Research in Marketing*, **4**, 173–86
Heilbrunn, B., 1995, 'My brand the hero? A semiotic analysis of the consumer–brand relationship', enlarged version of a paper presented at the European Marketing Academy Conference, Paris, May
Floch, J.-M., 1988, 'The contribution of structural semiotics to the design of a hypermarket', *International Journal of Research in Marketing*, **4**, 233–52

Introduction

The word semiology and its practice go back to Ancient Greek, and especially the Stoic philosophers who were the first to establish and form the concept of sign (*sêmeion*) as a combination of a signifier (*sêmainon*) and a signified (*sêmainomenon*) (Marin, 1978, pp. 658–9). Generally defined as the science of signs, semiology or semiotics is primarily concerned with the investigation and explication of meaning, that is, how meaning is created, transmitted and interpreted in various situations. More precisely, semiology 'aims to take in any system of signs, whatever their substance and limits: images, gestures, musical signs, objects and the complex associations of all these, which form the content of ritual, convention or public entertainment: these constitute, if not language, at least systems of signification' (Barthes, 1967). For a long time, semiology and semiotics have been considered as two different concepts, semiotics often being defined as the theory of non-linguistic signs, whereas semiology was said to focus on the study of textual structures. Some leading authors, such as Barthes, Jakobson and Lévi-Strauss, proposed in 1969 to adopt 'semiotics' as a general term that would comprise the fields of research in the traditions of both semiology and general semiotics, a decision which has been widely followed since, and which legitimized the use of 'semiotics' as a general concept for the study of signs systems (see Nöth, 1990, p. 14). The understanding of the functioning of consumption systems is related to the three main areas covered by semiotics, as described by Charles Morris (1946): *syntactics* which studies the relations between signs, *pragmatics* which is concerned with the relationships between signs and their users, and *semantics* which focus on the sign–object relations. Whereas pragmatics received recent attention only in consumer research, its use being generally confined to the areas of product design and advertising discourse, both syntactics and semantics have proved to play a determinant role in the semiotic study of consumption practices, as will be illustrated in the three articles presented in this chapter.

The syntactic approach is largely based on the assumption that cultural practices always reflect a deep unconscious structure, which can be decoded as a language system. This assumption is largely influenced by structuralism, which emerged through such sister disciplines as anthropology and structural semiotics. Based on the famous Jakobson's maxim that 'there are no things, only relations between things', a stream of research emerged mainly in Europe in the 1960s, which investigated the functioning of signifying systems such as clothes, food, commodities by privileging the linguistic approach. Mainly influenced by Jakobson and Lévi-Strauss, this approach refused to treat elements as independent entities, reinterpreting them instead in terms of their relations within a global system which operates according to generalizable laws. In this approach priority is given to the relations at the expense of elements, since only the relations between elements constitute a structure (Greimas, 1983). This assumption which grounds the structuralist approach to semiotics originally derives from the linguist Ferdinand de Saussure, who thought of language as a whole system of rules governing the selection and combination of the different signs out of which meaning was produced (Sinclair, 1987, p. 44). Such an approach allows us to analyze the functioning of systems of signs by comparison with linguistic systems, that is, through relations of oppositions and complementarity between constitutive elements of the system. The basis for this approach is the supposition that every object in our world is a sign, and that every sign is linguistic or trans-linguistic to the extent that its signification always involves its structural relation to other signs, and that this relation is determined by the hidden codes of a language system (Barthes, 1967; Kearney, 1988). Moreover, this approach is based on the assumption that cultural practices are governed by unconscious possibilities, which are always imbued with the symbolizing power of language.

Lévi-Strauss can be considered as representative of this innovative approach within the sciences of man. He successively studied kinship structures and goods exchange practices in primitive societies by applying the four following principles of analysis: (1) the shift from the study of conscious phenomena to the study of their unconscious infrastructure, (2) the shift from the terms to the relations between them, (3) the study of the whole system, and (4) the discovery of general laws within the system (Nöth, 1990, p. 302). His anthropological analysis of kinship structures is a good example of the analogies which exist between language and culture. For Lévi-Strauss, kinship structures can be viewed as elements which acquire meaning only once integrated into larger systems of signification. Kinship systems express rules of prohibited marriage (e.g. taboo, incest), and in some cultures prescribe some categories of relatives who should be married, and can therefore be interpreted as real systems of communication in primitive societies, in which the women are the messages exchanged between class, lineages or families (Lévi-Strauss, 1958; Nöth, 1990). As Lévi-Strauss puts it, 'although they belong to another order of reality, kinship phenomena are of the same type as linguistic phenomena' (Lévi-Strauss, 1958). The same approach has been applied to the exchange of goods, identified by Lévi-Strauss as another essential mode of social communication in any society. Hence, by equating the codes of kinship or goods systems with the codes of a linguistic system (as an interrelationship between minimal signifying units), this structural approach aims at 'relocating the structural origin of the commercial and sexual behaviour of primitive societies in the infrastructure of language itself' (Kearney, 1994, p. 256).

Applied to consumption goods, this approach infers that commodities can be viewed as the minimal units of a whole language system, which means they operate not in isolation but within a system of signifying relations that can be decoded in semiotic terms. Consumption goods thus have meaning through relations to other goods and through relations to other market actors. The first role of semiotics is to decode and understand these various relations and to point out the syntactic rules that govern consumption systems viewed as languages.

An alternative approach largely influenced by semantics and widely used in advertising, communication and consumer behaviour, is to analyze how meaning is both created and interpreted, but also what types of meanings are associated with products and brands as well as specific consumption practices. As early as 1959, Sidney Levy considered products as 'symbols for sale', which meant that products and brands have both a utilitarian or pragmatic value and a symbolic value. Even though the symbolic nature of consumption has long been acknowledged,[1] semiotics only became influential in marketing research in the late 1960s after the seminal works of outstanding and innovative semioticians such as Barthes, Eco and Greimas. The seminal work of Barthes (1964) postulated the universal semantization of usage whereby the use of an object is converted into a sign for that use. Goods such as clothes and food are used for functional purposes such as protection and nourishment. They might nevertheless also be used as signs, by an 'inevitable' process of semantization by which the utilitarian object becomes 'suffused with meaning' (Barthes, 1964; Nöth, 1990). Moles (1972) and Barthes (1964) have pointed out two types of meanings potentially associated with a commodity: the first one is a *denotative* meaning related to specific functional needs and expectations and essentially attached to the commodity itself (the commodity as a sign names directly a given object); the second layer of meanings can be defined as *connotative* in the sense a commodity might refer to a set of attributes that supposedly characterizes its customer and not the commodity itself. Commodities as signs may therefore refer to culturally determined implications or connotations which have additional meanings (the possession of a luxury brand may, for instance, connote a high social status). Thus the meaning of consumption objects involves higher levels of connotation that are linked in more substantive ways to cultural processes (Gottdiener, 1995).

This theory of universal semantization of usage, largely developed by Baudrillard, assumes that, with consumer society, objects lose their material and functional status by their integration into sign systems. Consuming is defined by Baudrillard as the organization of material substance into signifying substance: 'to become an object of consumption the objects must become a sign' (Baudrillard, 1968, p. 277). A commodity product can hence be conceived as a sign, that is, a relational term which refers to a perceiving subject but also to other entities within a semiotic system. Lefebvre describes 'the world of commodities' as constituting a system of signs, a language. As a sign, the commodity 'comprises a *signifier*, which is the object susceptible of exchange, and a *signified* which is the possible . . . satisfaction derived from its purchase' (Lefebvre, 1966, p. 342). Thus the sign relation of the commodity exists between the object as a mere material signifier and its use value as the signified, but the commodity also derives its semiotic value from its paradigmatic relationship to the system of commodities as a whole (Nöth, 1994, p. 5; Lefebvre, 1966, p. 343). In a semiotic perspective, an object is thus essentially a conjunction between a sign vehicle (a *signifier*) and its referent (a *signified*). Semiotics' main task is to analyze the articulations of these two dimensions of the commodity as a sign. The extreme limit of this semiotic approach to consumption is represented by Baudrillard who tends to view commodities solely in their semiotic essence to the neglect of their utilitarian function. His critical analysis of commodities defines both the use- and exchange-value of commodities as values within a system of commercial signs. According to him, commodities become signs within the process of consumption, which he defines as an 'activity of systematic sign manipulation' (Baudrillard, 1968). In this view, 'the material and functional object acquires meaning in an abstract systematic relation to all other objects as signs, . . . never in its materiality, but in its difference from all other commodities' (Baudrillard, 1968; Nöth, 1990, p. 444). A semiotic approach to consumption thus aims at decoding and understanding consumption practices as systems of signification which express cultural discourses and values.

The first article by Winfried Nöth presents various approaches to the semiotics of commodities. He contends that the language of commodities is perceived prototypically within three semiotic frames as utilitarian, commercial and socio-cultural signs. It is further argued that the meanings of such signs are not inherent from the physical products but derive from three interrelated spheres: (1) the producer's discourse about the product, (2) the consumer's interaction with the product, and (3) the consumer's assessment of the product against the background of the commodities system. Nöth then introduces a famous distinction between the two types of relations, *paradigmatic* and *syntagmatic*, which, in a given system, describe how signs are organized. Paradigmatic relations reveal oppositions and contrasts of products, that is it refers to the substitutability of products. A paradigmatic choice conveys meaning through the differences between the sign selected and those not selected (Mick, 1986). On the other hand, syntagmatic relations refer to the possible complementarity of products. The final argument made by Nöth is that, since competition tends to maximize differences and minimize similarities between products, the semiotic system of commodities has a marked paradigmatic structure and a weak syntagmatic dimension. This interesting approach may be fruitfully compared to the works of Kehret-Ward, who carried out research on the mechanism of articulation involved in most consumption practices by looking at the syntagmatic dimension of the language of commodities involved in functionally related products (Kehret-Ward, 1987, 1988).

The next two articles illustrate the application of structural semiotics to the study of consumption through the use of two important and representative tools: the narrative scheme and the semiotic square. The second article (Heilbrunn) provides a semiotic framework to conceptualize the relationship between the consumer and the brand. From the consumer's perspective, goods can be considered as value providers, which means they are endowed with a narrative programme within which they have to perform, that is, essentially to satisfy the consumer's expectations. The interactions existing between consumers and goods can thus be 'read' as a story in which the brand helps the consumer in his quest for value(s). The consumption process may thus be described as a narrative programme which develops itself through several possible interactions between the consumer and the brand called 'contact nodes'. This series of contacts is then semiotically decoded in a narrative perspective using the morphological approach proposed by Propp to study fairy tales. Four major stages in this relational process are examined: (1) the contract, (2) the acquisition of competence, (3) the performance, and (4) the sanction. This preliminary study ends considering a brand as a character who can thus perform various roles on the market. The article ends with a semiotic perspective which apprehends a brand in a structuralist perspective as a collective process within which the brand's value and meaning are co-constructed and negotiated by various market entities called *actants*.

The third article by Floch illustrates the use of the semiotic square to typologize supermarket shoppers by means of values ascribed to the store. Consumers, when asked about their expeditions to hypermarkets, express a diversity of experiences, behaviour patterns, and wishes which can be organized around the semantic axis 'practical' values vs 'mythical' values. In other words, a store can be endowed with practical values (speed, functionality, etc.) or, on the contrary, with fundamental 'life values' (friendliness, modernity, etc.). This first dichotomy can be enriched and developed through the use of a semiotic square considered as the visual representation of the relations which exists between the distinctive features constituting a semantic category. The semiotic square points out four types of valorizations potentially ascribed by consumers to a store. This typology of consumers has also been used by Floch to account for the expectations of consumers towards cars (Floch, 1990). This example illustrates the use of semiotics as a segmentation tool but it also provides an excellent example of the design conception of a hypermarket attempting to reconcile the desires expressed by consumers and the technical and managerial requirements drawn up by the company.

Note

1. See for instance Thorstein Veblen, *The Theory of the Leisure Class*, originally published in 1899.

References

Barthes, R. (1967), *Elements of Semiology*, New York: Hill & Wang. Original edition: *Eléments de Sémiologie*, Paris: Seuil, 1964.

Baudrillard, J. (1968), *Le Système des Objets*, Paris: Gallimard.

Eco, U. (1976), *A Theory of Semiotics*, Bloomington, IN: Indiana University Press.

Floch, J.-M. (1990), *Sous les Signes les Stratégies. Sémiotique, marketing et communication*, Paris: PUF.

Gottdiener, M. (1995), *Postmodern Semiotics*, Oxford: Basil Blackwell.

Greimas, A.-J. (1983), *Structural Semantics*, Lincoln, NB: University of Nebraska Press; originally published in France in 1966.

Kearney, R. (1988), 'Barthes', in *Modern Movements in European Philosophy*, Manchester: Manchester University Press, 319–31. (Second edition 1994).

Kehret-Ward, T. (1987), 'Combining products in use: How the syntax of products use affects product design and promotion', in J. Umiker-Sebeok (ed.), *Marketing and Semiotics. New Directions in the Study of Signs for Sale*, Berlin: Mouton de Gruyter, 219–38.

Kehret-Ward, T. (1988), 'Using a semiotic approach to study the consumptions of functionally related products', *International Journal of Research in Marketing*, 4, 187–200.

Lefebvre, H. (1966), *Le Langage et la Société*, Paris: Gallimard.

Levy, S. (1959), 'Symbols for sale', *Harvard Business Review*, 37, 117–24.

Marin, L. (1978), 'The semiotic approach', in J. Havet (ed.), *Main Trends of Research in the Social and Human Sciences* Part 2, Vol. 1, Paris: Mouton Publishers/Unesco.

Mick, D. (1986), 'Consumer research and semiotics: Exploring the morphology of signs, symbols and significance', *Journal of Consumer Research*, 13, 196–213.

Moles, A. (1972), *Théorie des Objets*, Paris: Editions Universitaires.

Morris, C. (1946), *Signs, Language and Behavior*, New York: Prentice-Hall.

Nöth, W. (1990), *Handbook of Semiotics*, Bloomington, IN: Bloomington University Press; original edition: *Handbuch der Semiotik*, Stuttgart: Metzler, 1985.

Nöth, W. (1994), 'The sign nature of commodities', unpublished working paper, University of Kassel.

Pinson, C. (1993), 'Marketing: Semiotics', in R.E. Asher (ed.-in-chief), *The International Encyclopedia of Language and Linguistics*, Vol. 1, London: Pergamon Press, 2384–8.

Pinson, C. (1988), 'Editorial: Introduction to the double special issue on semiotics and marketing communications research', *International Journal of Research in Marketing*, 4, 167–72.

Saussure, F. de (1915), *Course in General Linguistic*, New York: McGraw-Hill.

Sinclair, J. (1987), *Images Incorporated: Advertising as Industry and Ideology*, London: Routledge.

The language of commodities: Groundwork for a semiotics of consumer goods

●●●

Winfried Nöth

Professor, Department of English, University-Gesamthochschule Kassel, Germany

Summary

Consumer research has long since acknowledged the symbolic character of commodities but only recently is semiotics being discovered as a possible source of approaches to study the signs of the marketplace. After a survey of the state of the art in related fields of research, a semiotic model is proposed to show that commodities are prototypically perceived within three semiotic frames as utilitarian, commercial and as socio-cultural *signs*. The meanings of these signs are not inherent in the physical products. They are generated in the producer's discourse about the product, in the consumer's interaction with it or in his or her evaluation of it against the background of the system of commodities.

The system of commodities is a semiotic *system* (a language) par excellence, since competition tends to maximize differences and minimize similarities between products. In contradistinction to its marked paradigmatic structure, however, the semiotic system of commodities has only a weak syntagmatic dimension.

Metaphors, such as 'the language of clothes' (cf. Lurie, 1981), 'the language of the automobile' (cf. Aronoff, 1985), or the popular method of 'the language of flowers' suggest that the objects of the marketplace are not only signs but form also semiotic systems.

1. Semiotics of the commodity: State of the art

The sign character of commodities has been analyzed in explicitly semiotic studies (section 1.2) and in a number of implicitly semiotic approaches developed within marketing research (section 1.1), political economy (section 1.3) and anthropology (section 1.4).

From the *International Journal of Research in Marketing*, 4 (1988), 173–86.

1.1   Semiotics of the commodity in marketing research

In marketing research, semiotic aspects of commodities have been studied primarily within three complementary fields of research, advertising, brand image research and the theory of symbolic consumption. A review of research in these areas need not be given in this context, but the semiotic implications of these studies may be commented on briefly.

1.1.1   Advertising

From a semiotic point of view, advertising research studies *messages about commodities*. Such messages are the discourse of a producer or seller directed to a potential consumer. The message consists of verbal or visual signs, and the commodity is the *referential object* of those signs. Brand image and symbolic consumption research, on the other hand, study the communicative functions of *commodities as messages*.

1.1.2   Brand image research

From this perspective commodities are studied as signs whose meaning is the consumer's 'brand image'. Semantic components of a brand image, according to Levy (1978: 168), include 'technical matters', 'product characteristics', 'financial value' or 'social suitability'. Semiotically, such components constitute the *signified* (or content) of the product, while the material object is the *signifier* of the commodity as a *sign*.

1.1.3   Symbolic consumption research

Symbolic consumption (cf. Hirschman and Holbrooks, 1981a), already discovered by Veblen (1899) in the form of 'conspicuous consumption', is an act of communication, not between producer and consumer, but between the consumer and any other member of society, possibly also between the consumer and that consumer's self. The sign in symbolic consumption is less the commodity itself than the act of its consumption. As summarized by Belk *et al.* (1982: 6), the theory of symbolic consumption makes the following assumption about the meaning of such a sign: 'Whether or not consumption communicates status as clearly as was once the case, it is clear that there are still a number of inferences about people which are affected by the goods and services that they presumably have selected.' If inferences are thus made from goods (e.g. cars) to their users (e.g. their personality type) the commodities are interpreted as *indexical signs*. The meaning of such an index is not a characteristic feature of the commercial object itself (e.g. its usefulness or stylistic beauty). The commodity, taken as an index, refers to an attribute which supposedly characterizes its consumer. A language of commodities based on such indexical signs is a language about commodity users.

1.2   Semiotic approaches to the commodity

Since 'all this universe is perfused with signs' (Peirce, 1906, §5.448n) and semiotics is the 'science that studies the life of signs within society' (Saussure, 1916: 16), the discipline thus characterized by its modern founding fathers seems to be a tool predestined for the study of the signs of the marketplace. But consumer research has only recently discovered the methods of semiotics (cf. Mick, 1986; Umiker-Sebeok, 1987) although semioticians have been working in the field since the 1960s (cf. the survey in Nöth, 1985: 447–54).

By far the most extensive explicitly semiotic research in commodities has been made in the context of the semiotics of *advertising* (section 1.2.1), the study of messages *about* commodities. The study of commodities *as* messages has so far remained largely unexplored within semiotics. It is a branch of the more general semiotics of *objects* (reviewed by Krampen, 1979: 6–21). A central topic in this field of research has been the search for a 'semiotic threshold' (cf. Eco, 1976: 19–28) between the sphere of the non-semiotic objects and objects which function as signs. Two proposals for such thresholds, a higher (section 1.2.2) and a lower one (section 1.2.3), will be discussed below.

1.2.1 Advertising and commodity myths

The semiotics of advertising, messages *about* commodities, need not be studied in this context dealing with commodities *as* messages. (But for a survey, see Nöth, 1985: 447–54.) Advertising is nevertheless relevant to the topic under discussion. The public discourse *about* the commodity generates meanings which transform the commercial object into a sign. Once the consumer has learned its meanings, he or she is liable, at a certain level of consciousness, to rediscover this sign on the marketplace, i.e. within the system of commodities.

Among such textually generated meanings of commodities, semioticians have paid special attention to *connotations*, secondary meanings which have been interpreted as being, so to speak, engrafted in a parasitic fashion upon the primary meaning of the commodity. Systems of such meanings have been interpreted (following Barthes, 1964a,b) as *myths* (Langholz-Leymore, 1975) or *ideologies* (Williamson, 1978). (For mythical meanings of commodities see section 2.5.)

1.2.2 Socio-cultural semiotization

One of the first semiotic interpretations of commodities as signs was proposed by Barthes (1964a: 41–2). To him the threshold from the non-semiotic to the semiotic seems to lie above the 'utilitarian or functional' aspect of objects (although he calls these aspects of objects sign-functions (cf. *ibid.*: 41, 68)). Barthes acknowledges that commodities and other objects of culture 'have a substance of expression whose essence is not to signify', e.g. 'clothes are used for protection and food for nourishment even if they are also used as signs'. But in an 'inevitable' process of *semantization* this utilitarian object becomes 'pervaded with meaning': 'As soon as there is a society, every usage is converted into a sign of itself.' Barthes (*ibid.*: 41) discusses two aspects of this semiotization. The first might be called the *socio-cultural sign*. (His example: 'The use of a raincoat . . . cannot be dissociated from the very signs of an atmospheric situation.') The second might be called the *economic sign*. Its frame of reference is the system of commodities: 'Since our society produces only standardized, normalized objects, these objects are unavoidably realizations of a model . . . the substances of a significant form. To discover a non-signifying object, one would have to imagine a utensil absolutely improvised and with no similarity to an existing model' (*ibid.*: 41–2).

The semiotic threshold which Barthes sees between the utilitarian and the socio-cultural aspects of objects has been characterized similarly within various other theories of semiotics. In particular Mukařovský's (1978: 40) functional semiotics (developed in the 1930s and 1940s) draws a clear dividing line between the spheres of the *practical*, where an immediate use and manipulation of objects takes place, and the sphere of the *semiotic*, which is a mediated account-taking of objects. (A different view of this dichotomy is proposed in section 2.2.)

1.2.3   Semiotization of the utilitarian

The semiotic sphere has rarely been extended to the realm of functional utility, but Moles (1972) has proposed such an extension in his *theory of objects*. Moles (1972: 48) defines the meaning of an object as being 'largely attached to its *function*, its utility in relation to the repertoire of human needs'. To him, the practical function of a commodity is its *denotative* meaning. In his study of such meaning he combines principles of structural semantics with methods of psychosemantics. The meaning of an object thus discovered is similar to the lexicographical meaning of the *word* by which the object is designated. E.g., the meaning of the object 'knife', according to this theory, could be 'sharp blade with a handle, used as a cutting instrument'. In addition to this primary layer of meaning, Moles also studies secondary layers of meaning which he defines as 'aesthetic or connotative'. (A different view will be proposed in sections 2.1 and 3.1.)

1.3   Semiotics and political economy

Further semiotic approaches to consumer goods were developed within the framework of political economy where the semiotic essence of the commodity was first sought in its use-value or its exchange-value. Karl Marx had already used the metaphor of 'the language of commodities' (in which 'the linen conveys its thoughts': *Capital* I, 2.2).

In more explicitly semiotic terms, Lefebvre (1966: 342) argued that a commodity is a sign whose *signifier* is the 'object susceptible of exchange' and whose *signified* is the 'potential satisfaction' which the consumer might derive from it. Rossi-Landi (1975: 128), while accepting this *use-value* aspect of the commodity as 'a sign function which exists already at the product level', argued that the *specific* sign value of an object as commodity is its *exchange-value* because only by this value does a useful object become a commodity.

Baudrillard (1968, 1972) developed a semiotics of consumer goods which defines both the use- and the exchange-value of commodities as values within a system of commercial signs. According to Baudrillard (1968: 276–7), commodities become signs within the process of *consumption*, which he considers as 'an activity of systematic sign manipulation'. In this view, the material and functional object acquires meaning in an 'abstract systematic relation to all other object-signs . . ., never in its materiality, but in its difference' from all other commodities. Like linguistic signs whose value is determined by their differences from other elements of a language, commodities are thus defined as elements of a semiotic system. As in language, where the material (phonetic or written) substance of words is essentially irrelevant ('arbitrary') to their content, commodities are seen as signs whose material substance is equally arbitrary: 'Evidently, it is never the objects which are consumed, but it is . . . the *idea of the relation* which is consumed in the series of objects which give rise to this idea'. With this radical view of the semiotics of consumption, the semiotization of the commodity has reached an unsurpassable climax. The commodity has become a pure sign. There seems to be no material trace of practical functionality.

1.4 Anthropological approaches

Baudrillard's extreme insistence on the semiotic essence of commodities to the neglect of their utilitarian function (cf. Krampen, 1979: 7) is paralleled by theses proposed independently by anthropologists. As outlined by Sahlins (1976: 55), anthropological theory has for a long time oscillated between the two poles of a utilitarian and a symbolic account of goods and activities. The former pole is the one of culture while the latter is the one of *practical reason* (*ibid.*). While a cultural interpretation ascribes a sign value to goods, 'practical reason' interprets goods as having non-semiotic, utilitarian functions. Sahlin's (1976: 169) own position in this debate is that objects of consumption are always permeated by cultural meanings both in their practical utility and in their social and commercial context: 'The social meaning of an object that makes it useful to a certain category of persons is no more apparent from its physical properties than is the value it may be assigned in exchange. Use-value is not less symbolic or less arbitrary than commodity-value.'

This radical thesis of the semiotic character of commodities has no less vigorously been defended by Douglas and Isherwood (1979: 62) who programmatically declare that 'the essential function of consumption is its capacity to make sense. Forget the idea of consumer irrationality. Forget that commodities are good for eating, clothing, and shelter; forget their usefulness and try instead the idea that commodities are good for thinking; treat them as a non-verbal medium for the human creative faculty'.

Further non-utilitarian dimensions of objects of cultural exchange have been revealed by Csikszentmihalyi and Rochberg-Halton (1981) in their study of the social and psychological significance of the attachment which Americans have for objects in their homes. Wallendorf and Arnould (1988) provide a cross-cultural perspective of attitudes towards 'favorite things'. Anthropological research in the evolution of cultural values associated with commodities is presented by Appadurai (1986).

2. Commodities as signs: A pluralistic view

Approaches to the semiotics of commodities have suffered from one-sided perspectives and from false dichotomies. Consumer goods do not become signs in spheres beyond practical utility. As brand image research has shown, consumers certainly associate utilitarian or practical meanings with commodities. Such meanings are constituents of commodity-signs which the consumer has learned either through advertising or through his or her own practical experiences in individual acts of consumption. The semiotic essence of consumer goods can therefore not be exhausted in dichotomies such as 'utilitarian vs. semiotic' or 'sign vs. non-sign'. Nor is the denotation–connotation dichotomy a sufficient tool for the description of the plurality meanings associated with commodities.

2.1   The multi-framed sign: Basic assumptions

Instead of such dichotomous views a pluralistic approach to the semiotics of consumer goods will be proposed in the following. The basic assumption is that commodities are objects which are perceived by the consumer from *various semiotic perspectives* (cf. Eco, 1976: 24–7) or, in the terminology of cognitive science, within various *frames* (cf. Nöth, 1987a).

2.1.1   Semiotic frames of the commodity

Three prototypical frames of the commodity will be proposed in the following, the *utilitarian* (section 2.2), the *commercial* (section 2.3) and the *socio-cultural* frame in a narrower sense (cf. section 2.4). The spheres of meaning associated with these frames are not unknown in consumer and marketing research (see section 1.1), but semioticians have tended to neglect the utilitarian and the commercial frames (see section 1.2).

The number of possible frames which may determine the perception of commodities is not necessarily limited to three. One of the additional frames which could be set up by further differentiation would be a *psychological frame*. For subframes of the cultural frame see section 2.4. From a more philosophical view, there have been proposals to set up universal frames of world views ranging from three (Popper and Eccles's (1977) three worlds) to seven (Koch's (1986: 167) seven levels of semiogenesis).

2.1.2   The commodity as a multi-framed sign

Within each frame the commodity is seen as a *sign* consisting of a signifier and a signified. The *signifier* is the signifying substance and form of the commodity, the vehicle or means by which its message is conveyed. The *signified* is the *specific* content of each sign. In other words, it is argued that the multi-framed commodity-sign is typically associated with three semantic fields.

2.1.3   Actual and potential signs

Every commodity is only a *potential* sign and each of its four perspectives are only virtual semiotic dimensions. In situations of purchase or use, the commodity may appear within non-semiotic frames (see section 2.2). The commodity is neither always a sign nor always a non-sign *per se*. Only in a given pragmatic context does the potential sign become an actual sign. However, in marketing and advertising the focus is typically on the sign character of the commodity.

2.1.4   Sources of commodity meanings

There are three main sources of commodity meanings, (1) the producer's discourse (descriptions or advertisements) about the product and the interpretation of this discourse by the consumer (who may accept, reject or ignore the proposed meanings), (2) the consumer's personal preferences of or experiences with the product in his or her prior acts of consumption and (3) the consumer's knowledge of the system of commodities, which consists of his or her knowledge of the competing products of the market.

The meanings generated by the producer and the consumer reflect two antagonistic interests in and perspectives of the commodity (cf. Nöth, 1987a). While the producer's meanings are typically euphoric with respect to the product, never focusing on any of its possible negative features, the ideal critical consumer meets the producer's self-interested claims about the commodity with skepticism.

2.2 The utilitarian sign and the 'semiotic threshold'

To those who advocate a clear-cut separation between the practical and the semiotic or even define the semiotic as the non–utilitarian (cf. section 1.2.2), the 'utilitarian sign' must sound like a contradiction in terms.

2.2.1 The non-semiotic and the 'semiotic threshold'

In contradistinction to those who assume a semiotic 'threshold' between the spheres of the utilitarian and of the semiotic (see section 1.2), the present approach assumes that utilitarian objects can be perceived either as semiotic or as non-semiotic. The difference is not one of a 'threshold' between two classes of objects or events. It is one of the user's or perceiver's perspective: in a *utilitarian perspective*, the commodity is *used* (e.g. a screwdriver or a car) or it is *consumed* (e.g. a can of beer). Use and consumption involve an immediate manipulation or transformation of the object (cf. Mukařovský, 1978), but characteristics of use and of consumption may also be *referred to* in an act of semiosis.

2.2.2 The utilitarian sign

At the utilitarian level of semiosis, there are two perspectives of the commodity sign. In the consumer's perspective, the utilitarian commodity sign is associated with features related to its practical *use-value*. In addition, the producer's perspective includes such features as the amount of labor or material required for its production. The following discussion will concentrate on the consumer's perspective, though. To the consumer, the utilitarian commodity sign comprises such features as technical reliability, durability, practical usefulness, suitability, fit or taste (cf. section 2.2.3). A washing machine, e.g. whose brand image includes features such as 'high quality', 'reliability' or 'economy', has become a sign of those utilitarian concepts even though the sign user may never have used a machine of this brand. Further examples of utilitarian meanings are taste and nutritional values of food products, the body-protecting qualities of garments (cf. Holman, 1981a) and the characteristics for the care of textiles. These semiotic features do not necessarily have to coincide with any 'real' features or qualities of the product, as they may be revealed by a scientific test concerning the qualities of the product (cf. section 2.2.3).

2.2.3 Utilitarian facts and signs

The referential characteristics of the utilitarian sign are not identical with any utilitarian 'facts', the features and functions of the product in practical use. The non-semiotic status of those physical, technical, biochemical or other 'real facts' is not denied here. With all due skepticism about the possibility of attaining scientific objectivity, it may be said that product features revealed in a consumer report test come close to representing the non-semiotic utilitarian features of a commodity. Only the 'ideal critical consumer' who studies and learns these features develops a utilitarian *sign* of the commodity whose features correspond closely to these non-semiotic 'facts', but it is not a matter of semiotics whether a washing machine is really durable and reliable or not. It is only a matter of semiotics whether consumers are convinced of the durability of a particular brand of washing machine. On the level of semiosis, it has to be acknowledged that such convictions may be based on false assumptions. As Eco (1976: 7) points out, 'a sign is everything which can be taken as significantly substituting for something else. This something else does not necessarily have to exist or to actually be somewhere at the moment in which a sign stands in for it. Thus *semiotics is in principle the discipline studying everything which can be used in order to lie.*'

2.3   The commercial sign

As a commercial sign, a commodity signifies its exchange value, the commercial value in relation to other products of the system of commodities. The most direct indicator of this value is the price, but it also includes other factors which increase or decrease the producer's or consumer's costs, such as scarcity, rebates or service guarantees. Some products have an exchange value which is inherent in the consumer's brand image; e.g. Rolls-Royce connotes expensiveness while the Russian Lada is known to be an inexpensive car. Other commercial meanings are generated by the seller's pricing strategies (e.g. the promise of a 'good bargain' or the regretful concession that good quality 'has its price'). Many advertising campaigns for mass products omit the commercial perspective and create the image of a 'price-less' product. In those cases the commodity becomes a (potential) commercial sign only in the stores or supermarkets, which build up their own variable systems of commercial commodity signs.

2.4   The socio-cultural sign

The consumer (or advertiser) who perceives (or presents) a commodity as a socio-cultural sign relates the product to the social group or culture which in his or her view is typically associated with it. It must be emphasized that the term *culture* in this context is used in the narrower sense. In a broader sense, culture, of course, includes both the spheres of commerce and of practical utility (e.g. technology).

The socio-cultural frame comprises a large number of sub-frames or possibly super-frames whose precise interrelation cannot be specified in this paper. Two such socio-cultural frames can only be discussed briefly in sections 2.4.1 and 2.4.2. Other socio-cultural sub-frames of importance in the semiotization of commodities are, e.g., the *aesthetic* frame (cf. Nöth, 1987b) and the *sacred* frame (cf. Kopytoff, 1986: 73–76). Within both frames, the product ultimately loses its status of a commodity and is transformed into a non-commercial object.

2.4.1 The sociological sub-frame

Products may be consumed to indicate the consumer's affiliation to a certain sociological group (cf. Holman, 1981b). Even though the consumer may not *intend* such a sociological indexical sign, an observer will sometimes *decode* such acts of consumption in this way. In these cases the product functions as a sociological sign.

The social group to which a commodity is related may be small (e.g. when trying 'to keep up with the Joneses') or it may be a whole culture ('the American way of life'). More than other aspects of commodities, sociological signs are subject to historical change. Such changes may be fast, as with products depending on fashions and styles, or they may be slow, as with products related to national stereotypes.

Commodities frequently consumed or interpreted as sociological signs are cars, food or fashion products. Examples: pizza and hamburgers referring to the Italian or American way of life, and Rolls-Royce, Cadillac or Citroën referring to British, American or French styles and technological standards. Most evident is the sociological sign value of clothes (cf. Barthes, 1967; and Holman, 1981a). Their social dimensions extend from professions (the bowler hat of London businessmen) to regional folklore (Bavarian *lederhosen*) and mass cultures ('blue jeans culture').

As stated in section 2.1.3, no product is by definition consumed as a sign. Some products even *seem* to be wholly restricted to the non–semiotic utilitarian perspective. Tools such as hammers and pliers or nails and screws are typical examples of this category of commodities. But even these products may become socio–cultural signs. Hammers and pliers have a natural potential to be interpreted as referring to the sociological group of craftsmen (and not to academics or aristocrats). Further examples of a sociological semiotization of tools can be found in lexicology. Thus, the German language distinguishes some tools according to the trades with which they are typically associated. There is, for example, a cobbler's, a mason's, a locksmith's, and an American locksmith's hammer, and an English and a French wrench. ('Engländer' and 'Franzose' are two types of monkey wrenches.) Even screws relate to the *countries* of their origin; witness the difference between metrical threads, British Whitworth threads, and American Sellers threads. Notice that the technical features by which these types of screws differ are only potential utilitarian signs. Only when they are associated with the Continental European, British or American technologies do they become socio–cultural signs.

2.4.2 The mythical sign

The study of myths connected with commodities has been a favorite topic of research in the semiotics of advertising (cf. section 1.2.1). However, the definition of myth in this context has remained rather vague. Barthes (e.g. 1964a) and others have often discussed mythological meanings without differentiating them from simple connotations, and in particular, from ideological meanings. To avoid such vagueness, mythical meanings will be defined, in this paper, in a sense that is closer to the ancient Greek 'mythos', which meant 'a poetic or legendary tale' as opposed to a historical account: myth in this sense is a narrative with a secondary level of meaning in addition to a primary one. Mythical signs in this definition refer to stories or fragments of such stories with a metaphorical dimension of meaning.

There are old and new myths. The old ones have developed within the literary or religious traditions of a culture. The new ones are being created by our mass media, including advertising.

Examples of new myths can be found in advertising campaigns for products such as Marlboro or Camel cigarettes: every new advertisement brings a further episode from a seemingly endless story of adventures. The episodes of these sequels have often only the form of pictures. Their suggestive narrative content remains unwritten. It is the narrative of a solitary hero in a successful struggle with the forces of nature, be it a lassoing cowboy who proves his command over a wild herd of cattle or the courageous discoverer who reaches unknown exotic shores in his primitive boat. But, in spite of the changing scenery in the American Wild West or in exotic regions, the mythical message of these narratives remains unchanged: it is the myth of unbounded self-fulfilment in harmony with nature, which is the counter-image of real life within the confines of a polluted industrialized world.

Another recent modern myth with a historical, more precisely a pseudo-historical dimension, is being created in the many episodes of the current Virginia Slims campaign. The topic of this myth is the history of progress in the emancipation of women, a history which, in the self-interested perspective of the advertiser, is connected with the propagation of smoking. This false myth, epitomized by the slogan, 'You've come a long way baby', has rightly been rejected by the critical consumer who resents the predicate of progress for a development which results in smoking by a 'baby'.

Old myths refer to stories known independently of any association with the commodity. Some products refer to such myths by their brand name, e.g. 'Napoleon Cognac' or 'Highland Queen Scotch Whisky'. Often advertisements depict such myths in contiguity with the product with the aim of achieving a meaning transfer from the narrative (picture) to the product (cf. Nöth, 1977, 1987b). E.g. an advertisement for 'Highland Queen Scotch' shows the product against the background of a painting referring to a national myth of Scotland, 'Queen Mary of Scots acclaimed by her troops before Edinburgh Castle, 1561'.

2.5 Example

The four semiotic frames of a commodity-sign discussed so far can briefly be illustrated in a sample analysis which must remain restricted to the producer's perspective (cf. section 2.1.4). *TIME* magazine (12.8.1986: 1) presents the 'New Ford Thunderbird Sport' in an advertisement which need not be quoted at length since it is similar to many other ads of this type. The message is an attempt to create a multi-framed commodity sign: the main focus is on the utilitarian sign. It comprises semantic components such as 'Engine: 5.0 liter V-8 . . . Power: 150 hp. . . . Standard equipment: . . .' and many others. The *economic* sign consists of the offer of a '3-year unlimited powertrain warranty' and a 'free Lifetime Service Guarantee'. A *socio-cultural* sign is in the brand name's association with 'sports' and in the textual reference to 'touring'. A *mythical* sign is also related to the brand name, since Thunderbird is 'a mythical bird believed by American Indians to cause lightning and thunder' (Webster's Third International Dictionary). This sign also appears in the trademark in the form of a bird with outstretched wings. It is further implied in the slogan, 'Go like the wind'. Again these intended meanings are not inherent to the message. To consumers who are not, or only vaguely, acquainted with this Indian myth, the mythical sign is not actualized or will remain fragmentary. Those who know nothing about engines and other technical details will not develop a utilitarian sign.

3. Processes of commodity semiotization

After discussing the three most typical semiotic frames of commodities, the relationship of these frames in the process of commodity semiotization remains to be determined (cf. section 3.2). This relationship depends on the type of commodity and is discussed below in section 3.1.

3.1 Prototypical categories of products

Although it has been shown that all commodities can be decoded in principle within all three main frames, it will now be argued that there are *prototypical* semiotic frames for many categories of products even though there may be typological vagueness in some cases. Thus, there are *prototypically utilitarian* and *prototypically socio-cultural* products. The former category includes tools, machines and basic foods. The latter comprises products such as badges, booster buttons, eccentric fashion wear, flowers, souvenirs, novels, paintings or opera performances. The third major category, *prototypically commercial* products, comprising commodities such as stocks, bonds, foreign currencies or money in general, cannot be discussed in detail here.

The category to which a product prototypically belongs is not inherent in the product itself but empirically observable from the predominant mode of consumption and from the genetic or historical primacy in the evolution of the commodity. To a predominantly utilitarian product, the cultural dimension is secondary in actual use and/or in the history of the product. Thus, typewriters are prototypically utilitarian products. Their industrial design is secondary to their utility. Coins are prototypically commercial products. The fact that some individuals use pennies or dimes in the form of bracelets has little to do with the evolution and predominant use of this commodity. However, commodities may change their prototypical class. Thus, antique typewriters which are collected because of their old-fashioned industrial design have changed from the utilitarian to the socio-cultural category.

3.2 Prototypical processes of semiotization

The typical process of semiotization of predominantly utilitarian products, discussed in section 3.2.1, is different from the one of prototypically socio-cultural commodities. (For atypical processes, see section 3.3.)

3.2.1 Prototypically utilitarian products

The prototypical process in the genesis of primarily utilitarian commodity signs is in the order (1) utilitarian (u), (2) economic (e) and (3) socio–cultural ($s-c$) sign. Most discussions of commodity semiotization have so far only concentrated on the third phase of this process (cf. section 1.2.2). McCracken (1986: 74), for example, studies this phase of semiotization in his discussion of the transfer of cultural meaning to goods.

The prototypical semiotization of this category of products is characteristic of semiosis in an economic world of 'practical reason' (cf. section 1.4). It may best be illustrated by the example of simple tools and technical instruments (cf. section 2.4). If seen as signs at all (cf. section 2.2.1), hammers and nails are in the first place *utilitarian signs*. As *commercial signs*, they depend on their utilitarian qualities: a rational consumer evaluates their price on the basis of their use value. The producer also evaluates the commercial meaning of the commodity sign (i.e. costs and profits) in terms of a utilitarian semantics related to materials, production and retail. The rarer *socio-cultural* meanings associated with tools, such as nails or screws (see section 2.4), are a semantic addition (a tertiary connotation) to the other two levels. They presuppose the utilitarian sign (from whose technical features they are derived) and are secondary to the commercial sign.

Another utilitarian product which is prototypically semiotized in the order $u \rightarrow e \rightarrow s\text{-}c$ is milk: its nutritional value and taste (u) are primary (e.g. this is what counts to the infant), its price (e) is secondary (commerce with milk is later in the evolution of culture than its consumption) and socio-cultural connotations, such as 'country life' or 'nature' ($s\text{-}c$), are still later and thus tertiary in the evolution of this commodity. Not all foods follow the order of this prototypical semiotization. Soft drinks, for example, are commodities whose brand image is often created in a process of semiotization which is atypical of food products (compare section 3.3).

Some products which must fulfil a utilitarian function when in practical use are nevertheless not semiotized in the order of $u \rightarrow e \rightarrow s\text{-}c$ but in the order $u \rightarrow s\text{-}c \rightarrow e$. In this class of commodities, not only the practical utility (u) but also the style or industrial design ($s\text{-}c$) are essential factors determining the commercial value (e) of the product (e.g. fashionable furniture or ornamented chinaware). These utilitarian commodities are less prototypical. They are situated between the categories of prototypically utilitarian and socio-cultural objects.

3.2.2 Prototypically socio-cultural objects

The prototypical order of semiotization of this category of commodities is $s\text{-}c \rightarrow e$. For instance, badges or novels are primarily objects of culture and only in the second place commercial values. Sometimes there is a third phase of semiotization ($s\text{-}c \rightarrow e \rightarrow u$): a bound book has a higher practical utility (u) than a paperback edition. Booster buttons of one kind may be known to be durable, others may be known to break easily.

A practical utilitarian sign associated with a sculpture of clay (in contrast to one of bronze) is that it breaks easily. If this material object is predominant to a degree that it affects essentially its price (cf. a sculpture of gold), the order of semiotization may be $s\text{-}c \rightarrow u \rightarrow e$.

3.3   Deviant modes of commodity semiotization

Three deviant modes of commodity semiotization have to be discussed briefly, atypical (in section 3.3.1) fallacious (in section 3.3.2) and degenerate (in section 3.3.3) commodity semiotization.

3.3.1 Atypical commodity semiotization

This process can be found in the socio–cultural sphere. It characterizes objects whose status as a commodity is resented or rejected by societies or cultures. In this sense, a human being sold as a slave is an atypical commodity in this century. Sacred objects are equally atypical commodities in cultures which believe that relics or churches should not be sold ($s-c \rightarrow e$). To a certain degree, art objects are atypical commodities, too (cf. Nöth, 1987b). In contra-distinction to any other comparable commercial transaction, the sale of a Rembrandt to a foreign country, for example, is usually interpreted as an unpatriotic act.

In an extreme case of atypical semiotization, the object of art can even turn into a utilitarian sign ($s-c \rightarrow u$), namely, when it is considered from a purely practical point of view, for example, when a consumer buys a painting with the primary motive of hanging it on the wall in order to cover stains in the wallpaper.

3.3.2 Semiotic fallacies

Reversals of the order of semiotization in which the consumer takes the prototypically secondary commodity sign as the basis of evaluating the primary sign commit a semiotic fallacy. Veblen (1899) described one type of such fallacies: purchases of utilitarian com-modities according to the principle 'expensive, therefore good' ($e \rightarrow u$).

Another classic fallacy in the semiotization of commodities has been studied in connec-tion with the marketing of cola brands. It is the assumption that many consumers perceive certain cola brands primarily as socio-cultural signs (cf. Coca-Cola as the incarnation of the American myth) and evaluate their taste on this basis ($s-c \rightarrow u$). Even though most con-sumers may be unaffected by this fallacy (cf. Stanley, 1978), some consumers evidently do commit the fallacy of preferring a mythical cola brand whose taste they could not identify in a blind comparison taste test.

3.3.3 Degenerate semiotization

This mode of commodity semiotization is characterized by a conflict or even contradiction between primary and secondary semiotic features of commodities. The product is con-sumed because of positive secondary semiotic characteristics but *in spite of* considerable deficiencies of its prototypically primary features. For example, the socio-cultural com-modity sign is in conflict with the economic sign when the product is consumed *although* the consumer can really not afford it (e.g., the prestige car). There is a conflict between the utilitarian and the socio-economic sign when the product is consumed although it is impractical (e.g. tight fashion wear) or in spite of its disagreeable taste. For example, youngsters smoking cigarettes or drinking beer for the first time in order to be accepted by their peers consume a commodity as a socio-cultural sign which is in conflict with the utilitarian sign of taste (which first signals dislike).

4. The language of commodities as a system

If commodities deserve to be called a *language*, they should be analyzable in terms of *paradigmatic* and *syntagmatic* relations, those two basic types of relation which form the two classical axes of linguistic structure. While the paradigmatic axis of a language refers to the possible (e.g. lexical or semantic) *alternatives* of and *oppositions* to a sign, the syntagmatic axis refers to its *syntax*, the rules for the combination of the signs.

4.1   The paradigmatic dimension

Barthes (1964a: 63; 1967) was among the first to propose an analysis of the paradigmatic dimension of commodities. More recently American consumer research has begun with the empirical exploration of this dimension of the market (cf. Mick, 1986: 202–3). The study of the paradigmatic dimension of a semiotic system has to explore both *similarities* and *differences* between the objects under consideration. According to semantic likeness, the units of a system are grouped together to form *classes* of signs. The classification of commodities by brands and kinds of goods performed by any manager of a supermarket reflects a possible semiotic classification of commodities as *practical* (utilitarian) signs. By the differences between these signs, commodities enter into *oppositions* which constitute the structure of the semiotic *system*. In the language of commodities these structures of opposition are emphasized by the competition between brands and classes of goods. Saussure's thesis that a semiotic system, and with it the meanings of its signs, is only constituted by the differences between its elements is particularly true for the language of commodities. Since competition is the motor of a free market, it should be evident that the language of commodities is a *semiotic system par excellence*. In the intention of the advertisers and producers of goods, this language is even a system of a radically semiotic nature: *The language of commodities strives to maximize the differences and to minimize the similarities between competing goods.* The most convincing illustration of this thesis is the competition between the so–called generic brands and their materially identical counterparts sold in different packages, under different names and at higher prices.

4.2   The syntax of commodities

If commodities are combined by the producer and the consumer in a meaningful way, similar to the combination of words into sentences and texts, this combination will result in a commodity *message*. The rules which determine these combinations in space and time form the *syntagmatic* dimension of the language of commodities. Barthes (1964a: 63) has proposed to study such combinations of clothes into garments, foods into menus, or pieces of furniture into the furnishing of a room as syntagmatic structures. More recently, Kehret-Ward (1987), too, has proposed to study product combinations as the syntax of commodities.

However, the studies of product combinations have so far only resulted in the discovery of a very rudimentary commodity syntax. Except for some *cultural* and *aesthetic* rules and conventions which restrict the possibilities of combining products such as tableware, foods, clothes, pieces of furniture, or their colors, forms and sizes, there is little evidence for a systematic syntax of commodities. Notice that the transition from words to sentences in language leads to two essentially new dimensions in syntax, restrictions of *linear order* and *predication*, i.e. the formation of a new holistic meaning by the combination of an argument (e.g. a subject) with a predicate. In contradistinction to the linear syntax of language, the (weak) cultural and aesthetic rules of product syntax are essentially only rules of *combination*, which prescribe or restrict the order of elements in a possible pluridimensional commodity message. There seems to be nothing comparable to the principle of predication in commodity syntax. Product combinations are basically *additive*, even when their addition results in typical product constellations, such as 'knife and fork', 'cup and saucer', 'table and chair', or similar product combinations which are sometimes sold as a set only. In such product constellations of the type A + B, the cultural meaning of A is not specified or modified by B in the way the predicate 'golden' modifies its argument 'fork' in the predication 'The fork is golden'. In contrast to its highly structured paradigmatic dimension (cf. section 4.1), it must therefore be concluded that the language of commodities has only a rather weak syntax.

References

Appadurai, Arjun (ed.) (1986), *The Social Life of Things*. Cambridge: Cambridge University Press.

Aronoff, Mark (1985), 'Automobile semantics', in V.P. Clark *et al.* (eds.), *Language*. New York: St. Martin's Press (4th ed.), 401–21.

Barthes, Roland (1964a/1967), *Elements of Semiology*. London: Cape.

Barthes, Roland (1964b/1977), 'Rhetoric of the image', in R. Barthes (ed.), *Image-Music-Text*. New York: Hill and Wang, 32–51.

Barthes, Roland (1967/1983), *The Fashion System*. New York: Hill and Wang.

Baudrillard, Jean (1968), *Le Système des Objets*. Paris: Gallimard.

Baudrillard, Jean (1972/1981), *For a Critique of the Political Economy of the Sign*. St. Louis, MO: Telos.

Belk, Russell W., K.D. Bahn and R.N. Mayer (1982), 'Developmental recognition of consumption symbolism', *Journal of Consumer Research*, **9**, 4–17.

Csikszentmihalyi, Mihaly and Eugene Rochberg-Halton (1981), *The Meaning of Things*. Cambridge: Cambridge University Press.

Douglas, Mary and Baron Isherwood (1979/1982), *The World of Goods*. New York: Norton.

Eco, Umberto (1976), *A Theory of Semiotics*. Bloomington, IN: Indiana University Press.

Hirschman, Elizabeth C. and Morris B. Holbrook (eds.) (1981), *Symbolic Consumer Behavior*. Ann Arbor, MI: Association for Consumer Research.

Holman, Rebecca H. (1981a), 'Apparel as communication', in Elizabeth C. Hirschman and Morris B. Holbrook (eds.), *Symbolic Consumer Behavior*. Ann Arbor, MI: Association for Consumer Research, 7–15.

Holman, Rebecca H. (1981b), 'Product use as communication', *Review of Marketing*, **7**, 106–119.

Kehret-Ward, Trudy (1987), 'Combining products in use: How the syntax of product use affects marketing decisions', in Jean Umiker-Sebeok (ed.), *Marketing and Semiotics*. Berlin: Mouton de Gruyter, 219–238.

Koch, Walter A. (1986), *Philosophie der Philologie und Semiotik*. Bochum: Brockmeyer.

Kopytoff, Igor (1986), 'The cultural biography of things: Commodization as process', in Arjun Appadurai (ed.), *The Social Life of Things*. Cambridge: Cambridge University Press, 64–91.

Krampen, Martin (1979), *Meaning in the Urban Environment*. London: Pion.

Langholz-Leymore, Varda (1975), *Hidden Myth*. New York: Basic Books.

Lefebvre, Henri (1966), *Le Langage et la Société*. Paris: Gallimard.

Levy, Sidney J. (1978), *Marketplace Behavior*. New York: AMACOM.

Lurie, Alison (1981), *The Language of Clothes*. New York: Random.

McCracken, Grant (1986), 'Culture and consumption', *Journal of Consumer Research*, **13**, 71–81.

Mick, David G. (1986), 'Consumer research and semiotics', *Journal of Consumer Research*, **13**, 196–213.

Moles, Abraham A. (1972), *Théorie des Objects*. Paris: Ed. Universitaire.

Mukařovský, Jan (1978), *Structure, Sign, and Function*. New Haven, CT: Yale University Press.

Nöth, Winfried (1977), *Dynamik semiotischer Systeme. Vom a.e. Zauberspruch zum illustrierten Werbetext*. Stuttgart: Metzler.

Nöth, Winfried (1985), *Handbuch der Semiotik*. Stuttgart: Metzler. (English translation: *Handbook of Semiotics*, Bloomington, IN: Indiana University Press, in preparation.)

Nöth, Winfried (1987a), 'Advertising: The frame message', in Jean Umiker-Sebeok (ed.), *Marketing and Semiotics. New Directions in the Study of Signs for Sale*. Berlin: Mouton de Gruyter, 279–294.

Nöth, Winfried (1987b), 'Advertising, poetry, and art: Semiotic reflections on aesthetics and the language of commerce', *Kodikas/Code*, **10**, 53–81.

Peirce, Charles Sanders (1931/1958), *Collected Papers*, ed. C. Hartshorne, P. Weiss and A.W. Burks. Cambridge, MA: Harvard University Press.

Popper, Karl R. and John C. Eccles (1977), *The Self and its Brain: An Argument for Interactionism*. Heidelberg and New York: Springer.

Rossi-Landi, Ferruccio (1975), *Linguistics and Economics*. The Hague: Mouton.

Sahlins, Marshall (1976), *Culture and Practical Reason*. Chicago, IL: Chicago University Press.

Saussure, Ferdinand de (1916/1966), *Course in General Linguistics*. New York: McGraw-Hill.

Stanley, Thomas J. (1978), Cola preferences: Disguised taste vs. brand evaluations. *Advances in Consumer Research*, **5**, 19–21.

Umiker-Sebeok, Jean (ed.) (1987), *Marketing and Semiotics. New Directions in the Study of Signs for Sale*. Berlin: Mouton de Gruyter.

Veblen, Thorstein (1899/1934), *The Theory of the Leisure Class*. New York: Modern Library.

Wallendorf, Melanie and Eric J. Arnould (1988), 'My favorite things: A cross-cultural inquiry into object attachment, possessiveness and social linkage', *Journal of Consumer Research*, **14**, 531–547.

Williamson, Judith (1978), *Decoding Advertisements*. London: Boyars.

My brand the hero? A semiotic analysis of the consumer–brand relationship

● ●

Benoît Heilbrunn
Groupe ESC Lyon

Summary

This article provides a framework to conceptualize and improve our understanding of the relationship between the consumer and the brand by proposing a semiotic analysis of this relationship. The conceptual background of the demonstration is the semantization of the brand, which means that the brand is endowed with an array of meanings which largely overrides the functional aspects of the branded product or service. Among the metaphors commonly assigned to the brand, one is to consider the brand as a character, or a person, hence the fact that consumers can engage in a relationship with brands, which has some common features with interpersonal relationships. Two paradigms are then applied to this peculiar relationship. The first is the value chain concept, which helps to point out the general structure of this relationship by indicating a certain number of stages which play a role in the creation and the development of the relationship. The second paradigm considers buying decisions and consumption patterns as a text which will be interpreted accordingly using a semiotic approach. The morphological approach Propp used to study fairy tales is proposed as a means of understanding the structure of this relationship. Four major stages in this relational process are examined: (1) the contract, (2) the acquisition of competency, (3) the performance, and (4) the sanction. A brand can thus be assimilated to a character who performs various roles in the market. This preliminary study ends with a semiotic conceptualization of the brand, based on Greimas's actantial model, which understands the brand in a differential perspective as a co-construction of meaning and value among various actants.

Humanum genus est avidum nimis auricularum.
[Mankind loves to be told stories.]
(Lucretius, *De natura rerum*, IV, 598)

Paper presented at the European Marketing Academy Conference, Paris, May 1995.

370

Introduction

Brands have become so integrated into our daily life as a ubiquitous phenomenon that we are living in a rich 'brandscape' (Sherry, 1986). An average consumer is said to be able to recognize over 5,000 brands which makes him or her virtually speak a foreign language: the language of brands (Boutié, 1994: 9, 12). Familiar brands act as verbal and visual representations of physical characteristics, objects, concepts, relations which help consumers in the creation of a reassuring daily environment. Brands have thus become part of consumers' familiar environment, like the words of a mother tongue, and the consumer is thus often described as selecting from a 'brandscape of availability' a personal brandspace in which to live (Biel, 1993: 67). It is therefore widely recognized that consumers develop strong relationships with their familiar brands which go far beyond their functional aspects (Babin *et al.*, 1994). Most researchers on brands do not consider as crucial the relationship between the consumer and the brand. This relationship is hardly considered as an affective link, even though emotional ties have been proved to play an important role not only in the choice of a brand but also in loyalty patterns (Batra and Ahtola, 1990; McQueen *et al.*, 1993).

Brands can thus be understood in a linking and relational perspective, granted that they essentially play as mediators between various market actors. The brand has even acquired the status of a partner in its own right in the manufacturer–consumer relationship, and its linking function tends to increase due to the missing or weak link between the large company and the final consumer, and to the fact that links get loose in our modern society because of the rise of individualism and of severe social dissolution resulting in a rising need for a 'linking value' versus 'use value' (Cova and Kassis, 1994; Cova, 1995). This relational perspective on brands makes us consider a brand as part of a more general semiotic system and decode the relationships which potentially exist between the constitutive parts of this system. The aim of this article is (1) to point out the underlying premises of the relational metaphor, (2) to show the crucial and determinant role of this relationial paradigm to understand the value put on the brand by various market actors and especially by consumers, and (3) to propose a conceptual framework to understand and analyze the brand in a semiotic perspective.

1. The brand as part of a semiotic system

The first historical role assigned to brands was to represent the producer and to be a sign of reassurance and attest the origin and quality of the product. Initially, brands were introduced as a way for manufacturers to differentiate their goods from the retailers' commodities at a time when groceries were sold as commodity items, being usually produced by small manufacturers supplying a limited market; as retailers usually blended the produce of several suppliers, the quality varied by retailer. The brand thus historically implied a linguistic value imposed on goods, in the sense that the branded status of a product provides an identification between the basic commodity presented and its producer (Péninou, 1972; Lagneau, 1969). The first historical task of the brand was thus to transmit information on its source, its origin and thus its enunciator. Then, trademarks were used by guilds to attest quality and to control entry into particular trades; they were employed to single out the individual artisan, who manufactured or sold defective products (Wilkins, 1992: 70). Since then the brand, which was a sort of transparent sign to deliver information on the producer, has historically gained opacity, that is to say the brand has acquired some characteristics of its own (personality, identity, image, etc.) which contribute to give it a different mode of existence. The 'product plus approach' to branding traditionally considered the brand as a mere indexical sign added to the product (the brand as one dimension of the product) in order to signal to the consumer the source of the product. An alternative and somewhat opposed approach to branding, which has gained a wide importance, is the 'holistic approach' (Styles and Ambler, 1995), which views the brand as a more global entity, a symbol, which synthesizes the various functional and emotional attributes, promises and expectations that provide satisfaction to a consumer (the product as one dimension of the brand). In this perspective, brands are endowed with an array of meanings which largely overflow the functional aspects of the product or service they stand for. It is now widely accepted that branding goes beyond the simple fact of describing a product, 'it is providing a product with a personality which is so expressed as to encompass that product's uses, values, status, function, stature, usefulness' (Lamb, 1979: 22). This holistic view of brands largely derives from a process of semantization of objects and brands, a phenomenon widely acknowledged by various works in semiotics and anthropology which aim at providing a solid basis for understanding how consumers project and create meaning on the objects they live with. The seminal work of Barthes (1964) postulated the universal semantization of usage whereby the use of an object is converted into a sign for that use. Even though objects are thought of as being entirely absorbed in an end-use, a function, there is 'always a meaning which overflows the object's use' (Barthes, 1966: 182). This theory of universal semantization of usage was largely developed by Baudrillard in his book, *Le Système des Objets* (1968), in which he contended that, in a consumer society, objects lose their material and functional status by their integration into object systems. Consuming is, for instance, defined by Baudrillard as the organization of material substance into signifying substance: 'to become an object of consumption the objects must become a sign' (Baudrillard, 1968: 277). The brand has thus become a 'modern sign' in the sense it has gained opacity. This idea of the brand as a sign is consistent with Foucault's definition of modern language: 'it has nothing to say but itself, nothing to do but shine in the brightness of its being' (Foucault, 1970: 300). Therefore, nowadays the brand does not just exist through a manufacturer or a product, it has an existence of its own with its own traits, history and density. This identity of brands allows them to play a role of their own in the market which goes beyond their historical role of an indexical link between manufacturers and their customers. As Barthes reminds us, there is a kind of transitivity involved in the definition of any object or any brand, in the sense that 'the object . . . is what is thought of in relation to the subject' (Barthes, 1988: 180): hence the essential role of brands as mediators and partners. As the brand has become a partner of its own in the manufacturer–retailer–consumer relationship, a dual approach to the brand may be insufficient to understand the branding process. A relational approach of the brand might rather be substituted (see Table 1).

A brand, as a cultural entity essentially refers to a system of relations and interactions with other actors. This relational paradigm shifts the focus away from discrete transactions and towards the formation and maintenance of long-term relationships with the key actors

Table 1 A dual versus a relational view of a brand

Dual or Transactional View of Brand	Relational View of Brand
• The exchange surrounding the brand is a self-explained relationship	• The brand can induce effects which influence/concern third parties
• The exchange involves two actors (bilaterality)	• The 'game' surrounding the brand involves 2 or more actors in an interdependent relationship
• The exchange process has only one outcome: one gains what the other loses: zero-sum game	• The game may be a non-zero sum. Each participant may win or lose. Some may win or lose more than others
• The brand responds to a need	• The brand represents a different 'enjeu' for every actor and this may vary across situations
• To understand the exchange process, there is a need to understand the utilities of each partner and which utilities the brand is able to satisfy	• The exchange process and the brand status can be explained by observing the way actors appropriate the brand

Source: Translated and adapted from F. Dupuy and J.-C. Thoenig, 1989, 'La marque et l'échange', in J.-N. Kapferer and J.-C. Thoenig (eds.), *La Marque*, Paris: McGraw-Hill, p. 173.

relevant to the brand (Styles and Ambler, 1995: 588). A brand thus only gains existence, identity and visibility through its appropriation and description by the various actors. As Denzin puts it, first, 'human beings act towards things on the basis of the meanings that things have for them; second, that the meaning of things arise out of a process of social interaction; and third, that meanings are modified through an interpretive process which involves self-reflective individuals symbolically interacting with one another' (Denzin, 1992: XIV; Gottdiener, 1995: 57).

The role of a brand in a market can thus be decoded as a series of interactions between various market actors such as the brand manufacturer and its competitors, consumers, retailers and such other influential agents as the customers, prescribers, other brands available in the marketplace, etc.

It is therefore possible to consider a brand value in a linguistic perspective, in the sense it was first defined by Saussure (1969), that is, in a given system, meaning resides in the interactions and differences apprehended between the various elements of the system; the value of the elements is thus only relative and determined by the relations existing between the constituent elements of the system. As Barthes reminds us, 'to signify means that objects carry not only informations . . . but also constitute systems of signs, i.e., essentially systems of differences, of opposition, and of contrasts' (Barthes, 1988, 180). In a system, 'priority is given to relations at the expense of elements, since only differences (which are relations) between elements constitute a system' (Greimas, quoted in Nöth, 1990: 317). It is therefore essential to consider the brand, not as a single element, but as an elementary part of a more general system of signification made up of the various actors which contributes to give existence and identity to this brand. Brands can thus be regarded as unitary elements of a more general system which is organized and structured according to syntactic rules, as a linguistic system. Kehret-Ward further developed this syntactic approach to consumption by proposing that any consumption system is organized – as any linguistic system – thanks to paradigmatic relations (of opposition and contrast) and syntagmatic relations (of complementarity and substitutability) between its constitutive parts (Kehret-Ward, 1988; Mick, 1986). Brands can therefore be considered as actors in the market, i.e. entities which do not operate in isolation but within a system of signifying relations with other actors such as retailers, consumers, other brands, etc. Like linguistic signs, whose value is determined by their difference from other elements of a language, brands are defined as elements of a semiotic system and they mainly exist through syntagmatic and paradigmatic relationships to other brands but more generally through relations with market actors. Alongside a dual structure of this relationship represented by the manufacturer–customer relationship has emerged a more complex structure made of the relations existing between the manufacturer, the brand, the consumer, the intermediaries and the socio-economic environment (regrouped under the concept of influence agents). The branding process essentially involves a multi-level relationship between the manufacturer, the brand, the consumer and influence agents (see Figure 1).

Figure 1 illustrates that the brand exists only through a process of interactions between three sets of actors, who can be denominated under the concept of encyclopedias (Eco, 1979, 1990; Semprini, 1992b): the encyclopedia of production (manufacturers), the encyclopedia of reception (consumers) and the environment encyclopedia (influence agents). The concept of the encyclopedia refers to the theory of text interpretation and is used here to point out the complexity and the multidimensionality of each set of actors. An encyclopedia is much more than a mere transmitter or receiver of messages, it is 'a set of competencies, memories, relations, ideas, wills, structured by a common enunciative structure' (Semprini, 1992b: 40). The market can thus be seen as a network of value-laden relationships in between various actors – regrouped into three distinct encyclopedias – involved in the exchange process, i.e. who engage co-operatively to create value (Styles and Ambler, 1988: 588).

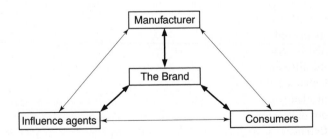

Figure 1   The branding process in a relational perspective.

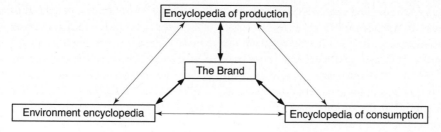

Figure 2   The brand in a semiotic perspective.
Source: adapted from Semprini (1992b).

The next step is to illustrate the fact that the value of a brand is in fact defined, created and transformed through a process of constant interactions between the three encyclopedias mentioned above and the brand.

2. Towards a relational approach to the brand

Even though the concept of brand value is hard to conceptualize because of the many dimensions involved in the evaluation process, philosophical inquiries into the complex concept of value have nevertheless pointed out two main properties of values which can be of use to our purpose:

- First, values are not elements of things but properties, qualities, *sui generis*, which certain objects that we may call valuable objects possess. Values belong to the class of objects which Husserl calls 'not independent', which means they do not possess substantiveness (Frondizi, 1971). A brand does not have an intrinsic value but rather both the consumer and the manufacturer project value onto the brand, through a meaning which they associate with it. In other words, value is dependent on an evaluator. Thus a brand itself does not have a value; its value depends on the evaluator.
- Secondly, the value of a thing depends partly on the circumstances under which it is evaluated: 'value is not a fixed, inherent property . . . A thing may have different values for different purposes, at different times, to different people, under different conditions (the physical environment in which the evaluator finds himself), and in different circumstances (the personal, physical, emotional, psychological, social, and political situation of the evaluator at the time he makes the valuation)' (Sinden and Worrell, 1979: 4–5). Value is 'all factors, both qualitative and quantitative, subjective and objective, that make up the complete shopping experience' (in Babin *et al.*, 1994). Therefore a strictly objective approach focusing on an object, its price, or the functional utility may be too narrow to account for all value provided by consumption experiences (Hirschman and Holbrook, 1982).

The underlying hypothesis is that the perceived value of a brand for a given market actor varies according to numerous criteria; time of the day/year, mood represent, for instance, situational variables which may affect a consumer's perception of a brand's value. This means that the brand does not have a value *per se*, but is rather submitted to an evaluation process by the consumer at different stages. This approach to a brand's value as an interaction process is consistent with one of the most comprehensive definitions of value given by Holbrook and Corfman: value is seen as an 'interactive relativistic preference experience . . . characterizing a subject's experience of interacting with some object. The object may be any thing or event' (in Babin *et al.*, 1994: 645). Thus a brand's value appears as the result of the various interactions between the different actors directly or indirectly affecting the branding process.

Hence it can be said that (1) a brand does not have a value in itself but is a value carrier, that is, it is endowed with a narrative programme which is to provide value to the various actors on the market (manufacturer, influence agents, consumers), and (2) the brand creates value through a system of differences. A brand's value can thus only be apprehended in a differential perspective because it is jointly co-constructed by various actors in the market. It seems thus important to analyze the brand in a relational perspective, as a complex system of interactions between the three encyclopedias mentioned above. It means that the brand's essence is to add value to the various partners in the economic exchange. The branding process can thus be read as the process by which value is generated, constructed and transformed through a system of interactions between various actors. In this perspective, the brand exists solely through the conjunction of three interdependent relations: the manufacturer–brand relationship, the retailer–brand relationship and the consumer–brand relationship, which all contribute to the construction of the brand's value. Each of these relations will now be decoded using the value chain concept.

2.1 The relationship between manufacturers and their brands

On the manufacturer's point of view, branding is often defined as the process aiming at creating, 'providing, communicating and delivering value' to the customer (Bradley, 1995). It follows that branding is essentially an exchange process with multiple stages. Therefore manufacturers develop a temporal relationship through the different stages of the process aiming at creating and delivering value to the consumer through a value delivery system (Bower and Garda, 1985, in Buell, 1986). Branding gives manufacturers a competitive advantage in the business system (Porter, 1985; Davis, 1986: 46) which can be summarized through the concept of the value chain (Table 2).

2.2 The relationship between retailers and brands

Among all the influence agents, retailers are chosen as an example to illustrate the value of a brand from an intermediary's point of view. Retailers – and in general all intermediaries in the branding process – have a relationship with brands which can also be decoded using the value chain concept. The main sources of value of brands for retailers are summarized in Table 3.

Table 3 illustrates the fact that a brand might be endowed with different values by a retailer along the sales process. The value of a brand from a retailer's perspective is

Table 2   The brand as a source of value for the manufacturer

Stages	Sources of value
Raw material sourcing	• Control of source supply • Access to better quality
Production	• Lower cost • More responsive to product changes • More reliable better quality
Sales and distribution	• Lower cost • Better service • Faster service
Communication to end users	• Established/dominant image • Creative breakthrough

Table 3   The brand as a source of value for retailers

Stages	Sources of value
Store traffic	• Well-known brands provide a guarantee of sales and act as a generator of store traffic • Brands provide a basis for customer loyalty
Sales and profitability	• Brands increase turnover • Brands can often command premium prices
Communication	• The brand assumes the responsibility and does the talking for the retailer

therefore not a fixed property but rather refers to an evaluative process. Anyhow, it would also be possible to analyze the reverse phenomenon, that is, the role of the retailer in the constitution of a brand's value.

2.3   The consumer–brand relationship

The relationship marketing literature, which generally applies to the service industry, shows that customers and companies establish links which can be described in terms of trust, commitment, etc. Nevertheless this terminology seems valid to understand the relationship between a consumer and a brand. The service literature provides interesting approaches on the importance of *customer contact* in the success or failure of new services (de Brentani, 1993). High contact affects the perceived quality of a new service and 'leads to longer-term and profitable service relationships' (Gummesson, 1987). On the other hand, it is widely recognized that a high degree of contact during service delivery means that the service quality can vary substantially from one service provider/occasion to another and this may have a negative effect on the perceived quality of the core service (Lovelock, 1984). It is possible to draw an analogy with the consumer–brand relationship. Relationships with the customer have long been viewed as an important aspect of a brand's equity. Farquhar states, for instance, that brand equity can be built in three ways: creating positive brand evaluations with a product quality, fostering accessible brand attitudes to have the most impact on consumer purchase behaviour, developing a consistent brand image to form a relationship with the customer (Farquhar, 1989: 29). As Blackston reminds us, 'The concept of a brand relationship is neither novel nor outrageous. It is readily understandable as an analogue – between brand and consumer – of that complex of cognitive, affective and behavioral process which constitute a relationship between 2 people' (Blackston, 1993: 115).

The value of a brand, therefore, depends considerably on the value created with customers along this relationship process. First, the brand truly exists and has a meaningful value because of the meaning consumers gradually come to project onto it. What makes a brand is that the physical result is combined with something else – symbols, images, feelings – to produce an idea, which is both more than and different from the sum of its parts (Cooper, 1979: 578). Both product and symbolism live and grow with one another in a partnership and mutual exchange. Cooper proposes calling this particular relationship *symbiosis*, which can be defined as the 'living together of two or more entities to their mutual benefit' (Cooper, 1979). This analogy is drawn from biology and refers to such realities as fungi and algae combining to produce lichen, a new organism capable of adapting to extremes. This symbiotic process seems pertinent to account for the relationship unifying the consumer and brands. First, it occurs through different stages constituted by various contact occasions, and the various meanings attached by consumers to their familiar brands so that meaning is lifted from the brand and transferred to the self through purchase and consumption rituals (McCracken, 1993: 127). Consumer behaviour can thus be read as a sequence of actions (Peter and Olson, 1993) which might include the examples of behaviours shown in Table 4.

Table 4 Various contact occasions between the consumer and the brand

Information contact	Read newspapers or billboards, listen to radio commercials, listen to salespersons
Product contact	Locate product in store, obtain product
Transaction	Exchange funds for product, take product to use location
Consumption	Consume/use product, dispose of packaging/used product, repurchase
Communication	Tell others of product experience, fill out warranty cards

Source: Adapted from Peter and Olson (1993).

Also, cognitive learning theories consider consumption as being first a problem to be solved (find the brand which best suits consumer needs) and learning as a process occurring through the discovering of meaningful patterns that enable the consumer to solve problems. Then the development of consumer scripts was proposed as a way to solve a problem (Rethans and Taylor, 1982). A script represents the series of events that consumers come to expect and permits them to predict the outcome of their actions (Assael, 1992: 152). Once a situation is identified (example: state of thirst and search for a refreshing drink) a script is defined, which might include the various stages leading the consumer to solve the problem: finding a store, entering the store, examining available drink brands, comparing prices, making a selection, paying, leaving the store, transporting, preparing and consuming the brand. This brief example shows that the concept of closure is crucial because as long as the consumer has not solved the problem, a state of incompleteness produces tension which motivates continued search for a solution.

Motivation is often defined as a key concept to understand why behaviours occur and what drives consumers to buy a particular product or brand. The term motivation, derived from the Latin verb *movere* (meaning to move), refers to the processes that move a consumer to behave in certain ways. In other words, motivation deals with 'how behaviour gets started, is energised, is sustained, is directed, and is stopped' (Wilkie, 1994: 123). This definition is interesting because it stresses the temporal perspective of consumption behaviour analysis and it points out the fact that behaviour is essentially a move, that is to say the individual goes through different stages. This idea of movement and the existence of different stages can be observed in the relationship consumers may have with some familiar products and brands.

Anthropological research (McCracken, 1988, 1993; Rook, 1985) has shown that consumers develop relations with products and brands by investing these with meaning, and that the relationship with these 'objects' is created and punctuated within a temporal process by various stages (acquisition, preparation, disposal). The consumer is to be seen as a dynamic human being who is not passive but actively constructs his reality, as Piaget would say. The consumer is thus not a passive recipient of a value already innate to a brand, rather he acts as a selector and organizer of this experience (White, 1966: 91). Thus the relationship with the brand is the result of a selective and temporal process in which the consumer chooses and organizes from the stimuli emerging from the brand and its environment a pattern that is significant (White, 1966: 91). It thus becomes possible to imagine an implicit value chain underlying any relationship consumers have with brands. The concept of a benefit chain has already been proposed (Young and Feigin, 1975) to evaluate the intangible benefits or 'pay-offs' consumers derive from a brand, or one of its specific attributes. The benefit or value chain proposed here is more general in the sense that it considers the benefits provided by the brand at each stage of the relationship. Indeed the brand represents a source of value for the consumers at each stage of the relationship.

- 'During the buying decision process, the brand makes it easier to decode and read the product. The brand identifies the product and reveals the facets of its differences' (Kapferer, 1992: 10). It thus provides a means of identification and helps the consumer to choose, reducing complexity by signifying which choice can be trusted (Corstjens, 1995: 58).

- During preparation and consumption, the brand provides a guarantee which decreases the level of risk (functional, psychological, social) associated with the use of the product; the brand can also enhance the consumer's self image by helping the consumer to express himself.
- After consumption, the brand still has a potential value for the consumer because it contributes to the existence of a familiar brandscape which helps overcome the uncertainty of the environment by providing a strong emotional link.

This value chain (Table 5) shows that:

1. the value of a brand is essentially a relational value with the consumer,
2. the relationship is essentially a dynamic process which has to be considered in a temporal horizon,
3. the relationship occurs through several contact occasions,
4. each contact occasion involves a specific conception of the value put by the consumer on the brand.

The purpose is now to propose a structural analysis for this value chain.

Table 5   A value chain from the consumer's perspective

Stages	Sources of Value
Buying decision	• Reduces search costs • Provides quick identification • Reduces choice complexity • Removes uncertainty • Makes the product easier to read • Provides reassurance
Preparation	• Meets the expectation level
Consumption	• Decrease in perceived risk (social, psychological, functional) • Enhance self-image • Provides a means of distinctivity
Post purchase evaluation	• Provides satisfaction • Brand's familiar traits provide an emotional value through the existence and enhancement of a familiar 'brandscape' • Fights the environment uncertainty • Provides a strong relational link

3 The interpersonal relationship metaphor

3.1 Brand as a person

3.1.1 The brand as a human character

As part of the symbolization function of the brand, one of the meanings often assigned to the brand is humanization (Péninou, 1972; Fournier, 1994). Anthropomorphism, which means the faculty of projecting onto external objects some human traits and characteristics, has been shown to be a common feature of the human mind and is widely applied to the brand. The anthropomorphic approach is intrinsic to the branding process and reflects the historical transition from an economy of production based on the realism of matter (products have a generic name) to an economy of the brand based on the symbolism of the person (the branded product is endowed with a proper name) (Péninou, 1972: 135). Thus the brand is a mediating phenomenon which allows branded objects to integrate the symbolic universe, so that brands have rapidly been perceived in a relationship that is analogous with people. The anthropological function of brands is in this perspective to project a human dimension onto the product. This humanization of brands has long been acknowledged by advertisers, who strongly contribute to projecting human characteristics onto brands: 'when probed deeply, consumers describe the products that they call brands in terms that we would normally expect to be used to describe people. They tell us that brands can be warm or friendly; cold; modern; old fashioned; romantic; practical; sophisticated; stylish and so on. They talk about a brand's persona, its image and its reputation – and this "aura" or "ethos" is what characterises the brand' (Saatchi and Saatchi Compton Worldwide, 1984 annual report; quoted in Watkins, 1986: 3). The brand is hence commonly assigned human characteristics and traits such as personality (Gardner and Levy, 1955; Lamb, 1979; Lannon and Cooper, 1983; Batra *et al.*, 1993; Blackston, 1993), identity (Kapferer, 1992), character, charisma (Smothers, 1993), and thus treated analogously as a person (Péninou, 1972). Brands are thus often associated with characteristics, or categories of meaning, usually used to define a person's identity, such as maleness or femaleness (the gender meaning), social standing (the status meaning), nationality (the country meaning) (McCracken, 1993: 126), etc. This human vocabulary is part of what McCracken defines as a 'displaced meaning', that is, a 'cultural meaning that has deliberately been removed from the daily life of a community and relocated in a distant cultural domain' (McCracken, 1988: 104).

3.1.2 Brand as part of the self

Brands are also humanized to the extent that consumers consider them to be an extension of themselves. This humanization of the brand is due first to the very nature of the exchange because, according to Mauss, an object exchanged between two persons infers a 'relationship between them of reciprocal obligations' (Mauss, 1967) and therefore 'the object carries person-like properties' (Miller, 1995: 23). The exchange of objects has been assimilated in many cultures to an exchange of persons – hence the importance of reciprocity in many non-market exchange situations – in the sense that people were literally giving part of themselves to other people. In his analysis of the Maori gift, Mauss (1967) states it was, for instance, believed that goods were made of both natural raw materials and the 'life force' of the person who had produced it. The process of objectification implies an 'organic unity' between people and things because people have deposited a part of themselves in the goods exchanged (Mauss, 1967; Jhally, 1990: 25).

Possession has also been shown to be an important component of self. In *Being and Nothingness* (1943), Sartre suggests that the only reason we want to have something is to enlarge our sense of self, and the only way we can know who we are is by observing what we have. In other words, 'having and being are distinct but inseparable. When an object becomes a possession, what were once self and non-self are synthetized and having and being merge' (Belk, 1988: 145). Allport (1937) also hypothesized that the process of gaining an identity progresses from infancy by extending the self through a continuously expanding set of things regarded as one's own. The idea that we make things a part of ourselves by creating or altering them appears to be a universal human phenomenon (Belk, 1988: 144), one reason being that we invest psychic energy in an object to which we have directed our effort, time and attention (Csikszentmihalyi and Rochberg-Halton, 1981). The theoretical basis for these notions derives from the interpersonal attraction literature in social psychology, which suggests that people tend to perceive others whom they like as being more similar to themselves than those whom they dislike. The congruence image theory also holds that consumers tend to project themselves in brands, which proves that brands are not solely considered as pure objects. A brand might be considered by consumers as a real *alter ego*. Consumers tend to choose brands according to the way their self-image is congruent with their perception of the brand's image, because a brand may serve as an expressive device by the individual, a way in which a person identifies his/her self-image to others; individuals will, therefore, prefer brands whose image is closest (that is to say, more congruent) to their own self-images. Brands, in so far as they can be considered to be part of the self (Csikszentmihalyi and Rochbert-Halton, 1981; Belk, 1988), are treated as persons and valued as such. Moreover, the confusion of objects and subjects has been said to be a major characteristic of the postmodern condition (see Van Raaij, 1993; Toffler, 1980). It is interesting to note that the personification of objects and brands is also parallel to a reification of persons, which has been said to be one of the main dangers of the postmodern condition.

3.2 The temporal horizon of the relationship

A relationship is usually based on a series of different interactions between the various actors involved in the relationship (Fournier, 1994). As Morgan and Hunt (1994: 20) remind us, understanding relationship marketing requires distinguishing between the discrete transaction, which has a 'distinct beginning, short duration, and sharp ending by performance', and relational exchange, which 'traces to previous agreements (and) is longer in duration, reflecting an ongoing process' (Dwyer *et al.*, 1987: 13). It is essential to consider the consumer–brand relationship in a temporal horizon because, as shown earlier, this relationship passes through different stages because the value assigned to a given brand is situational and thus the perception of value depends on the frame reference in which the consumer is making the evaluation. Time is, therefore, an inevitable characteristic of the consumer–brand relationship. No empirical study has so far been conducted to investigate the variation in value perceptions and evaluations contexts. The value of a brand may have various meanings at different stages, depending on the frame of reference of the consumer: point of purchase, preparation, consumption. Value means different things at different points. Zeithaml gives the example of orange juice: at the point of purchase value means low price, special offer or coupons; at the point of preparation, value involves some calculation about whether the product is easy to prepare and how much the consumer gets for what he or she paid; at consumption, value is judged in terms of whether the children will drink the beverage, how much will be wasted. It is thus necessary to explore the value of a brand in a temporal dimension (Zeithaml, 1988).

Therefore the relationship has more to do with contact occasions than with actually buying and consuming the product. The value of a brand can, for instance, be disconnected from its purchase (e.g. the increasing importance of browsing) and vicarious consumption might, for instance, provide hedonic value by allowing a consumer to enjoy a product's benefits without purchasing it (Babin *et al.*, 1994: 646; MacInnis and Price, 1987). Perceived enjoyment itself is an important hedonic benefit provided through shopping activities (Bloch *et al.*, 1986, quoted in Babin *et al.*, 1994: 646). It seems pertinent then to consider the various contact occasions the consumer has with the brand (advertising, purchase, preparation, consumption, etc.). The value is thus derived from one contact with a brand from a 'total experience' made of different 'contact modes' (looking, touching, preparing, consuming . . .) involved in the relationship between the consumer and the brand. The relationship might thus be decomposed into different stages which act as 'contact-nodes' between the consumer and the brand and helps create and sustain value to the brand. The rest of the article will now present a structural analysis of this relationship using a semiotic approach.

4. The consumer–brand relationship in a narrative perspective

4.1   Brand–consumer relationship as a text

The following assumptions have been worked out so far:

1. the brand can be assimilated to a character,
2. the brand and consumer can be considered as two partners in a dyadic relationship,
3. this relationship exists within a temporal process and therefore has different stages.

These assumptions are both necessary and sufficient to consider the consumer–brand relationship in a narrative perspective. It is now widely accepted among semioticians that the concept of text does not apply only to literary texts but can be expanded to other kinds of human production (Barthes, 1966, 1977; Eco, 1962; Greimas, 1966; Floch, 1990). For instance, Hirschman and Holbrook are the authors of a recent book whose main interest and originality might not at first glance lie in the subject matter nor in the title, *Postmodern Consumer Research*, but rather in the subtitle, *The study of consumption as text*. This exciting and innovative title reflects a fundamental move in consumer research in the sense that it gives some new insights into the use of such disciplines as hermeneutics, narratology, literary criticism and semiotics to study consumption patterns. This paper will now focus on the application of this new approach to the study of the brand–consumer relationship. This peculiar re'ationship can be assimilated to a story, a story being defined as 'the content or chain of events (actions, happiness) plus what may be called the existents (characters, items and settings)' (Chatman, 1974). Basically, a story can be defined as a series of events arranged in a time sequence. As Aristotle remarked in the *Poetics*, any story must be united by some interconnection of events, and therefore a mimetic drama should depict only such events as might 'probably' follow each other in causal sequence (Flechter, 1964: 181). Ricoeur has magnificently illustrated the fact that both time and causality are the basic dimensions of the narrative process (Ricoeur, 1983–84).

The consumer–brand relationship can thus be regarded as a text and therefore analyzed in a narrative perspective. First, this text has a closure which individualizes it as an autonomous totality and thus makes possible its structural organization and understanding. Then, the text can be segmented in a limited number of stages, these various stages being related to each other according to certain rules. Finally, the text is oriented and has a direction, in the sense that it is oriented towards a finalized end, which basically can be described as the satisfaction of a need or more generally the reduction of a state of tension from the consumer's perspective.

Moreover, personification is a narrative procedure which consists in attributing to an object properties which allow it to be considered as a subject with a narrative programme (Greimas and Courtès, 1979). The personification of the brand means an isotopic isomorphism between the brand and the consumer, who can thus be considered at the same narrative level. Barthes (1977) has detected a hierarchy of three levels forming a narrative. At the lowest level, there are the minimal units of the narrative; at the next level, that of actions, these elements are integrated in a functional syntax of actions; the third level is that of narrative communication between the narrator and the listener (Nöth, 1990). The structural analysis proposed further will now focus on the first two levels described by Barthes, that is, (1) the identification of the minimal units of this particular narrative, and (2) the functional organization of these events.

4.2 The consumer–brand relationship as a sequence of events

As mentioned earlier, the consumer, when buying a brand, is usually described as fulfilling a need, that is to say he or she is originally driven by a tension and the first function of the purchase is to reduce this state of tension. The same process also occurs within a narrative whose macro-structure usually includes a linear process starting with an original situation generally involving a problem (example: a character has been killed), the narrative being the process by which a solution will be found to solve the original problem (the necessity to find the murderer). The process of resolution, or sequence of actions, thus serves to build the plot of the narrative. Most narratologists agree that narratives essentially refer to sequences of events of which the final event is semantically connected with the initial event (Nöth, 1990). The action of a character in the tale is defined as 'a change of state brought about intentionally by a (conscious) human being in order to bring about a preferred state or state of change' (van Dick, 1976: 550). This sentence could without any alteration be transferred in another context to account for any consumption behaviour.

It seems essential in this context to adopt a structural approach, so as to determine the basic sequences of the narrative. Brémond has defined a triad of phases describing any narrative process. The process starts with (1) a situation opening a potentiality, then (2) its actualization (or the alternative, which is the lack of actualization); finally (3) the success (or its alternative, which is the failure) (Brémond, 1970: 249). Every function is seen as having a set of alternative consequences according to the principle of narrative alternatives. This simple process can implicitly be applied to the process leading a consumer to buy a given product or brand. Table 6 sets out the very basic structure of this particular narrative.

Let us now come to a more precise analysis of this process, using the morphological approach designed by Propp (1928).

4.3   The brand–consumer relationship as a sequence of functions

The Russian folklorist Vladimir Propp published in 1928 *Morfologija skazki* (*Morphology of the Folktale*) which had a decisive influence on the semiotics of narrative structures (Brémond, 1986). The author attempts to solve the historical problem of the origin and evolution of the fairy tale by working out a morphological description. Morphology, which is the study of forms, is considered to be very similar to botany in the sense that botany is 'the study of the components of a plant; their mutual relationship and the relation of the parts to the whole – in other words the study of a plant's structure.' The study of the structure of folk tales is closely linked to the problem of their classification. Wishing to understand the organizing principles of all narrative discourses, Propp soon hypothesized that there exist universal forms of narrative organizations.

The first thing Propp pointed out is the distinction between the variable and invariant parts of fairy tales. Propp rapidly came up with the idea that the variable part of the motif deals with the name and qualitative attributes of the *dramatis personae*, whereas the invariant

Table 6   Consumer–brand relationship as a narrative process

Stage in the Narrative Process	Stage in the Brand–Consumer Relationship
State of deficiency	• Consumer original need-drive
Procedure of improvement/degradation	• Buying decision and consumption process
Satisfactory/unsatisfactory state	• Decrease in perceived risk (social, psychological, functional) • Enhance self-image • Provides a means of distinctivity
Post-purchase evaluation	• Post-purchase evaluation

Source: Adapted from Brémond (1970: 251).

part deals with their actions. In other words, the question of knowing who performs which role and how does not concern the invariant part of any given tale. On the contrary, the invariant element of the motif consists of its function in the plot. Applying this principle to the study of a hundred Russian fairy tales, Propp pointed out a definite number (31) of functions in the plot. He searched for minimal units of the tale, called functions, which serve as stable, 'constant elements in a tale independent of how and by whom they are fulfilled' (Propp, 1928: 21). The plot consists in fact of a sequence of functions (absence, interdiction, violated interdiction . . .), which usually follow in a definite order for aesthetics' sake. Independently of their succession in the basic sequence, the functions can be united in two ways.

Propp was thus able to point out a certain number of common stages in the process of narratives. The structure of folklore tales revealed a number of recurrences and repetitions of moves, that is, a number of minimal invariant stages in the tale, considered as narrative minimal units which, when linked, would become the syntagmatic process, which is the tale. Thus the tale could be considered as having a direction, being oriented (Floch, 1990: 59). In fact, three main kinds of move can be stressed, which appear as the regularity that reveals the existence of a canonical narrative schema (Greimas and Courtès, 1979):

1. *A qualifying move*: the character has to acquire competency through trials, competitions and initiation rituals.
2. *A decisive move*: the character accomplishes himself by going through a certain number of actions.
3. *A glorifying move*: the character is recognized for what he has accomplished and thus for what he is.

Hence the structure of a narrative scheme is easy to point out (Floch, 1988; Heilbrunn, 1996):

1. *The acquisition of competency*: acquisition of the ability to accomplish the programme. The character proves its ability to perform.
2. *The contract*: within the framework of a given value system, proposal of a programme which the character has to carry out.
3. *The performance*: execution of the programme by conquering the object of one's desire. The character performs.
4. *The sanction*: comparison of the realized programme with the programme that had to be accomplished. The character's performance is assessed.

This scheme can be extended to all the forms a narrative can take in order to understand the underlying organization of a narrative, articulated around the performance of an actor.

4.4 Application of the narrative scheme to the consumer–brand relationship

The narrative scheme applied to the consumer–brand integrates the following functions:

1. *The acquisition of competency*: the brand acquires the ability required to carry out the programme.

2. *The contract*: proposal and acceptance of a programme the brand has to carry out.
3. *The performance*: the brand *performs*.
4. *The sanction: comparison* of the realized programme with the programme that had to be accomplished.

Thus the scheme can very easily be applied to a typical consumption process and can help decode the consumer–brand relationship chain established above (Table 5).

Table 7 points out the existence of several levels of contact occasions between the consumer and the brand, an idea which is consistent with the holistic approach to brands that has been adopted throughout this paper. Several types of brand contacts can be outlined, such as functional contacts with the tangible product, emotional contacts with the brand's symbol used as a self-expression device, etc. Before illustrating this morphological framework, an important remark needs to be made: all the functions need not be present within the process, and the functions do not always follow the same order. A child is, for example, very influenced in game choice by the toys he or she has seen at a friend's. The buying process of an electronic game or a robot is usually in the following temporal order, in which the brand has to accomplish the four functions:

1. First contact with the game through word of mouth or advertising
   → Acquisition of competency (of the brand)
2. Experience with the brand at a friend's house
   → Performance (of the brand)
3. Prescription towards the buyer (usually the parents)
   → Sanction
4. The parents (or Santa Claus) decide to buy the product
   → Contract

5. Interpreting the different stages in the consumer–brand relationship

5.1   The acquisition of competency

This stage deals with the initial contacts occurring between the consumer and the brand before the purchase. This involves communication contact (brand advertising), product contact in the store, or other kinds of contact such as what the consumer might hear about the brand through word-of-mouth communication. This stage is crucial because the brand promises a programme to accomplish and offers a promise of value. This refers to the 'feeling on the part of consumers that a brand offers certitudes . . .' (Staveley, 1987: 33, quoted in de Chernatony and McWilliam, 1988: 342). This implies a perception of value which is driven by the consumer's main expectation of the brand. The brand has to be a hero in the sense that it has to be perceived and accepted by the consumer as a valuable object of desire able to perform a narrative programme. The brand's value derives essentially from an *a priori* evaluation because it refers to all the *a priori* beliefs the consumer holds about the brand. That is why the brand's discourse has to be perceived as credible by the consumer. This is valid in three different situations:

Table 7 Consumer–brand contact occasions as a narrative chain

Contact Occasions with the Brand	Related Behaviours	Corresponding Stage in the Narrative Chain
Information contact	• Read newspapers or billboards • Listen to radio commercials • Listen to salespersons	Acquisition of competency
Brand contact	• Locate product in store • Obtain product	Acquisition of competency
Transaction	• Exchange funds for product • Take product to use location	Contract
Consumption	• Consume/use brand • Dispose of packaging/used product	Performance
Subsequent contacts	• Repurchase • Brand switching	Sanction
Communication	• Tell others of brand experience • Fill out complaint cards	Sanction

1. When a new brand is introduced, all the discourses surrounding the brand have to be perceived as credible and give a consistent image to the brand.

2. When a brand is bought on a regular basis, the brand essentially signals to the customer the source of the product, and protects both the customers and the producer from competitors who would attempt to provide products that appear to be identical. It acts as a sign of reassurance and guarantee for the consumer. McQueen *et al.* have pointed out the fact that most long-term loyal consumers – who buy brands almost exclusively in a given product category – believe that their brand is superior to other brands in a way that is meaningful to them (McQueen *et al.*, 1993: 239). In other words, the brand has to acquire a kind of legitimacy, that is appear as credible and valuable for target customers, through all brand discourses (advertising discourse, product discourse, packaging discourse, etc.).

3. In the case of a brand extension, a successful brand extension implies a perceived fit between the old product and the new product. Successful brands have core properties which their users value. Two requirements are usually mentioned for the success of a brand extension: consumers must associate the brand with high quality which means that the brand has already gained competency among its loyal customers, and there must be a perception fit between the two products, i.e. transference from the old to the new product. An interesting example is Persil, which has always been associated in the consumer's mind with one single value, 'caring', which declined over the years: caring about whiteness, clothes, skin, washing machines and mothers' reputations. In a recent reformulation, biological enzymes were introduced into the product to allow the levels of

some of Persil's basic active ingredients to be rebalanced. But biological enzymes are not seen by consumers as naturally associated with the concept of care, hence the failure of the new position.

It might also predict the success or failure of a brand extension. The process of brand extension is essentially the process of gaining competency and credibility to extend the product line. Aaker and Keller (1990) have shown that consumers are more likely to accept a brand extension when there is a fit of product complementarity or common attributes. The contract concept could then prove useful to understand the coherence and consistency of the brand's positioning strategy, the brand's message, the brand's ability to be extended.

5.2 The contract

Narrative discourse is often seen in the form of a circulation of objects of value. Its organization can thus be described as a series of transfers of values. A particular and complex mode of transfer is that of exchange of values. Such an operation implies that, whenever the values in exchange are not identical, they be primarily identified; a fiduciary contract must thus be established between the subjects who engage in the exchange; this contract has no other role but to fix the exchange value of the values in question (see Greimas and Courtès, 1979: 365–6). The contract hence usually concerns the purchase stage. During the transaction, the brand and the consumer can be seen as two partners involved in a mutual contract. The contract is usually seen in most influential political writings (Hobbes, Rousseau) as a voluntary and reversible choice made by each individual to associate rationally with others in a specified framework. Nevertheless the contractual scheme might be expanded to other kinds of entity than the individuals with whom man is likely to be linked. Serres has, for instance, proposed a new way of understanding the relationship between men and the earth based on a natural contract in which nature would become a contractor as a whole (Serres, 1993). The contract has also been used to account for the relationship between a company and its customers. This is consistent with the existence of a legal terminology associated with the brand. The concept of a 'consumer's franchise', for example, implicitly enables us to consider the relationship between the consumer and the brand in a contractual perspective. Staveley sees, for example, the brand as a 'compact' between the manufacturer (or distributor) and the consumer and he defines the compact as related to the consistency of formulation, of intrinsic quality and of other values, both extrinsic ('added values') and intrinsic (Staveley, 1987: 33, in de Chernatony and McWilliam, 1988: 342). The contract refers to the basic exchange process which involves an exchange of value. The underlying conception of value is 'Value is what I get for the price I pay' (Zeithaml, 1991: 42). The value of the brand, as perceived by the consumer, derives in this stage from a comparison between the 'give' components (time, effort, money) and the 'get' components. In this stage value plays the role of an intervening variable caused directly by consumer perceptions of quality, sacrifice and a brand's intrinsic and extrinsic attributes and resulting in brand choice (Babin et al., 1994; Dodds and Monroe, 1985). Value can thus be seen as a trade-off of the salient give and get components, that is to say an exchange value. Value is measured by what is given up by the consumer (concept of sacrifice). The concept of contract also helps to understand certain consumption behaviours such as browsing or *flânerie*, which involve a specific kind of consumer–brand relationship where the contract is missing, because there is no purchase.

5.3 The performance

The performance mainly deals with the consumption experience with the brand, that is to say the series of brand contacts which may involve such actions as storage and transport, preparation, consumption and disposal. The value put on the brand by the consumer at this stage is essentially a value in use, that is, the value provided by the brand to various users. This approach to the brand's value is very similar to the economist's definition of utility. Zeithaml has illustrated the fact that the value of the brand is defined according to what the consumer wants in the product/brand. The value of an orange juice brand might, for example, be described by a consumer as 'what my kids will drink', 'what is good for me', 'little containers because then there is no waste' or 'what is convenient', etc. (Zeithaml, 1988). Floch (1988, 1990) was, for instance, able to typologize the main values ascribed to such consumption objects as a supermarket or a car; the four values potentially ascribed to any brand are the following: utilitarian or practical values (money, time, effort required to purchase and consume the brand), existential or 'life' values (experience, adventure provided by the brand), ludic values (fun, fantasy, etc.) and critical values (value for money, perceived quality, etc.). It is important to note that the performance of a brand is not necessarily to a previous contract. As mentioned above, the performance of the brand is multidimensional because it is evaluated at different levels (functional level, emotional level, symbolic level, etc.), which refer to the various dimensions of the brand (tangible product, packaging, brand logo, etc.) seen in a holistic perspective.

5.4 The sanction

At this stage, the consumer compares what he or she got from the brand with what he or she expected. Brand value is perceived by the consumer as the difference between what he or she got and what he or she paid for. The brand's value is then seen as an *a posteriori* evaluation of the experience with the brand which can result in several outcomes. The brand's performance is evaluated according to the consumer's expectations and to the consumer's experiences with other brands. The consumer may be satisfied, satisfaction usually being defined as the 'level of a person's felt state resulting from comparing a product's perceived performance (or outcome) in relation to the person's expectations' (Kotler, 1994: 40). The resulting outcome can be a further purchase and loyal behaviour.

On the other hand, if the consumer is dissatisfied, the sanction can be the creation and development of negative attitudes towards the brand, and resulting behaviours such as brand switching, negative word-of-mouth communication, etc. Related areas of brand management involved with the sanction are brand loyalty, brand switching and other types of after-purchase behaviour.

Table 8   Decoding the consumer–brand relationship as a narrative process: a synthesis

Contact Occasions	Corresponding Stage in the Narrative Chain
Communication contact	Acquisition of competency
Purchase	Contract
Consumption and evaluation	Performance
Post-purchase behaviour	Sanction

5.5   My brand the hero?

Before concluding this exploratory investigation, another interesting point needs to be made in order to answer the original question which started this search for the brand as a hero. The narratological scheme helped us to understand the different phases of the consumer–brand relationship by reading it as a text. This approach also provides fruitful insights into the various roles played by the different characteristics present in a market.

Propp has remarked that the basic functions mentioned above can be divided into limited spheres of actions (7), each of them corresponding to a given type of *dramatis personae: villain, donor, helper, sought-for-person, dispatcher, hero, false hero*. It can then be shown that each of these seven spheres of actions are implicitly used by brand managers as positioning strategies.

Although being a character in the narrative process described above, the brand can play various roles in the narrative process and therefore does not always act as a hero. Seven major types of brand characters can thus be identified:

- The *villain* can be illustrated by positioning strategies based on very aggressive comparative advertising. The Irish supermarket chain, Dunnes Stores, for instance, which frequently initiates price wars against its competitors by using comparative advertising based on price differences, can be considered a villain brand.
- The *donor* represents a brand which provides wealth and distributes generosity. Airline companies and luxury hotels giving tangible benefits (frequent flyer miles programmes) and other kinds of incentives can be considered as 'donor brands'. Other examples include American Express, which provides courtesy lounges for their consumers in major international airports, and up-market department stores which provide very elaborate window displays suggesting opulence with an implicit reference to Aladdin's cave.
- The *helper* is a brand which is positioned according to the main benefits offered. Examples include such brands as Mars ('A Mars a day helps you work, rest and play') and the toothpaste Crest, positioned as a cavity fighter.
- The *sought-for-person* is a brand which is looked for by the consumer because it helps change a given situation. A good example is given by the Suzuki brand: 'The end of a dull day. The start of Suzuki'. Apple can also be considered as a sought-for-brand because its business philosophy is to provide friendly computers that enable users to

improve their personal development and to stimulate their imagination and intelligence (Rijkens, 1992: 17). The Club Méditerranée, whose motto is 'Happiness is our Business', is also intentionally positioned as a sought-for-brand.

- The *dispatcher* would be a brand which gives information and provides the consumer with advice. Financial service companies usually portray themselves as advisers. 'We trade in ideas, not just bonds' was, for instance, the recent advertising of one financial company.
- The *hero* is represented by such positioning strategies as the one used by Volvo which stressed safety and desirability, or Marlboro which is represented by a cowboy who is a 'hero [because] he controls the world around him' (Rijkens, 1992: 115). Lux toilet soap, which has long been advertised as 'The Beauty Soap of International Stars', explicitly positioned itself as a hero. Numerous luxury brands also position themselves as heroes. Examples include Joy by Jean Patou, Mont Blanc, etc.
- The *false-hero* is a brand which denies the right to be the hero of the story (i.e. the market leader). A good example is provided by Avis, which has long used the following advertising message in the United States: 'Avis is only No. 2 in rent a cars. So why go with us.' This is also generally the case with retailers' brands and generic brands, which are usually positioned as underdogs.

Before developing further a semiotic definition of the brand, several research areas can be suggested, as related to the spheres of action mentioned above.

The first one would be to provide a precise definition of each role by listing the sphere of actions related to it through a careful review of the literature on narratives. It would thus be valuable to investigate (1) the robustness of this narrative metaphor, that is, to what extent the roles generally used for the analysis of literary characters can be metaphorically applied to brands, (2) whether the roles identified by Propp account for all the possible roles a brand can play in a given market. In the first stage of the research process, the use of projective techniques within focus groups might help us to identify implicit personality traits, functions and roles around a set of representative brands.

The exact definition of each role and the corresponding sphere of actions would then allow a consideration of a possible methodology to classify brands in accordance with Propp's categorization. Content analysis, as a possible methodological approach, could be used. A range of brands within a given product category and different types of advertising campaigns would be considered. Advertising campaigns, which can be considered as explicit forms of expression of a brand's role, would be analyzed by means of content analysis.

Using the focus groups results, a sample of consumers would then be given a codebook with a precise definition of each possible role. Then they would be exposed to the various advertising messages and would be asked to assign a role to each brand. A validity check would be ensured through an agreement measure (Kripendorf, 1980) as well as an inter-judge reliability measure (for example: Cohen kappa). Such a methodology has, for instance, been suggested and used by Leigh (1994) to investigate the use of figures of speech in print advertising headlines.

The second possible step would be to investigate the various variables that lead to the definition of a brand's role in the market in order better to define and enhance brand strategy. This would lead to (1) the identification of all the variables contributing to the role definition of a brand on its market, and (2) the measure of their influences in the context of a role creation and/or role change.

6. Towards a semiotic reformulation of the brand

This narrative approach sets a number of philosophical and conceptual issues concerning the brand. First, it stresses the fact that a brand does not have a value *per se*, but that its value is only to be perceived in a relational perspective. This means that a brand can be decoded/interpreted as part of a system that exists only through a number of differences, oppositions and interactions. This assumption largely derives from the structuralist methodology which gradually permeated the social sciences following the pioneering works of Jakobson and Lévi-Strauss (1955, 1958). The most significant contribution made by this new approach was to refuse to treat elements as independent entities and to reinterpret them instead in terms of their relationships within a global system which operates according to generalizable laws. As Lévi-Strauss recognized, the most universal trait of human culture is the desire to have meaning and the human need for communication exchange through signs. Lévi-Strauss has, for instance, suggested that marriage regulations and kinship arrangements should be considered as a set of coded relations of exchange which performs as a language system, that is, as a signifying system of communication.

Brands, as cultural objects, also exist as constitutive parts of a market system within which they must accomplish a narrative programme. This programme is usually defined as being oriented towards a finalized end which basically can be described as the satisfaction of a need or, more generally, the reduction of a state of tension from the consumer's perspective. Brands in this perspective play the role of magic objects in fairy tales, in the sense that they provide the consumer with powers (invisibility, ubiquity, omniscience, etc.) and help or even replace him or her in the quest for values. In other words, brands do not have value *per se*, but they can only be understood as 'mediators between a mythical destinator and the man to whom they are provided' (Greimas, 1983: 20). Therefore, these objects can be mythically analyzed as degraded and figurative forms of the main spheres of divine sovereignty, that is, at an imaginative level, essential attributes of human competency which institute and justify human actions (see Greimas, 1983: 20; Dumézil, 1968: 541–2). This assumption led Greimas to reconsider the model proposed by Propp and to suggest the idea of actantial categories which are a redefinition of Propp's narrative functions as relationship between actants. This model (Figure 3), which was shown to decode the relationships between consumers and goods (see Heilbrunn, 1996), can also more specifically be applied to an understanding of the branding process in a relational and narrative perspective. This model is based on the following: a subject wants (i.e. desires) an object, encounters an opponent, finds a helper, obtains the object from a sender, and gives it to the receiver (Greimas, 1966, 1983; Nöth, 1990: 372).

This model functions if one keeps in mind the following rules (Everaert-Desmedt, 1988: 29):

• an object can be a material possession as well as a non-material value (e.g. quest for knowledge);

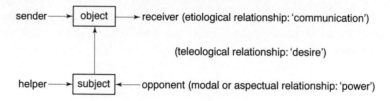

Figure 3   The actantial model.
Source: adapted from Greimas (1966) and Schleifer (1987).

- an actant is not an actor but rather a fictive narrative unity which exists at a more abstract level than the actor; an actantial role can be played by a human character but also by a material object;
- an actant can be represented by several actors;
- an actor can play several actantial roles;
- within a given narrative, the actantial model can appear at different levels, because several actants might be searching for objects simultaneously.

This model is based on the assumption that the object and the subject do not exist independently but are related by either *disjunction* or *conjunction*. In other words, any narrative is the process by which the subject and the object who are originally 'disjuncted' gradually come to be 'conjuncted'. This move from the *disjunction* to the *conjunction* of the subject and the object occurs through the various interactions between actants, which are 'characters' considered from the point of view of their narrative roles and their mutual relations. Any narrative can thus be interpreted as the coexistence of three axes: (1) a *desire axis*: the story of a subject in search of an object; (2) a *communication axis*: this object is also transmitted from a sender to a receiver; (3) a *power axis*: the helper helps the subject to obtain the object while the opponent is an obstacle to this quest.

This actantial model seems useful to understand the roles and functions of the brand in a semiotic perspective. As mentioned above, a brand can be seen in a *holistic* manner as 'a bundle of attributes that someone buys and that provide satisfaction' (Styles and Ambler, 1995: 583). Thus a brand can be viewed from a Greimasian perspective as an object that is essentially something which stands for values and is potentially desired by some individuals.

Let us consider the following consumer quote adapted from Wilkie (1994: 13):

> The woman came on a quest for a refill of detergent. But when her usual brand was no longer available, she was tossed into the chaos of the modern day world of detergents: 'I'd never use brand X [detergent brand]! My neighbour's child whose clothes have a yellowish tinge, which does not say much for her mother. She uses it. I'll use brand Y; it's the best one. I think it's one of the leading sellers, too, because they do not stop advertising on TV. Also my sister strongly recommended it to me. Furthermore it's on special offer today! I'll definitely get it!

This consumer's quote might easily be decoded in narrative terms by means of the actantial model. Semiotically, this story is the narrative programme of a *subject* (the consumer) who is searching for – state of *disjunction* – an *object* (a detergent brand and all the potential values she associates with it). The *subject* finds a potential *opponent* (her usual brand is not on the shelf) in her search for the *object*, but the *opponent*'s action is thwarted by various *helpers* (the sister's recommendations, brand Y is on special offer, etc.) who help the consumer to make her decision, that is, to find the object of value she's looking for. The *object* of her quest is potentially transmitted by a *sender* (brand Y manufacturer) to a *receiver* (the consumer) thanks to the conjunction of such elements as the presence of brand Y on the shelf (retailer's role as helper), as well as the ideological discourses which surround this particular brand in the marketplace (brand Y's advertising pressure, positive word-of-mouth communication, the neighbour's bad experience with brand X as perceived by the consumer). The story ends with the purchase of brand Y, that is the consumer found the *object* of value he/she was looking for, hence a state of *conjunction* between the *subject* and the *object* which closes the narrative process.

This very basic example is very interesting as regards the two following issues:

1. Actors in the market do not have fixed actantial roles; they can play different, alternative roles. As soon as the consumer cannot find the detergent brand she is looking for, she is faced with a multitude of brands on the shelf; these alternative brands act alternatively as *helpers* (they provide a potential substitution solution) and as *opponents* (brand Y is chosen against other brands). Therefore we propose replacing the concept of market-actor with the concept of market-actant, which allows us to take into consideration the various roles potentially played by a market entity within the branding process.

2. The brand can be considered as an object of desire which must fulfil a certain number of expectations from the consumer's point of view. Brand Y's value, as perceived by this consumer, is clearly distinct from its immediate utilitarian function (to wash clothes). A detergent brand is endowed with social values and literally intertwined with ideological connotations which are distinct from the material object itself. This consumer refuses to get brand X – the brand her neighbour uses – because she thinks it could leave her and her family with an unsatisfactory social image. The detergent brand is thus an *object* which is socially and not solely individually desired (or undesired) because it is potentially related to her image (own image and her family image) as an individual and not solely as a consumer. It illustrates the fact that the desire for a brand is socially constructed by the various actants. In other words, the value of an object, that is, its propensity to arouse desire, is created and negotiated by the various actants within the narrative process. A narrative can be understood as the story by which an object's value is created, transformed and appropriated by the various actants. Thus, the important consequence is that the value of a brand, conceived in a narrative perspective as its desirability, is co-constructed and negotiated by the various actants (see Heilbrunn, 1996). This approach refers to the theory of *mimetic rivalry* proposed by Girard (1972, 1977) to explain the way things are socially desired in so far as they are desired by a rival; there is no immediate desire for a given object; by desiring an object, the rival signifies to the subject what is desirable. 'In other words, a desire expressed towards an object is not constituted due to its representational role – as "standing for", being "symbol of", or representing something valued and desired. An object is desired only derivatively on the basis of an intimate relation to (an) other subject . . . or by adopting the other's desire and resulting in a rivalry concerning the other's object of desire' (Falk, 1994:

119). The conspicuous consumption of luxury brands provides a good illustration of the way a brand's value is collectively negotiated and constructed through an essential process of mimetic rivalry.

7. Main managerial implications

This brief overview of the possible roles played by market actants may constitute a valuable toolbox for brand managers to structure and enhance their branding strategy approach.

First, with regard to strategic brand management, the different roles provided by Propp's study help us to understand the positions of brands in a given market and the alternative relationships of brands in a product category. Owing to the rising hypersegmentation of markets, the need for a definite position is crucial for the success of any brand. This framework provided by the narrative approach offers a list of the possible positions a brand can have in the market in order to play a role in this market. A given market, which can be read as a text, exists only through the reassignment of roles among different characters. Hypersegmented markets such as detergents, toothpaste or shampoos intuitively provide good examples of markets in which different spheres of actions are being played by different brands. With regard to a brand launch, extension or repositioning, the set of different positions derived from Propp provides a useful framework for possible competitive moves. A brand can play different roles at different times, that is to say, its role might evolve from one sphere of actions to another. A good example is 'Marlboro Friday', that is 2 April 1993, when Philip Morris decided to slash the price of Marlboros by 20% to stave off the brand's market share deterioration. This was considered as an historic move simply because Marlboro, which has always played the role of a hero by raising its price twice a year with little consumer resistance (Bradley, 1995), had suddenly borrowed the sphere of actions of another character, that is, the villain. Brand extension is also often used by a company to play several roles simultaneously in a given market.

Second, with regard to brand image and brand identity, it illustrates the necessary consistency of the various ingredients which compose the brand strategy. In a narrative text, as Propp remarked, a function is often associated with another in a fixed pair (e.g. struggle–victory, pursuit–rescue . . .). Therefore, functions can often be grouped to define the sphere of actions of the *dramatis personae*. The functions of a character are what constitute the constant and repetitive elements of the fairy tale. For example, the sphere of action of a villain can generally be described by the following actions: villainy, struggle (with the hero), pursuit. Among the 31 principal functions identified by Propp, it seems obvious that most functions such as interdiction, transgression, information, deceit, complicity and mediation can easily be applied to the brand's universe. In other words, a brand expresses its role by various acts just as a character in a fairy tale is represented by a given sphere of action. A brand's role derives from its main functions in the market and this role is largely expressed through marketing variables such as the positioning strategy, the segmentation strategy, the promotional strategy, the advertising strategy, etc. Thus, it can be said that each brand possesses a sphere of action in order to play a definite role in a market. This sphere of action seems to be an important aspect of both brand identity and brand image.

Third, Greimas's actantial model gives an accurate account of the possible narrative roles of various actants involved in the branding process. A brand or a consumer might alternatively play several actantial roles in the definition of a brand's value. It shows that brand identity is not an *a priori* concept as is often naively believed, but rather derives from a process of construction and transformation by various actants who are part of an interdependent system. The branding process might thus be viewed as a temporal (that is evolving) system constituted by various actants which do not exist as isolated entities, but exist only through their mutual interactions, these interactions being governed by three kinds of force: desire, power and communication.

Conclusion

This brief overview of the narrative approach applied to the brand is only a starting point for further research and thought. Narrativity was presented as a key concept to account for the way brands become invested with value so as to become desirable objects. Consumption is the process by which value is created and transformed by various actants and the desirability of consumption objects (such as brands) narratively co-constructed. The narrative approach also provides good insights to decode and analyze this peculiar text which is the consumer–brand relationship. This relationship is in fact part of a semiotic system which implies the existence of several actors (the brand, consumers, manufacturers, influence agents) in a sequence of events which can be condensed to a set of four minimal functions: the acquisition of competency, the contract, the performance, the sanction. Each of the stages is related to a particular definition and perception of the brand's value from the consumer's perspective.

Each actor might successively or alternatively play several actantial roles; hence the suggestion to decode this semiotic system using the particular concept of *actant*, rather than the fictitious one of actor. The narrative approach views consumption as a system constituted by various actants who are in an interdependent situation: actants do not exist as isolated entities, but only through their interaction with other actants, these interactions being governed by three kinds of force which are *desire, power* and *communication*. The value of a brand, semiotically considered as an *object*, does not exist *per se*, but results from an interaction process between various tyupes of actants. This postulate is consistent with the main assumption which grounds structuralism, that is, meaning resides in the differences apprehended between the various elements of a system. A brand's value can thus only be apprehended in a differential perspective, which means it is endlessly constructed and transformed by the interactions of several actants.

References

Aaker, D. and Biel, A. (eds.) (1993), *Brand Equity and Advertising. Advertising's Role in Building Strong Brands*, Hillsdale, NJ: Lawrence Erlbaum.

Aaker, D.A. and Keller, K.L. (1990), 'Consumer evaluations of brand extensions', *Journal of Marketing*, **54**, January, 24–41.

Allport, G.W. (1937), *Personality: A Psychological Interpretation*, New York: Henri Holt.

Asa Burger, A. (1990), 'Semiological analysis', in O. Boyd Barret and P. Braham (eds.), *Media, Knowledge and Power*, London: Routledge, 132–55.

Assael, H. (1992), *Consumer Behavior and Marketing Action*, fourth edition, Boston: PWS-Kent Publishing Company.

Babin, B.J. *et al.* (1994), 'Work and/or fun: Measuring hedonic and utilitarian shopping value', *Journal of Consumer Research*, **20**, March, 644–56.

Barthes, R. (1964), 'Sémantique de l'objet', Colloquium at the Cini Foundation in Venice, reproduced in: *The Semiotic Challenge*, 1988, Berkeley: University of California Press, 179–90.

Barthes, R. (1966), 'Introduction à l'analyse structurale des récits', *Communications*, **8**, Paris, Seuil, 1–27.

Barthes, R. (1977), 'Introduction to the structural analysis of narratives', in R. Barthes, *Image-Music-Text*, New York: Hill & Wang, 79–124.

Batra, R. *et al.* (1993), 'The brand personality component of brand goodwill: Some antecedents and consequences', in D. Aaker and A. Biel (eds.), *Brand Equity and Advertising*, Hillsdale, NJ: Lawrence Erlbaum, 83–96.

Batra, R. and Ahtola, O.T. (1990), 'Measuring the hedonic and utilitarian sources of consumer attitudes', *Marketing Letters*, **2**(2), 159–70.

Baudrillard, J. (1968), *Le Système des objets*, Paris: Gallimard.

Baudrillard, J. (1972), *Pour une critique de l'economie politique du signe*, Paris: Gallimard.

Beaglehole, E. (1932), *Property: A Study in Social Psychology*, New York: Macmillan.

Belk, R.W. (1988), 'Possessions and the extended self', *Journal of Consumer Research*, **15**, September, 139–68.

Belk, R.W. (1991), 'The ineluctable mysteris of possessions', in F.W. Rudmin (ed.), *To Have Possessions: A handbook on ownership and property* (special issue), *Journal of Social Behavior and Personality*, **6**(6), 17–55.

Biel, A.L. (1993), 'Converting image into equity', in D. Aaker and A. Biel (eds.), *Brand Equity and Advertising*, Hillsdale, NJ: Lawrence Erlbaum, 67–82.

Blackston, M. (1993), 'Beyond brand personality: Building brand relationships', in D. Aaker and A. Biel (eds.), *Brand Equity and Advertising. Advertising's Role in Building Strong Brands*, Hillsdale, NJ: Lawrence Erlbaum, 113–24.

Boutié, P. (1994), 'The map is not the territory: Who will save the brands?', in *Building Successful Brands: The Need for an Integrated Approach*, ESOMAR seminar, Prague, 26–29 October, 9–22.

Bradley, F. (1995), *Marketing Management. Providing, Communicating and Delivering Value*, Englewood Cliffs, NJ: Prentice-Hall.

Brémond, C. (1966), 'La logique des possibles narratifs', *Communications*, **8**, Paris, Seuil, 60–76.

Brémond, C. (1970), 'Morphology of the French folkstale', *Semiotica*, **2**, 247–76.

Brémond, C. (1973), *Logique du récit*, Paris: Seuil.

Brémond, C. (1986), 'Propp', in T.A. Sebeok (ed.), *Encyclopedic Dictionary of Semiotics*, Berlin: Mouton de Gruyter, T.2, 771–3.

Buell, V.P. (1986), *Handbook of Modern Marketing*, New York: McGraw-Hill.

Chatman, S. (1974), 'Rhetoric & semiotics', in S. Chatman *et al.* (eds.), *A Semiotic Landscape*, The Hague: Mouton, 103–12.

Christopher, M. *et al.* (1991), *Relationship Marketing*, London: Butterworth-Heinemann.

Cooper, P. (1979), 'Symbiosis: the consumer psychology of branding', *ADMAP*, November, 578–86.

Corstjens, J. and M. (1995), *Store Wars. The Battle for Minspace and Shelfspace*, Chichester: Wiley.

Cova, B. (1995), *Au-delà du marché: Quand le lien importe plus que le bien*, Paris: L'Harmattan.

Cova, B. and J. Kassis (1994), 'Plurality of the social link and confusion in consumption', Proposal for the Sixth Annual Conference of the Society for the Advancement of Socio-Economics, Jouy-en-Josas, July.

Csikszentmihalyi, M. and Rochberg-Halton, E. (1981), *The Meaning of Things. Domestic symbols and the self*, Cambridge: Cambridge University Press.

Davis (1986), 'Does branding pay?', *ADMAP*.

de Brentani, U. (1993), 'The effects of customization and customer contact on the factors determining success and failure of new industrial services', in M. Baker, *Perspectives on Marketing Management*, Vol. 3, Chichester: Wiley, 275–98.

de Chernatony, L. and M.H.B. McWilliam (1989), 'The varying nature of brands as assets: theory and practice compared', *International Journal of Advertising*, 8(4), 339–49.

de Chernatony, L. and M. McWilliam (1992), *Creating Powerful Brands*, London: Butterworth-Heinemann.

Denzin, N. (1992), *Symbolic Interaction and Cultural Studies*, Oxford: Blackwell.

Dodds, W.B. and K.B. Monroe (1985), 'The effects of brand and price information on subjective product evaluations', *Advances in Consumer Research*, 12, 85–90.

Dolich, I.J. (1969), 'Congruence relationships between self-images and product brands', *Journal of Marketing*, 6 (February), 80–4.

Dumézil, G. (1968), *Mythe et epopée*, Paris: Gallimard.

Dupuy, F. and J.-C. Thoenig (1989), 'La marque et l'échange', in J.-N. Kapferer and J.-C. Thoenig (eds.) (1989), *La Marque*, Paris: McGraw-Hill.

Dwyer, F.R., P.H. Schurr and S. Oh (1987), 'Developing buyer-seller relationships', *Journal of Marketing*, 51 (April), 11–27.

Eco, U. (1962), *Opera Aperta*, Milan: Bompiani; French translation: *L'Oeuvre ouverte*, 1966, Paris: Seuil.

Eco, U. (1979), *A Theory of Semiotics*, Bloomington, IN: Indiana University Press.

Eco, U. (1979), *Lector in fabula*, Milano, Bompiani; French translation: *Le rôle du lecteur ou la Coopération interprétative dans les textes narratifs*, 1985, Paris: Grasset & Fasquelle.

Eco, U. (1990), *I Limiti Dell' Interpretazione*, Milano, Bompiani; French translation: *Les Limites de l'interprétation*, 1992, Paris: Grasset & Fasquelle.

Egan C. *et al.* (1992), 'The importance of brand names in industrial markets', in M.J. Baker, *Perspectives on Marketing Management*, Vol. 2, Chichester: Wiley, 307–24.

Everaert-Desmedt, N. (1988), *Sémiotique du récit*, De Boeck Université: Editions Universitaires.

Falk, P. (1994), 'Consuming desire', in P. Falk, *The Consuming Body*, London: Sage, 93–150.

Farquhar, P. (1989), 'Managing brand equity', *Marketing Research*, September, 24–33.

Flechter, A. (1964), *Allegory. The Theory of a Symbolic Mode*, New York: Cornell University Press.

Floch, J.-M. (1988), 'The contribution of structural semiotics to the design of a hypermarket', *International Journal of Research in Marketing*, 4, 233–252.

Floch, J.-M. (1990), *Sémiotique, marketing et communication*, Paris: PUF.

Foucault, M. (1970), *The Order of Things*, New York: Random House.

Fournier, S. (1994), 'A Consumer–Brand Relationship Framework for Strategic Brand Management', PhD dissertation, University of Florida.

Frondizi, R. (1971), *What is Value? An introduction to axiology*, 2nd edn, La Salle, IL: Open Court Publishing Company.

Gardner, B. and S. Levy (1955), 'The product and the brand', *Harvard Business Review*, 33, 33–9.

Girard, R. (1972), *La Violence et le sacré*, Paris: Grasset; English translation: *Violence and the Sacred* (1977), Baltimore: Johns Hopkins University Press.

Girard, R. (1977), *Des Choses cachées depuis la fondation du monde*, Paris: Grasset; English translation: *Things Hidden Since the Foundation of the World* (1987), London: Athlone.

Gottdiener, M. (1995), *Postmodern Semiotics. Material Culture and the Forms of Postmodern Life*, Oxford: Blackwell.

Greimas, A.J. (1966), 'Eléments pour une théorie de l'interprétation du récit mythique', *Communications*, 8, Paris: Seuil, 28–59.

Greimas, A.J. (1983), *Structural Semantics: An Attempt at a Method*, Lincoln, NB: University of Nebraska Press. Translation of *Sémantique structurale*, 1966, Paris: Larousse.

Greimas, A.J. and Courtès, J. (1979), *Semiotics and Language. An Analytical Dictionary*, Bloomington, IN: Indiana University Press.

Gummesson, E. (1987), 'The new marketing – developing long-term interactive relationships', *Long Range Planning*, 20(4), 10–20.

Heilbrunn, B. (1996), 'In search of the hidden go(o)d: A philosophical deconstruction and narratological revisitation of the eschatological metaphor in marketing', in Brown, S. *et al.* (eds), *Marketing Apocalypse: Eschatology, Escapology and the Illusion of the End*, London: Routledge.

Hirschman, E.C. and Holbrook, M.B. (1982) 'Hedonic consumption: Emerging concepts, methods and propositions', *Journal of Marketing*, **46** (Summer), 92–101.

Hirschman, E.C. and Holbrook, M. (1992), *Postmodern Consumer Research. The Study of Consumption as a Text*, Newbury Park, CA: Sage.

Jhally, S. (1990), *The Codes of Advertising. Fetichism and the Political Economy of Meaning in the Consumer Society*, London: Routledge.

Kapferer, J.N. (1992), *Strategic Brand Management*, London: Kogan Page.

Kearney, R. (1994), *Modern Movements in European Philosophy*, 2nd edition, Manchester: Manchester University Press.

Kehret-Ward, T. (1988), 'Using a semiotic approach to study the consumption of functionally related products', *International Journal of Research in Marketing*, **4**, 187–200.

Kotler, P. (1994), *Marketing Management, Analysis, Planning, Implementation, and Control*, 8th edition, Englewood Cliffs, NJ: Prentice-Hall.

Kripendorf, K. (1980), *Content Analysis: An Introduction to its Methodology*, Newbury Park, CA: Sage.

Lagneau, G. (1969), *Le faire savoir. Introduction à la sociologie des phénomènes publicitaires*, Paris: Sabri.

Lamb, D. (1979), 'The ethos of the brand', *ADMAP*, **15**, January, 19–24.

Lannon, J. and Cooper, P. (1983), 'Humanistic advertising. A holistic cultural perspective', *International Journal of Advertising*, **2**, 195–213.

Lash, S. and Urry, J. (1994), *Economies of Signs & Space*, London: Sage.

Leigh, J.A. (1994), 'The use of figures of speech in print ad headlines', *Journal of Advertising*, **23**(2), June, 17–33.

Lévi-Strauss, C. (1955), *Tristes Tropiques*, Paris: Plon.

Lévi-Strauss, C. (1958), *Anthropologie Structurale*, Paris: Plon.

Lovelock, C.H. (1984), *Services Marketing*, Englewood Cliffs, NJ: Prentice-Hall.

MacInnis, D.H. and Price, L.L. (1987), 'The role of imagery in information processing: Review and extensions', *Journal of Consumer Research*, **13**, 473–91.

Mauss, M. (1967), *The Gift: Forms and Functions of Exchange in Archaic Societies*, New York: Norton. Translated from: 'Essai sur de don: Forme et raison de l'échange dans les sociétés archaïques', *L'Année Sociologique*, **I** (1923–24), 30–186.

McCracken, G. (1981), 'Culture and consumption', *Journal of Consumer Research*, **13**, June, 71–84.

McCracken, G. (1988), *Culture and Consumption*, Bloomington, IN: Indiana University Press.

McCracken, G. (1993), 'The value of the brand: An anthropological perspective', in D. Aaker and A. Biel (eds.), *Brand Equity and Advertising*, Hillsdale, NJ: Lawrence Erlbaum, 125–39.

McQueen, J., Foley, C. and Deighton, J. (1993), 'Decomposing a brand's franchise into buyer types', in D. Aaker and A. Biel (eds.), *Brand Equity and Advertising. Advertising's Role in Building Strong Brands*, Hillsdale, NJ: Lawrence Erlbaum, 235–45.

Mélétinski, E. (1970), 'L'étude structurale et typologique du conte', in V. Propp, *Morphologie du conte*, 1973, Paris: Seuil, 202–54.

Mick, D. (1986), 'Consumer research and semiotics: Exploring the morphology of signs, symbols and significance', *Journal of Consumer Research*, **13**, 196–213.

Miller, D. (1995), 'Consumption as the vanguard of history', in D. Miller (ed.), *Acknowledging Consumption. A Review of New Studies*, London: Routledge, 1–57.

Morgan, R.M. and S.D. Hunt (1994), 'The commitment–trust theory of relationship marketing', *Journal of Marketing*, **58** (July), 20–38.

Nöth, W. (1990), *Handbook of Semiotics*, Bloomington, IN: Indiana University Press.

Péninou, G. (1972), *Intelligence de la publicité*, Paris: Robert Laffont.

Peter, J.P. and Olson, J.C. (1993), *Consumer Behavior and Marketing Strategy*, 3rd edition, Chicago, IL: Irwin.

Porter, M.E. (1985), *Competitive Advantage*, New York: Free Press.

Propp, V. (1928), *Morfologija skazkii*, coll. Voprosy poetiki, n°12, Gosudarstvennyj institut istorii iskusstava, Leningrad; English translation: *Morphology of the Folktale*, 1973, University of Texas Press; French translation, *Morphologie du conte*, 1973, Paris: Seuil.

Rethans, A.J. and Taylor, J.L. (1982), 'A script theoretic analysis of consumer decision making', in B.J. Walker (ed.), *Proceedings of the AMA Educator's Conference*, Series No. 48, 71–4.

Ricoeur, P. (1983–84), *Time and Narrative*, Chicago: Chicago University Press, 2 vols.

Rijkens, R. (1992), *European Advertising Strategies*, London: Cassel.

Rook, D.W. (1985), 'The ritual dimension of consumer behavior', *Journal of Consumer Research*, **12**, December, 251–64.

Sartre, J.-P. (1943), *Being and Nothingness: A Phenomenological Essay on Ontology*, New York: Philosophical Library.

Saussure, F. de (1969), *Courses in General Linguistic*, New York: McGraw-Hill; originally published in French in 1915.

Schleifer, R. (1987), *A.J. Greimas and the Nature of Meaning: Linguistics, Semiotics and Discourse Theory*, Lincoln: University of Nebraska Press.

Sebeok, T.A. (ed.) (1986), *Encyclopedic Dictionary of Semiotics*, Berlin: Mouton de Gruyter, 3 vols.

Semprini, A. (1992a), 'The brand audit', in *The Challenge of Branding Today and in the Future*, ESOMAR, Brussels, 28–30 October, 163–74.

Semprini, A. (1992b), *Le Marketing de la marque. Approche sémiotique*, Paris: Editions Liaisons.

Serres, M. (1993), *Le Contrat naturel*, Paris: Flammarion.

Sherry, J. (1986), 'Cereal Monogamy: Brand Loyalty as a Secular Ritual in Consumer Culture', paper presented at the Association for Consumer Research Annual Conference, Toronto, October.

Sinden, J.A. and Worrel, A.C. (1979), *Unpriced Values. Decisions without Market Prices*, Chichester: Wiley.

Smothers, N. (1993), 'Can products and brands have charisma?', in D. Aaker and A. Biel (eds.), *Brand Equity and Advertising*, Hillsdale, NJ: Lawrence Erlbaum, 97–112.

Styles, C. and Ambler, T. (1995), 'Brand management', in S. Crainer (ed.), *The Financial Times Handbook of Management*, London: Pitman Publishing, 581–93.

Toffler, A. (1980), *The Third Wave*, Toronto: Bantam Books.

van Dick, T.A. (1976), 'Narrative macro structures: logical and cognitive foundations', *PTL: Journal for Descriptive Poetics and Theory of Literature*, **1**, 547–68.

Van Raaij, W.F. (1993), 'Postmodern consumption', *Journal of Economic Psychology*, **14**, 541–63.

Watkins, T. (1986), *The Economics of the Brand. A Marketing Analysis*, London: McGraw-Hill.

White, I.S. (1966), 'The perception of value in products', in J.W. Newman, *On Knowing the Consumer*, Chichester: Wiley, 90–106.

Wilkie, W. (1994), *Consumer Behaviour*, 3rd edition, Chichester: Wiley.

Wilkins, M. (1992), 'The neglected intangible asset: The influence of the trade mark on the rise of the modern corporation', *Business History*, **34**, 66–95.

Young, S. and Feigin, B. (1975), 'Using the benefit chain for improved strategy formulation', *Journal of Marketing*, July, 72–4.

Zeithaml, V. (1988), 'Consumer perceptions of price, quality and value: A means–end model and synthesis of evidence', *Journal of Marketing*, **52** (July), 2–22.

The contribution of structural semiotics to the design of a hypermarket

●●●

Jean-Marie Floch
Director of the Visual Semiotics Workshop, Groupe de Recherches Sémio-Linguistiques, École des Hautes Etudes en Sciences Sociales, Centre National de la Recherche Scientifique, Paris

Summary

During the planning phase of the construction of a new hypermarket, a study was conducted of the discourse of consumers taken from the catchment area of the hypermarket. The author demonstrates how the identification of different types of values ascribed by the consumers to this commercial site was used to help establish zoning and define the interior architecture. This semiotic study employed the structural approach developed by the Groupe de Recherches Sémio–Linguistiques (directed by A.J. Greimas).

1. Introduction

A hypermarket in the 'Mammouth' chain was opened by Cofradel[1] at Dardilly, in the north-western outskirts of the French city of Lyons, on 1 October 1986. The 7,500-square-metre hypermarket and the shopping centre in which it is housed fulfilled a long-standing need in this part of the Lyons suburbs, where shopping facilities on this scale were inadequate. This hypermarket has been regarded as a concrete illustration of the type of contribution that semiotics can make to the definition of a new type of hypermarket.[2] The approach used in the design conception was based on the principle of attempting to reconcile the desires expressed by consumers drawn from the catchment area, taking part in discussion groups, and the requirements drawn up by the technical and management teams within the company. Furthermore, a semiotic approach was used to perform a discourse analysis of the consumers' wishes and then to define the general layout of the hypermarket. Semiotics thus played a twin role in the conception and design of the Lyons hypermarket.

Firstly, semiotics provided an interpretative model for consumers' representations and expectations of the hypermarket. The use of such a model allowed the identification of the

From the *International Journal of Research in Marketing*, **4** (1988), 233–52.

different values which are ascribed to hypermarkets and the revelation of the logic underlying the rejections or expectations associated with certain types of layout, certain atmospheres, etcetera.

Secondly, semiotics contributed to the actual design concept of the hypermarket itself, supplying concrete and precise information as to the formal nature of lighting, zoning, signing and itineraries, so providing an interior layout which corresponded to the consumers' wishes.

2. The theoretical and methodological framework

The results of the consumer discussion groups were analysed according to a structural semiotic approach, as designed and developed by the Paris-based Semio-Linguistic Research Group (*Groupe de Recherches Sémio-Linguistiques*), directed by Professor A.J. Greimas. Such an approach aims at elucidating the conditions in which meaning can be produced and perceived. Therefore its concerns exceed signs alone, but rather involve the recognition of systems of signification manifested by both verbal and non-verbal languages. There are three aspects of this approach which proved particularly valuable for this study.

(1) The approach being of a structural nature, the terms, themselves matter less than the relations which inter-define them. It is less in the study of the actual signs than in that of their contextual values that the approach brings out the relations between the various representations and expectations of the consumers with regard to hypermarkets. A semiotic description therefore moves from the recording of the various observable differences in hypermarket layouts and the way the consumers speak about their use of them, to the definition of relations accounting for the logical compatibilities or contradictions which exist between the values ascribed to this type of space.

(2) The approach is also of a generative nature: in other words, it first identifies different layers constituting meaning, ranks them hierarchically, and then enriches meaning by showing increasing articulation and complexity. The production of meaning can thus be conceived as a 'pathway' which starts from abstract relations ensuring the minimal conditions for signification, and progresses to the complex patterns which underlie any manifestation of discourse, whether verbal or otherwise. Along these lines, it was possible to establish a structural relation between the logic of the services which were expected by the consumers or the organisation of time and space and the 'deeper' system of the major elements of hypermarket design. Moreover, this logic determined the perceptible and material qualities forming the physical manifestation of distinct zones and atmospheres.

The identification and ranking effected between the 'deep' system of the major elements of hypermarket design, the logic of services and the organisation of time and space, and the physical manifestation of distinct zones and atmospheres were all achieved with reference to the model of the 'generative process of signification' elaborated by Greimas (1979).

Two distinct kinds of steps occur along the pathway of the generative process: semio-narrative structures and discursive structures. Discursive structures are the steps by which meaning is conveyed as of the moment that the formulator of the discourse selects and orders the virtualities offered by the system. They are the points at which he chooses to have one or more characters fulfil a particular narrative function, and at which he decides whether his utterance will remain abstract or take a figurative form. Semio-narrative structures are the 'virtualities' which the formulator adopts and exploits. They therefore precede discursive structures in the generative process of signification. 'Different differences' are established at a fundamental level, and these are the root of meaning. They also determine the rules which allow transformations, or passages, between positions thus established. The semiotic square is the representation of what takes place on this level, and the principle will be explained and illustrated shortly. But let us first take a look at the diagram showing an outline of the 'generative process' and the key elements which occur in our study (see Figure 1).

(3) Finally, the structural semiotic approach, with its focus on the expression of the logic of discourse, has always taken a particular interest in the narrative forms governing discourse, going far beyond textual segmentation into paragraphs or sentences. The semiotic work which has been achieved in the field of narratology was fully exploited in this study in the analysis of consumers' accounts of their 'expeditions' to the hypermarket, which are tales of '*getting the shopping done as quickly as possible*' or '*taking your time*', '*queuing at the checkout*', '*paying*', '*loading the car*' or else '*staying for lunch*' or '*wandering around in the clothes department*' . . . so many micro-tales with structures and sequences lending themselves to semiotic analysis, so long as they are analysed as complex programmes of action performed in function of value systems. The extent to which it is necessary for the value systems to be accepted consciously is immaterial.

Each expedition to the hypermarket described or related in the group discussion sessions was analysed according to the 'narrative schema'. This schema, developed by narrative semiotics from the work of Propp (1928, 1958), may be considered as a model capable of dealing with the different forms that a narrative can take: folk tale, parable or – in our case – a trip to the hypermarket. The narrative schema is the logical sequence of the four major 'episodes' which comprise the basic structure of all tales. It is the model of reference

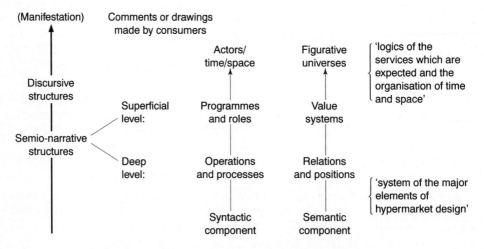

Figure 1 The generative process of signification.

representing the underlying organisation of the narrative, articulated around the performance of the subject and his implicit *competence*, which itself determines the action of the narrative. But the subject can only accomplish his performance, indeed even acquire the competence to accomplish it, in function of an initial contract which he must fulfil. Symmetrically, once the performance has been accomplished, the subject may receive a sanction, positive or negative, reflecting how closely his performance has complied with the original contract. The analysis therefore works on the premise that each *action* can be preceded by *manipulation* (leading to a *contract*) and concluded by judgement (leading to a *sanction*). Not all 'episodes' are necessarily developed or exploited, but the existence of one leads to the logical presence of the others (see Figure 2).

3. Structuring the logics of consumers' discourses

While the accounts related by consumers of expeditions to hypermarkets clearly showed a genuine diversity of experiences and situations, the number of behaviour patterns, criticisms and wishes identified by the analysis was nevertheless fairly limited. These could be organised, or rather their inter-relations could be defined, according to the handful of key values which consumers ascribe, whether implicitly or explicitly, to the hypermarket, which they look on as a space fulfilling a function as much social as economic. Going to the hypermarket can be '*doing the week's shopping*' or '*stocking up in the least possible time*'. People want to '*find the product quickly, always enough in stock, always on the same shelf*'. A hypermarket visit is the accomplishment of a programme of action which is highly logistical and pragmatic: there is '*transporting*', '*filling up the trolley*', '*loading*' or '*unloading*', and

CONTRACT	COMPETENCE	PERFORMANCE	SANCTION
Within the framework of a value system, proposal and acceptance of a programme to carry out.	Acquiring the ability required to carry out the programme. The ability breaks down into four models: – 'having to' (one's duties) – 'wanting to' (one's wishes) – 'knowing how to' (one's experience) – 'being able to' (the means at one's disposal)	Carrying out the programme: conquering the object of value of one's desire.	Comparing the programme carried out with the contract which was to be fulfilled.

As applied to the various phases of a visit to the hypermarket:

Temptation, brand image appeal, special offers, or the image of the sales outlet itself.	Car-park, day nursery, cloak-room, trolleys, etc. – the 'means' given to the consumer to achieve his performance.	Accomplishment of the act of shopping.	Especially at the checkout: friendly acknowledgement of the customer by the cashier.

Figure 2   The narrative schema.

'*going round*' with a maximum degree of efficiency. '*Why on earth do you think we go to a hypermarket if not to cut down on the time factor? Why don't they make a hypermarket which we could shop in even more quickly? They could build multi-storey car-parks so that it takes up less space, so you'd be even nearer the products. You'd need a system to take the trolleys up and down. It would work very well.*'

It is the semiotician's task to identify recurrent patterns in the narratives, similarities within different programmes of action, and identical values being ascribed to the hypermarket, and to discover how these are negated by other programmes of action, other ways of using hypermarkets. Thus – even for the same consumers, though as an afterthought – the hypermarket can be a place where the very concepts of functionality and practicality are contradicted: '*I get the basic stuff out of the way first, and then I give myself a little treat (. . .) I go browsing in the book department.*' People talk of '*strolling*', of '*a break from the chore*'. The intimacy that some consumers seek in the hypermarket implies the negation of the basic necessity and usefulness of the shopping outing, although this was not clearly expressed: '*You have to really want to go to the hypermarket, feel at home when you're there, and have something to do other than just filling up your trolley with what you need.*' In the light of such a negation of the fundamental utilitarianism of the hypermarket, it is not surprising to find narrations and descriptions in which consumers endow the hypermarket with the capacity to 'embody' other values, life values, as it were, such as human proportions, friendliness, etcetera. '*I like being somewhere on a human scale, and not somewhere vast and overwhelming.*' '*Hypermarkets today aren't friendly. That word's important to me. You ought to really want to go there. That doesn't happen with me (. . .) I go because I have to. Ideally, in a friendly hypermarket, there'd be a place right in the middle where you can have a sit, talk to people, and eat crepes.*'

Another consumer from the same group session replied to this idea, '*I go shopping with my husband. He isn't interested in frills and friendliness (. . .) He's only bothered about his wallet. He looks at the quality of the products, and at the price. Anyway, everybody knows you don't get the same warmth in a hypermarket as you get in the local butcher's or grocer's.*' In the same manner as we have seen for values of functionality and practicality, life values can also be negated in such a way that the emphasis returns to functionality and practicality: '*Whatever improvements you're going to make to presentation and to the atmosphere, it mustn't have any effect on prices.*' '*I wouldn't want anything exotic or "olde worlde". I'd want the hypermarket staff to be easily identifiable so I can ask them for information when I need it, and I don't want there to be anything to get in my way when I'm in a hurry.*'

So, whether the discourse is in expanded form (long descriptions, detailed narratives) or in concise form (an adjective, a verb, a comparison made in passing), the semiotic analysis sets about recognising the various forms of narrative programmes and the 'objects of value' which recur within them, and it defines them in relation to one another. There is a fundamental category[3] which here articulates the field of the various recurrent values present in the consumers' discourses: the hypermarket can either be seen as a place to stock up rapidly, efficiently and economically or, on the contrary, it can be a space representing a new way of life, an ultra-modern version of the market or fair, both mythical symbols of 'friendliness'. To put this another way, in either real or potential terms, the hypermarket can be endowed with practical values (speed, functionality, etcetera) or, on the contrary, with fundamental 'life' values: friendliness, modernity, or the balance (at last made feasible) between nature and culture (one group of consumers actually imagined the hypermarket of the future as a kind of giant greenhouse in which different zones, cultural spaces and product displays would be defined and linked by streams and copses). The fact that this category is capable of organising all of these discourses both ensures a minimal organisation of their common elements, and provides the basis for a potential consumer typology, according to the emphasis which consumers give to any particular term or to any particular value with which the hypermarket is endowed. For example, some consumers – whether loving it or loathing it – define a hypermarket as exclusively utilitarian, others maintain that it allows and promotes a particular way of life, and still others reckon that it is a more or less successful compromise between the utilitarian and the enjoyable, between necessity and pleasure.[4]

We will return to the potential consumer typology shortly. In the meantime, we are going to take the 'practical values/basic values' category further, and see it as the foundation for general discourse about the hypermarket. From the premise that practical (or utilitarian) values and life (or basic) values form a semantic category, we can go on 'project' the category onto a semiotic square. We shall thus be able to inter-define four positions of meaning, and hence four potential positionings.

4. The semiotic square

The first point to be made about the semiotic square is that it represents a scientific legacy. Taking Saussure's (1916) assertion that there is no meaning without difference, and Hjelmslev's (1943, 1971) that language – indeed, all systems of signification – is a system of relations and not a system of signs, we must go on to consider the various types of potential difference which may create meaning. In structural semiotics, relations are primordial; terms are never more than the points at which relations intersect.

The semiotic square (Greimas and Courtès, 1979, 1985; Floch, 1983) is a visual representation of the relations which exist between the distinctive features constituting a given semantic category. Its construction depends on one of the fundamental discoveries which semiotics has borrowed from structural linguistics, the identification of the two different types of opposition at work in languages: privative relations and qualitative relations, otherwise known as contradiction and contrariety. This can perhaps best be explained through an example: the opposition of male and female. This relation may be regarded as a semantic axis in which either term presupposes the other. That is to say that the two terms are in a qualitative relation, or in contrariety. But individually, either term of the category can also be involved in a privative relation: each term, marked by the presence of a distinctive feature, contradicts the term which may be defined by the absence of this feature. In this example, female/non-female and male/non-male are the two contradictions.

In the final stage of composing a semiotic square, after the definition of contradictory terms by an operation of negation, we turn to an operation of assertion: What happens when one of the two contradictory terms is maintained against the contrary from which it has been projected? In this case, the other contrary is considered a non-reciprocal presupposition: the proposition that a being is not female implies its potential maleness, and the proposition that a being is not male implies its potential femaleness. The female/non-male and male/non-female relations are called relations of complementarity, and the operation which constitutes them is known as an implication.

Figure 3 features the semiotic square illustrating our example.

The semiotic square we have drawn represents the relational organisation of the various 'sexual states', or, one might say, of the cultural category of sexuality, relative to epochs and to societies. It allows us to 'position' men and women, hermaphrodites and even angels (which we shall presume, for the sake of this example, to be sexless!).

The interest of the semiotic square clearly lies in its ability to organise a conceptual universe coherently, even one which is not recognised as 'rational'. It allows the anticipation both of the ways that meaning may follow, and of positions of meaning which are logically present but not yet in force. Above all, the themes, images, concepts and expressions 'positioned' on the semiotic square always exist in defined logico–semantic relations.

5. The axiology of a hypermarket

Having taken a brief look at the rules governing the composition of a semiotic square, we now return to the category of 'practical values versus "life" values', which organises discourse on the hypermarket on a deep level. The projection of this category onto a semiotic square immediately shows up four types of valorisation of the hypermarket which can be logically anticipated, and, in point of fact, they are all to be found in the consumers' discourse [Figure 4]. As we saw earlier, some consumers, even among those whose primary concern may well be speed and functionality, stressed the occasional pleasure they could get by '*strolling*', '*daydreaming*', even meandering, taking advantage of the time they could save by not wasting time when '*shopping for the staples*'. Others essentially denied any form of personal or ideological investment in the hypermarket, and strongly stated their constant concern with destroying the 'myth' of the hypermarket, and using it '*as an informed*

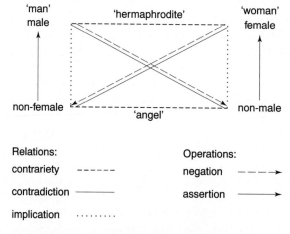

Figure 3   The semiotic square (example).

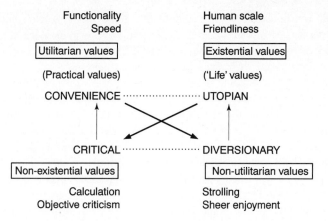

Figure 4   The major values ascribed to the hypermarket.

purchaser, not a naive consumer'. For argument's sake, let us call the practical values 'utilitarian' and the life values 'existential'. The first group endow the hypermarket with 'non-utilitarian' values (such as relaxation, free admission, etcetera), and the second group endow the hypermarket with 'non-existential' values (objective criticism, obsessive calculation of good and bad value for money, or linking of itinerary and gestures).

We may now proceed to present this axiology (i.e. a value system revealed and organised by a semiotic approach) in the form of a semiotic square. Let us name the types and the positions which define them as follows:

– utilitarian values (practical values): 'convenience' position;
– existential values ('life' values): 'utopian' position;
– non-utilitarian values (negation of practical values): 'diversionary' position;
– non-existential values (negation of 'life' values): 'critical' position.

It must be emphasised that the four terms, 'convenience', 'utopian',[5] 'diversionary'[6] and 'critical', are merely somewhat arbitrary denominations imposed by the analyst in order to designate the four positions. In semiotic terminology, they are known as 'metaterms', and could easily be replaced by other terms which certain readers – or specialists in particular fields – might find either more appropriate or less ambiguous.

We shall now illustrate each type of value with extracts from consumers' discourse already quoted above. These quotations constitute the 'surface' manifestation of the logics of expectations and representations of the hypermarket, interdefined on a deep, immanent level by the semiotic square.

The four types of valorisation of the hypermarket brought out by the analysis of the consumers' descriptions and narratives exist on a deep, relatively abstract, level of discourse: they are semio-narrative structures. With reference to the generative process of signification, as presented above, it will be understood that to these four types correspond, on the level of discursive structures, different times, spaces, actors and also figurative universes. It is not only abstract values which take on meaning in function of their correlations with a particular logic, but also zones, atmospheres, services, and so on. Thus the 'concrete' dimension of the consumers' discourse becomes meaningful, and can be analysed to provide information which, to take just one example, can be exploited to make spatial and visual characteristics of the hypermarket conform to the wishes of local consumers (Figure 5).

The consumers talked a lot about the space of the hypermarket, and drew many images of it (it should be remembered that one of the objectives of the semiotic analysis was precisely to contribute to the interior design of the hypermarket). A number of urban metaphors repeatedly came up: '*malls*', '*opening shops*', '*granting permission for a market*', or an indicator board pointing the way to '*a roundabout*', '*a public garden*' or '*wide avenues*'. The semiotic analysis considers these various places as genuine motifs,[7] i.e., as units of discourse constituted as fixed blocks, with their own relatively autonomous syntax and semantics (which explains the phenomenon of their '*migration*', studied chiefly in art history). The study of the micro-tales which these motifs represent makes clear how each of them could illustrate particular functions of the hypermarket, and imply such-and-such a type of values, since each motif occurred as part of a narrative relating one of the programmes of action

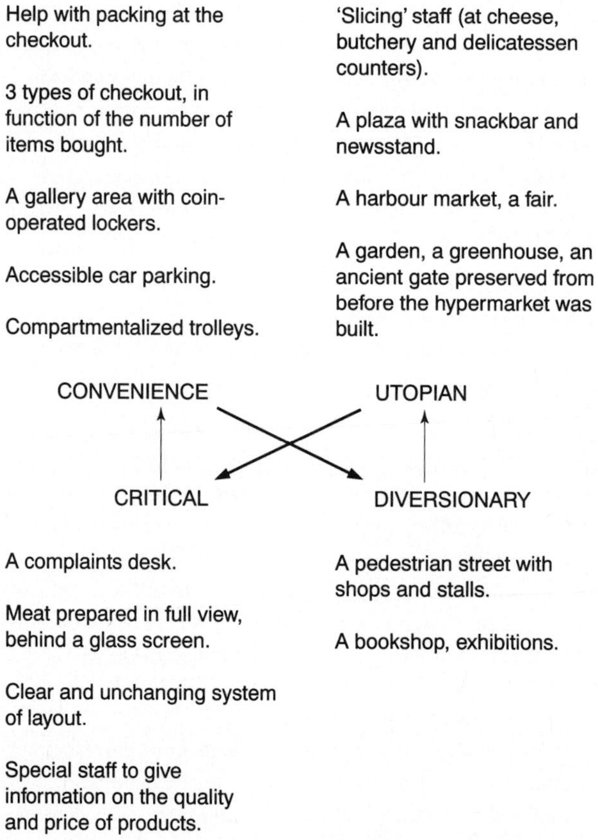

Help with packing at the checkout.	'Slicing' staff (at cheese, butchery and delicatessen counters).
3 types of checkout, in function of the number of items bought.	A plaza with snackbar and newsstand.
A gallery area with coin-operated lockers.	A harbour market, a fair.
Accessible car parking.	A garden, a greenhouse, an ancient gate preserved from before the hypermarket was built.
Compartmentalized trolleys.	

A complaints desk.	A pedestrian street with shops and stalls.
Meat prepared in full view, behind a glass screen.	A bookshop, exhibitions.
Clear and unchanging system of layout.	
Special staff to give information on the quality and price of products.	

Figure 5 The expectations of consumers corresponding to major types of values.

corresponding to a type of value. In this way, each of the positions on the semiotic square can be assigned an urban expression (see Figure 6).

In the course of the group discussion sessions, each urban motif in turn was 'explored', and its spatial qualities specified. This meant that spatial qualities common to the figures corresponding to all our types of values could be systematically identified. For example, a 'roundabout' and an 'orientation map' are characterised by panoptic vision, all-embracing and immediate, suggesting spatial organisation which is circular and allows no obstacle to impede the eye. Consumers who followed up this particular urban metaphor imagined that '*all departments should be arranged around the single basic principle of the roundabout*'. Alternatively, they envisaged, in the very centre of the hypermarket, '*a transparent booth, a kind*

'Find the product quickly, always enough in stock, always on the same shelf'.

'Why on earth do you think we go to a hypermarket if not to cut down on the time factor? Why don't they make a hypermarket which we could shop in even more quickly? They could build multi-storey car-parks so that it takes up less space, so you'd be even nearer the products. You'd need a system to take the trolleys up and down. It would work very well.'

'I like being somewhere on a human scale, and not some-where vast and overwhelming.'

'Hypermarkets today aren't friendly. That word's important to me. You ought to really want to go there. That doesn't happen with me, I go because I have to. Ideally, in a friendly hypermarket, there'd be a place right in the middle where you can have a sit, talk to people, and eat crêpes.'

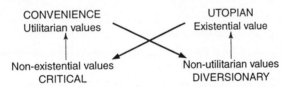

CONVENIENCE
Utilitarian values

UTOPIAN
Existential value

Non-existential values
CRITICAL

Non-utilitarian values
DIVERSIONARY

'My husband isn't interested in frills and friendliness ... He's only bothered about his wallet. He looks at the quality of the products, and at the price.'

'I wouldn't want anything exotic or "olde worlde". I'd want the hypermarket staff to be easily identifiable so I can ask for information when I need it, and I don't want there to be anything to get in my way when I'm in a hurry.'

'I get the basic stuff out of the way first, then I give myself a little treat ... I go browsing in the book department.'

'You have to really want to go to the hypermarket, feel at home when you're there, and have something to do other than just filling up your trolley with what you need.'

Figure 5   (continued).

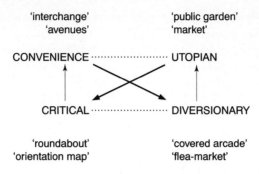

Figure 6 Urban motifs.

of transparent column, which would have one or two hostesses to answer questions about products or prices'. Diametrically opposed to the panoptic vision corresponding to the notion of objective criticism in the face of the hypermarket and all it offers, there is the wish (a wish for 'diversion', according to the terms of our square) of other consumers for a *'labyrinth'* or a *'fairly remote, quiet, covered place, with none of the normal hubbub of a hypermarket'*: a place *'full of surprises and discoveries'*, where you can *'take your time and snoop around'*. In place of the wish to conquer space with one glance, we here have the pleasure of being lost and being 'seduced', in the etymological sense of the word, i.e., led astray or off the track. The flea-market, which was mentioned a number of times, is a predictable configuration in this scenario: it is the place, *par excellence*, where people 'browse' and where it is impossible to plan one's itinerary 'in reverse', i.e., with one's arrival at a specific objective in mind when one sets out.

The village fair and the harbour market were mentioned either as illustrations of the ideal hypermarket or as a means of describing lively, warm and 'human' zones of certain existing hypermarkets. An analysis of their figurative dimension puts them in the same grouping as the references to a *'greenhouse'*, a *'plaza with a snackbar and a newsstand'* and even an *'archipelago'*. In each case, spatial organisation is characterised by complexity, segmentation and contrast. The recurrence of such spatial qualities in utopian configurations is even more remarkable in so far as they clearly contradict the spatial qualities of the 'convenience' hypermarket, i.e., simplicity and continuity. The hypermarket is *'a three-lane motorway with trolleys moving at different speeds'* or *'a marshalling yard with the platforms at the right height for car boots simplify the unloading of trolleys. Whatever the product, you take the packet or the jar but then you don't have to deal with it again, you go through and it goes off along a rail into your car, or maybe even straight to your home'*. The practical consumer, a logistician at heart, dreams of continuity and fluidity, perhaps even of the shopping space being immediately adjacent to the place of consumption.

6. A potential consumer typology

It was stated earlier that a consumer typology [Figure 7] was suggested by the composition of the semiotic square of values ascribed to the hypermarket, established according to the

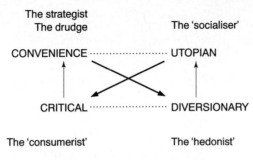

Figure 7   A consumer typology.

type of values that consumers single out, sometimes peremptorily. According to the principle of reciprocal pre-supposition between subject and object, it will be understood that different consumer-subjects are pre-supposed by differences in values ascribed to the hypermarket. The terms which are employed to designate these subjects have been borrowed from available case studies, in which definitions of different types of hypermarket users conform with the positions defined by the semiotic square. Only the two designations used for the type corresponding to the 'convenience' position are derived from the discourse of the Lyons consumer groups, since they seem more expressive and thoughtful, one carrying positive implications, the other negative.

The advantage of using types taken from available case studies was to allow a comparison to be made between the weightings and socio-demographic definitions of other kinds of studies with those based on a semiotic analysis. Furthermore, since each consumer type can be considered and studied as a formulator of discourse, the tape recordings of each group session were systematically replayed in order to enumerate characteristic items for each type, and in this way it was possible to provide valid quantitative market research information regarding the expectations of consumers in the catchment area of the new hypermarket.

The typology has been termed 'potential' because the types have been constructed out of 'pure' positions, each considered in isolation. However, it is more than likely that any consumer would actually invest the hypermarket with values of various types, either at the same moment or at different moments of his visit.

7. The spatial and visual dimensions of the hypermarket

Although semiotics could conceivably have bowed out from the conception of the Lyons hypermarket after the discourse analysis of the local consumers, it did, in reality, have a larger role to play. At the request of Cofradel, visits were made to a number of hypermarkets in the surrounding Rhône-Alpes region. This allowed us ample opportunity to discuss architecture, itineraries, behaviour typology, actions and semiotic studies in this field. In these circumstances, it was possible to observe on site, and analyse very concretely, a whole series of problems confronting not only those who design commercial sites, but also those who manage them. Problems included the juxtaposition of adjacent zones or product-environments; the 'staging' and display of products; the unity and rhythm over the space

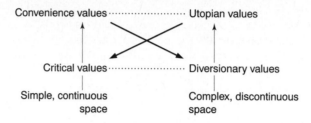

Figure 8 Correlation between spatial qualities and values ascribed to the hypermarket.

taken as a whole; and the correlation between the product-environments and the types of valorisation which we had already brought out. The problems were all the more acute for the fact that not only our discourse analysis, but also a quantitative research survey, had demonstrated that the hypermarket, for it to comply with what the customers 'expected' – not even their 'ideal' hypermarket – would necessarily have to embrace all four types of values. Clearly, it would have been surprising had the results indicated expectations of a diversionary and utopian hypermarket. A large number of people interviewed did indeed rank convenience and critical values as their chief expectations, but, as the semiotic analysis of the discussion groups and other available studies all implied, expectations of 'basic' values could not be neglected, given the scores achieved by items corresponding to them.[8]

In view of this, the first phase in the design conception of the Lyons hypermarket was to find a distinct spatial delineation to allow for the coexistence of two pairs of complementary values: convenience and critical values on the one hand, and utopian and diversionary values on the other. This was done in function of two spatial categories correlating with the values in the consumers' discourse: simple, continuous space corresponded to convenience and critical values, and complex, discontinuous space corresponded to utopian and diversionary values.

These two spatial categories (simple versus complex, continuous versus discontinuous) were not selected haphazardly to express the design concept of the Lyons Mammouth. They are the categories which, on a profound level, organise the various spatial characteristics not only of the urban motifs which were analysed above, but also of the zones and departments mentioned by consumers to illustrate a specific programme of action undertaken during a visit to a hypermarket.

Hence, the urban motifs of the alleyway, the avenue, the interchange or the market acquired full significance, as the various types of itineraries described in discussion groups or observed in other hypermarkets: *'doing the flea-market'*, going straight into *'buying in the basics'*, then stopping off at a *'local bar'*, and so on.

The correlations

CONTINUOUS, SIMPLE SPACE

vs.

DISCONTINUOUS, COMPLEX SPACE

CONVENIENCE AND CRITICAL VALUES

vs.

UTOPIAN AND DIVERSIONARY VALUES

imply a 'paradigmatic' approach to space, which aims to make the 'system' of the space evident, i.e., to structure it in such a way that the system becomes visible. Another complementary approach can, and should, be applied: the 'syntagmatic' approach, which looks at space rather as a process or sequence. Any phenomenon taken as an object of analysis may be considered under two aspects, that of the system and that of the process. The system is the complete set of relations of difference and resemblance which define the potentials implied by the effective organisation of the object being analysed; the process is the complete set of arrangements of selected elements in combination, the collective presence of which constitutes the object. So, provided that we consider it as a semiotic object, i.e., as a signifying whole, an object can be studied in terms either of its system, according to the paradigmatic axis, or of its process, according to the syntagmatic axis. The paradigmatic axis is characterised by a hierarchy of relations of the 'either . . . or . . .' type, and the syntagmatic axis by a hierarchy of relations of the 'both . . . and . . .' type.

The syntagmatic approach tends to suggest general orientation or direction; it organises sequence, progression and series of tensions and rhythms between the various zones and kinds of space. In the layout of the Lyons hypermarket as proposed after the analysis (plan 1), for example, the gondolas of the entire 'convenience' area, leading from the main entrance, were set at an oblique angle in order to create an orientation towards, or a link-up with, the 'utopian' and 'diversionary' zones. A majority of consumers would seek all four principal values in the hypermarket, but envisaged that they would satisfy their utopian and diversionary values (e.g. browsing or enjoying the medieval experience of the alleyway or the market) only once they had made their 'basic' purchases. The diversionary, even the utopian, experience of the hypermarket pre-supposed for them the prior accomplishment of the practical, utilitarian experience. The angled layout would have had the further advantage of allowing the minority who came to the hypermarket solely '*to enjoy looking round*' to enter and leave the diversionary and utopian zones directly, since the general plan of the hypermarket was to include a secondary entrance.

Such an abstract conception of space still had to be converted into the concrete space that is the reality of the hypermarket for the consumer, who perceives it principally as an arrangement of shelves, aisles, 'mini-shops' and countless product displays. The various departments and product families were described and represented by the consumer discussion groups, and analysed as semantic groups which could be articulated, globally, according to the four types of values. The discourse was systematically reviewed to discover which product families and which departments were mentioned when consumers were relating a 'convenience' programme of action, a 'diversionary' programme or a 'utopian' one. Hence, the book, perfume and fashion departments came out as the figurative universes corresponding to the diversionary. We have already seen one woman's remark: '*I get the basic stuff out of the way first, and then I give myself a little treat . . . I go browsing in the book department.*' Another made a similar point: '*I go to the hypermarket once a week, on a Saturday, because I go out to work and I don't fancy going shopping in the evening. I know the shop very well, and I make a list of everything I want, then I go around taking the things I need. But after that, if I feel like spending some time, I go to other departments, such as clothing or perfume.*' By common accord, 'shopping' involves only the practical and the functional: it includes cleaning products, basic groceries and drinks, with the exception of wines. Certain departments came to be considered in two, or even three, different programmes of action or different types of values. The meat department, for instance, falls under utopian values when consumers talk about fresh slicing, or the presence of a master butcher at the counter to give advice and information, but under critical values when they talk about prepacked meat or having the preparation area on view through a glass screen. So the different departments and product families were not considered in isolation or according to the customary logics of store management and merchandising, but defined and articulated in relation to one another according to the logic of the consumers' discourse. A new approach to zoning resulted, with distinctions such as convenience/utopian or convenience/ diversionary cutting across the more traditional delimitations of product universes. This happened chiefly with textiles, household goods and consumer products. Plan 1 shows a representation of this zoning.

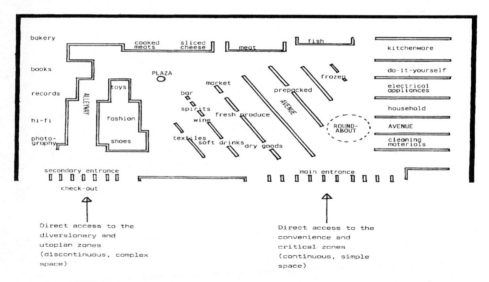

Plan 1 Zoning based on analysis of consumers' discourse.

This floor plan is a sort of visual synthesis of the results of analysing the narrative programmes of shopping which were related in the group sessions. It shows an organised progression along the angled gondolas from heavy products and consumer products to more 'festive' products, suggesting a higher degree of status, enclosing the small triangular plaza formed by the market, the stalls along the back wall and the shop-spaces along the alleyway-arcade.

It should also be said that this zoning was designed for clarity and legibility not only in terms of different spatial qualities, but also of different lighting qualities. The convenience zone, in line with the wishes of consumers, receives the strong, uniform lighting of the traditional hypermarket; the diversionary zone is lit more softly and diffusely, giving it the more 'intimate' atmosphere of a closed passage; and the utopian zone is given the closest possible effect to daylight, the light of an open, outdoor space.

8. How zoning was actually implemented

Referring back to the generative process of signification, we may say that the Lyons Mammouth hypermarket was conceived, in terms of its semio-narrative structure, for the coexistence of the four principal types of values ascribed to it by the consumers, and that it was to possess, in terms of its discursive structure, spaces, times, actors and figures from the commercial universe, all promoting the establishment of relatively new services and zoning. Several weeks elapsed as attempts were made to convert the conception of the 'ideal' hypermarket as defined by the local consumers into the exact, concrete, definitive design, which necessarily had to take account not only of technical and logistical constraints, but also draconian public security and safety regulations and the commercial demands of a style of merchandising which is based at least as much on management as on appeal. To examine the divergencies between the original conception and the final design, it will be helpful to distinguish between two factors: technical constraints in setting up and servicing a hyper-market, and anything which implies other, more 'professional', logics.

A glance at the floor plan (Plan 2) shows that the obliquely angled gondolas of the convenience zone are missing (it proved impossible to provide enough linear metres of shelving for the various departments in this zone), and, indeed, the convenience zone has been divided into two major areas. The first, and larger, part includes groceries, textiles and linen. Dry goods and drinks to one side, and cheeses, delicatessen and frozen food to the other surround the fruit and vegetable counters and loose goods, which are set in a utopian area 'attracting' the customer towards the back wall as soon as he comes in through the secondary entrance. The second part of the convenience zone is located immediately to the right of the main entrance, and includes household goods. The utopian and diversionary zones are situated towards the rear of the general space, with only two departments (the markets for the utopian zone and perfumery and fashion for the diversionary zone) set forward in such a way as to attract customers entering the hypermarket.

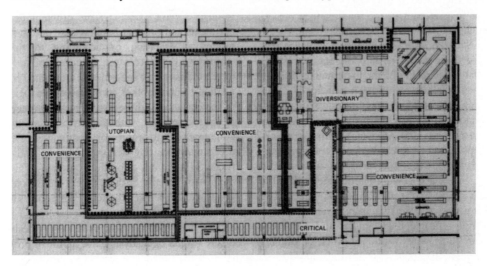

Plan 2

The 'convenience' zone, the part of the hypermarket in which the customer demands to be able to accomplish his shopping rapidly and in optimal conditions, is treated in a traditional way, with wide, rectilinear aisles. This zone contains the departments of current consumer products, such as dry goods, drinks, fresh produce self-service, hardware and household goods, cleaning materials, etcetera. The distribution of products takes account of consumers' needs, and where possible products are grouped by 'universe'. The 'utopian' zone contains fresh produce and 'stalls'. The 'fruit and vegetables' area is designed to resemble an open market place.

Loose goods are in a special zone, designed to suggest an old-fashioned grocer's shop, near the luxury food and health food departments. The utopian zone dispenses with the large indicator signs suspended above the shelves in the rest of the hypermarket. Here, the department is able to perform its own act of signalling. So, for example, the fresh fish department is indicated by blue tiling, a bluish light and a clear, fully visible stall display.

The 'diversionary' zone has been divided in specialised zones rather like those that are found in a pedestrian precinct in a town centre: tableware, sportswear, light fittings, gifts, hifi, photography, etcetera. Everything is arranged to encourage browsing, looking and selecting in peace and tranquility. The gondolas are not arranged in continuous rows, and they are not all of uniform height. Indeed, the choice of display furniture varies noticeably from department to department. In the textile department, for example, the presentation is modelled on that normally found in a department store.

Finally, the 'critical' zone consists essentially of a 'focal' point, located at the intersection of the main access aisle into the hypermarket and the central cross-aisle (it is a desk at which a hostess can give information to customers and summon a department manager for assistance with more technical or contentious matters at any time thanks to a network of radio bleepers), and the checkout, which is equipped with laser readers. The cashier only has to hand the customer a chit: payment is made at a separate cash-desk (one for every two tills), set further back.

Before paying, though, the customer is able to pack his purchases in a 'free' area, where plastic carriers are available from automatic dispensers, and where he can take his time, check the articles against the till-slip, and choose his form of payment. When he is ready, he can proceed to the cash-desk.

In its final form, is the design of the Lyons hypermarket really particularly original? Perhaps the representation of the general organisation as shown on the floor plan will deceive a reader unversed in the traditional spatial distribution of hypermarkets, or too sensitive to the graphic aspect of a plan or a schema (and therefore liable to underestimate the decisive contribution of the third dimension to an architectural space). The most immediately striking feature of the various plans drawn to represent the 'clients' hypermarket' (as constructed from their discourse) is certainly the oblique angles. It is true that they were intended to play an important role: the creation of orientation within the space, and of the contrast and unity needed to ensure a dynamic perception of the hypermarket. It is also true that they helped to define the space of a 'plaza' and, more generally, they were symbolic of the more novel aspects of the Lyons Mammouth.

But, effects of different locations and the dynamic unity of the space were subsequently achieved through the use of light and varying heights. The coupling of values ascribed to the hypermarket and aspects of its spatial qualities is accomplished through the choice of materials and chromatic colour schemes, this being effective not only in terms of the mutual differentiation of the four zones, but also for product staging within each zone.

As a result of the syntagmatic approach to the design concept, and the articulated linking of spatial and visual qualities, Christian Bessette, the interior designer, was able to conceive a general pattern for the heights of zones. The natural wood false ceiling over the market area and the three-dimensional structures forming a canopy over the diversionary zone (fashion, perfumery, books, photography and hifi departments) create low 'depressions' by comparison with the height of the three parts of the convenience zone. Plan 3 is an axonometric projection which gives an indication of the general flow of zone height, and of the rhythmic links that are set up between the different spaces.

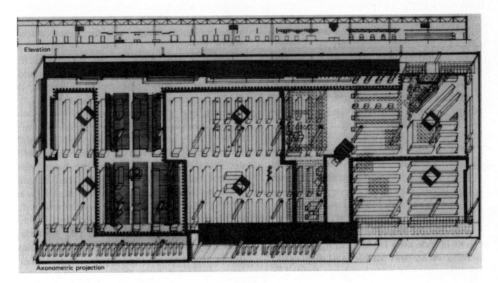

Plan 3

9. Conclusion

This experiment was not entirely without precedent. Concrete articulations between a semiotic study of the expectations and representations of the target public of a 'commercial space' on the one hand, and the definition of an architectural design concept depending on the prior results of a semiotic analysis on the other hand, had already been performed a number of times, most notably for banks and luxury boutiques. However, this particular project was the first time that such an articulation had been attempted for the conception of such a vast sales outlet, and one involving so many products. This was also the first time that so much prominence was given to the reflections and proposals of potential customers.

In semiotic terms, the principles of a semiosis, i.e., the relation between *signified* (or content) and *signifier* (or expression), were laid down. The principal function of the semiotician during the meetings held during the period of definition of the design concept was to make sure that the features of expression and content which would endow the hypermarket with a degree of originality were effectively implemented, and that any given modification which had to be made owing to technical considerations would not fundamentally impair the project as accepted. It was therefore the semiotician's job to distinguish clearly between what related to the 'form of expression' or the 'form of content' of the hypermarket (the project's invariables, which determined the basis of its layout and the essential part of its appeal) and what related to the 'substance' of each plan (which constituted the project's variables of expression and content). Here, previous work undertaken in plastic semiotics (Floch, 1985) was exploited. Plastic semiotics takes as its object visual languages constituted by a correlation termed 'semi-symbolic' between a category of expression and a category of content.[9] These languages act to reorganise the figurative dimension of paintings, posters and films, 'corrupting' it to produce a quite different discourse, both more abstract and, more often than not, of an ideological nature.

A considerable amount of evidence could be produced – derived from analyses of paintings, architecture and films – to demonstrate that, for example, meaning was not conveyed by colours themselves, but by chromatic figures; in other words, by sets of distinctive features (e.g. saturated + pale + matt or non-saturated + dark + matt), each of which could be produced in different colours or colour combinations according to the materials, surfaces and lighting of the zone in question.

The fact that the semiotic study was undertaken throughout the definition and creation process of the Lyons hypermarket clearly had the beneficial effect of allowing the integration of the expectations of potential catchment area customers, to the extent that their logics were brought out and formalised and that these logics could bestow meaning onto very complete indications or notations concerning atmospheres, itineraries, store furniture, services, etcetera. Another beneficial effect, though, was that the study allowed both the Cofradel project management team and the designers to work with the same model of reference and the same schema of reflection, on the basis of which all parties could explicit, formulate and communicate their ideas, preoccupations and experience. Through the explication and formalisation of the discourse – or discourses – of the consumers, the study provoked considerable reaction from management and designers alike, and thereby stimulated them to formalise their own discourse(s).

In this way, the study contributed to a better elucidation of a problematic common to the different specialist skills and levels of responsibility involved in this group project. Even so, the actual success of the Lyons Mammouth hypermarket will obviously not depend on this study. Nevertheless, the study does raise two fundamental points:

– Should the embodiment of the four major types of values be confined to the hypermarket itself, or rather to the entire shopping centre? This question is perhaps all the more relevant for the fact that the overall form of the hypermarket remained the traditional 'box' shape (the parallelepiped). In the future, should this type of study not be undertaken as of the earliest surveys for new shopping centres, and the results communicated to the developers? In this way, the whole building, or perhaps the group of buildings, constituting the shopping centre would reflect the four types of values and encourage their coexistence.

– With its design specifically intended to make the new distribution of space as legible as possible, will the Lyons Mammouth in point of fact demand a particular effort – a 'semiotic' effort, so to speak – from local consumers who are all too accustomed to the 'hypermarket code', powerfully represented by the Carrefour hypermarket in the neighbouring suburb of Ecully? Let us assume that more and more local consumers will be willing to 'learn' the code of the new hypermarket,/which is particularly novel chiefly because it closely corresponds to their own logics, and/that they will do so only so long as the reality of the services and prices proposed does not disqualify it by comparison with traditional hypermarkets, and as the publicity it has received has an enduring effect on its originality and on its future.

Notes

1. Cofradel ('*Compagnie Française du Grand Delta*') is a retail distribution group based in south-eastern France, operating 1,000 local grocery shops, 35 supermarkets and six Mammouth hypermarkets.
2. See the October 1986 *Points de vente* article, 'Un Mammouth de la nouvelle génération à la porte de Lyon' and 'Mammouth Porte de Lyon, la sémiotique au service de l'hypermarché', from the October 1986 Libre-service-Actualités 1044.
3. In line with the principles of structuralism, the term 'category' designates a relation, i.e., a semantic axis, and not the elements resulting from such a relation. Thus the category of gender, for instance, can only be conceived in so far as it is articulated as masculine/feminine.
4. Such a compromise is held not only to be desirable but also possible by other actors in the economic process of retail distribution. Bernard Lacan, Chief Executive of Sopad-Nestlé, has spoken of merchandising as follows:
   'Producers and distributors alike, we must see, together, to what extent and by what means commercial outlets can be better exploited in terms of merchandising management, with more appropriate range and supply of goods for the consumer, and better exploited in terms of merchandising appeal, so that the act of purchasing remains, or rebecomes, an act of pleasure for the customer. The 'rational' and 'aesthetic' sides have become too separate.' (International symposium, *Le Printemps du Merchandising*, Paris, June 1986).
5. 'Utopian' is not intended to have the sense of the illusory, but suggests a 'final aim'. In narrative semiotics, a 'utopian' or 'utopic space' is the space in which the hero achieves victory, the place where performances are accomplished, and where the subject is united with his own basic values.
6. The term used in the original semiotic analysis was '*ludique*', which literally means 'relating to play- or game-activities'. The term 'diversionary' replaces '*ludique*' throughout this English text, and conveys in particular the quality of gratuitousness suggested by the French term. (Trans.)
7. See Courtès (1985) for a structural study of motifs in ethnoliterature and a semiotic critique of the definition of the motif in art history.
8. A survey was carried out by DOMAS-IPSOS in June 1986 on a representative sample of 400 consumers from the catchment area of the new Lyons Mammouth, and the main results are given in Table 1.
9. Hjelmslev (1943, 1971) first pointed out the distinction between symbolic systems from semiotic systems proper. Symbolic systems are languages whose two planes are in total conformity: this means that to each element of expression there corresponds one, and only one, element of content. Indeed, there is no value in analysing such a system on the levels both of expression and content, since they have one and the same form. In this sense, formal languages, such as semaphore and traffic lights, are examples of symbolic systems. Semiotic systems proper are languages whose two planes are not in conformity, where expression and content must be distinguished and studied separately. 'Natural languages', i.e. French, Russian, etcetera, are classic examples of such semiotic systems. Recent work on poetry and the plastic arts has brought to light the importance of a third

Table 1   Main results of June 1986 consumer survey (see Note 8)

The ideal hypermarket is a hypermarket:	Essential	Ranking				Average ranking
		1st	2nd	3rd	Other	
Which is light, clean, orderly	74%	19%	31%	13%	11%	2.2
Where everything is done to waste the least time possible	97%	63%	21%	8%	5%	1.5
Where I can find the information I need to choose	67%	6%	20%	26%	15%	2.8
Where I can stroll around in pleasure	45%	4%	7%	9%	25%	3.5
Which has a personality, a soul	42%	2%	10%	12%	18%	3.4
Where we can share out the shopping	28%	1%	2%	9%	16%	3.7
Where I must be able to find a place to relax	26%	3%	5%	7%	11%	3.4
Where I can meet people, like at the market	15%	1%	2%	2%	10%	4.0

type of language: semi-symbolic systems, which are defined by the conformity not between individual elements on the two planes, but between categories of expression and categories of content. The visual spatial category 'right/left' in medieval tympans representing the Last Judgement, for instance, corresponds to a semantic category 'reward/punishment'. Such systems are much more current than we imagine: think, for example of the coupling of the 'yes/no' ('affirmation/negation') category and the category of head movements 'verticality/horizontality'.

References

Courtès, Jean (1985), *Le Conte populaire: Poétique et mythologie*. Paris: Presses Universitaires de France.

Floch, Jean-Marie (1983), 'Le carré semiotique: Pour une topographie du sens', in Institut de Recherches et d'Etudes sur la Publicité, *Sémiotique et publicité* II. Paris: IREP.

Floch, Jean-Marie (1985), *Petites mythologies de l'oeil et de l'esprit*. Paris and Amsterdam: Hades Benjamines.

Greimas, A.J. and Jean Courtès (1979, 1985), *Sémiotique – dictionnaire raisonné de la théorie du langage*, Vols 1 and 2. Paris: Hachette Université. [English translation by Larry Crist, Daniel Patte and Gary Phillips, *Semiotics and Language, an Analytical Dictionary*. Bloomington: Indiana University Press.]

Hjelmslev, Louis (1943, 1971), *Prolégomènes à une théorie du langage* (2nd edn). [French translation by Una Canger and Annick Ewer (*Prolegmena to a Theory of Language*). Paris: Editions de Minuit.

Propp, Vladimir (1928, 1958), *Morphology of the Folktale*. (translated by Laurence Scott.) Austin: Texas Univesity Press.

Saussure, Ferdinand de (1916), *Cours de linguistique général*. Paris: Payot.

Un Mammouth de la nouvelle génération à la porte de Lyon. Points de vente. 1 October 1986.

Mammouth Porte de Lyon, la sémiotique au service de l'hypermarché, Libre-service-Actualités 1044, October 1986.

Epilogue

● ●

In conclusion, it seems appropriate to mention emerging fields of research which can be considered as representative of both current and future directions in Europe. From the many new research topics which have permeated consumer behaviour over the last ten years, the globalization of markets, the study of cross-cultural differences and similarities, interactive media for consumer information or the experiential approach, to name only a very few, offer rich research perspectives.

An interesting stream of research, which is very popular in Northern European countries, deals with environmentally conscious consumers, which illustrates a decisive move in the way both manufacturers and consumers perceive their role in the consumption process. Marketing has traditionally been loosely defined as having the role only of gathering resources from the environment, and transforming these resources into products and services which could profitably satisfy consumers (see Sheth *et al.*, 1988). Both manufacturers and consumers are now beginning to perceive that the right to produce and consume goods is intimately connected to major societal responsibilities towards the resources involved in the whole production–distribution–consumption process. Consumers have gradually begun to understand that the consumption of goods is not only related to a right to consume, but also to societal responsibilities in the sense that consumption places a strain on the environment and therefore has a major impact on the quality of life.

Pioneer studies mostly dealt with the impact of excessive use or disposal of goods on the environment, and especially recycling behaviours. The field of research is now getting wider and the link between consumption and the environment is now being studied in greater detail. Most of these studies are conducted in countries such as Germany, the Netherlands and Scandinavia where the environmental conscience has traditionally been more important than in other European countries.

A representative example is the work of Lavik and Enger (1995), which aims at finding pertinent variables in which environmentally conscious consumers can be analyzed and segmented and variations in environmental consciousness can be explained and predicted.

Another emerging topic of interest is the importance of the time factor in consumer behaviour. Consumption may be understood as an exchange of values. Traditionally, buying behaviour has essentially been perceived as a monetary transaction, that is, the only types of values to be considered from the consumer's perspective were monetary resources. But, any buying decision involves other resources such as psychic and physical energy, feelings and emotions, and time.

Time also refers to the influence of culture on behaviour. Two approaches to time can be found throughout Europe. Some cultures such as Switzerland and Germany and especially Northern Europe have a monochronic and economic approach to time, that is, time is essentially perceived as a scarce resource which is quantitative and thus measurable. In this perspective, time can be sliced into discrete units and consumers generally undertake tasks successively, according to a preset schedule. In these cultures, time has a monosemic meaning, that is, the time display is precise and time is imposed (Voirol, 1976; Hall, 1959).

On the other hand, countries such as Italy, Spain and France have a polychronic and anti-economic approach to time, that is, time is perceived as an abundant resource which is qualitative and therefore not measurable. Time is seen as a whole and tasks can therefore be undertaken simultaneously. The time display is imprecise. This polysemic conception of time means that time is not imposed but can be negotiated (Voirol, 1976; Hall, 1959). These two approaches to time can readily be perceived by looking at the difference in the way consumers queue at a cinema or at a bank till in two different countries such as Germany and France. This distinction also allows the better understanding of the way consumers shop and the differences to be noted in terms of store displays in different countries.

Time also presupposes another associated concept, that is, the concept of space which plays a complementary role to time in the consumption of place (Urry, 1995). Space and especially the way it is perceived by consumers in its consumable dimension is gaining a wide interest. Numerous studies focus on the emergence of new forms of subjectivity and the rise of social practices in the context of time and space (see Shields, 1992, for varied and insightful approaches on this topic). Space is analyzed in its propensity to create meaning for consumers. Marin (1984) was, for instance, one of the first to analyze Disneyland in semiotic terms, by showing it could be decoded as a text whose themes could be dissected, to show that it represents a model of a degenerate Utopia. Gottdiener (1995) went further by applying a socio-semiotic analysis to this park in order to point out that the meaning emerging from such places was due to the careful organization of sociospatial codes. Numerous studies have focused on new spatial and cultural forms of consumption and especially shopping malls where the design and layout of stores inform, offer visual pleasures, but also incite consumers to new forms of consumption such as *flânerie* (see Tester, 1994 for an interesting review).

Another fascinating stream of research considers alternative ways of delivering messages to consumers than the visual senses on which most studies in the field of communication have been centred. Hornik (1994), for instance, provides an interesting and new type of communication: tactile communication. Companies are beginning to communicate with their customers through the five senses and not only predominantly through the visual sense as used to be the case. This move is important because it shows that marketers are looking at new ways to communicate with their customers in an era that is said to be polluted with visual and verbal messages. Tactile stimuli, as well as olfactory stimuli, represent new ways of delivering messages. The emergence of these new senses suggests new forms of communication research, due to the fact that most communication theories are largely influenced by a visual conception of communication.

This approach is consistent with the fact that situational variables are said to play a determinant role in purchase behaviour. The concept of 'atmospherics' represents, for instance, the efforts involved in the design of spatial sale environments which enable the creation of specific sensory effects which are likely to increase customers' likelihood to purchase. The focus on the different senses is important, especially if one accepts the fact that consumption is essentially lived by the consumer as an experience in which hedonic and emotional desires prevail over utilitarian and rational motivations (see, for instance, Hirschman and Holbrook, 1982).

A final innovative and original stream of research which has gained popularity in both Europe and North America deals with deviant behaviour. A representative example is the research on the addictive aspects of consumption (Elliott, 1994). Based on the assumption developed in chapter 6 by Featherstone and van Raaij that postmodernity is a major paradigm which largely influences and dictates consumption choices, the nature of addiction is analyzed as regards its infusion into consumption behaviour. This type of study is very interesting in the way it looks at behaviours which do not derive from a normative framework; these behaviours have long been said to be dysfunctional, i.e. beyond normality. As Elliott defines it, addiction is a behaviour which is atypical, being 'under the control of an irresistible urge to buy [and] involv[ing] the extension of normal behavior into a pathological habit'.

Whereas most studies on consumer behaviour traditionally focused on normalized types of behaviour in order to be able to explain and predict reactions and choices expressed by consumers in normal situations, the study of compulsive behaviour, and especially the nature and meaning of addiction as regards consumption, is interested in ways of behaving whose focus is that they differ from the norm. This type of investigation reveals that we can no longer rely on traditional categories because most consumption choices, such as the category of 'addictive consumption', illustrate forms of consumption that do not necessarily conform to the established codes of behaviour. It is very tempting to draw a parallel between the study of 'deviant' consumption behaviours such as compulsive or addictive buying and insanity. In *Madness and Civilization* (1961), Foucault shows how Western societies invented the category of madness to keep themselves pure by proclaiming the necessity of purging themselves of these undesirable elements of difference which threatened their sense of legitimacy. He also explains how insanity became an acknowledged object of scientific knowledge, the distinction between reason and unreason being itself undetermined. With the rise of humanistic psychology in the nineteenth century, the thin line separating rational and non-rational behaviour was increasingly blurred. The culmination of the modern era of science witnessed a subtle erosion of the conventional division between the categories of rationality and irrationality (Kearney, 1994).

Such approaches urge us, in order to understand the variety of consumption practices, to subvert the established distinctions between sane and insane, normal and abnormal, conscious and unconscious, and to disclose the unthought collusion which exists between these conventional oppositions of thought. As Foucault recommends, we must acknowledge the madness and the deviance that lie in every consumer practice, rather than banishing them. Therefore, the study of consumption should place more emphasis on those types of behaviour considered deviant, even though they are in fact part of most of our daily consumption acts.

References

Elliott, R. (1994), 'Addictive consumption: Function and fragmentation in postmodernity', *Journal of Consumer Policy*, **17**(2), 159–79.

Foucault, M. (1965), *Madness and Civilization: A History of Insanity in the Age of Reason*, New York: Random House.

Gottdiener, M. (1995), 'Disneyland: A utopian urban space', in M. Gottdiener, *Postmodern Semiotics. Material Culture and the Forms of Postmodern Life*, Oxford: Blackwell, 99–118.

Graham, R. (1981), 'The role of perception of time in consumer research', *Journal of Consumer Research*, **7** (March), 335–42.

Hall, E.T. (1959), *The Silent Language*, New York: Doubleday.

Hirschman, E. and Holbrook, M. (1982), 'Hedonic consumption: Emerging concepts, methods and propositions', *Journal of Marketing*, **46** (Summer), 92–101.

Holbrook, M. and Hirschman, E. (1982), 'The experiential aspects of consumption: Consumer fantasies, feelings and fun', *Journal of Consumer Research*, **9**, 132–40.

Hornik, J. (1992), 'Tactile communication and consumer response', *Journal of Consumer Research*, **19**(3), 449–58.

Kearney, R. (1994), *Modern Movements in European Philosophy*, 2nd edition, Manchester: Manchester University Press.

Lavik, R. and Enger, A. (1995), 'Environmentally conscious consumers. Who are they, and what explains the variation in environmental consciousness?', in E. Sto (ed.), *Sustainable Consumption*, Lysaker, Norway: SIFO, 245–86.

Marin, L. (1984), *Utopics: The Semiological Play of Textual Spaces*, Atlantic Highlands, NJ: Humanities Press.

Sheth, J.N., Gardner, D.M. and Garrett D.E. (1988), *Marketing Theory. Evolution and Evaluation*, New York: Wiley.

Shields, R. (ed.) (1992), *Lifestyle Shopping. The Subject of Consumption*, London: Routledge.

Tester, K. (ed.) (1994), *The Flâneur*, London: Routledge.

Urry, J. (1995), 'Time and space in the consumption of space', in J. Urry, *Consuming Places*, London: Routledge.

Voirol, M.-A. (1976), 'Un problème d'évolution du produit horloger', in *Les Apports de la Sémiotique au Marketing et à la Publicité*, IREP Seminar.

Index